W9-BGW-281

ROCK ON

By the same author

Rock On: The Illustrated Encyclopedia of Rock n' Roll:
The Modern Years (Volume 2)

The Illustrated Encyclopedia of Rock n' Roll

The Solid Gold Years

Updated Edition

NORM N. NITE

Special Introduction by
DICK CLARK

JUN 27 1983

COOK MEMORIAL LIBRARY
413 N. MILWAUKEE AVE.
LIBERTYVILLE, ILLINOIS 60048

HARPER & ROW, PUBLISHERS, New York
Cambridge, Philadelphia, San Francisco, London,
Mexico City, São Paulo, Sydney

This book is dedicated to my mother, Jean,
and especially to the memory of my father, Jim,
whose inspiration and guidance enabled this book to
become a reality.

ROCK ON and **MR. MUSIC** are registered trademarks of Norm N. Nite. All rights reserved.

ROCK ON, Volume 1 (*Updated Edition*). Copyright © 1974, 1982 by Norm N. Nite. All rights reserved. Printed in the United States of America. No part of this book may be used or reproduced in any manner whatsoever without written permission except in the case of brief quotations embodied in critical articles and reviews. For information address Harper & Row, Publishers, Inc., 10 East 53rd Street, New York, N.Y. 10022. Published simultaneously in Canada by Fitzhenry & Whiteside Limited, Toronto.

Library of Congress Cataloging in Publication Data

Nite, Norm N
  Rock on.

  Includes index.
  Discography: p.
  1. Rock music—Bio-bibliography. I. Title.
ML105.N49   784′.092′2 [B]   82–48240
ISBN 0–06–181642–6

82 83 84 85 86 10 9 8 7 6 5 4 3 2 1

Contents

Acknowledgments   vi

Introduction by Dick Clark   viii

Preface to the Updated Edition   ix

Author's Foreword   x

Performers   1

Index of Song Titles   675

Photo Credits   721

Acknowledgments

Putting this monumental work together could never have been done without the cooperation of many dear friends who took the time to make this book what it is. I am grateful for their help, but more than that, pleased at how they all extended themselves, in my demands from them, in wanting to make this the music industry's best book ever compiled about the artists who made the music we have listened to all these years. Through our many discussions both on the phone and in person, the result is the definitive study of an unbelievable era of music.

I wish to thank Jim Brown, Steve Popovich, Jerry Wexler, Jerry Leiber and Mike Stoller, Art Laboe, Norman Petty, Joe Rock, George Motola, the late Irving Michanik, Jules Bihari, Richard Nader, Billy Vera, Bobby Miller, John Apostol, Don Imus, Dick Fox and Milt Gabler. I also wish to thank Dick and Kari Clark, Russ Sanjek, Pat Fabbio, Donald Mott, Tina Gulli, Steve Flam, Bob Galgano, Phil Groia, Marcia Vance, "Big" Bob Czartoryski, Bob and Gene Schwartz, Eliot Greenberg, Ernie Maresca, Tom Long, Robert Golubski, Vince DeFini, Jim Pewter, Frank Guida, Jonny Meadow, Dave Appel, Charles Grean and John Zacherle. Thanks to Harold Lipsius, Michael Lynne, Ray Haughn, the late Sheldon P. Weitzman and Paul Ackerman; Robert "Bumps" Blackwell, Jim Maderitz, Smokey Robinson, Dick Liberatore, Leroy Kirkland, Suzy Baldwin, Suzy Phalin and my original editor, Jay Acton.

Thanks also to Ursula Kadziella, Sanford Fisher, Tony DeLauro, Donald Durma, Barbara and Rich Durma, Carolyn and Joe Lascko, Marc Wiener, Frank Lanziano, Joe Contorno, Kevin G. McCoy, Peter DePietro, Charles Scimeca, Larry Lynn, Dr. Arch, Michael Dainard, Byron N. Rowland, Michel Landron, Tom Jones, Jay Riggio, Lou O'Neill Jr., Jimmy "JP" Pullis, Bob VanDerheyden, Joe McCoy, Miami Steve Van Zandt, Jeff Thompson, Phil Dunning, Chuck Collier, Adam Berg, Jim Swingos, Mel Phillips, Chuck Lester, Joe Senkiewicz, Rick Newman, Rich Fields, Richard Turk, Inga Freed, Jack Thayer, Brian Bierne, Wolfman Jack, Don Kelly, Don Kirshner, Judy Phelps, Michael Purcell and to my editor, Buddy Skydell, whose efforts made this updated volume a reality.

Special thanks to those who supplied me with priceless photos.

Thanks to the late Tommy Edwards, formerly of WERE Radio, Cleveland, Allen Levy of United Artists Records, Ron Juliano of Columbia Records, Esmond Edwards of Chess/Janus Records, Freddy Bienstock of King Records, Bob Rolontz of Atlantic Records, Steve Holden of RCA Records, Jim Bland of James J. Kreigsman Copy Art, Mike Gormley of Mercury Records, Art Rupe of Specialty Records, Fred Bailin of Roulette Records, Dootsie Williams of Dooto Records, Dave Zaan of Banner Talent, Leonard Korobkin of ABC/Dunhill Records, Don Robey of Duke/Peacock Records, Mike Shavelson of Warner Brothers Records, Jon Doyle of The Walter Reade Organization, Ted and Steve Petryszyn, Art Berlowitz, Henry Kier of Kier Photo New York, Dave Rick, and Ann Martin.

And finally to the hundreds of recording artists that have supplied their personal recollections of their music and their own careers, which, in our discussions over the years, have been the basis for a very lasting friendship and the material from which to write my book.

Introduction by Dick Clark

Longer ago than I care to remember, my good friend Norm N. Nite asked me to write an introduction to his book . . . now, that's all I need . . . write an introduction to a book . . . Norm, have you any idea what that means right now? In the next sixty days, I'll be participating in 108 TV programs—half of them will have something to do with rock n' roll music. Come to think of it . . . that's apropos to this subject material.

Do you realize how long it's taken for rock n' roll to become legitimate? Back in the rock stone age when I was but a callow youth, I was branded a purveyor of pornographic sounds . . . the czar of the switchblade set . . . the kingpin of the teen-age mafia. All of a sudden, now . . . rock n' roll is an art form!

Now, along comes a guy with a dream—a disc jockey—a full-out rock freak, and this crazy guy has put it all down . . . in an interesting, scholarly manner. (Norm, has anybody ever told you, you need help!)

Nite sez to me, "Put your introduction down as if somebody stopped you on the street corner and asked you to reflect on *your* years with 'rock.'"

I sez to Norm, "Hey, dummy, that's my book!" Someday, I'm gonna sit down and apply myself . . . look over the diary notes and swap stories with my old cronies and come up with "Dick Clark's Reflections on the Inside of Rock." In the meantime, what the hell am I doing giving away this valuable contribution to history to my legitimate, nice, warm, sincere, rock nut? SCHMUCK! You think I put in all those dues-paying years to introduce this scholarly treatise? Norm, you'd better introduce MY book when the time comes!

Seriously, what follows is a gem. If I were half as serious a student about the world of rock . . . if I had more attention span than that of the average flea . . . I'd have done it myself. My hat is off to you, oh, great one from Cleveland (later to emigrate to the "fun city"—New York) . . . you've done it!

This is the research we needed. This is the encyclopedia. This is the definitive study.

Norm, it's a great contribution. I kid you, because I envy your phenomenal devotion to a subject I love. Thank you for putting it all together for all of us who love rock n' roll!

Dick Clark

Preface to the Updated Edition

When this book was first released in late 1974, I did not realize what an impact it would make on both the public and the music industry. I was very pleased to see that many considered it the "bible" of the record business for information regarding the artists who helped launch rock 'n' roll during the fifties. Although I was grateful for this acknowledgment, I realized I now had a greater responsibility in maintaining the high standards this book had already established. In fact, I had to continue my research with the hope that someday there would be an updated edition in which I could include information that was not in the original book.

After the release of *Rock On: The Modern Years* (Volume 2) in late 1978, my publisher approached me with the idea of updating this book, *Rock On: The Solid Gold Years* (Volume 1). It would include not only all the performers who had died, like Elvis and Bill Haley, along with additional songs that were released since then, but an all-important song index, listing, alphabetically, all the songs in the book.

After months of research, the book was completed, updating all discographies and biographical information and adding some additional information not contained in the original book. It has been updated through December 1981.

At this point I would like to thank all of you for the support you have given my *Rock On* books, making them the true definitive sources dealing with the artists who started and shaped rock 'n' roll music. Thank you all, and may the music continue to Rock On.

Author's Foreword

I became interested in rock n' roll while growing up in Cleveland in the early 1950's. At that time, Cleveland got a heavier dose of the music than the rest of the country, thanks to the late Alan Freed who was then a disc jockey on Station WJW. It was Alan, in concert with his good friend, Leo Mintz, proprietor of the Record Rendezvous in Cleveland, who coined the term "rock n' roll."

Alan left Cleveland in the summer of 1954 to work at WINS Radio in New York. I was sad that he was leaving, but I knew it was only a matter of time before the rest of the country was introduced to rock n' roll. Shortly thereafter, his show, "Rock n' Roll Party," became the biggest thing on New York radio. Rock n' roll was here to stay. Disc jockeys all over the country followed Alan's lead and soon rock 'n roll was a national madness.

In 1955 Alan began producing a series of live stage shows in New York, featuring artists he played on his program. The television networks, among others, watched with great interest as Alan carefully nurtured rock n' roll. On August 5, 1957, a new TV show premiered on ABC called "American Bandstand." It was hosted by a twenty-seven-year-old newcomer named Dick Clark, and emanated from Philadelphia. There's no need to recount the success of "American Bandstand" here. It's only important to note that it was probably the single most influential rock n' roll vehicle of the late fifties. If it could be said that Alan Freed moved rock n' roll through its infancy, Dick Clark certainly has a claim of right as its guardian during its childhood and adolescence. There is no question in my mind that Alan Freed and Dick Clark were the two most important forces in the growth of rock n' roll.

During the fifties, I was simply an observer—the typical teen-age record collector. Each record recalls a particular time or memory for me. By the mid-sixties I was keenly aware of the fact that, although most people could locate the records of the rock n' roll era in space and time, they knew little about the artists who recorded the songs or the stories behind the songs themselves.

Out of curiosity I began going through some of the record trade periodicals of the fifties, gathering facts about the artists and the songs. I compiled a notebook on the material I extracted and began sharing some of this information with my friends. For about five years, I collected this data anywhere I could find it—from the trade papers, interviews with the artists themselves, and discussions with people in the music industry. I had accumulated a wealth of information that I and my friends enjoyed going through. These fascinating and little-known tidbits I had garnered became a very popular feature of my "Nite Train" radio show on Station WHK in Cleveland. The show prominently featured the music of the fifties. My listeners encouraged me to do a book on the rock n' roll era that would be the most comprehensive work of its kind. This I set out to do.

I interviewed hundreds of recording artists, among them Paul Anka, Chuck Berry, Fats Domino, Bill Haley, Little Richard, Dion, Neil Sedaka, and Pat Boone. I talked to record company executives and the top DJ's from all areas of the country, as well as music writers and critics. It took me nearly five years of systematic research to get my basic material assembled.

In April of 1973, I moved to New York to work for WCBS-FM Radio. A few months of intensively checking my material and updating some of the later entries, and the project was completed. The result is, hopefully, the most comprehensive book of its kind, due in large measure to the help I received from hundreds of friends in the music business. Some data may be missing on some artists but this is only because long and diligent research has indicated that it is not available.

The book contains primarily rock artists, but it also contains any artist who was on the charts during the fifties and early sixties with a hit record. I've done this so that the reader can see how various strains of popular music were integrated during that time. There are Country artists, R & B artists, the novelty songs, and truly pop singers like Johnny Mathis and Andy Williams. If their records made the weekly top 100 of the national trade magazines, you'll find them included here.

A few terms, "trade lingo" if you will, are used throughout the text and it might be helpful to explain them here. A "cover" record refers to the industry practice of having a white artist record a hit that a black artist originally recorded successfully. A "dub" is a duplicate of a recording already made. "R & B" is rhythm and blues. "A & R" is an artist and repertoire man who works with the singer and his material. A "demo" or demonstration record is usually made by a singer to get a feel of how the recorded song will sound. A "master" is the original recording of a song on a reel of tape.

Throughout the rockin' fifties we laughed and cried, grew up, got married, had families, went off to college or the military. Regardless of where we've gone, we all cherish the music of our teens. It's a very personal part of our lives. These artists provided us with many fond memories through their music. Since I cannot sing or write music, I would like to offer this book in tribute to the greatest music ever recorded and the artists who made it possible. This book is a testimonial to them for making that music what it was and is today.

Norm N. Nite

A

JOHNNY ACE

THE ACCENTS

The Accents had only one national hit, a song that came out during the "sack" dress fad. The song "Wiggle, Wiggle," which was released in November 1958, contended that a girl did not have to be pretty, or wear nice clothes; all she had to do was wear a "sack" dress and "wiggle" where it showed the most.

November 1958   WIGGLE, WIGGLE   Brunswick

JOHNNY ACE

Real Name: Johnny Marshall Alexander, Jr.
Born: June 9, 1929, Memphis, Tennessee
Died: December 25, 1954, Houston, Texas

Johnny began his career as a singer after serving in the Navy during World War II. In 1949, Johnny played the piano in Memphis, with a band led by Adolph Duncan. The band's vocalist at the time was a nineteen-year-old named Robert Calvin Bland, who later became a top singer in his own right as Bobby Bland.

In 1952, Johnny began recording for Don Robey's Duke records out of Houston, Texas. He recorded a song in 1954 written by Robey and Ferdinand Washington called "Pledging My Love." On Christmas Eve of that year, while on a promotional tour of concerts, Johnny was playing Russian roulette backstage at the City Auditorium in Houston, and accidently shot himself. He died the next day and his song went on to become one of the top hits of 1955.

August	1952	MY SONG	Duke
January	1953	CROSS MY HEART	Duke
June	1953	THE CLOCK	Duke
January	1954	SAVING MY LOVE FOR YOU	Duke
June	1954	PLEASE FORGIVE ME	Duke
January	1955	PLEDGING MY LOVE	Duke
July	1955	ANYMORE	Duke

FAYE ADAMS

Real Name: Faye Scruggs

In 1953, Faye was singing with the Joe Morris band and doing local engagements in the New York area. Morris had just left Atlantic records and was looking to sign with a new label when he met Al Silver, who had just taken control of Herald records. Al went to an audition to hear Joe play, since he was looking for new talent for his label. At this session he heard the unique blues style of Faye and decided to sign her to his label. In July 1953, she recorded a song Morris had written called "Shake a Hand," which became her first hit. It was also the first hit for Herald under Al Silver. After that hit Faye was known as "Atomic Adams."

July	1953	SHAKE A HAND	Herald
November	1953	I'LL BE TRUE	Herald
August	1954	HURTS ME TO MY HEART	Herald

CHUCK ALAIMO

In the mid-fifties, the saxophone was probably the most popular and exciting musical instrument in rock and roll because of such stylists as Red Prysock, Rusty Bryant, Sil Austin, Jimmy Wright, Sam "the Man" Taylor, Charlie Calhoun, Al Sears, and King Curtis. There were many instrumental hits during this time like "Honky Tonk," "Slow Walk,"

"Hand Clappin'," "All Nite Long," and "7-11," which all featured the tenor saxophone.

In this honorable tradition, Chuck Alaimo with his group recorded a throbbing sound in March 1957 called "Leap Frog," featuring himself on the saxophone. The song was released on MGM records and became his only national hit.

March	1957	LEAP FROG	MGM

STEVE ALAIMO

Born: December 6, 1940
Hometown: Rochester, New York

Steve was accepted to three medical schools but decided on singing as a career. While working with his own musical group, The Redcoats, at the University of Miami, he became interested in the blues, first as a guitar player, then as a singer. He tried his hand at recording and had a regional hit in Miami, in the late fifties.

His first national break was on Dick Clark's "American Bandstand" where he performed and backed up some of the other performers on the

STEVE ALAIMO

show with his group. On the show he introduced his moderately popular hit "I Want You to Love Me." He then left the show to take a job with a local record distributor to learn more about the record business. In the evening he played night club dates during the Twist rage. In 1962, he took his group to the Eden Roc in Miami, and played there for six months. It was at this time that he signed a contract with Checker records of Chicago. In 1963, he had his first major hit with "Every Day I Have to Cry." Today Steve is a staff producer for Steady records based in Jamaica.

February	1962	MASHED POTATOES	Checker
January	1963	EVERY DAY I HAVE TO CRY	Checker
October	1963	MICHAEL	Checker
November	1963	GOTTA LOTTA LOVE	Imperial
March	1965	REAL LIVE GIRL	ABC
June	1965	CAST YOUR FATE TO THE WIND	ABC
June	1971	WHEN MY LITTLE GIRL IS SMILING	Entrance
April	1972	AMERICAN MUSIC	Entrance

ARTHUR ALEXANDER

Hometown: Sheffield, Alabama

Arthur started singing by entering amateur contests in 1957. While working as a bellhop in a hotel in late 1961, he was discovered by Dot records' A & R man Noel Ball. His first release was a hit in early 1962 called "You Better Move On."

February	1962	YOU BETTER MOVE ON	Dot
April	1962	WHERE HAVE YOU BEEN ALL MY LIFE	Dot
September	1962	ANNA	Dot
September	1975	EVERYDAY I HAVE TO CRY SOME	Buddah

LEE ALLEN & HIS BAND

Lee was a tenor saxophone player who worked as a studio musician. In the mid-fifties he alternated with Herbert Hardesty as the featured sax player on many of Fats Domino's recordings. In late 1957, Lee recorded an instrumental song called "Walkin' With Mr. Lee," which was sold to Ember records. Al Silver of Ember records sent the demo of the song to Dick Clark of "American Bandstand" and Dick played the song on his show in December 1957. The song took off and became a hit, and all of a sudden Lee Allen was a star. He made numerous appearances on "American Bandstand" and other rock shows around the country.

| January | 1958 | WALKIN' WITH MR. LEE | Ember |
| September | 1958 | TIC TOC | Ember |

REX ALLEN

Born: December 31, 1924
Hometown: Willcox, Arizona

Rex was raised in the cattle country of Arizona, where he learned to ride a horse and rope a calf. For recreation, he still enjoyed playing his guitar and singing.

In the 1940s he got a job at a radio station in Trenton, New Jersey, and became a local star. He spent five successful years on the "National Barn Dance" radio show in Chicago in the late 1940s. By 1950, he had his own TV show and had signed with Decca records.

During the fifties Rex signed with Republic pictures and made several dozen films as a singing cowboy. In the early sixties he signed with Mercury records and in September 1962, recorded his only "pop" chart hit, "Don't Go Near the Indians."

Today Rex makes appearances at rodeos, does some work for the Walt Disney organization, and manages a hotel he owns in Acapulco.

September 1962	DON'T GO NEAR THE INDIANS	Mercury

HERB ALPERT AND THE TIJUANA BRASS

Born: March 31, 1935
Hometown: Los Angeles, California

Herb began working with West Coast acts such as Dante and The Evergreens ("Alley-Oop"), Jan and Dean, and Sam Cooke in the late fifties. In 1962, while attending a bullfight he got an idea for an instrumental group which he called The Tijuana Brass. Herb and his friend Jerry Moss then decided to start a label called A & M records (Herb Alpert & Jerry Moss), which they operated out of a small garage. In October of 1962, Herb premiered his new group with the song "The Lonely Bull," which became their first hit.

Since that time his group has had many hit records and A & M has become a major record company.

October	1962	THE LONELY BULL	A & M
April	1963	MARCHING THRU MADRID	A & M
April	1964	MEXICAN DRUMMER MAN	A & M
June	1964	THE MEXICAN SHUFFLE	A & M
February	1965	WHIPPED CREAM	A & M
September	1965	TASTE OF HONEY	A & M
December	1965	ZORBA THE GREEK	A & M
December	1965	TIJUANA TAXI	A & M
March	1966	WHAT NOW MY LOVE	A & M
March	1966	SPANISH FLEA	A & M

June	1966	THE WORK SONG	A & M
September	1966	FLAMINGO	A & M
November	1966	MAME	A & M
March	1967	WADE IN THE WATER	A & M
April	1967	CASINO ROYALE	A & M
July	1967	THE HAPPENING	A & M
September	1967	A BANDA	A & M
January	1968	CARMEN	A & M
April	1968	CABARET	A & M
November	1968	MY FAVORITE THINGS	A & M
March	1969	ZAZUERA	A & M
October	1970	JERUSALEM	A & M
March	1973	LAST TANGO IN PARIS	A & M
May	1974	FOX HUNT & Tijuana Brass	A & M

HERB ALPERT AS A SOLO PERFORMER

May	1968	THIS GUY'S IN LOVE WITH YOU	A & M
September	1968	TO WAIT FOR LOVE	A & M
June	1969	WITHOUT HER	A & M
July	1979	RISE	A & M
November	1979	ROTATION	A & M
June	1980	BEYOND	A & M
September	1981	MAGIC MAN	A & M

THE AMES BROTHERS

Members:

Joe Ames—May 3, 1924
Gene Ames—February 13, 1925
Vic Ames—May 20, 1926; died: January 23, 1978
Ed Ames—July 9, 1927
Hometown: Malden, Massachusetts

The brothers started singing together in high school and in a short time won a few amateur contests. They were spotted by an executive from Coral records in late 1948. In March of 1949, they launched their career for Coral with the song "You, You, You Are the One."

They left Coral in 1952 and went with RCA Victor, where in June of 1953, they had their first hit for RCA with "You You You." The group sang together until the late fifties when they disbanded.

Ed decided to maintain his singing status as a solo performer. In the late sixties he had hits like "Try to Remember" and "My Cup Runneth Over" for RCA. (See *Rock On: The Modern Years.*) He also played the role of Mingo on the TV series "Daniel Boone." Today Ed lives in Los Angeles where he is very active singing and performing. Vic died in an auto crash in Nashville, Tennessee.

March	1949	YOU, YOU, YOU ARE THE ONE	Coral
January	1950	RAG MOP	Coral
January	1950	SENTIMENTAL ME	Coral
March	1950	MUSIC! MUSIC! MUSIC!	Coral
August	1950	CAN ANYONE EXPLAIN?	Coral

THE AMES BROTHERS

July	1951	WANG WANG BLUES	Coral
September	1951	HAWAIIAN WAR CHANT	Coral
January	1952	I WANNA LOVE YOU	Coral
September	1952	STRING ALONG	Coral
June	1953	YOU YOU YOU	RCA Victor
March	1954	THE MAN WITH THE BANJO	RCA Victor
November	1954	THE NAUGHTY LADY OF SHADY LANE	RCA Victor
August	1955	MY BONNIE LASSIE	RCA
February	1956	FOREVER DARLING	RCA
April	1956	IT ONLY HURTS FOR A LITTLE WHILE	RCA
August	1956	49 SHADES OF GREEN	RCA
August	1956	SUMMER SWEETHEART	RCA
November	1956	I SAW ESAU	RCA
June	1957	ROCKIN SHOES	RCA
June	1957	TAMMY	RCA
September	1957	MELODIE D'AMOUR	RCA
February	1958	LITTLE GYPSY	RCA
April	1958	A VERY PRECIOUS LOVE	RCA
August	1958	STAY	RCA
October	1958	PUSSY CAT	RCA
October	1958	NO ONE BUT YOU	RCA
January	1959	RED RIVER ROSE	RCA
May	1959	SOMEONE TO COME HOME TO	RCA
February	1960	CHINA DOLL	

**LEE ANDREWS
AND THE HEARTS**

Standing center: Lee Andrews

LEE ANDREWS AND THE HEARTS

Members:
    Lee Andrews—lead
    Roy Calhoun—first tenor
    Tammey Currey—second tenor
    Ted Weems—baritone
    Wendell Calhoun—bass
Hometown: Philadelphia, Pennsylvania

The group first got together in Philadelphia, while they were in high school. While singing at various local functions they were discovered by Barry Goldner, an executive with Mainline records. In June of 1957, they recorded a song called "Long Lonely Nights" which was sold to Chess records in Chicago, and went on to be the group's first national hit.

Their second national hit was the song called "Tear Drops," released in late 1957. In 1958, they signed with United Artists where they had only one hit, "Try the Impossible" in May of 1958.

Today Lee still lives in Philadelphia, where he operates a clothing boutique. He sings in occasional rock "revival" shows with two young ladies as Lee Andrews and The Hearts.

June	1957	LONG LONELY NIGHTS	Chess
November	1957	TEAR DROPS	Chess
May	1958	TRY THE IMPOSSIBLE	United Artists

THE ANGELS

Members:
Linda Jansen—lead—replaced by Peggy Santiglia (May 4, 1944) in 1962
Barbara Allbut—September 24, 1940
Phyllis "Jiggs" Allbut—September 24, 1942
Hometown: Orange, New Jersey

Barbara and her sister Jiggs sang together in their high school choir and decided to form a singing group. With a friend, Linda Jansen from nearby Hillside, New Jersey, they formed a group called the Starlits. In 1961, they went to New York to do some work as background singers. At

THE ANGELS
Left to right: Peggy Santiglia, Barb Allbut, Jiggs Allbut

this time they were heard by record executives from Caprice records and were signed to a contract.

The company had them record two songs: " 'Til" and "Cry Baby Cry." After the recordings they had the girls change the name of the group. They threw a bunch of names into a hat and drew out the name Blue Angels, which was eventually shortened to The Angels.

In September 1961 " 'Til" was released and became the group's first national hit. In January 1962 "Cry Baby Cry" was released and also became a hit. Shortly after those two songs, Linda left the group and Peggy became the new lead singer.

The Angels signed with Smash records in 1963. In June of that year they recorded a song called "My Boyfriend's Back" which became a number one national song and the group's biggest hit.

Today Jiggs (Allbut) Meister is divorced and lives in Fairfield, Connecticut. Barbara (Allbut) Levine is divorced and lives in Brooklyn Heights, New York. Peggy (Santiglia) Davison has remarried and lives in Baltimore, Maryland, and Linda Jansen lives with her husband in New York City. Peggy, Barbara, and Jiggs still sing together as The Angels and perform in many shows around the country.

September	1961	'TIL	Caprice
January	1962	CRY BABY CRY	Caprice
June	1963	MY BOYFRIEND'S BACK	Smash
October	1963	I ADORE HIM	Smash
December	1963	THANK YOU AND GOODNIGHT	Smash
January	1964	WOW WOW WEE	Smash

PAUL ANKA

Born: July 30, 1941
Hometown: Ottawa, Ontario, Canada

At the age of twelve, Paul made his first public appearance—as an impersonator. Several years later he made his first night club appearance as a singer in Gloucester, Massachusetts. In the mid-fifties, at the age of fourteen, Paul's father financed a trip to Hollywood, where Paul made his first attempt at pursuing a singing career. He met Ernie Freeman of Modern records, who helped him with a recording in September of 1956 called "I Confess." The record was not too successful so Paul returned to Canada.

In early 1957, Paul won a contest for collecting the most soup wrappers and his prize was a trip to New York, where he stayed at the Y.M.C.A. When he returned to Canada, he borrowed some money from his father and returned to New York. In May of 1957, Paul was staying with some friends called The Rover Boys, who were from Canada, and

PAUL ANKA

who were recording for ABC Paramount records. They suggested that he go to ABC and see Don Costa. Paul made an appointment and played a song for Don about a girl that Paul knew in Canada, who was twenty when Paul was only fifteen. She was a girl who never noticed him. Costa liked the song and had Paul record it. The song "Diana" became Paul's first hit for ABC during the summer of 1957, and it launched his long and successful career.

Paul wrote just about all the songs he recorded, like "Puppy Love" in February of 1960, which reflected how he felt about Annette Funicello, whom he was dating at the time. His number one hit "Lonely Boy" in the summer of 1959, told his fans, even though he was successful and traveling all over the country, he was still very lonely inside.

In 1962, Paul left ABC Paramount for RCA records. Paul has written not only many hits for himself, but hits for others like "My Way" for Frank Sinatra and "She's a Lady" for Tom Jones. Paul also wrote the title song for the film "The Longest Day" and the theme song for Johnny Carson's "Tonight" show.

On February 16, 1963, Paul married Marie Ann DeZogheb in Paris. Today he lives with his wife and four children in Las Vegas.

Paul has become one of pop music's true superstars.

July	1957	DIANA	ABC
November	1957	I LOVE YOU BABY	ABC
January	1958	YOU ARE MY DESTINY	ABC
April	1958	CRAZY LOVE	ABC
April	1958	LET THE BELLS KEEP RINGING	ABC
July	1958	MIDNIGHT	ABC
October	1958	JUST YOUNG	ABC
December	1958	(ALL OF A SUDDEN MY HEART SINGS)	ABC
April	1959	I MISS YOU SO	ABC

June	1959	LONELY BOY	
September	1959	PUT YOUR HEAD ON MY SHOULDER	ABC
November	1959	IT'S TIME TO CRY	ABC
February	1960	PUPPY LOVE	ABC
May	1960	MY HOME TOWN	ABC
June	1960	SOMETHING HAPPENED	ABC
August	1960	HELLO YOUNG LOVERS	ABC
August	1960	I LOVE YOU IN THE SAME OLD WAY	ABC
October	1960	SUMMER'S GONE	ABC
January	1961	THE STORY OF MY LOVE	ABC
March	1961	TONIGHT MY LOVE, TONIGHT	ABC
June	1961	DANCE ON LITTLE GIRL	ABC
September	1961	KISSIN' ON THE PHONE	ABC
September	1961	CINDERELLA	ABC
February	1962	LOVE ME WARM AND TENDER	ABC
May	1962	A STEEL GUITAR & A GLASS OF WINE	RCA
August	1962	EVERY NIGHT	RCA
November	1962	ESO BESO	RCA
January	1963	LOVE MAKES THE WORLD GO 'ROUND	RCA
April	1963	REMEMBER DIANA	RCA
June	1963	HELLO JIM	RCA
December	1963	DID YOU HAVE A HAPPY BIRTHDAY	RCA
January	1969	GOODNIGHT MY LOVE	RCA
March	1969	IN THE STILL OF THE NIGHT	RCA
May	1969	SINCERELY	RCA
November	1969	HAPPY	RCA
September	1971	DO I LOVE YOU	RCA
March	1972	JUBILATION	Buddah
January	1974	LET ME GET TO KNOW YOU	Buddah
July	1974	(YOU'RE) HAVING MY BABY	Fame
November	1974	ONE MAN WOMAN/ONE WOMAN MAN (with Odia Coates)	United Artists
March	1975	I DON'T LIKE TO SLEEP ALONE	United Artists
July	1975	I BELIEVE THERE'S NOTHING STRONGER THAN OUR LOVE (with Odia Coates)	United Artists
November	1975	TIMES OF YOUR LIFE	United Artists
April	1976	ANYTIME (I'LL BE THERE)	United Artists
December	1976	HAPPIER	United Artists
April	1977	MY BEST FRIEND'S WIFE	United Artists
July	1977	EVERYBODY OUGHT TO BE IN LOVE	United Artists
October	1978	THIS IS LOVE	RCA
April	1981	I'VE BEEN WAITING FOR YOU ALL MY LIFE	RCA

ANNETTE

Real Name: Annette Funicello
Born: October 22, 1942
Hometown: Utica, New York

The family moved from Utica to California in 1946. Annette's major break came when she became a Mouseketeer in October 1955. In late 1958, the Disney organization decided that she had such appeal with teen-agers, especially with the boys, that they decided to let her try a recording career. Her first release, in January 1959, was a hit called "Tall Paul" on Disneyland records. The rest of her recordings were released on the Vista label.

Today Annette does many national TV commercials, while appearing with Frankie Avalon on occasional Dick Clark "American Bandstand" anniversary shows.

January	1959	TALL PAUL	Disneyland
April	1959	JO-JO THE DOG-FACED BOY	Vista
June	1959	LONELY GUITAR	Vista
October	1959	FIRST NAME INITIAL	Vista
October	1959	MY HEART BECAME OF AGE	Vista
February	1960	O DIÒ MIO	Vista
June	1960	TRAIN OF LOVE	Vista
August	1960	PINEAPPLE PRINCESS	Vista
December	1960	TALK TO ME BABY	Vista
February	1961	DREAM BOY	Vista

ANN-MARGRET

Real Name: Ann-Margret Olson
Born: 1941
Hometown: Stockholm, Sweden

The only child of electrician Gustave Olson, Ann-Margret moved in 1946 to Wilmette, Illinois. In June 1960, after one year at Northwestern Uni-

ANN-MARGRET

versity, she moved to Hollywood. It was there that she auditioned for George Burns, who took her to Las Vegas. She was spotted by movie scout Bob Goldstein of 20th Century-Fox, who got her a screen test and a contract. Dick Pierce of RCA signed her and she debuted on the label with "Lost Love."

In 1961, she had a hit with "I Just Don't Understand."

Her special on-stage presence has made Ann-Margret a top entertainer. She suffered a serious accident in Las Vegas in 1973, when she was injured on stage, but is today performing again in top form.

| July | 1961 | I JUST DON'T UNDERSTAND | RCA |
| October | 1961 | IT DOES ME SO GOOD | RCA |

RAY ANTHONY

Born: January 22, 1922
Hometown: Cleveland, Ohio

Ray began playing the trumpet as a youngster in Cleveland, hoping someday to have his own band. After playing with several groups he finally formed his own band in 1946. He signed with Capitol records in 1950, and in May of that year had his first hit with the label, an instrumental called "Sentimental Me." Throughout the early fifties Ray and his orchestra were very popular and recorded many instrumental hits.

May	1950	SENTIMENTAL ME	Capitol
July	1950	COUNT EVERY STAR	Capitol
September	1950	CAN ANYONE EXPLAIN?	Capitol
October	1950	HARBOR LIGHTS	Capitol
October	1950	NEVERTHELESS	Capitol
February	1952	AT LAST	Capitol
August	1953	DRAGNET	Capitol
September	1954	SKOKIAAN	Capitol
January	1959	PETER GUNN	Capitol
June	1962	WORRIED MIND	Capitol

THE APPELLJACKS

Dave Appell
Born: March 24, 1922
Hometown: Philadelphia, Pennsylvania

Dave worked as an arranger and producer in Philadelphia, in the fifties. He recorded for a while on Decca records as The Dave Appell Four, until

Paul Cohen of Decca suggested he change the group name to The Appell-jacks.
After working for a while as the studio band on the Ernie Kovaks show in Philly, Dave went to Cameo Parkway records as an arranger-producer. It was while at Cameo that he worked with many of the top artists for the label and wrote many top hits.

In the summer of 1958, he got an idea for a song from the Philadelphia String Band of a marching-type song with a dance beat. He wrote a song called "The Mexican Hat Rock" that he had his studio band record. The song was released on Cameo that fall and became a big dance hit on "American Bandstand."

Today Dave works in New York with Hank Medress (formerly of The Tokens).

September 1958	MEXICAN HAT ROCK	Cameo
December 1958	ROCKA-CONGA	Cameo
February 1959	BUNNY HOP	Cameo

THE AQUATONES

Members:
Larry Vannata—lead vocal—organ
Barbara Lee—vocals—bass guitar
Vic Castel—vocals—guitar
Russ Nagy—drums
Mike Roma—trumpet
Tom ViVona—sax
Hometown: Valley Stream, Long Island, New York

The group was formed in 1957, playing local engagements. They were discovered at a local talent show that year and signed by Fargo records. In March 1958 they recorded a song that Larry had written called "You" which became the group's only major hit.

March 1958	YOU	Fargo

TONI ARDEN

Real Name: Antoinette Aroizzone
Hometown: New York, New York

Toni's father sang with the Metropolitan opera but rather than follow in his classical footsteps, Toni opted for pop music. Her big break came in 1949 when Ed Sullivan featured her on his "Talk of the Town" television program. Her first hit, "Kiss of Fire," was released by Columbia in 1952.

| June | 1952 | KISS OF FIRE | Columbia |
| May | 1958 | PADRE | Decca |

RUSSELL ARMS

Born: February 3, 1929

In the 1950s "The Hit Parade" was a very popular TV show that starred Dorothy Collins, Gisele MacKenzie, Snooky Lanson, and Russell Arms. The four of them would sing the top ten songs of the week on their weekly show.

Due to the popularity of the foursome and the show itself, by the mid-fifties they each had signed with a major recording company to record the songs they sang on the TV show. Dorothy signed with Coral, Gisele with "X" and later with Vik, Snooky with Dot, and Russell with Era records. They each had a few moderately popular hits with Russell having his one chart entry with "Cinco Robles" in late 1956.

| December 1956 | CINCO ROBLES | Era |

LOUIS ARMSTRONG

Born: July 4, 1900
Died: July 6, 1971
Hometown: New Orleans, Louisiana

Born in the "cradle of jazz," New Orleans, Louis was weaned on the music of Basin Street. On New Year's Eve, 1913, he was celebrating by firing a gun and was arrested for carrying a weapon. He was placed in the Waifs' Home for a year and it was there his interest in music began. He was given a bugle and a trumpet and began to play by ear. At the end of the year he was a leader of a band and wanted to become a musician.

During the next few years he sold papers and worked odd jobs while he studied the work of his idols Bunk Johnson and Joseph "King" Oliver. He later studied with King Oliver. Under King's tutelage, Louis developed his unique style. In 1918, when King Oliver left the Kid Ory band, Louis took his place. Louis went to Chicago in 1922 to join King Oliver's new band.

In the 1920s Louis worked with many great jazz leaders and by 1930 he took over the Luis Russell orchestra. By 1935, he signed with Decca records and became a recording star.

Although he had many hits, Louis got the biggest of his career in early 1964, when he recorded the title song from the Broadway show *Hello Dolly*; it became a number one national hit for him on Kapp records.

Louis was an incredibly versatile musician and singer who became a legend in music. On July 6, 1971, he died in his sleep of a heart attack in New Orleans.

September	1949	THAT LUCKY OLD SUN	Decca
August	1951	I GET IDEAS	Decca
October	1951	A KISS TO BUILD A DREAM ON	Decca
October	1952	TAKES TWO TO TANGO	Decca
January	1956	A THEME FROM THE THREEPENNY OPERA	Columbia
October	1956	BLUEBERRY HILL	Decca
February	1964	HELLO, DOLLY!	Kapp
June	1964	I STILL GET JEALOUS	Kapp
October	1964	SO LONG, DEARIE	Mercury
May	1966	MAME	Mercury

EDDY ARNOLD

Born: May 15, 1918
Hometown: Nashville, Tennessee

Eddy grew up on a farm in Tennessee, and as a youngster admired singers like Bing Crosby and especially Gene Autry. In the forties he began to

EDDY ARNOLD

pursue a career as a singer and appeared in the Grand Ole Opry. The host of the show, George D. Hay, felt that Eddy needed a nickname so he became the "Tennessee Plowboy."

Eddy signed with RCA records in 1945. About this time he met Colonel Tom Parker (Elvis Presley's manager) and the two became very friendly. Tom Parker then became Eddy's personal manager for the next eight years. During the early "Eddy Arnold Years" he recorded such country hits as "Cattle Call," "Anytime," and "Bouquet of Roses." His first major TV break came in 1949, on Milton Berle's show.

Tom Parker and Eddy parted ways in 1953 and it wasn't until 1964, when he met his new manager Jerry Pursell, that Eddy's career matched its earlier peaks. In 1965, Eddy suggested to Pursell recording a song that he had heard Timi Yuro record called "Make the World Go Away." He recorded the song, released it as a single, and it became a top-ten hit record. Of all the songs Eddy has recorded since 1954, he says "I Really Don't Want to Know" remains his favorite.

Today Eddy lives with his wife in Nashville. He continues to record for RCA and make TV and concert appearances all over the country.

May	1949	ONE KISS TOO MANY	RCA
November	1956	MUTUAL ADMIRATION SOCIETY	RCA
May	1957	GONNA FIND ME A BLUEBIRD	RCA
March	1959	CHIP OFF THE OLD BLOCK	RCA
July	1959	TENNESSEE STUD	RCA
December	1962	DOES HE MEAN THAT MUCH TO YOU	RCA
May	1965	WHAT'S HE DOING IN MY WORLD	RCA
October	1965	MAKE THE WORLD GO AWAY	RCA
February	1966	I WANT TO GO WITH YOU	RCA
May	1966	THE LAST WORD IN LONESOME IS ME	RCA
July	1966	THE TIP OF MY FINGERS	RCA
October	1966	SOMEBODY LIKE ME	RCA
March	1967	LONELY AGAIN	RCA
May	1967	MISTY BLUE	RCA
August	1967	TURN THE WORLD AROUND	RCA
December	1967	HERE COMES HEAVEN	RCA
February	1968	HERE COMES THE RAIN, BABY	RCA
May	1968	IT'S OVER	RCA
September	1968	THEN YOU CAN TELL ME GOODBYE	RCA
December	1968	THEY DON'T MAKE LOVE LIKE THEY USED TO	RCA

SIL AUSTIN

Real Name: Sylvester Austin
Born: 1929
Hometown: Donnellon, Florida

Sil Austin grew up in Florida, where he began to play the tenor sax at the age of fifteen. Around 1946, he left for New York and entered a talent show at the Apollo theater in Harlem. He won the contest playing his favorite song, "Danny Boy."

Bandleader Ron Jefferson saw him and gave him a job. From there he got a job with Cootie Williams, and then with Ray Bradshaw. It was while playing with Bradshaw that Sil wrote a song called "Ping Pong" that Ella Fitzgerald recorded. Ella then tagged Sil with the nickname "Ping Pong." After he left Bradshaw in the mid-fifties, Sil signed with Mercury records and had his first hit in October of 1956, called "Slow Walk."

May	1956	TITANIC	Wing
October	1956	SLOW WALK	Mercury
February	1957	BIRTHDAY PARTY	Mercury
June	1959	DANNY BOY	Mercury

FRANKIE AVALON

Born: September 18, 1940
Hometown: Philadelphia, Pennsylvania

Frankie's initial ambition was to be a boxer. After seeing the movie *Young Man with a Horn* (six or seven times), he switched that to trumpet

FRANKIE AVALON

player. His father got him a trumpet and he was soon playing with a local group called Rocco and the Saints.

Chancellor records in Philly had Frankie cut a few vocals like "Teacher's Pet" and "Cupid," which were notably unsuccessful. As a lark at a recording session, Frankie pinched his nose to get a nasal effect. He used the gimmick successfully on "Dede Dinah," which became his first big record.

Songwriter Al Marshall, after a visit to Al Martino's house, stopped at Frankie's to play a song for him he had just written. Frankie liked the tune, recorded it immediately and it became his first number one record. The song: "Venus."

Frankie, who lived in Philadelphia, where Dick Clark's "American Bandstand" originated, had the benefit of constant exposure on the TV show. As a result he became one of the first of the country's teen idols.

Today, Frankie lives with his wife and family in Los Angeles. He plays concert dates around the country and also does some summer stock.

January	1958	DEDE DINAH	Chancellor
April	1958	YOU EXCITE ME	Chancellor
June	1958	GINGER BREAD	Chancellor
October	1958	I'LL WAIT FOR YOU	Chancellor
February	1959	VENUS	Chancellor
May	1959	BOBBY SOX TO STOCKINGS	Chancellor
May	1959	A BOY WITHOUT A GIRL	Chancellor
August	1959	JUST ASK YOUR HEART	Chancellor
August	1959	TWO FOOLS	Chancellor
November	1959	WHY	Chancellor
December	1959	SINGIN' ON A RAINBOW	Chancellor
March	1960	DON'T THROW AWAY ALL THOSE TEARDROPS	Chancellor
June	1960	WHERE ARE YOU	Chancellor
September	1960	TOGETHERNESS	Chancellor
December	1960	A PERFECT LOVE	Chancellor
February	1961	ALL OF EVERYTHING	Chancellor
June	1961	WHO ELSE BUT YOU	Chancellor
October	1961	TRUE TRUE LOVE	Chancellor
March	1962	YOU ARE MINE	Chancellor
July	1962	A MIRACLE	Chancellor
January	1976	VENUS	De-Lite

B

LA VERN BAKER

DOC BAGBY

The instrumental record with the jitterbug dance beat was extremely popular during the mid-fifties of rock and roll at many of the teen canteens around the country. If the song had a beat and was easy to dance to, it became a hit. In September 1957, Doc Bagby recorded an instrumental called "Dumplin's." It was his only national hit for Okeh records.

September 1957   DUMPLIN'S   Okeh

LA VERN BAKER

Born: November 11, 1929
Hometown: Chicago, Illinois

La Vern was reared in a Baptist Church choir and made her singing debut at the age of twelve. By age seventeen, after singing in Chicago night clubs like the Club DeLisa, she was known as "Little Miss Sharecropper." She was responsible for teaching Johnnie Ray to sing the blues at "The Flame" show bar in Detroit in the early fifties.

Her manager until his death in December 1957 was Al Green, who first got her a recording contract with Columbia records. She then signed with Atlantic records and recorded a song called "Soul on Fire." Her first major hit for Atlantic was in December 1954, a song called "Tweedlee Dee," which originally was to be the "B" side of the record. At the same time, Georgia Gibbs of Mercury records had a very successful cover version of La Vern's hit. The song stayed on the charts well into 1955, making it one of the top records of the year.

Today La Vern resides in Japan; she has done no singing in the United States for a number of years.

December	1954	TWEEDLEE DEE	Atlantic
April	1955	BOP-TING-A-LING/THAT'S ALL I NEED	Atlantic
October	1955	PLAY IT FAIR	Atlantic
September	1956	I CAN'T LOVE YOU ENOUGH	Atlantic
November	1956	JIM DANDY	Atlantic
December	1956	TRA LA LA	Atlantic
June	1957	JIM DANDY GOT MARRIED	Atlantic
September	1957	HUMPTY DUMPTY HEART	Atlantic
December	1958	I CRIED A TEAR	Atlantic
April	1959	I WAITED TOO LONG	Atlantic
August	1959	SO HIGH SO LOW	Atlantic
November	1959	TINY TIM	Atlantic
May	1960	WHEEL OF FORTUNE	Atlantic
November	1960	BUMBLE BEE	Atlantic
April	1961	SAVED	Atlantic
December	1962	SEE SEE RIDER	Atlantic
February	1965	FLY ME TO THE MOON	Atlantic

KENNY BALL AND HIS JAZZ BAND

Members:
    Kenny Ball—May 22, 1937
    Johnny Bennett—trombone—1938
    Dave Jones—clarinet—1936
    Colin Bates—piano—1938
    Vic Pitts—bass—1937
    Ron Bowden—drums—1935
    Diz Disley—banjo—1939
Hometown: London, England

The group was first formed in December 1958, and made their debut at a British resort. They later played dates for the BBC radio and TV network. They were discovered at an audition by British vocalist Lonnie

Donnegan. He got them a contract at Pye records in England. Their big 1962 hit "Midnight in Moscow"was released in this country on Kapp records.

January	1962	MIDNIGHT IN MOSCOW	Kapp
April	1962	MARCH OF THE SIAMESE CHILDREN	Kapp
June	1962	GREEN LEAVES OF SUMMER	Kapp

HANK BALLARD

Born: November 18, 1936
Hometown: Detroit, Michigan

Hank was discovered by writer-producer Johnny Otis in the early fifties. Soon after he joined a group called the Royals, who changed their name to the Midnighters and were signed by Federal records. In 1954 the group recorded a song that Hank had written called "Work with Me Annie," the first of the sexually oriented songs. After that came another Ballard song called "Sexy Ways" and Henry Glover's song "Annie Had a

HANK BALLARD

Baby." The year 1954 really launched this new wave of suggestive songs which were banned by radio stations but sold very well in record stores.

Hank remained with the Midnighters as their lead singer until late 1958, after which he went out as a solo singer on the parent label, King records. In early 1959, he wrote a song called "The Twist" that was to be released as the "B" side of a record. Instead it got air play, and by March of 1959 he had himself a hit. The flip side, "Teardrops on Your Letter," also was a mild hit for him.

One year later, this same song was recorded by Chubby Checker and it not only became Chubby's biggest hit, but it also set the pace for the dance trend songs of the sixties. In 1960, Hank went on to write and record "Finger Poppin' Time" and his favorite "Let's Go, Let's Go, Let's Go."

Today Hank lives in Miami, Florida, where he is writing new songs and performing in occasional rock shows.

March	1959	THE TWIST	King
March	1959	TEARDROPS ON YOUR LETTER	King
April	1959	KANSAS CITY	King
May	1960	FINGER POPPIN' TIME	King
July	1960	THE TWIST	King
September	1960	LET'S GO, LET'S GO, LET'S GO	King
November	1960	THE HOOCHIE COOCHIE COO	King
January	1961	LET'S GO AGAIN	King
March	1961	THE CONTINENTAL WALK	King
June	1961	THE SWITCH-A-ROO	King
June	1961	THE FLOAT	King
August	1961	NOTHING BUT GOOD	King
August	1961	KEEP ON DANCING	King
February	1962	DO YOU KNOW HOW TO TWIST	King

CHRIS BARBER'S JAZZ BAND

During the fifties, trombone player Chris Barber was very popular in England with his five-piece jazz band, which had a distinctive New Orleans-type sound. In late 1958, the group was looking for a final song for their album. Clarinet player Sidney Bechet proposed a simple melody he had written called "Petite Fleur" (Little Flower), which the group decided to do, even though it was a deviation from the kind of material they ordinarily did. When the album was released, "Petite Fleur" started getting tremendous reaction all over Europe.

A record promoter took the disc to New York, and met with Bob Schwartz, the president of Laurie records, who liked the song and released it in this country on his own label. By January 1959, "Petite Fleur" was on its way to becoming as big a hit in America as in Europe.

| January | 1959 | PETITE FLEUR | Laurie |

BOBBY BARE

BOBBY BARE

Born: April 7, 1935
Hometown: Irontown, Ohio

Bobby started singing professionally in Charleston, West Virginia, at the age of seventeen. In the late fifties, Bobby was at a recording session with his good friend Bill Parsons, where Bill recorded several songs and had Bobby record a couple. At that session Bobby recorded a song called "The American Boy" which was a take-off on Elvis' career.

After that session Bobby entered the Army and the tapes of the session were sold to Fraternity Records of Cincinnati. The tapes were all listed as Bill Parsons, so when they found the cut "The All American Boy" Harry Carlson of Fraternity Records thought that it was Bill Parsons who had recorded the song. Bobby did not realize this mistake until he heard the song on the radio being billed as Bill Parsons' hit. Bobby and Bill remained friends even after the mishap, but to this day the song is still credited to Bill Parsons.

In 1962, Bobby signed with RCA Records and had the first of his hit under his new label with a song called "Shame On Me."

June	1962	SHAME ON ME	RCA
June	1963	DETROIT CITY	RCA

October	1963	500 MILES AWAY FROM HOME	RCA
January	1964	MILLER'S CAVE	RCA
May	1964	HAVE I STAYED AWAY TOO LONG	RCA
October	1964	FOUR STRONG WINDS	RCA

H. B. BARNUM

Hometown: Los Angeles, California

At one time H.B. sang on the West Coast with a group called the Robins. He worked as a producer and musical arranger for many artists on the West Coast, including Lou Rawls. In January 1961, he played piano on the instrumental hit "Lost Love," which was his only national hit.

Today he works in Los Angeles as a producer-arranger.

| January | 1961 | LOST LOVE | Eldo |

RICHARD BARRETT

Hometown: Philadelphia, Pennsylvania

In the early fifties Richard was the lead voice with a group called the Valentines. The group recorded for Rama records and recorded songs like "Woo Woo Train," "Lily Mae Belle," and "Don't Say Goodnight," which were East Coast hits. The group broke up in 1958, and Richard concentrated on his A. & R work for Rama records. He was responsible for discovering, developing, and working with groups like Frankie Lymon and The Teenagers, the Chantels, and Little Anthony and The Imperials, for his associated labels, such as Gee and End records.

Today Richard lives and works in Philadelphia, developing many young acts in that area.

| July | 1959 | SUMMER'S LOVE (with the Chantels) | Gone |

RAY BARRETTO

Born: April 1939
Hometown: Brooklyn, New York

After his discharge from the Army, Ray held a number of odd jobs. His first real break came when he became a percussionist with Tito Puente. He stayed with Tito for three years and then joined Herbie Mann's group. After a few months with Herbie, Ray formed his own group and began working in New York City. He cut an album for Tico records in New York, called "Charanga Moderna." Disc jockeys all liked one cut on the album called "El Watusi." It got so much air play in the spring of 1963 that Tico records released it as a single, and it became a national hit.

| April | 1963 | EL WATUSI | Tico |

JOE BARRY

Real Name: Joe Barios
Hometown: Cut Off, Louisiana

Joe began singing with gospel groups in Louisiana and, in 1952, he began his professional career by playing a guitar. In 1955, Joe started singing and was encouraged by his music teachers, Al Hirt and Pete Fountain. Joe's personal manager, Huey P. Meaux, got him a contract with Smash records, and in early 1961 he had his own band back him up on his only real hit, "I'm a Fool to Care."

| April | 1961 | I'M A FOOL TO CARE | Smash |
| August | 1961 | TEARDROPS IN MY HEART | Smash |

BARRY & THE TAMERLANES

The group's one hit, a simple song about a guy who's lost his girl and, still pining for her, wonders what she's doing "Tonight," was written by Barry DeVorzon. The record had a kind of pre-Association sound. (The Association recorded for Valiant some three years later. One of their big hits in the same idiom was "Along Comes Mary.")

| October | 1963 | I WONDER WHAT SHE'S DOING TONIGHT | Valiant |

EILEEN BARTON

Born: November 24, 1929
Hometown: New York, New York

Eileen started out in show business at the age of two and a half and did vaudeville until she was eleven. In her teens she sang on various radio programs and eventually wound up with her own show on NBC called "Teen Timers" during the late forties.

After her radio show Eileen spent a year touring. While appearing in Indianapolis she saw some sheet music of a tune she thought was catchy on top of a piano in a theater where she was working. The song was "If I

EILEEN BARTON

Knew You Were Comin' I'd've Baked a Cake." She recorded it in January 1950. A short time later it was released on National records and became a number one national hit.

| February | 1950 | IF I KNEW YOU WERE COMIN' I'D'VE BAKED A CAKE | National |
| February | 1953 | PRETEND | Coral |

LES BAXTER

Born: March 14, 1922
Hometown: Mexia, Texas

Les was hired as a musical arranger for Capitol in the early fifties. In July of 1951, he had an instrumental hit with a version of the Tony Bennett standard "Because Of You." Not only did he compose many hits for himself, but he also wrote songs that other artists were successful with like "Quiet Village" for Martin Denny in 1959. His biggest number for Capitol was in January of 1956—"The Poor People of Paris" which became a number one national hit.

July	1951	BECAUSE OF YOU	Capitol
March	1952	BLUE TANGO	Capitol
March	1953	APRIL IN PORTUGAL	Capitol
May	1953	RUBY	Capitol
July	1954	THE HIGH AND THE MIGHTY	Capitol
March	1955	UNCHAINED MELODY	Capitol
August	1955	WAKE THE TOWN AND TELL THE PEOPLE	Capitol
January	1956	THE POOR PEOPLE OF PARIS	Capitol
March	1956	THE TROUBLE WITH HARRY	Capitol
May	1956	TANGO OF THE DRUMS	Capitol
October	1956	GIANT	Capitol
December	1956	LEFT ARM OF BUDDHA	Capitol

B. BUMBLE AND THE STINGERS

Members:

B. Bumble (real name: William Bumble)—guitar—Ada, Oklahoma

Ron Brady—drums—California

Fred Richard—piano—California

William, or Billy as he preferred to be called, first played in his brother's small band at high school dances. In July of 1960, he formed his own trio and called the group the "Stingers" to go along with his name B. Bumble. The group was noticed by Ron Pierce and Gordon Wolf of Rendezvous records at a dance. They liked them and signed them to a contract. Their first record for the label was released in April of 1961, with a song entitled "Bumble Boogie," which went on to be a national hit.

April	1961	BUMBLE BOOGIE	Rendezvous
July	1961	BOOGIE WOOGIE	Rendezvous
February	1962	NUT ROCKER	Rendezvous

THE BEACH BOYS

Members:

Mike Love—lead vocalist—sax—March 15, 1941

Brian Wilson—keyboard and bass—June 20, 1942

Carl Wilson—guitar—December 21, 1946

Dennis Wilson—drums—December 4, 1944

David Marks—rhythm guitar—replaced by Al Jardine (1963)—September 3, 1942

Hometown: Hawthorne, California

The California-generated Beach Boys form a bridge between the great rock and roll years of the fifties and the Beatles-led British invasion of the early sixties. Dennis Wilson had long wanted to write a song about the

THE BEACH BOYS

Clockwise from top:
Brian Wilson, Carl
Wilson, Mike Love,
Al Jardine, Dennis
Wilson

popular West Coast sport of surfing, so he convinced his brother Brian and his cousin Mike Love to give him a hand. The result was a tune called "Surfin'," which was released on Candix, a local label, and the song became a regional hit early in 1962.

Nick Venet, a producer for Capitol records, heard the group, liked its sound, and signed them to the label. In July 1962 The Beach Boys had their first national hit with "Surfin' Safari." They followed this inital pair of surfing songs with other songs teen-agers could relate to about cars and racing, the West Coast, and girls.

In the mid-sixties the group had an incredible number of hits, including three number-one records: "I Get Around," "Help Me, Rhonda," and "Good Vibrations." Mike Love sang lead on most of their songs. A few records featured either Brian Wilson or Alan Jardine.

After recording hits for more than two decades, The Beach Boys are as popular as ever, playing to capacity crowds all over the country. Although Carl and Mike have done solo recording projects, the original five still play together for concerts, making them the only rock band still performing with all its original members.

January	1962	SURFIN'	Candix
August	1962	SURFIN' SAFARI	Capitol
October	1962	409	Capitol
December	1962	TEN LITTLE INDIANS	Capitol
March	1963	SURFIN' U.S.A.	Capitol
April	1963	SHUT DOWN	Capitol
August	1963	SURFER GIRL	Capitol

August	1963	LITTLE DEUCE COUPE	Capitol
November	1963	BE TRUE TO YOUR SCHOOL	Capitol
November	1963	IN MY ROOM	Capitol
February	1964	FUN, FUN, FUN	Capitol
May	1964	I GET AROUND	Capitol
May	1964	DON'T WORRY BABY	Capitol
September	1964	WHEN I GROW UP (TO BE A MAN)	Capitol
October	1964	WENDY	Capitol
October	1964	LITTLE HONDA	Capitol
November	1964	DANCE, DANCE, DANCE	Capitol
February	1965	DO YOU WANNA DANCE	Capitol
April	1965	HELP ME, RHONDA	Capitol
July	1965	CALIFORNIA GIRLS	Capitol
November	1965	THE LITTLE GIRL I ONCE KNEW	Capitol
January	1966	BARBARA ANN	Capitol
April	1966	SLOOP JOHN B	Capitol
July	1966	WOULDN'T IT BE NICE	Capitol
August	1966	GOD ONLY KNOWS	Capitol
October	1966	GOOD VIBRATIONS	Capitol
August	1967	HEROES AND VILLAINS	Brother
October	1967	WILD HONEY	Capitol
December	1967	DARLIN'	Capitol
April	1968	FRIENDS	Capitol
July	1968	DO IT AGAIN	Capitol
December	1968	BLUEBIRDS OVER THE MOUNTAIN	Capitol
March	1969	I CAN HEAR MUSIC	Capitol
July	1969	BREAK AWAY	Capitol
March	1970	ADD SOME MUSIC TO YOUR DAY	Reprise
October	1971	LONG PROMISED ROAD	Reprise
February	1973	SAIL ON SAILOR	Reprise
May	1973	CALIFORNIA SAGA	Reprise
August	1974	SURFIN' U.S.A.	Capitol
March	1975	SAIL ON SAILOR	Warner/Reprise/Brother
June	1976	ROCK AND ROLL MUSIC	Warner/Reprise/Brother
August	1976	IT'S O.K.	Brother/Reprise
September	1978	PEGGY SUE	Brother/Reprise
March	1979	HERE COMES THE NIGHT	Caribou
April	1979	GOOD TIMIN'	Caribou
April	1980	GOIN' ON	Caribou
July	1981	THE BEACH BOYS MEDLEY	Capitol
November	1981	COME GO WITH ME	Caribou

THE BEAU-MARKS

Members:

> Joey Frechette—piano and lead vocal—1939
> Ray Hutchinson—lead guitar—1941
> Mike Robitaille—bass guitar—1940
> Gilles Tailleur—drums—1941

Hometown: Montreal, Canada

The group started out in Montreal in June of 1958 as The Del-Tones. They eventually signed a recording contract with a Canadian label, Quality records, and had a Canadian hit, "Moonlight Party." They debuted in the United States as The Beau-Marks on Shad records with "Clap Your Hands" in May of 1960. It was their only hit.

May	1960	CLAP YOUR HANDS	Shad

BOB BECKHAM

Bob Beckham's "Just as Much as Ever" crossed from the country and western charts to the pop charts in the summer of 1959. The same tune became a big hit for Bobby Vinton in the mid-sixties.

August	1959	JUST AS MUCH AS EVER	Decca
December	1959	CRAZY ARMS	Decca

HARRY BELAFONTE

Real Name: Harold George Belafonte, Jr.
Born: March 1, 1927
Hometown: New York, New York

In 1944, Harry joined the Navy for two years of active duty. After his discharge he got a job as a maintenance man in New York, but never forgot his first love, which was singing. An audition at the Royal Roost night club in New York resulted in a twenty-week contract. After this engagement, he got a job in a Greenwich Village restaurant where he discovered folk material. By 1950, he began working with guitarists Millard Thomas and Craig Work and built a repertoire of old and modern folk ballads. Later that year he was booked at the Village Vanguard which got him his first real recognition; it resulted in a contract with RCA records.

By the fall of 1956, he had his first chart record with the Calypso-flavored "Jamaica Farewell." In January 1957 he recorded his biggest hit, "Banana Boat."

Today Harry does occasional concerts and special dramatic roles for television. However, he is most active in civil and voting rights and peace throughout the world.

October	1956	JAMAICA FAREWELL	RCA
December	1956	MARY'S BOY CHILD	RCA
January	1957	BANANA BOAT	RCA
February	1957	HOLD 'EM JOE	RCA
March	1957	MAMA LOOK AT BUBU	RCA
April	1957	DON'T EVER LOVE ME	RCA
May	1957	ISLAND IN THE SUN	RCA
May	1957	COCOANUT WOMAN	RCA

HARRY BELAFONTE

THE BELL NOTES

Members:
> Carl Bonura—sax—dual lead
> Ray Ceroni—guitar—dual lead
> Lenny Giamblavo—bass
> Pete Kane—piano
> John Casey: drums

Hometown: Long Island, New York

New York disc jockey Alan Frederics heard the fellows playing on Long Island, and became interested in the group. He arranged an audition with Time records in New York, where they were eventually signed to a contract. Their first release in February of 1959, called "I've Had It," became a solid smash for the group.

February	1959	I'VE HAD IT	Time
May	1959	OLD SPANISH TOWN	Time
August	1960	SHORTNIN' BREAD	Madison

THE BELMONTS

Members:

    Angelo D'Aleo—first tenor—February 3, 1940
    Fred Milano—second tenor—August 22, 1939
    Carlo Mastrangelo—bass—October 5, 1938—replaced by Frank
        Lyndon in May 1962

Hometown: Bronx, New York

The group got their name from Belmont Avenue in the Bronx. They all
lived around Belmont Avenue, Garden Street, and Prospect Avenue—the
same neighborhood Bobby Darin and The Regents ("Barbara-Ann")
came from. The Belmonts, along with Dion DiMucci, formed at Roosevelt

THE BELMONTS

Left to right: Angelo D'Aleo,
Fred Milano, Carlo
Mastrangelo

High in the Bronx. In March of 1958, they launched their careers with "I Wonder Why," which was their first release for the newly formed Laurie records. Songs like "Teenager in Love" and "Where or When" were to follow over the years.

In the summer of 1960, they recorded their last song with Dion as the lead, called "In the Still of the Night." Dion then went out as a soloist with "Lonely Teenager" in the fall of 1960, also on Laurie records. The Belmonts left Laurie and eventually signed with Sabina records. Their first hit, in May of 1961, was "Tell Me Why," on which Carlo sang lead. Carlo also sang lead on "I Need Someone" and "Come On Little Angel." He left the group in May of 1962, and was replaced by Frank Lyndon. Today Carlo lives in the Bronx, while Fred and Angelo live on Long Island, New York. Fred, along with two new members, still performs at local rock shows, while they also record with Freddy Cannon.

See also Dion; Dion & The Belmonts.

May	1961	TELL ME WHY	Sabina
August	1961	DON'T GET AROUND MUCH ANYMORE	Sabina
December	1961	I NEED SOMEONE	Sabina
July	1962	COME ON LITTLE ANGEL	Sabina
October	1962	DIDDLE-DE-DUM	Sabina
April	1963	ANN-MARIE	Sabina

JESSE BELVIN

Born: December 15, 1933, in Texarkana, Arkansas
Died: February 6, 1960
Hometown: Los Angeles, California

Jesse moved to Los Angeles at the age of five. In L.A. he attended Jefferson High School and Compton Junior College. At age seven, he sang in his mother's church choir, and at sixteen, he joined Big Jay McNeely's band and made his first recording. In 1953, he went into the Army and was stationed at Fort Ord, California. He was later assigned to Germany. It was at this time that he wrote a classic song, along with Curtis Williams and Gaynel Hodge, called "Earth Angel" which became a fantastic hit for the Penguins in 1954.

Jesse sang with Marvin Phillips, as Marvin and Jesse, for Specialty records with songs like "Dream Girl" in the mid-fifties. Then he went on his own and had a big hit for Modern records in Los Angeles called "Goodnight My Love," which became a national hit for him. It was disc jockey Alan Freed's closing song on his radio program every night on

JESSE BELVIN

WINS in New York. Jesse was brought east by Alan Freed, and eventually signed a contract with RCA in late 1958. His biggest hit for the label was a song that Jesse's wife Jo Ann wrote called "Guess Who."

Jesse died in an automobile accident on February 6, 1960.

November	1956	GOODNIGHT MY LOVE	Modern
January	1959	FUNNY	RCA
April	1959	GUESS WHO	RCA

BOYD BENNETT

Born: December 7, 1924, Nashville, Tennessee
Hometown: Muscle Shoals, Alabama

Boyd organized a high school band in Tennessee and played around the state. He then became a disc jockey at a station in Kentucky. In the mid-fifties he signed with King records of Cincinnati, and was known as Boyd Bennett and The Rockets. He had two big hits for the label in 1955, "Seventeen" and "My Boy Flat Top." Four years later he signed with Mercury records and had only one popular release, "Boogie Bear." After that he moved to Indianapolis, and bought a night club called The Thunderbird.

Today Boyd lives in Dallas, Texas, and is a surgical gauze salesman.

June	1955	SEVENTEEN	King
September	1955	MY BOY FLAT TOP	King
April	1956	BLUE SUEDE SHOES	King
September	1959	BOOGIE BEAR	Mercury

JOE BENNETT AND THE SPARKLETONES

During the fifties, many songs were written about hot rod racing and going steady embodying typical teen-age expressions like "Daddy Cool" and "Daddy-O." In the summer of 1957, Joe Bennett wrote a song about the attire of a "cool" teen-age boy called "Black Slacks" in which he emphasized that when you wore them you stood out as number one with your friends. He also utilized a lot of typical teen-age expressions in the song like "cool-breeze," "crazy little mamma," "hep-cat," "cool Daddy-O," and "rarin' to go." The song was recorded and sold to ABC records, and by August 1957 it became a national hit, because of the exposure it got on Dick Clark's "American Bandstand" show.

August   1957   BLACK SLACKS   ABC

BOYD BENNETT (Center front)

TONY BENNETT

TONY BENNETT

Real Name: Anthony Dominick Benedetto
Born: August 3, 1926
Hometown: Queens, New York

Tony's first public appearance was at a church at the age of seven. He sang in Army bands while in the service and studied singing when he was discharged. Bob Hope heard him singing in a night club and invited him to sing in the supporting cast in a traveling show.

In March 1950, Mitch Miller of Columbia records heard one of his audition records and immediately signed him to a contract. His dual release of "Be My Love" and "Cold, Cold Heart" sold one million copies in 1951. It was fast on the heels of his first number one record for Columbia, "Because of You," in September 1951. "Because of You" was also Tony's first million seller. In the summer of 1962, he recorded his most popular song—"I Left My Heart in San Francisco."

Today Tony travels between New York and Los Angeles while performing in front of capacity crowds.

June	1951	BECAUSE OF YOU	Columbia
June	1951	I WON'T CRY ANYMORE	Columbia
July	1951	COLD, COLD HEART	Columbia
October	1951	BLUE VELVET	Columbia
November	1951	SOLITAIRE	Columbia
May	1952	HERE IN MY HEART	Columbia
August	1952	HAVE A GOOD TIME	Columbia
September	1953	RAGS TO RICHES	Columbia

December	1953	STRANGER IN PARADISE	Columbia
March	1954	THERE'LL BE NO TEARDROPS TONIGHT	Columbia
July	1954	CINNAMON SINNER	Columbia
April	1956	CAN YOU FIND IT IN YOUR HEART	Columbia
August	1956	HAPPINESS STREET	Columbia
August	1956	FROM THE CANDY STORE ON THE CORNER TO THE CHAPEL ON THE HILL	Columbia
October	1956	JUST IN TIME	Columbia
October	1956	THE AUTUMN WALTZ	Columbia
May	1957	ONE FOR MY BABY	Columbia
July	1957	IN THE MIDDLE OF AN ISLAND	Columbia
August	1957	I AM	Columbia
November	1957	CA C'EST L'AMOUR	Columbia
June	1958	YOUNG AND WARM AND WONDERFUL	Columbia
September	1958	FIREFLY	Columbia
August	1959	SMILE	Columbia
December	1959	CLIMB EV'RY MOUNTAIN	Columbia
August	1962	I LEFT MY HEART IN SAN FRANCISCO	Columbia
January	1963	I WILL LIVE MY LIFE FOR YOU	Columbia
January	1963	I WANNA BE AROUND	Columbia
May	1963	THE GOOD LIFE	Columbia
June	1963	SPRING IN MANHATTAN	Columbia
July	1963	THIS IS ALL I ASK	Columbia
July	1963	TRUE BLUE LOU	Columbia
October	1963	DON'T WAIT TOO LONG	Columbia
December	1963	THE LITTLE BOY	Columbia
March	1964	WHEN JOANNA LOVED ME	Columbia
July	1964	IT'S A SIN TO TELL A LIE	Columbia
August	1964	A TASTE OF HONEY	Columbia
October	1964	WHO CAN I TURN TO	Columbia
February	1965	IF I RULED THE WORLD	Columbia
July	1965	FLY ME TO THE MOON	Columbia
November	1965	LOVE THEME FROM THE SANDPIPER	Columbia
July	1966	GEORGIA ROSE	Columbia
October	1967	FOR ONCE IN MY LIFE	Columbia

BROOK BENTON

Real Name: Benjamin Franklin Peay
Born: September 19, 1931
Hometown: Camden, South Carolina

In the early fifties Brook joined Bill Landford's Spiritual Quartet and traveled across the country. Brook met songwriter Clyde Otis and the two of them collaborated on several hits in 1958, "Looking Back" for Nat "King" Cole, and "Lover's Question" for Clyde McPhatter.

Brook's real success as a singer did not occur until early 1959, when he signed with Mercury records and released the first of many hits for the label, called "It's Just a Matter of Time," a song that he wrote with Clyde Otis and Belford Hendricks. His biggest chart record came in May of 1961, with another song that he had written with Clyde Otis, called "The

BROOK BENTON

Boll Weevil Song." In 1960, with Dinah Washington he recorded two chart hits that both he and Clyde Otis had written called "Baby (You Got What It Takes)" and "A Rockin' Good Way." In January of 1970, he came back with another top-ten hit on Cotillion records, written by Tony Joe White, called "Rainy Night in Georgia."

Brook has had eighteen gold records and was one of the early artists who wrote his own material. Today he lives with his wife and family in New York, but has chosen to get involved with religious music.

February	1958	A MILLION MILES FROM NOWHERE	Vik
January	1959	IT'S JUST A MATTER OF TIME	Mercury
April	1959	ENDLESSLY	Mercury
April	1959	SO CLOSE	Mercury
July	1959	THANK YOU PRETTY BABY	Mercury
October	1959	SO MANY WAYS	Mercury
March	1960	THE TIES THAT BIND	Mercury
August	1960	KIDDIO	Mercury
August	1960	THE SAME ONE	Mercury
November	1960	FOOLS RUSH IN	Mercury
February	1961	FOR MY BABY	Mercury
February	1961	THINK TWICE	Mercury
May	1961	THE BOLL WEEVIL SONG	Mercury
August	1961	FRANKIE AND JOHNNY	Mercury
October	1961	IT'S JUST A HOUSE WITHOUT YOU	Mercury
November	1961	REVENGE	Mercury
January	1962	SHADRACK	Mercury
February	1962	WALK ON THE WILD SIDE	Mercury

May	1962	HIT RECORD	Mercury
August	1962	LIE TO ME	Mercury
November	1962	HOTEL HAPPINESS	Mercury
March	1963	I GOT WHAT I WANTED	Mercury
June	1963	MY TRUE CONFESSION	Mercury
September	1963	TWO TICKETS TO PARADISE	Mercury
January	1964	GOING GOING GONE	Mercury
May	1964	TOO LATE TO TURN BACK NOW	Mercury
May	1964	ANOTHER CUP OF COFFEE	Mercury
July	1964	A HOUSE IS NOT A HOME	Mercury
October	1964	LUMBERJACK	Mercury
December	1964	DO IT RIGHT	Mercury
July	1965	LOVE ME NOW	Mercury
November	1965	MOTHER NATURE, FATHER TIME	RCA
August	1967	LAURA (WHAT'S HE GOT THAT I AIN'T GOT)	Reprise
October	1968	DO YOUR OWN THING	Cotillion
July	1969	NOTHING TAKES THE PLACE OF YOU	Cotillion
January	1970	RAINY NIGHT IN GEORGIA	Cotillion
April	1970	MY WAY	Cotillion
May	1970	DON'T IT MAKE YOU WANT TO GO HOME	Cotillion
December	1970	SHOES	Cotillion

BROOK BENTON and DINAH WASHINGTON

| January | 1960 | BABY (YOU'VE GOT WHAT IT TAKES) | Mercury |
| May | 1960 | A ROCKIN' GOOD WAY | Mercury |

**BROOK BENTON and
DINAH WASHINGTON**

ROD BERNARD

Born: August 12, 1940
Hometown: Opelousas, Louisiana

At nine, Rod joined the cast of "The Blue Room" radio show on KSLO radio in Opelousas. He stayed on as a featured singer for seven years. At seventeen, he was hired as a disc jockey at KSLO. At the same time he joined a band called The Twisters and cut a song with the group called "This Should Go on Forever" which was sold to Jin records. The master recording was then sold to Argo records in Chicago, and the song became a hit for Rod in early 1959. It was the only real hit he ever had.

March	1959	THIS SHOULD GO ON FOREVER	Argo
November	1959	ONE MORE CHANCE	Mercury

CHUCK BERRY

Real Name: Charles Edward Anderson Berry
Born: October 18, 1926
Hometown: Wentzville, Missouri

Chuck's parents were members of the Antioch Baptist church choir in St. Louis. He had three sisters and two brothers. While he was in the Sumner High School glee club singing bass, he bought a six-string Spanish guitar. His music teacher, Julia Davis, encouraged him to play it as much as he could. In 1952, Chuck started his own group called the Chuck Berry combo and began playing local clubs in east St. Louis. At this time, Chuck was contemplating a career as either a hairdresser, a singer, or a photographer.

A vacation trip to Chicago in 1955 was the deciding factor in Chuck's eventual decision. It was during this trip that Chuck met blues singer Muddy Waters, who encouraged Chuck to go and see Leonard and Phil Chess, the two brothers who owned Chess records. Chuck auditioned for them with a song he had written called "Ida Red." They liked the song, but suggested he change the title. Remembering the name of a cow from a third grade story, Chuck renamed the song "Maybellene." The song was recorded, a contract was signed, and the beginning of a legend was launched in July 1955, with his first of many hits.

Chuck defines his music as giving a feeling of adventure or joy. In some of his songs he would write of personal experiences, like "School Days," which were experiences from his own high school days. Other songs related true life incidents, like "Sweet Little Sixteen," which was about something that happened in Denver, Colorado, in late 1957, during

CHUCK BERRY

one of the touring rock and roll shows that Chuck was on. He wrote about one little eleven-year-old at the show who was busy collecting autographs for her wallet. The song became one of his biggest hits in early 1958. Later that same year he wrote and recorded a song that is said to be a musical autobiography—"Johnny B. Goode." Chuck feels that music is a "food for mood" and he likes all kinds of music depending upon his mood. He is a true rock 'and roll giant, who has been acknowledged by today's superstars like John Lennon of The Beatles and Keith Richards of The Rolling Stones. Chuck has been a tremendous influence on guitar players around the world.

Chuck still headlines major rock 'n' roll reunion shows such as the one he did at New York's Madison Square Garden on October 23, 1981. He truly is one of rock 'n' roll's legends and superstars.

| July | 1955 | MAYBELLENE | Chess |
| October | 1955 | THIRTY DAYS | Chess |

February	1956	NO MONEY DOWN	Chess
June	1956	ROLL OVER BEETHOVEN	Chess
October	1956	TOO MUCH MONKEY BUSINESS/	
		BROWN EYED HANDSOME MAN	Chess
March	1957	SCHOOL DAY	Chess
July	1957	OH BABY DOLL	Chess
October	1957	ROCK & ROLL MUSIC	Chess
February	1958	SWEET LITTLE SIXTEEN	Chess
April	1958	JOHNNY B. GOODE	Chess
June	1958	REELIN' AND ROCKIN'	Chess
July	1958	BEAUTIFUL DELILAH	Chess
August	1958	CAROL	Chess
October	1958	MEMPHIS	Chess
November	1958	SWEET LITTLE ROCK AND ROLL	Chess
December	1958	RUN, RUDOLPH, RUN	Chess
December	1958	MERRY CHRISTMAS, BABY	Chess
January	1959	LITTLE QUEENIE	Chess
February	1959	ANTHONY BOY	Chess
April	1959	ALMOST GROWN	Chess
June	1959	BACK IN THE U.S.A.	Chess
February	1960	TOO POOPED TO POP	Chess
March	1964	NADINE	Chess
May	1964	NO PARTICULAR PLACE TO GO	Chess
August	1964	YOU NEVER CAN TELL	Chess
October	1964	LITTLE MARIE	Chess
December	1964	PROMISED LAND	Chess
April	1965	DEAR DAD	Chess
August	1972	MY DING-A-LING	Chess
December	1972	ROLLIN' AND ROCKIN'	Chess

THE BIG BOPPER

Real Name: Jape Richardson
Born: 1935
Died: February 3, 1959
Hometown: Beaumont, Texas

Jape did not like his real first name, so he abbreviated it to J.P. Richardson. He worked as a disc jockey at station KTRM in Beaumont, as well as writing many songs for his friends in the area. In fact one of the songs he wrote was for his good friend from Port Arthur, Texas, Johnny Preston, called "Running Bear." J.P. got the inspiration to write the song from a Dove soap commercial. In fact, J.P. is even heard on the record making sounds like an Indian.

J.P., who preferred to be known as the "Big Bopper," signed with Mercury records. In 1958 he recorded a song he had written called "Chantilly Lace." The record took off in August of that year and The Big Bopper became a singing star. He had to take various leaves of absence from his radio job to go on promotional tours. It was on one such leave that he, along with Buddy Holly and Ritchie Valens, chartered a Beechcraft Bonanza to take them to Fargo, North Dakota, after finishing an

THE BIG BOPPER

engagement in Clear Lake, Iowa. The plane took off into the snowy darkness on the morning of February 3, 1959, only to crash in a field a few miles from the airport. All the passengers on the plane were killed.

August	1958	CHANTILLY LACE		Mercury
December	1958	LITTLE RED RIDING HOOD		Mercury
December	1958	BIG BOPPER'S WEDDING		Mercury

ACKER BILK

Hometown: Somerset, England

Acker Bilk was the son of a church organist. He took up the clarinet while in the British Army. After his discharge, he became a blacksmith, but soon went back to playing a clarinet. He joined the Ken Colyer group in Britain for several years. In 1958, he formed his own group called The Paramount Jazz Band. In late 1961, he recorded a song, "Stranger on the Shore," that not only became a top record in Europe, but when it was

ACKER BILK

released by Atco records in the United States in March 1962, eventually became the number one song for the entire year.

March	1962	STRANGER ON THE SHORE	Atco
July	1962	ABOVE THE STARS	Atco
December	1962	LIMELIGHT	Atco
February	1963	ONLY YOU	Atco

BILLY JOE & THE CHECKMATES

In late 1961 Billy Joe wrote "Percolator" in which a xylophone created the novel sound of coffee perking. When the song was released in early 1962 it was subtitled "Percolator (Twist)" because of its dance beat which was easily adaptable to the biggest craze of the time—the Twist.

January	1962	PERCOLATOR (TWIST)	Dore

BILLY & LILLIE

Real Names:
    Billy Ford—March 9, 1925—Bloomfield, New Jersey
    Lillie Bryant—February 14, 1940—Newburg, New York

Billy credits his success to two valuable years with Cootie Williams singing in vocal groups and collaborating with other writers. Ford left Williams to form his own group, The Thunderbirds, a group of seven, which featured comedy, choreography, and vocals. The group appeared in spots like The Hollywood Brown Derby and New York's Paramount theater. Lillie Bryant, the youngest member of the group, became his singing partner in 1957. That same year, they signed a recording contract with Swan records of Philadelphia, and recorded a cha-cha number called "La Dee Dah," which went straight up the charts in January of 1958.

Today Billy has a group called The Billy Ford Thunderbirds, which plays the New York area. Lillie lives in Newberg with her six children, where she is an assistant housing manager and an N.A.A.C.P. advisor.

December	1957	LA DEE DAH	Swan
April	1958	HAPPINESS	Swan
December	1958	LUCKY LADYBUG	Swan
July	1959	BELLS, BELLS, BELLS	Swan

BILLY FORD'S THUNDERBIRDS

Center front: Billy Ford and Lillie Bryant
Rear, left to right: Freddy Pinkard, Frisco Bombay,
Alma Fortez, Jimmy Holmes, Frederick "Money" Johnson

BILL BLACK

Born: September 17, 1926
Died: October 21, 1965
Hometown: Memphis, Tennessee

Bill was an original member of Elvis's trio, which consisted of Scotty Moore on guitar, D. J. Fontanna on drums, with Bill on bass. He backed up Elvis on his early hits on Sun records and RCA.

Leaving Elvis, Bill formed The Bill Black Combo in 1959, and was signed to Hi records. In December of 1959, he released the first of many hit records, called "Smokie—Part 2."

December	1959	SMOKIE—Part 2	Hi
February	1960	WHITE SILVER SANDS	Hi
June	1960	JOSEPHINE	Hi
September	1960	DON'T BE CRUEL	Hi
November	1960	BLUE TANGO	Hi
February	1961	HEARTS OF STONE	Hi
June	1961	OLE BUTTERMILK SKY	Hi
September	1961	MOVIN'	Hi
December	1961	TWIST-HER	Hi
May	1962	TWISTIN' WHITE SILVER SANDS	Hi
August	1962	SO WHAT	Hi
April	1963	DO IT-RAT NOW	Hi
October	1963	MONKEY-SHINE	Hi
January	1964	COMIN' ON	Hi
May	1964	TEQUILA	Hi
October	1964	LITTLE QUEENIE	Hi
December	1964	SO WHAT	Hi

JEANNE BLACK

Born: October 25, 1937
Hometown: Mount Baldy, California

In early 1960 C & W singer Jim Reeves had a top hit called "He'll Have to Go." Jeanne Black, who also sang C & W, had a big answer-record to Reeves's number called "He'll Have to Stay." It became one of the first answer-records. Later, Damita Jo recorded "I'll Save The Last Dance for You" in answer to the Drifters' "Save the Last Dance For Me."

May	1960	HE'LL HAVE TO STAY	Capitol
July	1960	LISA	Capitol
January	1961	OH HOW I MISS YOU TONIGHT	Capitol

BILLY BLAND

Born: April 5, 1932
Hometown: Wilmington, North Carolina

Billy began singing as a youngster throughout the South, and eventually headed for New York in the late fifties. In late 1959, he met Hy Weiss of Old Town records and was signed to a contract and in January 1960, he recorded a song that became his biggest hit, called "Let the Little Girl Dance."

January	1960	LET THE LITTLE GIRL DANCE	Old Town
July	1960	BORN TO BE LOVED	Old Town
October	1960	HARMONY	Old Town
August	1961	MY HEART'S ON FIRE	Old Town

BOBBY "BLUE" BLAND

Real Name: Robert Calvin Bland
Born: January 27, 1930
Hometown: Rosemark, Tennessee

Bobby's family moved to Memphis, where Bobby began singing. At the age of eighteen, Bobby met Billy "Red" Love, a pianist in Memphis, who taught him to sing. Rosco Gordon and B. B. King introduced Bobby to Saul Bihari of Modern records in Los Angeles, and Bobby signed a contract with them. Bobby was in the Army from 1951 until 1954. After his discharge, he signed with Duke records and began a new career with songs like "Army Blues," "Lovin' Blues," and "It's My Life."

July	1957	FARTHER UP THE ROAD	Duke
January	1960	I'LL TAKE CARE OF YOU	Duke
November	1960	CRY, CRY, CRY	Duke
February	1961	I PITY THE FOOL	Duke
August	1961	DON'T CRY NO MORE	Duke
December	1961	TURN ON YOUR LOVE LIGHT	Duke
February	1962	WHO WILL THE NEXT FOOL BE	Duke
August	1962	YIELD NOT TO TEMPTATION	Duke
September	1962	STORMY MONDAY BLUES	Duke
January	1963	CALL ON ME	Duke
January	1963	THAT'S THE WAY LOVE IS	Duke
July	1963	SOMETIMES YOU GOTTA CRY A LITTLE	Duke
December	1963	THE FEELING IS GONE	Duke
March	1964	AIN'T NOTHING YOU CAN DO	Duke
June	1964	SHARE YOUR LOVE WITH ME	Duke
October	1964	AIN'T DOING TOO BAD	Duke
January	1965	BLIND MAN	Duke
April	1965	AIN'T NO TELLING	Duke
August	1965	THESE HANDS (SMALL BUT MIGHTY)	Duke
January	1966	I'M TOO FAR GONE (TO TURN AROUND)	Duke
May	1966	GOOD TIME CHARLIE	Duke
September	1966	POVERTY	Duke
April	1967	YOU'RE ALL I NEED	Duke
March	1968	DRIFTIN' BLUES	Duke
November	1968	ROCKIN' IN THE SAME OLD BOAT	Duke

June	1969	GOTTA GET TO KNOW YOU	Duke
September	1969	CHAINS OF LOVE	Duke
February	1970	IF YOU'VE GOT A HEART	Duke
December	1970	KEEP ON LOVING ME (YOU'LL SEE THE CHANGE)	Duke
June	1971	I'M SORRY	Duke
November	1973	THIS TIME I'M GONE FOR GOOD	Dunhill
March	1974	GOIN' DOWN SLOW	Dunhill
August	1974	AIN'T NO LOVE IN THE HEART OF THE CITY	Dunhill
November	1974	I WOULDN'T TREAT A DOG (THE WAY YOU TREATED ME)	Dunhill

MARCIE BLANE

Born: May 21, 1944
Hometown: Brooklyn, New York

After she graduated from high school in June 1962, Marcie was discovered by Marv Holtzman, an A & R man from Seville records in New York. Marv had her signed to a contract, and in October 1962 she had her only hit for the label, called "Bobby's Girl."

October	1962	BOBBY'S GIRL	Seville
January	1963	WHAT DOES A GIRL DO	Seville

ARCHIE BLEYER

Born: June 12, 1909
Hometown: Corona, New York

Archie began playing the piano at the age of seven and sang in a church choir. He entered Columbia College in 1927 to be an electrical engineer, but changed his major to music during his sophomore year. He left college when he was a junior to become a musical arranger.

In 1934, Archie organized a band and began playing around the New York area. He went to Hollywood in 1938, and got a job conducting an orchestra. He returned to New York as a conductor for several Broadway shows in 1940.

Shortly after that Archie accepted a job with CBS radio as a musical conductor and began to work on the Arthur Godfrey Show in the same capacity. Archie formed his own record company in 1952 called Cadence Records, and signed Julius La Rosa as his first artist. Archie left the Godfrey Show in 1953. His label did well with hits like La Rosa's "Eh Cumpari," the Chordettes' "Mr. Sandman," and his own hits like "Hernando's Hideaway" and "The Naughty Lady of Shady Lane" in 1954.

In 1964, Archie retired from the business.

May	1954	HERNANDO'S HIDEAWAY	Cadence
November	1954	THE NAUGHTY LADY OF SHADY LANE	Cadence
June	1956	ROCKIN' GHOST	Cadence

THE BLUE BELLES

"I Sold My Heart to the Junkman" was the first and only hit for the group who later became Patti LaBelle and the Blue Belles.

April   1962   I SOLD MY HEART TO THE JUNKMAN   Newtown

THE BLUE JAYS

In the summer of 1961, the group recorded a tender love ballad called "Lover's Island." The song had the same premise as an earlier recording by the Sheppards called "Island of Love." The Blue Jays' recording was primarily successful because of lead singer Leon Peel's high falsetto.

August   1961   LOVER'S ISLAND   Milestone

THE BLUE NOTES

Members:
    Theodore Pendergrass—lead
    Harold Melvin
    Bernard Wilson
    Lawrence Brown
    Lloyd Parks
Hometown: Philadelphia, Pennsylvania

In 1959 when the members were all between twenty-one and twenty-five years old, Harold Melvin formed a group called the Blue Notes which began working in the Philadelphia area. In a short time they signed with Brooke records and had a national chart record with a song called "I Don't Know What It Is" in November of that year. After some more moderate hits they signed with Value records and had another national hit with "My Hero" in September of 1960. For a while the Blue Notes were a lounge act; then they signed to have Kenny Gamble and Leon Huff produce them in 1972. They called themselves Harold Melvin and The Blue Notes (even though Harold does not sing lead—he manages the group along with singing with them) and had Theodore Pendergrass sing lead. Theodore was a drummer with James Brown and then the Blue Notes. They started having hits like "If You Don't Know Me By Now" and "The Love I Lost" and have become a super group of today.

Teddy Pendergrass left the group in the mid-seventies and has become a major solo performer for Philadelphia International records, while Harold Melvin & The Bluenotes continue to perform and record as a group.

November	1959	I DON'T KNOW WHAT IT IS	Brooke
September	1960	MY HERO	Value
July	1972	I MISS YOU	Philadelphia International
November	1972	IF YOU DON'T KNOW ME BY NOW	Philadelphia International
March	1973	YESTERDAY I HAD THE BLUES	Philadelphia International
September	1973	THE LOVE I LOST	Philadelphia International
April	1974	SATISFACTION GUARANTEED	Philadelphia International
November	1974	WHERE ARE ALL MY FRIENDS	Philadelphia International
March	1975	BAD LUCK (Part 1)	Philadelphia International
July	1975	HOPE THAT WE CAN BE TOGETHER SOON	Philadelphia International
November	1975	WAKE UP EVERYBODY (Part 1)	Philadelphia International
April	1976	TELL THE WORLD HOW I FEEL ABOUT 'CHA BABY	Philadelphia International
February	1977	REACHING FOR THE WORLD	ABC

THE BOBBETTES

Members:
>Heather Dixon—1945
>Jannie Pought—1945
>Emma Pought—1944
>Helen Gathers—1944
>Laura Webb—1943

Hometown: New York, New York

The Bobbettes all attended P.S. 109 in New York City, and sang together as a group to entertain friends and schoolmates at parties in the mid-fifties. A neighbor-friend of the girls, James Dailey, took them under his wing and worked with them, for he thought they had great potential. At the time they began this serious attempt at singing in early 1957, all the girls in the group ranged from twelve to fourteen years old. That same year, the girls wrote a song about their principal as a gag and began to sing it everywhere they went. Finally they signed with Atlantic records. The record was released in June of 1957, and within a few months "Mr. Lee" of P.S. 109 was a nationally known figure.

July	1957	MR. LEE	Atlantic
July	1960	I SHOT MR. LEE	Triple-X
October	1960	HAVE MERCY BABY	Triple-X
October	1960	DANCE WITH ME GEORGIE	Triple-X
September	1961	I DON'T LIKE IT LIKE THAT	Gone

BOB B. SOXX & THE BLUE JEANS

Members:
>Darlene Love—lead
>Fanita James

Bobby Sheen—bass
Hometown: Los Angeles, California

In 1962, while record producer Phil Spector was on the West Coast, he was intrigued by the singing voices of Fanita James and especially Darlene Love, who were being used as background singers with a group called The Blossoms. He took the girls and added the male voice of Bobby Sheen and called the group Bob B. Soxx & The Blue Jeans. The first song that Phil had the group cut was a song, featured in a Walt Disney film *Song of the South*, called "Zip-A-Dee-Doo-Dah." Phil used Billy Strange as the solo guitarist and only a bass drum as the major instruments with a lot of redubbing. The result, in October of 1962, was a national hit on Spector's Philles records.

A few months earlier, Phil used Darlene to sing lead with the Crystals on their number one hit "He's a Rebel." It was the only time she sang with the group. In 1963, Darlene became a solo singer with "Today I Met the Boy I'm Gonna Marry" also on Philles records. Today, Darlene is a background singer for Dionne Warwicke.

October	1962	ZIP-A-DEE DOO-DAH	Philles
February	1963	WHY DO LOVERS BREAK EACH OTHERS HEARTS	Philles
June	1963	NOT TOO YOUNG TO GET MARRIED	Philles

JOHNNY BOND

Real Name: Cyrus Whitfield Bond
Born: June 1, 1915
Died: June 12, 1978, Burbank, California
Hometown: Enville, Oklahoma

Johnny's career started with a ninety-eight-cent ukelele ordered from a Montgomery Ward catalog. After finishing high school Johnny switched from the uke to the guitar and began playing various ballrooms and theaters in the Southwest. In 1940 while singing with the Jimmy Wakely trio he was discovered by Gene Autry. The group was signed to Autry's CBS radio show. Sometime later the trio broke up but Johnny remained with the show as special guitar accompanist.

Johnny had many C & W hits on Columbia records but in the summer of 1960 he had a top pop record called "Hot Rod Lincoln," a novelty song about a father whose son is driving him to drinkin' because he won't stop drivin' that hot rod Lincoln. The song became a big success a decade later for Commander Cody and His Lost Planet Airmen.

| August | 1960 | HOT ROD LINCOLN | Republic |
| March | 1965 | 10 LITTLE BOTTLES | Starday |

GARY "U.S." BONDS

GARY "U.S." BONDS

Real Name: Gary Anderson—then changed to Ulysses Samuel Bonds
Born: June 6, 1939
Hometown: Jacksonville, Florida

Gary started singing as a youngster. At three, his family moved to Norfolk, Virginia, where he lived until he was twenty-one. It was while Gary was in Norfolk that he met a man named Frank Guida who liked Gary's singing style and wanted to record him. Frank had his own label (Legrand records) and had written a song that he felt Gary would be a natural on. Frank also suggested Gary change his name to "U.S." Bonds as a gimmick. So in the fall of 1960, Gary signed with Legrand and recorded "New Orleans," which became a smash hit for him. Gary's next hit, "Quarter to Three," which was a number one song for him, was recorded accidentally. A group known as Daddy G had a song out called a "Night With Daddy G." Gary and his group played almost the identical music track, while Gary improvised some words and the group started a jam session. No one knew the tape recorder was on, and they accidently recorded Gary's biggest hit. In just a short time, it was the number one song all across the country during the summer of 1961.

Early in 1981, Bruce Springsteen worked with Gary on producing a new album called *Dedication* which resulted in the hit "This Little Girl."

October	1960	NEW ORLEANS	Legrand
May	1961	QUARTER TO THREE	Legrand
July	1961	SCHOOL IS OUT	Legrand
October	1961	SCHOOL IS IN	Legrand
January	1962	DEAR LADY TWIST	Legrand
March	1962	TWIST, TWIST SENORA	Legrand
June	1962	SEVEN-DAY WEEKEND	Legrand
August	1962	COPY CAT	Legrand
April	1981	THIS LITTLE GIRL	EMI-America
July	1981	JOLE BLON	EMI-America

THE BONNIE SISTERS

Members:
    Pat Bonnie
    Jean Bonnie
    Sylvia Bonnie
Hometown: New York, New York

All three of the Bonnie Sisters were nurses at Bellevue Hospital in New York when they decided to pursue a singing career on the side. In December of 1955, they had an audition with Rainbow records in New York. They were then signed to a contract and cut their first release called "Cry Baby." Mickey "Guitar" Baker, who would later go on and record "Love Is Strange" with Sylvia Vanderpool, used his orchestra for the recording. The girls left their jobs as nurses to pursue a career as singers. The song was released in January of 1956, and it became their only hit.

January   1956   CRY BABY   Rainbow

JAMES BOOKER

James Booker helped break the instrumental monopoly of guitars and saxophones on records with his unique organ sound on "Gonzo." The song was a top-forty number for Peacock records in the fall of 1960.

November 1960   GONZO   Peacock

BOOKER T. & THE MG'S

Members:
    Booker T. Jones—organ—November 12, 1944
    Steve Cropper—guitar—October 21, 1941
    Donald "Duck" Dunn—bass guitar—November 24, 1941
    Al Jackson—drums—November 27, 1935; died: October 1, 1975 (re-
        placed by Willie Hall)
Hometown: Memphis, Tennessee

Booker began working at Stax records in Memphis as a staff musician in 1960, since he was able to play the organ, piano, sax, guitar, and bass very well. He backed such artists as Otis Redding and Sam & Dave.

Booker then joined a combo known as The Triumphs. He stayed with them for a while, then he left to join the Mar-Keys, who had a big hit in 1961 with a song on Satellite records called "Last Night." Also in the Mar-Keys at the time were Steve Cropper and "Duck" Dunn. In early

BOOKER T. & THE MG's

Left to right: Donald "Duck" Dunn, Booker T. Jones,
Steve Cropper, Al Jackson

1962, Booker persuaded Steve and "Duck" to leave the Mar-Keys to join a group he wanted to form. They added drummer Al Jackson and called themselves The Memphis Group or simply The MG's. They established their Memphis sound with their first song for Stax records called "Green Onions," a song that Booker, Steve, and Al had written. By the fall of 1962, Booker T. & The MG's were national stars.

Booker says he was greatly influenced by his idol Ray Charles. Today Booker is a producer working with new acts. Steve and Don have worked as back-up musicians for John Belushi and Dan Aykroyd's Blues Brothers Band; Al was shot to death in Memphis, Tennessee.

August	1962	GREEN ONIONS	Stax
December	1962	JELLY BREAD	Stax
July	1963	CHINESE CHECKERS	Stax
February	1964	MO' ONIONS	Stax
August	1964	SOUL DRESSING	Stax
June	1965	BOOT-LEG	Stax
August	1966	MY SWEET POTATO	Stax
March	1967	HIP HUG-HER	Stax
August	1967	GROOVIN'	Stax
July	1968	SOUL-LIMBO	Stax
November	1968	HANG 'EM HIGH	Stax
March	1969	TIME IS TIGHT	Stax
June	1969	MRS. ROBINSON	Stax
July	1970	SOMETHING	Stax
March	1971	MELTING POT	Stax

PAT BOONE

Real Name: Charles Eugene Pat Boone
Born: June 1, 1934
Hometown: Nashville, Tennessee

Pat is a descendant of frontiersman Daniel Boone. In high school in Nashville, he was a member of the baseball, basketball, and track teams. He was president of the student body and elected the most popular boy. It was while living in Nashville that he married Western star Red Foley's daughter Shirley.

Pat went to David Lipscomb College in Nashville in the early fifties, but then transferred to North Texas State. It was while he was in Texas that he won a local talent show and was encouraged to audition for Ted Mack's Amateur Hour, which he did and won. He then went to Arthur Godfrey's Talent Scout show in 1954, and won, and became a regular on the show.

Pat's early recording career began on Republic records in Nashville, with songs like "Until You Tell Me So," but it wasn't until his good friend Hugh Cherry of WMAK radio Nashville introduced him to Randy Wood, president of Dot records, that things started to happen. Randy was impressed with Pat's voice and clean-cut image so he signed him to a recording contract. They flew to Chicago in February of 1955, and recorded his first record for Dot called "Two Hearts, Two Kisses." It wasn't until November of the same year that Pat had any success, which he found in a Fats Domino song called "Ain't that a Shame."

His white buck shoes that were his trademark were used quite accidentally. Pat wore those shoes on TV every week at the beginning, because they were the only shoes he had. When they caught on, he continued to wear them as part of his clean-cut image.

His two favorite songs are "Love Letters in the Sand" and "Speedy Gonzales."

March	1955	TWO HEARTS	Dot
June	1955	AIN'T THAT A SHAME	Dot
September	1955	AT MY FRONT DOOR	Dot
September	1955	NO OTHER ARMS	Dot
October	1955	GEE WHITTAKERS!	Dot
January	1956	TUTTI' FRUTTI	Dot
January	1956	I'LL BE HOME	Dot
April	1956	LONG TALL SALLY	Dot
May	1956	I ALMOST LOST MY MIND	Dot
September	1956	CHAINS OF LOVE	Dot
September	1956	FRIENDLY PERSUASION	Dot
December	1956	DON'T FORBID ME	Dot
December	1956	ANASTASIA	Dot
March	1957	WHY BABY WHY	Dot
March	1957	I'M WAITING JUST FOR YOU	Dot
May	1957	LOVE LETTERS IN THE SAND	Dot
May	1957	BERNARDINE	Dot
August	1957	REMEMBER YOU'RE MINE	Dot
August	1957	THERE'S A GOLD MINE IN THE SKY	Dot
October	1957	APRIL LOVE	Dot
November	1957	WHEN THE SWALLOWS COME BACK TO CAPISTRANO	Dot
February	1958	A WONDERFUL TIME UP THERE	Dot
February	1958	IT'S TOO SOON TO KNOW	Dot
April	1958	SUGAR MOON	Dot
May	1958	CHERIE, I LOVE YOU	Dot
July	1958	IF DREAMS CAME TRUE	Dot
July	1958	THAT'S HOW MUCH I LOVE YOU	Dot
September	1958	FOR MY GOOD FORTUNE	Dot
September	1958	GEE, BUT IT'S LONELY	Dot
November	1958	I'LL REMEMBER TONIGHT	Dot
January	1959	WITH THE WIND AND THE RAIN IN YOUR HAIR	Dot
January	1959	GOOD ROCKIN' TONIGHT	Dot
March	1959	FOR A PENNY	Dot
April	1959	THE WANG DANG TAFFY-APPLE TANGO	Dot
June	1959	TWIXT TWELVE AND TWENTY	Dot
September	1959	THE FOOL'S HALL OF FAME	Dot
December	1959	BEYOND THE SUNSET	Dot
February	1960	(WELCOME) NEW LOVERS	Dot
March	1960	WORDS	Dot
May	1960	WALKING THE FLOOR OVER YOU	Dot
June	1960	SPRING RAIN	Dot
August	1960	CANDY SWEET	Dot
August	1960	DELIA GONE	Dot

October	1960	DEAR JOHN	Dot
October	1960	ALABAM	Dot
January	1961	THE EXODUS SONG	Dot
May	1961	MOODY RIVER	Dot
August	1961	BIG COLD WIND	Dot
November	1961	JOHNNY WILL	Dot
January	1962	I'LL SEE YOU IN MY DREAMS	Dot
February	1962	PICTURES IN THE FIRE	Dot
May	1962	QUANDO, QUANDO, QUANDO	Dot
June	1962	SPEEDY GONZALES	Dot
September	1962	TEN LONELY GUYS	Dot
March	1963	MEDITATIONS	Dot
September	1964	BEACH GIRL	Dot
October	1966	WISH YOU WERE HERE, BUDDY	Dot

EARL BOSTIC

Born: April 25, 1920
Died: October 28, 1965

Earl was one of the great alto sax men in the early fifties when he recorded many great instrumental hits for King records.

January	1951	FLAMINGO	King
December	1951	SLEEP	King

EARL BOSTIC

JIMMY BOWEN

JIMMY BOWEN

Born: 1937
Hometown: Santa Rita, New Mexico

Jimmy's family moved to Dumas, Texas, when he was eight. It was while living in Dumas that he joined the church choir and the glee club at Dumas High. While at school he met guitarist Don Lanier, who became a close friend. They both later enrolled at West Texas State College, where they met guitarist Buddy Knox and drummer Dave Alldred. They formed their own group called The Rhythm Orchids. Jimmy played bass guitar and Don also played guitar. After graduation, several songs that Jimmy and Buddy had written together came to the attention of New York music publisher Phil Kahl. He had the boys fly to New York and record the songs for Roulette records. In January 1957 the group recorded a Bowen-Knox song called "Party Doll" for which Buddy sang the lead, and they also recorded another Bowen-Knox song called "I'm Stickin' with You," on which Jimmy sang lead. Both songs were released simultaneously and became individual hits for each of them in 1957.

Today Jimmy is head of Elektra/Asylum records' Nashville division, dealing with some of today's biggest country artists.

February	1957	I'M STICKING WITH YOU	Roulette
February	1957	EVER-LOVIN' FINGERS	Roulette
May	1957	WARM UP TO ME BABY	Roulette
July	1958	BY THE LIGHT OF THE SILVERY MOON	Roulette

JAN BRADLEY

Born: July 6, 1944
Hometown: Byhalia, Mississippi

Jan started a singing career at the age of six. Years later, in a talent show in Chicago in 1959, Don Talty spotted her singing with four fellows in a group called The Passions. At Talty's suggestion, she began studying singing, dancing and modeling.

In 1962, Jan cut her first record for Formal records called "We Girls," which went nowhere. Shortly thereafter she signed with Chess records and recorded "Mama Didn't Lie," which was a big national hit for her in early 1963.

January	1963	MAMA DIDN'T LIE	Chess
February	1965	I'M OVER YOU	Chess

BOB BRAUN

Real Name: Robert Earl Brown
Born: April 20, 1929
Hometown: Ludlow, Kentucky

Bob started, in 1957, as an emcee-singer on the "Ruth Lyon's 50-50 Club" on WLW-TV Cincinnati. He had a local hit with "Til Tomorrow." He then signed with Decca records, and in the summer of 1962 had a national hit with "Til Death Do Us Part."

Today Bob works as a talk-show host at WLW-TV in Cincinnati.

July	1962	TILL DEATH DO US PART	Decca

WALTER BRENNAN

Born: July 25, 1894
Died: September 21, 1974
Hometown: Lynn, Massachusetts

After serving in the Army during the First World War, Walter began to pursue an acting career. By 1924, he had appeared in his first motion picture. During his very successful movie career he won three academy awards for best supporting actor—*Come and Get It*, 1936; *Kentucky*, 1938; and *The Westerner*, 1940. He starred in several television series, probably best known for his role as Grandpa on "The Real McCoys."

He recorded a narrative in 1960 called "Dutchman's Gold," which became a national hit in May of that year. Two years later he signed with Liberty and recorded his biggest hit, "Old Rivers."

May	1960	DUTCHMAN'S GOLD	Dot
April	1962	OLD RIVERS	Liberty
August	1962	HOUDINI	Liberty
October	1962	MAMA SANG A SONG	Liberty

TERESA BREWER

Real Name: Theresa Breuer
Born: May 7, 1931
Hometown: Toledo, Ohio

Teresa grew up in a family with four younger brothers who had no singing talent whatsoever. At two years of age, she was entered by her mother on "The Uncle August Kiddie Show" on WSPD radio in Toledo, where she was a hit. By age seven, she became a regular on "The Major Bowes Amateur Hour" and stayed with them until she was twelve, traveling around the country.

At twelve, Teresa stopped her show biz career to finish high school. After graduation, she left for New York with her aunt, and entered a talent contest. She won first prize, which was a two-week engagement at the Latin Quarter. After that she worked various night clubs around New York's Times Square at the tender age of sixteen.

One year later, she married her first husband, Bill Monahan, who was a customer at one of the clubs she worked at. In late 1949, at the age of eighteen, she signed with Coral records and had the first of her many hits with "Music! Music! Music!" which became a number one song in early 1950. In October of 1972, she married Bob Thiele.

Teresa Brewer became the "little lady with the uniquely big voice" who became known for her happy, fun, bright songs of the early fifties. Today Teresa appears in night clubs around the country.

January	1950	MUSIC! MUSIC! MUSIC!	London
April	1950	CHOO'N GUM	London
September	1951	LONGING FOR YOU	London
September	1952	YOU'LL NEVER GET AWAY (Don Cornell)	Coral
December	1952	TILL I WALTZ AGAIN WITH YOU	Coral
October	1953	RICOCHET	Coral
February	1954	BELL BOTTOM BLUES	Coral
April	1954	JILTED	Coral
December	1954	LET ME GO, LOVER!	Coral
March	1955	PLEDGING MY LOVE	Coral

September	1955	SHOOT IT AGAIN	Coral
February	1956	A TEAR FELL	Coral
February	1956	BO WEEVIL	Coral
May	1956	A SWEET OLD FASHIONED GIRL	Coral
September	1956	I LOVE MICKEY	Coral
October	1956	MUTUAL ADMIRATION SOCIETY	Coral
March	1957	EMPTY ARMS	Coral
June	1957	TEARDROPS IN MY HEART	Coral
November	1957	YOU SEND ME	Coral
August	1958	PICKLE UP A DOODLE	Coral
October	1958	THE HULA HOOP SONG	Coral
January	1959	ONE ROSE	Coral
March	1959	HEAVENLY LOVER	Coral
February	1960	PEACE OF MIND	Coral
August	1960	ANYMORE	Coral
December	1960	HAVE YOU EVER BEEN LONELY	Coral
May	1961	MILORD	Coral

LILLIAN BRIGGS

Lillian was a former laundry-truckdriver. The late Alan Freed thought she had a tremendous stage presence and he included Lillian on the bill in many of the shows he produced in New York at this time. She would come out on stage in a skin-tight silver or gold lamé dress which she seemed to have been poured into, and then proceed to break up the audience with her trombone-playing and her singing. Her biggest hit was a vocal, "I Want You to Be My Baby," released in the fall of 1955.

September 1955	I WANT YOU TO BE MY BABY	Epic

LILLIAN BRIGGS

DONNIE BROOKS

Hometown: Dallas, Texas

Donnie began singing as a boy soprano in churches in Ventura, California. In early 1960, Herb Newman of Era records was listening to some demo records in his office and heard one of Donnie's. He called him to the studio, listened some more, then offered him a contract. By June of that year Donnie released his biggest hit, "Mission Bell."

June	1960	MISSION BELL	Era
December	1960	DOLL HOUSE	Era
March	1961	MEMPHIS	Era

THE BROTHERS FOUR

Members:
    Bob Flick—bass fiddle
    Mike Kirkland—banjo

THE BROTHERS FOUR

Left to right: John Paine, Mike Kirkland, Richard Foley, Bob Flick

John Paine—guitar
Richard Foley—bongos and cymbals
Hometown: Seattle, Washington

They met at the University of Washington in the fall of 1958, during fra-
ternity rush week. When they were pledging to join the Phi Gamma
Delta fraternity, they got together to work as an entertainment feature.
Later they started playing clubs on campus, calling themselves The
Brothers Four since they were all fraternity brothers.

Their first date was at the Colony Club in Seattle, but their big break
came when Dave Brubeck's manager saw them perform at the Hungry I
in San Francisco. He signed them to a personal management contract in
late 1959, and then got them signed to Columbia records. In February
1960, The Brothers Four released their first hit, a song written by Terry
Gilkyson (formerly with The Easy Riders, who had sung "Marianne")
called "Greenfields," which became their biggest hit for Columbia.

February	1960	GREENFIELDS	Columbia
June	1960	MY TANI	Columbia
October	1960	THE GREEN LEAVES OF SUMMER	Columbia
April	1961	FROGG	Columbia
January	1962	BLUE WATER LINE	Columbia
December	1963	HOOTENANNY SATURDAY NIGHT	Columbia

BUSTER BROWN

Born: August 11, 1914
Hometown: Criss, Georgia

Buster Brown began to sing the blues and play the harmonica at talent
shows in the South in the 1950s. He worked in clubs in Georgia and Florida, before moving north to New York in the late fifties. While appearing
at a night club in New York, he was asked by an executive from Fire
records to cut a demo record. He cut the song in December of 1959, a
contract was signed, and "Fannie Mae" went on to be a fairly big national
hit in 1960.

| January | 1960 | FANNIE MAE | Fire |
| September | 1960 | IS YOU IS OR IS YOU AIN'T MY BABY | Fire |

JAMES BROWN

Born: May 3, 1928
Hometown: Macon, Georgia

James comes from the same town as Little Richard. In the mid-fifties he
formed a group called the Famous Flames and had one of their demo

records presented to Syd Nathan, the president of King records in Cincinnati, Ohio. Syd liked James's emotional style and signed him to the label. In March of 1956, Syd's subsidiary label, Federal records, released James's first song, a tune that James had written called "Please, Please, Please," which launched the James Brown sound.

"Soul Brother Number 1," or "Mr. Dynamite," as he has been called, switched to the parent label, King records, in 1961, and then in 1968, was billed simply as James Brown. Today James records for Polydor records.

April	1956	PLEASE, PLEASE, PLEASE	Federal
November	1958	TRY ME	Federal
April	1959	I WANT YOU SO BAD	Federal
February	1960	I'LL GO CRAZY	Federal
June	1960	THINK	Federal
September	1960	THIS OLD HEART	Federal
November	1960	THE BELLS	King
March	1961	BEWILDERED	King
May	1961	I DON'T MIND	King
August	1961	BABY, YOU'RE RIGHT	King
December	1961	LOST SOMEONE	King
April	1962	NIGHT TRAIN	King
July	1962	SHOUT AND SHIMMY	King
September	1962	MASHED POTATOES U.S.A.	King
December	1962	THREE HEARTS IN A TANGLE	King
February	1963	EVERY BEAT OF MY HEART	King
April	1963	PRISONER OF LOVE	King
July	1963	THESE FOOLISH THINGS	King
October	1963	SIGNED, SEALED & DELIVERED	King
January	1964	OH BABY DON'T YOU WEEP	King
February	1964	PLEASE, PLEASE, PLEASE	King
December	1964	HAVE MERCY BABY	King
July	1965	PAPA'S GOT A BRAND NEW BAG	King
November	1965	I GOT YOU (I FEEL GOOD)	King
February	1966	I'LL GO CRAZY	King
March	1966	AIN'T THAT A GROOVE	King
April	1966	IT'S A MAN'S MAN'S MAN'S WORLD	King
July	1966	MONEY WON'T CHANGE YOU	King
October	1966	DON'T BE A DROP-OUT	King
January	1967	BRING IT UP	King
March	1967	KANSAS CITY	King
May	1967	LET YOURSELF GO	King
July	1967	COLD SWEAT	King
October	1967	GET IT TOGETHER	King
December	1967	I CAN'T STAND MYSELF	King
January	1968	THERE WAS A TIME	King
March	1968	I GOT THE FEELIN'	King
May	1968	AMERICA IS MY HOME	King
May	1968	LICKING STICK-LICKING STICK	King
July	1968	I GUESS I'LL HAVE TO CRY, CRY, CRY	King
September	1968	SAY IT LOUD—I'M BLACK & I'M PROUD	King
November	1968	GOODBY MY LOVE	King
December	1968	TIT FOR TAT	King
January	1969	GIVE IT UP OR TURNIT A LOOSE	King
April	1969	I DON'T WANT NOBODY TO GIVE ME NOTHING	King

May	1969	THE POPCORN	King
June	1969	MOTHER POPCORN (Part 1)	King
August	1969	LOWDOWN POPCORN	King
September	1969	WORLD	King
October	1969	LET A MAN COME IN AND DO THE POPCORN (Part 1)	King
November	1969	AIN'T IT FUNKY NOW	King
December	1969	LET A MAN COME IN AND DO THE POPCORN (Part 2)	King
February	1970	IT'S A NEW DAY	King
March	1970	FUNKY DRUMMER (Part 1)	King
May	1970	BROTHER RAPP (Part 1)	King
July	1970	GET UP I FEEL LIKE BEING LIKE A SEX MACHINE	King
October	1970	SUPER BAD	King
January	1971	GET UP, GET INTO IT, GET INVOLVED	King
February	1971	SOUL POWER	King
March	1971	SPINNING WHEEL	King
May	1971	I CRIED	King
June	1971	ESCAPE-ISM	People
July	1971	HOT PANTS (SHE GOT TO USE WHAT SHE GOT TO GET WHAT SHE WANTS)	People
August	1971	MAKE IT FUNKY	Polydor
October	1971	MY PART/MAKE IT FUNKY	Polydor
November	1971	I'M A GREEDY MAN	Polydor
May	1972	THERE IT IS	Polydor
June	1972	HONKY TONK	Polydor
July	1972	GOOD FOOT	Polydor
November	1972	I GOT A BAG OF MY OWN	Polydor
December	1972	WHAT MY BABY NEEDS NOW IS A LITTLE MORE LOVIN'	Polydor
January	1973	I GOT ANTS IN MY PANTS	Polydor
March	1973	DOWN AND OUT IN NEW YORK CITY	Polydor
May	1973	THINK	Polydor
August	1973	SEXY, SEXY, SEXY	Polydor
November	1973	STONED TO THE BONE	Polydor
March	1974	THE PAYBACK (Part 1)	Polydor
June	1974	MY THANG	Polydor
August	1974	PAPA DON'T TAKE NO MESS PART 1	Polydor
November	1974	FUNKY PRESIDENT (PEOPLE IT'S BAD)	Polydor
February	1975	REALITY	Polydor
May	1975	SEX MACHINE (Part 1)	Polydor
August	1976	GET UP OFFA THAT THING	Polydor
February	1977	BODY HEAT (Part 1)	Polydor

MAXINE BROWN

Hometown: Kingstree, South Carolina

Around 1960, a local group named the Manhattans (not the current group with that name) was looking for a tenor, but after hearing Maxine, they quickly changed their minds and asked her to join the group. It was while she was with the Manhattans that Maxine wrote the song that was destined to become her biggest seller, "All in My Mind."

Maxine left the Manhattans after a short time, but continued to sing for her own enjoyment while she kept her job as a medical stenographer.

But she had the "bug." One night she was asked to get up and sing one number at a club in Jamaica, Long Island. She was no more than halfway through "Misty" when the booking agent asked her to come back every weekend. It wasn't long before word of this incredible young talent spread and that small club was jammed each weekend.

Today, Maxine is still active, recording and doing club dates.

January	1961	ALL IN MY MIND	Nomar
April	1961	FUNNY	Nomar
April	1963	ASK ME	Wand
January	1964	COMING BACK TO YOU	Wand
October	1964	OH NO, NOT MY BABY	Wand
February	1965	IT'S GONNA BE ALRIGHT	Wand
July	1965	ONE STOP AT A TIME	Wand
December	1965	IF YOU GOTTA MAKE A FOOL OF SOMEBODY	Wand

NAPPY BROWN

Real Name: Napoleon Brown
Hometown: Charlotte, North Carolina

Nappy left Charlotte with a gospel group to go to Newark, New Jersey. He was heard by James Evans who took him to Herman Lubinsky's Savoy Records. In the spring of 1955 Nappy recorded his first major hit, "Don't Be Angry," written by Rose Marie McCoy. He remained with the label till the end of the fifties, during which time Rose Marie wrote most of his hits. Today, he lives in North Carolina and is still active as a recording artist.

April	1955	DON'T BE ANGRY	Savoy
July	1955	PITTER PATTER	Savoy
January	1957	LITTLE BY LITTLE	Savoy
October	1958	IT DON'T HURT NO MORE	Savoy
December	1959	I CRIED LIKE A BABY	Savoy

RUTH BROWN

Born: January 30, 1928
Hometown: Portsmouth, Virginia

Ruth was brought up to sing spirituals in her father's church. As she grew up she began to admire Billie Holiday and Ella Fitzgerald. During World War II, as a teen-ager, Ruth sang at various soldiers' clubs in Virginia. In 1948, she landed a job with Lucky Millinder's band. It was during this time that Blanche Calloway, Cab's sister, heard Ruth sing in Washington,

RUTH BROWN

at The Crystal Caverns. She was so impressed with her that she asked to
be her manager.

Blanche quickly set up an audition for Ruth at Atlantic records in
New York, along with a debut engagement at the Apollo theater in
Harlem. On her way to New York, Ruth was involved in an auto accident
and was hospitalized in Chester, Pennsylvania, for months with serious
internal injuries and two broken legs. When she finally left the hospital,
she wore leg braces and had five thousand dollars in medical bills.

Ruth went to New York and auditioned for Atlantic, and got a contract with them. Her first recording for the label was a song called "So
Long." Because of her singing style she was given the name "Miss
Rhythm." She had her first major hit for Atlantic in 1952, with a song
called "5-10-15 Hours."

It wasn't until 1957, that her fame finally spread from the R & B
charts to the pop charts with a song called "Lucky Lips," which was writ-

ten by Jerry Leiber and Mike Stoller. Today she lives in Long Island, New York, and sings occasionally at jazz festivals.

September	1949	SO LONG	Atlantic
October	1950	TEARDROPS FROM MY EYES	Atlantic
March	1951	I'LL WAIT FOR YOU	Atlantic
July	1951	I KNOW	Atlantic
April	1952	5-10-15 HOURS	Atlantic
August	1952	DADDY DADDY	Atlantic
February	1953	(MAMA) HE TREATS YOUR DAUGHTER MEAN	Atlantic
June	1953	WILD WILD YOUNG MEN	Atlantic
July	1954	OH WHAT A DREAM	Atlantic
October	1954	MAMBO BABY	Atlantic
June	1955	AS LONG AS I'M MOVING/I CAN SEE EVERYBODY'S BABY	Atlantic
September	1955	IT'S LOVE, BABY	Atlantic
February	1957	LUCKY LIPS	Atlantic
September	1958	THIS LITTLE GIRL'S GONE ROCKIN'	Atlantic
June	1959	JACK O' DIAMONDS	Atlantic
October	1959	I DON'T KNOW	Atlantic
March	1960	DON'T DECEIVE ME	Atlantic
June	1962	SHAKE A HAND	Philips

THE BROWNS

Members:
    Jim Edward Brown—March 1, 1934
    Maxine Brown—April 27, 1932
    Bonnie Brown—June 7, 1936
Hometown: Pine Bluff, Arkansas

Brother and sister Jim and Maxine started as a team when they won an amateur contest on "The Barnyard Frolics" in Little Rock. Later they appeared on the radio show "Louisiana Hayride."

Kid sister Bonnie joined the act in 1955. They eventually signed with RCA and premiered on the label with "I Take the Chance" in April of 1956. They had a series of unsuccessful records until August of 1959, when they released a number one record, "The Three Bells."

Today Maxine and Bonnie operate their own recording studio in Little Rock, Arkansas, while brother Jim Ed Brown is a very popular country and western vocalist for RCA records.

August	1959	THE THREE BELLS	RCA
November	1959	SCARLET RIBBONS	RCA
March	1960	THE OLD LAMPLIGHTER	RCA
April	1960	TEEN-EX	RCA
November	1960	SEND ME THE PILLOW YOU DREAM ON	RCA
December	1960	BLUE CHRISTMAS	RCA
April	1961	GROUND HOG	RCA

AL BROWN'S TUNETOPPERS

Al Brown—born: May 22, 1934

"The Madison" was released in the spring of 1960 on the heels of Chubby Checker's recording of "The Twist." The country was in the midst of a huge dance craze and the Madison, like its predecessor, caught on quickly.

The song was released as a two-parter. The first part of the song received the most air play and became the hit side of the record.

April   1960   THE MADISON   Amy

DAVE BRUBECK

Born: December 6, 1920
Hometown: Concord, California

Dave, the youngest of three sons, started playing the piano as a youngster. He got plenty of encouragement because his mother was one of the

DAVE BRUBECK

leading piano teachers in the San Francisco area. At college Dave became interested in classical piano and jazz.

During the Second World War, he played with the Army radio band. It was at this time that he married Lola Marie Whitlock, whom he had met in college. In 1946, Dave returned to Oakland, where he formed a jazz group known as The 8. It was at a concert of The 8 that Brubeck was first discovered by disc jockey Jimmy Lyons. In 1951, Jimmy introduced Dave and his trio to jazz audiences at the Blackhawk club.

Dave added another member in 1953, and they became known as the Dave Brubeck Quartet. By the mid-fifties, his group was described as the "most exciting jazz artists at work at the time." Dave became the most widely known jazz musician in the country as his quartet toured college campuses around the entire United States. In September 1961, the group made jazz a pop winner as well when they recorded "Take Five," which group member Paul Desmond had written for Columbia records. (Paul died May 30, 1977, of lung cancer in New York at the age of fifty-two.)

Today Dave and his wife, Lola, reside in California with their six children. He travels around the country with his three sons: Darius, who plays piano; Chris, who plays bass; and Danny, who plays drums. With Dave himself, who plays piano, they are known as Two Generations of Brubeck.

September	1961	TAKE FIVE	Columbia
December	1961	UNSQUARE DANCE	Columbia
January	1963	BOSSA NOVA U.S.A.	Columbia

ANITA BRYANT

Born: March 25, 1940
Hometown: Tulsa, Oklahoma

At age nine, Anita was the "Red Feather Girl" in Oklahoma. She studied in Oklahoma City, and made her TV debut there. Her popularity on Tulsa stations brought her to the attention of Arthur Godfrey, and she sang on his show.

In 1958, Anita became Miss Oklahoma, and was the second runner-up to Miss America. In 1959, she signed with Carlton records and released her first hit that summer, which was from the show "The Music Man," a song called "Til There Was You." The song began her professional recording career. In 1960, she married a Miami disc jockey named Bob Green.

ANITA BRYANT

Today Anita resides in Florida, separated from her husband, and has become a controversial figure because of her outspoken statements against the gay liberation movement.

July	1959	TILL THERE WAS YOU	Carlton
September	1959	SIX BOYS AND SEVEN GIRLS	Carlton
January	1960	PROMISE ME A ROSE	Carlton
April	1960	PAPER ROSES	Carlton
July	1960	IN MY LITTLE CORNER OF THE WORLD	Carlton
October	1960	ONE OF THE LUCKY ONES	Carlton
December	1960	WONDERLAND BY NIGHT	Carlton
February	1961	A TEXAN & A GIRL FROM MEXICO	Carlton
May	1961	I CAN'T DO IT BY MYSELF	Carlton
May	1964	THE WORLD OF LONELY PEOPLE	Columbia

RAY BRYANT

Ray did a cover version of Al Brown's Madison song called "Madison Time." He recorded many jazz pieces for Columbia, and his Madison number marked his first successful foray into the pop vein.

| April | 1960 | MADISON TIME | Columbia |
| September | 1967 | ODE TO BILLIE JOE | Cadet |

RUSTY BRYANT

Hometown: Columbus, Ohio

Rusty played tenor sax for many bands, including Lionel Hampton, before forming his own band in 1953. He took his band to the Carolyn Club in Columbus, whose owner, Lou Wilson, later began to manage the group. Shortly after appearing at the Carolyn Club Rusty signed with Dot records. He never took his band into a studio for a recording session; instead, he made his recordings before a live audience at the Carolyn Club. It was there in 1955 that he recorded such classics as "Pink Champagne," "Hot Fudge," "Back Street," and "All Night Long." This last song was used as an occasional theme song for Alan Freed at WINS radio in New York.

June	1955	ALL NIGHT LONG	Dot
October	1955	BACK STREET	Dot
January	1956	HOT FUDGE	Dot

BUCHANAN & GOODMAN

Members:
>   Bill Buchanan—1935
>   Dickie Goodman—April 19, 1934

Hometown: New York, New York

In June of 1956, Bill and Dickie came up with an idea to put together a novel recording, using excerpts from the songs that were popular at the time. They came up with the recording "The Flying Saucer Parts 1 & 2," which they released on their Luniverse label that summer. The result was an unbelievable response to the novel record, making it an overwhelming national hit.

The problems arose, however, with many lawsuits by the record companies whose material they used. After a long legal entanglement, they finally made an out-of-court settlement.

Today Dickie is still going strong with his novelty records, recording them under the name Dickie Goodman.

July	1956	THE FLYING SAUCER	Luniverse
November	1956	BUCHANAN & GOODMAN ON TRIAL	Luniverse
July	1957	FLYING SAUCER THE 2ND	Luinverse
December	1957	SANTA & THE SATELLITE	Luniverse

BUD & TRAVIS

Real Names:
> Bud Dashiel—born in Paris, moved to Virginia
> Travis Edmonson—Long Beach, California

After being in the Army for seven years, Bud enrolled in art school in Los Angeles and supported himself by playing various club dates with his guitar. Travis began playing the guitar and singing in college. After graduation he took to the road for three years and then went into the service for four years.

They joined forces in 1958, while Travis was appearing in San Francisco at The Hungry I and Bud was across the street at The Purple Onion. The two began appearing together after that as Bud & Travis. They signed a recording contract with Liberty records in 1960, releasing their first hit, "Ballad of The Alamo," in October of that year. It was while appearing at New York's St. Regis hotel in December of the same year that the duo split up, at the peak of their career with a hot selling record.

October	1960	BALLAD OF THE ALAMO	Liberty

SOLOMON BURKE

Born: 1935
Hometown: Philadelphia, Pennsylvania

At nine, Solomon started singing in church; by age twelve, he was known as "The Wonder-Boy Preacher" and had his own church, later on called "Solomon's Temple," from which he broadcast a weekly radio show. Mrs. Kae Williams, wife of a Philadelphia disc jockey, heard him and told her husband about him. Kae got Solomon to sign with Apollo records. In 1960, Solomon signed with Atlantic records and had a big hit for the label in the fall of 1961, with a country-flavored song, "Just Out of Reach." Today Solomon records for MGM and is very popular in England.

September	1961	JUST OUT OF REACH	Atlantic
January	1962	CRY TO ME	Atlantic
May	1962	DOWN IN THE VALLEY	Atlantic
September	1962	I REALLY DON'T WANT TO KNOW	Atlantic
April	1963	IF YOU NEED ME	Atlantic
July	1963	CAN'T NOBODY LOVE YOU	Atlantic
November	1963	YOU'RE GOOD FOR ME	Atlantic
February	1964	HE'LL HAVE TO GO	Atlantic
April	1964	GOODBYE BABY (BABY GOODBYE)	Atlantic
July	1964	EVERYBODY NEEDS SOMEBODY TO LOVE	Atlantic
October	1964	YES I DO	Atlantic
November	1964	THE PRICE	Atlantic

SOLOMON BURKE

March	1965	GOT TO GET YOU OFF MY MIND	Atlantic
May	1965	TONIGHT'S THE NIGHT	Atlantic
August	1965	SOMEONE IS WATCHING	Atlantic
November	1965	ONLY LOVE (CAN SAVE ME NOW)	Atlantic
January	1966	BABY COME ON HOME	Atlantic
April	1966	I FEEL A SIN COMING ON	Atlantic
February	1967	KEEP A LIGHT IN THE WINDOW TILL I COME HOME	Atlantic
July	1967	TAKE ME (JUST AS I AM)	Atlantic
May	1968	I WISH I KNEW	Atlantic
May	1969	PROUD MARY	Bell
May	1971	THE ELECTRONIC MAGNETISM (THAT'S HEAVY, BABY)	MGM
April	1972	LOVE'S STREET AND FOOL'S ROAD	MGM

DORSEY BURNETTE

Born: December 28, 1932
Died: August 19, 1979
Hometown: Memphis, Tennessee

Dorsey sang with his brother Johnny and friend Paul Burlison in the Johnny Burnette Trio from around 1956 until 1959. In 1959, he left the trio and signed with Era records. He had his first hit with the label in February of 1960, with "Tall Oak Tree."

Dorsey died of a heart attack in Los Angeles, California, but his name is still active with record buyers because of his son Billy who is following in his late father's footsteps as a recording artist.

DORSEY BURNETTE

| February | 1960 | TALL OAK TREE | Era |
| June | 1960 | HEY LITTLE ONE | Era |

JOHNNY BURNETTE

Born: March 25, 1934
Died: August 14, 1964
Hometown: Memphis, Tennessee

Growing up as a youngster in Memphis in the early fifties, Johnny became a golden gloves boxing champ. He always had an interest in music, which eventually led to his forming a musical trio consisting of his brother Dorsey on bass guitar and a friend of his, Paul Burlison, on electric guitar. They became known as the Johnny Burnette trio. The three played together part time and worked full time as electricians in Memphis. They worked for the same electric company that employed a schoolmate of theirs as a truckers' helper. His name was Elvis Presley.

In 1956, after playing at a few fairs, they left Memphis for New York and entered the Ted Mack competitions, where they won top honors on the shows. At this point they met Henry Jerome, who became their manager and got them a recording contract with Coral records. One of their first hits for the label, in 1956, was a song called "The Train Kept-A-Rollin'," which had moderate success.

After a few years together, the trio split up. Dorsey signed with ERA records by late 1959, and Johnny signed with Liberty records about the same time. By the summer of 1960, Johnny had his first national hit with "Dreamin'."

Although Johnny died in a fishing accident in Clear Lake, California, in 1964, his son, Rocky, is keeping the Burnette name alive with songs like the 1980 hit "Tired of Toein' The Line" for EMI-America records.

July	1960	DREAMIN'	Liberty
November	1960	YOU'RE SIXTEEN	Liberty
February	1961	LITTLE BOY SAD	Liberty
May	1961	BIG BIG WORLD	Liberty
October	1961	GOD, COUNTRY AND MY BABY	Liberty

JERRY BUTLER

Born: December 8, 1939
Hometown: Sunflower, Mississippi

As an infant, Jerry moved from Mississippi to Chicago. Later he attended trade school, majoring in restaurant management. At first he wanted to be a chef and ice sculptor.

After graduation in June 1957, Jerry met Curtis Mayfield and Sam Gooden at the Traveling Souls Spiritualistic Church. They decided to form a singing group after singing together a couple of times. They added Fred Cash to the group and called themselves The Roosters. Later in 1957, Eddie Thomas began to manage the group and called them The Impressions. At a personal appearance at a swank fashion show in Chicago, they met Mrs. Vi Muzinski who was so impressed with them that she took them to Vee Jay records, where they eventually wound up with a recording contract.

The group had one big hit in the summer of 1958, which was a song that Jerry had written called "For Your Precious Love," which was released on Vee Jay's subsidiary label, Falcon records. In June of 1958, Falcon records was changed to Abner records after Ewart Abner, the General Manager of Vee Jay, because there was a Falcon records in Texas. After the one hit, Jerry left the group to go on his own and Curtis Mayfield became the new lead voice of The Impressions.

It wasn't until November of 1960 that Jerry had his first national hit as a single artist for Vee Jay. It was "He Will Break Your Heart," a song that he cowrote with Curtis Mayfield.

**JOHNNY
BURNETTE**

Today the "Ice Man," as he is known, does occasional concerts; however, his primary interest is working with new talent.

November	1960	HE WILL BREAK YOUR HEART	Vee Jay
March	1961	FIND ANOTHER GIRL	Vee Jay
July	1961	I'M A-TELLING YOU	Vee Jay
October	1961	MOON RIVER	Vee Jay
July	1962	MAKE IT EASY ON YOURSELF	Vee Jay
October	1962	YOU CAN RUN	Vee Jay
December	1962	THEME FROM TARAS BULBA	Vee Jay
March	1963	WHATEVER YOU WANT	Vee Jay
November	1963	NEED TO BELONG	Vee Jay
April	1964	GIVING UP ON LOVE	Vee Jay
August	1964	I STAND ACCUSED	Vee Jay
March	1965	GOOD TIMES	Vee Jay
March	1966	FOR YOUR PRECIOUS LOVE	Vee Jay
January	1967	I DIG YOU BABY	Mercury
October	1967	MR. DREAM MERCHANT	Mercury
December	1967	LOST	Mercury

May	1968	NEVER GIVE YOU UP	Mercury
August	1968	HEY, WESTERN UNION MAN	Mercury
December	1968	ARE YOU HAPPY	Mercury
March	1969	ONLY THE STRONG SURVIVE	Mercury
May	1969	MOODY WOMAN	Mercury
August	1969	WHAT'S THE USE OF BREAKING UP	Mercury
November	1969	DON'T LET LOVE HANG YOU UP	Mercury
January	1970	GOT TO SEE IF I CAN'T GET MOMMY (TO COME BACK HOME)	Mercury
March	1970	I COULD WRITE A BOOK	Mercury
August	1970	WHERE ARE YOU GOING	Mercury
March	1971	IF IT'S REAL WHAT I FEEL	Mercury
July	1971	HOW DID WE LOSE IT BABY	Mercury
October	1971	WALK EASY MY SON	Mercury
September	1972	CLOSE TO YOU	Mercury
November	1972	ONE NIGHT AFFAIR	Mercury
March	1977	I WANNA DO IT TO YOU	Motown

RED BUTTONS

Real Name: Aaron Chwatt
Born: February 5, 1919
Hometown: New York, New York

Red has had an extensive career in burlesque, Broadway, and television. He has had a night club act, has done summer stock, and has appeared in a number of films, including *The Longest Day* and *Hatari*. He won an Oscar for his 1958 performance in *Sayonara*. Both of his hit records, "The Ho Ho Song" and "Strange Things Are Happening," were helped by the exposure they received on his television program in the early fifties. Today he lives with his wife, Alicia, and daughter, Amy, in Los Angeles, where he continues to make movies.

April	1953	THE HO HO SONG	Columbia
May	1953	STRANGE THINGS ARE HAPPENING	Columbia

EDWARD BYRNES

Born: July 30, 1938
Hometown: Los Angeles, California

Eddie, who played the role of Kookie on the popular TV series "77 Sunset Strip" in 1959, wound up with a hit record that year when he teamed up with Connie Stevens and recorded "Kookie Kookie (Lend Me Your Comb)" for Warner Brothers in April 1959. Recently he has been doing some TV commercials for men's styling combs.

April	1959	KOOKIE, KOOKIE (LEND ME YOUR COMB)	Warner Bros
August	1959	LIKE I LOVE YOU	Warner Bros.

THE CADETS & THE JACKS

Clockwise from top: Willie Davis, Dub Jones,
Aaron Collins, Ted Taylor, Lloyd McGraw

THE CADETS

Members:
     Aaron Collins—lead
     George Hollis—second tenor—replaced by Willie Davis
     Will "Dub" Jones—bass
     Ted Taylor—baritone
Hometown: Los Angeles, California

The group was formed in the mid-fifties and signed with Saul Bihari's
Modern records. Their first release for the label was "Don't Be Angry,"
which was moderately popular. A short time later The Cadets did a version of the Jay Hawks' "Stranded in the Jungle," which became a hit in
1956. A year prior to this hit, the group had recorded under another name,
The Jacks, (which included Lloyd McGraw) and had a hit on RPM records (owned by Modern records), called "Why Don't You Write Me."

    When the group disbanded a short time later, bass singer Will Jones
went on to sing with The Coasters on most of their major hits, while lead
singer Aaron Collins, whose sisters Betty and Rosie were the original

Teen Queens of "Eddie My Love" fame, went on to form The Flares with George Hollis and a few others, and had a hit in 1961, called "Foot Stomping Part 1."

June   1956   STRANDED IN THE JUNGLE   Modern

THE CADILLACS

Members:
> Earl Carroll—lead—born: November 2, 1937
> Robert Phillips—1935
> Laverne Drake—1938
> Gus Willingham—replaced by Charles Brooks—1937
> Papa Clark—replaced by Earl Wade—1937

Hometown: New York, New York

Earl, Laverne, and Robert, with Gus Willingham first formed the singing group in Harlem in 1953 and called themselves the Carnations. After practicing for a year, they went downtown to audition for a writer named Esther Navarro, who was also a manager and musical arranger. She liked the sound of the group and signed them to a personal recording contract. She had them change the name of the group to the Cadillacs, after the automobile, because there were too many groups with the names of birds at the time.

The group added another singer at this time known as Papa Clark, and in 1954, Esther took them to Beltone studios in New York and had them record four songs. With Rene Hall's band backing them, they recorded "I Wonder Why," "Gloria," "Wishing Well," and "I Want to Know About Love." "Gloria" became the most famous of these songs, a ballad that Esther had written about Gloria Smith, a singer she was managing at the time.

Esther took the recordings to Jerry Blaine of Jubilee records, who released "I Wonder Why" and "Gloria" on his Josie label. At this time Gus and Papa left the group and were replaced by Charles Brooks and Earl Wade.

Esther had the fellows work up a stage presentation. She also made sure that they wore flashy outfits that would make them a visual act. This idea set the trend for many other groups in the years to follow.

In late 1955, Esther wrote a song about the group's lead singer, Earl Carroll, whom everyone called "Speedo." The line that began the famous song was "Everybody calls me Speedo but my real name is Mr. Earl." The song "Speedo" turned out to be the group's biggest hit.

THE CADILLACS
Top: Earl Carroll
Left to right: Earl Wade, Robert Phillips,
Charles Brooks, Laverne Drake

In 1958, Earl Carroll left the group for good, to join the Coasters, with whom he is currently singing. He lives in New York.

June	1954	GLORIA/I WONDER WHY	Josie
October	1955	SPEEDO	Josie
January	1956	ZOOM	Josie
March	1956	WOE IS ME	Josie
December	1956	RUDOLPH THE RED-NOSED REINDEER	Josie
March	1957	MY GIRL FRIEND	Josie
November	1958	PEEK-A-BOO	Josie
January	1959	JAY WALKER	Josie
March	1959	PLEASE MR. JOHNSON	Josie

AL CAIOLA

Born: September 7, 1920
Hometown: Jersey City, New Jersey

Al began as a studio musician, and he worked at United Artists as a musical arranger and conductor. In late 1960 he recorded "The Magnificent Seven," the theme from the movie of that name, and the song became a national chart hit. Shortly, after that he recorded the theme from the popular TV series "Bonanza" and this song also became a hit.

| November | 1960 | THE MAGNIFICENT SEVEN | United Artists |
| April | 1961 | BONANZA | United Artists |

GLEN CAMPBELL

Born: March 22, 1936
Hometown: Delight, Arkansas

Glen was a very popular studio musician in the late fifties and early sixties and played with many different groups at different sessions. In October of 1961, he recorded a song that Jerry Capehart (writer of many of Eddie Cochran's hits including "Summertime Blues") had written, called "Turn Around, Look At Me," for Crest records. It was a mild hit. (The same song became a big hit for the Vogues in the late sixties.) In 1962, Glen signed with Capitol and premiered with "Too Late to Worry, Too Blue to Cry" in August of that year.

It wasn't until Glen got together with songwriter Jimmy Webb that things started to happen. Glen recorded one of Jimmy's songs called "By the Time I Get to Phoenix" in October 1967. It was a very big hit for him and it moved his career into high gear.

Today Glen is a major draw in Las Vegas.

November	1961	TURN AROUND, LOOK AT ME	Crest
August	1962	TOO LATE TO WORRY, TOO BLUE TO CRY	Capitol
September	1965	UNIVERSAL SOLDIER	Capitol
July	1967	GENTLE ON MY MIND	Capitol
October	1967	BY THE TIME I GET TO PHOENIX	Capitol
January	1968	HEY LITTLE ONE	Capitol
April	1968	I WANNA LIVE	Capitol
July	1968	DREAMS OF THE EVERYDAY HOUSEWIFE	Capitol
September	1968	GENTLE ON MY MIND	Capitol
November	1968	WICHITA LINEMAN	Capitol
March	1969	GALVESTON	Capitol
May	1969	WHERE'S THE PLAYGROUND SUSIE	Capitol
July	1969	TRUE GRIT	Capitol
October	1969	TRY A LITTLE KINDNESS	Capitol

January	1970	HONEY COME BACK	Capitol
April	1970	OH HAPPY DAY	Capitol
July	1970	EVERYTHING A MAN COULD EVER NEED	Capitol
September	1970	IT'S ONLY MAKE BELIEVE	Capitol
March	1971	DREAM BABY (HOW LONG MUST I DREAM)	Capitol
June	1971	THE LAST TIME I SAW HER	Capitol
March	1973	I KNEW JESUS (BEFORE HE WAS A STAR)	Capitol
February	1974	HOUSTON (I'M COMIN' TO SEE YOU)	Capitol
May	1975	RHINESTONE COWBOY	Capitol
November	1975	COUNTRY BOY	Capitol
March	1976	DON'T PULL YOUR LOVE / THEN YOU CAN TELL ME GOODBYE	Capitol
February	1977	SOUTHERN NIGHTS	Capitol
July	1977	SUNFLOWER	Capitol
October	1978	CAN YOU FOOL	Capitol
May	1980	SOMETHIN' BOUT YOU BABY I LIKE (with Rita Coolidge)	Capitol
January	1981	I DON'T WANT TO KNOW YOUR NAME	Capitol
August	1981	I LOVE MY TRUCK	Mirage

JO-ANN CAMPBELL

Born: July 20, 1938
Hometown: Jacksonville, Florida

Jo-Ann was a drum majorette at Fletcher High School in Jacksonville. At sixteen, she traveled through Europe with the USO as a dancer. When she came to New York in the mid-fifties, she decided to quit dancing and try her luck at singing. She was a smash success at New York's Apollo in Harlem. This led to a recording contract with Eldorado records, where she recorded a song she wrote called "Come On Baby" in January of 1957. She then went to Gone records where she premiered with "Wait A

JO-ANN CAMPBELL

Minute" in December of 1957. Her biggest hit, "Kookie Little Paradise," was with ABC records in the fall of 1960.

Today Jo-Ann lives with her husband, Troy Seals (a record producer for Atlantic records), in Hendersonville, Tennessee. These days she does not do any singing.

August	1960	KOOKIE LITTLE PARADISE	ABC
August	1962	I'M THE GIRL FROM WOLVERTON MOUNTAIN	Cameo
April	1963	MOTHER, PLEASE	Cameo

ACE CANNON

Born: May 5, 1934
Hometown: Grenada, Mississippi

Ace began playing the alto sax at age ten and continued playing through high school. After dropping out of college, he began playing night clubs in the South. In 1959, Ace joined a combo that began touring the country and appearing on national TV. In late 1961, he formed his own group and eventually signed with Hi records. He recorded one of his own compositions called "Tuff," and it became a hit in early 1962.

November	1961	TUFF	Hi
April	1962	BLUES STAY AWAY FROM ME	Hi
June	1963	COTTONFIELDS	Hi
February	1964	SEARCHIN'	Hi

FREDDY CANNON

Real Name: Fredrick Anthony Picariello
Born: December 4, 1940
Hometown: Revere, Massachusetts

Freddy started singing in 1957 in Lynn, Massachusetts, and eventually formed his own group. Jack McDermott, a disc jockey in Boston, saw Freddy perform and encouraged him to pursue a recording career. While working as a truck driver, Freddy recorded a song that his mother had written called "Tallahassee Lassie." The tape was sent to Swan records in Philadelphia. Frank Slay and Bob Crewe worked with the raw tape and added some things to it. The records were sent to Freddy who took them to disc jockey Arnie Ginsberg of station WMEX in Boston. Arnie played the records that afternoon, and the response was unbelievable. Freddy immediately quit his job as a truck driver and began to pursue his new

FREDDY CANNON

career. The song became a smash in May of 1959, and established the Freddy Cannon sound.

Everyone started calling him "Boom Boom" because of his driving beat, the "whoos" that he would yell in the records, and because his last name was Cannon. He stayed with Swan until the end of 1963, after which he signed with Warner Brothers and had his first hit for them in February of 1964, called "Abigail Beecher."

Freddy has teamed up with The Belmonts, of Dion & The Belmonts fame, and has embarked on a brand new recording career.

May	1959	TALLAHASSEE LASSIE	Swan
August	1959	OKEFENOKEE	Swan
November	1959	WAY DOWN YONDER IN NEW ORLEANS	Swan
January	1960	CHATTANOOGA SHOE SHINE BOY	Swan
May	1960	JUMP OVER	Swan
July	1960	HAPPY SHADES OF BLUE	Swan
October	1960	HUMDINGER	Swan
January	1961	THE MUSKRAT RAMBLE	Swan
April	1961	BUZZ BUZZ A-DIDDLE-IT	Swan
August	1961	TRANSISTOR SISTER	Swan
October	1961	FOR ME AND MY GAL	Swan
February	1962	TEEN QUEEN OF THE WEEK	Swan
May	1962	PALISADES PARK	Swan
September	1962	WHAT'S GONNA HAPPEN WHEN SUMMER'S GONE	Swan
November	1962	IF YOU WERE A ROCK & ROLL RECORD	Swan

May	1963	PATTY BABY	Swan
August	1963	EVERYBODY MONKEY	Swan
February	1964	ABIGAIL BEECHER	Warner Bros.
August	1965	ACTION	Warner Bros.
February	1966	THE DEDICATION SONG	Warner Bros.

WITH THE BELMONTS

September 1981	LET'S PUT THE FUN BACK IN ROCK'N'ROLL	MIA Sound

THE CAPRIS

Members:
> Nick Santo—real name: Santamaria—lead—1941
> Mike Miniceli—first tenor—1941
> Frank Reina—second tenor—1940
> Vin Naccarato—baritone—1941
> John Cassese—bass—1941

Hometown: Ozone Park, New York

The Capris met while playing baseball for St. Anthony's High in New York City in 1957. They called themselves The Capris, after the Isle of Capri in Italy. They sang together for a while in the New York area in late 1960, and then met Hy Weiss of Old Town records who signed them to a recording contract. In January of 1961, they released the group's only real national hit record, "There's a Moon Out Tonight."

Today the fellows live around the New York city area, with Mike being the only original member to be singing with a group called the Capris. Lead singer Nick Santo (Santamaria) is a policeman in New York City.

January	1961	THERE'S A MOON OUT TONIGHT	Old Town
March	1961	WHERE I FELL IN LOVE	Old Town
September	1961	GIRL IN MY DREAMS	Old Town

THE CARAVELLES

Members:
> Andrea Simpson—1946
> Lois Wilkinson—1944

Hometown: London, England

Until April of 1963, the two girls worked for an English brokerage firm. While they were performing at an office party, they were encouraged to turn professional. They began to rehearse evenings and eventually made a home recording of a song, which they took to B.P.R. records in London. The record became a hit in England, and was released on the Smash label in the United States in November of 1963. Their recording of "You Don't Have to be a Baby to Cry" made the two girls a worldwide success.

They chose their name, the Caravelles, after the famous French jet airliner.

| November | 1963 | YOU DON'T HAVE TO BE A BABY TO CRY | Smash |
| February | 1964 | HAVE YOU EVER BEEN LONELY | Smash |

CATHY CARR

Born: June 28, 1936

In the mid-fifties Jo Stafford, Kay Starr, Patti Page, and Gail Storm had many hits with the major recording companies. Cathy, however, recorded for the less well-known Fraternity Records in Cincinnati. Her biggest hit was the ballad "Ivory Tower," which was released in February 1956.

February	1956	IVORY TOWER	Fraternity
July	1956	HEART HIDEAWAY	Fraternity
January	1959	FIRST ANNIVERSARY	Roulette

JOE "FINGERS" CARR

Real Name: Lou Busch
Born: 1910
Hometown: Louisville, Kentucky

In the late forties Joe worked as arranger for Capitol artists like Kay Starr and Dean Martin. With his piano he created a ragtime honky-tonk sound, which produced a number of successful releases including "Sam's Song."

June	1950	SAM'S SONG	Capitol
October	1951	DOWN YONDER	Capitol
May	1956	PORTUGESE WASHERWOMEN	Capitol

ANDREA CARROLL

Real Name: Andrea Lee DeCapite
Born: October 3, 1946
Hometown: Cleveland, Ohio

At age three, she made her first appearance at The Alpine Village in Cleveland. From there she eventually won titles of Little Miss Cleveland and Little Miss Ohio. In 1954, she won the Cleveland News Star Night

Contest, which was judged by Perry Como, Patti Page, and Nat "King" Cole. A year later she won the Walt Disney National Talent Contest. She then became a regular on local TV's "Gene Carroll Show" from 1959 until 1961.

At fourteen, Andrea signed with Epic records and had local hits "Young And Lonely" and "Please Don't Talk to the Lifeguard" in July 1961. Her only real national hit came in the summer of 1963, when she recorded "It Hurts to Be Sixteen" for Big Top records.

July	1961	PLEASE DON'T TALK TO THE LIFEGUARD	Epic
July	1963	IT HURTS TO BE SIXTEEN	Big Top

DAVID CARROLL

Born: October 15, 1913
Hometown: Chicago, Illinois

David signed with Mercury records in Chicago in the early fifties as an arranger-conductor. He was the one who backed up and arranged most of the hits on Mercury during this period for artists like the Crew Cuts, The Diamonds, Georgia Gibbs, The Gaylords and others. In late 1954, David had a hit of his own, the instrumental record, "Melody of Love."

December	1954	MELODY OF LOVE	Mercury
October	1955	IT'S ALMOST TOMORROW	Mercury
February	1957	THE SHIP THAT NEVER SAILED	Mercury
August	1957	FASCINATION	Mercury
February	1962	THE WHITE ROSE OF ATHENS	Mercury

KIT CARSON

Kit had only one major hit during his recording career. Unfortunately for him, Don Cherry recorded the song "Band of Gold" for Columbia and Don's version became the bigger of the two.

September 1955	BAND OF GOLD	Capitol

MINDY CARSON

Born: July 16, 1927
Hometown: New York, New York

After high school Mindy got a job as a secretary in a candy company and worked her way up to be an assistant sales manager. During the mid-forties, while on vacation in Florida, she visited a small night club in Miami, where she was invited to sing with the band. She did, was a hit, and the club owner offered her a job. When she returned to New York, she considered singing professionally and met Eddie Joy, manager of a music publishing firm. Eddie signed her to a management contract

By 1946, Mindy became a featured vocalist on Paul Whiteman's radio show "Stairway to the Stars." In July 1949, she had star billing at New Yorks' Copacabana at only twenty-two. Shortly after that she married Eddie Joy, got a contract to star on NBC network radio, and signed with RCA Victor by 1950. She had a number of chart records during the early fifties.

March	1950	CANDY AND CAKE	RCA Victor
April	1950	MY FOOLISH HEART	RCA Victor
August	1955	WAKE THE TOWN AND TELL THE PEOPLE	RCA Victor

MEL CARTER

Born: April 22, 1943
Hometown: Cincinnati, Ohio

Mel's singing career began at age four. By sixteen, he was performing with Lionel Hampton and Jimmy Scott and Paul Gayton's band. While in the service he joined the Robert Anderson singers and won a scholarship to the Cincinnati Conservatory of Music. He then became the leading soloist and the assistant director of the greater Cincinnati youth and young adult choral union.

In 1957, Mel won the award as the nation's top choral tenor. In 1959, he formed his own gospel group, The Carvetts. He moved to California in 1960, where he began performing at various clubs. Three years later he signed with Derby records and had his first national hit, "When a Boy Falls in Love." He signed with Imperial records in 1965, and had his first of many hits with them, called "Hold Me, Thrill Me, Kiss Me."

Today Mel lives on the West Coast and records for Romar records. He is being produced by Bob Marcucci, former owner of Chancellor records and former manager of Frankie Avalon.

June	1963	WHEN A BOY FALLS IN LOVE	Derby
June	1965	HOLD ME, THRILL ME, KISS ME	Imperial
October	1965	ALL OF A SUDDEN MY HEART SINGS	Imperial
January	1966	LOVE IS ALL WE NEED	Imperial
March	1966	BAND OF GOLD	Imperial
July	1966	YOU YOU YOU	Imperial
October	1966	TAKE GOOD CARE OF HER	Imperial

THE CASCADES

Members:
  John Gummoe
  Eddie Snyder
  Dave Stevens
  Dave Wilson
  Dave Zabo
Hometown: San Diego, California

In late 1962, while The Cascades were playing at a club in San Diego called The Peppermint Stick, an executive from Warner Brothers heard them and liked the group well enough to want to audition them for the label. They signed with Valiant records, a subsidiary of Warner Brothers, and released their first and only real hit with the label in January of 1963, called "Rhythm of the Rain," a song John Gummoe had written.

January	1963	RHYTHM OF THE RAIN	Valiant
May	1963	THE LAST LEAF	Valiant
December	1963	FOR YOUR SWEET LOVE	RCA

JOHNNY CASH

Born: February 26, 1932
Hometown: Kingsland, Arkansas

Johnny grew up on a farm where he began singing and writing songs in between his chores. During high school he sang at radio station KLCN in Blytheville, Arkansas.

In 1955, following Johnny's discharge from the Air Force, he got a job working in Memphis as a salesman. At this time he met guitarist Luther Perkins and bass player Marshall Grant, and Johnny formed the "Tennessee Two." They went to see Sam Phillips, the president of Sun records in Memphis, for an audition. He recorded Johnny's group doing a song Johnny wrote called "Cry, Cry, Cry." It was released and became a hit in the South. In the fall of 1956, Johnny had his first major hit for Sun records with "I Walk the Line."

After a string of hits for Sun, Johnny signed with Columbia records in 1958, and began another long and successful career, which has included many hits with his wife, June Carter.

Although Johnny still does concerts and recordings, he is more involved with watching the development of the recording career of his daughter Rosanne.

| September | 1956 | I WALK THE LINE | Sun |
| June | 1957 | NEXT IN LINE | Sun |

JOHNNY CASH

October	1957	HOME OF THE BLUES	Sun
January	1958	BALLAD OF A TEENAGE QUEEN	Sun
May	1958	GUESS THINGS HAPPEN THAT WAY	Sun
August	1958	THE WAYS OF A WOMAN IN LOVE	Sun
December	1958	IT'S JUST ABOUT TIME	Sun
July	1959	KATY TOO	Sun
February	1960	STRAIGHT A's IN LOVE	Sun
July	1960	DOWN THE STREET TO 301	Sun
January	1961	OH LONESOME ME	Sun
October	1969	GET RHYTHM	Sun
October	1958	ALL OVER AGAIN/WHAT DO I CARE	Columbia
October	1958	WHAT DO I CARE	Columbia
January	1959	DON'T TAKE YOUR GUNS TO TOWN	Columbia
April	1959	FRANKIE'S MAN, JOHNNY	Columbia
August	1959	I GOT STRIPES	Columbia
December	1959	THE LITTLE DRUMMER BOY	Columbia
July	1960	SECOND HONEYMOON	Columbia
November	1961	TENNESSEE FLAT-TOP BOX	Columbia
September	1962	BONANZA	Columbia
May	1963	RING OF FIRE	Columbia
October	1963	THE MATADOR	Columbia
February	1964	UNDERSTAND YOUR MAN	Columbia
October	1964	IT AIN'T ME BABE	Columbia
February	1965	ORANGE BLOSSOM SPECIAL	Columbia
February	1966	THE ONE ON THE RIGHT IS ON THE LEFT	Columbia
July	1966	EVERYBODY LOVES A NUT	Columbia
January	1968	ROSANNA'S GOING WILD	Columbia
May	1968	FOLSOM PRISON BLUES	Columbia
December	1968	DADDY SANG BASS	Columbia
July	1969	A BOY NAMED SUE	Columbia
November	1969	BLISTERED/SEE RUBY FALL	Columbia
April	1970	WHAT IS TRUTH	Columbia
August	1970	SUNDAY MORNING COMING DOWN	Columbia
December	1970	FLESH AND BLOOD	Columbia
March	1971	MAN IN BLACK	Columbia
April	1976	ONE PIECE AT A TIME	Columbia

THE CASTELLS

Members:
> Bob Ussery—Santa Rosa, California
> Tom Hicks—Santa Rosa, California
> Chuck Girard—Santa Rosa, California
> Joe Kelly—Petaluma, California

The group originally started with three members in November of 1958. Bob Ussery was added to the group in February of 1959. Joe Kelly joined the group that same summer after one of the other members left.

   While singing in the Santa Rosa area they met disc jockey Dan Dillon, who asked the group to cut a demo record. Dillon took the record to Herb Newman of Era records and the group got a contract with the label. Their first record, "Little Sad Eyes," was only a local hit. Their first national hit came in the summer of 1961, with the song "Sacred."

May	1961	SACRED	Era
October	1961	MAKE BELIEVE WEDDING	Era
April	1962	SO THIS IS LOVE	Era
August	1962	OH WHAT IT SEEMED TO BE	Era

THE CASUALS

Members:
> Gary Mears—lead vocals
> Jay Joe Adams
> Paul Kearney
Hometown: Dallas, Texas

In one of those strange stories of music history, The Casuals found themselves with one-half a hit record. They came from the New York area and their version of "So Tough" was a hit on the East Coast at the same time the Kuf-Linx were making the song popular on the West Coast.

| January | 1958 | SO TOUGH | Back Beat |

GEORGE CATES

Born: October 19, 1911
Hometown: New York, New York

Motion picture music became very popular in the mid-fifties—"Unchained Melody" from the film *Unchained*, "Love Is a Many Splendored Thing" from the film of the same name, and "Rock Around the Clock" from *Blackboard Jungle*. George Cates, a musical conducter for Coral records, recorded the song, "Moonglow" from the picture *Picnic*, and it was a big hit in 1956. The lyrics of the song were written by TV personality Steve Allen.

| March | 1956 | MOONGLOW & THEME FROM PICNIC | Coral |
| September | 1956 | WHERE THERE'S LIFE | Coral |

CATHY JEAN & THE ROOMMATES

This group from the New York City area recorded "Please Love Me Forever." Their high, shrill harmony resembled an earlier song called "Angel Baby," which was recorded by Rosie and the Originals. "Please Love Me Forever" became a top-ten hit in early 1961.

| February | 1961 | PLEASE LOVE ME FOREVER | Valmor |

THE CELLOS

Members:
    Robert Thomas
    Cliff Williams
    Alton Campbell
    William Montgomery
    Alvin Williams
Hometown: Jamaica, Queens, New York

The Cellos started singing while attending the Charles Evans Hughes High School in New York City. They got a recording contract with Apollo records in 1957. In April of that year they recorded their only hit for the label called "Rang Tang Ding Dong."

| May | 1957 | RANG TANG DING DONG | Apollo |

RICHARD CHAMBERLAIN

Real Name: George Richard Chamberlain
Born: March 31, 1935
Hometown: Los Angeles, California

Actor Richard Chamberlain, the star of the popular TV show of the early sixties called "Dr. Kildare," pursued a singing career in May 1962. The theme song of the show, "Theme from Dr. Kildare," became a hit on MGM for him.

Today he is a serious actor doing movies and TV.

May	1962	THEME FROM DR. KILDARE	MGM
October	1962	LOVE ME TENDER	MGM
February	1963	ALL I HAVE TO DO IS DREAM	MGM
February	1963	HI-LILI, HI-LO	MGM
July	1963	I WILL LOVE YOU	MGM
September	1963	BLUE GUITAR	MGM

THE CHAMPS

Members:

> Dave Burgess—lead guitar—Lancaster, California
> Dale Norris—guitar—Springfield, Mississippi
> Chuck Rio—sax—replaced by Jimmy Seals—Rankin, Texas
> Ben Norman—bass guitar—replaced by Bobby Morris—Tulsa, Oklahoma
> Gen Alden—drums—replaced by Dash Crofts—Cisco, Texas

Dave, Dale, Chuck, Ben, and Gen originally formed the group and played around the West Coast area in the late fifties. In late 1957, they signed with Challenge records and recorded one of sax player Chuck Rio's compositions called "Tequila," which became a number one record for the group in early 1958. After the group's second hit, "El Rancho Rock," Chuck Rio left the group to go on his own.

Of the group, Jimmy Seals and Dash Crofts have become superstars today, recording as the popular duo Seals and Crofts.

January	1958	TEQUILA	Challenge
May	1958	EL RANCHO ROCK	Challenge
October	1958	CHARIOT ROCK	Challenge
January	1960	TOO MUCH TEQUILA	Challenge
February	1962	TEQUILA TWIST	Challenge
May	1962	LIMBO ROCK	Challenge
October	1962	LIMBO DANCE	Challenge

GENE CHANDLER

Real Name: Eugene Dixon
Born: July 6, 1937
Hometown: Chicago, Illinois

As a youngster growing up in Chicago, Gene admired a group from his town called The Spaniels, especially their lead singer "Pookey" Hudson.

Gene's professional career began in 1960, when Mrs. Bruce Williams heard him sing and signed him to a contract. She then took him to Bill Sheppard, a Chicago talent agent, who got him a recording contract with Nat records singing with The Du-Kays.

At a recording session in late 1961 in Chicago, the group cut a song called "Nite Owl" and a song that Gene had cowritten with two of his friends called "Duke of Earl." Calvin Carter of Vee Jay records flipped over Gene's singing style, and he persuaded Gene to leave the group and go on as a single artist on Vee Jay records. Gene listened to him, and by early 1962 he had a number one song with "Duke of Earl." It turned out to be the only real hit he had with the label.

Gene came back with another top hit during the summer of 1970, when he recorded "Groovy Situation" for Mercury.

Today he is active as a performer, while also looking to write new songs and produce young talent.

January	1962	DUKE OF EARL	Vee Jay
April	1962	WALK ON WITH THE DUKE	Vee Jay
January	1962	YOU THREW A LUCKY PUNCH	Vee Jay
January	1963	RAINBOW	Vee Jay
August	1963	MAN'S TEMPTATION	Vee Jay
April	1964	SOUL HOOTENANNY	Constellation
July	1964	JUST BE TRUE	Constellation
September	1964	BLESS OUR LOVE	Constellation
December	1964	WHAT NOW	Constellation
April	1965	NOTHING CAN STOP ME	Constellation
August	1965	GOOD TIMES	Constellation
November	1965	RAINBOW '65	Constellation
March	1966	I'M JUST A FOOL FOR YOU	Constellation
November	1966	I FOOLED YOU THIS TIME	Checker
May	1967	TO BE A LOVER	Checker
February	1967	GIRL DON'T CARE	Brunswick
September	1967	THERE GOES THE LOVER	Brunswick
September	1968	THERE WAS A TIME	Brunswick
July	1970	GROOVY SITUATION	Mercury
November	1970	SIMPLY CALL IT LOVE	Mercury
January	1979	GET DOWN	20th Century
October	1979	WHEN YOU'RE #1	20th Century

BRUCE CHANNEL

Hometown: Jacksonville, Texas

Bruce began singing and playing the guitar at age five. His family moved to Dallas and, while attending high school in the city, Bruce appeared on benefit shows and local gatherings.

His big break came when he went with his father to Shreveport, Louisiana for an audition with Tillman Franks for the radio show "Louisiana Hayride." He was signed for the show and remained on it for six months.

In 1961, Bruce signed with Smash records and recorded a song he had written along with a friend of his, Margaret Cobb. The song was released in January 1962 and within weeks "Hey! Baby" became a number one national hit.

In December of 1980 there was a major pop song on the charts called "Giving It Up For Your Love," which was recorded by Delbert McClinton. Delbert was the fellow who, back in 1962, played the harmonica on "Hey! Baby."

January	1962	HEY! BABY	Smash
April	1962	NUMBER ONE MAN	Smash
July	1962	COME ON BABY	Smash
February	1964	GOING BACK TO LOUISIANA	LeCam

THE CHANNELS

Members:

     Earl Lewis—lead—born February 11, 1941
     Larry Hampden—first tenor
     Billy Morris—second tenor
     Edward Doulphin—baritone
     Clifton Wright—bass
Hometown: New York, New York

In 1956, Billy, Edward, and Larry were singing with two other fellows as the Channels. When the two members left, Earl and Clifton, who had just left a group called the Latharios, joined the Channels. In the summer of 1956, they recorded the song "The Closer You Are" for Whirlin' Disc records and it became the first major hit for the group, featuring Earl's unique high falsetto lead.

Earl still resides in New York, and sings with a new group of Channels consisting of John Fernandez, Jack Brown, and John Felix.

July	1956	THE CLOSER YOU ARE	Whirlin Disc
September	1956	THE GLEAM IN YOUR EYE	Whirlin Disc
April	1957	THAT'S MY DESIRE	Gone
September	1957	BYE BYE BABY	Fire
April	1959	MY LOVE WILL NEVER DIE	Fury

THE CHANTAYS

Members:

     Brian Carman—1946
     Bob Marshall—1945

EARL LEWIS & THE CHANNELS

Clockwise from top: Larry Hampden, Billy Morris,
Edward Doulphin, Cliff Wright, Earl Lewis

> Warren Waters—1944
> Bob Spickard—1946
> Bob Welch—1946
Hometown: Santa Ana, California

The group was formed in 1961, when they were all attending Santa Ana High in California. In early 1963, Bill and Jack Wenzel heard the fellows playing a song that Bob Spickard and Brian Carman had written called "Pipeline." They liked the song so much that they signed the fellows to record the song for their local label called Downey records. The record became such a big local hit that Randy Wood of Dot records decided to buy the master recording and release it on his label. It was released in March 1963, and became the group's only national hit.

March   1963   PIPELINE   Dot

THE CHANTELS

Left to right: Arlene Smith, Lois Harris,
Reene Minus, Sonia Goring, Jackie Landry

THE CHANTELS

Members:
  Arlene Smith—lead—born: October 5, 1941
  Sonia Goring—1940
  Lois Harris—1940
  Jackie Landry—1940
  Reene Minus—1943
Hometown: Bronx, New York

The girls formed the group in 1956, while singing together in the school choir at St. Anthony of Padua in the Bronx. Richard Barrett, an A & R man with Gone records, heard the girls and signed them to a contract with one of his company's affiliated labels, End records.

The Chantels' first major release was in September 1957 with "He's Gone." Their next release, which came in January 1958, established their sound nationally with "Maybe." Both of these songs were written by Arlene.

They stayed with End records for only a few years, and in 1961 signed with Carlton records. Their first release for the new label in September of that year became their biggest hit for Carlton, called "Look in My Eyes." Arlene was not with the group when they recorded for Carlton. Back in the summer of 1959, they sang with the man who discovered them, Richard Barrett & The Chantels with "Summer's Love" on Gone records.

The girls chose the name of their group from a rival basketball team, St. Francis deChantelle.

Today Arlene lives and teaches in the Bronx. Lois, Sonia, Jackie, and Reene are all married and live in the New York area. Arlene and two new girls perform as The Chantels at local rock shows.

September	1957	HE'S GONE	End
October	1957	THE PLEA	End
January	1958	MAYBE	End
March	1958	EVERY NIGHT	End
May	1958	I LOVE YOU SO	End
September	1961	LOOK IN MY EYES	Carlton
November	1961	WELL I TOLD YOU	Carlton

THE CHANTERS

Teen voices were especially popular in the fifties. The Chanters, with lead singer Larry Pendergass, Buddy Johnson, and four of their friends, emulated the "Doo-Wop" sound, the close-knit street corner harmony practiced in ghetto areas. Their big hit was "No, No, No," released by Deluxe records in 1961.

| June | 1961 | NO, NO, NO, | Deluxe |
| September | 1961 | MY DARLING | Deluxe |

JIMMY CHARLES

Born: 1942
Hometown: Paterson, New Jersey

At age eleven, Jimmy started singing in church and at civic affairs. When he was sixteen he entered the amateur contest at the Apollo theater in Harlem, where he won four straight weeks. In 1960, when Jimmy was eighteen, his uncle brought him to songwriter Phil Medley, who had just written a song that he wanted to hear Jimmy record. His rendition of the song was so good that a demo of the record was given to Promo records. They liked what they heard, signed Jimmy to a contract, and by September of 1960, he had a national hit with "A Million to One."

| August | 1960 | A MILLION TO ONE | Promo |
| December | 1960 | THE AGE FOR LOVE | Promo |

RAY CHARLES

Real Name: Ray Charles Robinson
Born: September 23, 1930
Hometown: Albany, Georgia

As a baby, Ray's family moved to Greenville, Florida. At the age of six, he was struck with an illness that left him totally blind. He then learned braille and began playing the piano when he reached his teens. He was orphaned at age fifteen in St. Augustine, Florida. By age seventeen, he organized a musical trio and traveled to Seattle.

In 1952, Ray signed with Atlantic records and recorded "Roll with My Baby." His first national hit came in 1955 with his own composition "I've Got a Woman." His biggest hit for Atlantic was in the summer of 1959 with "What'd I Say."

Ray left Atlantic for ABC records in 1960, where he went into a country-oriented sound with Hoagy Carmichael's "Georgia on My Mind" in the fall of that year, which became his first number one pop hit. It was the first of many hits he was to enjoy on ABC Paramount records.

RAY CHARLES

Today the "genius of soul" is bigger than ever and continues to attract large crowds as he travels around the country doing concerts.

He is currently recording for Crossover records, his own company, and lives in Los Angeles with his wife Delle and their three children.

March	1951	BABY LET ME HOLD YOUR HAND	Swing Time
March	1952	KISS ME BABY	Swing Time
March	1954	IT SHOULD'VE BEEN ME	Atlantic
August	1954	DON'T YOU KNOW	Atlantic
January	1955	I'VE GOT A WOMAN/COME BACK	Atlantic
June	1955	A FOOL FOR YOU/THIS LITTLE GIRL OF MINE	Atlantic
October	1955	BLACKJACK/GREENBACKS	Atlantic
February	1956	DROWN IN MY OWN TEARS	Atlantic
June	1956	HALLELUJAH I LOVE HER SO	Atlantic
October	1956	LONELY AVENUE	Atlantic
February	1957	AIN'T THAT LOVE	Atlantic

October	1957	SWANEE RIVER ROCK	Atlantic
December	1958	ROCKHOUSE II	Atlantic
February	1959	THE RIGHT TIME	Atlantic
July	1959	WHAT'D I SAY	Atlantic
November	1959	I'M MOVIN' ON	Atlantic
January	1960	LET THE GOOD TIMES ROLL	Atlantic
December	1960	COME RAIN OR COME SHINE	Atlantic
February	1961	ONE MINT JULEP	Impulse
June	1961	I'VE GOT NEWS FOR YOU	Impulse
June	1960	STICKS AND STONES	ABC
October	1960	GEORGIA ON MY MIND	ABC
November	1960	RUBY	ABC
January	1961	THEM THAT GOT	ABC
September	1961	HIT THE ROAD JACK	ABC
December	1961	UNCHAIN MY HEART	ABC
February	1962	BABY IT'S COLD OUTSIDE	ABC
April	1962	HIDE 'NOR HAIR	ABC
May	1962	I CAN'T STOP LOVING YOU	ABC
May	1962	BORN TO LOSE	ABC
July	1962	YOU DON'T KNOW ME	ABC
November	1962	YOU ARE MY SUNSHINE	ABC
November	1962	YOUR CHEATING HEART	ABC
February	1963	DON'T SET ME FREE	ABC
April	1963	TAKE THESE CHAINS FROM MY HEART	ABC
June	1963	NO ONE	ABC
June	1963	WITHOUT LOVE (THERE IS NOTHING)	ABC
September	1963	BUSTED	ABC
December	1963	THAT LUCKY OLD SUN	ABC
February	1964	BABY DON'T YOU CRY	ABC
February	1964	MY HEART CRIES FOR YOU	ABC
May	1964	MY BABY DON'T DIG ME	ABC
July	1964	NO ONE TO CRY TO	ABC
August	1964	A TEAR FELL	ABC
September	1964	SMACK DAB IN THE MIDDLE	ABC
December	1964	MAKIN' WHOOPEE	ABC
February	1965	CRY	ABC
April	1965	I GOTTA WOMAN	ABC
July	1965	I'M A FOOL TO CARE	ABC
December	1965	CRYING TIME	ABC
March	1966	TOGETHER AGAIN	ABC
May	1966	LET'S GO GET STONED	ABC
August	1966	I CHOSE TO SING THE BLUES	ABC
November	1966	PLEASE SAY YOU'RE FOOLING	ABC
March	1967	I WANT TO TALK ABOUT YOU	ABC
May	1967	HERE WE GO AGAIN	ABC
August	1967	IN THE HEAT OF THE NIGHT	ABC
November	1967	YESTERDAY	ABC
February	1968	THAT'S A LIE	ABC
June	1968	ELEANOR RIGBY	ABC
June	1968	UNDERSTANDING	ABC
September	1968	SWEET YOUNG THING LIKE YOU	ABC
May	1969	LET ME LOVE YOU	ABC
March	1970	LAUGHIN & CLOWNIN	ABC
October	1970	IF YOU WERE MINE	ABC
March	1971	DON'T CHANGE ON ME	ABC
August	1971	FEEL SO BAD	ABC

December	1971	WHAT AM I LIVING FOR	ABC
July	1972	LOOK WHAT THEY'VE DONE TO MY SONG, MA	ABC/TRC
June	1973	I CAN MAKE IT THROUGH THE DAY	ABC
November	1973	COME LIVE WITH ME	Crossover
September	1975	LIVING FOR THE CITY	Cross Over

THE CHARMS

Back in 1954 a group from the West Coast called the Jewels had a hit on Imperial records called "Hearts of Stone." Sid Nathan, president of King records, was sitting in his Cincinnati office one day looking for a group to do a follow-up version of that hit. He saw a group of guys playing baseball in a vacant lot across the street. He called them over to his office and asked them if they had ever done any singing. They said yes. He had them learn "Hearts of Stone," recorded it with Otis Williams featured as lead singer, and released the song on his Deluxe label in October 1954. The Charms' version of the song became a number one record. Later, the Fontane Sisters had a hit with the record on Dot. Otis Williams is now a single act and plays many engagements in the Midwest.

October	1954	HEARTS OF STONE	DeLuxe
January	1955	LING, TING, TONG	DeLuxe
February	1955	TWO HEARTS	DeLuxe

THE CHARTS

Members:
> Joseph Grier—lead
> Leroy Binns—first tenor
> Steven Brown—second tenor
> Glenmore Jackson—baritone
> Ross Buford—bass

Hometown: New York, New York

The Charts began singing on the street corners in Harlem while they were in their teens in the mid-fifties. They decided to call themselves the Charts because they were always scanning the record charts of the various trade magazines.

In 1957 lead singer Joseph, while only seventeen, the oldest of the group, wrote a song which they took to their friend Les Cooper (who had a hit of his own in 1962, called "Wiggle Wobble"). Les liked the song and took them to Everlast records where they signed a contract. In the summer of 1957, the song "Deserie" became their first and biggest hit.

July	1957	DESERIE / ZOOP	Everlast
September	1957	DANCE GIRL	Everlast

CHUBBY CHECKER

CHUBBY CHECKER

Real Name: Ernest Evans
Born: October 3, 1941
Hometown: Philadelphia, Pennsylvania

During his high school days Ernest Evans was employed as a chicken plucker at a poultry shop. He would entertain his customers with singing and humor. The owner of the store thought he had talent so he introduced young Ernest to Kal Mann of Parkway records. Kal signed him to the label in early 1959.

Since Ernest admired Fats Domino a lot, and since Ernest was kind of heavy himself, his friends began calling him "Chubby." It was Dick Clark's wife who thought of calling him Checker, after she saw him on her husband's show "American Bandstand."

Chubby's first record for Parkway, "The Class," in which he did singing impersonations, was a fairly successful record in the summer of 1959. But it was his next record, released nearly a year later, that brought him worldwide success. It was while the kids were dancing on "Bandstand" to a new dance called the Twist, which Hank Ballard had written and recorded, that Kal Mann and Bernie Lowe of Cameo/Parkway records thought that the song could be a hit for Chubby if he recorded the same song note for note. They were right, for in August 1960, when the song hit the national charts, it became the biggest dance in the country for the next three years, making Chubby Checker a worldwide star. The song was so popular that not only was it a number one song in 1960, but it came back to be a number one song in 1961 as well.

Because of that one song, Chubby became the innovator of all kinds of new dances such as the Hucklebuck, the Pony, the Fly, and the Limbo.

In December 1963, Chubby married Catharina Lodders of Holland, the former Miss World of 1962. Today Chubby still lives in Philadelphia, and is still actively recording. Chubby has been busier than most over the past two decades, and his hit "The Twist" holds the distinction as the only single in the history of the pop music charts ever to hit number one on the national charts two different times.

May	1959	THE CLASS	Parkway
August	1960	THE TWIST	Parkway
October	1960	THE HUCKLEBUCK	Parkway
October	1960	WHOLE LOTTA SHAKIN' GOIN' ON	Parkway
January	1961	PONY TIME	Parkway
April	1961	DANCE THE MESS AROUND	Parkway
June	1961	LET'S TWIST AGAIN	Parkway
October	1961	THE FLY	Parkway
November	1961	THE TWIST	Parkway
November	1961	LET'S TWIST AGAIN	Parkway
February	1962	SLOW TWISTIN'	Parkway
June	1962	DANCIN' PARTY	Parkway
September	1962	LIMBO ROCK	Parkway
September	1962	POPEYE THE HITCHHIKER	Parkway
February	1963	LET'S LIMBO SOME MORE	Parkway
February	1963	TWENTY MILES	Parkway
May	1963	BIRDLAND	Parkway
July	1963	SURF PARTY	Parkway
July	1963	TWIST IT UP	Parkway
November	1963	LODDY LO	Parkway
December	1963	HOOKA TOOKA	Parkway
March	1964	HEY BOBBA NEEDLE	Parkway
June	1964	LAZY ELSIE MOLLY	Parkway
August	1964	SHE WANTS T'SWIM	Parkway
January	1965	LOVELY, LOVELY	Parkway
April	1965	DO THE FREDDIE	Parkway
July	1966	HEY YOU LITTLE BOO-GA-LOO	Parkway
April	1969	BACK IN THE U.S.S.R.	Buddah

THE CHEERS

Members:
    Gil Garfield
    Bert Convy
    Sue Allen
Hometown: Los Angeles, California

This was a vocal group that Jerry Leiber and Mike Stoller put together on the West Coast in the mid-fifties to sing demo records of the songs that Jerry and Mike had written. One of their demos called "(Bazoom) I

Need Your Lovin',", which Jerry and Mike had written, and the Cheers recorded, found its way to Capitol records. The group was signed to the label and the song was released in September of 1954.

In September of 1955, The Cheers had their biggest hit with a song about a rebel type character (in the James Dean mold) who wore "Black Denim Trousers," which became a national hit for the group. They had another hit in March of 1956 with a car song about two autos racing toward each other in a game called "Chicken."

Today Bert is an accomplished actor and has starred in *Cabaret* and the TV series "Love Of Life" playing the role of Glen Hamilton.

September 1954	(BAZOOM) I NEED YOUR LOVIN'	Capitol
September 1955	BLACK DENIM TROUSERS	Capitol
March 1956	CHICKEN	Capitol

DON CHERRY

Born: January 11, 1924
Hometown: Wichita, Texas

DON CHERRY

After serving in the Army in the 1940s, Don became interested in singing. He went back to Texas where he practiced singing along with his first love, golf. In 1950, he worked a club in Dallas where he also had his own radio show on WFAA and played in local golf competitions. On May 5, 1950, while playing in the Western Amateur Golf Tournament in Dallas, he was given a recording contract from Decca Records. He withdrew from the tournament and flew to New York to begin his singing career.

Don became a popular vocalist for both Decca and Columbia until the mid-fifties when he gave up singing to pursue a golfing career. He turned pro and has been doing very well with it ever since.

September	1950	THINKING OF YOU	Decca
July	1951	VANITY	Decca
September	1955	BAND OF GOLD	Columbia
March	1956	WILD CHERRY	Columbia
July	1956	GHOST TOWN	Columbia
September	1956	NAMELY YOU	Columbia

THE CHIFFONS

Members:
> Judy Craig—lead—1946
> Barbara Lee—May 16, 1947
> Patricia Bennett—April 7, 1947
> Sylvia Peterson—September 30, 1946

Hometown: Bronx, New York

The group was brought together in 1960 by Ronald Mack. They first signed a recording contract that same year with Big Deal records and had a small hit with "Tonight's the Night." But it wasn't until early 1963, when the girls signed with Laurie records, that they really reached success with their only number one song, the first one they released for Laurie, called "He's So Fine," that their manager Ronald Mack had written. Today Barbara, Patricia and Sylvia still sing as the Chiffons around the New York area.

September	1960	TONIGHT'S THE NIGHT	Big Deal
February	1963	HE'S SO FINE	Laurie
June	1963	ONE FINE DAY	Laurie
September	1963	A LOVE SO FINE	Laurie
November	1963	I HAVE A BOYFRIEND	Laurie
August	1964	SAILOR BOY	Laurie
June	1965	NOBODY KNOWS WHAT'S GOIN' ON	Laurie
May	1966	SWEET TALKIN' GUY	Laurie
August	1966	OUT OF THIS WORLD	Laurie
October	1966	STOP LOOK AND LISTEN	Laurie

THE CHIMES

Members:
  Len Cocco—lead
  Pat DePrisco—first tenor
  Richard Mercado—second tenor
  Joseph Croce—baritone
  Pat McGuire—bass
Hometown: Brooklyn, New York

The group was first formed in Brooklyn in 1959. They sang locally for a while until Andy Leonetti, the president of Tag records, heard them. He liked them so well that he signed them to his label. In November 1960, they recorded and released a song that was an old standard hit many years ago. "Once in a While" became their biggest-selling hit.

| November | 1960 | ONCE IN AWHILE | Tag |
| March | 1961 | I'M IN THE MOOD FOR LOVE | Tag |

THE CHIPMUNKS

Originator: David Seville—real name: Ross Bagdasarian
Born: January 27, 1919
Died: January 1972
Hometown: Fresno, California

Through experimenting with speeding up a tape, David was able to create a high-pitched voice. He utilized this effect in recording a song he wrote called "Witch Doctor" in March 1958, which became a number one song. Later that year he used the same effect and created three voice characters named Alvin, Theodore, anl Simon, who Dave called The Chipmunks. He wrote a song for them called "The Chipmunk Song" which became a Christmas hit in December of 1958, and has been a Christmas classic ever since. Seville named Alvin and Simon after Al Bennett and Si Warnoker, the heads of Liberty at the time, while Theodore was named after Ted Keep, the recording engineer at the session.

December	1958	THE CHIPMUNK SONG	Liberty
February	1959	ALVIN'S HARMONICA	Liberty
July	1959	RAGTIME COWBOY JOE	Liberty
February	1960	ALVIN'S ORCHESTRA	Liberty
September	1960	ALVIN FOR PRESIDENT	Liberty
December	1960	RUDOLPH THE RED NOSED REINDEER	Liberty
March	1962	THE ALVIN TWIST	Liberty

THE CHORDETTES
Left to right: Jinny Osborn, Lynn Evans, Carol Bushman, Janet Ertel

THE CHORDETTES

Members:
      Dorothy Schwartz—replaced by Lynn Evans (January 1952)
      Jinny Osborn—replaced by Margie Needham (June 1953)
      Janet Ertel
      Carol Bushman
Hometown: Sheboygan, Wisconsin

Dorothy, Jinny, Janet and Carol organized the group in their hometown of Sheboygan in the early fifties. After working on their barbershop harmony, they began to do many local engagements.

In 1949, the group had success on a national scale when they won Arthur Godfrey's Talent Scout contest and then became part of the regular show.

In 1953, Dorothy and Jinny left the group to be replaced by Lynn and Margie. On Godfrey's show they met musical director Archie Bleyer who signed them to his Cadence label in 1954 where they had their first big hit called "Mr. Sandman."

October	1954	MR. SANDMAN	Cadence
December	1955	THE WEDDING	Cadence
February	1956	EDDIE MY LOVE	Cadence
May	1956	BORN TO BE WITH YOU	Cadence
September	1956	LAY DOWN YOUR ARMS	Cadence
August	1957	JUST BETWEEN YOU AND ME	Cadence
February	1958	LOLLIPOP	Cadence
May	1958	ZORRO	Cadence
March	1959	NO OTHER ARMS, NO OTHER LIPS	Cadence
August	1959	A GIRL'S WORK IS NEVER DONE	Cadence
June	1961	NEVER ON SUNDAY	Cadence

THE CHORDS

THE CHORDS

Members:
>Carl Feaster—lead; died: January 23, 1981
>Claude Feaster
>James Keyes
>Floyd McRae
>James Edwards

Hometown: New York, New York

The fellows got together in the mid-fifties and began to sing at small local functions. In May 1954, they went into a recording studio and recorded a song that they all had written called "Sh-Boom." They took the recording and sold it to Cat records, a subsidiary of Atlantic records, and the song was released that summer.

The song started to take off until a Canadian group called the Crew Cuts did a "cover" version of the record. The Crew Cuts, who recorded for Mercury, wound up with a number one national hit while the Chords' version got moderate play.

"Sh-Boom" has been considered by music experts as one of the first rock and roll songs to go from R & B to pop charts, and a song that helped to pave the way for many other hits after it. It has become an all-time classic.

James Keyes keeps the group active in the New York area with all new members. Carl Feaster died of cancer in early 1981.

June   1954   SH-BOOM   Cat

LOU CHRISTIE

Real Name: Lugee Sacco
Born: February 19, 1943
Hometown: Glen Willard, Pennsylvania

LOU CHRISTIE

Lou started singing in high school with a group called the Classics. In 1960, he began to do some recording in Pittsburgh, but nothing ever happened with the songs. A couple of years later he signed with a production firm in Pittsburgh called C & C records, owned by Nick Cenci.

In October 1962, Lou recorded a song he and Twyla Herbert had written called "The Gypsy Cried," which was released on C & C records and became a big local hit. The song was unique, for it featured Lou's high falsetto voice, which was to become his trademark. A few months later the song was sold to Roulette records in New York, and by January 1963 it became a national hit.

After "Two Faces Have I" and several other songs in 1963, which Twyla and Lou had written, Lou left Roulette records. In 1965, he signed with MGM records and had a number one national hit in December 1965 called "Lightnin' Strikes."

Today Lou lives in Pittsburgh and performs on the rock 'n' roll reunion shows around the country.

January	1963	THE GYPSY CRIED	Roulette
February	1963	TWO FACES HAVE I	Roulette
July	1963	HOW MANY TEARDROPS	Roulette
December	1965	LIGHTNIN' STRIKES	MGM
March	1966	RHAPSODY IN THE RAIN	MGM
June	1966	PAINTER	MGM
February	1966	OUTSIDE THE GATES OF HEAVEN	Co & Co
March	1966	BIG TIME	Colpix
April	1967	SHAKE HANDS AND WALK AWAY CRYING	Columbia
August	1969	I'M GONNA MAKE YOU MINE	Buddah
December	1969	ARE YOU GETTING ANY SUNSHINE	Buddah
February	1974	BEYOND THE BLUE HORIZON	Three Brothers

EUGENE CHURCH

Born: January 23, 1938

In late 1958, Eugene Church and his group, The Fellows, had a top forty hit called "Pretty Girls Everywhere." The song had a great R & B beat and was just right for doing the jitterbug. The song expressed how most teen-age boys felt at the time—everywhere they went pretty girls were in abundance. You could look but you couldn't touch. Eugene's voice bellowed this frustration into a hit record. The follow-up, "Miami," used the same idea. It had Eugene pining away for all the pretty girls in that fair city.

December	1958	PRETTY GIRLS EVERYWHERE	Class
August	1959	MIAMI	Class

JIMMY CLANTON

JIMMY CLANTON

Born: September 2, 1940
Hometown: Baton Rouge, Louisiana

In high school Jimmy formed a band called The Rockets, playing at all the local dances. After graduation he appeared in local clubs and on "Teen-Town Rally," a local radio show.

In 1958, the Rockets went to New Orleans to make a record at a studio owned by Cosimo Matassa. Matassa was so impressed with Jimmy's voice that he took him for an audition to see his friend Johnny Vincent, the president of Ace records. Vincent then signed Jimmy, while Matassa became Jimmy's personal manager.

In the summer of 1958, Jimmy wrote a song that was to be his first hit on Ace records. The song, "Just a Dream," became his biggest hit.

Today Jimmy is active as a performer once again, performing in many clubs throughout the country.

June	1958	JUST A DREAM	Ace
October	1958	A LETTER TO AN ANGEL	Ace
November	1958	A PART OF ME	Ace
August	1959	MY OWN TRUE LOVE	Ace
December	1959	GO, JIMMY, GO	Ace
April	1960	ANOTHER SLEEPLESS NIGHT	Ace
August	1960	COME BACK	Ace
January	1961	WHAT AM I GONNA DO	Ace
August	1962	VENUS IN BLUE JEANS	Ace
January	1963	DARKEST STREET IN TOWN	Ace
November	1969	CURLY	Laurie

CLAUDINE CLARK

Born: April 26, 1941
Hometown: Macon, Georgia

Claudine studied music composition at Coombs College in Philadelphia. She became interested in writing and singing and eventually signed with Herald records, and then Gotham records. It wasn't until the summer of 1962, when she signed with Chancellor records of Philadelphia, that she really achieved fame. She recorded a song she had written called "Party Lights," which became her only national hit.

June   1962   PARTY LIGHTS   Chancellor

DEE CLARK

Real Name: Delectus Clark
Born: November 7, 1938
Hometown: Blythsville, Arkansas

DEE CLARK

Dee's family moved to Chicago when he was a child. At age fourteen, he sang with a group called The Hambone Kids and recorded a song on Okeh records called "Hambone." In 1955, he won a talent contest in Chicago, and disc jockey Herb Kent took him over to Vee Jay records. They signed him to their subsidiary label Falcon records, which was later changed to Abner records.

On Falcon in 1957, Dee had such small hits as "Kangaroo Hop" and "24 Boy Friends." This was also the year that he took over rock singer Little Richard's band The Upsetters when Richard gave up singing to go into the ministry. It wasn't until December 1958 that Dee had his first national hit with "Nobody But You."

December	1958	NOBODY BUT YOU	Abner
May	1959	JUST KEEP IT UP	Abner
August	1959	HEY LITTLE GIRL	Abner
December	1959	HOW ABOUT THAT	Abner
March	1960	AT MY FRONT DOOR	Abner
August	1960	YOU'RE LOOKING GOOD	Vee Jay
February	1961	YOUR FRIENDS	Vee Jay
May	1961	RAINDROPS	Vee Jay
October	1962	I'M GOING BACK TO SCHOOL	Vee Jay
November	1963	CROSSFIRE TIME	Constellation

SANFORD CLARK

Hometown: Phoenix, Arizona

Sanford was born in Oklahoma, but his family later moved to Phoenix, Arizona. In Phoenix, he began appearing on radio and TV in the mid-fifties. At this time he met a disc jockey named Lee Hazlewood, who began to manage Sanford. This is the same Lee Hazlewood who would later work on writing and producing hits for Duane Eddy and Nancy Sinatra. Lee wrote a song in 1956, and he got guitarist Al Casey and his combo to back up Sanford on it in the recording session. Al Casey was the one who eventually taught Duane Eddy to play the guitar and later played in Duane's group for many years.

After the recording session, Lee took the master recording to Randy Wood, president of Dot records, who bought it and released it on his label. In the summer of 1956, Lee Hazlewood's composition "The Fool" became Sanford Clark's only real hit.

| July | 1956 | THE FOOL | Dot |
| November | 1956 | THE CHEAT | Dot |

THE CLASSICS

Left to right: John Gambale, Emil Stucchio,
Jamie Troy, Tony Victor

THE CLASSICS

Members:
      Emil Stucchio—lead—born: April 9, 1944
      Tony Victor—first tenor—born: April 11, 1943
      Johnny Gambale—second tenor—born: February 4, 1942
      Jamie Troy—bass—born: November 22, 1942
Hometown: Brooklyn, New York

The group first formed in 1958 as the Perennials and began singing on street corners. While appearing at a club in Brooklyn one night, the emcee of the show they were on had difficulty introducing the group by name. Out of frustration he called them the Classics, a name that stuck with the group.

In 1959, friends of theirs from Brooklyn called the Passions (of "Just to Be with You" fame) introduced the group to their manager, Jim Gribble, who got them a recording contract with Dart records. They remained with Dart until 1961, when they recorded several songs for Mercury. In early 1963, they recorded a standard song, "Til Then," which was sold to Music Note records and went on to become a national hit for the group by June 1963.

Today Emil lives in Long Island, New York, and is a transit policeman, Jamie lives in Brooklyn, and is in the scrap iron business, Johnny is a commercial artist in New York, and Tony has a seat on the New York Stock Exchange. Emil sings with Albie Galione and Lou Rotondo (both former members of the Passions) on occasional rock shows around New York, as the Classics.

June   1963   TIL THEN   Music Note

THE CLEFTONES

Members:
    Herbie Cox—lead—May 6, 1939
    Berman Patterson—second tenor—1938
    Warren Corbin—bass—1939
    Charles James—first tenor—1940
    William McClain—baritone—1938—replaced by Gene Pearson in 1959
Hometown: Jamaica, Queens, New York

THE CLEFTONES

Left to right: Herb Cox, Berman Patterson,
Charles James, Warren Corbin, Buzzy McClain

Formed at Jamaica High School in Queens in 1955 for a school function, they first called themselves The Silvertones. Then they changed the name to The Cleftones. George Goldner of Rama records heard the group and signed them to a contract in late 1955. Their first song, which was written by Berman Patterson of the group, called "You Baby You" was used as the record to launch Rama's new subsidiary label called Gee records in January 1956. The group's next release several months later, a song written by lead singer Herbie Cox, called "Little Girl of Mine" established them as a top group in the rock and roll period.

Today Herbie lives in Flushing, New York, and is employed as a computer analyst. Berman lives in the same area and works for the Department of Correction and Rehabilitation, while Charles is an IBM technician in New York City. Herbie, Charles and Tony Gaines are still active on weekends in the New York area, singing as The Cleftones.

January	1956	YOU BABY YOU	Gee
April	1956	LITTLE GIRL OF MINE	Gee
June	1956	CAN'T WE BE SWEETHEARTS	Gee
September	1956	STRING AROUND MY HEART	Gee
November	1956	WHY DO YOU DO ME LIKE YOU DO	Gee
April	1958	LOVER BOY	Gee
May	1961	HEART AND SOUL	Gee
August	1961	I LOVE YOU FOR SENTIMENTAL REASONS	Gee

BUZZ CLIFFORD

Real Name: Reese Francis Clifford III
Born: October 8, 1942
Hometown: Berwyn, Illinois

At age six, Buzz became interested in cowboy singers. Three years later his parents gave him a guitar and he started composing and singing. In high school he not only sang but also was involved in sports, becoming the captain of the varsity football team. When he was eighteen, Buzz entered an amateur contest at the Morris County Fair in New Jersey, when he was pressured into it by his friends. He won the contest, and a short time later signed a recording contract with Columbia records.

In late 1960, he recorded a Johnny Parker novelty song called "Baby Sittin' Boogie," which became a top-selling song for him after it was released in January 1961. It was Buzz's only hit record.

Today Buzz is a popular country and western artist.

| January | 1961 | BABY SITTIN' BOOGIE | Columbia |

BUZZ CLIFFORD

MIKE CLIFFORD

Born: November 6, 1943
Hometown: Los Angeles, California

Mike was born to a musical family. His father was a professional trumpet player who would take him to many of his engagements. Because of Mike's interest in music, his parents started him on voice lessons.

MIKE CLIFFORD

At sixteen, while appearing in a night club in Los Angeles, he met Mrs. Helen Noga, the woman who managed the career of Johnny Mathis for many years. She liked Mike's style and decided to manage him. She booked him for his debut on "The Ed Sullivan Show." He then traveled in the United States and abroad.

In July 1962, Mike signed with United Artists records and a few months later had his first hit, "Close to Cathy."

Mike, at one time, enjoyed success portraying the role of Teen-Angel in the smash Broadway show *Grease*.

September	1962	CLOSE TO CATHY	United Artists
December	1962	WHAT TO DO WITH LAURIE	United Artists
May	1963	ONE BOY TOO LATE	United Artists

PATSY CLINE

Real Name: Virginia Patterson Hensley
Born: September 8, 1932
Died: March 5, 1963
Hometown: Winchester, Virginia

Patsy's first big break came when Wally Fowler of the Grand Ole Opry signed her for an appearance on the Nashville show. From there she went on to win Arthur Godfrey's Talent Scout show in early 1957, which led to a recording contract with Decca records. Her first hit was in February of that year with "Walkin' After Midnight."

More than a year later in May 1961, she had her next big pop record with "I Fall to Pieces." A month later, on June 14, she was involved in an auto crash in Madison, Tennessee, where she sustained a fractured hip and head injuries.

Several years later, on Tuesday, March 5, 1963, Patsy, along with country stars Cowboy Copas and Hawkshaw Hawkins, was returning from Kansas City, Missouri, where the three of them had just staged a benefit show for the widow of disc jockey Cactus Jack Call. (Cactus Jack had been killed in an auto crash.) The single-engine plane, carrying the singers and pilot Randy Hughes, had just gassed up at 6:00 P.M. that evening at Dyersburg, Tennessee, and was on its last hop to Nashville, when a crash occurred, killing everyone aboard.

February	1957	WALKIN' AFTER MIDNIGHT	Decca
May	1961	I FALL TO PIECES	Decca
October	1961	CRAZY	Decca
January	1962	SHE'S GOT YOU	Decca
February	1962	STRANGE	Decca

May	1962	WHEN I GET THROUGH WITH YOU	Decca
August	1962	SO WRONG	Decca
October	1962	HEARTACHES	Decca
January	1963	LEAVIN' ON YOUR MIND	Decca
April	1963	SWEET DREAMS (OF YOU)	Decca
August	1963	FADED LOVE	Decca

THE CLIQUES

Originator: Jesse Belvin
Born: December 15, 1933
Died: February 6, 1960
Hometown: Los Angeles, California

Actually the Cliques was a creation of singer Jesse Belvin, for he recorded his voice four times to create the effect of a four-man group, and released the song "Girl of My Dreams" on Modern records in April 1956. No one knew this was one man doing four voices. Later Jesse would go on to record solo hits like "Goodnight My Love" and "Guess Who" before his untimely death in 1960.

| April | 1956 | GIRL OF MY DREAMS | Modern |

ROSEMARY CLOONEY

Born: May 23, 1928
Hometown: Cincinnati, Ohio

Rosemary was born in Maysville, Kentucky, where, when she was only a few years old, she began her career by singing for her grandfather to help him in his race for mayor. She and her sister won an amateur contest while growing up in Cincinnati as the Clooney Sisters. This led them to being regulars on radio station WLW in Cincinnati seven nights a week. They later went on to join Tony Pastor's orchestra in the forties as vocalists and toured with him for two and a half years.

In 1949, Rosemary became a soloist and signed with Columbia records. Her first major hit with the label was in 1951, when she had a number one record called "Come On-a My House." The song was written by William Saroyan and Ross Bagdasarian (later known as David Seville of the singing Chipmunk fame) in the late thirties, and took over ten years to become a hit.

Rosemary's biggest years for Columbia were from 1951 until 1955, during which she enjoyed other hits like "Botch-a-Me" and "Half as

Much" in 1952, "Hey There," "Mambo Italiano," and "This Ole House" during 1954 and 1955.

She got involved in motion pictures in the fifties, starring in such films as *White Christmas, Deep in My Heart, Red Garters, Here Come the Girls,* and *The Stars Are Singing.* In 1954 Rosemary married actor Jose Ferrer. They were divorced in 1962, remarried in 1963, separated in 1966, and divorced again in 1967. Rosemary is active, performing on some nostalgia shows throughout the country with other vocalists like Margaret Whiting and Helen O'Connell.

February	1951	BEAUTIFUL BROWN EYES	Columbia
June	1951	COME ON-A MY HOUSE	Columbia
September	1951	IF TEARDROPS WERE PENNIES	Columbia
February	1952	BE MY LIFE'S COMPANION	Columbia
March	1952	TENDERLY	Columbia
May	1952	HALF AS MUCH	Columbia
June	1952	BOTCH-A-ME	Columbia
August	1952	TOO OLD TO CUT THE MUSTARD	Columbia
September	1952	BLUES IN THE NIGHT	Columbia
July	1954	HEY THERE	Coiumbia
July	1954	THIS OLE HOUSE	Columbia
November	1954	MAMBO ITALIANO	Columbia
September	1955	PET ME, POPPA	Columbia
January	1956	MEMORIES OF YOU	Columbia
May	1956	I COULD HAVE DANCED ALL NIGHT	Columbia
May	1956	I'VE GROWN ACCUSTOMED TO YOUR FACE	Columbia

ROSEMARY CLOONEY

THE CLOVERS

From top: Harold Lucas, Matthew McQuater, John Bailey
Harold Winley, Bill Harris

THE CLOVERS

Members:
    John "Buddy" Bailey—dual lead tenor
    Billy Mitchell—dual lead tenor—joined group in 1953
    Matthew McQuater—second tenor
    Harold "Hal" Lucas, Jr.—baritone
    Harold Winley—bass
    Bill Harris—guitarist
Hometown: Washington, D.C., and Baltimore, Maryland, area

Lou Krefetz discovered the fellows singing at the Rose Club in Washington, D.C., in the late forties, while they were all in high school. Lou began to manage the group and eventually got them a contract with Atlantic records around 1950.

The first really big hit they had for the label was in 1951, with a song that was written by the president of Atlantic, Ahmet Ertegun, called "Don't You Know I Love You." Then came other songs like "Hey, Miss Fannie," "I Played the Fool," "Middle of the Night," "One Mint Julep," and "Your Cash Ain't Nothing but Trash," which were R & B hits from 1951 until 1954.

Several of The Clovers' biggest hits came in 1956 with "Devil or Angel," along with "From the Bottom of My Heart" and one of their first pop tune hits, "Love, Love, Love." In 1959, the group signed with United Artists records and had their biggest pop hit in the fall of that year with a Lieber and Stoller song "Love Potion No. 9."

The Clovers are considered one of the first rock and roll singing groups, along with The Dominoes. In the late forties it was the Ravens who enjoyed popularity, followed in the early fifties by The Clovers, The Dominoes, The Orioles, The "5" Royales, The Midnighters, and the thousands of black vocal groups that were to follow.

June	1951	DON'T YOU KNOW I LOVE YOU	Atlantic
September	1951	FOOL, FOOL, FOOL	Atlantic
April	1952	ONE MINT JULEP	Atlantic
July	1952	TING-A-LING	Atlantic
October	1952	HEY, MISS FANNIE	Atlantic
October	1952	I PLAYED THE FOOL	Atlantic
March	1953	CRAWLIN'	Atlantic
July	1953	GOOD LOVIN'	Atlantic
March	1954	LOVEY DOVEY	Atlantic
July	1954	I'VE GOT MY EYES ON YOU	Atlantic
July	1954	YOUR CASH AIN'T NOTHIN' BUT TRASH	Atlantic
March	1955	BLUE VELVET	Atlantic
September	1955	NIP SIP	Atlantic
January	1956	DEVIL OR ANGEL/HEY, DOLL BABY	Atlantic
June	1956	LOVE, LOVE, LOVE	Atlantic
October	1956	FROM THE BOTTOM OF MY HEART	Atlantic
December	1959	LOVE POTION NO. 9	United Artists

THE COASTERS

Members:

Carl Gardner—lead—born: April 29, 1928

Billy Guy—first tenor—June 20, 1936

Leon Hughes—second tenor—replaced by Young Jessie—replaced by Cornell Gunther—replaced by Earl "Speedo" Carroll (November 2, 1937) in 1960

Bobby Nunn—bass—replaced by Will "Dub" Jones in 1958—replaced by Ronnie Bright (October 18, 1938) in the 1960s

THE COASTERS, 1957–1958

Clockwise from top left: Bobby Nunn, Carl Gardner,
Billy Guy, Leon Hughes

Adolph Jacobs—guitarist—joined group in late 1955
Hometown: Los Angeles, California

In the early fifties, songwriters Jerry Leiber and Mike Stoller formed a record label in Los Angeles called Spark records. They signed a group to record for them called The Robins. In 1955, The Robins recorded a Leiber and Stoller song called "Smokey Joe's Cafe," on which Carl Gardner sang lead. It was a hit for Spark records on the West Coast, and it eventually came to the attention of Atlantic records. Lieber and Stoller made an agreement with Atlantic to sell the master to their subsidiary label, the newly founded Atco records. They also agreed to produce The Robins for Atco as independent producers. This was one of the first such contracts ever signed, for it meant that they would not be employees of Atlantic; instead, they would act independently as producers. This created some friction with some of the members of The Robins; conse-

THE COASTERS, 1958–1960

Left to right: Will "Dub" Jones, Carl Gardner,
Cornell Gunther, Billy Guy, Adolph Jacobs

quently, Leiber and Stoller convinced lead singer Carl Gardner and bass singer Bobby Nunn to leave The Robins to form a new group. Carl and Bobby got friends Billy Guy and Leon Hughes to form a new group in February 1956. They decided to call themselves The Coasters, because they all came together on the West Coast. The remaining Robins went on to record for Whippet records and released a song called "Cherry Lips." The Coasters' first song for Atco was "Down in Mexico," which was similar to "Smokey Joe's Cafe." Then they released "One Kiss Led to Another" to round out 1956. It wasn't until April 1957 that things changed for them. Leiber and Stoller wrote a couple of songs for them, which they released on a single record. Initially the "A" side, "Young Blood," began to climb the pop music charts and wound up in the top ten; then the flip side, "Searchin'," which Billy Guy sang lead on, began getting air play and became a hit as well. This double-sided hit became the first of many hits to follow, from 1957 until around 1961.

Almost every one of the Coasters' hits was written by Leiber and Stoller. The team became known as the comedy group of rock and roll because of their songs and funny stage routines.

Bass singer Bobby Nunn, who worked at one time with the Johnny Otis band and had a hit on Savoy records with "Double-Crossin' Blues," was replaced in The Coasters by Will "Dub" Jones around 1958. "Dub" Jones is the bass voice on all the Coasters' big hits. "Dub" was replaced by Ronnie Bright in the 1960s. (Ronnie was the bass singer in Johnny Cymbal's hit "Mr. Bass Man" in 1963.)

Second tenor Leon Hughes, once a member of The Four Flames, was replaced by Young Jessie, who was then replaced by Cornell Gunther. Cornell was then replaced by Earl "Speedoo" Carroll, onetime lead voice of The Cadillacs in 1955.

Today Carl, Earl Carroll, Ronnie Bright, and a new member Jimmy Norman, sing as The Coasters. They all reside in New York and are very active performing. Cornell Gunther has another group he travels with, billed as Cornell Gunther & The Coasters, with him being the only original member.

March	1956	DOWN IN MEXICO	Atco
September	1956	ONE KISS LED TO ANOTHER	Atco
April	1957	YOUNG BLOOD	Atco
May	1957	SEARCHIN'	Atco
October	1957	IDOL WITH THE GOLDEN HEAD	Atco
May	1958	YAKETY YAK/ZING WENT THE STRINGS OF MY HEART	Atco
January	1959	CHARLIE BROWN	Atco
May	1959	ALONG CAME JONES	Atco
August	1959	POISON IVY	Atco
September	1959	I'M A HOG FOR YOU	Atco
December	1959	RUN RED RUN	Atco
April	1960	BESAME MUCHO	Atco
June	1960	WAKE ME, SHAKE ME	Atco
October	1960	SHOPPIN' FOR CLOTHES	Atco
February	1961	WAIT A MINUTE	Atco
April	1961	LITTLE EGYPT	Atco
August	1961	GIRLS, GIRLS, GIRLS	Atco
March	1964	T'AIN'T NOTHIN' TO ME	Atco
December	1971	LOVE POTION NO. 9	King

EDDIE COCHRAN

EDDIE COCHRAN

Born: October 3, 1938, in Albert Lea, Minnesota
Died: April 17, 1960
Hometown: Oklahoma City, Oklahoma

Eddie was the youngest of five children. He started playing the guitar at the age of twelve. In 1953, his family left Oklahoma for Bell Gardens, California. Two years later, at a music store in Bell Gardens, Eddie met a songwriter named Jerry Capehart, who asked Eddie to record some songs for him. This marked the beginning of a very important friendship.

In 1956, Si Warnoker of Liberty records heard of Eddie's talents and signed him up to record for the label. At the time, Eddie was recording for Jerry Capehart's label, Ekko records, with a friend named Hank Cochran (no relation) as The Cochran Brothers. Hank left for Nashville and began writing songs, and Eddie went with Liberty.

Eddie was offered a cameo role in the film *The Girl Can't Help It*, in which he sang the song "Twenty Flight Rock." This was to be Eddie's first release for Liberty in 1956. However, before it was released, Liberty chose a John D. Loudermilk song called "Sittin' in the Balcony" for him to record. The song became a hit for Eddie in early 1957, but it really wasn't the particular sound that he was trying to capture; it leaned too much toward an Elvis imitation.

It wasn't until the spring of 1958 that Eddie really found his sound with a song that he and Jerry wrote called "Summertime Blues." In the song, Eddie utilized a sort of "King Fish" voice for the low, answering portions of the song. It became his biggest hit that summer, and it established his sound with acoustic guitars, hand clapping, and the driving beat. H.s follow-up song that fall was a song that Eddie and Jerry wrote called "C'mon Everybody," which was originally recorded as "Let's Get Together." In 1959, Eddie began to write another song with a young lady named Sharon Sheeley, the same girl who wrote "Poor Little Fool" for Rick Nelson. The result was "Somethin' Else." Sharon became a close friend of Eddie's during this time.

While touring England in early 1960, Eddie met his untimely death. On Sunday, April 17, 1960, Eddie was motoring in the early morning hours to London, after a week at the Bristol Hippodrome, ending a ten-week British tour. In the limousine with him, as they were heading toward the airport, were Sharon Sheeley, Gene Vincent (of "Be-Bop-a-Lula" fame), and his chauffer. A tire blew out on the limo, causing a collision near Chippenham, Wiltshire, where Eddie sustained severe head injuries. He died in Bath Hospital in England, a short time after the crash. His body was flown to California, where he was buried in Hollywood.

February	1957	SITTIN' IN THE BALCONY	Liberty
September	1957	DRIVE IN SHOW	Liberty
February	1958	JEANNIE, JEANNIE, JEANNIE	Liberty
August	1958	SUMMERTIME BLUES	Liberty
November	1958	C'MON EVERYBODY	Liberty
March	1959	TEENAGE HEAVEN	Liberty
September	1959	SOMETHIN' ELSE	Liberty

COZY COLE

Real Name: William Cole
Born: October 17, 1907
Died: January 29, 1981
Hometown: East Orange, New Jersey

Cozy made his recording debut with Jelly Roll Morton in the late 1920s, then worked with Cab Calloway and later with Louis Armstrong's All-Stars. He and Gene Krupa formed the "Krupa and Cole School of Drumming" in New York in the 1950s. In the summer of 1958 he had a

132

COZY COLE

smash with "Topsy II," the only drum feature ever to sell more than a million records. On January 29, 1981, he died of cancer in Columbus, Ohio.

August	1958	TOPSY II	Love
September	1958	TOPSY I	Love
November	1958	TURVY II	Love

NAT "KING" COLE

Real Name: Nathaniel Adams Cole
Born: March 17, 1919, in Montgomery, Alabama
Died: February 15, 1965, in Santa Monica, California

Nat was the second son of a Baptist minister in a family of six children. He began playing the piano at four, at the Regal theater in Chicago, where his family had moved. When he was eleven, Nat played the organ in his father's church, the True Light Baptist Church. At sixteen, he formed his own band called The Royal Dukes. Later he joined his brother Eddie in a group called The Rogues of Rhythm.

In the forties, Bob Lewis hired Nat and the trio that he had formed to play at his club in Hollywood, called the Swanee Inn. Nat's group was known as the Nat Cole Swingsters Three. At this time Nat began to write songs and wrote "Straighten Up and Fly Right." It was while Nat was playing at the Swanee Inn that a customer persuaded him to sing "Sweet Lorraine," which launched his singing career. He eventually wound up with a recording contract.

Nat "King" Cole became one of the hottest selling artists through the forties, fifties, and sixties. He became a legend with his fantastic sound. On December 8, 1964, he entered St. John Hospital in Santa Monica, California, for lung cancer. On January 25, 1965, his left lung was removed. His career ended with his death on February 15, 1965.

| May | 1944 | STRAIGHTEN UP AND FLY RIGHT | Capitol |
| November | 1946 | (I LOVE YOU) FOR SENTIMENTAL REASONS | Capitol |

NAT "KING" COLE

December	1946	THE CHRISTMAS SONG	Capitol
April	1948	NATURE BOY	Capitol
May	1950	MONA LISA	Capitol
September	1950	ORANGE COLORED SKY (Stan Kenton)	Capitol
March	1951	JET	Capitol
April	1951	TOO YOUNG	Capitol
July	1951	RED SAILS IN THE SUNSET	Capitol
October	1951	UNFORGETTABLE	Capitol
May	1952	SOMEWHERE ALONG THE WAY	Capitol
June	1952	WALKIN' MY BABY BACK HOME	Capitol
September	1952	BECAUSE YOU'RE MINE	Capitol
October	1952	FAITH CAN MOVE MOUNTAINS	Capitol
January	1953	PRETEND	Capitol
April	1953	CAN'T I	Capitol
February	1954	ANSWER ME, MY LOVE	Capitol
September	1954	SMILE	Capitol
November	1954	HAJJI BABA	Capitol
February	1955	DARLING JE VOUS AIME BEAUCOUP	Capitol
February	1955	THE SAND AND THE SEA	Capitol
April	1955	A BLOSSOM FELL/ IF I MAY	Capitol
June	1955	MY ONE SIN	Capitol
September	1955	FORGIVE MY HEART	Capitol
September	1955	SOMEONE YOU LOVE	Capitol
December	1955	TAKE ME BACK TO TOYLAND	Capitol
January	1955	ASK ME	Capitol
March	1956	TOO YOUNG TO GO STEADY	Capitol
June	1956	THAT'S ALL THERE IS TO THAT	Capitol
October	1956	NIGHT LIGHTS	Capitol
October	1956	TO THE ENDS OF THE EARTH	Capitol
January	1957	BALLERINA	Capitol
April	1957	WHEN ROCK 'N' ROLL COMES TO TRINIDAD	Capitol
June	1957	SEND FOR ME	Capitol
September	1957	WITH YOU ON MY MIND	Capitol
January	1958	ANGEL SMILE	Capitol
April	1958	LOOKING BACK	Capitol
July	1958	COME CLOSER TO ME	Capitol
October	1958	NON DIMENTICAR	Capitol
January	1959	MADRID	Capitol
May	1959	YOU MADE ME LOVE YOU	Capitol
August	1959	MIDNIGHT FLYER	Capitol
February	1960	TIME AND THE RIVER	Capitol
August	1960	MY LOVE	Capitol
January	1961	IF I KNEW	Capitol
July	1961	TAKE A FOOL'S ADVICE	Capitol
September	1961	LET TRUE LOVE BEGIN	Capitol
August	1962	RAMBLIN' ROSE	Capitol
November	1962	DEAR LONELY HEARTS	Capitol
December	1962	THE CHRISTMAS SONG	Capitol
March	1963	ALL OVER THE WORLD	Capitol
April	1963	THOSE LAZY-HAZY-CRAZY DAYS OF SUMMER	Capitol
August	1963	THAT SUNDAY, THAT SUMMER	Capitol
February	1964	MY TRUE CARRIE LOVE	Capitol
April	1964	I DON'T WANT TO BE HURT ANY MORE	Capitol
September	1964	I DON'T WANT TO SEE TOMORROW	Capitol
September	1964	L-O-V-E	Capitol
August	1966	LET ME TELL YOU BABE	Capitol

THE COLTS

Members:
    Joe Crundy
    Rubin Crundy
    Carl Moland
    Leroy Smith
Hometown: Los Angeles, California

The fellows met around 1955 while attending Los Angeles City College. They began singing together and came to the attention of Buck Ram, the manager of the Platters. Buck signed them with Vita records and wrote their first release, which became their biggest hit. Although the song "Adorable" was a hit for the Colts, the Drifters' version was the much bigger hit.

October	1955	ADORABLE	Vita

PERRY COMO

Born: May 18, 1912
Hometown: Canonsburg, Pennsylvania

Being one of thirteen children of Pietro and Lucia Como, Perry became a barber at the age of fourteen in order to help his family. Some seven years later, while he was still a barber, he went to Cleveland, Ohio, to audition for Freddy Carlone's orchestra. The audition resulted in a job with Freddy's band. At the same time Perry married his sweetheart, Roselle Belline, on July 31, 1933, and they began to travel on the road with the band.

Perry stayed with Freddy until 1936 when he joined the Ted Weems band and remained with them until 1942. After that, Perry was planning to return to Canonsburg, but he received an offer with CBS radio in New York, and also a radio contract with RCA Victor.

By 1944, Perry had launched his career with RCA with "Long Ago (and Far Away)."

Semi-retired, he makes only rare TV appearances.

April	1944	LONG AGO (AND FAR AWAY)	Victor
January	1945	I DREAM OF YOU	Victor
July	1945	IF I LOVED YOU	Victor
August	1945	I'M GONNA LOVE THAT GAL	Victor
August	1945	TILL THE END OF TIME	Victor
November	1945	DIG YOU LATER (A HUBBA-HUBBA-HUBBA)	Victor
January	1946	I'M ALWAYS CHASING RAINBOWS	Victor

PERRY COMO

March	1946	PRISONER OF LOVE	RCA Victor
June	1946	THEY SAY IT'S WONDERFUL	RCA Victor
June	1946	SURRENDER	RCA Victor
December	1946	WINTER WONDERLAND	RCA Victor
May	1947	CHI-BABA CHI-BABA	RCA Victor
August	1947	WHEN YOU WERE SWEET SIXTEEN	RCA Victor
August	1947	I WONDER WHO'S KISSING HER NOW	RCA Victor
March	1948	BECAUSE	RCA Victor
July	1948	RAMBLING ROSE	RCA Victor
January	1949	FAR AWAY PLACES	RCA Victor
January	1949	N'YOT N'YOW (THE PUSSYCAT SONG)	RCA Victor
February	1949	BLUE ROOM	RCA Victor
February	1949	FOREVER AND EVER	RCA Victor
May	1949	I DON'T SEE ME IN YOUR EYES ANYMORE	RCA Victor
March	1949	"A"—YOU'RE ADORABLE	RCA Victor
April	1949	SOME ENCHANTED EVENING	RCA Victor
May	1949	BALI HA'I	RCA Victor
July	1949	JUST ONE WAY TO SAY I LOVE YOU	RCA Victor
July	1949	LET'S TAKE AN OLD-FASHIONED WALK	RCA Victor
September	1949	GIVE ME YOUR HAND	RCA Victor
October	1949	A DREAMER'S HOLIDAY	RCA Victor
November	1949	I WANNA GO HOME	RCA Victor
December	1949	THE LORD'S PRAYER	RCA Victor
December	1949	AVE MARIA	RCA Victor
January	1950	BIBBIDI-BOBBIDI-BOO (Fontane Sisters)	RCA Victor

April	1950	HOOP-DEE DOO (Fontane Sisters)	RCA Victor
August	1950	I CROSS MY FINGERS (Fontane Sisters)	RCA Victor
September	1950	PATRICIA	RCA Victor
October	1950	A BUSHEL AND A PECK (Betty Hutton)	RCA Victor
December	1950	YOU'RE JUST IN LOVE (Fontane Sisters)	RCA Victor
January	1951	IF	RCA Victor
June	1951	THERE'S A BIG BLUE CLOUD	RCA Victor
December	1951	IT'S BEGINNING TO LOOK LIKE CHRISTMAS (Fontane Sisters)	RCA Victor
January	1952	TULIPS AND HEATHER	RCA Victor
June	1952	MAYBE (Eddie Fisher)	RCA Victor
November	1952	DON'T LET THE STARS GET IN YOUR EYES	RCA Victor
January	1953	WILD HORSES	RCA Victor
April	1953	SAY YOU'RE MINE AGAIN	RCA Victor
June	1953	NO OTHER LOVE	RCA Victor
October	1953	YOU ALONE	RCA Victor
February	1954	WANTED	RCA Victor
June	1954	HIT AND RUN AFFAIR	RCA Victor
September	1954	PAPA LOVES MAMBO	RCA Victor
November	1954	THE THINGS I DIDN'T DO	RCA Victor
December	1954	HOME FOR THE HOLIDAYS	RCA Victor
January	1955	KO KO MO	RCA Victor
June	1955	TINA MARIE	RCA
October	1955	ALL AT ONCE YOU LOVE HER	RCA
February	1956	HOT DIGGITY	RCA
February	1956	JUKE BOX BABY	RCA
May	1956	GLENDORA	RCA
June	1956	MORE	RCA
July	1956	SOMEBODY UP THERE LIKES ME	RCA
October	1956	MOONLIGHT LOVE	RCA
January	1957	ROUND AND ROUND	RCA
May	1957	THE GIRL WITH THE GOLDEN BRAIDS	RCA
August	1957	DANCIN'	RCA
October	1957	JUST BORN	RCA
October	1957	IVY ROSE	RCA
December	1957	JINGLE BELLS	RCA EPA
January	1958	CATCH A FALLING STAR/MAGIC MOMENTS	RCA
January	1958	MAGIC MOMENTS	RCA
March	1958	KEWPIE DOLL	RCA
July	1958	MOON TALK	RCA
October	1958	LOVE MAKES THE WORLD GO 'ROUND	RCA
November	1958	MANDOLINS IN THE MOONLIGHT	RCA
February	1959	TOMBOY	RCA
June	1959	I KNOW	RCA
February	1960	DELAWARE	RCA
January	1961	MAKE SOMEONE HAPPY	RCA
November	1961	YOU'RE FOLLOWING ME	RCA
March	1962	CATERINA	RCA
June	1963	I LOVE YOU DON'T YOU FORGET IT	RCA
April	1965	DREAM ON LITTLE DREAMER	RCA
July	1965	OOWEE, OOWEE	RCA
May	1967	STOP! AND THINK IT OVER	RCA
March	1968	FATHER OF GIRLS	RCA
April	1969	SEATTLE	RCA
November	1970	IT'S IMPOSSIBLE	RCA
March	1971	I THINK OF YOU	RCA
April	1973	AND I LOVE YOU SO	RCA
December	1974	CHRISTMAS DREAM	RCA

BOBBY COMSTOCK

Born: December 28, 1943
Hometown: Ithaca, New York

Bobby learned to play the guitar at five. At the age of twelve, he formed a rock band which played the Ithaca area. A few years later he joined a group called the Counts. The group went to New York in early 1959 with one hundred dollars to record a song called "Tennessee Waltz." They recorded the song and took it to Herb Abramson (onetime owner of Atlantic records), who liked it. Herb had the fellows recut the song and released it on his Blaze records in October 1959. The song went on to be a national hit.

Today Bobby still lives in Ithaca and backs up many of the rock and roll shows at Radio City Music Hall and Madison Square Garden, in New York City.

October	1959	TENNESSEE WALTZ	Blaze
March	1960	JAMBALAYA	Atlantic
February	1963	LET'S STOMP	Lawn

RAY CONNIFF

Born: November 6, 1916
Hometown: Attleboro, Massachusetts

While in high school, Ray began playing the trombone and became interested in arranging music. After graduation he went to Boston, where he worked with an orchestra for a while. In 1938, he joined the Bunny Berigan band, and from there worked with Bob Crosby and later Artie Shaw. While with Artie, Ray arranged such hits as "Prelude in C-Sharp Major," " 'S Wonderful," and others.

After some time in the Army in the mid-forties, he returned to civilian life and worked as an arranger for Harry James. Ray's work eventually came to the attention of Mitch Miller of Columbia records and Ray was signed to the label as a conductor-arranger. In January 1956, he was signed to the label as an artist. That same year he had his group record the " 'S Wonderful" album, which launched the Ray Conniff sound.

Today Ray still records for Columbia, using only eight voices but utilizing the over-dub technique. He resides in Mt. Olympus, California (which overlooks Hollywood), with his wife Vera and their daughter Tamara. He still continues to record and do concerts all over the world.

| February | 1957 | 'S WONDERFUL | Columbia |
| October | 1960 | MIDNIGHT LACE | Columbia |

RAY CONNIFF AND THE SINGERS

July	1964	INVISIBLE TEARS	Columbia
June	1966	SOMEWHERE MY LOVE	Columbia
October	1966	LOOKIN' FOR LOVE	Columbia

CHRIS CONNOR

Born: November 8, 1930
Hometown: Kansas City, Missouri

Chris was very much influenced by the jazz style of Anita O'Day. Her biggest break came in 1952, when June Christy recommended her to sing with the Stan Kenton band. She began to record jazz numbers for Bethlehem records but in 1956 switched to Atlantic records. Chris's jazz style developed at Atlantic and in the fall of 1956 she had her first hit on the pop charts with "I Miss You So."

Today Chris continues to perform in various clubs around the country.

| October | 1956 | I MISS YOU SO | Atlantic |
| June | 1957 | TRUST IN ME | Atlantic |

THE CONTOURS

Members:
    Billy Gordon
    Billy Hoggs
    Joe Billingslea
    Sylvester Potts
    Hubert Johnson
    Huey Davis
Hometown: Detroit, Michigan

Billy Gordon, Billy Hoggs, Joe, and Sylvester originally formed The Contours in 1959. When Hubert joined the group, he became the link to the group's first audition with Motown records. Hubert called upon a distant cousin of his, Jackie Wilson, to listen to the group. Jackie then called his friend Berry Gordy, Jr., the president of Motown, to work with the group. This led to a contract with Berry's label Gordy records. The Contours' first release in 1962, "Whole Lotta Woman," went nowhere. Guitarist Huey Davis then joined the group in March 1962. The group's next release, which came that summer, became their biggest hit. It was a song that Berry Gordy, Jr., had written for the group called "Do You Love Me."

July	1962	DO YOU LOVE ME	Gordy
December	1962	SHAKE SHERRY	Gordy
April	1963	DON'T LET HER BE YOUR BABY	Gordy
March	1964	CAN YOU DO IT	Gordy
December	1964	CAN YOU JERK LIKE ME	Gordy
August	1965	FIRST I LOOK AT THE PURSE	Gordy
May	1966	JUST A LITTLE MISUNDERSTANDING	Gordy
April	1967	IT'S SO HARD BEING A LOSER	Gordy

SAM COOKE

Born: January 22, 1935
Died: December 11, 1964
Hometown: Chicago, Illinois

One of eight children, Sam began his singing career as a gospel singer in his father's church as a youngster. While attending Wendell Phillips High

SAM COOKE

in Chicago, he began to sing with his brother in a gospel group called The Highway Q.C.'s. In the fifties, he joined a gospel group called The Soul Stirrers with Roy Crain, Paul Foster, Bob King, R. B. Robinson, Jesse J. Farley, and T. L. Bruster. Sam was the lead voice on such songs as "Touch the Hem of His Garment" and "Pilgrim of Sorrow" when the group was recording for Specialty records in Los Angeles.

In 1956, Sam became interested in pop music and recorded several pop tunes for Specialty, including "I'll Come Running Back to You" and "Forever." He wanted to record more pop material, but the label did not go along with his thinking; consequently, along with his friend and producer Bumps Blackwell, he left Specialty to sign with the newly formed Keen records in 1957. His first hit for the label was a song that Sam's brother, L. C. Cooke had written called "You Send Me," It became a number one song by late 1957. In October 1959, Sam married his high school sweetheart, Barbara Campbell, in Los Angeles.

In early 1960, Sam signed with RCA records and released his first hit for the new label called "Teenage Sonata," which was mildly popular. His next release, later that summer, was a blockbuster called "Chain Gang," which he had written. Sam wrote most of his hits except for a few, like "Wonderful World" which was written by Lou Adler and Herb Alpert (of the Tijuana Brass).

At the age of twenty nine, while in Los Angeles for a Christmas vacation, Sam was shot by a woman at a motel.

October	1957	YOU SEND ME	Keen
October	1957	SUMMERTIME	Keen
December	1957	(I LOVE YOU) FOR SENTIMENTAL REASONS	Keen
December	1957	DESIRE ME	Keen
February	1958	LONELY ISLAND	Keen
February	1958	YOU WERE MADE FOR ME	Keen
August	1958	WIN YOUR LOVE FOR ME	Keen
November	1958	LOVE YOU MOST OF ALL	Keen
March	1959	EVERYBODY LIKE TO CHA CHA CHA	Keen
June	1959	ONLY SIXTEEN	Keen
November	1959	THERE I'VE SAID IT AGAIN	Keen
May	1960	WONDERFUL WORLD	Keen
March	1960	TEENAGE SONATA	RCA
August	1960	CHAIN GANG	RCA
December	1960	SAD MOOD	RCA
February	1961	THAT'S IT—I QUIT—I'M MOVIN' ON	RCA
June	1961	CUPID	RCA
October	1961	FEEL IT	RCA
January	1962	TWISTIN' THE NIGHT AWAY	RCA
May	1962	HAVING A PARTY	RCA
June	1962	BRING IT ON HOME TO ME	RCA
September	1962	NOTHING CAN CHANGE THIS LOVE	RCA
January	1963	SEND ME SOME LOVIN'	RCA
April	1963	ANOTHER SATURDAY NIGHT	RCA

July	1963	FRANKIE AND JOHNNY	RCA
October	1963	LITTLE RED ROOSTER	RCA
January	1964	GOOD NEWS	RCA
May	1964	GOOD TIMES	RCA
May	1964	TENNESSEE WALTZ	RCA
September	1964	COUSIN OF MINE	RCA
January	1965	SHAKE	RCA
January	1965	A CHANGE IS GONNA COME	RCA
April	1965	IT'S GOT THE WHOLE WORLD SHAKIN'	RCA
June	1965	WHEN A BOY FALLS IN LOVE	RCA
July	1965	SUGAR DUMPLING	RCA
February	1966	FEEL IT	RCA
April	1966	LET'S GO STEADY	RCA

THE COOKIES

Members:
> Dorothy Jones
> Margaret Ross
> Earljean McCree

Hometown: Brooklyn, New York

The Cookies worked as background singers for many artists like Carole King and Neil Sedaka in the early sixties. They were also used to back up Little Eva on her hit "Loco-motion." Don Kirshner, who owned the publishing firm where Carole King and her husband Gerry Goffin worked, assigned Gerry the task of writing a hit for these unknown background singers. In late 1962, a few months after Little Eva's hit, which Gerry and Carole had written, they wrote the first hit for The Cookies called "Chains," which was a hit on Dimension records.

November	1962	CHAINS	Dimension
February	1963	DON'T SAY NOTHIN' BAD	Dimension
June	1963	WILL POWER	Dimension
November	1963	GIRLS GROW UP FASTER THAN BOYS	Dimension

EDDIE COOLEY & THE DIMPLES

Eddie was a New York songwriter who penned a hit in the mid-fifties called "Fever" for Little Willie John. In 1956, he wrote a song called "Priscilla." He enjoyed the song so much that he got together with three young ladies, called them the Dimples, and recorded the song himself. It was released on Royal Roost records in October 1956 and became the group's only national hit.

October	1956	PRISCILLA	Royal Roost

LES COOPER

Hometown: Norfolk, Virginia

Les came to New York City in the fifties and first formed a singing group called The Empires. A short time later he became an arranger at Everlast records in New York.

During the summer of 1957, he brought the Charts to the label and managed them when they had their hit "Desirie." In October 1962, he had his only major hit as a performer, with the instrumental hit "Wiggle Wobble."

October 1962 WIGGLE WOBBLE   Everlast

JILL COREY

Real Name: Norma Jean Speranza
Born: September 30, 1935
Hometown: Avonmore, Pennsylvania

Jill was the youngest of five children of an Italian coal miner. In August 1953, while Jill was appearing with a dance band in Pittsburgh, the man-

JILL COREY

ager of one of the local radio stations heard her and was impressed with her style. Later he got her to tape a few numbers and mailed the tape to Mitch Miller of Columbia records in New York. Mitch liked what he heard and had Jill fly to New York, where she was auditioned and signed to the label.

Although she recorded songs like "He Is a Man" and "Number One Boy," it wasn't until late 1956 that she had her first national chart hit.

November	1956	I LOVE MY BABY	Columbia
April	1957	LET IT BE ME	Columbia
July	1957	LOVE ME TO PIECES	Columbia
August	1958	BIG DADDY	Columbia

DON CORNELL

Born: 1924
Hometown: New York, New York

In 1940, Don began singing with Bobby Hayes. A year later, while Don was singing with the MacFarland twins' band, Sammy Kaye heard him on the radio and sent him a wire asking him to join his band. In January 1942, Don joined Sammy's band, but mainly as a guitar player. Later that year he entered the Army Air Corps. Upon his discharge in 1946, he rejoined Sammy.

By 1949, Don left Sammy to go out as a solo, and within a couple of years signed with Coral records. By February 1952, he had his first major hit for the label with "I'll Walk Alone."

Today Don performs in clubs around the country and still has that big booming voice.

February	1952	I'LL WALK ALONE	Coral
April	1952	I'M YOURS	Coral
July	1952	THIS IS THE BEGINNING OF THE END	Coral
October	1952	I	Coral
November	1953	HEART OF MY HEART	
		(Johnny Desmond, Alan Dale)	Coral
September	1954	HOLD MY HAND	Coral
May	1955	MOST OF ALL/THE DOOR IS STILL	
		OPEN TO MY HEART	Coral
August	1955	THE BIBLE TELLS ME SO	Coral
August	1955	LOVE IS A MANY-SPLENDORED THING	Coral
November	1955	YOUNG ABE LINCOLN	Coral
February	1956	TEENAGE MEETING	Coral
April	1956	ROCK ISLAND LINE	Coral
October	1956	SEE-SAW	Coral
April	1957	MAMA GUITAR	Coral

THE CORSAIRS

Members:
    Jay Uzzell—lead—born: July 13, 1942
    James Uzzell—born: December 1, 1940
    Moses Uzzell—born: September 13, 1939
    George Wooten—born: January 16, 1940
Hometown: La Grange, North Carolina

The three brothers, along with their cousin George, attended the same high school and grew up together. They sang together in the glee club at school and at talent shows under the name The Gleems. They went to Newark, New Jersey in the early sixties to audition for various record companies but they had no success at this so they decided to stay in Newark, playing the local clubs.

    In the summer of 1961, Abner Spector and Chuck Fly caught their act at a club and liked them enough to get them a contract with Tuff records. They changed the name of the group to The Corsairs and took them to a studio to record. The result was "Smoky Places," which became a hit in January 1962.

| December | 1961 | SMOKY PLACES | Tuff |
| April | 1962 | I'LL TAKE YOU HOME | Tuff |

DAVE "BABY" CORTEZ

Real Name: David Cortez Clowney
Born: 1939
Hometown: Detroit, Michigan

Dave attended North Western High in Detroit. His father, a pianist, encouraged Dave to pursue a musical career. Dave played the piano for ten years, then switched to the organ.

    In late 1958, while Dave was singing with The Pearls, Clock records offered him a recording contract to come up with a song for the label. The result was "The Happy Organ," a song that went up to the number one spot on the national charts in March 1959. It took over three years for him to come up with another hit, and it happened in the summer of 1962, on Chess records with "Rinky Dink."

March	1959	THE HAPPY ORGAN	Clock
June	1959	THE WHISTLING ORGAN	Clock
July	1962	RINKY DINK	Chess

DAVE "BABY" CORTEZ

October	1962	HAPPY WEEKEND	Chess
March	1963	HOT CAKES (1ST SERVING)	Chess
August	1963	ORGAN SHOUT	Chess
June	1966	COUNT DOWN	Roulette

DON COSTA

Born: 1925
Hometown: Boston, Massachusetts

In the late fifties he was A & R director for ABC Paramount records and was responsible for the success of artists like Paul Anka.

Don formed his own record label DCP records (Don Costa Productions) in the mid-sixties, on which Little Anthony and The Imperials had hits like "I'm on the Outside Looking In," "Hurt So Bad," and "Goin' Out of My Head."

November	1959	I'LL WALK THE LINE	United Artists
April	1960	THEME FROM THE UNFORGIVEN	United Artists
August	1960	NEVER ON SUNDAY	United Artists

DON COSTA

DON COVAY & THE GOODTIMERS

Hometown: Washington, D.C.

Don began singing in Washington during the mid-fifties, with a group called the Rainbows. Two other members were Marvin Gaye and Billy Stewart.

Throughout the fifties, Don worked as a writer, singer, and musician with many of the top artists of the period. At one time he sang under the name of Pretty Boy for Atlantic records.

In early 1961, due to the enormous dance craze interest in the country, Don recorded a song called "Pony Time" for Arnold records. Unfortunately for Don, a young man from Philadelphia named Chubby Checker had a number one national hit at the same time called "Pony Time."

Today Don does some occasional soul shows with performers like Solomon Burke, Wilson Pickett, and Joe Tex performing under the name The Soul Clan.

January	1961	PONY TIME	Arnold
December	1962	POPEYE WADDLE	Cameo
August	1964	MERCY, MERCY	Rosemart
December	1964	TAKE THIS HURT OFF ME	Rosemart
July	1973	I WAS CHECKIN' OUT, SHE WAS CHECKIN' IN	Mercury

FLOYD CRAMER

Born: October 27, 1933
Hometown: Shreveport, Louisiana

When he was five, Floyd's family bought him a piano and he began to play almost every chance he had. After high school he joined radio station KWKH for the show "Louisiana Hayride." By 1955, he joined RCA at the suggestion of Chet Atkins and moved to Nashville to join the Grande Ole Opry. He became very busy as a studio musician playing for many dates with Elvis Presley, Jim Reeves, and The Browns.

FLOYD CRAMER

In 1958, RCA released a single with Floyd as a featured artist called "Flip, Flop and Bop," which went nowhere. Then in the fall of 1960, he recorded his own composition called "Last Date," which became a national hit and his biggest all-time seller. This recording established the "Cramer style," which is like a lonesome cowboy sound.

April	1958	FLIP, FLOP AND BOP	RCA
October	1960	LAST DATE	RCA
February	1961	ON THE REBOUND	RCA
June	1961	SAN ANTONIO ROSE	RCA
October	1961	YOUR LAST GOODBYE	RCA
January	1962	CHATTANOOGA CHOO CHOO	RCA
April	1960	LOVESICK BLUES	RCA
July	1962	HOT PEPPER	RCA
December	1962	JAVA	RCA

JOHNNY CRAWFORD

Real Name: John Ernest Crawford

Johnny began entertaining at age four. One year later he became one of the original Mouseketeers. Later on he starred with Chuck Connors in "The Rifleman" on ABC-TV as Chuck's son Mark.

In 1961, Bob Keene of Del Fi records convinced Johnny's father to let his son pursue a recording career. The result was "Daydreams" in the summer of 1961.

June	1961	DAYDREAMS	Del Fi
February	1962	PATTI ANN	Del Fi
May	1962	CINDY'S BIRTHDAY	Del Fi
July	1962	YOUR NOSE IS GONNA GROW	Del Fi
November	1962	RUMORS	Del Fi
January	1963	PROUD	Del Fi
September	1963	CINDY'S GONNA CRY	Del Fi
January	1964	JUDY LOVES ME	Del Fi

THE CRESCENDOS

In late 1957 a group from Nashville, Tennessee, called the Crescendos recorded "Oh, Julie," which featured the lead voice of Dale Ward, whose singing style was reminscient of an Elvis Presley with background singers. The song's success can be attributed primarily to the unique sound this combination generated. Today, Dale Ward is a solo C & W artist recording for Dot.

December	1957	OH JULIE	Nasco

THE CRESTS

Members:

Johnny Maestro (real name: Mastrangelo)—lead—Brooklyn, New York—May 7, 1939

Jay Carter (1939)—bass—Brooklyn, New York—replaced by Eddie Wright in 1960

Harrold Torres (1940)—second tenor—Staten Island, New York—replaced by Chuck Foote in 1960

Tommy Gough (1940)—first tenor—Staten Island, New York—replaced by Leonard Alexander in 1960.

The group first formed in the late fifties and signed with Joyce records. In 1958 they signed with George Paxton, the president of Coed records, and recorded "Pretty Little Angel." In November of that year they had their first smash hit, "Sixteen Candles," which carried into 1959 as their biggest hit.

Johnny left the group in 1961 to go as a single artist on Coed with "Model Girl." His career without the Crests went downhill. It wasn't until 1968, when he formed another group, The Brooklyn Bridge, and became their lead voice, that his career went back on the upswing.

Today Johnny sings lead with The Brooklyn Bridge (of "The Worst that Could Happen" fame) and resides outside of New York City.

July	1957	SWEETEST ONE	Joyce
October	1957	MY JUANITA	Joyce
September	1958	PRETTY LITTLE ANGEL	Coed
November	1958	16 CANDLES	Coed
February	1959	SIX NIGHTS A WEEK	Coed
June	1959	FLOWER OF LOVE	Coed
August	1959	THE ANGELS LISTENED IN	Coed
November	1959	A YEAR AGO TONIGHT	Coed
February	1960	STEP BY STEP	Coed
June	1960	TROUBLE IN PARADISE	Coed
September	1960	JOURNEY OF LOVE	Coed
October	1960	ISN'T IT AMAZING	Coed

THE CREW CUTS

Members:

John Perkins—lead—August 28, 1931

Pat Barrett—tenor—September 15, 1933

Rudi Maugeri—baritone—January 27, 1931

Ray Perkins—bass—November 28, 1932

Hometown: Toronto, Canada

Ray and his brother John got together with their friends Pat and Rudi to form the group in the early fifties, calling themselves The Canadaires

THE CREW CUTS

Clockwise from top: Rudi Maugeri, Pat Barrett,
Ray Perkins, John Perkins

since they were all from Canada. They got their first major break when
they drove from Canada to Cleveland, Ohio, to appear on Gene Carroll's
TV show in 1954. After their appearance, their manager, Fred Strauss,
introduced them to Cleveland disc-jockey Bill Randle, who suggested,
due to their hair style, that they change their name to The Crew Cuts.
Randle then called the head of Mercury records in Chicago and set up
an audition. This led to a recording contract and their first hit, "Crazy
'Bout You Baby," which Rudi and Pat wrote in 1954. After that they
recorded their biggest hit, "Sh-Boom," a song that had been originally
recorded as a blues hit for The Chords on Cat records earlier that same
year. The Crew Cuts' cover version of the song became a number one
hit on the pop music charts, while The Chords' version was a hit on the
R & B charts. The song has been considered as one of the pioneer rock
songs of all time.

Today Rudi is vice-president and music director of Radio Arts Syndi-
cation in California; John works for a newspaper near New Orleans; Pat is

in the automobile business in New Jersey, and Ray is in real estate in California. They recently got together and recorded a fifties-type nostalgia album for Seattle-based First American records.

April	1954	CRAZY 'BOUT YOU, BABY	Mercury
June	1954	SH-BOOM	Mercury
September	1954	OOP-SHOOP	Mercury
January	1955	KO KO MO	Mercury
January	1955	EARTH ANGEL	Mercury
April	1955	DON'T BE ANGRY/CHOP CHOP BOOM	Mercury
June	1955	A STORY UNTOLD	Mercury
August	1955	GUM DROP	Mercury
October	1955	ANGELS IN THE SKY	Mercury
November	1955	MOSTLY MARTHA	Mercury
January	1956	SEVEN DAYS	Mercury
June	1956	TELL ME WHY	Mercury
December	1956	YOUNG LOVE	Mercury

BOB CREWE

Real Name: Stanley Robert Crewe
Born: November 12, 1931
Hometown: Belleville, New Jersey

Bob was born in Newark, but his family moved to Belleville while he was a youngster. He became interested in the music business and wanted to become an entertainer. In the mid-fifties he went to Detroit to pursue a career as a vocalist. He signed with Spotlight records and recorded "Penny, Nickel, Dime, Quarter," which was moderately popular. After a few unsuccessful recordings, he went to Philadelphia, where he met piano player Frank Slay at a party. They formed their own label called XYZ records and signed an unknown group called the Rays. In late 1957, Bob and Frank wrote a song called "Silhouettes," which the Rays made a national hit. Subsequently, Frank and Bob wrote many hits for artists like the Rays, Billie and Lilly, and Freddy Cannon to name a few. In the early sixties Bob and Frank split up. Bob began working with a group called the Four Seasons, where he coauthored such songs with group member Bob Gaudio as "Big Girls Don't Cry" and "Walk Like a Man."

In November 1965, Bob signed Mitch Ryder and The Detroit Wheels to his new label, New Voice. They premiered with "Jenny Take a Ride." In 1969, he got Oliver (of "Jean" fame) to sign with his Crewe records.

Today he lives in New York, and works as a writer-producer for many of today's pop acts.

February	1956	PENNY NICKEL DIME QUARTER	Spotlight
February	1960	THE WHIFFENPOOF SONG	Warwick
December	1966	MUSIC TO WATCH GIRLS BY	Dyno Voice
October	1967	BIRDS OF BRITAIN	Dyno Voice

THE CRICKETS

Members:
  Buddy Holly—lead vocalist and guitarist—died: February 3, 1959
  Niki Sullivan—rhythm guitar—replaced by Tommy Allsup in 1959
  Joe B. Mauldin—bass
  Jerry Allison—drums
Hometown: Lubbock, Texas

In 1957, Buddy formed the group and took them to Clovis, New Mexico, to the studios of producer Norman Petty. They recorded a song that Buddy and Jerry had written called "That'll Be the Day." Petty then sent the demos to Roulette records in New York. They were sent back, because Roulette already had Jimmy Bowen and Buddy Knox under contract. Since both Jimmy and Buddy were from the same area of Texas as The Crickets, and since the company felt the sound was somewhat similar, they decided against signing the group.

Petty then sent the tapes to Peer-Southern Publishing in New York, where they were forwarded to Bob Thiele at Brunswick records. Thiele liked what he heard so much that he signed the group to the label and released the song in June 1957. The song took off and began to climb up the charts, becoming a national hit. A few months later, the group recorded their second hit, entitled "Oh Boy!," and Buddy recorded "Peggy Sue," for Jerry Allison's girl friend, as a solo artist for Coral records.

After the recording "Maybe Baby," Niki Sullivan left the group and was later replaced by Tommy Allsup in 1959. In later 1958, Jerry Allison recorded "Real Wild Child" for Coral under the name of Ivan, with Buddy playing lead guitar on the song.

After Buddy got married in August of 1958, the relationship between him and the rest of the group began to change. By mid-October, Buddy flew to Lubbock and decided to end his relationship with producer Petty. Allison and Mauldin decided to remain with Petty, so Holly chose to go out as a solo.

In January 1959, Buddy was booked for a big tour, so he got Waylon Jennings and another guitar player Tommy Allsup, along with drummer Charles Bunch, to accompany him. His pregnant wife, Maria, did not accompany Buddy on this tour. Later Maria was to lose the baby. It was on this tragic tour that Buddy, along with Ritchie Valens and the Big Bopper, were killed in a plane crash in Iowa on February 3, 1959.

July	1957	THAT'LL BE THE DAY	Brunswick
November	1957	OH, BOY!	Brunswick
February	1958	MAYBE BABY	Brunswick

July	1958	THINK IT OVER	Brunswick
September	1958	IT'S SO EASY	Brunswick

THE CROWS

Members:
>   Daniel "Sonny" Norton—lead (deceased)
>   Harold Major—tenor
>   William Davis—baritone
>   Gerald Hamilton—bass (deceased)

Hometown: New York, New York

In the late forties, the four fellows got together with guitar player Mark Jackson and decided to form a singing group. They called themselves The Crows because other groups they admired at the time had names of birds, like "The Ravens," "The Orioles," "The Cardinals," and "The Flamingos."

After singing on the street corners of Harlem for a while, they decided to enter a talent contest at the Apollo theater on their Wednesday night amateur nights. They were spotted by Cliff Martinez, a talent agent, who took an interest in the group. He worked with them for a while until he felt they were ready for an audition.

Cliff took the group in early 1954 to meet a friend of his by the name of George Goldner. George had just put together a new label called Rama records and was looking for new talent for the label. George heard the group and liked their sound, and wanted to know if they had any original material. William presented a song he had just written called "Gee" and they decided to record it.

The song was recorded and released in March 1954, and went on to become a classic in the annals of rock and roll, for it was one of the first songs to bridge the gap between R & B and pop music. The song went on to become a national hit and is considered by historians as one of the first rock and roll records to gain popularity on a national level and to be played on white radio stations

Due to the success of the record "Gee" in 1954, George Goldner began a new label in January 1956 called Gee records, premiering with the Cleftones and the song "You Baby You." It was also the same label Frankie Lymon & The Teenagers had so many hits on.

Daniel and Gerald are deceased. Harold and William still live in Harlem working regular jobs. They have not done any singing since the group disbanded in the mid-fifties.

March	1954	GEE	Rama
June	1954	HEARTBREAKER	Rama
August	1954	UNTRUE	Rama

THE CROWS

Center front: Gerald Hamilton
Left to right: William Davis, Harold Major, Sonny Norton

September	1954	MISS YOU	Rama
January	1955	BABY DOLL	Rama
March	1955	MAMBO SHEVITZ	Tico

THE CRYSTALS

Members:
    Mary Thomas—1946
    Dee Dee Kenniebrew—1945
    Lala Brooks—1946
    Barbara Alston—1945
    Pat Wright—1945
Hometown: Brooklyn, New York

The Crystals started singing together in high school. Their big break came in 1961 when they met Phil Spector in New York during an audi-

THE CRYSTALS

tion. He liked them and signed them to his label, Philles records. Their first release was "There's No Other," in November of 1961. Then came "Uptown" in early 1962, and their only number one song, "He's a Rebel," in the fall of 1962, a song that was written by Gene Pitney. On that song, producer Phil Spector used Darlene Love to sing lead. Darlene went on to other hits, like "Today I Met the Boy I'm Gonna Marry."

Today The Crystals sing at occasional rock shows and still reside in the New York area.

November	1961	THERE'S NO OTHER	Philles
March	1962	UPTOWN	Philles
September	1962	HE'S A REBEL	Philles
December	1962	HE'S SURE THE BOY I LOVE	**Philles**
April	1963	DA DOO RON RON	Philles
August	1963	THEN HE KISSED ME	Philles
January	1964	LITTLE BOY	Philles
August	1964	ALL GROWN UP	Philles

KING CURTIS

Real Name: Curtis Ousley
Died: August 13, 1971
Hometown: New York, New York

A tremendous talent on the tenor sax, King could be heard featured on many of the hits on Atco (such as many of the Coasters' hits) and Atlantic records, for he was a staff musician for the labels. He even enjoyed a career of his own as a featured performer on Capitol and Atco records. King met an untimely death in the summer of 1971, when he was stabbed to death in front of his own apartment building in New York Curity.

February	1962	SOUL TWIST	Enjoy
July	1962	BEACH PARTY	Capitol
August	1963	DO THE MONKEY	Capitol
February	1964	SOUL SERENADE	Capitol
December	1965	SPANISH HARLEM	Atco
April	1967	JUMP BACK	Atco
August	1967	MEMPHIS SOUL STEW	Atco
September	1967	ODE TO BILLIE JOE	Atco
November	1967	FOR WHAT IT'S WORTH	Atco
December	1967	I WAS MADE TO LOVE HER	Atco
February	1968	SITTIN' ON THE DOCK OF THE BAY	Atco
May	1968	VALLEY OF THE DOLLS	Atco
August	1968	I HEARD IT THROUGH THE GRAPEVINE	Atco
October	1968	HARPER VALLEY P.T.A.	Atco

KING CURTIS

BOBBY CURTOLA

Born: April 17, 1944
Hometown: Port Arthur, Ontario, Canada

He was a Canadian star on Tartan records and had nine hit singles in Canada by 1960. In 1962, Bob Keene, the president of Del Fi records in Los Angeles, signed him and acted as his United States manager. In May 1962, Bobby recorded his only big hit for the label, called "Fortune Teller."

May	1962	FORTUNE TELLER	Del Fi
October	1962	ALADDIN	Del Fi

JOHNNY CYMBAL

Hometown: Cleveland, Ohio

In early 1963, Johnny recorded a song he wrote called "Mr. Bass Man." The bass man on the record was Ronnie Bright (former bass with the Valentines and current bass with the Coasters). In October 1968, he called himself Derek and had a hit with "Cinnamon."

Today Johnny is a record producer on the West Coast.

February	1963	MR. BASS MAN	Kapp
May	1963	TEENAGE HEAVEN	Kapp
August	1963	DUM DUM DEE DUM	Kapp
October	1968	CINNAMON	Bang
February	1969	BACK DOOR MAN	Bang

VIC DAMONE

DALE & GRACE

Real Names:
  Dale Houston—Baton Rouge, Louisiana—1944
  Grace Broussard—Prairiville, Louisiana—1944

Dale and Grace had been solos in local clubs in Baton Rouge before they teamed up. They met at the recording studio of producer Sam Montel and did an impromptu session. Montel was so impressed with the song that they did, "I'm Leaving It Up to You," that he recorded it. He released the song, an old rock song originally written and recorded by Don "Sugarcane" Harris and Dewey Terry (Don & Dewey) on his own label, Montel records, and sold the master to Jamie/Guyden records for national distribution. The song was released in September 1963, and in just a short time became a number one national hit.

October	1963	I'M LEAVING IT UP TO YOU	Montel
January	1964	STOP AND THINK IT OVER	Montel
April	1964	THE LONELIEST NIGHT	Montel

VIC DAMONE

Real Name: Vito Farinola
Born: June 12, 1928
Hometown: Brooklyn, New York

While he was an usher at the New York Paramount theater, Vic stopped the elevator between floors to sing for Perry Como. He later won an audition on Arthur Godfrey's Talent Scout show, where Milton Berle heard him and arranged an engagement at the La Martinique club.

In 1947, Damone signed a two-year radio contract. Later he got a studio contract with MGM. Shortly afterward Vic recorded his first million seller, "You're Breaking My Heart."

His career started to wane until he signed with Columbia records in the mid-fifties. He came back strong in early 1956, with a top seller from the Broadway show *My Fair Lady* called "On the Street Where You Live." After doing some radio commercials for Coppertone suntan lotion in the fifties, Vic has lately confined himself to occasional night club appearances in Las Vegas, after filing for bankruptcy in 1971 for back taxes.

August	1947	I HAVE BUT ONE HEART	Mercury
March	1949	AGAIN	Mercury
June	1949	YOU'RE BREAKING MY HEART	Mercury
August	1949	MY BOLERO	Mercury
October	1949	WHY WAS I BORN?	Mercury
June	1950	VAGABOND SHOES	Mercury
July	1950	TZENA, TZENA, TZENA	Mercury
August	1950	JUST SAY I LOVE HER	Mercury
December	1950	MY HEART CRIES FOR YOU	Mercury
May	1951	MY TRULY, TRULY FAIR	Mercury
July	1951	LONGING FOR YOU	Mercury
September	1951	CALLA CALLA	Mercury
May	1953	APRIL IN PORTUGAL	Mercury
March	1956	ON THE STREET WHERE YOU LIVE	Columbia
September	1956	WAR AND PEACE	Columbia
March	1957	DO I LOVE YOU	Columbia
August	1957	AN AFFAIR TO REMEMBER	Columbia
April	1958	GIGI	Columbia
April	1965	YOU WERE ONLY FOOLING	Warner Bros.

VIC DANA

Born: August 26, 1942
Hometown: Buffalo, New York

Vic started dancing at age nine. When he was eleven and performing in Buffalo, Sammy Davis, Jr. caught Vic's act. Davis wanted to handle him, but Vic's parents thought he was too young. However, he convinced Vic's parents they should go to California, where there was more opportunity. They moved there, where Vic worked hard on his dancing and began to do some singing.

In 1960, he went on tour as a solo act, appearing on the same bill as The Fleetwoods. Dolton records signed Vic to a recording contract shortly thereafter. His first hit for the label, "Little Altar Boy," was at

Christmas 1961. It has since become a Christmas classic, getting play each holiday season.

November	1961	LITTLE ALTAR BOY	Dolton
March	1962	I WILL	Dolton
May	1963	DANGER	Dolton
August	1963	MORE	Dolton
March	1964	SHANGRI-LA	Dolton
June	1964	LOVE IS ALL WE NEED	Dolton
October	1964	GARDEN IN THE RAIN	Dolton
January	1965	RED ROSES FOR A BLUE LADY	Dolton
May	1965	BRING A LITTLE SUNSHINE	Dolton
August	1965	MOONLIGHT AND ROSES	Dolton
December	1965	CRYSTAL CHANDELIER	Dolton
May	1966	I LOVE YOU DROPS	Dolton
August	1966	A MILLION AND ONE	Dolton
January	1970	IF I NEVER KNEW YOUR NAME	Liberty
May	1970	RED RED WINE	Liberty

THE DANLEERS

Hometown: Brooklyn, New York

The group's only big hit came with Mercury records during the summer of 1958. It was called "One Summer Night" and it was written by the group's manager, Danny Webb, and featured the lead voice of Jimmy Weston.

June	1958	ONE SUMMER NIGHT	Mercury

THE DANLEERS

DANNY AND THE JUNIORS

Members:

Danny Rapp—lead—born: May 10, 1941
Dave White (September 1940)—first tenor—replaced by Bill Carlucci
Frank Maffei—second tenor—born: November 1940
Joe Terranova—baritone—born: January 30, 1941
Hometown: Philadelphia, Pennsylvania

The group was formed in Philadelphia in 1957, while its members were in high school. A short time later they signed with a local label called Singular records and called themselves The Juvenairs. Artie Singer of Singular records, along with a local disc jockey named Larry Brown, decided to change the name of the group to Danny & The Juniors.

In late 1957, Singer, John Medora, and group member Dave White wrote a song that they called "Do the Bop" to accommodate a new dance called The Bop that many teen-agers were doing on Dick Clark's "American Bandstand" TV show. Dick Clark heard the song and suggested they change the name to "At the Hop." The group went back into the studio with only a piano, bass, and drums and after about one hour emerged with the finished product. The song was released on Singular records in November 1957, and after it started to sell it was sold to ABC Paramount records, where it went on to become a number one national hit.

Their follow-up song in February of 1958, "Rock and Roll Is Here to Stay," written by Dave White, is a classic today, for it expresses how everyone today feels about rock and roll and the revival movement.

Today the fellows all live in Philadelphia. Only Joe and Bill, with several new members, travel around the country as Danny and The Juniors.

November	1957	AT THE HOP/SOMETIMES WHEN I'M ALL ALONE	ABC
February	1958	ROCK AND ROLL IS HERE TO STAY / SCHOOL BOY'S ROMANCE	ABC / Paramount
May	1958	DOTTIE	ABC
September	1960	TWISTIN' U.S.A.	Swan
February	1961	PONY EXPRESS	Swan
September	1961	BACK TO THE HOP	Swan
January	1962	TWISTIN' ALL NIGHT LONG	Swan
April	1962	DOIN' THE CONTINENTAL WALK	Swan
January	1963	OO-LA-LA-LIMBO	Guyden

DANTE & THE EVERGREENS

Members:

Dante Drowty—lead—born: September 8, 1941
Tony Moon—first tenor—born: September 21, 1941

Frank Rosenthal—bass—born: November 12, 1941
Bill Young—second tenor—born: May 25, 1942
Hometown: Los Angeles, California

The group got together while they were all in high school. They had a
chance to cut a couple of tapes, which Lou Adler heard. He liked what he
heard and let his friend Herb Alpert (of Tijuana Brass fame) listen. Herb
also liked the group, so they both decided to manage the fellows. They
got them a recording contract with Madison records and the group
recorded a song called "Alley-Oop" in May 1960, which became their first
big hit. Their version of the song, however, did not get as big as the version by The Hollywood Argyles, which went to number one. Dante & The
Evergreens' version only went as high as number fifteen on the national
charts.

| May | 1960 | ALLEY-OOP | Madison |
| September | 1960 | TIME MACHINE | Madison |

JOE DARENSBOURG & THE DIXIE FLYERS

The New Orleans-type jazz sound of this group helped catapult "Yellow
Dog Blues" onto the national charts in January 1958.

| January | 1958 | YELLOW DOG BLUES | Lark |

BOBBY DARIN

Real Name: Walden Robert Cassotto
Born: May 14, 1936
Died: December 20, 1973
Hometown: Bronx, New York

Bobby was born in a tough area of the Bronx, where he grew up a skinny,
sickly kid. His father died before Bobby was born and his mother lived
on welfare. But as a child he learned to play the drums, piano, and guitar.
In the mid-fifties, Bobby enrolled at Hunter College in New York and
took up drama. It was while a freshman at college that he decided to get
into show business. He changed his name from Cassotto to Darin by picking his new name from the phone book.

In 1956, Bobby signed with Decca records and made some obscure
recordings like "Blue-Eyed Mermaid." In 1957, he signed with Atco
records and premiered with "Million Dollar Baby," which was followed
with "Don't Call My Name" and "Just in Case You Change Your Mind."
In May 1958, while sitting at a piano, he got an idea for a song from New

York disc jockey Murray the "K's" mother. In about ten minutes he wrote "Splish Splash," which went on to be his first national hit.

After hits like "Queen of the Hop," "Plain Jane," and "Dream Lover," he recorded Kurt Weill's "Mack the Knife" in July 1959, and it not only became a number one song and his biggest hit, but it opened a new area for Bobby that changed his image and style.

In 1960, Bobby began a motion picture career with *Come September*. In December 1960, he married Sandra Dee, and two years later had a son named Dodd. In 1963, he was nominated for Best Supporting Actor for his role in *Captain Newman M.D.*

By the mid-1960s his career had begun to run downhill. In 1967, he divorced Sandra Dee. In 1970, he changed his name to Bob Darin and tried to create a new image with an antiwar act aimed at the new teen audiences.

Bobby, who had a history of heart trouble dating back to his boyhood days when he suffered from rheumatic fever, was admitted to Cedars of Lebonan Hospital in Los Angeles on December 12, 1973, for an examination. Tests shows that one of the two artificial valves inserted in his heart in 1971 was not functioning properly, necessitating surgery. On December 20, 1973, at 12:15 A.M., after almost seven hours on the operating table, Bobby Darin died.

May	1958	SPLISH SPLASH	Atco
October	1958	QUEEN OF THE HOP	Atco
January	1959	PLAIN JANE	Atco
April	1959	DREAM LOVER	Atco
August	1959	MACK THE KNIFE	Atco
January	1960	BEYOND THE SEA	Atco
March	1960	CLEMENTINE	Atco
May	1960	WON'T YOU COME HOME BILL BAILEY	Atco
September	1960	BEACHCOMBER	Atco
September	1960	ARTIFICIAL FLOWERS	Atco
September	1960	SOMEBODY TO LOVE	Atco
December	1960	CHRISTMAS AULD LANG SYNE	Atco
January	1961	CHILD OF GOD	Atco
January	1961	LAZY RIVER	Atco
June	1961	NATURE BOY	Atco
September	1961	YOU MUST HAVE BEEN A BEAUTIFUL BABY	Atco
December	1961	IRRESISTIBLE YOU	Atco
December	1961	MULTIPLICATION	Atco
March	1962	WHAT'D I SAY	Atco
June	1962	THINGS	Atco
September	1962	BABY FACE	Atco
December	1962	I FOUND A NEW BABY	Atco
May	1964	MILORD	Atco
September	1962	IF A MAN ANSWERS	Capitol
January	1963	YOU'RE THE REASON I'M LIVING	Capitol
May	1963	18 YELLOW ROSES	Capitol
August	1963	TREAT MY BABY GOOD	Capitol

BOBBY DARIN

November	1963	BE MAD LITTLE GIRL	Capitol
March	1964	I WONDER WHO'S KISSING HER NOW	Capitol
October	1964	THE THINGS IN THIS HOUSE	Capitol
January	1965	HELLO DOLLY	Capitol
April	1966	MAME	Atlantic
September	1966	IF I WERE A CARPENTER	Atlantic
December	1966	THE GIRL THAT STOOD BESIDE ME	Atlantic
January	1967	LOVIN' YOU	Atlantic
April	1967	THE LADY CAME FROM BALTIMORE	Atlantic
July	1967	DARLING BE HOME SOON	Atlantic
February	1967	LONG LINE RIDER	Direction
June	1973	HAPPY	Motown

JAMES DARREN

Real Name: James Ercolani
Born: October 3, 1936
Hometown: Philadelphia, Pennsylvania

James went to Epiphany School and Southern High in Philadelphia. He was spotted by Joyce Selznick of Screen Gems and she signed him to a contract with Columbia pictures in the late fifties. While appearing in the film *Gidget* he sang the title song, which was released on Colpix records in April 1959 and became his first hit for the label. His first real hit came in September 1961, with "Goodbye Cruel World."

April	1959	GIDGET	Colpix
August	1959	ANGEL FACE	Colpix
October	1961	GOODBYE CRUEL WORLD	Colpix
January	1962	HER ROYAL MAJESTY	Colpix
April	1962	CONSCIENCE	Colpix
June	1962	MARY'S LITTLE LAMB	Colpix
October	1962	HAIL TO THE CONQUERING HERO	Colpix
February	1963	PIN A MEDAL ON JOEY	Colpix
January	1967	ALL	Warner Bros.
March	1977	YOU TAKE MY HEART AWAY	Private Stock

THE DARTELLS

DeeDee Sharp's "Mashed Potatoes" was the first of the improbable "food" hits. She followed that with "Gravy." The Dartells got into the act with "Hot Pastrami" in April 1963.

April	1963	HOT PASTRAMI	Dot
August	1963	DANCE, EVERYBODY, DANCE	Dot

HUTCH DAVIE

Hutch Davie was a much-sought-after musical arranger for all the major labels in the mid-fifties. While he was working for Atco records in May 1958 he arranged and recorded his own hit—an instrumental called "Woodchoppers Ball."

May	1958	WOODCHOPPERS BALL	Atco

SAMMY DAVIS, JR.

Born: December 8, 1925
Hometown: New York, New York

Sammy's parents, Sammy, Sr. and Elvira, were member's of his uncle Will Mastin's vaudeville act, "Holiday in Dixieland," in the early twenties. As Sammy grew older he became a large part of the vaudeville act with his father and uncle, and the threesome was billed as The Will Mastin Trio.

Sammy spent the war years touring with a special services unit. In 1946 he rejoined his father and uncle in an engagement at Slapsie Maxie's in Hollywood. It was around this time that Sammy's good friend Frank Sinatra urged him to pay more attention to his singing career.

In 1954 following an appearance at New York's Copacabana, Sammy was signed by Decca records. Sammy recorded two albums for the label, out of which came his first chart record, "Hey There" (from the Broadway smash *Pajama Game*), in the summer of 1954.

In November of that year after a Vegas engagement, Sammy was returning to Hollywood for a recording session. He was in an automobile accident which cost him the loss of one eye. In January 1955, undaunted, Sammy made his return to the stage at Ciro's in Hollywood, wearing an eyepatch and joking about his handicap.

Sammy's career has not been limited strictly to the recording studio. In addition to his live performances, he has worked in films and television and has starred in a number of Broadway plays including *Golden Boy*.

In late 1968, he was sent a song by Steve Lawrence that Steve sang in the Broadway show *Golden Rainbow*. The song "I've Gotta Be Me" has become Sammy's song over the years and best depicts his career. Although he collapsed from exhaustion in Las Vegas, in 1970, he still maintains a busy schedule that keeps him involved with all areas of entertainment.

Sammy truly is Mr. Entertainment, for he excels in everything he does.

August	1954	HEY THERE	Decca
May	1955	SOMETHING'S GOTTA GIVE/LOVE ME OR LEAVE ME	Decca
June	1955	THAT OLD BLACK MAGIC	Decca
September	1955	I'LL KNOW	Decca
August	1956	EARTHBOUND	Decca
November	1956	NEW YORK'S MY HOME	Decca
August	1962	WHAT KIND OF FOOL AM I	Reprise
January	1963	AS LONG AS SHE NEEDS ME	Reprise
November	1963	THE SHELTER OF YOUR ARMS	Reprise
May	1967	DON'T BLAME THE CHILDREN	Reprise
May	1968	LONELY IS THE NAME	Reprise
December	1968	I'VE GOTTA BE ME	Reprise
March	1972	CANDY MAN	MGM
October	1972	PEOPLE TREE	MGM

SKEETER DAVIS

Real Name: Mary Frances Penick
Born: December 30, 1931
Hometown: Dry Ridge, Kentucky

Skeeter got her nickname as a youngster from her grandfather, who thought she was so active that she buzzed around like a mosquito. When

SKEETER DAVIS

she was in her early twenties, Skeeter appeared on WSM's Grand Ole Opry in Nashville and the Ernest Tubb show with her good friend Bee Jay (Betty Jack) Davis. In fact, she took Bee Jay's last name and they billed themselves as the Davis Sisters. When Bee Jay died in an auto crash in the mid-fifties, Skeeter was persuaded for several years by Steve Sholes of RCA records to go on as a solo.

In 1960, Skeeter married all-night disc jockey Ralph Emery of WSM, a marriage that lasted only a couple of years. Around 1961, she was presented with a song by Slyvia Dee, the same lady who wrote "Too Young" for Nat "King" Cole in 1951. The song was "The End of the World." (Sylvia Dee had first started to write the song after her father died. But nearly forty years elapsed before she completed it.)

Chet Atkins felt Skeeter should record the song. So Skeeter did—in memory of Bee Jay. In January 1963 it was released and became her biggest hit. Later in 1963, she recorded a Carole King song called "I Can't Stay Mad at You," which was another hit for her.

Today Skeeter lives in Nashville, still records for RCA, and continues to travel around the states in Country & Western shows.

August	1960	(I CAN'T HELP YOU) I'M FALLING TOO	RCA
December	1960	MY LAST DATE WITH YOU	RCA

January	1963	THE END OF THE WORLD	RCA
April	1963	I'M SAVING MY LOVE	RCA
August	1963	I CAN'T STAY MAD AT YOU	RCA
January	1964	HE SAYS THE SAME THINGS TO ME	RCA
April	1964	GONNA GET ALONG WITHOUT YOU NOW	RCA

BOBBY DAY

Real Name: Robert Byrd
Born: 1934
Hometown: Los Angeles, California

Bobby formed a group in 1957 called the Satellites, who sang around Los Angeles. He had the group back him up on a song called "Little Bitty Pretty One," a song that he wrote. The song was released on Class records in October 1957, and became Bobby's first hit. (Another version of the song was recorded by Thurston Harris for Aladdin records at about the same time. It outsold Bobby's version.)

Shortly after that, Bobby recorded another song with the Hollywood Flames called "Buzz-Buzz-Buzz," which was released on Ebb records in October 1957, becoming a national hit. In July 1958, as a solo performer for Class records, he recorded his biggest seller with the song "Rockin' Robin." The flip side, called "Over and Over," was also a hit.

October	1957	LITTLE BITTY PRETTY ONE	Class
July	1958	ROCKIN' ROBIN/OVER AND OVER	Class
December	1958	THE BLUEBIRD, THE BUZZARD AND THE ORIOLE	Class
March	1959	THAT'S ALL I WANT	Class

DORIS DAY

Real Name: Doris Kappelhoff
Born: April 3, 1924
Hometown: Cincinnati, Ohio

Doris sang with Les Brown's orchestra in the late forties. She signed with Columbia records in 1948, and had her first release with Buddy Clark called "Love Somebody." She became a top vocalist with Columbia during the early fifties, due in part to her popularity as an actress. In fact, her movie *Calamity Jane* presented her with a number one national hit in January 1954, with a tune from the movie, called *Secret Love*. She had other hits from motion pictures, including "Whatever Will Be Will Be," "Teacher's Pet," and "Tunnel of Love."

Today Doris lives in Los Angeles, but has retired from films and TV.

DORIS DAY

May	1948	LOVE SOMEBODY (Buddy Clark)	Columbia
June	1948	CONFESS (Buddy Clark)	Columbia
July	1948	IT'S MAGIC	Columbia
April	1949	AGAIN	Columbia
September	1949	NOW THAT I NEED YOU	Columbia
October	1949	CANADIAN CAPERS	Columbia
October	1949	BLUEBIRD ON YOUR WINDOWSILL	Columbia
February	1950	QUICKSILVER	Columbia
February	1950	I SAID MY PAJAMAS (AND PUT ON MY PRAYERS)	Columbia
April	1950	BEWITCHED	Columbia
May	1950	HOOP-DEE-DOO	Columbia
June	1950	I DIDN'T SLIP—I WASN'T PUSHED—I FELL	Columbia
January	1951	A BUSHEL AND A PECK	Columbia
February	1951	WOULD I LOVE YOU (LOVE YOU, LOVE YOU)	Columbia
June	1951	SHANGHAI	Columbia
February	1952	A GUY IS A GUY	Columbia
June	1952	SUGARBUSH (Frankie Laine)	Columbia
January	1953	MISTER TAP TOE	Columbia
January	1954	SECRET LOVE	Columbia
September	1954	IF I GIVE MY HEART TO YOU	Columbia
July	1955	I'LL NEVER STOP LOVING YOU	Columbia
December	1955	LET IT RING	Columbia
May	1956	WHATEVER WILL BE, WILL BE	Columbia
October	1956	LOVE IN A HOME	Columbia

December	1956	THE PARTY'S OVER	Columbia
April	1957	TWELVE O'CLOCK TONIGHT	Columbia
April	1958	TEACHER'S PET	Columbia
July	1958	EVERYBODY LOVES A LOVER	Columbia
November	1958	TUNNEL OF LOVE	Columbia
February	1960	ANYWAY THE WIND BLOWS	Columbia
April	1962	LOVER COME BACK	Columbia

JIMMY DEAN

Real Name: Seth Ward
Born: August 10, 1928
Hometown: Plainview, Texas

After getting out of the service in 1948, Jimmy formed a group in the Washington, D.C., area called The Texas Wildcats. Eventually he got his own morning TV show.

In the late fifties he signed with Columbia records and placed his first pop song on the charts in the fall of 1957 called "Deep Blue Sea." While flying to a recording session in Nashville, Jimmy wrote a song called "Big Bad John." The song went on to become a number one national hit in 1961.

Although Jimmy does occasional TV commercials, he leads a life of semi-retirement.

JIMMY DEAN

October	1957	DEEP BLUE SEA	Columbia
December	1957	LITTLE SANDY SLEIGHFOOT	Columbia
September	1961	BIG BAD JOHN	Columbia
January	1962	DEAR IVAN	Columbia
January	1962	TO A SLEEPING BEAUTY	Columbia
January	1962	THE CAJUN QUEEN	Columbia
March	1962	P. T. 109	Columbia
June	1962	STEEL MEN	Columbia
August	1962	LITTLE BLACK BOOK	Columbia
November	1962	GONNA RAISE A RUCKUS TONIGHT	Columbia
June	1965	THE FIRST THING EV'RY MORNING	Columbia
May	1976	I.O.U.	Casino

DEAN & JEAN

Real Names:
     Dean—Welton Young
     Jean—Brenda Lee Jones
Hometown: Dayton, Ohio

In the fall of 1963, Dean and Jean came to the offices of Laurie records in New York with some material they had written. They auditioned for Elliot Greenberg; he liked what he heard and signed them to Laurie's subsidiary label Rust records. "Tra La La La Suzy" became a national hit in October 1963.

October	1963	TRA LA LA LA SUZY	Rust
February	1964	HEY JEAN, HEY DEAN	Rust
May	1964	I WANNA BE LOVED	Rust

THE DE CASTRO SISTERS

Members:
     Peggy De Castro—Dominican Republic
     Babette De Castro—Havana, Cuba
     Cherie De Castro—New York, New York

The girls were raised on their father's sugar plantation in Cuba. They eventually came to New York, and began singing as a group. They signed with Abbott records and had a big hit with "Teach Me Tonight" in 1954.

September	1954	TEACH ME TONIGHT	Abbott
April	1955	BOOM BOOM BOOMERANG	Abbott
October	1955	TOO LATE NOW	Abbott
December	1955	SNOWBOUND FOR CHRISTMAS	Abbott
October	1956	IT'S YOURS	RCA
August	1958	WHO ARE THEY TO SAY	ABC
January	1959	TEACH ME TONIGHT CHA CHA	ABC

JIMMY DEE

Hometown: San Antonio, Texas

Girls' names have always been fair game as record subjects and titles. Chuck Berry had "Maybellene," Little Richard had "Lucille," and Buddy Holly had "Peggy Sue," among others. Jimmy Dee went far afield to pick a name probably no one else would have thought of using as a song title. The rasp sound of this West Coast vocalist earned him a big hit with "Henrietta" back in December 1957.

December 1957	HENRIETTA		Dot

JOEY DEE & THE STARLIGHTERS

Members:

> Joey Dee—real name: Joe DiNicola—lead—born: June 11, 1940—Passaic, New Jersey
> Carlton Latimor—organist—1939
> Willie Davis—drummer—1940
> Larry Vernieri—tenor—1940
> David Brigati—tenor—1940

After working as the house band for over a year at The Peppermint Lounge on West Forty-fifth Street in New York City, an interesting phenomenom occurred in late 1961. Some society people came in one night to dance the Twist and this caused some newspaper reporters in the place at the time to write a story about what had happened. Consequently, the place became the focal point for the "in" crowd of New York.

Joey, along with Henry Glover, wrote a song about the place called the "Peppermint Twist," which was released on Roulette records in the fall of 1961. It went right up the charts to the number one spot and made the Peppermint Lounge a nationally known spot.

In the summer of 1962, Joey cut a song as a single without the group, called "What Kind of Love Is This." However, he knew that his success was with the group so he bolstered the Starlighters by adding different members. At one time the Ronettes were in his revue. In 1963, three of the original Rascals were Starlighters, and in 1966, Joey hired a guitar player named Jimi Hendrix.

Today Joey lives in Winter Park, Florida, and does an occasional rock show.

November	1961	PEPPERMINT TWIST	Roulette
February	1962	HEY, LET'S TWIST	Roulette
March	1962	SHOUT	Roulette
August	1962	WHAT KIND OF LOVE IS THIS	Roulette

October	1962	I LOST MY BABY	Roulette
February	1963	BABY YOU'RE DRIVING ME CRAZY	Roulette
April	1963	HOT PASTRAMI WITH MASHED POTATOES	Roulette
July	1963	DANCE, DANCE, DANCE	Roulette

JOHNNY DEE

Johnny Dee recorded a song with which Eddie Cochran had launched his career on Liberty called "Sittin' in the Balcony." Johnny's hit was the only one he had for Colonial records.

February	1957	SITTIN' IN THE BALCONY	Colonial

LENNY DEE

Organ player Lenny Dee developed a large following of fans during the time he recorded for Decca, but it wasn't until he recorded a swinging version of "Plantation Boogie" that his popularity took on a national character. The song, which was released in January 1955, was his only major hit for Decca.

January	1955	PLANTATION BOOGIE	Decca

TOMMY DEE

Born: July 15, 1940

Following the tragic plane crash in February 1959 that claimed the lives of Buddy Holly, The Big Bopper, and Ritchie Valens, Tommy recorded a song he wrote called "Three Stars," a sort of musical epitaph. The song was his only hit.

March	1959	THREE STARS	Crest

THE DE JOHN SISTERS

Real Names:
    Julie DeGiovanni—born: March 18, 1931
    Dux DeGiovanni—born: January 21, 1933
Hometown: Chester, Pennsylvania

The sisters started singing at the age of sixteen but only on weekends. They worked for Sears, Roebuck during the week. Instead of going into the family business (a dry cleaning store), their ambition was to go on stage. Their big break came in the early fifties when another group from Chester called the Four Aces were signed by Decca. The Aces left the Ukrainian club where they had been playing and the De John sisters replaced them on the bill. In the mid-fifties they were signed by Epic records, and in late 1954 "No More" became a top-ten hit for them. It was the first time a hiccup song made the hit parade. The sisters would sing: "My baby don't love (stutter) ah me, no more."

| December 1954 | (MY BABY DON'T LOVE ME) NO MORE | Epic |
| September 1955 | C'EST LA VIE | Epic |

THE DELLS

Members:
>   Johnny Funches—lead—replaced by Johnny Carter
>   Marvin Junior—first tenor
>   Verne Allison—second tenor
>   Mike McGill—baritone
>   Chuck Barksdale—bass

Hometown: Harvey, Illinois

The group attended Thornton Township High in Harvey, Illinois, which is just south of Chicago. They began by singing gospel music in the church choir. In 1954, they called themselves the El Rays and went to Chicago to audition for Phil and Leonard Chess of Chess records. They signed them to their Checker label and the El Rays recorded "Darling I Know," which was a disaster. The group continued to play local clubs in Chicago, and worked on improving their sound.

In 1955, they auditioned for Vivian Carter of Vee Jay records and were signed to a recording contract. She also suggested they change their name to the Dells. Their first release, in the spring of 1955, was "Tell the World." In the summer of 1956, the fellows went to a party some girls had thrown and the next day Johnny and Marvin were reminiscing about the previous evening. Johnny exclaimed, "Oh! what a night," to which Marvin said that sounded like a great line for a song. They wrote some lyrics about the evening and then went into a studio to record the song. A few weeks later "Oh, What A Night" was released and became the Dells' biggest hit.

Today The Dells have the same group they started with back in 1954, with the exception of Johnny Carter who has replaced Johnny

THE DELLS

Clockwise from top: Chuck Barksdale, Mike McGill,
Verne Allison, Johnny Carter, Marvin Junior

Funches. They all still live in the Chicago area and now record for Cadet
records. They continue to perform for audiences all over the country.

April	1955	TELL THE WORLD	Vee Jay
August	1956	OH, WHAT A NIGHT	Vee Jay
October	1956	MOVIN' ON	Vee Jay
January	1957	A DISTANT LOVE	Vee Jay
May	1957	THE SPRINGER	Vee Jay
February	1958	JEEPERS CREEPERS	Vee Jay
May	1965	STAY IN MY CORNER	Vee Jay
November	1967	O-O, I LOVE YOU	Cadet
February	1968	THERE IS	Cadet
May	1968	WEAR IT ON OUR FACE	Cadet
June	1968	STAY IN MY CORNER	Cadet
October	1968	ALWAYS TOGETHER	Cadet
January	1969	DOES ANYBODY KNOW I'M HERE	Cadet

March	1969	I CAN'T DO ENOUGH	Cadet
May	1969	I CAN SING A RAINBOW/LOVE IS BLUE	Cadet
August	1969	OH, WHAT A NIGHT	Cadet
October	1969	ON THE DOCK OF THE BAY	Cadet
January	1970	OH WHAT A DAY	Cadet
April	1970	OPEN UP MY HEART/NADINE	Cadet
July	1970	LONG LONELY NIGHTS	Cadet
January	1971	THE GLORY OF LOVE	Cadet
August	1971	THE LOVE WE HAD (STAYS ON MY MIND)	Cadet
April	1973	GIVE YOUR BABY A STANDING OVATION	Cadet
October	1973	MY PRETENDING DAYS ARE OVER	Cadet
January	1974	I MISS YOU	Cadet
July	1974	I WISH IT WAS ME YOU LOVED	Cadet
October	1974	BRING BACK THE LOVE OF YESTERDAY	Cadet

THE DEL VIKINGS

Members:

> Norman Wright—lead—Philadelphia, Pennsylvania—October 21, 1937
> Corinthian "Kripp" Johnson—first tenor—Cambridge, Maryland
> Donald "Gus" Bakus—second tenor—Southampton, Long Island, New York
> David Lerchey—baritone—New Albany, Indiana
> Clarence E. Quick—bass—Brooklyn, New York

The five fellows formed a singing group in 1955, while they were all stationed in the Air Force in Pittsburgh, Pennsylvania. They practiced in the service club each day as they began to develop their sound. In late 1956, Clarence wrote a song at the piano in five minutes called "Come Go with Me," which he suggested the group record. This was at the same time that they had won the "Tops in Blues" show sponsored by the Air Force.

They went to the home of a friend named Barry Kaye, a Pittsburgh disc jockey, and recorded the song in his basement. The room was so small and poorly equipped acoustically that some of the members had to get into a closet to get the sound they were looking for.

After they recorded the song, they sold it to Fee-Bee records in Pittsburgh, where it became an instant hit. A few months later, in early 1957, Dot records purchased the recording and released it nationally, and signed the group to the label. The fellows chose to call themselves the Del Vikings after going through some books in a library and running across the accounts of the Vikings. They took that name and just added "Del" to it. The Del Vikings, which had Dave and Gus, two white members, and Kripp, Norman, and Clarence, who were black, were one of the few mixed groups with a hit recording.

After "Come Go with Me" became a national hit, Mercury records tried to lure the group to record for them when most of the fellows got their discharge from the Air Force. All of them except Kripp had been under twenty-one when they signed with Dot so, except for Kripp, they were not legally bound to Dot. So when Mercury offered more money, they all left for the new label. Kripp remained with Dot and formed another Del Vikings group with all black members, while the other four members went to Mercury and added another black member named

THE DEL VIKINGS

Top: Kripp Johnson
Bottom: Norman Wright
Center, left to right: Gus Bakus,
Clarence Quick, Dave Lerchey

William Blakely. At Mercury they recorded "Cool Shake," on which Gus sang lead, and "Sunday Kind of Love," on which Norman sang lead. These were the two biggest hits they had for Mercury. Dot released "Whispering Bells," another Clarence Quick composition, on which Kripp sang lead. Consequently, during the summer of 1957, there were two Del Vikings' hits on the charts, "Whispering Bells" on Dot and "Cool Shake" on Mercury, at the same time. This led to many legal entanglements to be resolved.

By December 1, 1957, Mercury got complete control of the group name. Kripp left Dot that same month to work for Fee-Bee music in Pittsburgh, and Chuck Jackson, an unknown at the time in Kripp's group, began a solo career that would get him hits on Wand records in 1961, with songs like "I Don't Want to Cry." The Mercury Del Vikings continued, but with no other major hits.

Today Gus lives in Europe, Norman in New York City, Clarence in Brooklyn, and Kripp in Pittsburgh. Norman and Clarence sang with two other members as the Del Vikings at a show in New York several years ago, but have not sung together since. Today only Clarence keeps the group working, with all new members.

January	1957	COME GO WITH ME	Dot
June	1957	WHISPERING BELLS	Dot
July	1957	COOL SHAKE	Mercury
September	1957	SUNDAY KIND OF LOVE	Mercury

THE DIMENSIONS

Members:
> Phil Del Giudice—lead—1938
> Lenny Dell—second tenor—1944
> Howie Margolin—baritone—1943
> Marisa Martelli—soprano—1944

Hometown: Bronx, New York

Howie and Lenny sang together in Bronx High's choral group in early 1960. They asked Marisa, a schoolmate, to join them. Phil, five years older than the rest, was asked to join the group as lead singer. Lenny's father, Lou, a professional musician, helped the group polish their style. He then introduced them to executives of Mohawk records during the summer of 1960. This led to a contract and the recording "Over the Rainbow," which became their only real hit.

| June | 1960 | OVER THE RAINBOW | Mohawk |
| February | 1963 | MY FOOLISH HEART | Coral |

MARTIN DENNY

Members:
Martin Denny—piano—born: April 10, 1921—New York, New York
Julius Wechter—vibes and marimba
August Colon—birdcalls, bongos, and congas
Harvey Ragsdale—string bass and marimbula

Martin started playing classical music on the piano at the age of ten. After college he began touring South America with a jazz group. During an engagement at Don the Beachcomber's in Honolulu in the late fifties, Martin decided to settle in Hawaii.

He formed a jazz group with Julius (who later would form his own group The Baja Marimba Band in the 1960s), August, and Harvey. They specialized in exotic sounds with birdcalls and other way-out sound effects. In early 1959, an executive from Liberty records heard the group and decided to sign them to the label. Their version of Les Baxter's composition "Quiet Village" became a smash hit in the United States that summer.

April	1959	QUIET VILLAGE	Liberty
July	1959	MARTINIQUE	Liberty
October	1959	THE ENCHANTED SEA	Liberty
July	1962	A TASTE OF HONEY	Liberty

JACKIE DeSHANNON

Born: August 21, 1944
Hometown: Hazel, Kentucky

Jackie was born in Kentucky, where both her parents were entertainers who sang folk and country blues. At the age of six, she had her own radio show. As she grew older she also began to write songs and acquired proficiency in this area. Brenda Lee recorded her "Dum Dum" in June 1961.

Jackie signed with Liberty records in 1962 and recorded "Faded Love," which became her first hit in February 1963. In May 1965, she recorded a Burt Bacharach and Hal David song called "What the World Needs Now Is Love," which was nominated for four Grammys. Jackie has written over six hundred songs, many of which have been hits for other performers from Brenda Lee to the Byrds. She continues to record and has written a number of successful songs for herself, including the million seller "Put a Little Love in Your Heart." Her biggest was the 1981 song she co-wrote for Kim Carnes called "Bette Davis Eyes."

February	1963	FADED LOVE	Liberty
May	1963	NEEDLES AND PINS	Liberty
January	1964	WHEN YOU WALK IN THE ROOM	Liberty

May	1965	WHAT THE WORLD NEEDS NOW IS LOVE	Imperial
September	1965	A LIFETIME OF LONELINESS	Imperial
May	1966	COME AND GET ME	Imperial
September	1966	I CAN MAKE IT WITH YOU	Imperial
August	1968	THE WEIGHT	Imperial
June	1969	PUT A LITTLE LOVE IN YOUR HEART	Imperial
October	1969	LOVE WILL FIND A WAY	Imperial
March	1970	BRIGHTON HILL	Imperial
May	1970	MEDLEY—YOU KEEP ME HANGIN' ON/HURT SO BAD	Imperial
August	1970	IT'S SO NICE	Liberty
October	1977	DON'T LET THE FLAME BURN OUT	Amherst
March	1980	I DON'T NEED YOU ANYMORE	RCA

THE DIABLOS

Members:
> Nolan Strong—lead
> Jimmy Strong—first tenor
> George Scott—baritone
> Willie Hunter—bass
> Bob Edwards—guitar

Hometown: Detroit, Michigan

The Diablos had a big hit with "The Wind" in 1954, a song that Nolan had written. Nolan called the group The Diablos because of a book he was reading in high school at the time called *El Nino Diablo*. Nolan, who is a cousin to Barret Strong ("Money," 1960) recorded the song "The Wind" with his group in 1954 for Fortune records in Detroit, and it became their only national hit.

April	1954	THE WIND	Fortune

THE DIAMONDS

Members:
> Dave Somerville—lead
> Bill Reed—bass—replaced by Evan Fisher in 1959—California
> Ted Kowalski—tenor—replaced by John Felton in 1959—California
> Phil Leavitt—baritone—replaced by Mike Douglas in 1959—Canada

Hometown: Ontario, Canada

Ted Kowalski came up with the name The Diamonds as the group were walking to their first job in the basement of a church at St. Thomas Aquinas in 1953, in Canada. In 1955, while working at The Alpine Village club in Cleveland, Ohio, disc jockey Bill Randle of station WERE heard the group and suggested they record. Randle was instrumental in getting them a contract with Mercury records in Chicago a few days later.

THE DIAMONDS

Clockwise from top: Mike Douglas, Bill Reed,
Dave Somerville, Ted Kowalski

By February 1956, The Diamonds released their first record, "Why Do Fools Fall in Love," a cover version of Frankie Lymon & The Teenagers' big hit on Gee records. Their next release was a cover version of a song by another black vocal group, The Willows, "Church Bells May Ring," which was fairly successful. They followed by doing versions of "Love, Love, Love" and The G-Clefs' 'Ka-Ding-Dong." In essence, The Diamonds offered white teen-agers a white version of a hit made popular by black singing groups.

In early 1957, while at a recording session, the group's manager, Nat Goodman, found a recording called "Little Darlin'," which had been recorded by the Gladiolas on Excello records. (The Gladiolas' lead singer and writer of "Little Darlin'" was Maurice Williams, who three years later would find fame with another song that he would write and record called "Stay.") David Carroll of Mercury had been listening to the song and had left it on his desk. Nat took the song to the hotel where The Diamonds were staying and he had them learn the song note by note. They practiced all night long and later that afternoon they recorded the song. It became their first real hit in early 1957, even though it was a "cover" version (not too many people knew the Gladiolas' version existed, for it was an R & B hit, primarily in the South).

The Diamonds scored big with another original in late 1957, a dance song called "The Stroll," which everyone was doing on Dick Clark's "American Bandstand" TV show.

Today only Dave is active singing. Up until a couple of years ago, he was singing with Bruce Belland (former lead voice of the Four Preps). The duo did TV shows and summer concert tours.

February	1956	WHY DO FOOLS FALL IN LOVE	Mercury
March	1956	CHURCH BELLS MAY RING	Mercury
June	1956	LOVE, LOVE, LOVE	Mercury
August	1956	KA-DING-DONG	Mercury
September	1956	SOFT SUMMER BREEZE	Mercury
February	1957	LITTLE DARLIN,	Mercury
June	1957	WORDS OF LOVE	Mercury
August	1957	ZIP ZIP	Mercury
October	1957	SILHOUETTES	Mercury
December	1957	THE STROLL	Mercury
April	1958	HIGH SIGN	Mercury
July	1958	KATHY-O	Mercury
November	1958	WALKING ALONG	Mercury
February	1959	SHE SAY (OOM DOOBY DOOM)	Mercury
July	1961	ONE SUMMER NIGHT	Mercury

DICK AND DEEDEE

Members:

    Dick St. John—1944

    DeeDee Sperling—1945

Hometown: Los Angeles, California

Dick was singing as a solo in Los Angeles in the early 1960s without much success. DeeDee, a friend since grammar school, joined him and they began appearing as a duo. In 1961, they got a contract with Liberty records to cut a song, so Dick wrote a tune called "I Want Someone" and they recorded it. He was thinking of an idea for the flip side of the record when he won a scholarship to the Los Angeles Art Institute for his sketch of a mountain. While looking at the sketch he got the idea for the song "The Mountains High" which they recorded as the flip side. "The Mountains High" started getting fantastic response in San Francisco that summer, so Liberty decided to make that the "A" side, and it went on to be their first and biggest hit.

DICK AND DEEDEE

In 1962, they left Liberty and signed with Warner Brothers and released "Young and in Love" in early 1963 as their first hit with their new label.

July	1961	THE MOUNTAIN'S HIGH	Liberty
March	1962	TELL ME	Liberty
March	1963	YOUNG AND IN LOVE	Warner Bros
October	1963	WHERE DID THE GOOD TIMES GO	Warner Bros.
November	1963	TURN AROUND	Warner Bros
February	1964	ALL MY TRIALS	Warner Bros.
November	1964	THOU SHALT NOT STEAL	Warner Bros
March	1965	BE MY BABY	Warner Bros.

BO DIDDLEY

Real Name: Ellas McDaniels
Born: December 30, 1928
Hometown: McComb, Mississippi

When Bo was a small boy his family moved to Chicago. It was while in grammar school that he got the nickname Bo Diddley, which he began using as an amateur boxer. At the age of ten, he got a guitar as a Christmas present and began playing it daily. He was influenced to play the guitar by John Lee Hooker when he heard the song "Boogie Children."

In 1951, Bo started playing at the 708 Club in Chicago. In 1955, he auditioned for Phil and Leonard Chess of Chess records with a song he wrote called "Uncle John." The brothers liked what they heard so they signed Bo to an exclusive contract and decided to record the song. They felt the title of the song should be changed, so Bo named it after himself, "Bo Diddley." Bo used maracas in the song to emphasize the beat and the sound he was trying to create. It took thirty-five takes in the recording studio, but they finally had the sound and song they wanted. It became his biggest hit in 1955, and established his guitar sound.

Four years later, in 1959, while at a recording session, Bo came up with another classic hit. It was during a coffee break that Bo and his maracas player Jerome Green started to kid each other while they were playing their guitars. Ron Maylow of Chess records was in the control room at the time, and he turned on the recorder to capture the spontaneous humor. After about ten minutes of the kidding he turned off the recorder and told Bo he had recorded their conversation. Bo, somewhat surprised, could not figure out why Ron would want to record what they had just been doing. After much editing, the song was released that fall and "Say Man" became a hit.

In the mid-fifties, when Bo played the Apollo theater in Harlem, a young man named Elvis Presley would come to watch him work whenever he was in town.

BO DIDDLEY

Today Bo lives on a ranch in Los Lunas, New Mexico, and travels around the country appearing in various rock shows. He still records for Checker's parent company, Chess records.

April	1955	BO DIDDLEY/I'M A MAN	Checker
July	1955	DIDDLEY DADDY	Checker
March	1959	I'M SORRY	Checker
July	1959	CRACKIN UP	Checker
August	1959	SAY MAN	Checker
December	1959	SAY MAN, BACK AGAIN	Checker
April	1960	ROAD RUNNER	Checker
August	1962	YOU CAN'T JUDGE A BOOK BY THE COVER	Checker
January	1967	OOH BABE	Checker

MARK DINNING

Born: 1933
Hometown: Grant County, Oklahoma

Mark was one of nine children, whose father was an Evangelist minister. His sisters were the famous Dinning Sisters trio of the forties. After his tour of duty in the military in 1957, Mark went to Nashville to start a singing career. That same year he was signed by MGM records. He had a couple of small hits, but it wasn't until November 1959 that he really found success with a song called "Teen Angel," which went to the number one spot on the national charts and became his biggest hit.

November	1959	TEEN ANGEL	MGM
April	1960	A STAR IS BORN	MGM
August	1960	LOVIN' TOUCH	MGM
February	1961	TOP 40, NEWS, WEATHER & SPORTS	MGM

KENNY DINO

Born: February 12, 1942
Hometown: New York, New York

Kenny was the second of five children. He went to high school in New York and, after graduation in 1958, he joined the Navy for two years as an aircraft mechanic. After his discharge in October 1960, Kenny decided to concentrate on singing. In early 1961, he signed with Musicor records. In October of the same year he recorded his only hit, "Your Ma Said You Cried in Your Sleep Last Night."

October	1961	YOUR MA SAID YOU CRIED IN YOUR SLEEP LAST NIGHT	Musicor

PAUL DINO

Born: March 2, 1939
Hometown: Philadelphia, Pennsylvania

Paul began singing in his high school glee club. After high school he went to barber school. But since he had talent in music, being able to play the sax, piano, drums, and accordion, he decided to pursue a musical career. He went to Bill Lasly of Promo records and auditioned with a song he had written. Bill liked the song and signed Paul. "Ginnie Bell" was released in January 1961, and became Paul's only hit.

January	1961	GINNIE BELL	Promo

DION

Real Name: Dion DiMucci
Born: July 18, 1939
Hometown: Bronx, New York

Dion's father was an entertainer, which inspired Dion to become involved in show business. He made his professional debut at age eleven on Paul Whiteman's radio show. In early 1958, Dion formed a group with Freddie Milano, Carlos Mastrangelo, and Angelo D'Aleo; they called themselves Dion & The Belmonts. (The Belmonts' name came from Belmont Avenue, a street in the Bronx.)

Dion remained with the group until the middle of 1960, when he went on his own as a solo performer on Laurie records. His first hit as a single was "Lonely Teenager" in the fall of 1960. His first major hit, which became his only number one record, was a song he wrote with his good friend Ernie Maresca (of "Shout, Shout Knock Yourself Out" fame) about a girl Dion eventually went on to marry named Sue. The song "Runaround Sue" became his biggest hit.

Dion remained with Laurie records until 1963, after which he joined Columbia for five years before returning to Laurie records in 1968.

Today Dion resides with his wife and family in Florida, and has become a Born Again Christian, doing gospel music while refusing either to sing his old hits or appear on any rock shows.

See also The Belmonts; Dion & The Belmonts.

October	1960	LONELY TEENAGER	Laurie
January	1961	HAVIN' FUN	Laurie
May	1961	KISSIN' GAME	Laurie
October	1961	RUNAROUND SUE	Laurie

DION

November	1961	THE WANDERER	Laurie
November	1961	THE MAJESTIC	Laurie
April	1962	LOVERS WHO WANDER	Laurie
April	1962	(I WAS) BORN TO CRY	Laurie
June	1962	LITTLE DIANE	Laurie
November	1962	LOVE CAME TO ME	Laurie
February	1963	SANDY	Laurie
June	1963	COME GO WITH ME	Laurie
January	1963	RUBY BABY	Columbia
April	1963	THIS LITTLE GIRL	Columbia
June	1963	BE CAREFUL OF STONES THAT YOU THROW	Columbia
September	1963	DONNA THE PRIMA DONNA	Columbia
November	1963	DRIP DROP	Columbia
August	1964	JOHNNY B. GOODE	Columbia
October	1968	ABRAHAM, MARTIN AND JOHN	Laurie
January	1969	PURPLE HAZE	Laurie
April	1969	BOTH SIDES NOW	Laurie
June	1970	YOUR OWN BACK YARD	Warner Bros.

DION & THE BELMONTS

Members:

Dion DiMucci—lead—born: July 18, 1939
Angelo D'Aleo—first tenor—born—February 3, 1940

Freddie Milano—second tenor—born: August 22, 1939
Carlo Mastrangelo—bass—born: October 5, 1938
Hometown: Bronx, New York

They got the name of the group from Belmont Avenue in the Bronx. All the members came from around Belmont Avenue, Garden Street, and Prospect Avenue, the same neighborhood The Regents ("Barbara-Ann") and Bobby Darin were from. Dion, Angelo, Freddie, and Carlo formed the group at Roosevelt High in the Bronx in early 1958. In April of that year, they launched their careers with the song "I Wonder Why," which was the first release for the newly formed Laurie records.

After a few moderate hits, the group recorded one of their biggest numbers in early 1959, a song that Doc Pomus and Mort Shuman had written called "A Teenager in Love." (Shortly after this song Angelo left the group and joined the Navy.) Their biggest hit and their favorite recording was the Rodgers and Hart classic "Where or When." A few months later, after "In the Still of the Night," Dion left the group to go on as a solo performer.

In 1961, after Angelo got out of the Navy, he got together with Carlo and Freddie and they signed with Sabina records as The Belmonts. Carlo became their new lead voice. Their first hit was "Tell Me Why."

Today Dion records religious music; Freddie sings with two new members backing up Freddy Cannon; while Carlo and Angelo are involved in their own separate careers.

See also The Belmonts; Dion.

April	1958	I WONDER WHY	Laurie
August	1958	NO ONE KNOWS	Laurie
December	1958	DON'T PITY ME	Laurie
April	1959	A TEENAGER IN LOVE	Laurie
September	1959	EVERY LITTLE THING I DO	Laurie
January	1960	WHERE OR WHEN	Laurie
April	1960	WHEN YOU WISH UPON A STAR	Laurie
July	1960	IN THE STILL OF THE NIGHT	Laurie

THE DIXIEBELLS

Members:
    Shirley Thomas
    Mary Hunt
    Mildred Pratcher
Hometown: Memphis, Tennessee

The Dixiebells grew up in Memphis and attended high school there. After graduation they decided to form a vocal group. They began backing up other singers on recording dates in Memphis and New Orleans. In 1963, they met Bill Justis (who had recorded "Raunchy") and he signed them to Sound Stage 7 records. That summer they recorded their biggest hit, a song called "Down at Papa Joe's."

| August | 1963 | DOWN AT PAPA JOE'S | Sound Stage 7 |
| January | 1964 | SOUTHTOWN, U.S.A. | Sound Stage 7 |

CARL DOBKINS, JR.

Born: January 1941
Hometown: Cincinnati, Ohio

While a high school junior in Cincinnati, appearing in the TV show The Sunday Swing Dance at Castle Farm, Carl was spotted by Harry Silverstein of Decca records, who signed him to a recording contract. In early 1959, he recorded a song which became his biggest hit called "My Heart Is an Open Book."

April	1959	MY HEART IS AN OPEN BOOK	Decca
October	1959	IF YOU DON'T WANT MY LOVIN'	Decca
November	1959	LUCKY DEVIL	Decca
May	1960	EXCLUSIVELY YOURS	Decca

BILL DOGGETT

Born: February 16, 1916
Hometown: Philadelphia, Pennsylvania

Bill first worked for Jimmy Gorman and his orchestra. In 1938, he formed his own band, but sold it to Lucky Millinder when the physical strain became too great. He went to Los Angeles in 1947 and arranged music for Lionel Hampton, Louis Jordan, Count Basie, and Louis Armstrong. He also played piano for the Ink Spots for a while.

Bill formed his own combo in 1952 and signed with King records. In a short time he became known as one of the fathers of the swinging organ. In the summer of 1956, he recorded his biggest all-time seller, the instrumental "Honky Tonk (Parts 1 and 2)."

Today Bill lives on Long Island but makes occasional appearances at rock shows in the New York area.

| July | 1956 | HONKY TONK | King |
| October | 1956 | SLOW WALK | King |

BILL DOGGETT

January	1957	RAM-BUNK-SHUSH	King
October	1957	SOFT	King
July	1958	BLIP BLOP	King
November	1958	HOLD IT	King
January	1960	SMOKIE (PART 2)	King
January	1961	HONKY TONK (PART 2)	King

FATS DOMINO

Real Name: Antoine Domino
Born: February 26, 1928
Hometown: New Orleans, Louisiana

Born in New Orleans, Fats was one of nine children. As a youngster, he became interested in playing the piano. After working on an ice truck for a while, he had another job that almost ended his musical aspirations. While working at a bedspring factory, one of the heavy springs fell and gashed his hand. Several stitches were necessary to close the wound, and there was question as to whether he would be able to move the hand again. By exercise and willpower he regained the use of his fingers and

FATS DOMINO

was able to resume his piano playing again. The greatest influence on Fats's style at the time were songs like "Chicken Shack Boogie" by Amos Milburn.

In 1949, while playing at The Hideaway club in New Orleans, Lew Chudd, the president of Imperial records, along with Dave Bartholemew and Al Young, came in to hear Fats play. This meeting resulted in a recording contract with Imperial. Shortly thereafter, Fats and Dave co-wrote the song "The Fat Man," which resulted in Fats's first big hit and the origin of his nickname. Fats started off with Dave Bartholemew's band in 1949, but by 1951 he had formed his own.

His next really big hit didn't come until May 1955, with "Ain't It a Shame," which also became a hit for Pat Boone. The ideas for his songs came from everyday expressions like "Ain't It a Shame," "I'm in Love Again," "I Gotta Whole Lotta Lovin'," "Poor Me," and "Be My Guest." Fats's biggest hit, "Blueberry Hill, which was recorded in the summer of 1956, was a song he had always wanted to record, ever since he heard Louie "Satchmo" Armstrong recording of it years before.

Although Fats had many hit records, he never had a number one song on the pop music charts.

Fats lives with his wife and eight children (four boys and four girls) in New Orleans, but he is constantly on the road appearing in Las Vegas and other spots throughout the country.

January	1950	THE FAT MAN	Imperial
November	1950	EVERY NIGHT ABOUT THIS TIME	Imperial
December	1951	ROCKIN' CHAIR	Imperial
April	1952	GOIN' HOME	Imperial
December	1952	HOW LONG	Imperial
April	1953	GOIN' TO THE RIVER	Imperial
July	1953	PLEASE DON'T LEAVE ME	Imperial
October	1953	ROSE MARY	Imperial
December	1953	SOMETHING'S WRONG	Imperial
March	1954	YOU DONE ME WRONG	Imperial
March	1955	DON'T YOU KNOW	Imperial
May	1955	AIN'T IT A SHAME	Imperial
September	1955	ALL BY MYSELF	Imperial
November	1955	POOR ME	Imperial
February	1956	BO WEEVIL	Imperial
April	1956	I'M IN LOVE AGAIN	Imperial
April	1956	MY BLUE HEAVEN	Imperial
July	1956	WHEN MY DREAMBOAT COMES HOME	Imperial
July	1956	SO-LONG	Imperial
September	1956	BLUEBERRY HILL	Imperial
December	1956	BLUE MONDAY	Imperial
January	1957	WHAT'S THE REASON I'M NOT PLEASING YOU	Imperial
February	1957	I'M WALKIN'	Imperial
May	1957	VALLEY OF TEARS	Imperial
May	1957	IT'S YOU I LOVE	Imperial
August	1957	WHEN I SEE YOU	Imperial
October	1957	WAIT AND SEE	Imperial
October	1957	I STILL LOVE YOU	Imperial
December	1957	THE BIG BEAT	Imperial
December	1957	I WANT YOU TO KNOW	Imperial
February	1958	YES, MY DARLING	Imperial
April	1958	SICK AND TIRED	Imperial
June	1958	LITTLE MARY	Imperial
September	1958	YOUNG SCHOOL GIRL	Imperial
November	1958	WHOLE LOTTA LOVING	Imperial
February	1959	WHEN THE SAINTS GO MARCHING IN	Imperial
February	1959	TELLING LIES	Imperial
May	1959	I'M READY	Imperial
May	1959	MARGIE	Imperial
July	1959	I'M GONNA BE A WHEEL SOME DAY	Imperial
July	1959	I WANT TO WALK YOU HOME	Imperial
October	1959	BE MY GUEST	Imperial
October	1959	I'VE BEEN AROUND	Imperial
January	1960	COUNTRY BOY	Imperial
April	1960	TELL ME THAT YOU LOVE ME	Imperial
June	1960	WALKING TO NEW ORLEANS	Imperial
June	1960	DON'T COME KNOCKIN'	Imperial
September	1960	THREE NIGHTS A WEEK	Imperial
September	1960	PUT YOUR ARMS AROUND ME HONEY	Imperial

October	1960	MY GIRL JOSEPHINE	Imperial
November	1960	NATURAL BORN LOVER	Imperial
January	1961	WHAT A PRICE	Imperial
January	1961	AIN'T THAT JUST LIKE A WOMAN	Imperial
March	1961	SHU RAH	Imperial
March	1961	FELL IN LOVE ON MONDAY	Imperial
May	1961	IT KEEPS ON RAININ'	Imperial
July	1961	LET THE FOUR WINDS BLOW	Imperial
October	1961	WHAT A PARTY	Imperial
December	1961	I HEAR YOU KNOCKING	Imperial
December	1961	JAMBALAYA	Imperial
February	1962	YOU WIN AGAIN	Imperial
May	1962	MY REAL NAME	Imperial
June	1962	NOTHING NEW (SAME OLD THINGS)	Imperial
October	1962	DID YOU EVER SEE A DREAM WALKING	Imperial
May	1963	THERE GOES MY HEART AGAIN	ABC
September	1963	RED SAILS IN THE SUNSET	ABC
January	1964	WHO CARES	ABC
February	1964	LAZY LADY	ABC
September	1964	SALLY WAS A GOOD OLD GIRL	ABC
October	1964	HEARTBREAK HILL	ABC
September	1968	LADY MADONNA	Reprise

THE DOMINOES

Members:

Clyde McPhatter—lead—replaced by Jackie Wilson in 1953
Charlie White—second tenor—replaced by James Van Loan in 1952
Joe Lamont—baritone
Bill Brown—bass—replaced by David McNeil in 1952
Billy Ward—piano

Hometown: New York, New York

In 1950, Billy Ward first formed the group as a gospel ensemble and they appeared on the Arthur Godfrey show. After a while, due to Clyde's unique singing voice, the group started singing more blues numbers. Later that year they signed with Federal records and recorded their first chart record late that year called "Do Something for Me." In May 1951, they recorded the classic "Sixty Minute Man," featuring the bass voice of Bill Brown.

In 1952, Charlie and Bill left the group and were replaced by James and David respectively. Clyde left the group in 1953 to form his own group The Drifters, who went on to record "Money Honey" for Atlantic records, among many other hits. Clyde was replaced by Jackie Wilson from Detroit, who remained with the group until 1957, when he went on to a solo career with Brunswick records with hits like "Lonely Teardrops" and "Baby Workout" and so many others.

THE DOMINOES

Clockwise from top right:
Bill Brown, Charlie White,
Clyde McPhatter, Joe
Lamont, Billy Ward

**BILLY WARD &
HIS DOMINOES**

Top middle: Billy Ward
Top right: Jackie Wilson

The Dominoes were one of the pioneer and premier groups of rock, for they not only produced two great lead voices, Clyde McPhatter and Jackie Wilson, but they had a style that was to be copied by many groups for years to come.

Of the group Clyde, Charlie, and Bill have died, while Jackie is in a comatose state in a New Jersey hospital after suffering a heart attack in 1975.

January	1951	DO SOMETHING FOR ME	Federal
May	1951	SIXTY MINUTE MAN	Federal
November	1951	I AM WITH YOU	Federal
April	1952	THAT'S WHAT YOU'RE DOING TO ME	Federal
May	1952	HAVE MERCY BABY	Federal

DON & DEWEY

Real Names:
    Don "Sugarcane" Harris—guitar
    Dewey Terry—piano
Hometown: Los Angeles, California

They got together as a duo in the fifties, with Dewey singing lead on most of their songs. They wrote and recorded hits like "Justine," "Big Boy Pete" (later a hit for the Olympics), and "I'm Leavin' It All Up to You" (a hit for Dale & Grace).

| June | 1958 | JUSTINE | Specialty |

DON & JUAN

Real Names:
    Don—Roland Trone
    Juan—Claude Johnson
Hometown: New York, New York

The two met in 1961 while they were both employed as house painters in a New York City apartment building. They would both sing as they worked; inevitably a tenant told agent Peter Paul about them. Peter met the boys, became their manager, and took them to Big Top records, where he got them a recording contract. They recorded a song that Claude wrote called "What's Your Name," which was released in January 1962 and became their biggest hit.

The two of them got together for the first time in years to do the Royal New York Doo Wopp Show in New York City in May of 1981.

| January | 1962 | WHAT'S YOUR NAME | Big Top |
| October | 1962 | MAGIC WAND | Big Top |

DON & JUAN

LONNIE DONEGAN

Real Name: Anthony James Donegan
Born: April 29, 1931
Hometown: Glasgow, Scotland

Lonnie was a top British artist with a "skiffle" (English banjo sound) music group. He first came to the attention of American fans in early 1956, with his "Rock Island Line" on London records. Mannie Greenfield, his personal manager, brought him to the United States in 1959, where Lonnie played during the intermission show for the Harlem Globetrotters.

In 1958, he recorded a song for Pye records called "Does Your Chewing Gum Lose Its Flavor," which became a hit in England. Dot records bought the master and released it in the United States. First time out, it was a flop. But in 1961, disc jockey Arnie Ginsburg of WMEX in Boston received a copy of the record from two Englishmen and began playing it. The response was overwhelming and it became a big hit in the United States for Lonnie.

February	1956	ROCK ISLAND LINE	London
May	1956	LOST JOHN	Mercury
July	1961	DOES YOUR CHEWING GUM LOSE ITS FLAVOR	Dot

RAL DONNER

Born: February 10, 1943
Hometown: Chicago, Illinois

At the age of ten, Ral began singing in a church choir. He formed his own band at thirteen. Shortly after that he took top prize in a local talent show. At fifteen, he was booked in Chicago clubs like the Chez Paree and New York's Apollo theater. In early 1961, Ral signed a contract with Gone records in New York, and had his first hit that year with "Girl of My Best Friend." That was followed a few months later with his biggest hit, "You Don't Know What You've Got."

Ral was the narrator, doing Elvis's voice, in the 1981 movie *This Is Elvis.*

April	1961	GIRL OF MY BEST FRIEND	Gone
July	1961	YOU DON'T KNOW WHAT YOU'VE GOT	Gone
September	1961	PLEASE DON'T GO	Gone
December	1961	SHE'S EVERYTHING	Gone
March	1962	(WHAT A SAD WAY) TO LOVE SOMEONE	Gone

DICKEY DOO & THE DON'TS

Members:
> Dickey Doo—real name: Gerry Granahan—leader and tenor—June 17, 1939
> Jerry Grant—lead
> Harvey Davis—baritone
> Al Ways—bass
> Ray Gangi—tenor

Hometown: Philadelphia, Pennsylvania

Dick and Jerry wrote a song one night while riding on a train. They took the tune to their friend Dick Clark, who played it for Bernie Bennick, the president of Swan records. In January 1958, Dickey Doo & The Don'ts recorded the song they wrote for Swan records and the song "Click-Clack" became their first major hit.

January	1958	CLICK-CLACK	Swan
April	1958	NEE NEE NA NA NA NA NU NU	Swan
May	1958	FLIP TOP BOX	Swan
October	1958	LEAVE ME ALONE	Swan

HAROLD DORMAN

Harold's only hit was a song he wrote and recorded for Rita records in February 1960 called "Mountain of Love." The song also became a hit for Johnny Rivers a few years later.

| February | 1960 | MOUNTAIN OF LOVE | Rita |

JIMMY DORSEY

Born: February 29, 1904
Died: June 12, 1957
Hometown: Shenandoah, Pennsylvania

When Jimmy was eight, his father taught him to play the coronet. He also learned to play the saxophone and clarinet, and by age eighteen had his own band called the Dorsey Novelty Band, which played in the Reading, Pennsylvania, area. In the early 1920s Jimmy got a job playing sax and clarinet with a band called the Scranton Sirens. He talked the band's leader into giving his younger brother Tommy a job, and in a short time the Dorsey Brothers began their rise to fame.

By 1933, the Dorsey Brothers Orchestra was known throughout the country. Shortly after that, musical differences led to the brothers going their separate ways. In 1953, however, they became the Dorsey Brothers again. This new association lasted until 1956 when Tommy died.

In January of 1957, Jimmy, after many years of success with Decca records, signed with Fraternity records and recorded a big hit with the instrumental "So Rare."

January	1957	SO RARE		Fraternity
August	1957	JUNE NIGHT		Fraternity

LEE DORSEY

Hometown: Portland, Oregon

Lee started out as a prizefighter and was known as Kid Chocolate when he boxed around the Portland area. After four years in the Navy he returned to the ring and began traveling around the country. He was so good that he became a contender for the light-heavy weight title.

He met a man named Allen Toussaint, a very successful songwriter ("Mother-in-Law" for Ernie K. Doe in 1961) at a party in New Orleans. Allen convinced Lee to pursue a recording career and wanted to record him. In the summer of 1961, Lee recorded a song he had written called "Ya Ya." It wound up as Lee's first national hit that fall.

In July 1966, Lee recorded Allen Toussaint's "Working in the Coal Mine," which became his biggest hit to date.

September	1961	YA YA	Fury
December	1961	DO-RE-MI	Fury
June	1965	RIDE YOUR PONY	Amy
January	1966	GET OUT OF MY LIFE, WOMAN	Amy
July	1966	WORKING IN THE COAL MINE	Amy
October	1966	HOLY COW	Amy
May	1967	MY OLD CAR	Amy
October	1967	GO-GO GIRL	Amy

TOMMY DORSEY

Born: November 10, 1905
Died: November 26, 1956
Hometown: Shenandoah, Pennsylvania

While Tommy was still a youngster, his father, an accomplished musician, taught him to play all the brass instruments. At age twelve, much to Tommy's dismay, he was given the trombone to play. By the early 1920s, he and his brother Jimmy were playing in the same band called the Scranton Sirens. For about ten years they played together, or in different bands like Paul Whiteman's, Rudy Vallee's, or Andre Kostelanetz's. By 1933, they formed their own band, with members like drummer Ray McKinley, trombonist Glenn Miller, and vocalist Bob Crosby, each of whom went on to form their own bands.

After a couple of years together, the brothers formed their own bands. Tommy hired many vocalists who became stars in their own right like Frank Sinatra, Jo Stafford, and Connie Haines.

Tommy died at his Greenwich, Connecticut, home in late 1956. After many hits on Decca during the thirties and forties, his band had another chart hit in August 1958 with "Tea for Two Cha Cha."

August	1958	TEA FOR TWO CHA CHA	Decca
December	1958	I WANT TO BE HAPPY CHA CHA	Decca

THE DOVELLS

Members:
    Len Barry—lead—born: June 12, 1942
    Jerry Summers—first tenor—born: December 29, 1942
    Mike Dennis—second tenor—born: June 3, 1943
    Arnie Satin—baritone—born: May 11, 1943
    Danny Brooks—bass—April 1, 1942
Hometown: Philadelphia, Pennsylvania

The group was formed in 1957, and they sang at local school functions. They wrote several tunes as a group like "No, No, No," which gained some recognition in Philadelphia. After little success, the group disbanded.

In December 1960, they got together again to audition for Dave Appell, the A & R director of Parkway records in Philly. He signed them to the label. In the summer of 1961, they recorded a composition of Dave

Appell and Kal Mann's called "The Bristol Stomp," which became their biggest hit.

Len Barry left the group in 1963, and a couple of years later, while recording as a solo artist on Decca, he had a hit with the song "1-2-3."

Today Len works as a bartender in a Philadelphia bar, while the others reside in the area pursuing individual careers. Two new fellows carry on the name of The Dovells, doing occasional rock shows.

September	1961	BRISTOL STOMP	Parkway
January	1962	DO THE NEW CONTINENTAL	Parkway
May	1962	BRISTOL TWISTIN' ANNIE	Parkway
August	1962	HULLY GULLY BABY	Parkway
October	1962	THE JITTERBUG	Parkway
April	1963	YOU CAN'T SIT DOWN	Parkway
August	1963	BETTY IN BERMUDAS	Parkway
October	1963	STOP MONKEYIN' AROUN'	Parkway

JOE DOWELL

Born: 1940
Hometown: Bloomington, Illinois

Joe's interest in music began at the age of seven when he composed songs on the family piano; later he composed on the guitar. He joined the high school choir and glee club. In 1961, while a junior at the University of Illinois, majoring in Radio & TV, he decided to drive down to Nashville and pursue a singing career. He met songwriter-producer Shelby Singleton of Smash records, who liked his voice and style and signed him to the label.

After final exams in June 1961, Joe received a call from Shelby about a song he wanted him to come to Nashville to record. Shelby felt that the Bert Kaempfert song "Wooden Heart," which Elvis had recorded and sung in the film *G.I. Blues*, would be a natural for Joe since RCA had not yet released the song as a single in the United States. Joe bought the soundtrack album and learned the German part of the song phonetically, just as Elvis sang it on the record, and the next day recorded the song. The result was his first hit and a number one song.

After a couple of years with Smash, Joe decided to leave the label and began a career recording radio commercials for advertising agencies.

Today Joe lives in Louisville, Kentucky, and is very successful in the advertising business.

June	1961	WOODEN HEART	Smash
October	1961	BRIDGE OF LOVE	Smash
June	1962	LITTLE RED RENTED ROWBOAT	Smash

CHARLIE DRAKE

Born: June 19, 1925
Hometown: London, England

Charlie left school at fourteen, to go into show business. He worked various jobs before going into the Royal Air Force for four years. After his discharge, he went into radio, and later into TV. In late 1961, he recorded a nonsense song called "My Boomerang Won't Come Back," which was purchased by United Artists records and released in the United States in January 1962. It became Charlie's only United States hit.

January	1962	MY BOOMERANG WON'T COME BACK	United Artists

RUSTY DRAPER

Hometown: Kirksville, Ohio

By age ten the young redhead had begun playing the guitar and taking an interest in singing. When he was twelve, his family moved to Tulsa, Oklahoma, where he got a job singing on a local radio show on station KTUL. His family moved to San Francisco in 1942, where he got jobs singing at local clubs. He stayed in the Bay area until 1949, after which he moved east.

In 1953, Rusty signed with Mercury records and had a hit in February of that year with "No Help Wanted," which was followed by "Gambler's Guitar."

February	1953	NO HELP WANTED	Mercury
June	1953	GAMBLER'S GUITAR	Mercury
July	1955	SEVENTEEN	Mercury
October	1955	THE SHIFTING, WHISPERING SANDS	Mercury
March	1956	HELD FOR QUESTIONING	Mercury
August	1956	IN THE MIDDLE OF THE HOUSE	Mercury
February	1957	TIGER LILY	Mercury
January	1957	LET'S GO CALYPSO	Mercury
May	1957	FREIGHT TRAIN	Mercury
July	1960	PLEASE HELP ME I'M FALLING	Mercury
September	1961	SIGNED, SEALED AND DELIVERED	Mercury
September	1963	NIGHT LIFE	Monument

THE DREAMLOVERS

Members:
    Tommy Ricks—first tenor
    Cleveland Hammock—second tenor

Cliff Dunn—baritone
Morris Gardner—baritone
Ray Dunn—bass
Hometown: Philadelphia, Pennsylvania

The Dreamlovers began singing together in 1956, and began appearing at various high school functions. After four years of talent shows, benefits, and local club dates, their big break came when they were selected to back Chubby Checker on his recording of "The Twist." Jerry Ross and Murray Wecht of Heritage records heard them at this session and signed them to a long-term contract.

Their debut disc on Heritage in the summer of 1961 was a song written by Donny Hogan, an earlier member of the group, called "When We Get Married."

| July | 1961 | WHEN WE GET MARRIED | Heritage |
| June | 1962 | IF I SHOULD LOSE YOU | End |

THE DREAMWEAVERS

Hometown: Miami, Florida

This trio of two guys and a girl began singing in college in Florida in the mid-fifties, and decided to record a song called "It's Almost Tomorrow." They recorded the song themselves and then had it played on the college radio station. The ballad became so popular that it came to the attention of a Decca records distributor, who had a copy sent to Milt Gabler, the head of A & R for Decca in New York. Milt liked the song and purchased the disc for Decca, releasing it on the label in September 1955. The song went on to become the group's biggest hit.

September	1955	IT'S ALMOST TOMORROW	Decca
February	1956	INTO THE NIGHT	Decca
April	1956	A LITTLE LOVE CAN GO A LONG, LONG WAY	Decca

THE DRIFTERS

Members 1953–1958:
   Clyde McPhatter—lead—replaced by David Baughan in 1954, replaced by Johnny Moore in 1955, replaced by Bobby Hendricks in 1957
   Gerhart Thrasher—tenor
   Andrew Thrasher—baritone—replaced by Charlie Hughes in 1956

    Bill Pinckney—bass—replaced by Tommy Evans (September 1, 1927)
    in 1956; replaced by Bill Pinckney rejoining group in 1957
    Jimmy Oliver—guitarist
Members 1959–1966:
    Ben E. King—real name: Benjamin Nelson—lead—replaced by Rudy
    Lewis (August 23, 1936) in 1961, replaced by Johnny Moore in
    1964
    Charley Thomas—tenor and lead—April 7, 1937
    Doc Green—baritone—October 8, 1934
    Elsberry Hobbs—bass—January 17, 1936
Hometown: New York, New York

In 1953, when Clyde McPhatter left The Dominoes after such hits as "Have Mercy Baby" and "Sixty Minute Man," he got together with a gospel group known as the Civitones and asked the members Gerhart and Andrew Thrasher to join him and Bill Pinckney to form a new singing group. They called themselves The Drifters, because each member drifted from one singing group to another.

They signed with Atlantic records in New York and, in September 1953 had their first hit with a Jesse Stone song called "Money Honey." This song was followed with hits like "Honey Love" (which Clyde wrote), "Bip Bam," and the Irving Berlin classic, "White Christmas."

In April 1954, Clyde went into the Army and was replaced for a while by David Baughan, who sounded almost like Clyde. In 1955, Johnny Moore became the lead on such hits as "Adorable," "Ruby Baby," "Soldier of Fortune," "I Gotta Get Myself a Woman," and "It Was a Tear." In 1957, Johnny was drafted into the Army and was replaced by Bobby Hendricks (who later had solo hits with "Itchy Twitchy Feeling" and "Psycho"). Bobby sang lead on "Moonlight Bay" and "Drip Drop" in 1958. During the summer of 1958, the original Drifters disbanded.

George Treadwell, the group's original manager, wanted to keep the name going, so in late 1958, he signed a group that he saw perform at New York's Apollo theater called The Five Crowns (of "Kiss and Make Up" fame). The group consisted of Benny Nelson (Ben E. King), Doc Green, Charley Thomas, and Elsberry Hobbs. With Benny as the new lead of The Drifters, they recorded their initial hit for Atlantic in the summer of 1959, which Benny and George Treadwell had written, called "There Goes My Baby." It was the first rock recording to incorporate strings. After that came hits like "Dance with Me," "This Magic Moment," "Lonely Winds," "Save the Last Dance for Me," and "I Count the Tears" (the last song Benny recorded with the group).

In 1960, Ben E. King went on his own as a single artist with the song "Spanish Harlem." He was replaced on the next Drifters' hit, "Some Kind of Wonderful," by Rudy Lewis. Rudy became lead on all the Drifters' hits

THE DRIFTERS, 1953–1958

Clockwise from top: Charlie Hughes,
Johnny Moore, Gerhart Thrasher,
Tommy Evans, Jimmy Oliver

THE DRIFTERS, 1959–1961

Left to right: Charley
Thomas, Ben E. King, Doc
Green, Ellsberry Hobbs

THE DRIFTERS, 1961–1964

Clockwise from top: Doc Green,
Rudy Lewis, Tommy Evans, Charley
Thomas

from 1960 until late 1963, except for "Sweets for My Sweet" and "When My Little Girl Is Smiling," on which Charley Thomas sang lead. "Vaya Con Dios" was the last song Rudy recorded with the group. Johnny Moore again joined the group and became the lead voice on "One Way Love," "Under the Boardwalk," "I've Got Sand in My Shoes," and "Saturday Night at the Movies."

Of all the hits the group had from 1953 until 1966, only one record made it to the number one spot on the pop music charts. That was in the fall of 1960, when Ben E. King sang lead on "Save the Last Dance for Me."

The group's manager, George Treadwell, died in 1967, so his wife, Faye, began to manage them. Faye Treadwell has a Drifters group that features Johnny Moore. There is another group that operates out of New York, consisting of Charley Thomas, Doc Green, Elsberry Hobbs, and Al Banks (former lead voice of The Turbans, of "When You Dance" fame).

Ben E. King now resides in New Jersey and sings as a solo performer throughout the New York area. Clyde McPhatter died in 1972. Rudy Lewis died in 1963. Bill Pinckney, the original bass, has a group he travels with called The Bill Pinckney Drifters.

| September | 1953 | MONEY HONEY | Atlantic |
| February | 1954 | SUCH A NIGHT | Atlantic |

February	1954	LUCILLE	Atlantic
May	1954	HONEY LOVE	Atlantic
November	1954	BIP BAM	Atlantic
December	1954	WHITE CHRISTMAS	Atlantic
March	1955	WHAT'CHA GONNA DO	Atlantic
October	1955	ADORABLE/STEAMBOAT	Atlantic
May	1956	RUBY BABY	Atlantic
August	1956	I GOTTA GET MYSELF A WOMAN	Atlantic
February	1957	FOOLS FALL IN LOVE	Atlantic
June	1957	HYPNOTIZED	Atlantic
June	1958	MOONLIGHT BAY	Atlantic
August	1958	DRIP DROP	Atlantic
May	1959	THERE GOES MY BABY	Atlantic
October	1959	DANCE WITH ME	Atlantic
November	1959	TRUE LOVE, TRUE LOVE	Atlantic
February	1960	THIS MAGIC MOMENT	Atlantic
May	1960	LONELY WINDS	Atlantic
September	1960	SAVE THE LAST DANCE FOR ME	Atlantic
December	1960	I COUNT THE TEARS	Atlantic
March	1961	SOME KIND OF WONDERFUL	Atlantic
May	1961	PLEASE STAY	Atlantic
September	1961	SWEETS FOR MY SWEET	Atlantic
December	1961	ROOM FULL OF TEARS	Atlantic
February	1962	WHEN MY LITTLE GIRL IS SMILING	Atlantic
May	1962	STRANGER ON THE SHORE	Atlantic
November	1962	UP ON THE ROOF	Atlantic
March	1963	ON BROADWAY	Atlantic
June	1963	RAT RACE	Atlantic
August	1963	I'LL TAKE YOU HOME	Atlantic
January	1964	VAYA CON DIOS	Atlantic
May	1964	ONE WAY LOVE	Atlantic
June	1964	UNDER THE BOARDWALK	Atlantic
September	1964	I'VE GOT SAND IN MY SHOES	Atlantic
November	1964	SATURDAY NIGHT AT THE MOVIES	Atlantic
January	1965	AT THE CLUB	Atlantic
April	1965	COME ON OVER TO MY PLACE	Atlantic
April	1965	CHAINS OF LOVE	Atlantic
June	1965	FOLLOW ME	Atlantic
August	1965	I'LL TAKE YOU WHERE THE MUSIC'S PLAYING	Atlantic
March	1966	MEMORIES ARE MADE OF THIS	Atlantic
November	1966	BABY WHAT I MEAN	Atlantic

THE DUALS

Members:

Henry Bellinger—guitar—Colorado—1942
Johnny Lageman—guitar—New Orleans, Louisiana—1942

Henry and Johnny lived on the same street in Los Angeles. In the summer of 1961, they recorded a song called "Stick Shift," which was sold to Sue records and released a short time later. It became their only hit for the label.

| August | 1961 | STICK SHIFT | Sue |

THE DUBS

Left to right: William Carlisle, James Miller,
Richard Blandon, Cleveland Still, Tommy Grate

THE DUBS

Members:

    Richard Blandon—lead—Montgomery, Alabama—September 16, 1934

    Cleveland Still—first tenor—New York, New York—October 1934

    Cordell Brown—second tenor—Charlotte, North Carolina—1935—replaced by William Carlisle

    Tommy Grate—bass—Beaufort, South Carolina—1934

    James Miller—baritone

The group was organized in early 1957 by their manager Hiram Johnson, after Richard got out of the Air Force. They called themselves The Dubs because the group had made so many *dub* (more than one) recordings. Later in 1957, Gone records in New York bought their first recording, "Don't Ask Me to Be Lonely," which Richard had written. Several months later, in the fall of 1957, the group recorded another Richard Blandon classic, "Could This Be Magic," a song Richard wrote about a girl he thought of while in the Air Force. It became the group's biggest hit.

Today Richard and Cleveland Still sing with two other fellows as The Dubs in the New York area at many rock oldie concerts.

June	1957	DON'T ASK ME TO BE LONELY	Gone
October	1957	COULD THIS BE MAGIC	Gone
February	1958	BESIDE MY LOVE	Gone
May	1958	BE SURE MY LOVE	Gone
August	1959	CHAPEL OF DREAMS	Gone

DAVE DUDLEY

Born: March 3, 1928
Hometown: Spencer, Wisconsin

Dave learned to play a guitar when he was a youngster, and he played in his high school band. But even though he loved music, he pursued his first love, which was to be a professional baseball player.

In the late forties, though, Dave injured his pitching arm playing semipro ball in Wisconsin. So he began to play the guitar again and got a chance to sing on radio station WTWT. After that, he formed a trio and began touring the Midwest.

Some years later, in April 1963, he recorded a song he liked called "Six Days on the Road." The song was sold to Golden Wing records and became a national hit by May of that year. The song became very popular with truck drivers, and Dave was known as a great singer of trucking songs.

| May | 1963 | SIX DAYS ON THE ROAD | Golden Wing |
| October | 1963 | COWBOY BOOTS | Golden Wing |

THE DUPREES

Members:
 Joe Vann (Canzano)—lead—born: April 3, 1943—replaced by Mike Kelly—April 19, 1943
 Joe Santollo—first tenor—born: July 23, 1943; died: June 3, 1981
 John Salvato—second tenor—born: July 9, 1940
 Mike Arnone—baritone—born: September 19, 1943
 Tom Bialaglow—bass—born: November 5, 1940
Hometown: Jersey City, New Jersey

The group first got together in the early sixties and began singing around their neighborhood in Jersey City. They first called themselves The Parisians and began playing local clubs. In the spring of 1962, they went to New York to audition for George Paxton, the president of Coed records. They sang "You Belong to Me," a ballad that had been a big hit ten years earlier for Jo Stafford.

George liked the song but did not like the name of the group, so he asked them to change it. Since they knew of a singer in New Jersey known simply as "Dupree," and since it was a French-sounding name that was close to Parisians, they decided to call themselves The Duprees. The song was released in July 1962, and it became a national hit and the group's biggest selling record.

Joe Canzano left the group around 1964, and Mike Kelly became the new lead voice.

Today John keeps the group active in the New York area with several new members. Joe Santollo died in Jersey City, New Jersey, of a heart attack in 1981.

July	1962	YOU BELONG TO ME	Coed
October	1962	MY OWN TRUE LOVE	Coed
January	1963	I'D RATHER BE HERE IN YOUR ARMS	Coed
March	1963	GONE WITH THE WIND	Coed
August	1963	WHY DON'T YOU BELIEVE ME	Coed
October	1963	HAVE YOU HEARD	Coed
January	1964	IT'S NO SIN	Coed
July	1965	AROUND THE CORNER	Columbia

THE DUPREES

Clockwise from top: Joe Santollo, Mike Arnone, Mike Kelly, John Salvato

THE EARLS

Left to right: Robert Del Din,
John Wray, Eddie Harder,
Larry Chance

THE EARLS

Members:

> Larry Chance (real name: Larry Figueiredo)—lead—Philadelphia,
> Pennsylvania—born: October 19, 1940
> Robert Del Din—first tenor—Bronx, New York—1942
> Eddie Harder—second tenor—Bronx, New York—1942
> Larry Palumbo—baritone—Bronx, New York—1941; died: 1959
> John Wray—bass—Bronx, New York—1939

Larry Chance formed the group in the Bronx in the late fifties, shortly after his family moved there from Philadelphia. After singing at various local functions he decided to call this new group the Earls, after finding the word in the dictionary to mean "noblemen of high rank."

After more work on creating their own style, the Earls decided to record a song that was once a hit for the Harptones in 1954, called "Life

Is but a Dream." The group went into a studio with only two musicians and an investment of forty-five dollars, and recorded the song with an up-tempo arrangement. The resulting recording was sold to Rome records in 1961, and became the group's first hit.

Shortly after they recorded "Lookin' for My Baby," also for Rome records. In November of 1962, they recorded "Remember Then," for Old Town records, which went on to be the group's biggest hit.

The Earls were able to create their unique sound with a repetition of nonsensible lyrics that sounded almost like baby talk during certain parts of the song.

When baritone Larry Palumbo was killed in the paratroopers in 1959 when his chute failed to open during one of his jumps, the group recorded the song "I Believe" in his honor. Although the song never became a national hit, it is always used during the group's performances and has become one of the most popular songs in the New York area.

Today Larry lives in Loch Shelldrake, Long Island, New York, and sings with Bob Tribuzzio and T. J. "Butch" Barbella as The Earls. He has also developed a new career on NBC radio in New York, as the fictional station manager Geraldo Santana Banana.

April	1961	LIFE IS BUT A DREAM	Rome
September	1961	LOOKIN' FOR MY BABY	Rome
January	1962	MY HEARTS DESIRE	Rome
November	1962	REMEMBER THEN	Old Town
March	1963	NEVER	Old Town
July	1963	EYES	Old Town
June	1964	KISSIN'/CRY CRY CRY	Old Town
October	1964	I BELIEVE	Old Town
June	1965	REMEMBER ME BABY	Old Town
June	1966	IF I COULD DO IT OVER AGAIN	"Mr. G."
October	1969	LONG TIME COMING	ABC

THE ECHOES

Members:
> Tommy Duffy—lead—born: February 1, 1944
> Harry Boyle—1948
> Tom Morrissey—1943

Hometown: Brooklyn, New York

In late 1960, Sam Guilino, a Long Island music teacher, and Val Lageux, an assistant principal, penned a song called "Baby Blue," which they gave to the Echoes to practice with. They took the group to a friend named Jack Gold, who had the tune recorded for Seg-Way records. It was released in February 1961, and became a national hit for the group.

Today Harry Boyle sings with a buddy under the name Red Hook and performs in many New York clubs. The other two fellows are pursuing separate careers.

| February | 1961 | BABY BLUE | Seg-Way |
| June | 1961 | SAD EYES | Seg-Way |

DUANE EDDY

Born: April 26, 1938
Hometown: Phoenix, Arizona

Duane started playing the guitar at the age of five. By fifteen he was playing various dances around Phoenix. In 1957 he met disc jockey Lee Hazlewood, who became his producer. (In the late sixties Hazlewood wrote and produced for stars like Dean Martin and Nancy Sinatra.)

Al Casey began working with Duane on his guitar style and by January of 1958 Duane was looking for a recording contract. He asked Casey, Larry Knecktall (who played piano) and Steve Douglas (whose specialty was the sax) to become his back-up group. He dubbed them the Rebels.

DUANE EDDY

Their first song was "Movin' 'n Groovin'," which they recorded in Phoenix and mailed to Harry Finfer, the president of Jamie records in Philadelphia. This resulted in a contract with the label. It wasn't until later that summer that he had his first real hit, with "Rebel-Rouser."

Lester Sill, Lee Hazlewood's partner at the time, came up with the word *Twangy*, after which Duane Eddy was referred to as "Mr. Twang," or Duane Eddy and his twangy guitar.

Duane stayed with Jamie records until 1962, when he left to join RCA.

February	1958	MOOVIN' 'N GROOVIN'	Jamie
June	1958	REBEL-'ROUSER	Jamie
August	1958	RAMROD	Jamie
October	1958	CANNONBALL	Jamie
January	1959	THE LONELY ONE	Jamie
March	1959	YEP	Jamie
June	1959	FORTY MILES OF BAD ROAD	Jamie
October	1959	SOME KIND-A EARTHQUAKE	Jamie
January	1960	BONNIE CAME BACK	Jamie
March	1960	SHAZAM	Jamie
May	1960	BECAUSE THEY'RE YOUNG	Jamie
August	1960	KOMMOTION	Jamie
October	1960	PETER GUNN	Jamie
December	1960	PEPE	Jamie
March	1961	THEME FROM DIXIE	Jamie
May	1961	RING OF FIRE	Jamie
July	1961	DRIVIN' HOME	Jamie
August	1961	MY BLUE HEAVEN	Jamie
April	1962	DEEP IN THE HEART OF TEXAS	RCA
July	1962	THE BALLAD OF PALADIN	RCA
October	1962	DANCE WITH THE GUITAR MAN	RCA
January	1963	BOSS GUITAR	RCA
May	1963	LONELY BOY, LONELY GUITAR	RCA
August	1963	YOUR BABY'S GONE SURFIN'	RCA
January	1964	THE SON OF REBEL ROUSER	RCA

THE EDSELS

Members:
George Jones, Jr.—lead—October 5, 1936
Larry Green—1937
Harry Green—1936
James Reynolds—1937
Marshall Sewell—bass—1936
Hometown: Youngstown, Ohio

In early 1958, Jim Maderitz, a Youngstown music publisher, had heard of a group that was really popular in the Youngstown area. He decided to

THE EDSELS
Left to right: Marshall Sewell, Larry Green,
George Jones, Jr., Harry Green, James Reynolds

meet them. At a record store in Youngstown, Jim auditioned the group in a listening booth. The group did an a cappella rendition of a song that lead singer George had written called "Rama Lama Ding Dong." Jim liked the song so well that he decided to record the group. Then he took the master to record companies to try to sell it. No one was interested. He had just about given up on it when he met a fellow named Foster Johnson, who was starting a record company in Little Rock. Johnson's newly formed Dub records put the song out during the summer of 1958. Inadvertently, Johnson's company printed the labels of the record, as "Lama Rama Ding Dong" instead of the original title "Rama Lama Ding Dong."

After some spotty airplay, the song finally broke in Baltimore, where the song became a local hit. After that the song died, (probably because its sound was a little premature); the Edsels (named after the automobile) went back to Youngstown and disbanded a short time later.

In early 1961, a group from Pittsburgh, called the Marcels, had a number one hit with "Blue Moon," which had a unique bass voice intro. A disc jockey in New York, remembering a similar effect on "Rama," found an old copy of the Edsels' song and began playing it. The response was phenomenal. Maderitz then made a deal with Sam and Hy Weiss of Old Town records to release the song on their Twin records label. They did, and by May 1961, the song was on its way to becoming a national hit under the correct title "Rama Lama Ding Dong."

Today George Jones, Jr., sings with a group called the New Affair, while the other members have regular jobs in Youngstown.

| June | 1958 | LAMA RAMA DING DONG | Dub |
| April | 1961 | RAMA LAMA DING DONG | Twin |

BOBBY EDWARDS

Real Name: Robert Moncrief
Hometown: Anniston, Alabama

Bobby began singing throughout the South in the late fifties. In 1961 he and his group, The Four Young Men, collaborated on a song "You're the Reason," which they recorded and sold to Los Angeles—based Crest records. The song was released that summer and quickly became a national hit.

| August | 1961 | YOU'RE THE REASON | / | Crest |
| January | 1962 | WHAT'S THE REASON | | Capitol |

TOMMY EDWARDS

Born: March 27, 1923
Died: July 24, 1981
Hometown: Milwaukee, Wisconsin

Tommy began in radio as a disc jockey at KICD in Spencer, Iowa, in 1945, and worked there until 1949. From there he went to WOKY in Milwaukee, where he worked for a couple of years. In the summer of 1951, he ventured to Cleveland, Ohio, where he began working at station WERE.

While songwriter Buddy Kaye was making a tour through Cleveland, in late 1956, he talked with Tommy about an idea Tommy had about a narrative song relating the trials and tribulations of the parents of a teen-age girl. They recorded the narrative with music, called "What Is A Teen-age Girl" for Coral records, and it became a national hit in early 1957.

Tommy continued to work at WERE, where he was very much responsible for the success of many early artists of the fifties, including

TOMMY EDWARDS, D-J

Elvis Presley. He left WERE in 1959 to go to WADC in Akron, Ohio. In 1962, he returned to Cleveland to open a record store called Record Heaven. Tommy, while hospitalized in Cleveland, Ohio, died of an aneurysm of the brain during the summer of 1981.

| January | 1957 | WHAT IS A TEEN AGE GIRL | Coral |
| January | 1957 | WHAT IS A TEEN AGE BOY | Coral |

TOMMY EDWARDS

Born: February 17, 1922
Died: October 22, 1969
Hometown: Richmond, Virginia

In the early 1940s Tommy had a radio show in Richmond, on which he sang and played the piano. In 1946, he wrote "That Chick's Too Young to Fry," which became a hit for Louis Jordan.

Tommy moved to New York in 1950, where he got a job singing demo records. A year later he was signed by MGM records and recorded "The Morning Side of the Mountain," which became a hit that summer.

During the fall of 1951, he recorded the song "It's All in the Game," the music of which was written by onetime vice-president of the United States, Charles Dawes, which became a national hit. The same song was rereleased in 1958, and went on to become a number one national hit for him.

On October 22, 1969, at the age of forty-seven, Tommy died in Henrico County, Virginia.

August	1958	IT'S ALL IN THE GAME	MGM
September	1958	PLEASE LOVE ME FOREVER	MGM
October	1958	LOVE IS ALL WE NEED	MGM
February	1959	PLEASE MR. SUN	MGM
February	1959	THE MORNING SIDE OF THE MOUNTAIN	MGM
May	1959	MY MELANCHOLY BABY	MGM
August	1959	I'VE BEEN THERE	MGM
November	1959	NEW IN THE WAYS OF LOVE	MGM
February	1960	DON'T FENCE ME IN	MGM
May	1960	I REALLY DON'T WANT TO KNOW	MGM
October	1960	IT'S NOT THE END OF EVERYTHING	MGM

THE EL DORADOS

Members:
> Pirkle Lee Moses, Jr.—lead
> Jewell Jones—first tenor
> Louis Bradley—second tenor
> James Maddox—baritone
> Richard Nickens—bass

Hometown: Chicago, Illinois

The fellows first got together at Engelwood High School in Chicago and called themselves the Five Stars. In 1954, the group entered a talent show at a local club and won first prize. A local disc jockey took the group to Vee Jay records where owner Vivian Carter signed them. They changed their name to the El Dorados and recorded their first song called "My Lovin' Baby" in 1954.

After a couple of other moderately popular songs, they recorded their biggest hit in 1955, "At My Front Door." Their follow-up was also a hit, "I'll Be Forever Loving You."

The group broke up in 1957, with Pirkle remaining in Chicago, while the other four members went off to the West Coast. The popular song the group recorded in 1956, called "Bim Bam Boom" became the title of the New York based oldies magazine on popular music of the fifties, when the magazine was launched in 1971.

August	1954	MY LOVIN' BABY	Vee Jay
September	1955	AT MY FRONT DOOR	Vee Jay
November	1955	I'LL BE FOREVER LOVING YOU	Vee Jay
March	1956	BIM BAM BOOM	Vee Jay

THE ELEGANTS

Clockwise from top
Frank Fardogno, Carman
Romano, Jimmy Moschella,
Vito Picone, Artie Venosa

THE ELEGANTS

Members:
    Vito Picone—lead—born: March 17, 1940
    Artie Venosa—first tenor—born: September 3, 1940
    Frankie Fardogno—second tenor—born: September 18, 1941
    Carman Romano—baritone—born: August 17, 1939
    Jimmy Moschella—bass—born: May 10, 1938
Hometown: Staten Island, New York

The group got together in 1957 and began singing at local functions in Staten Island. They chose the name of the group from a Schenley's whiskey bottle, where the word "Elegance" appeared. They changed the name from "Elegance" to "Elegants."

In 1958, Vito and Artie wrote a song which the group recorded and took to Hull records in New York. Hull referred them to ABC Paramount, who in turn leased the record to the Apt label, one of their subsidiaries. In the summer of 1958, "Little Star" became a number one national hit.

Today, Vito, Nino Amato, Freddy Redmond, and Bruce Copp sing as

The Elegants, performing in many shows, especially a major show like the one at Radio City Music Hall in October of 1981.

June	1958	LITTLE STAR	Apt
September	1958	LITTLE BOY BLUE	Apt
December	1958	GOODNIGHT	Apt

JIMMY ELLEDGE

Born: 1944
Hometown: Nashville, Tennessee

Jimmy started playing the piano at age six. In the second grade he was the conductor of the grammar school's little orchestra. His mother, Mae Carter Elledge, encouraged her son in his musical interest. He signed with RCA in the early sixties and premiered with a song he wrote called "Send Me a Letter." In October 1961, RCA released his biggest hit, "Funny How Time Slips Away," which was also his only real hit for the label.

October	1961	FUNNY HOW TIME SLIPS AWAY	RCA

JIMMY ELLEDGE

SHIRLEY ELLIS

SHIRLEY ELLIS

Born: 1941
Hometown: Bronx, New York

Shirley began singing with her family as a youngster. In the fifties she wrote a song called "One, Two, I Love You" for the Heartbreakers who recorded it for Vik. Later on, Alicia Evelyn introduced her to songwriter Lincoln Chase ("Jim Dandy" for LaVern Baker and "Such a Night" for the Drifters), and they began working together. Lincoln then wrote a song called "The Nitty Gritty," which he wanted Shirley to record. He took her to Hal Fein of Roosevelt Music, who vetoed doing the song. Next stop was Trinity Music, where Bobby Darin opined that Shirley sounded too old on the song.

Finally, in 1963, Charlie Singleton introduced Lincoln to Al Galico of Galico Publishing, who liked the song. Next door to Galico's office was Kapp records' newly acquired Congress records. Congress released the song in the fall of 1963, and it went on to become a top-ten national hit.

In late 1964, another Lincoln Chase song, "The Name Game,"

became Shirley's biggest hit. Today Lincoln is still writing and lives in the Bronx. Shirley, who has given up singing and writing for now, also still lives in the Bronx.

October	1963	THE NITTY GRITTY	Congress
February	1964	THAT'S WHAT THE NITTY GRITTY IS	Congress
December	1964	THE NAME GAME	Congress
March	1965	THE CLAPPING SONG	Congress
May	1965	THE PUZZLE SONG	Congress
February	1967	SOUL TIME	Columbia

PRESTON EPPS

Hometown: Los Angeles, California

He learned to play the bongos in Okinawa during the Korean War. In the late fifties, disc jockey Art Laboe of KPOP in Los Angeles heard Preston playing in a coffeehouse. He got him a contract with Original Sound records, and in May 1959, Preston had a national hit with "Bongo Rock."

May	1959	BONGO ROCK	Original Sound
August	1960	BONGO, BONGO, BONGO	Original Sound

THE ESSEX

Members:
Anita Humes—Harrisburg, Pennsylvania—1941
Walter Vickers—New Brunswick, New Jersey—1942
Rodney Taylor—Gary, Indiana—1942
Billie Hill—Princeton, New Jersey—1942
Rudolph Johnson—New York, New York—1942

The group began singing together while they were in the U.S. Marine Corps. The group was started by Walter and Rodney while they were stationed in Okinawa. When they returned to Camp LeJeune, North Carolina, they added Billie and Rudy. They worked together as a foursome for a while, until they heard Anita sing at the Non-Commissioned Officers' Club. She then became a permanent member of the group.

In 1963, they were signed by Roulette records. The recorded "Easier Said than Done," which became a big hit that summer. They made all their hit recordings while still in the service. In fact, they had to get special permission to travel around on promotion tours, during which they would wear their uniforms.

THE ESSEX

May	1963	EASIER SAID THAN DONE	Roulette
August	1963	A WALKIN' MIRACLE	Roulette
October	1963	SHE'S GOT EVERYTHING	Roulette

THE ETERNALS

This Bronx-based group developed a local following in the late fifties. Lead singer Charlie Girona felt the group would have to write its own material to make it big. Their first effort was about a neighborhood friend who was getting married. They called it "Babalu's Wedding Day." At this point they met Bill Martin, who became their manager and got them a contract with Hollywood records. Their first few releases were big local hits. In the summer of 1959, their "Rockin' in the Jungle," which featured novel animal calls, became their only national hit.

| July | 1959 | ROCKIN' IN THE JUNGLE | Hollywood |

PAUL EVANS

PAUL EVANS

Born: 1938
Hometown: St. Albans, Queens, New York

Paul initially was a writer. He wrote the hit "When" for the Kalin twins in 1958. In 1959, he signed with Guaranteed records and recorded with two girls named Sue Singelton and Sue Terry who were from Perry Como's chorale group. The girls were known as The Curls, and they all recorded a song called "Seven Little Girls Sitting in the Back Seat," which was Paul's biggest hit after it was released in the fall of 1959.

Paul also wrote his third hit, "Happy-Go-Lucky Me." He has continued to spend most of his energies in the record business on writing, coming up with "Roses Are Red, My Love" for Bobby Vinton in 1961 and, a few years later, with "Happiness Is" for the Ray Coniff Singers, a song that was eventually used for four years as the Kent cigarette jingle.

September	1959	SEVEN LITTLE GIRLS SITTING IN THE BACK SEAT	Guaranteed
January	1960	MIDNITE SPECIAL	Guaranteed
April	1960	HAPPY-GO-LUCKY-ME	Guaranteed
August	1960	BRIGADE OF BROKEN HEARTS	Guaranteed

THE EVERLY BROTHERS

Members:
    Don Everly—born: February 1, 1937—Brownie, Kentucky
    Phil Everly—born: January 19, 1939—Chicago, Illinois

The Everlys' parents, Ike and Margaret, were well-known country music artists. When Don was eight, and Phil six, they made their first public appearance on radio station KMA in Shenandoah, Iowa. When they graduated from high school, they moved to Nashville, and signed their first recording contract thanks to Chet Atkins. They, along with singer Gordon Terry, were the first country artists on the label.

THE EVERLY BROTHERS

Left to right: Don Everly, Phil Everly

The Everly Brothers met Boudeleaux Bryant and his wife Felice and developed a close relationship with these two writers. The Bryants penned the Everlys' first hit in May of 1957, "Bye, Bye Love." Their next release came a few months later in September with "Wake Up Little Suzie," which became a number one song. There was some controversy between the Everlys and the president of Cadence, Archie Blyer, for he thought the lyrics were suggestive with "Susie sleeping with someone at a drive-in show."

In 1959, Don wrote a song called " 'Til I Kissed You" while he was in Australia. He returned to Nashville, where they got Buddy Holly's old group The Crickets to record the song with them. Jerry Allison was on drums, using a whole set of drums including tom-toms for the arrangement. This was a first, for prior to this all drummers in the studio used only snare drums and brushes. Joe Mauldin was on bass and Sonny Curtis on guitar. The song became a smash when it was released that summer. On December 15, 1959, they recorded "Let It Be Me" in New York City. It was the first time they recorded out of Nashville and the first time they used strings in an arrangement.

In 1960, they left Cadence to sign with Warner Brothers. Their first release for Warner Brothers, in April 1960, became their biggest all-time seller, "Cathy's Clown."

In 1962, Don and Phil joined the Marine Corps reserve and served six months active duty. In 1973, the brothers split up the act and pursued individual recording careers.

May	1957	BYE, BYE LOVE	Cadence
September	1957	WAKE UP LITTLE SUSIE	Cadence
January	1958	THIS LITTLE GIRL OF MINE	Cadence
April	1958	ALL I HAVE TO DO IS DREAM	Cadence
April	1958	CLAUDETTE	Cadence
July	1958	BIRD DOG	Cadence
July	1958	DEVOTED TO YOU	Cadence
November	1958	PROBLEMS	Cadence
November	1958	LOVE OF MY LIFE	Cadence
March	1959	TAKE A MESSAGE TO MARY	Cadence
March	1959	POOR JENNY	Cadence
August	1959	'TIL I KISSED YOU	Cadence
January	1960	LET IT BE ME	Cadence
May	1960	WHEN WILL I BE LOVED	Cadence
October	1961	LIKE STRANGERS	Cadence
July	1961	ALL I HAVE TO DO IS DREAM	Cadence
October	1962	I'M HERE TO GET MY BABY OUT OF JAIL	Cadence
April	1960	CATHY'S CLOWN	Warner Bros.
August	1960	SO SAD	Warner Bros.
August	1960	LUCILLE	Warner Bros.
January	1961	EBONY EYES	Warner Bros.
January	1961	WALK RIGHT BACK	Warner Bros.
June	1961	TEMPTATION	Warner Bros.

October	1961	DON'T BLAME ME	Warner Bros.
January	1962	CRYING IN THE RAIN	Warner Bros.
May	1962	THAT'S OLD FASHIONED	Warner Bros.
October	1962	DON'T ASK ME TO BE FRIENDS	Warner Bros.
June	1964	THE FERRIS WHEEL	Warner Bros.
October	1964	GONE, GONE GONE	Warner Bros.
May	1967	BOWLING GREEN	Warner Bros.

THE EXCELLENTS

Lead singer John Kuse formed the group in Brooklyn in 1960. In 1961, the group recorded "Red Robin" for Vinnie Catalano's Murmaid records. The song was a small local success, and the group gained confidence.

They went back into the studio and recorded two songs, the Cleftones' big hit "You Baby You" and a song that Vinnie Catalano had written, called "Coney Island Baby." Vinnie released the songs on his Blast label in the summer of 1961, with "You Baby You" as the "A" side. The song got some local airplay, but it never made the national charts.

Almost one year later, in late 1962, the flip side, "Coney Island Baby," was picked up by a number of disc jockeys. In a short time it became a national hit.

November 1962	CONEY ISLAND BABY/YOU BABY YOU	Blast

THE EXCITERS

Members:
>Brenda Reid—lead—1945
>Carol Johnson—1945
>Lilian Walker—1945
>Herbert Rooney—1941

Hometown: Jamaica, Queens, New York

As high school juniors in 1962, Brenda, Carol, and Lilian were singing in Jamaica, New York. Herb, who was a few years older and working as a record producer, was singing with a group of fellows. When both groups disbanded, Herb joined Brenda, Carol, and Lilian to form the Exciters.

A few months later they landed a contract with United Artists records and recorded a Bert Russell song called "Tell Him," which became a big hit for the group in 1963, the same year the girls graduated from high school.

November	1962	TELL HIM	United Artists
February	1963	HE'S GOT THE POWER	United Artists
June	1963	GET HIM	United Artists
January	1964	DO-WAH-DIDDY	United Artists
January	1965	I WANT YOU TO BE MY BOY	Roulette
January	1966	A LITTLE BIT OF SOAP	Bang

FABIAN

SHELLY FABARES

Real Name: Michele Fabares
Born: January 19, 1944
Hometown: Santa Monica, California

Shelly started her career as a dancer. Her big break came in 1953 when she appeared on a Frank Sinatra TV spectacular. In 1955, she appeared in the film *Never Say Goodbye*, followed by *Rock, Pretty Baby* and *Summer Love.*

Shelly, the niece of comedian Nanette Fabray, gained her popularity by playing the role of Donna Reed's daughter in the early sixties on "The Donna Reed Show." In 1961, she signed a recording contract with Colpix records, and in February 1962 released her first major hit, which went to the number one position on the national charts, "Johnny Angel." It was to be her only number one record.

Today, Shelly is very active on TV.

February	1962	JOHNNY ANGEL	Colpix
May	1962	JOHNNY LOVES ME	Colpix
September	1962	THE THINGS WE DID LAST SUMMER	Colpix
April	1963	RONNIE CALL ME WHEN YOU GET A CHANCE	Colpix

FABIAN

Real Name: Fabiano Forte
Born: February 6, 1943
Hometown: Philadelphia, Pennsylvania

When Fabian was fifteen, and a sophomore at Southern High in Philly, Bob Marcucci, who was Frankie Avalon's manager at the time, went to see Fabian at Frankie's suggestion. Frankie had told Bob that Fabian was a cross between Elvis and Rick Nelson. Bob signed him to a contract with Chancellor records.

Fabian's first release in 1958 was a local hit called "Lillie Lou," but in January 1959 he had his first major hit with "I'm a Man." A few months later he established himself with "Turn Me Loose."

Due to his popularity with teen-age girls around the country, he began to make motion pictures in late 1959, with his first film *Hound Dog Man*. The title song also became a hit single for him in November 1959.

Today Fabian lives on the West Coast and has made occasional appearances during the past couple of years at various rock shows in Philadelphia and New York. He does some acting and would like to become more active with his recording career.

January	1959	I'M A MAN	Chancellor
March	1959	TURN ME LOOSE	Chancellor
June	1959	TIGER	Chancellor
September	1959	COME ON AND GET ME	Chancellor
September	1959	GOT THE FEELING	Chancellor
November	1959	HOUND DOG MAN	Chancellor
November	1959	THIS FRIENDLY WORLD	Chancellor
February	1960	STRING ALONG	Chancellor
February	1960	ABOUT THIS THING CALLED LOVE	Chancellor
October	1960	KISSIN' AND TWISTIN'	Chancellor

BENT FABRIC

Born: 1927

He was the head of Metronome records in Denmark, along with being a composer-pianist and a TV personality. He was called the Danish Perry Como. Bent would play at many formal parties at the Royal Palace in Copenhagen for the royal Danish family.

In 1962, he wrote and recorded a song that became a big hit in Europe for which he did a solo at the piano. The recording was sold to Atco records to be released in the United States and by the summer Bent had a national hit with "Alley Cat."

July	1962	ALLEY CAT	Atco
December	1962	CHICKEN FEED	Atco

TOMMY FACENDA

TOMMY FACENDA

Born: November 10, 1939
Hometown: Portsmouth, Virginia

Frank Guida, the owner of the Birdland record shop in Norfolk (the same Frank Guida who would go on to write and manage the hits and career of Gary "U.S." Bonds a few years later) saw Tommy at a club in Norfolk and asked to be his manager. Tommy tried to launch his career with a song called "Little Baby" on Nasco records in 1958, without much success.

In late 1959, Frank wrote a song for Tommy about the various schools in the area. It was a success, and the idea was sold to Atlantic records to record various versions of the song specifically aimed at high schools in major cities where the record was to be released. At first they were only going to record about a dozen versions, but due to the song's popularity after its release in October 1959, forty-six versions of "High School U.S.A." were eventually cut. The song turned out to be Tommy's only real hit.

October   1959   HIGH SCHOOL U.S.A.   Atlantic

PERCY FAITH

Born: April 7, 1908
Died: February 9, 1976
Hometown: Toronto, Canada

In 1933, Percy was appointed staff conductor for the Canadian Broadcasting Company. By 1940, he moved to the United States and joined Columbia records as a musician-composer.

In the early fifties, he became the arranger and conductor of the staff orchestra at Columbia for many artists including Tony Bennett on recordings like "Because of You" and "Cold, Cold Heart."

He started having hits under his own name around 1950, with songs like "I Crossed My Fingers" and "All My Love." In early 1952, he had his first major hit called "Delicado," which became a number one song. A year later, in March 1953, he recorded a motion picture song called "The Song from Moulin Rouge," subtitled "Where Is Your Heart," on which Felicia Sanders did the vocal solo. The song was a million seller and became another number one hit for Percy.

Seven years later he recorded a Max Steiner theme from a motion picture and it gave Percy another gold record. "Theme from a Summer

PERCY FAITH

Place" was launched in January 1960, and remained on the pop music charts for twenty-one weeks. It eventually became a number one song. Percy died of cancer in Los Angeles in early 1976.

May	1950	I CROSS MY FINGERS	Columbia
September	1950	ALL MY LOVE	Columbia
May	1951	ON TOP OF OLD SMOKY	Columbia
April	1952	DELICADO	Columbia
March	1953	SONG FROM MOULIN ROUGE (Felicia Sanders)	Columbia
January	1956	VALLEY VALPARAISO	Columbia
March	1956	WE ALL NEED LOVE	Columbia
July	1956	WITH A LITTLE BIT OF LUCK	Columbia
April	1957	TILL	Columbia
January	1960	THE THEME FROM A SUMMER PLACE	Columbia
May	1960	THEME FOR YOUNG LOVERS	Columbia

THE FALCONS

Members:
   Eddie Floyd—lead
   Joe Stubbs—tenor
   Bonny Rice—baritone
   Willie Schoefield—bass
   Lance Finnie—guitar
Hometown: Detroit, Michigan

Bonny Rice formed the group in early 1959 in Detroit, and they began to get some local engagements. A short while later, guitarist Lance Finnie and bass singer Willie Schoefield wrote a song which the group began to practice with. They finally got a recording contract with Unart records, and decided to record Lance and Willie's song as their first endeavor. "You're So Fine" was released in April 1959 and became a national hit.

In late 1961, a young unknown singer named Wilson Pickett joined the group as lead singer. The group signed a new contract with a new company, LuPine records and recorded their only other real hit. "I Found a Love," which was released in March 1962, was the song Wilson Pickett sang lead on. He left the group shortly after that to go on his own. He signed with Double-L records in 1963, and later with Atlantic in 1965.

Eddie Floyd signed with Stax records in 1966, and began a successful career with that label by recording "Knock on Wood" in August of that year, which was the first of many hits. Joe Stubbs of the group was the brother of Levi Stubbs, the lead singer of the Four Tops.

| April | 1959 | YOU'RE SO FINE | Unart |
| March | 1962 | I FOUND A LOVE | LuPine |

THE FALCONS

THE FENDERMEN

Members:
    Jim Sundquist—born: November 26, 1937—Niagra, Wisconsin
    Phil Humphrey—born: November 26,1937—Madison, Wisconsin

Jim and Phil, who both had bands of their own, combined the two groups in late 1959. Then they recorded a song which was written by country and western great Jimmie Rodgers many years ago called "Mule Skinner Blues." The song was purchased by Soma records and released nationally in May 1960. In a short time Jim and Phil, who called themselves The Fendermen because they played Fender guitars, were on their way to having their first and only hit.

May   1960   MULE SKINNER BLUES   Soma

JOHNNY FERGUSON

Born: March 22, 1937
Hometown: Nashville, Tennessee

Johnny went to Hillsboro High, and attended Peabody College for a year. While in high school he worked part-time at radio station WNAH in Gallatin, Tennessee, and WAGG in Franklin, Tennessee. In the summer of 1958, he went to work as a disc jockey at WJAT in Swainsboro, Georgia.

He signed a recording contract with MGM in late 1959, and by February of 1960 had his first and only hit with "Angela Jones."

February	1960	ANGELA JONES	MGM

FERRANTE & TEICHER

Members:

Arthur Ferrante—piano—New York, New York
Louis Teicher—piano—Wilkes Barre, Pennsylvania

The two first met when they were six years old and attended the Juilliard School of Music.

After a long friendship, they joined forces as the Twin Pianos and signed with United Artists. In the summer of 1960, they had their first national hit with the title song from "The Theme from the Apartment," a motion picture that starred Jack Lemmon and Shirley MacLaine.

July	1960	THEME FROM THE APARTMENT	United Artists
October	1960	EXODUS	United Artists
March	1961	LOVE THEME FROM ONE EYED JACK	United Artists
May	1961	THEME FROM GOODBYE AGAIN	United Artists
October	1961	TONIGHT	United Artists
February	1962	SMILE	United Artists
June	1962	LISA	United Artists
January	1963	THEME FROM LAWRENCE OF ARABIA	United Artists
June	1963	ANTHONY & CLEOPATRA THEME	United Artists
November	1969	MIDNIGHT COWBOY	United Artists
April	1970	LAY LADY LAY	United Artists

ERNIE FIELDS

Ernie was a very popular arranger on the West Coast in the mid-fifties. He worked with many of the big artists. In September 1959, he recorded a swinging version of Glenn Miller's great song "In the Mood." It became a big hit on the Rendezvous label. He followed that hit with swinging versions of other standards.

September	1959	IN THE MOOD	Rendezvous
February	1960	CHATTANOOGA CHOO CHOO	Rendezvous
June	1961	THE CHARLESTON	Rendezvous

THE FIESTAS

Members:

Tommy Bullock—first tenor
Eddie Morris—second tenor
Sam Ingalls—baritone
Preston Lane—bass
Hometown: Newark, New Jersey

The Fiestas grew up together and began singing as a group in 1958. After much practice they went to Jim Gribble's studio in Newark to make a demo record. Gribble was so impressed with the disc that he immediately took it to his friend Hy Weiss, the president of Old Town records. Weiss signed the group and released the song "So Fine" in April 1959, and it went on to become a national hit.

April	1959	SO FINE	Old Town
August	1962	BROKEN HEART	Old Town

LARRY FINNEGAN

Real Name: Lawrence Finnegan
Born: 1941
Hometown: New York, New York

In November 1961, while attending Notre Dame college, Larry returned to New York City with a demo record of a song he had written and recorded. Old Town records liked the song and released "Dear One" in February 1962. It became Larry's only hit.

February	1962	DEAR ONE	Old Town

THE FIREBALLS

Members:

George Tomsco—leader—Raton, New Mexico
Stan Lark—bass guitar—Raton, New Mexico
Jimmy Gilmer—piano—LaGrange, Illinois
Eric Budd—drums—Raton, New Mexico

The group was formed in 1959, and got Norman Petty to manage them. Norman also managed The Crickets with Buddy Holly and owned his own recording studio in Clovis, New Mexico. Norman secured a recording contract for The Fireballs with Top Rank records and they had their first national hit in October 1959 with an instrumental called "Torquay." The group's piano player, Jimmy Gilmer, gained national fame in 1963 with the top song of the year called "Sugar Shack."

October	1959	TORQUAY	Top Rank
January	1960	BULLDOG	Top Rank
August	1960	VAQUERO	Top Rank
July	1961	QUITE A PARTY	Warwick
December	1967	BOTTLE OF WINE	Atco
March	1968	GOIN' AWAY	Atco
October	1968	COME ON, REACT	Atco
February	1969	LONG GREEN	Atco

THE FIREFLIES

Members:
Ritchie Adams—lead
Lee Reynolds
Frankie Manderino—replaced by Johnny Viscelli
Carl Giracelli—replaced by Paul Giacalone

In September 1959, the group recorded a song for Ribbon records that Paul Giacalone had written called "You Were Mine," which became a national hit. In 1961, Ritchie Adams wrote the song "Tossin' and Turnin" which became the top song of the year for Bobby Lewis.

September 1959	YOU WERE MINE	Ribbon
January 1960	I CAN'T SAY GOODBYE	Ribbon

EDDIE FISHER

Real Name: Edwin Jack Fisher
Born: August 10, 1928
Hometown: Philadelphia, Pennsylvania

Eddie was one of seven children, whose father supported the family by selling vegetables from his cart. By age seven, Eddie began entering amateur singing contests in Philadelphia. After high school Eddie continued singing at local clubs in his hometown, looking for a break. In the late forties he got a job singing at Grossinger's resort hotel in the Catskills. On Labor Day of 1949, Eddie Cantor heard Fisher sing and asked Eddie to join him on tour.

By 1950, Fisher signed a recording contract with RCA Victor which in the fall of that year released his first hit, "Thinking of You." In 1951, he entered the Army for two years, but continued to record. It was at this

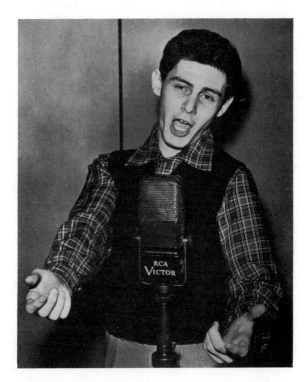

EDDIE FISHER

time that squealing teen-age girls began to swoon for Eddie. He became one of the most popular recording artists on the music scene during the early fifties with a long string of hits. On September 26, 1955, Eddie married Debbie Reynolds and their romance made headlines. Three years later he made headlines again by leaving Debbie for Liz Taylor. Subsequently, Liz married Richard Burton. Eddie's last big chart record was a top forty tune called "Game That Lovers Play" in 1966.

October	1950	THINKING OF YOU	RCA Victor
January	1951	BRING BACK THE THRILL	RCA Victor
April	1951	UNLESS	RCA Victor
June	1951	I'LL HOLD YOU IN MY HEART	RCA Victor
September	1951	TURN BACK THE HANDS OF TIME	RCA Victor
November	1951	ANY TIME	RCA Victor
December	1951	TELL ME WHY	RCA Victor
March	1952	FORGIVE ME	RCA Victor
April	1952	I'M YOURS	RCA Victor
July	1952	WISH YOU WERE HERE	RCA Victor
September	1952	LADY OF SPAIN	RCA Victor
January	1953	EVEN NOW	RCA Victor
February	1953	DOWNHEARTED	RCA Victor
April	1953	I'M WALKING BEHIND YOU	RCA Victor
July	1953	WITH THESE HANDS	RCA Victor
October	1953	MANY TIMES	RCA Victor
December	1953	OH! MY PAPA	RCA Victor

March	1954	A GIRL, A GIRL	RCA Victor
March	1954	ANEMA E CORE	RCA Victor
June	1954	MY FRIEND	RCA Victor
August	1954	I NEED YOU NOW	RCA Victor
October	1954	COUNT YOUR BLESSINGS	RCA Victor
January	1955	A MAN CHASES A GIRL	RCA Victor
May	1955	HEART	RCA Victor
August	1955	SONG OF THE DREAMER/DON'T STAY AWAY TOO LONG	RCA Victor
October	1955	MAGIC FINGERS	RCA
November	1955	DUNGAREE DOLL	RCA
March	1956	WITHOUT YOU	RCA
May	1956	ON THE STREET WHERE YOU LIVE	RCA
August	1956	OH MY MARIA	RCA
October	1956	CINDY, OH CINDY	RCA
January	1957	SOME DAY SOON	RCA
April	1957	TONIGHT MY HEART WILL BE CRYING	RCA
June	1957	SUNSHINE GIRL	RCA
November	1961	TONIGHT	Seven Arts
October	1966	GAMES THAT LOVERS PLAY	RCA
February	1967	PEOPLE LIKE YOU	RCA

TONI FISHER

Toni was petite and had a powerful voice, but she was popular primarily because of a special reverb effect on the guitars that backed her up. In November 1959 she had a top ten record: "The Big Hurt."

November	1959	THE BIG HURT	Signet
April	1960	HOW DEEP IS THE OCEAN	Signet
May	1962	WEST OF THE WALL	Big Top

THE FIVE BLOBS

"The Blob" was written by Burt Bacharach during the early part of his career. It was based on a motion picture called *The Blob*. The song was sung by one person who had his voice rerecorded five times to sound like a group. Whew, Burt. Some start for a career.

October	1958	THE BLOB	Columbia

THE FIVE DISCS

Members:
> Mario D'Androtti—lead—replaced by Eddie Pardocchi
> Paul Abano—first tenor
> Tony Basile—second tenor—replaced by Frank Arnone
> Joe Barsalona—baritone
> Charles DiBella—bass

Hometown: Brooklyn, New York

THE FIVE DISCS

The group was first formed in 1958 and sang at various high school functions in Brooklyn. They all combined in writing a song called "I Remember" in 1958, which they took to Gene Schwartz of Laurie records. Gene liked the song and released it on his subsidiary label, Emge records. When the song became popular in New York, RCA purchased the song and released it on their subsidiary label, Vik records. When Vik went bankrupt, it was released on the Rust label, subsidiary of Laurie. The record had the distinction of coming out on three different labels.

June	1958	I REMEMBER	Emge, Vik, Rust
September	1958	ADIOS	Calo
April	1961	NEVER LET YOU GO	Cheer

THE FIVE DU-TONES

In the midst of the dance craze, this group recorded a song called "Shake a Tail Feather." In early 1963, the song became a national hit. The song was in the same genre as "Do the Bird" and "The Bird Is the Word."

| May | 1963 | SHAKE A TAIL FEATHER | One-derful |

THE FIVE KEYS

Top: Rudy West
Bottom: Joe Jones
Center, left to right:
Ripley Ingram, Dickie
Smith, Maryland
Pierce, Bernie West

THE FIVE KEYS

Members:
    Maryland Pierce—lead—1933
    Rudy West—born: July 25, 1933—replaced by Ulysses K. Hicks in
        1953—replaced by Rudy West in 1956
    Dickie Smith—replaced by Ramon Loper in 1953
    Ripley Ingram—1933
    Bernie West—baritone—1932
    Joe Jones—pianist
Hometown: Newport News, Virginia

The group was first formed in 1950 with Rudy and Bernie West, and
Raphael and Ripley Ingram, as the Sentimental Four. In 1951, Raphael
went into the Army and was replaced by Maryland Pierce and Dickie
Smith was added. At this point they called themselves The Five Keys
after the keys on a piano.

That same year, while the group was appearing at the Apollo theater
in New York, Eddie Mesner of Aladdin records heard them and signed

them to his label. They first recorded "With a Broken Heart," and followed it up that summer with their first national hit, "Glory of Love." In 1953, Dickie and Rudy went into the Army and were replaced by Ramon Loper and Ulysses K. Hicks. Hicks died in 1954, and when Rudy finished the military in 1956, he rejoined the group.

In 1954, they signed with Capitol records and first recorded "Ling Ting Tong" which became their first hit for the label. Maryland sang lead on "Ling Ting Tong" and "Close Your Eyes," while Rudy sang lead on "Out Of Sight, Out Of Mind," "Wisdom Of A Fool" and many of the other Five Keys' hits.

Today Rudy sings with three new members. On October 3, 1981, they headlined the Royal New York Doo Wopp Show at New York's Radio City Music Hall. This was the first time in the fifty-year history of the great hall that singing groups of the fifties played there. They all reside in Hamton, Virginia, and work for the post office.

July	1951	THE GLORY OF LOVE	Aladdin
December	1954	LING, TING, TONG	Capitol
February	1955	CLOSE YOUR EYES	Capitol
July	1956	THE VERDICT	Capitol
September	1956	OUT OF SIGHT, OUT OF MIND	Capitol
November	1956	WISDOM OF A FOOL	Capitol
March	1957	LET THERE BE YOU	Capitol

THE "5" ROYALES

Members:
  Lowman Pauling—lead
  Clarence Pauling
  Johnny Tanner
  Obediah Carter
  Johnny Moore
Homestate: North Carolina

The group, which originally sang gospel, was first formed in 1948; they were known as the Royal Sons. By 1952, they had changed their name to the "5" Royales, and by December of that year they had their first national R & B hit with a song called "Baby, Don't Do It," written by Lowman Pauling.

In 1954, the group signed with King records. Four years later they had a big hit with another song Lowman had written with Ralph Bass called "Dedicated to the One I Love." The same song became a big hit for the Shirelles in 1961 as well.

December	1952	BABY, DON'T DO IT	Apollo
May	1953	HELP ME SOMEBODY	Apollo

THE "5" ROYALES

Top: Lowman Pauling
From left: Obediah Carter, Johnny Tanner,
Clarence Pauling, Johnny Moore

May	1963	CRAZY, CRAZY, CRAZY	Apollo
September	1953	TOO MUCH LOVIN'	Apollo
September	1957	THINK	King
April	1958	DEDICATED TO THE ONE I LOVE	King

THE FIVE SATINS

Members:

Fred Parris (March 26, 1936)—lead—replaced by Bill Baker on "To
the Aisle" in 1957

Rich Freeman—tenor—December 1940

West Forbes—second tenor—1937

Lewis Peeples—harmony—1937

Sy Hopkins—bass—1938

Hometown: New Haven, Connecticut

In 1954 Fred Parris was the leader of a group called the Scarletts. He was also partial to a group called the Velvets. It's not hard to see how Fred picked "Satin" as the name for the new group he formed in 1956. Guard duty in the Army at three A.M. inspired Fred to write the group's greatest hit, "In the Still of the Night." The record was first released on a small Connecticut label and later sold to Ember records in New York. Ironically, that tune was the "B" side of the record. The long-forgotten "A" side was "The Jones Girl."

By the early sixties the group had quit touring and recording and returned to the New Haven area to pursue their respective livelihoods.

In 1969 the members got back together for a rock and roll revival show at Madison Square Garden in New York. The response to their appearance was so great they have been singing together ever since.

Today Fred does limited appearances with new members as The Five Satins.

July	1956	IN THE STILL OF THE NIGHT/THE JONES GIRL	Ember
October	1956	WONDERFUL GIRL	Ember
June	1957	TO THE AISLE	Ember
October	1959	SHADOWS	Ember
April	1960	I'LL BE SEEING YOU	Ember

THE FLAMINGOS

Members:
> Nathaniel Nelson—lead—born: April 10, 1932—Chicago, Illinois
> John Carter—replaced by Tommy Hunt—second tenor—born: June 18, 1933—Pittsburgh, Pennsylvania
> Terry Johnson—tenor—born: November 12, 1935—Baltimore, Maryland—joined in 1956
> Ezekiel Carey—second tenor—born: January 24, 1933—Bluefield, West Virginia—not in group 1956-1958
> Paul Wilson—baritone—born: January 6, 1935—Chicago, Illinois
> Jacob Carey—bass—born: September 9, 1926—Pulaski, Virginia
> Sollie McElroy—left in 1954

In 1952, the group started appearing around Chicago. In a short time, Ralph Leon noticed them and signed them to a managerial contract. By 1953, they had their first hit with "Golden Teardrops" on which Sollie McElroy sang lead.

In January 1956, they recorded their first national hit with "I'll Be Home" (which also became a hit for Pat Boone) and followed it with "A Kiss from Your Lips," on both of which Nate Nelson sang lead.

In 1956, John Carter and Zeke Carey went into the Army and were

THE FLAMINGOS

Bottom row: Nate Nelson,
Zeke Carey
Top row: Jake Carey,
Johnny Carter, Paul Wilson

replaced by Tommy Hunt and Terry Johnson. The group signed with Decca records in 1957 and had a hit with "Ladder of Love."

By 1958, Zeke rejoined the group and they signed with End records in New York. They recorded a whole string of hits beginning with "Lovers Never Say Goodbye" in October 1958. After that came songs like "I Only Have Eyes for You" and "Love Walked In."

In April 1960, they swapped their ballad format for an up-tempo number written by Sam Cooke called "Nobody Loves Me Like You," which became a smash. Nate Nelson sang lead on most of the hits on End records.

Today Nate lives in Southboro, Massachusetts, while Zeke and Jake reside in the New York area. In May 1981 Nate joined Zeke and Jake on stage on the Royal New York Doo Wopp Show. This was the first time they sang together in twenty years. Otherwise, Zeke and Jake perform as The Flamingos with several new members.

August	1953	GOLDEN TEARDROPS	Chance
January	1956	I'LL BE HOME	Checker
March	1956	A KISS FROM YOUR LIPS	Checker
January	1957	THE LADDER OF LOVE	Decca
October	1958	LOVERS NEVER SAY GOODBYE	End
May	1959	I ONLY HAVE EYES FOR YOU	End
September	1959	LOVE WALKED IN	End
April	1960	NOBODY LOVES ME LIKE YOU	End
July	1960	MIO AMORE	End
December	1960	YOUR OTHER LOVE	End
March	1961	POKOMO	End
June	1961	TIME WAS	End
February	1966	THE BOOGALOO PARTY	Philips
March	1970	BUFFALO SOLDIER	Polydor

THE FLARES

Members:
   George Felton Hollis—born: March 24, 1937—San Antonio, Texas
   Thomas Miller—born: April 25, 1938—Los Angeles, California
   Eddie King—born: April 1, 1938—New York, New York
   Robbie Robinson—born: June 5, 1930—Greensboro, North Carolina
   Beverly Harris—born: June 8, 1937

The group, originally formed in 1959, worked at various clubs getting their act down. In 1961, they signed with Felsted records and recorded "Foot Stomping—Part I," which hit the national charts that September. It was the group's only hit.

September 1961   FOOT STOMPING—PART I   Felsted

THE FLEETWOODS

Members:
   Gary Troxel—born: November 28, 1939—Centralia, Washington
   Barbara Ellis—born: February 20, 1940—Olympia, Washington
   Gretchen Christopher—born: February 29, 1940—Olympia,
      Washington

The trio met in 1958, when they were seniors at Olympia High in Washington. The group initially was formed as a duo with Barbara and Gretchen, but they asked Gary to join them playing trumpet. Gary's vocal talents also became apparent. They called themselves Two Girls and a Guy.

   In late 1958, the three collaborated on a song which came to the

THE FLEETWOODS

Left to right:
Gretchen Christopher,
Gary Troxel,
Barbara Ellis

attention of Bob Reisendorff, a record distributor in Seattle. He set up a recording session with Dolton records. The company signed them.

Bob felt the song would be a hit, so he decided to have the group change their name from Two Girls and a Guy to something that was more catchy. One day, while on the phone with Barbara, he accidently mentioned that they should change their name to something simple like his telephone exchange—FLeetwood. The rest is history.

When their song "Come Softly to Me" was released in early 1959, it became a national number one hit. Later that year they had another number one record: "Mr. Blue."

Today Gary lives with his wife in Anacortes, Washington, and works at a plywood mill. Gretchen is married and she teaches jazz dancing at Evergreen State College in Olympia, Washington, while Barbara is also married and is a housewife in Placentia, California.

February	1959	COME SOFTLY TO ME	Dolton
May	1959	GRADUATION'S HERE	Dolton
September	1959	MR. BLUE	Dolton
February	1960	OUTSIDE MY WINDOW	Dolton
May	1960	RUNAROUND	Dolton
October	1960	LAST ONE TO KNOW	Dolton
April	1961	TRAGEDY	Dolton
September	1962	HE'S THE GREAT IMPOSTER	Dolton
October	1962	LOVERS BY NIGHT, STRANGERS BY DAY	Dolton
May	1963	GOODNIGHT MY LOVE	Dolton

SHELBY FLINT

Hometown: North Hollywood, California

Shelby was first signed as a writer by music publisher Barry DeVorzon. Barry later agreed to manage her as a vocalist. In 1958, she recorded "I Will Love You" on Cadence records. Later she formed a folk trio and recorded "Angel on My Shoulder" for Valiant records. It became a big hit for her in early 1961.

| January | 1961 | ANGEL ON MY SHOULDER | Valiant |
| August | 1966 | CAST YOUR FATE TO THE WIND | Valiant |

THE FONTANE SISTERS

Members:
    Marge Fontane—lead
    Bea Fontane—low harmony
    Geri Fontane—harmony
Hometown: New Milford, New Jersey

The sisters were coached by their mother, who was a choral director and organist. They signed with Dot records in the mid-fifties and first recorded "Happy Days and Lonely Nights." Their first gold record came in 1954, with "Hearts of Stone," which was a cover version of the hit by Otis Williams & The Charms. After that they went high on the charts with "Rock Love" and "Seventeen."

January	1951	TENNESSEE WALTZ	RCA Victor
November	1954	HEARTS OF STONE	Dot
February	1955	ROCK LOVE	Dot
August	1955	SEVENTEEN	Dot
October	1955	DADDY-O/ADORABLE	Dot
December	1955	NUTTIN' FOR CHRISTMAS	Dot
February	1956	EDDIE MY LOVE	Dot
May	1956	I'M IN LOVE AGAIN	Dot
July	1956	VOICES	Dot
October	1956	PLEASE DON'T LEAVE ME	Dot
December	1956	THE BANANA BOAT SONG	Dot
May	1957	I'M STICKIN' WITH YOU	Dot
May	1958	CHANSON D'AMOUR	Dot
November	1958	JEALOUS HEART	Dot

FRANKIE FORD

Hometown: Fretna, Louisiana

Frankie went to Holy Name of Mary High School and won a musical scholarship to Southeastern College in Hammond, Louisiana. In January 1959, Frankie recorded a song that Huey "Piano" Smith had written and given to Frankie to record. The result was the song "Sea Cruise," which became a top twenty song for Frankie in January 1959.

Today Frankie is making a musical comeback on ABC records.

January	1959	SEA CRUISE	Ace
July	1959	ALIMONY	Ace
January	1960	TIME AFTER TIME	Ace
October	1960	YOU TALK TOO MUCH	Imperial
March	1961	SEVENTEEN	Imperial

TENNESSEE ERNIE FORD

Born: February 13, 1919
Hometown: Bristol, Tennessee

As a youngster, Ernie became an aficionado of country music. In 1937, he got a job as a radio announcer in Bristol, Tennessee. A year later he entered the Cincinnati Conservatory of Music to study music. During World War II he enlisted in the Air Force, and while stationed in California he married Betty Jean Heminger. After his discharge he became a disc jockey in San Bernadino, and then moved on to a Country station in Pasadena. A good friend of Ernie's named Cliffie Stone arranged an audition with Capitol records in late 1949. Ernie was signed, and he recorded "Mule Train" that year. After that he got his own CBS-TV show and by 1955 was a national star.

In 1955, he recorded a Merle Travis song called "Sixteen Tons," which became a number one national hit by the fall of 1955 and his biggest hit. Ernie, with his "Howdy, pea-pickers" greeting, has been a star of TV, radio, and records ever since.

November	1949	MULE TRAIN	Capitol
February	1950	THE CRY OF THE WILD GOOSE	Capitol
March	1951	SHOTGUN BOOGIE	Capitol
March	1955	BALLAD OF DAVY CROCKETT	Capitol
September	1955	SIXTEEN TONS	Capitol
February	1956	THAT'S ALL	Capitol
May	1956	ROVIN' GAMBLER	Capitol
October	1956	FIRST BORN	Capitol
February	1956	WATERMELON SONG	Capitol
August	1957	IN THE MIDDLE OF AN ISLAND	Capitol
August	1958	SUNDAY BARBECUE	Capitol
March	1959	GLAD RAGS	Capitol

THE FOUR ACES

Members:
    Al Alberts—lead
    Dave Mahoney—tenor
    Sod Vaccaro—baritone
    Lou Silvestri—bass
Hometown: Philadelphia, Pennsylvania

After singing around Philadelphia in the late forties, the fellows decided to record a song. So in 1951, they pooled their finances and recorded "Sin," which was released on Victoria records that summer. Decca records became interested in the group and signed them to the label a few months later.

That fall the group recorded "Tell Me Why," which became their first hit. This song launched their sound, which for the next five years set the precedent for male singing groups. The Four Aces became one of the most popular singing groups of the early fifties. Their songs were featured as title songs in four motion pictures. In 1955, they recorded the title song from the motion picture *Love Is a Many Splendored Thing*, which became a number one national hit.

Al left the group to go out as a solo in the mid-fifties.

Recently, the original members got together and have been doing night club shows and selected concerts.

August	1951	SIN	Victoria
November	1951	TELL ME WHY	Decca
November	1951	A GARDEN IN THE RAIN	Decca
February	1952	PERFIDIA	Decca
May	1952	I'M YOURS	Decca
August	1952	SHOULD I	Decca
October	1952	HEART AND SOUL	Decca
November	1953	STRANGER IN PARADISE	Decca
November	1953	THE GANG THAT SANG HEART OF MY HEART	Decca
May	1954	THREE COINS IN THE FOUNTAIN	Decca
May	1954	WEDDING BELLS (ARE BREAKING UP THAT OLD GANG OF MINE)	Decca
October	1954	IT'S A WOMAN'S WORLD	Decca
November	1954	MISTER SANDMAN	Decca
January	1955	MELODY OF LOVE	Decca
May	1955	HEART	Decca
August	1955	LOVE IS A MANY SPLENDORED THING	Decca
October	1955	A WOMAN IN LOVE	Decca
January	1956	IF YOU CAN DREAM	Decca
April	1956	TO LOVE AGAIN	Decca
July	1956	I ONLY KNOW I LOVE YOU	Decca
September	1956	FRIENDLY PERSUASION	Decca
November	1956	SOMEONE TO LOVE	Decca
March	1957	BAHAMA MAMA	Decca
March	1958	ROCK AND ROLL RHAPSODY	Decca
November	1958	THE WORLD OUTSIDE	Decca
March	1959	NO OTHER ARMS, NO OTHER LIPS	Decca

THE FOUR COINS

Members:
George Mantalis
Jim Gregorakis
Michael James
George James
Hometown: Canonsburg, Pennsylvania

The Four Coins grew up in the same town that spawned Perry Como and Bobby Vinton. In the mid-fifties, vocal quartets were very popular. The simple, clear sound of the group proved very successful around the Pittsburgh area.

They were noticed by an executive from Epic records and a short time later they were signed to the label. In July 1954, The Four Coins recorded their first song, "We'll Be Married (in the Church in the Wildwood)"

THE FOUR COINS

which went on to establish their smooth, bouncy beat. Next came their double-sided hit "Maybe" and "I Love You Madly" in December 1954.

Although there is a Four Coins group presently appearing around the country, none of the members are from the original quartet.

January	1955	I LOVE YOU MADLY/MAYBE	Epic
August	1955	MEMORIES OF YOU	Epic
May	1957	SHANGRI-LA	Epic
September	1957	MY ONE SIN	Epic
September	1958	WENDY WENDY	Epic
November	1958	THE WORLD OUTSIDE	Epic
June	1959	ONE LOVE, ONE HEART	Epic

THE FOUR DEUCES

Hometown: Salinas, California

In 1955, Luther McDaniel met Orvis Lee Teamer and two other servicemen from Fort Ord at a club in Salinas. They decided to form a singing group, and called themselves the Four Deuces. At this time Luther liked to drink white port wine and some lemon juice, which he simply called W-P-L-J. Luther then wrote a song about this drink, which he took to Ray Dobard of Music City records in Oakland. Ray signed the group and after about forty takes they had the version of "W-P-L-J" that they wanted.

The song was released a few weeks later and became the group's only major hit. The group broke up shortly thereafter, since several of the members were getting their discharge from the service and wanted to return home.

June   1955   W-P-L-J   Music City

THE FOUR ESQUIRES

Members:
  Bill Courtney—lead—drums
  Frank Mahoney—tenor—bass guitar
  Bob Golden—baritone—trombone
  Wally Gold—bass—alto sax
Hometown: Boston, Massachusetts

The Four Esquires formed their group at Boston University in the early fifties. After several years together, they came to the attention of London records, where they were signed to a recording contract. In March 1956, they had their first national hit, and their only hit for London, with the song "Look Homeward Angel."

March	1956	LOOK HOMEWARD ANGEL	London
October	1957	LOVE ME FOREVER	Paris
September	1958	HIDEAWAY	Paris

THE FOUR FELLOWS

Members:
  Harold "Hal" Miller
  Davey Jones
  Teddy Bell
  Jim McGowan
Hometown: New York, New York

The group was formed in 1955 and had one major hit for Glory records, "Soldier Boy," in June of that year.

Shortly thereafter, Hal and Davey left the group and got together with Walter Ford and Harry James and formed the Rays, who recorded "Silhouettes" in 1957.

Today Hal and Davey live and work in Brooklyn, New York.

June   1955   SOLDIER BOY   Glory

THE FOUR FRESHMEN

Members:

  Bob Flanigan—born: August 22, 1926—Greencastle, Indiana—lead
  Ross Barbour—born: December 31, 1928—Columbus, Indiana—third voice
  Hal Kratzch—replaced by Ken Errair (January 23, 1930)—replaced in 1956 by Ken Albers—born: Pitman, New Jersey—bass voice
  Don Barbour (April 19, 1929)—born: Greencastle, Indiana—second voice—replaced by Bill Comstock in 1960—replaced by Ray Brown in 1973

In 1947, while attending Butler University in Indianapolis, Ross Barbour, his brother Don, with their cousin Bob Flanigan and good friend Hal Kratzsch formed a quartet called The Toppers. By 1948, they were very popular on campus and decided to go on the road to make a name for themselves. Their booking agency decided to change the name of the group from The Toppers to The Four Freshmen because the four fellows were freshmen in college.

In 1950 their major break occurred. While they were playing a club in Dayton, Ohio, some local disc jockeys brought in bandleader Stan Kenton to hear the Freshmen. Stan was so impressed with their sound that he telephoned Capitol records and arranged a recording contract for them. They first recorded "Now You Know," and "Pick Up Your Tears" and several other songs that were only mildly popular. By 1952, Capital was ready to drop the group from the label when they recorded "It's a Blue World" during the summer of 1952. The record went on to be a national hit. Other big hits were to follow like "Day by Day," "Candy," and their classic, "Graduation Day."

Hal Kratzsch left the group in 1953, and was replaced by Ken Errair, who was replaced by Ken Albers in 1956. Don Barbour left the group in 1960, and was replaced by Bill Comstock. Ray Brown replaced him in 1973. The Four Freshmen were innovators of the tight harmony sound and had a great influence on many of the vocal groups of the fifties.

Today Bob, Ross, and Ken live in Granada Hills, California, while Ray lives in Fort Walters Beach, Florida. After over twenty-five years together as a group, they continue to travel all over the world singing in the style that has made them famous. They have had thirty-four hit albums for Capitol over the years.

August	1952	IT'S A BLUE WORLD	Capitol
September	1955	DAY BY DAY	Capitol
October	1955	CHARMAINE	Capitol
April	1956	GRADUATION DAY	Capitol

THE FOUR KNIGHTS

Members:
> Gene Alford—lead
> John Wallace—tenor and guitar
> Clarence Dixon—baritone
> Oscar Broadway—bass

Hometown: Charlotte, North Carolina

The Four Knights got their start at a local radio station in Charlotte. Next came Arthur Godfrey's show on CBS. In 1948, they appeared on the Red Skelton radio show. They got a recording contract with Capitol in 1951, and in October of that year had their first hit with "(It's No) Sin."

October	1951	(IT'S NO) SIN	Capitol
January	1953	OH, HAPPY DAY	Capitol
January	1954	I GET SO LONELY	Capitol
January	1959	O' FALLING STAR	Coral

THE FOUR LADS

Members:
> Frank Busseri—baritone
> Bernard Toorish—second tenor
> James Arnold—first tenor
> Connie Codarini—bass

Hometown: Toronto, Canada

The former choirboys were signed by Columbia records in the early fifties as background singers for many of the solo artists on the label. They backed Johnny Ray in late 1951 on his smash hit "Cry." They began their career as artists in the summer of 1952 with "The Mocking Bird." From there they had "Istanbul" and "Skokiaan." In late 1955, they had one of their biggest hits with "Moments to Remember," which was written by Bob Allen and Al Stillman. They also wrote the group's follow-up hit, "No, Not Much," and several hits for Johnny Mathis, including "Chances Are" and "It's Not for Me to Say."

THE FOUR LADS

Left to right: Frankie Busseri, Jimmy Arnold,
Connie Codarini, Bernie Toorish

Today Bernie lives in Cleveland, Ohio, and sings with the Vince Mastro Quartet. Jimmy and Frank sing with two other members as the Four Lads.

July	1952	THE MOCKING BIRD	Okeh
October	1953	ISTANBUL	Columbia
August	1954	SKOKIAAN	Columbia
May	1955	MOMENTS TO REMEMBER	Columbia
January	1956	NO, NOT MUCH	Columbia
February	1956	I'LL NEVER KNOW	Columbia
March	1956	STANDING ON THE CORNER	Columbia
March	1956	MY LITTLE ANGEL	Columbia
August	1956	THE BUS STOP SONG	Columbia
August	1956	A HOUSE WITH LOVE IN IT	Columbia
January	1957	WHO NEEDS YOU	Columbia
April	1957	I JUST DON'T KNOW	Columbia
November	1957	PUT A LIGHT IN THE WINDOW	Columbia
March	1958	THERE'S ONLY ONE OF YOU	Columbia
June	1958	ENCHANTED ISLAND	Columbia
November	1958	THE MOCKING BIRD	Columbia
January	1959	THE GIRL ON PAGE 44	Columbia
April	1959	FOUNTAIN OF YOUTH	Columbia
November	1959	HAPPY ANNIVERSARY	Columbia

THE FOUR LOVERS

Members:

  Frankie Valli—real name: Frank Castelluccio—drums—born: May 3, 1937

  Tommy DeVito—lead guitar—born: June 19, 1936

Nick DeVito—guitar—replaced by Bob Gaudio—born: November 17, 1942

Hank Majewski: bass guitar—replaced by Nick Massi—real name: Nicholas Macioci—born: September 19, 1935

Hometown: Newark, New Jersey

The group was first formed in Newark as the Varietones, and they played various local clubs. In 1956, they changed their names to The Four Lovers and signed with RCA records. They made the charts with "Apple of My Eye."

Four years later Hank decided to leave the group and was replaced by Nick Massi. A short time after that, Nick DeVito left the group and was replaced by an organ player named Bob Gaudio, who had just left a group called the Royal Teens of "Short Shorts" fame.

By 1961, Frankie, Tommy, Nick, and Bob had changed the name of the group to The Four Seasons (after a bowling alley that they had played). In 1962, with Vee Jay records, that group began its very successful career with the song "Sherry."

May   1956   YOU'RE THE APPLE OF MY EYE   RCA

THE FOUR PREPS

Members:
    Bruce Belland
    Glen Larson
    Ed Cobb
    Marv Ingram
Hometown: Hollywood, California

They attended Hollywood High School together and sang in the school choir. While singing at a dance at U.C.L.A. in 1956, a friend of theirs, Howard Adelman, made tapes of their performance, and, without their knowing it, sent the tapes to Capitol records. Capitol contacted the group and put them under contract.

The first national release for the group came in November 1956 with "Dreamy Eyes," but it wasn't until January 1958 that they had their first real hit, "26 Miles."

The Four Preps were the "Pat Boone" of the vocal groups, because of their clean-cut image.

Today the fellows live on the West Coast. Bruce sings with Dave Sommerville, former lead of the Diamonds, as a duo.

November 1956   DREAMY EYES   Capitol
January   1958   26 MILES   Capitol

April	1958	BIG MAN	Capitol
August	1958	LAZY SUMMER NIGHT	Capitol
October	1958	CINDERELLA	Capitol
September	1959	I AIN'T NEVER	Capitol
January	1960	DOWN BY THE STATION	Capitol
April	1960	GOT A GIRL	Capitol
January	1961	CALCUTTA	Capitol
August	1960	MORE MONEY FOR YOU AND ME	Capitol
March	1962	THE BIG DRAFT	Capitol
March	1964	A LETTER TO THE BEATLES	Capitol

THE FOUR SEASONS

Members:

Frankie Valli—real name: Frank Castelluccio—lead—born: May 3, 1937

Nick Massi—real name: Nicholas Macioci—born: September 19. 1935

Tommy DeVito—born: June 19, 1936

Bob Gaudio—born: November 17, 1942

Hometown: Newark, New Jersey

All the members except Gaudio had been singing since 1956 as The Four Lovers on RCA records. Gaudio, one-time member of The Royal Teens, left in the early sixties, after writing and recording hits like "Short Shorts," to join the Four Lovers. After working at a bowling alley one night, they decided to change the name of the group; thinking the name of the bowling alley would be fitting, they named themselves The Four Seasons.

Bob Crewe worked with the group and got them a contract with Vee Jay records. Their first release in 1962, "Bermuda," went nowhere, but in September of the same year the group recorded a song written by Bob Gaudio that went to the number one spot on the national charts. The song "Sherry" established the Four Seasons' sound.

Today Frankie keeps the group active with new members that have been together since 1975. The popularity of the group is bigger than ever.

August	1962	SHERRY	Vee Jay
October	1962	BIG GIRLS DON'T CRY	Vee Jay
December	1962	SANTA CLAUS IS COMING TO TOWN	Vee Jay
January	1963	WALK LIKE A MAN	Vee Jay
April	1963	AIN'T THAT A SHAME	Vee Jay
June	1963	CANDY GIRL	Vee Jay
June	1963	MARLENA	Vee Jay
October	1963	NEW MEXICAN ROSE	Vee Jay
January	1964	STAY	Vee Jay
June	1964	ALONE	Vee Jay

THE FOUR SEASONS

Clockwise from top:
Frankie Valli, Nick
Massi, Bob Gaudio,
Tom DeVito

August	1964	SINCERELY	Vee Jay
January	1964	DAWN	Philips
April	1964	RONNIE	Philips
June	1964	RAG DOLL	Philips
August	1964	SAVE IT FOR ME	Philips
October	1964	BIG MAN IN TOWN	Philips
January	1965	BYE, BYE BABY	Philips
March	1965	TOY SOLDIER	Philips
June	1965	GIRL COME RUNNING	Philips
October	1965	LET'S HANG ON	Philips
December	1965	LITTLE BOY (IN GROWN UP CLOTHES)	Vee Jay
January	1966	WORKING MY WAY BACK TO YOU	Philips
May	1966	OPUS 17 (DON'T YOU WORRY 'BOUT ME)	Philips
August	1966	I'VE GOT YOU UNDER MY SKIN	Philips
December	1966	TELL IT TO THE RAIN	Philips
February	1967	BEGGIN'	Philips
June	1967	C'MON MARIANNE	Philips
October	1967	WATCH THE FLOWERS GROW	Philips
February	1968	WILL YOU LOVE ME TOMORROW	Philips
December	1968	ELECTRIC STORIES	Philips
March	1969	SOMETHING'S ON HER MIND	Philips
March	1969	IDAHO	Philips
August	1969	AND THAT REMINDS ME	Crewe
August	1975	WHO LOVES YOU	Warner/Curb
December	1975	DECEMBER, 63 (OH, WHAT A NIGHT)	Warner/Curb
June	1976	SILVER STAR	Warner/Curb
July	1977	DOWN THE HALL	Warner/Curb
December	1980	SPEND THE NIGHT IN LOVE	Warner/Curb

THE FOUR TUNES

The Four Tunes were a group who originally recorded for RCA Victor in the late forties. They were four black singers who sounded as though they were white. Their material and style was more pop oriented than gospel or R & B. In 1953, they signed with Jubilee records and had their first chart record with the standard "Marie" in October 1953.

October	1953	MARIE	Jubilee
May	1954	I UNDERSTAND JUST HOW YOU FEEL	Jubilee

THE FOUR VOICES

The popularity of male quartets in the mid-fifties caused many major record labels to sign groups with soft, sweet harmony. Columbia had the Four Lads and the Four Coins on their sister label Epic. Then they signed the Four Voices, who sounded closer to the Lads, a blend of voices with no particular lead.

The group's biggest success was in early 1956 with "Lovely One."

February	1956	LOVELY ONE	Columbia
March	1958	DANCING WITH MY SHADOW	Columbia

THE FOUR VOICES

CONNIE FRANCIS

INEZ FOX

Born: September 9, 1942
Hometown: Greensboro, North Carolina

Inez started singing in a church choir with the Gospel Tide chorus in Greensboro. While with the gospel group she was discovered by Clarence Fuller. He got her an engagement at a local club called the ABC Club. In 1959, she went to New York City to audition for Brunswick records. They signed her and she recorded "A Feeling" for them. In 1963, she signed with Symbol records and had her biggest hit that summer with "Mockingbird."

June	1963	MOCKINGBIRD	Symbol
November	1963	HI DIDDLE DIDDLE	Symbol
January	1964	ASK ME	Symbol
April	1964	HURT BY LOVE	Symbol

CONNIE FRANCIS

Real Name: Constance Franconero
Born: December 12, 1938
Hometown: Belleville, New Jersey

Connie began playing the accordion at the age of four and made her first professional appearance playing and singing at eleven. At age twelve, she was singing on NBC's "Startime Show" on radio. Later she entered and won on Arthur Godfrey's Talent Scout show. It was Arthur who suggested that she change her name.

While she was in her teens, Connie signed with MGM records. She spent two years recording songs like "Forgetting," which went nowhere. Finally, in late 1957, Connie's father suggested she record an old standard that was one of his favorites. Although she was reluctant to do so at first, she finally gave in and in November 1957 recorded "Who's Sorry Now," which went on to be a million seller and her first big hit on MGM. It became one of the top songs of 1958. Later that summer she had a hit with a song that Neil Sedaka had written called "Stupid Cupid." Her first number one record came in May 1960 with "Everybody's Somebody's Fool." Connie has been married three times, but today lives by herself on the West Coast.

A sad incident happened to Connie when she was raped on November 8, 1974. However, she is making a comeback by appearing on stage for the first time in years.

January	1958	WHO'S SORRY NOW	MGM
April	1958	I'M SORRY I MADE YOU CRY	MGM
July	1958	STUPID CUPID	MGM
October	1958	FALLIN'	MGM
December	1958	MY HAPPINESS	MGM
February	1959	IF I DIDN'T CARE	MGM
May	1959	LIPSTICK ON YOUR COLLAR	MGM
May	1959	FRANKIE	MGM
August	1959	YOU'RE GONNA MISS ME	MGM
November	1959	AMONG MY SOUVENIRS	MGM
February	1960	MAMA	MGM
May	1960	EVERYBODY'S SOMEBODY'S FOOL	MGM
May	1960	JEALOUS OF YOU	MGM
August	1960	MY HEART HAS A MIND OF ITS OWN	MGM
October	1960	MANY TEARS AGO	MGM
January	1961	WHERE THE BOYS ARE	MGM
April	1961	BREAKIN' IN A BRAND NEW BROKEN HEART	MGM
June	1961	TOGETHER	MGM
October	1961	HE'S MY DREAMBOAT	MGM
November	1961	WHEN THE BOY IN YOUR ARMS	MGM
January	1962	DON'T BREAK THE HEART THAT LOVES YOU	MGM
April	1962	SECOND HAND LOVE	MGM
July	1962	VACATION	MGM
October	1962	I WAS SUCH A FOOL	MGM
December	1962	I'M GONNA BE WARM THIS WINTER	MGM
February	1963	FOLLOW THE BOYS	MGM
May	1963	IF MY PILLOW COULD TALK	MGM
August	1963	DROWNIN' MY SORROWS	MGM
October	1963	YOUR OTHER LOVE	MGM
December	1963	IN THE SUMMER OF HIS YEARS	MGM
February	1964	BLUE WINTER	MGM
April	1964	BE ANYTHING BUT BE MINE	MGM

July	1964	LOOKING FOR LOVE	MGM
October	1964	DON'T EVER LEAVE ME	MGM
January	1965	**WHOSE HEART ARE YOU BREAKING TONIGHT**	MGM
February	1965	FOR MAMA	MGM
May	1965	WISHING IT WAS YOU	MGM
June	1965	FORGET DOMANI	MGM
September	1965	ROUNDABOUT	MGM
November	1965	JEALOUS HEART	MGM
March	1965	LOVE IS ME, LOVE IS YOU	MGM
November	1966	SPANISH NIGHTS AND YOU	MGM
April	1967	TIME ALONE WILL TELL	MGM

ARETHA FRANKLIN

Born: March 25, 1943
Hometown: Buffalo, New York

Aretha started singing in her father's gospel group. Mahalia Jackson adopted her as a protégé. Aretha was discovered by Columbia records' A & R executive John Hammond in 1960 and signed to a contract. Her first recording with the label in March 1961 was "Won't Be Long."

In 1967, she left Columbia to join Atlantic records. Her greatest hits came with the help of executive producer Jerry Wexler. Aretha's first hit for the label was "I Never Loved a Man (The Way I Love You)." Her next release, "Respect," a couple of months later, went to the number one position on the national charts. Today she is more popular than ever.

March	1961	WON'T BE LONG	Columbia
October	1961	**ROCK-A-BYE YOUR BABY WITH A DIXIE MELODY**	Columbia
January	1962	I SURRENDER DEAR	Columbia
July	1962	DON'T CRY BABY	Columbia
September	1962	TRY A LITTLE TENDERNESS	Columbia
December	1962	TROUBLE IN MIND	Columbia
September	1964	RUNNIN' OUT OF FOOLS	Columbia
January	1965	CAN'T YOU JUST SEE ME	Columbia
August	1967	TAKE A LOOK	Columbia
December	1967	MOCKINGBIRD	Columbia
March	1967	I NEVER LOVED A MAN (THE WAY I LOVE YOU)	Atlantic
April	1967	RESPECT	Atlantic
July	1967	BABY I LOVE YOU	Atlantic
September	1967	A NATURAL WOMAN	Atlantic
November	1967	CHAIN OF FOOLS	Atlantic
February	1968	**(SWEET SWEET BABY) SINCE YOU'VE BEEN GONE**	Atlantic
April	1968	AIN'T NO WAY	Atlantic
August	1968	THE HOUSE THAT JACK BUILT	Atlantic
August	1968	I SAY A LITTLE PRAYER	Atlantic
November	1968	SEE SAW	Atlantic
November	1968	MY SONG	Atlantic
February	1969	THE WEIGHT	Atlantic
April	1969	I CAN'T SEE MYSELF LEAVING YOU	Atlantic

May	1969	THINK	Atlantic
August	1969	SHARE YOUR LOVE WITH ME	Atlantic
November	1969	ELEANOR RIGBY	Atlantic
January	1970	CALL ME	Atlantic
May	1970	SPIRIT IN THE DARK	Atlantic
July	1970	DON'T PLAY THAT SONG	Atlantic
November	1970	BORDER SONG	Atlantic
January	1971	YOU'RE ALL I NEED TO GET BY	Atlantic
June	1971	BRAND NEW ME	Atlantic
July	1971	SPANISH HARLEM	Atlantic
October	1971	ROCK STEADY	Atlantic
January	1972	OH ME OH MY	Atlantic
April	1972	DAYDREAMING	Atlantic
June	1972	ALL THE KING'S HORSES	Atlantic
August	1972	WHOLY HOLY	Atlantic
February	1973	MASTER OF EYES	Atlantic
July	1973	ANGEL	Atlantic
November	1973	UNTIL YOU COME BACK TO ME	Atlantic
April	1974	I'M IN LOVE	Atlantic
August	1974	AIN'T NOTHING LIKE THE REAL THING	Atlantic
November	1974	WITHOUT LOVE	Atlantic
September	1975	MR. D.J. (5 FOR THE D.J.)	Atlantic
June	1976	SOMETHING HE CAN FEEL	Atlantic
October	1976	JUMP	Atlantic
February	1977	LOOK INTO YOUR HEART	Atlantic
June	1977	BREAK IT TO ME GENTLY	Atlantic
December	1980	UNITED TOGETHER	Atlantic
May	1981	COME TO ME	Arista
August	1981	LOVE ALL THE HURT AWAY (with George Benson)	Arista

STAN FREBERG

Born: August 7, 1926
Hometown: Los Angeles, California

Stan grew up and went to school in Los Angeles. After he finished college, he made a guest appearance on Stuart Hamblen's program "Lucky Stars" over KFWB in Los Angeles. There he met Cliff Stone and accepted an offer to appear on his morning radio show doing impersonations.

In 1947, after his discharge from the Army, Stan got a job driving a truck, but went back into radio when a job opened up. Eventually, Stan teamed again with Cliff Stone. His reputation grew to the point where he was doing cartoon voices for Warner Brothers, Walt Disney, Paramount, and Columbia studios.

After a stint as a radio disc jockey, he got a job doing the voices for a TV puppet show called "Time for Beany."

In 1950, he signed with Capitol records and recorded a satire on soap operas called "John and Marsha," which became a national hit by January 1951. Today, Stan produces some of the most creative radio and television commercials around.

January	1951	JOHN AND MARSHA	Capitol
July	1951	I'VE GOT YOU UNDER MY SKIN	Capitol
March	1952	TRY	Capitol
September	1953	ST. GEORGE AND THE DRAGONET	Capitol
October	1953	LITTLE BLUE RIDING HOOD	Capitol
December	1953	CHRISTMAS DRAGNET	Capitol
May	1954	POINT OF ORDER	Capitol
June	1955	YELLOW ROSE OF TEXAS	Capitol
December	1955	NUTTIN' FOR CHRISTMAS	Capitol
June	1956	HEARTBREAK HOTEL	Capitol
March	1957	BANANA BOAT	Capitol
October	1957	WUN'ERFUL, WUN'ERFUL	Capitol
January	1959	GREEN CHRISTMAS	Capitol
February	1960	THE OLD PAYOLA ROLL BLUES	Capitol

BOBBY FREEMAN

Born: June 13, 1940
Hometown: San Francisco, California

At age fourteen, Bobby sang in a vocal group called the Romancers around the San Francisco area. He subsequently formed another group

BOBBY FREEMAN

called the Vocaleers. In 1958, while Bobby was still in high school, Jubilee record executive Mortimer Palitz on his honeymoon in San Francisco, heard Bobby sing at a club. He was so taken by the talent of this young man that he signed him to a recording contract. In April 1958, Bobby recorded a song he had written called "Do You Want to Dance," which became his biggest hit. It was released on Josie records, a subsidiary of Jubilee, and made Bobby a national star.

His follow-up hit, "Betty Lou Got a New Pair of Shoes," was also a hit for Bobby while he was still in high school. In fact, he was a singing sensation right up until his graduation from high school in February 1959.

April	1958	DO YOU WANT TO DANCE	Josie
August	1958	BETTY LOU GOT A NEW PAIR OF SHOES	Josie
November	1958	NEED YOUR LOVE	Josie
May	1959	MARY ANN THOMAS	Josie
December	1959	EBB TIDE	Josie
August	1960	(I DO THE) SHIMMY-SHIMMY	King
June	1964	C'MON AND SWIM	Autumn
October	1964	S-W-I-M	Autumn

ERNIE FREEMAN

Born: August 1923
Died: May 15, 1981
Hometown: Cleveland, Ohio

Ernie was a successful free-lance producer-arranger on the West Coast in the mid-fifties. He was the first to work with Paul Anka when the aspiring singer went to the Coast to try to get his career off the ground. (That attempt failed but subsequently Anka became a huge success.) In 1957 Ernie did two cover versions on Imperial, "Dumplin's" and "Raunchy," which had been hits for Doc Bagby and Bill Justis respectively.

Ernie died of a heart attack in North Hollywood, California, in 1981.

August	1957	DUMPLIN'S	Imperial
October	1957	RAUNCHY	Imperial
June	1958	INDIAN LOVE CALL	Imperial
October	1960	THEME FROM THE DARK AT THE TOP OF THE STAIRS	Imperial
January	1962	THE TWIST	Imperial

DON FRENCH

Born: 1940
Hometown: Wayne, Pennsylvania

Don learned to play the guitar by ear before he was ten. While attending Radnor High in Wayne, Pennsylvania, he got four of his friends to form a combo known as the Falcons. In May 1959, Don signed a contract with Lancer records and recorded "Lonely Saturday Night," which became his only hit. After that he enrolled at the University of Virginia in Charlottesville and joined the Sigma Nu fraternity.

May	1959	LONELY SATURDAY NIGHT	Lancer

THE FROGMEN

"Underwater," an instrumental hit by this group in 1961, was punctuated with the novel sound of a frog. A tough way to crack the charts.

March	1961	UNDERWATER	Cadix

JERRY FULLER

Jerry was a moderate success as a singer in the late fifties and early sixties. He's best known for his writing and producing of hits for Rick Nelson and Gary Puckett and The Union Gap, among others. For Rick he wrote songs like "Travelin' Man" and "Young World," while for Gary he wrote "Over You" and "Young Girl."

August	1959	BETTY, MY ANGEL	Challenge
October	1959	TENNESSEE WALTZ	Challenge
April	1961	SHY AWAY	Challenge
October	1961	GUILTY OF LOVING YOU	Challenge

GABRIEL & THE ANGELS

"That's Life," the group's only hit, was a gimmick song in which Gabriel would shout out a remark and his backup men would answer with some "in" expression of the time. Sample: "What's Life." Answer: "Life's a magazine." You get the idea.

October   1962   THAT'S LIFE (THAT'S TOUGH)   Swan

THE GALLAHADS

In 1956 an unknown writer named Lee Hazlewood wrote a song called "The Fool," which he had his good friend Sanford Clark record. The song was a hit for Clark in the summer of 1956. The Gallahads, an East Coast group, recorded the same song and had a moderately popular Atlantic Coast version at the same time on Jubilee records.

July   1956   THE FOOL   Jubilee

FRANK GALLOP

Frank Gallop, the popular radio and television announcer, did a novelty narrative hit called "Got a Match," and he followed it up some years later with a recording in a similar vein, the "Ballad of Irving," a kind of takeoff on "Big Bad John."

| May | 1958 | GOT A MATCH | ABC |
| April | 1966 | THE BALLAD OF IRVING | Kapp |

DON GARDNER & DEE DEE FORD

In the fifties there were many male-female duos who sang ballads and moderate-tempo songs, like Mickey and Sylvia ("Love Is Strange"), Shirley and Lee ("Let the Good Times Roll"), and Johnnie and Joe ("Over the Mountain"). In 1960, a new duo, the raucous, screeching sound of Ike and Tina Turner, burst upon the scene with "A Fool in Love." Gardner and Ford worked in this idiom. Their biggest hit: "I Need Your Loving" in the spring of 1962.

May	1962	I NEED YOUR LOVING	Fire
August	1962	DON'T YOU WORRY	Fire
August	1962	GLORY OF LOVE	KC

FRANK GARI

Born: April 1, 1942
Hometown: New York, New York

Frank began his professional career as an actor and appeared in several films. Then he signed with Ribbon records and recorded "Li'l Girl." Sy Muskin, president of Crusade records, signed Frank to the label. In December 1960, Frank had his first hit for Crusade called "Utopia."

December	1960	UTOPIA	Crusade
March	1961	LULLABY OF LOVE	Crusade
July	1961	PRINCESS	Crusade

MARVIN GAYE

Born: April 2, 1939
Hometown: Washington, D.C.

Marvin began singing in his father's church choir as a youngster. His father, Reverend Marvin Gaye, Sr., encouraged his son to sing and to play the organ. After graduating from Cardoza High in Washington, Marvin enlisted in the Air Force. When he was discharged he began a singing career and joined The Moonglows in the early sixties. The group had hits like "Sincerely," "See Saw," and "The Ten Commandments of Love" in the fifties.

After a while with them he left to go on as a solo performer. It was while he was appearing at a club in Detroit in 1962 that Berry Gordy, Jr., saw Marvin perform and was intrigued with his style. Berry immediately offered him a contract with his label, Tamla records. In October 1962, Marvin's career was launched with "Stubborn Kind of Fellow," which became his first hit. After a long list of hit records, he finally got a number one national hit in November 1968, when he recorded a song written by Barrett Strong (onetime singer of the hit "Money" in 1960) and Norman Whitfield called "I Heard It Through the Grapevine."

Marvin also had hits singing as a duo with singers like Tammi Terrell, Mary Wells, and Kim Weston.

After being on the road so much and not being able to spend time with his wife, Anna, and his son, Marvin III, he began to do some soul-searching as to what he really wanted to accomplish in life. The result of the soul-searching was the song "What's Going On," which became a big hit for him in January 1971. He also wrote "Mercy Mercy Me" and "Inner City Blues," all three of which became million sellers for him and were included in the album he produced and for which he wrote most of the material.

Marvin still lives with his family in Detroit, and although he went into a self-imposed exile from live performances several years ago, he has still managed to record hit records. It has only been recently that he has considered making any kind of concert appearances. Marvin Gaye, the singer-poet-philosopher, has become a gigantic talent today, truly making him a superstar.

October	1962	STUBBORN KIND OF FELLOW	Tamla
January	1963	HITCH HIKE	Tamla
May	1963	PRIDE AND JOY	Tamla
October	1963	CAN I GET A WITNESS	Tamla
February	1964	YOU'RE A WONDERFUL ONE	Tamla
June	1964	TRY IT BABY	Tamla
September	1964	BABY DON'T YOU DO IT	Tamla
December	1964	HOW SWEET IT IS TO BE LOVED BY YOU	Tamla
March	1965	I'LL BE DOGGONE	Tamla
June	1965	PRETTY LITTLE BABY	Tamla
October	1965	AIN'T THAT PECULIAR	Tamla
February	1966	ONE MORE HEARTACHE	Tamla
May	1966	TAKE THIS HEART OF MINE	Tamla
August	1966	LITTLE DARLING (I NEED YOU)	Tamla
July	1967	YOUR UNCHANGING LOVE	Tamla
January	1968	YOU	Tamla
September	1968	CHAINED	Tamla
November	1968	I HEARD IT THROUGH THE GRAPEVINE	Tamla
April	1969	TOO BUSY THINKING ABOUT MY BABY	Tamla
August	1969	THAT'S THE WAY LOVE IS	Tamla
January	1970	HOW CAN I FORGET/GONNA GIVE HER ALL THE LOVE I'VE GOT	Tamla

May	1970	THE END OF OUR ROAD	Tamla
February	1971	WHAT'S GOING ON	Tamla
June	1971	MERCY MERCY ME (THE ECOLOGY)	Tamla
September	1971	INNER CITY BLUES (MAKE ME WANNA HOLLER)	Tamla
December	1972	TROUBLE MAN	Tamla
July	1973	LET'S GET IT ON	Tamla
November	1973	COME GET TO THIS	Tamla
January	1974	YOU SURE LOVE TO BALL	Tamla
April	1974	MY MISTAKE	Tamla
July	1974	DON'T KNOCK MY LOVE (with Diana Ross)	Motown
September	1974	DISTANT LOVER	Tamla
April	1976	I WANT YOU	Tamla
August	1976	AFTER THE DANCE	Tamla
April	1977	GOT TO GIVE IT UP PT. 1	Tamla
January	1979	POPS, WE LOVE YOU	Motown

MARVIN GAYE AND TAMMI TERRELL

May	1967	AIN'T NO MOUNTAIN HIGH ENOUGH	Tamla
September	1967	YOUR PRECIOUS LOVE	Tamla
December	1967	IF I COULD BUILD MY WHOLE WORLD AROUND YOU	Tamla
March	1968	IF THIS WORLD WERE MINE	Tamla
April	1968	AIN'T NOTHING LIKE THE REAL THING	Tamla
July	1968	YOU'RE ALL I NEED TO GET BY	Tamla
October	1968	KEEP ON LOVIN' ME, HONEY	Tamla
February	1969	GOOD LOVIN' AIN'T EASY TO COME BY	Tamla
November	1969	WHAT YOU GAVE ME	Tamla
April	1970	THE ONION SONG/CALIFORNIA SOUL	Tamla

MARVIN GAYE AND MARY WELLS

June	1964	ONCE UPON A TIME	Motown
May	1964	WHAT'S THE MATTER WITH YOU BABY	Motown

MARVIN GAYE AND KIM WESTON

October	1964	WHAT GOOD AM I WITHOUT YOU	Tamla
January	1967	IT TAKES TWO	Tamla

THE GAYLORDS

Members:
    Ronnie Gaylord—standup bass
    Burt Bonaldi—lead and guitar
    Don Rea—piano
Hometown: Detroit, Michigan

The group got together when they were all students at the University of Detroit. They began playing at local clubs in Detroit, and wound up doing their own TV show on WXYZ five days a week called "Melodies in Money." After that they began to travel around the country and were spotted by a representative from Mercury records who signed them to the label. In late 1952, they had their first national hit, "Tell Me You're Mine," and in the summer of 1954 had their biggest hit called "The Little Shoemaker."

December	1952	TELL ME YOU'RE MINE	Mercury
March	1953	SPINNING A WEB	Mercury
January	1954	FROM THE VINE CAME THE GRAPE	Mercury
April	1954	ISLE OF CAPRI	Mercury
June	1954	THE LITTLE SHOEMAKER	Mercury
May	1955	NO ARMS CAN EVER HOLD YOU	Mercury
August	1958	MA-MA-MA MARIE	Mercury
October	1958	FLAMINGO L'AMORE	Mercury

PAUL GAYTEN

Paul was a staff musician who worked with many top groups in the fifties. (He backed up the Tuneweavers of "Happy, Happy Birthday, Baby" fame.) Many of his records came from jam sessions with leftover studio time other groups had accumulated. One such result was "Nervous Boogie."

November	1957	NERVOUS BOOGIE	Argo
June	1958	WINDY	Argo
October	1959	THE HUNCH	Anna

THE G-CLEFS

Members:
Teddy Scott
Chris Scott
Timmy Scott
Arnold Scott
Ray Gibson
Hometown: Roxbury, Massachusetts

The group started out singing gospel music. In 1956, Jack Gould of Pilgrim records heard them at a record hop and signed them to a contract. They recorded a song called "Ka-Ding Dong" which featured a fifteen-year-old guitar player named Freddy Cannon (later to record "Tallahassee Lassie"). "Ka-Ding Dong" was a hit for the group in the summer of 1956.

After a while, the traveling became too much for the fellows, and they returned to Boston to finish their education. In the summer of 1961, Jack Gould took them back into the studio and had them record a song that was sold to Terrace records. "I Understand (Just How You Feel)" became a smash hit for the group.

June	1956	KA-DING-DONG	Pilgrim
November	1956	CAUSE YOU'RE MINE	Pilgrim
September	1961	I UNDERSTAND (JUST HOW YOU FEEL)	Terrace
February	1962	A GIRL HAS TO KNOW	Terrace

GENE & EUNICE

Aladdin records signed Gene & Eunice and Shirley & Lee almost simultaneously, looking for the right male-female duo. Although on the popular charts, Shirley & Lee were more popular, the duos were about ever on the R & B side.

January	1955	KO KO MO	Aladdin
April	1955	THIS IS MY STORY	Aladdin
August	1959	POCO-LOCO	Case

THE GENIES

Members:
    Claude "Sonny" Johnson
    Roland Trone
    Fred Jones
    Estelle Williams
Hometown: Brooklyn, New York

In March 1959, this high school quartet recorded their only national hit, "Who's That Knockin'." Claude Johnson and Roland Trone became Don & Juan and recorded "What's Your Name" for Big Top records in January 1962.

| March | 1959 | WHO'S THAT KNOCKIN' | Shad |

BARBARA GEORGE

Born: August 16, 1942
Hometown: New Orleans, Louisiana

Barbara began singing in a church choir in New Orleans at seventeen. She later began appearing at local clubs. In late 1961, she was signed by AFO records. "I Know," her first and biggest hit was released in October of that year. Barbara had written the song herself.

October	1961	I KNOW	AFO
March	1962	YOU TALK ABOUT LOVE	AFO
August	1962	SEND FOR ME	Sue

STAN GETZ AND CHARLIE BYRD

Sax player Stan Getz and guitar player Charlie Bird created a bossa nova sound in 1962 called "Desafinado," easy dancing and listening music all the way.

| September 1962 | DESAFINADO | Verve |

GEORGIA GIBBS

Real Name: Fredda Lipson
Born: August 26, 1926
Hometown: Worchester, Massachusetts

Georgia began singing at thirteen, and was touring with bands by age fifteen. In 1943, after she had won an audition for the Jimmy Durante radio show, Gary Moore gave her the nickname "Her Nibs." She had her first pop hit in 1950 with "If I Knew You Were Comin' I'd've Baked a Cake."

In 1951, Georgia signed with Mercury, where she had her biggest hits. Her first smash for Mercury was "Kiss of Fire" in the spring of 1952. In 1955, she had cover version hits of "Tweedle Dee" (La Vern Baker's hit) and "Dance with Me Henry" (Etta James's hit).

Today Georgia occasionally appears in Las Vegas, but lives in Italy with her husband, Frank Gervasi.

March	1950	IF I KNEW YOU WERE COMIN' I'D'VE BAKED A CAKE	Coral
January	1951	I STILL FEEL THE SAME ABOUT YOU	Coral
August	1951	WHILE YOU DANCED, DANCED, DANCED	Mercury
March	1952	KISS OF FIRE	Mercury
October	1952	MY FAVORITE SONG	Mercury
February	1953	SEVEN LONELY DAYS	Mercury
January	1955	TWEEDLE DEE	Mercury
March	1955	DANCE WITH ME HENRY	Mercury
September	1955	I WANT YOU TO BE MY BABY	Mercury
October	1955	GOODBYE TO ROME	Mercury
February	1956	ROCK NIGHT	Mercury
May	1956	KISS ME ANOTHER	Mercury
July	1956	HAPPINESS STREET	Mercury
November	1956	TRA LA LA	Mercury
February	1957	SILENT LIPS	Mercury
May	1957	I'M WALKING THE FLOOR OVER YOU	RCA
October	1958	HULA HOOP SONG	Roulette

DON GIBSON

Born: March 3, 1928
Hometown: Shelby, North Carolina

Don grew up in a country music environment and became interested in singing as a youth. In early 1958, he recorded a song that he wrote called "I Can't Stop Loving You," which was a mild pop hit. The song, however, became a giant hit for Ray Charles some six years later. The flip side was another song he wrote called "Oh Lonesome Me," which became his biggest all-time seller.

DON GIBSON

Today Don is still active as a recording artist for Hickory records.

February	1958	OH LONESOME ME/I CAN'T STOP LOVING YOU	RCA
June	1958	BLUE BLUE DAY	RCA
September	1958	GIVE MYSELF A PARTY	RCA
January	1959	WHO CARES	RCA
April	1959	LONESOME OLD HOUSE	RCA
August	1959	DON'T TELL ME YOUR TROUBLES	RCA
February	1960	JUST ONE TIME	RCA
July	1960	FAR, FAR AWAY	RCA
November	1960	SWEET DREAMS	RCA
February	1961	WHAT ABOUT ME	RCA
June	1961	SEA OF HEARTBREAK	RCA
December	1961	LONESOME NUMBER ONE	RCA

TERRY GILKYSON

Real Name: Hamilton Henry Gilkyson
Born: 1928
Hometown: Phoenixville, Pennsylvania

Terry attended the University of Pennsylvania and majored in music, but by his second year, he left for New Mexico, where he bought a guitar and

TERRY GILKYSON & THE EASY RIDERS
Left to right: Rudy Dehr, Frank Miller, Terry Gilkyson

began to write folk-oriented songs. After working on a ranch in Tucson, Arizona, he wrote a song called "The Cry of the Wild Goose," which he recorded for Decca records. While with Decca he sang for a while with the famous Weavers folk group ("Good Night Irene" and "On Top of Old Smokey").

In the mid-fifties Terry formed a trio with Frank Miller and Rudy Dehr called the Easy Riders and they recorded a song called "Marianne," which became a national hit in January 1957.

Today he lives happily in Mexico.

January   1957   MARIANNE   Columbia

JIMMY GILMER & THE FIREBALLS

Born: 1940
Hometown: Amarillo, Texas

Jimmy began singing as a youngster in LaGrange, Illinois. In 1951, the family moved to Amarillo, Texas, where Jimmy studied music for four years at the Musical Arts Conservatory. In 1957, he organized his own band and played at local functions while attending Amarillo College, where he was majoring in engineering.

It was at the Norman Petty studios in Clovis, New Mexico, that Jimmy met a group called the Fireballs. The Fireballs (who consisted of George Tomsco, Stan Lark, and Eric Budd) already had some success with a song called "Torquay." They asked Jimmy to team up with them. In the summer of 1963, the group signed with Dot records and with Jimmy as lead recorded a song called "Sugar Shack." It became the number one song for the entire year.

August	1963	SUGAR SHACK	Dot
December	1963	DAISY PETAL PICKIN'	Dot
February	1964	AIN'T GONNA TELL NOBODY	Dot

THE GLADIOLAS

Maurice Williams wrote and originally recorded the song "Little Darlin' " with his group the Gladiolas, but the Diamonds covered the record for Mercury and wound up with the bigger hit. In late 1960, Maurice wrote another song called "Stay," which he recorded with the Zodiacs. It was a number one hit on Herald records that fall.

March	1957	LITTLE DARLIN'	Excello

TOM GLAZER & THE CHILDREN'S CHORUS

"On Top of Spaghetti" was a parody of the Weavers' successful fifties hit "On Top of Old Smokey." An inane idea with inane lyrics to match. Yecch!

May	1963	ON TOP OF SPAGHETTI	Kapp

JIMMY GILMER

THE GLENCOVES

Folk was *in* in 1963. To capitalize on the boom, the group recorded a rather simple song called "Hootenanny," which became a top-forty record for them.

June   1963   HOOTENANNY   Select

BOBBY GOLDSBORO

Born: January 18, 1942 in Marianna, Florida
Hometown: Dothan, Alabama

After two years at Auburn University, Bobby joined Roy Orbison as a guitar player in January 1962. Later that year, Bobby signed with Laurie records and released a song called "Molly" in November. He stayed with Orbison's band as a collaborator on songs until 1963. In late 1963, Bobby signed with United Artists records. His composition "See The Funny Little Clown" in January 1964 became the first of many hits for him.

Although a few years back he hosted a syndicated TV show, today he enjoys his first love, writing and recording new songs.

December 1962   MOLLY   Laurie
January   1964   SEE THE FUNNY LITTLE CLOWN   United Artists

BOBBY GOLDSBORO

March	1964	WHENEVER HE HOLDS YOU	United Artists
August	1964	ME JAPANESE BOY I LOVE YOU	United Artists
January	1965	LITTLE THINGS	United Artists
April	1965	VOODOO WOMAN	United Artists
September	1965	IF YOU'VE GOT A HEART	United Artists
November	1965	BROOMSTICK COWBOY	United Artists
February	1966	IT'S TOO LATE	United Artists
May	1966	I KNOW YOU BETTER THAN THAT	United Artists
August	1966	IT HURTS ME	United Artists
November	1966	BLUE AUTUMN	United Artists
March	1968	HONEY	United Artists
June	1968	AUTUMN OF MY LIFE	United Artists
October	1968	THE STRAIGHT LIFE	United Artists
January	1969	GLAD SHE'S A WOMAN	United Artists
April	1969	I'M A DRIFTER	United Artists
August	1969	MUDDY MISSISSIPPI LINE	United Artists
January	1970	MORNIN MORNIN	United Artists
March	1970	CAN YOU FEEL IT	United Artists
December	1970	WATCHING SCOTTY GROW	United Artists
April	1971	AND I LOVE YOU SO	United Artists
July	1971	COME BACK HOME	United Artists
September	1972	WITH PEN IN HAND	United Artists
August	1973	SUMMER.....	**United Artists**

THE GONE ALL-STARS

The Buddy Lucas studio orchestra for Gone records recorded "7-11" at a jam session in late 1957. It went on to become a national hit in early 1958, due to the exposure given the record by Alan Freed at radio station WINS in New York.

January	1958	"7-11"	Gone

DICKIE GOODMAN

Born: April 19, 1934
Hometown: Hewlett, New York

Dickie was part of the novelty team of Buchanan and Goodman of "The Flying Saucer" fame in 1956. He continued on his own with novelty songs and continues to do them today.

February	1961	THE TOUCHABLES	Mark-X
April	1961	THE TOUCHABLES IN BROOKLYN	Mark-X
December	1961	SANTA AND THE TOUCHABLES	Rori
June	1962	BEN CRAZY	Diamond
May	1966	BATMAN & HIS GRANDMOTHER	Red Bird
June	1969	ON CAMPUS	Cotique
June	1973	WATERGATE	Rainy Wednesday
February	1974	ENERGY CRISIS 74	Rainy Wednesday
June	1974	MR. PRESIDENT	Rainy Wednesday
September	1975	MR. JAWS	Cash
February	1977	KONG	Shock 6

RON GOODWIN

"Swinging Sweetheart," Ron's only popular hit, was ahead of its time in that it utilized a heavy string section to back a very simple melody. Nice, easy listening music.

August	1957	SWINGIN' SWEETHEARTS	Capitol

BARRY GORDON

"Nuttin' For Christmas" had a run on the national charts around Christmas of 1955. Who can forget: "I'm getting nothing for Christmas, cause I ain't been nothing but bad."

December	1955	NUTTIN' FOR CHRISTMAS	MGM
January	1956	ROCK AROUND MOTHER GOOSE	MGM

LESLEY GORE

Born: May 2, 1946
Hometown: Tenafly, New Jersey

Lesley became interested in singing as a youngster when her cousin Alan introduced her to his jazz record collection. Her favorites were June Christy, Chris Connor, and Anita O'Day.

In early 1963, while a senior in high school, Lesley was heard singing with her cousin's band by Quincy Jones of Mercury records. She was signed to the label. A few months later, while Lesley and Quincy were going over some demo records, they found a song that seemed right for her. They recorded it and released it in April 1963, and in a short time "It's My Party" became a number one national hit.

After a string of hits with Quincy Jones as her producer, she left Mercury in late 1967. She signed with Bob Crewe in 1968 after he started his own label.

In 1971, she began writing her own material and a year later she signed with Mowest records, a division of Motown. She released her first album with them in August of 1972.

Today Lesley is very active as a songwriter. She, along with her brother, Michael, wrote the music for the hit movie *Fame*.

May	1963	IT'S MY PARTY	Mercury
June	1963	JUDY'S TURN TO CRY	Mercury
September	1963	SHE'S A FOOL	Mercury
December	1963	YOU DON'T OWN ME	Mercury
March	1964	THAT'S THE WAY BOYS ARE	Mercury

LESLEY GORE

May	1964	I DON'T WANNA BE A LOSER	Mercury
July	1964	MAYBE I KNOW	Mercury
October	1964	HEY NOW	Mercury
December	1964	LOOK OF LOVE	Mercury
June	1965	SUNSHINE LOLLIPOPS AND RAINBOWS	Mercury
August	1965	MY TOWN, MY GUY AND ME	Mercury
November	1965	I WON'T LOVE YOU ANYMORE	Mercury
February	1966	WE KNOW WE'RE IN LOVE	Mercury
March	1966	YOUNG LOVE	Mercury
January	1967	CALIFORNIA NIGHTS	Mercury
June	1967	SUMMER AND SANDY	Mercury
October	1967	BRINK OF DISASTER	Mercury

EYDIE GORME

Born: August 16, 1931
Hometown: Bronx, New York

Eydie began singing at the age of three on a Saturday-morning radio
show. Her parents did not take her singing seriously, so she was given no
musical training. A Spanish major in high school, she worked after graduation for two years as an interpreter. Trumpet player Ken Greengrass
convinced her to leave her job and make singing her full-time occupation.

After years of trying, she finally got a recording contract in 1953 with

EYDIE GORME

Coral records and at the same time was signed to make regular appearances on Steve Allen's "Tonite" Show. It was on this show she met Steve Lawrence. They were married in Las Vegas in December 1957. After Steve's discharge from the Army in 1960 the couple became a popular night club act.

In 1962, Eydie signed with Columbia records, and in January 1963, had her biggest hit with "Blame It on the Bossa Nova."

March	1956	TOO CLOSE FOR COMFORT	ABC
July	1956	MAMA, TEACH ME TO DANCE	ABC
March	1957	I'LL TAKE ROMANCE	ABC
June	1957	YOUR KISSES KILL ME	ABC
May	1958	YOU NEED HANDS	ABC
August	1958	GOTTA HAVE RAIN	ABC
January	1959	VOICE IN MY HEART	ABC
January	1963	BLAME IT ON THE BOSSA NOVA	Columbia
May	1963	DON'T TRY TO FIGHT IT BABY	Columbia
September	1963	EVERYBODY GO HOME	Columbia
July	1964	I WANT YOU TO MEET MY BABY	Columbia
August	1964	CAN'T GET OVER (THE BOSSA NOVA)	Columbia
November	1969	TONIGHT I'LL SAY A PRAYER	RCA

ROBERT GOULET

Born: November 26, 1933
Hometown: Lawrence, Massachusetts

Bob's first major professional job came in 1949 at the age of sixteen when he appeared at the Summer Pops concert in Alberta, Canada. In the early

ROBERT GOULET

sixties, while working in Toronto doing a weekly TV variety show, a good friend of his told him of auditions being held in New York for a new Lerner and Lowe musical. Bob asked Don Hudson if he could go to New York and audition. He auditioned and was awarded the role of Lancelot in the play *Camelot,* which starred Richard Burton and Julie Andrews.

A major break occurred at that time when he was asked to do "The Ed Sullivan Show" on TV. From this show his popularity as a handsome singer spread all over the country. He was signed by Columbia records as a singer and recorded "What Kind of Fool Am I" as his first major chart hit in September 1962. While doing *Camelot,* he met Carol Lawrence, whom he married in August 1963.

Today, Bob and Carol are divorced, but he is still very active doing TV and some concert appearances.

September	1962	WHAT KIND OF FOOL AM I	Columbia
October	1964	MY LOVE FORGIVE ME	Columbia
May	1965	SUMMER SOUNDS	Columbia

CHARLIE GRACIE

Born: January 12, 1936
Hometown: Philadelphia, Pennsylvania

Charlie was taught to play the guitar by his father, Sam Gracie. He graduated from South Philly High and passed up offers to the University of

Pennsylvania and Temple University to pursue a singing career. He played various clubs in the Philadelphia area and had his own TV show in Pittsburgh. In late 1956, Charlie signed with Cameo records and recorded a song written by Bernie Lowe and Kal Mann called "Butterfly." It became a hit in January 1957.

January	1957	BUTTERFLY	Cameo
April	1957	FABULOUS	Cameo
July	1957	I LOVE YOU SO MUCH IT HURTS	Cameo

BILLY GRAMMER

Born: August 28, 1925
Hometown: Benton, Illinois

The son of a coal miner and one of thirteen children, Billy became interested in music early in life. Around 1947, he played in the Baltimore and Washington, D.C., area for about a year and a half. He then became the featured guitarist and vocalist on "The Jimmy Dean Show" on CBS-TV. In 1958, he signed with Monument records and decided to record a song that originated in the British Isles over a hundred years ago. In November 1958, "Gotta Travel On" became his first and biggest hit.

November	1958	GOTTA TRAVEL ON	Monument
April	1959	BONAPARTE'S RETREAT	Monument

GERRY GRANAHAN

Gerry was a New York songwriter, who supplied many local groups with their material. In May 1958, he tried it as a vocalist with the recording "No Chemise Please," which became a hit on Sunbeam records.

May	1958	NO CHEMISE, PLEASE	Sunbeam

ROCCO GRANATA

In the fall of 1959, Bob Schwartz of Laurie records in New York discovered a European recording on his desk called "Marina," which he liked. The song was released that fall and became Rocco's only major hit for Laurie.

October	1959	MARINA	Laurie

EARL GRANT

Born: 1931
Died: June 11, 1970
Hometown: Oklahoma City, Oklahoma

Earl studied at the Kansas City Conservatory of Music, the University of Southern California, the New Rochelle Conservatory in New York, and DePaul University in Chicago. After his discharge from the Army, he returned to the University of Southern California as a graduate student. While working on his thesis and playing local clubs in Los Angeles, Earl was offered a recording contract with Decca records. He signed with the label and in September 1958 had his first hit with "The End."

Earl died of injuries received in an automobile accident in 1970.

September	1958	THE END	Decca
January	1959	EVENING RAIN	Decca
March	1960	HOUSE OF BAMBOO	Decca
May	1962	SWINGIN' GENTLY	Decca
August	1962	SWEET SIXTEEN BARS	Decca
October	1965	STAND BY ME	Decca

GOGI GRANT

Real Name: Audrey Brown
Born: 1936
Hometown: Philadelphia, Pennsylvania

Philadelphia-born Gogi grew up in Los Angeles, California, where she admired the music of artists like Russ Columbo, Ben Bernie, and Ruth Etting. It was while in high school that she began to think about becom-

GOGI GRANT

ing a singer. She entered a statewide contest for teen singers and won. After graduation she got a job as a clerk-typist, but still thought of singing professionally. She entered some TV talent shows and won them, too, convincing herself this was the profession she should pursue.

In the mid-fifties she was signed to Era records. In the spring of 1956, she recorded a Herb Newman song called "The Wayward Wind," which became a number one national hit.

October	1955	SUDDENLY THERE'S A VALLEY	Era
January	1956	WHO ARE WE	Era
March	1956	THE WAYWARD WIND	Era
August	1956	YOU'RE IN LOVE	Era
August	1958	STRANGE ARE THE WAYS OF LOVE	RCA

JANIE GRANT

Born: 1945
Hometown: New York, New York

Janie was discovered at a party by Sunbeam recording artist Gerry Granahan ("No Chemise, Please"). Gerry took her to Caprice records where she signed a contract. In April 1961, only sixteen and a junior in high school, she had her first hit called "Triangle."

April	1961	TRIANGLE	Caprice
August	1961	ROMEO	Caprice
June	1962	THAT GREASY KID STUFF	Caprice

BILLY GRAVES

The Shag mirrored the dance craze phenomenon which was given wide exposure by "American Bandstand." It was not as popular as the Twist, the Madison, and the Stroll.

January	1959	THE SHAG	Monument

BUDDY GRECO

Real Name: Armando Greco
Born: August 14, 1926
Hometown: Philadelphia, Pennsylvania

The composer, arranger, and singer had his own trio from 1944 to 1949. For the next three years he was a pianist and arranger with Benny Goodman. His biggest hit in 1962 was a vocal written by Bobby Vinton, "Mr.

BUDDY GRECO

Lonely." Ironically, Bobby released the song himself two years later and it became a number one hit record.

September	1962	MR. LONELY		Epic

BOBBY GREGG & HIS FRIENDS

Bobby's two hits came at the height of the Twist fever. "The Jam" was a top forty record, while "The Potato Peeler" was somewhat less popular.

February	1962	THE JAM		Cotton
June	1962	POTATO PEELER		Cotton

VINCE GUARALDI TRIO

Born: 1929
Died: February 6, 1976

Vince's group recorded an album of the music from the film *Black Orpheus.*

　　　Vince died of a heart attack in San Francisco, California, in 1976.

November	1962	CAST YOUR FATE TO THE WIND		Fantasy

BONNIE GUITAR

Bonnie recorded "Dark Moon" for Dot records in March 1957, which was covered by another Dot artist, Gale ("My Little Margie") Storm. Ironically, "Dark Moon" was the last in a long series of hits for Gale Storm but only the first of several for Bonnie Guitar.

March	1957	DARK MOON		Dot
October	1957	MISTER FIRE EYES		Dot
December	1959	CANDY APPLE RED		Dolton

BILL HALEY & THE COMETS

Top left to right: Rudy
Pompelli, Al Rex, Bill Haley
Bottom left to right: Ralph
Jones, John Grande
Francis Beecher, Billy
Williamson

BILL HALEY & THE COMETS

Members:

   Bill Haley (William John Clifton Haley, Jr.)—guitar—born: July 6,
      1925, Highland Park, Michigan; died: February 9, 1981

   John Grande—accordion and piano

   Billy Williamson—steel guitar

   Rudy Pompelli—sax—1928; died: February 5, 1976

   Al Rex—bass

   Francis Beecher—Spanish guitar

   Don Raymond—drums—replaced by Ralph Jones in 1955

Hometown: Chester, Pennsylvania

Bill came from a musical family. His mother was a church organist and
his dad played the banjo. Both encouraged Bill to learn the guitar. At
fifteen Bill left home to travel with the Down Homers. Later he became
musical director and head of his own band which played on a small radio
station in Chester, Pennsylvania. The aggregation was known as Bill
Haley's Saddlemen, and in 1951 they began to record for Essex records.
One of their first recorded efforts: "We're Going to Rock this Joint
Tonight."

   In 1952 the name of the group was changed to the Comets. A couple
of moderate hits followed: "Dance with the Dolly" and "Patty Cake."

   About this time, Bill wrote a song for a friend named Danny Ceda-
rone, who was then heading up a group called The Esquire Boys. The song

"Rock-a-Beatin' Boogie" was a hit for the group. When Bill Haley and the Comets recorded the same song, Alan Freed, who worked for WJW radio in Cleveland, Ohio, at the time, was so intrigued by the song's words, "Rock, Rock, Rock Everybody, Roll, Roll, Roll Everybody," that it is said he coined the phrase rock and roll.

In May 1953, the group had their first major hit for Essex records with the song "Crazy Man Crazy." The group had their first of many hits for Decca records in 1954 with "Shake, Rattle and Roll." In 1955, they had their biggest all-time seller, and the song that has sold more records than any other single pop hit, over 20 million copies since 1955, "Rock Around the Clock." (The song was featured in *Blackboard Jungle*.)

Bill's identifying trademark was the little spit curl that he always tumbled over his forehead. Bill died in Rio Grande Valley Town, of Harlingen, Texas, of a heart attack in 1981. A private man, he lived in semiseclusion for several years with his wife, Martha, refusing either to perform or grant interviews. He was, however, a rock 'n' roll pioneer, considered by many the "Father of Rock 'N' Roll."

May	1953	CRAZY MAN, CRAZY	Essex
July	1954	SHAKE, RATTLE AND ROLL	Decca
October	1954	DIM, DIM THE LIGHTS	Decca
February	1955	MAMBO ROCK	Decca
March	1955	BIRTH OF THE BOOGIE	Decca
April	1955	ROCK AROUND THE CLOCK	Decca
July	1955	RAZZLE-DAZZLE/TWO HOUND DOGS	Decca
September	1955	BURN THAT CANDLE	Decca
December	1955	SEE YOU LATER ALLIGATOR	Decca
March	1956	R-O-C-K	Decca
March	1956	THE SAINTS ROCK 'N ROLL	Decca
May	1956	HOT DOG BUDDY BUDDY	Decca
July	1956	RIP IT UP	Decca
October	1956	RUDY'S ROCK	Decca
March	1957	FORTY CUPS OF COFFEE	Decca
June	1957	BILLY GOAT	Decca
March	1958	SKINNY MINNIE	Decca
August	1958	LEAN JEAN	Decca
October	1959	JOEY'S SONG	Decca
January	1960	SKOKIAAN	Decca
March	1974	ROCK AROUND THE CLOCK	MCA

LARRY HALL

Born: June 30, 1941

"Sandy" was a simple, syrupy ballad which used that female name as a title gambit. The song made the top twenty in the country in late 1959. It was Larry Hall's only chart record.

November 1959	SANDY	Strand

THE HALOS

Members:
Harold Johnson—lead
Al Cleveland
Phil Johnson
Arthur Crier—bass
Hometown: Bronx, New York

During the summer of 1961, The Halos were hired by Morty Craft, the president of Warwick records, as background singers for Shirley & Lee, who were recording for the label at the time. The Halos were also used as the back-up group on Curtis Lee's 1961 hit "Pretty Little Angel Eyes" for Dunes records.

Morty liked their sound so much that he had them record the song "Nag." He released the song during June 1961 on the 7 Arts label and it went on to become the group's only major hit. "Nag" was written by bass singer Arthur Crier.

July   1961   NAG   7 Arts

THE HALOS

GEORGE HAMILTON IV

GEORGE HAMILTON IV

Born: July 19, 1937
Hometown: Winston-Salem, North Carolina

The president of WTOB-TV secured George an audition on Arthur Godfrey's Talent Scout show and George was signed to appear for one week. He later became a regular on the Grand Ole Opry. In the fall of 1956, George recorded his first major hit, called "A Rose and a Baby Ruth," on Colonial records, which was then sold to Am-Par records.

October	1956	A ROSE AND A BABY RUTH	ABC
January	1957	ONLY ONE LOVE	ABC
July	1957	HIGH SCHOOL ROMANCE	ABC
November	1957	WHY DON'T THEY UNDERSTAND	ABC
March	1958	NOW AND FOR ALWAYS	ABC
May	1958	I KNOW WHERE I'M GOIN'	ABC
August	1958	WHEN WILL I KNOW	ABC
July	1959	GEE	ABC
June	1963	ABILENE	RCA

ROY HAMILTON

Born: April 16, 1929
Died: July 20, 1969
Hometown: Leesburg, Georgia

Roy started singing in church choirs at the age of six. When he was fourteen, his family moved to Jersey City, New Jersey, where he attended

ROY HAMILTON

Lincoln High and majored in commercial art. He also became an amateur heavyweight boxer. Roy sang regularly at the Central Baptist Church in Jersey City. One evening, while Roy was performing in a small night club in Newark, a disc jockey named Bill Cook heard him. Bill liked his act and introduced him to the people at Epic records. This resulted in a recording contract and Roy recorded Rodgers and Hammerstein's "You'll Never Walk Alone," which launched his career in 1954. After that came the hit "Unchained Melody" in April 1955, and songs like "Ebb Tide" and "Don't Let Go."

Roy died of a stroke in July 1969 in New Rochelle, New York, leaving a wife and two sons.

February	1954	YOU'LL NEVER WALK ALONE	Epic
May	1954	IF I LOVED YOU	Epic
August	1954	EBB TIDE	Epic
December	1954	HURT	Epic
April	1955	UNCHAINED MELODY	Epic
July	1955	WITHOUT A SONG	Epic
November	1955	EVERYBODY'S GOT A HOME BUT ME	Epic
January	1958	DON'T LET GO	Epic
November	1958	PLEDGING MY LOVE	Epic
April	1959	I NEED YOUR LOVIN'	Epic
August	1959	TIME MARCHES ON	Epic
February	1961	YOU CAN HAVE HER	Epic
May	1961	YOU'RE GONNA NEED MAGIC	Epic

JOE HARNELL

Joe Harnell added a bossa nova beat to a Frank Sinatra hit of the fifties called "Fly Me to the Moon" and the song became a hit for him in 1962. For many years, Joe was the musical director of the Mike Douglas television show.

| December | 1962 | FLY ME TO THE MOON BOSSA NOVA | Kapp |
| April | 1963 | DIANE | Kapp |

SLIM HARPO

Slim was a black guitar player whose blues singing style had an influence on many artists of the late fifties and early sixties. His first national hit came in 1961 with "Rainin' in My Heart."

May	1961	RAININ' IN MY HEART	Excello
January	1966	BABY SCRATCH MY BACK	Excello
June	1967	TIP ON IN	Excello
March	1968	TE-NI-NEE-NI-NU	Excello

THE HARPTONES

Members:
   William Winfield—lead tenor—born: August 24, 1929
   William (Dempsey) James—first tenor—1946
   William (Dicey) Galloway—second tenor—replaced in 1954 by Jimmie Beckum
   Bill Brown—1936
   Nicky Clark—1943
   Raoul Cita—organizer and arranger—February 11, 1928
Hometown: New York, New York

The group was first formed in early 1953 by Raoul Cita and called the Harps. They admired the group sounds of The Five Keys, The Larks, and The Swallows and were influenced greatly by them. They would practice on street corners in Harlem, trying to perfect their own sound.

   In 1953, the group changed their name to the Harptones, because there was another group that called themselves the Harps. Raoul, the group's manager, got them a contract with Morty Craft's Bruce records and they recorded their first hit, "A Sunday Kind of Love."

   The group's second tenor, Bill Galloway, was drafted into the Army in 1954 and was replaced by Jimmie Beckum. During that year they had their first hit for Paradise records with the song "Life Is But a Dream." In 1956 Bill Brown died.

THE HARPTONES

Top: Willie Winfield
Bottom: Raoul Cita
Center, left to right:
William "Dempsey"
James, Nicky Clark,
Billy Brown, William
"Dicey" Galloway

Even though the group had poor exposure and some contract difficulties, they have remained one of the East Coast's favorite rhythm and blues groups over the past twenty years. Several of their songs have become R & B classics. Today Willie Winfield is a funeral director in New York, but sings with another fellow and a girl as the Harptones on various rock bills in the New York area.

October	1953	A SUNDAY KIND OF LOVE/I'LL NEVER TELL	Bruce
December	1953	MY MEMORIES OF YOU	Bruce
March	1954	LIFE IS BUT A DREAM	Paradise
February	1956	THREE WISHES/THAT'S THE WAY IT GOES	Rama
May	1956	ON SUNDAY AFTERNOON/THE MASQUERADE IS OVER	Rama
September	1956	SHRINE OF ST. CECELIA	Rama
January	1957	CRY LIKE I CRIED	Gee

EDDIE HARRIS

Eddie did an instrumental jazz version of the theme from the motion picture *Exodus*, the same song that Ferrante and Teicher did so nicely with.

April	1961	EXODUS	Vee Jay
June	1968	LISTEN HERE	Atlantic

ROLF HARRIS

Hometown: Sydney, Australia

Rolf effected the unique sound he used on his big hit record "Tie Me Kangaroo Down, Sport" by accident. He had just finished a portrait on board instead of canvas and had placed the still-wet board on his stove to dry. The board got red hot so Rolf picked it up and began flapping it to cool it off. That's when it began making the strange noise he used to such advantage on the record to simulate the hopping of a kangaroo. This Australian hit became a United States hit in the summer of 1963.

March	1963	SUN ARISE	Epic
May	1963	TIE ME KANGAROO DOWN, SPORT	Epic

THURSTON HARRIS

Thurston sang with the Lamplighters and the Sharps before going out as a single. In September 1957, he recorded a song that Robert Byrd had written called "Little Bitty Pretty One," which went on to be a national hit. (Robert Byrd is better known as "Bobby Day" who recorded "Rockin' Robin.")

September	1957	LITTLE BITTY PRETTY ONE	Aladdin
January	1958	DO WHAT YOU DID	Aladdin
August	1958	OVER AND OVER	Aladdin

WILBERT HARRISON

Born: January 6, 1929
Hometown: Charlotte, North Carolina

Wilbert was one of a family of twenty-three. After almost four years in the Navy, he became interested in show business. In 1953, in Miami, he won first prize in an amateur show singing "Mule Train." Eventually he got a recording contract with Rockin' records where he recorded "This Woman of Mine."

Wilbert left Miami in 1957, and went to Newark, New Jersey, where he worked local clubs seven nights a week. He took "K.C. Lovin' " to his good friend Herman Lubinsky of Savoy records and told him he wanted to record it. Herman suggested that Wilbert take the song to Bobby Robinson, the head of Fury records. Wilbert recorded the song in March 1959 (retitled "Kansas City") and in a short time it became a number one national hit.

Today Wilbert lives in Queens, New York and does occasional appearances in the New York area at various rock shows.

April	1959	KANSAS CITY	Fury
December	1969	LET'S WORK TOGETHER	Sue
March	1971	MY HEART IS YOURS	SSS Intl.

DALE HAWKINS

Born: August 30, 1938
Hometown: Bossier, Louisiana

Guitar-playing Dale got a chance to go into a recording studio in 1957. He recorded a song he had written with two other friends called "Susie-Q." It was sold to Checker records of Chicago, and went on to become his first hit in May 1957.

May	1957	SUSIE-Q	Checker
August	1958	LA-DO-DADA	Checker
October	1958	A HOUSE, A CAR AND A WEDDING RING	Checker
March	1959	YEAH YEAH	Checker

DALE HAWKINS

SCREAMIN' JAY HAWKINS

RONNIE HAWKINS

Members:
    Ronnie Hawkins—vocals—Huntsville, Arkansas
    Will Jones—piano
    Levon Helm—drums
    Ray Paulman—guitar

Ronnie got his early training while touring Canada. In the summer of 1959, he had his first major hit for Roulette records with "Forty Days." A few months later came his biggest hit, "Mary Lou."

June	1959	FORTY DAYS	Roulette
August	1959	MARY LOU	Roulette
January	1970	DOWN IN THE ALLEY	Cotillion

SCREAMIN' JAY HAWKINS

Real Name: Jalacy Hawkins
Born: July 18, 1929
Hometown: Cleveland, Ohio

Jay became interested in boxing at an early age. He was a Golden Gloves amateur champ and went on to beat middleweight champ Billy McCan of Alaska in 1949. Shortly thereafter, Jay gave up the ring.

    That same year he turned to singing and was discovered by Tiny

Grimes in Atlantic City, New Jersey, where Jay was appearing. While Jay was on stage one evening, a lady in the audience yelled to him to "scream the song." She kept up with her cries for him to scream and he began to do so. After this he began to call himself "Screamin' Jay Hawkins."

In the mid-fifties he was signed to Okeh records where he came across a song called "I Put a Spell on You." The song was originally a ballad and this is how Jay was to record it: Prior to the recording session, Jay, along with the musicians, began drinking to get in the right mood. Jay recorded the song while under the influence. The result was a wild rendition of the song. The song was released in November 1956 and became a hit. Since he recorded the song while he was drunk, he had to learn that style in order to perform it on stage.

His next major hit was a Leiber and Stoller song called "Alligator Wine" in April 1958. Although he had only two major hits, his wild characterizations, with coffins, skulls, and capes on stage, have established him as a very popular performer.

Today Jay lives with his wife in New York City, and works at local clubs and concerts.

| November | 1956 | I PUT A SPELL ON YOU | Okeh |
| April | 1958 | ALLIGATOR WINE | Okeh |

DEAN HAWLEY

In the summer of 1960, Dean had a brief stay in the limelight with "Look for a Star," from the motion picture *Circus of Horrors*. This moderate-tempo ballad was a top-forty hit but Dean was not heard from again.

| June | 1960 | LOOK FOR A STAR | Dore |
| October | 1961 | POCKETFUL OF RAINBOWS | Liberty |

BILL HAYES

Born: June 5, 1926
Hometown: Harvey, Illinois

Bill got his start with a three-year stint on television's "Your Show of Shows." In 1951 the talented vocalist headlined the Roxy in New York for five weeks. He made his film debut in an unsuccessful adaptation of a Damon Runyon story. One day in 1955 Bill dropped into the record store in the Long Island suburb where he lived to check some of the new releases. He ran into Archie Bleyer, formerly of the Arthur Godfrey show and then musical director of Cadence records. A couple of months later

Archie got Bill to record "The Ballad of Davy Crockett." Within seven weeks of its release Bill had his own special niche in musical history: The song was number one on the charts and had sold over a million copies.

| January | 1955 | THE BALLAD OF DAVY CROCKETT | Cadence |
| January | 1957 | WRINGLE, WRANGLE | ABC |

RICHARD HAYMAN

Born: March 27, 1920
Hometown: Winthrop, Massachusetts

Richard taught himself to play the harmonica and the accordion when he was a young man. He played in several local bands before moving to the West Coast. Bit parts in several Betty Grable pictures came next. While at MGM, he learned the fine art of composing background music for motion pictures. After a stint with Vaughan Monroe's organization, he formed his own band.

Today he plays the piano in nightclub engagements around the country.

March	1953	RUBY	Mercury
April	1953	APRIL IN PORTUGAL	Mercury
September	1953	STORY OF THREE LOVES (Jerry Murad)	Mercury
January	1956	A THEME FROM THE THREEPENNY OPERA	Mercury
September	1961	NIGHT TRAIN	Mercury

THE HEARTBEATS

Members:
    James "Shep" Sheppard—lead—died: January 24, 1970
    Wally Roker
    Vernon Seavers
    Robbie Brown
    Albert Crump
Hometown: Jamaica, Queens, New York

Shep formed the group in the mid-fifties and they began singing on street corners to develop their unique harmonies. In 1956, Shep recorded a song with his group called "Crazy for You." They took the song to Hull records in New York, who signed the group.

Later that year, when Shep's girl friend moved to Texas, he wrote a song about how this separation made him feel. "A Thousand Miles Away" was recorded and released in late 1956, and it became the group's biggest

THE HEARTBEATS
Left to right: Robbie Brown, Wally Roker, James Sheppard, Vernon Seavers, Albert Crump

all-time seller. The group remained together for only a couple of years, disbanding in the late fifties.

In 1961 Shep formed another group called Shep & the Limelites and had another national hit with "Daddy's Home."

On January 24, 1970, Shep was found dead in his automobile on the Long Island Expressway, after having been beaten and robbed.

January	1956	CRAZY FOR YOU	Hull
March	1956	DARLING HOW LONG	Hull
July	1956	PEOPLE ARE TALKING / YOUR WAY	Hull
November	1956	A THOUSAND MILES AWAY	Hull also on Rama
February	1957	WEDDING BELLS	Rama
June	1957	EVERYBODY'S SOMEBODY'S FOOL	Rama
November	1957	AFTER NEW YEAR'S EVE	Gee
April	1958	DOWN ON MY KNEES	Roulette

THE HEARTS

Members:
    Joyce James—lead
    Joyce Peterson
    Baby Washington
    Rex Garvin
Hometown: Bronx, New York

The three girls got together with Rex Garvin (Rex later wrote "Over the Mountain" for Johnnie & Joe) and formed their group, singing around the New York area. In the spring of 1955, they recorded a song called "Lonely Nights," which became a national hit on Baton records.

| March | 1955 | LONELY NIGHTS | Baton |
| October | 1963 | DEAR ABBY | Tuff |

JOHNNY HEARTSMAN

Hometown: Los Angeles, California

Johnny's band, the House Rockers, backed up artists like the Four Deuces, who recorded for Music City records. In early 1957, during some extra time at a recording session, Johnny had the band record the song "Johnny's House Party." Music City liked the session so much that they decided to release the song and it became a national hit that year.

| May | 1957 | JOHNNY'S HOUSE PARTY | Music City |

BOBBY HELMS

Born: August 15, 1933
Hometown: Monroe County, Indiana

Bobby Helms was only on the recording scene for one year, but in that

BOBBY HELMS

short time he recorded two classics. The first was "My Special Angel" and the second was the perennial favorite, "Jingle Bell Rock."

June	1957	FRAULEIN	Decca
September	1957	MY SPECIAL ANGEL	Decca
December	1957	JINGLE BELL ROCK	Decca
May	1958	JACQUELINE	Decca
August	1958	BORROWED DREAMS	Decca
December	1958	THE FOOL AND THE ANGEL	Decca

JOE HENDERSON

"Big" Joe Henderson, with his deep Brook Benton-type voice, had his biggest hit in the summer of 1962, when he recorded the ballad "Snap Your Fingers" for Todd records. If it were not for the fact that he sounded similar to Brook, he might have been a bigger star.

| May | 1962 | SNAP YOUR FINGERS | Todd |
| September | 1962 | BIG LOVE | Todd |

BOBBY HENDRICKS

Born: February 22, 1938
Hometown: Columbus, Ohio

Bobby started singing in Columbus, with a group called the Five Crowns. Next he sang with the Swallows. He left the group to sing as lead singer with the Drifters for about eight months. He sang lead on "Moonlight Bay," and "Drip Drop." In 1958, Bobby and guitar player Jimmy Oliver wrote "Itchy Twitchy Feeling." Sue records released the record that summer. His only other major hit came in November 1960 with a song called "Psycho."

| July | 1958 | ITCHY TWITCHY FEELING | Sue |
| November | 1960 | PSYCHO | Sue |

CLARENCE "FROGMAN" HENRY

Born: 1937
Hometown: Algiers, Louisiana

Clarence's first professional job was as singer-pianist with Bobby Mitchell's band in 1955. Pascal Marcello, owner of the Joy Lounge in New Orleans, introduced Clarence to Leonard Chess of Chess records. This resulted in a contract with Chess's subsidiary Argo records. In October 1956, he recorded a song called "Ain't Got No Home," his first hit for the label. He got his nickname "Frogman" because he sang in three different voices in the song, the lowest voice sounding like a frog.

October	1956	AIN'T GOT NO HOME	Argo
February	1961	I DON'T KNOW WHY, BUT I DO	Argo
May	1961	YOU ALWAYS HURT THE ONE YOU LOVE	Argo
August	1961	LONELY STREET	Argo
November	1961	ON BENDED KNEES	Argo
January	1962	A LITTLE TOO MUCH	Argo

EDDIE HEYWOOD

Born: December 4, 1926

Piano-playing Eddie was the son of a jazz musician. His father influenced him a lot in the piano styling he created in the mid-fifties.

Eddie's first major hit was his own idiosyncratic version of "Begin the Beguine." He wrote and recorded the popular "Canadian Sunset" and followed it with "Soft Summer Breeze," which spent seven months on the national charts.

| June | 1956 | SOFT SUMMER BREEZE | Mercury |

EDDIE HEYWOOD

AL HIBBLER

AL HIBBLER

Born: August 16, 1915
Hometown: Little Rock, Arkansas

Al was born blind. He sang in the church choir in Little Rock, then attended the Arkansas state school for the blind and sang in the glee club. He was encouraged to enter the amateur contest at the Palace theater in Memphis, where he won for ten weeks in a row.

In 1941, Charlie Parker took Al to New York, where he was signed by Jay McShane to tour the country. He finally got a recording contract with Decca records in the forties.

He then won a spot as vocalist with Duke Ellington's band for eight years. Around 1950, he left Duke to go out as a single and recorded for RCA, Columbia, and Atlantic.

Al returned to Decca records and had a smash hit with them in early 1955 from the motion picture *Unchained* with the song "The Unchained Melody."

Today Al continues to work clubs and make concert appearances.

April	1955	UNCHAINED MELODY	Decca
October	1955	HE	Decca
January	1956	11TH HOUR MELODY	Decca
May	1956	NEVER TURN BACK	Decca
July	1956	AFTER THE LIGHTS GO DOWN LOW	Decca
January	1957	TREES	Decca

ERSEL HICKEY

ERSEL HICKEY

The former locksmith left home at fifteen to join a carnival. He impersonated Johnny Ray and won a $500 prize in a talent contest.

In 1958, he got a contract with Epic and recorded a song he had written called "Bluebirds Over The Mountain" which became his only hit.

Ersel lives in Queens, New York, and works today as a writer-producer.

April   1958   BLUEBIRDS OVER THE MOUNTAIN   Epic

THE HIGHWAYMEN

Members:
    Steve Butts—New York, New York—1940
    Chan Daniels—Buenos Aires, Brazil—1940; died: August 2, 1975
    Bobby Burnett—Mystic, Connecticut—1940
    Steve Trott—Mexico City, Mexico—1940
    Dave Fisher—New Haven, Connecticut—1940

The group met while attending Wesleyan University in Middletown, Connecticut. They got their act together doing various fraternity gigs. They went to New York in November 1960, where they met Ken Greengrass, who became their manager. He got them a contract with United Artists records. In the summer of 1961, they recorded the traditional folk song "Michael," which became a number one national hit.

June	1961	MICHAEL	United Artists
November	1961	COTTON FIELDS	United Artists
April	1962	I'M ON MY WAY	United Artists
July	1962	THE BIRD MAN	United Artists

JESSIE HILL

Jessie was a pianist who worked a lot in New Orleans. Working with Allen Toussaint, Jessie recorded a song he wrote called "Ooh Poo Pah Doo, Parts 1 & 2" in the spring of 1960. The record was released on the New Orleans label Minit. The chanting sounds and rhythmic beat made the Part 2 side of the record a national hit.

Today Jessie continues to write and has written a song called "Qualify" for Dr. John and his group.

| March | 1960 | OOH POO PAH DOO—PART II | Minit |
| July | 1960 | WHIP IT ON ME | Minit |

THE HILLTOPPERS

Members:
    Jimmy Sacca—lead
    Seymour Speigelman—tenor
    Don McGuire—bass
    Billy Vaughn—baritone—replaced by Doug Cardoza
Homestate: Kentucky

While a student at Western Kentucky College in Bowling Green, Kentucky, Jimmy wanted to start a singing group. One day while at a local club, he heard a piano player named Billy Vaughan (a former graduate) playing a song that Jimmy liked. Jimmy said he would like to try and record the song. So he got Billy and two classmates, Seymour and Don, to record the song, called "Trying," with Billy playing the piano as well. They then decided to give their newfound group a name and decided on The Hilltoppers, which was the college nickname.

They took the tape to local disc jockey Bill Stamps, who had a local radio show called "Whistling in the Dark," which was heard evenings from 10:30 P.M. until midnight. The song got so many calls when he played it that Bill sent the tape to his friend Randy Wood, the president of a newly founded label called Dot records, located in Gallatin, Tennessee, some fifty miles from the college. Randy liked the tape so much that he went to the college and had the fellows rerecord the song in the college auditorium, using the piano as the only musical instrument and only one microphone.

The song was released in the summer of 1952, and after a slow start began to generate sales, initially in Cleveland and Cincinnati, Ohio. By September 1952, the group was asked to go to New York to appear on "The Ed Sullivan Show." Since they had no money or wardrobe, they wore their college sweaters with a big "W" on the chest, and they bought beanies for a dollar apiece. Their outfits were such a hit that they became the group's trademark. In May 1953, they went to Nashville and recorded a song that Gordon Jenkins and Johnny Mercer had written called "P.S.: I Love You," which went on to become the group's biggest hit.

In 1955, Billy left the group to become the musical arranger for Dot records. The group continued together until around 1963 when they broke up, due in part to the fact that Jimmy was having trouble with his voice. They all accepted jobs with Dot records, and Jimmy went to New York as a distributor for Dot. He stayed with the company until around 1967. In 1968, Jimmy reformed a new Hilltoppers group, and even today, travels around the country singing with them.

August	1952	TRYING	Dot
May	1953	P. S.: I LOVE YOU	Dot
October	1953	TO BE ALONE	Dot
October	1953	LOVE WALKED IN	Dot
January	1954	TILL THEN	Dot
January	1954	FROM THE VINE CAME THE GRAPE	Dot
April	1954	POOR BUTTERFLY	Dot
July	1955	THE KENTUCKIAN SONG	Dot
September	1955	SEARCHING	Dot
November	1955	ONLY YOU	Dot
December	1955	MY TREASURE	Dot
August	1956	KA-DING-DONG	Dot
January	1957	MARIANNE	Dot
April	1957	I'M SERIOUS	Dot
July	1957	A FALLEN STAR	Dot
November	1957	THE JOKER	Dot

JOE HINTON

A onetime gospel singer, Joe adapted his vocal styling from that idiom. In 1963, he signed with the Texas-based Back Beat records and had several moderate hits. His biggest record was "Funny," in the summer of 1964.

May	1963	YOU KNOW IT AIN'T RIGHT	Back Beat
October	1963	BETTER TO GIVE THAN TO RECEIVE	Back Beat
July	1964	FUNNY	Back Beat

EDDIE HODGES

EDDIE HODGES

Born: March 5, 1947
Hometown: Hattiesburg, Mississippi

In 1953, Eddie and his family moved to New York, where he began his professional career. He appeared on many TV shows, including "The Jackie Gleason Show." He also appeared on "Name That Tune," where he won twenty-five thousand dollars and a contract to appear in the Broadway show *The Music Man*. After the show, he played Frank Sinatra's son in the movie *A Hole in the Head*. In June 1961, Eddie had his first hit for Cadence records, "I'm Gonna Knock on Your Door."

June	1961	I'M GONNA KNOCK ON YOUR DOOR	Cadence
January	1962	BANDIT OF MY DREAMS	Cadence
June	1962	(GIRLS, GIRLS, GIRLS) MADE TO LOVE	Cadence
June	1965	NEW ORLEANS	Aurora

RON HOLDEN

Born: August 7, 1939
Hometown: Seattle, Washington

Ron's mother and father, as well as his eight brothers and sisters, were all musicians. During his high school years Ron played with a group called the Thunderbirds. In early 1960, he signed with Donna records and recorded a song he wrote called "Love You So," which became his only hit.

| March | 1960 | LOVE YOU SO | Donna |

EDDIE HOLLAND

Born: February 17, 1941
Hometown: Detroit, Michigan

After graduating from high school Eddie found a job in Detroit at a music publishing house. It was while working there that he had the chance to do a demo record for Berry Gordy, Jr., the president of Motown records. This resulted in a contract and his first hit "Jamie" in January 1962. In the mid-sixties, Eddie with his brother Brian and good friend Lamont Dozier became a song-writing trio, turning out such hits as "Baby, I Need Your Loving" for the Four Tops, "Baby Love" for the Supremes, and dozens more for other Motown artists.

January	1962	JAMIE	Motown
January	1964	LEAVING HERE	Motown
May	1964	JUST AIN'T ENOUGH LOVE	Motown
August	1964	CANDY TO ME	Motown

BUDDY HOLLY

Real Name: Charles Hardin Holley
Born: September 7, 1936
Died: February 3, 1959
Hometown: Lubbock, Texas

Buddy entered his first talent contest at the age of five. At eight he was studying piano and violin, but soon switched to acoustic guitar. By the time he was thirteen, he and his friend Bob Montgomery were a popular local duo. They called their music "Western Bop" and they were increasingly in demand.

At a rock show in Lubbock that featured Bill Haley and the Comets, Buddy and Bob opened the show. A scout for Decca saw them and signed Buddy to the label. The first few cuts were not encouraging so Buddy returned to Lubbock to work further on his material.

He continued recording with a new group he formed called the Crickets at studios in Clovis, New Mexico, which were owned by Norman Petty. In early 1957, they decided to record a song that Buddy and drummer Jerry Allison had written called "That'll Be the Day." Petty then sent the tapes to Roulette records in New York, where they were turned down. The label had already signed Buddy Knox and Jimmy Bowen from the same area of Texas. The tapes were then sent to Peer-Southern, a New York publishing house, who forwarded them to Bob Thiele at Brunswick records. Thiele liked what he heard. He signed the group and released the recording in June 1957. In a short time it became a national hit.

BUDDY HOLLY

With Jerry Allison (drums), Nicki Sullivan (rhythm guitar), and Joe Mauldin (bass), Buddy Holly and his Crickets recorded "Oh Boy!" a few months later, and it became their second hit later that fall. Buddy recorded "Peggy Sue," Allison's girl friend's name, and it was released as Buddy's solo recording debut on Coral records. By late 1957, "Oh Boy!" by the Crickets and "Peggy Sue" by Buddy were challenging each other on the charts.

In the summer of 1958, while playing in New York, Buddy went to see his publishers Peer-Southern, where he met Maria Elena Santiago. After two weeks of dating, Buddy married her in Lubbock, August 15, 1958. After the wedding they moved to New York City. During the fall of that year, Buddy terminated his relationship with Norman Petty and the Crickets.

He recorded a few more songs including "Raining in My Heart" and Paul Anka's "It Doesn't Matter Anymore."

In January 1959, he began a tour for General Artists Corporation with Ritchie Valens, The Big Bopper, and Dion & The Belmonts. They traveled by bus throughout the tour. On Monday, February 2, the show just finished playing Clear Lake, Iowa, and Buddy decided to charter a plane to their next engagement in order to save some time. Valens and the Big Bopper decided to go with him. The next morning, Tuesday, February 3, the plane crashed on takeoff, killing all the occupants of the plane.

The crash ended the career of this twenty-two-year-old singing sensation who created a sound that completely took the music world by storm in the late fifties.

| November | 1957 | PEGGY SUE | Coral |
| May | 1958 | RAVE ON | Coral |

July	1958	EARLY IN THE MORNING	Coral
January	1959	HEARTBEAT	Coral
February	1959	IT DOESN'T MATTER ANYMORE	Coral
February	1959	RAINING IN MY HEART	Coral

THE HOLLYWOOD ARGYLES

Members:
    Gary Paxton
    Bobby Rey
    Ted Marsh
    Gary Webb—drums
    Deary Weaver—guitar
    Ted Winters—bass guitar
Hometown: Los Angeles, California

Bobby Rey, who was a member of The Phantom's Band, the group that backed up The Safaris ("Image Of A Girl") and played the wood block on the record which made the sound of the clock, formed The Hollywood Argyles with Gary Paxton (Gary previously was Flip of Skip & Flip, whose hits included "It Was I" and "Cherry Pie"). In the summer of 1960 the group signed with Lute records and recorded a Dallas Frazier song called "Alley-Oop," which became a number one record and the group's only hit.

| May | 1960 | ALLEY-OOP | Lute |

THE HOLLYWOOD FLAMES

The group was first formed in Los Angeles as The Satellites. In late 1957, they backed up Bobby Day on his recording of "Little Bitty Pretty One" for Class records. It was while backing Bobby that they changed their name to The Hollywood Flames and recorded "Buzz-Buzz-Buzz," their only national hit.

| October | 1957 | BUZZ-BUZZ-BUZZ | Ebb |

LEROY HOLMES

Real Name: Alvin Holmes
Born: September 22, 1913
Hometown: Pittsburgh, Pennsylvania

Leroy was the musical conductor at MGM who backed up artists like Joni James, Tommy Edwards, and Connie Francis. In the mid-fifties he utilized his studio orchestra to record the theme song from the film *The High and the Mighty*. It was a national hit for him in the summer of 1954.

July	1954	THE HIGH AND THE MIGHTY	MGM
July	1956	THEME FROM THE PROUD ONES	MGM
August	1956	WHEN THE WHITE LILACS BLOOM AGAIN	MGM

THE HONEYCONES

In 1958, on the "American Bandstand" TV show, many of the regulars began to use the expression *Op*. Ember records had one of their studio groups record the song to capitalize on the expression. Consequently, the Honeycones recorded "Op" in July 1958, and it went on to be a national hit.

July	1958	OP	Ember

JOHN LEE HOOKER

Born: 1915
Hometown: Memphis, Tennessee

John Lee's stepfather taught him to play the guitar. John did not like farm work so he ran off to live with an aunt in Memphis. There he worked as a theater usher and jammed with other blues men. By the early forties he had moved to Detroit and taken successive jobs as a hospital orderly and janitor. In his spare time he played in many of the Hastings Street clubs.

John Lee began his recording career in the late forties on Modern records. He recorded on various other labels under different names: John Lee Booker on Chance, Birmington Sam on Regent, Texas Slim on King, and Johnny Williams on Staff. His work was in great demand but the various companies were afraid of glutting the market if all the releases bore the name of John Lee Hooker.

April	1949	HOBO BLUES	Modern
November	1949	CRAWLING KING SNAKE BLUES	Modern
October	1951	I'M IN THE MOOD	Modern
November	1958	I LOVE YOU HONEY	Vee Jay
July	1960	NO SHOES	Vee Jay
June	1962	BOOM BOOM	Vee Jay

JOHNNY HORTON

JOHNNY HORTON

Born: April 30, 1927
Died: November 5, 1960
Hometown: Tyler, Texas

Johnny grew up in Rusk, Texas, and then moved to Shreveport, Louisiana, where he was a star for eight years on the Louisiana Hayride radio show. In May 1959, he recorded a Jimmy Driftwood song called "The Battle of New Orleans," which became a number one song and wound up being the number one song for the entire year.

Johnny was killed in an auto crash on November 5, 1960, on U.S. Route 70 near the small town of Milano, Texas. He was returning from an engagement in Austin, Texas. His widow, Billy Joe, was the former wife of Hank Williams, who also met his death in an auto crash in 1953.

May	1959	THE BATTLE OF NEW ORLEANS	Columbia
August	1959	JOHNNY REB	Columbia
February	1960	SINK THE BISMARCK	Columbia
July	1960	JOHNNY FREEDOM	Columbia
September	1960	NORTH TO ALASKA	Columbia
March	1961	SLEEPY-EYED JOHN	Columbia

THE HOT-TODDYS

In the springtime of 1959, the Hot-Toddys recorded an instrumental hit called "Rockin' Crickets," in which they utilized a picking guitar to create the sound of chirping crickets. The song was sold to Shan-Todd records and became a national hit a short time after its release.

March	1959	ROCKIN' CRICKETS	Shan-Todd

HUGO & LUIGI

Members:
  Hugo Peretti
  Luigi Creatore

In the fifties Hugo & Luigi were two of the most talented record producers in the business, working with artists like Jimmie Rodgers, Jimmy Bowen, the Isley Brothers, and Della Reese. Today they own Avco Embassy records and continue to turn out hits.

November	1955	YOUNG ABE LINCOLN	Mercury
May	1959	LA PLUME DE MA TANTE	RCA
December	1959	JUST COME HOME	RCA

IVORY JOE HUNTER

Born: October 10, 1922
Died: 1976
Hometown: Kirbyville, Texas

Ivory Joe's father, Dave Hunter, was a guitarist, and his mother a spiritual singer. Ivory had nine brothers and four sisters. In grade school he started playing the piano in the Fats Waller style. He was the program director of KFDM radio in Beaumont, Texas.

By 1942, he left Texas and went to Oakland, California, where he started his own label called Ivory records. Later he signed with King records. He signed with MGM in 1949 and then around 1954 he signed with Atlantic and recorded "It May Sound Silly" and "A Tear Fell." He recorded a song he wrote in late 1956 called "Since I Met You Baby," which won him a gold record.

October	1949	GUESS WHO	King
October	1949	LANDLORD BLUES	King
December	1949	I QUIT MY PRETTY MAMA	King
January	1950	I ALMOST LOST MY MIND	MGM

IVORY JOE HUNTER

February	1950	S.P. BLUES	MGM
April	1950	I NEED YOU SO	MGM
November	1956	SINCE I MET YOU BABY	Atlantic
March	1957	EMPTY ARMS/LOVE'S A HURTING GAME	Atlantic
October	1958	YES I WANT YOU	Atlantic

TAB HUNTER

Real Name: Arthur Andrew Kelm
Born: July 11, 1931
Hometown: New York, New York

A proficient ice skater and horseman, Tab was discovered by Dick Clayton, who persuaded him to take a screen test. He received less than passing grades for some of his movie performances, but he had better luck on television and his singing career was even more of a success. In January 1957 he had a knockout of a number one hit, "Young Love," which spent six months on the national charts.

January	1957	YOUNG LOVE	Dot
January	1957	RED SAILS IN THE SUNSET	Dot
April	1957	NINETY-NINE WAYS	Dot
October	1958	JEALOUS HEART	Warner Bros.
January	1959	APPLE BLOSSOM TIME	Warner Bros.
May	1959	THERE'S NO FOOL LIKE A YOUNG FOOL	Warner Bros.

FERLIN HUSKY

Born: December 3, 1927
Hometown: St. Louis, Missouri

Ferlin spent five years in the Merchant Marines and became a disc jockey at station KXLW in St. Louis. He went west in 1949, and became a disc jockey in Bakersfield, California. Eventually he got a recording contract with Capitol records in the fifties. In early 1957, Ferlin recorded a Smokey Rogers country song that went onto the pop music charts as well. The record "Gone" became his biggest hit. Ferlin has also recorded comedy material under the name of Simon Crum.

January	1957	GONE	Capitol
June	1957	A FALLEN STAR	Capitol
November	1960	WINGS OF A DOVE	Capitol

BRIAN HYLAND

Born: November 12, 1943
Hometown: Woodhaven, Queens, New York

Brian started singing at the age of nine in the church choir. At twelve, he organized a vocal group called the Delphis. He made a demo record that Kay Twomey liked and took to Dave Kapp of Kapp records. Brian debuted on Leader records, a subsidiary of Kapp, with "Rosemary" in February 1960.

As a sophomore at Franklin K. Lane High in Brooklyn, Brian recorded a Paul Vance and Lee Pockriss novelty song called "Itsy Bitsy Teenie Weenie, Yellow Polka Dot Bikini," which became a number one song during the summer of 1960.

June	1960	ITSY BITSY TEENIE WEENIE YELLOW POLKA DOT BIKINI	Leader
October	1960	FOUR LITTLE HEELS	Kapp
July	1961	LET ME BELONG TO YOU	ABC
November	1961	I'LL NEVER STOP WANTING YOU	ABC
February	1962	GINNY COME LATELY	ABC
June	1962	SEALED WITH A KISS	ABC
September	1962	WARMED OVER KISSES	ABC
November	1962	I MAY NOT LIVE TO SEE TOMORROW	ABC
February	1963	IF MARY'S THERE	ABC
June	1963	I'M AFRAID TO GO HOME	ABC
March	1966	3,000 MILES	Philips
June	1966	THE JOKER WENT WILD	Philips
October	1966	RUN, RUN, LOOK AND SEE	Philips
February	1967	HUNG UP IN YOUR EYES	Philips

BRIAN HYLAND

August	1967	GET THE MESSAGE	Philips
January	1969	TRAGEDY	Dot
April	1969	A MILLION TO ONE	Dot
July	1969	STAY AND LOVE ME ALL SUMMER	Dot
August	1970	GYPSY WOMAN	Uni
January	1971	LONELY TEARDROPS	Uni

DICK HYMAN

Born: March 8, 1927
Hometown: New York, New York

Dick Hyman is a multitalented man: composer, conductor, pianist, organist, and arranger. He studied at Columbia with Teddy Wilson and later toured Europe with Benny Goodman. He also played with Lester Young, Mitch Miller, and Percy Faith, as well as being musical director at a number of New York radio stations. In January of 1956 his jazz trio had a top-ten hit with "Moritat."

| January | 1956 | MORITAT (A THEME FROM THE THREE PENNY OPERA) | MGM |
| March | 1956 | HI LILI HI LO | MGM |

THE IKETTES

FRANK IFIELD

Born: November 1937
Hometown: Coventry, England

Frank began his career at the age of fifteen in Australia. In 1959, he went to England and signed with Columbia records. In July 1960, he recorded "I Remember You," which became to top British hit.

In September of 1962, it was released in the United States on Vee Jay records and became a big hit over here as well.

September	1962	I REMEMBER YOU	Vee Jay
November	1962	LOVESICK BLUES	Vee Jay
August	1963	I'M CONFESSIN'	Capitol
November	1963	PLEASE	Capitol

THE IKETTES

Members:
Alice Faye
Robbie Johnson
Josse Armstead

The group was originally formed as background singers for the Ike and Tina Turner Revue. One night they were called on to do a tune of their own, which brought down the house.

In January 1962, they recorded "I'm Blue," which became a hit on Atco records.

January	1962	I'M BLUE	Atco
February	1965	PEACHES 'N' CREAM	Modern
July	1965	I'M SO THANKFUL	Modern

THE IMPALAS

Members:
    Joe "Speedo" Frazier—lead—September 5, 1943
    Tony Carlucci—tenor
    Lenny Renda—baritone
    Richie Wagner—baritone
Hometown: Brooklyn, New York

Richie, Tony, and Lenny formed a trio in the Canarsie section of Brooklyn and practiced at a candy store in the neighborhood. They added Joe

THE IMPALAS

Top to bottom: Joe Frazier, Richie Wagner, Lenny Renda, Tony Carlucci

Frazier from Manhattan and began working harder on their style. They then began looking for a group name and finally decided on the Impalas after Lenny's father bought a new Chevy Impala.

One night in early 1959, Artie Zwirn heard the group and then Alan Freed arranged an audition with Cub records. This resulted in a recording contract and the recording of a song that Artie had written called "(Sorry) I Ran All The Way Home," which became the group's first and biggest national hit during March 1959.

Today "Speedo" is still living in Brooklyn, singing with all new members as The Impalas, while Lenny works for the New York Police Department and Richie moved to Arizona. No one knows the whereabouts of Tony.

| March | 1959 | SORRY (I RAN ALL THE WAY HOME) | Cub |
| June | 1959 | OH WHAT A FOOL | Cub |

THE IMPRESSIONS

Members:

Curtis Mayfield—lead—Chicago, Illinois—1940
Samuel Gooden—bass—Chattanooga, Tennessee—1939
Fred Cash—tenor—Chattanooga, Tennessee—1940
Jerry Butler—1939

Sam and Fred left Chattanooga and went to Chicago, where they met Jerry Butler and Curtis Mayfield. In 1957, the four of them formed a group called the Roosters. Later that year, Eddie Thomas began to manage the group and changed the group's name to the Impressions. They got a recording contract with Falcon records and in May 1958 recorded "For Your Precious Love." A few months after their first hit, Jerry left the group to go on his own. Curtis then became the new lead voice.

In 1961, the group signed with ABC Paramount records, and in October of the same year Curtis wrote the group's first hit in a long string: "Gypsy Woman."

In 1968, Curtis formed his own label, Curtom, which the group recorded for. In 1970, Curtis left the group to go out as a solo artist. Today Curtis writes movie soundtracks and records for Buddah records. He still produces material for the Impressions.

Today the group consists of four men with new members Reggie Torain and Ralph Johnson, as the lead voice.

| October | 1961 | GYPSY WOMAN | ABC |
| January | 1962 | GROW CLOSER TOGETHER | ABC |

July	1962	LITTLE YOUNG LOVER	ABC
January	1963	I'M THE ONE WHO LOVES YOU	ABC
May	1963	SAD, SAD GIRL AND BOY	ABC
September	1963	IT'S ALL RIGHT	ABC
January	1964	TALKING ABOUT MY BABY	ABC
March	1964	I'M SO PROUD	ABC
May	1964	KEEP ON PUSHING	ABC
September	1964	YOU MUST BELIEVE ME	ABC
November	1964	AMEN	ABC
January	1965	PEOPLE GET READY	ABC
March	1965	WOMAN'S GOT SOUL	ABC
June	1965	MEETING OVER YONDER	ABC
August	1965	I NEED YOU	ABC
October	1965	JUST ONE KISS FROM YOU	ABC
November	1965	YOU'VE BEEN CHEATIN'	ABC
February	1966	SINCE I LOST THE ONE I LOVE	ABC
September	1966	CAN'T SATISFY	ABC
February	1967	YOU ALWAYS HURT ME	ABC
September	1967	I CAN'T STAY AWAY FROM YOU	ABC
December	1967	WE'RE A WINNER	ABC
April	1968	WE'RE ROLLING ON	ABC
July	1968	I LOVED AND I LOST	ABC
November	1968	DON'T CRY MY LOVE	ABC
September	1968	FOOL FOR YOU	Curtom
November	1968	THIS IS MY COUNTRY	Curtom
April	1969	SEVEN YEARS	Curtom
June	1969	CHOICE OF COLORS	Curtom
October	1969	SAY YOU LOVE ME	Curtom
May	1970	CHECK OUT YOUR MIND	Curtom
September	1970	(BABY) TURN ON TO ME	Curtom
February	1971	AIN'T GOT TIME	Curtom
July	1971	LOVE ME	Curtom
May	1974	FINALLY GOT MYSELF TOGETHER	Curtom
July	1975	SOONER OR LATER	Curtom
November	1975	SAME THING IT TOOK	Curtom

JORGEN INGMANN

Born: 1932
Hometown: Copenhagen, Denmark

**JORGEN INGMANN
AND WIFE GRETA**

Many of Jorgen's solo guitar songs were released in Europe on the Metronome label. He supported himself by working as a public relations consultant. To get the special effects he sought on his recordings, he would multi-track his work. He did this on a number called "Apache." Atco records released the song here and it became a big hit in January 1961.

| January | 1961 | APACHE | Atco |
| May | 1961 | ANNA | Atco |

THE INNOCENTS

Members:
    Jim West—lead—born: January 7, 1941
    Al Candaleria—bass—born: March 7, 1941
    Darron Stankey—tenor—born: July 5, 1942
Hometown: Sun Valley, California

In 1958, at a party, Jim asked to join Al and Darron, who had been singing as a duo. They worked together as a trio and went to Indigo records for an audition in 1960. This led to a recording contract and their first release in August 1960, "Honest I Do." After that song they backed up Kathy Young, on the same label, on the song "A Thousand Stars."

| August | 1960 | HONEST I DO | Indigo |
| November | 1961 | GEE WHIZ | Indigo |

THE INTRUDERS

Members:
    George Mitchell—lead guitar—born: 1942
    Augie Mitchell—guitar—born: 1930
    Joe Rebardo—drums—born: 1939

They were discovered at a Holiday Inn in New Jersey, by Lee Gallo and Larry Bennet. In March 1959, they had their only hit, the instrumental "Fried Eggs."

| March | 1959 | FRIED EGGS | Fame |

THE ISLEY BROTHERS

Members:
    Ronald Isley—lead—May 21, 1941
    Rudolph Isley—April 1, 1939
    O'Kelly Isley—December 25, 1937

THE ISLEY BROTHERS

Left to right: Ronald,
O'Kelley and Rudolph

Hometown: Cincinnati, Ohio

The Isleys began as a quartet, but the youngest brother, Vernon, was killed in an auto crash. Three other brothers—Ernest, who arranges their material, Marvin, who plays bass, and Chris, who plays piano—round out the family act.

The brothers recorded several songs ("Angels Cried" for Teenage, "Everybody's Gonna Rock 'n' Roll" for Gone, and "This Is the End" for Cindy) before they cracked the big time. RCA producers Hugo and Luigi signed the group, and they racked up a big hit with "Shout" in September 1959, a song the brothers wrote.

Today, the Isleys live in New York and record for their own label, T Neck records.

September	1959	SHOUT	RCA
November	1959	RESPECTABLE	RCA
May	1962	TWIST AND SHOUT	Wand
September	1962	TWISTIN' WITH LINDA	Wand
February	1966	THIS OLD HEART OF MINE	Tamla
May	1966	TAKE SOME TIME OUT FOR LOVE	Tamla
July	1966	I GUESS I'LL ALWAYS LOVE YOU	Tamla
May	1967	GOT TO HAVE YOU BACK	Tamla
February	1969	IT'S YOUR THING	T Neck
May	1969	I TURNED YOU ON	T Neck
August	1969	BLACK BERRIES	T Neck
September	1969	WAS IT GOOD TO YOU	T Neck
January	1970	KEEP ON DOIN'	T Neck
July	1970	GIRLS WILL BE GIRLS, BOYS WILL BE BOYS	T Neck
October	1970	GET INTO SOMETHING	T Neck
January	1971	FREEDOM	T Neck
June	1971	LOVE THE ONE YOU'RE WITH	T Neck
October	1971	SPILL THE WINE	T Neck
December	1971	LAY LADY LAY	T Neck

April	1972	LAY-AWAY	T Neck
July	1972	POP THAT THANG	T Neck
October	1972	WORK TO DO	T Neck
July	1973	THAT LADY	T Neck
December	1973	WHAT IT COMES DOWN TO	T Neck
March	1974	SUMMER BREEZE (Part 1)	T Neck
July	1974	LIVE IT UP PART 1	T Neck
January	1975	MIDNIGHT SKY PART 1	T Neck
June	1975	FIGHT THE POWER PT. 1	T Neck
November	1975	FOR THE LOVE OF YOU (Part 1 & 2)	T Neck
May	1976	WHO LOVES YOU BETTER PART 1	T Neck
August	1976	HARVEST FOR THE WORLD	T Neck
May	1977	THE PRIDE (Part 1)	T Neck
June	1977	LIVIN' IN THE LIFE	T Neck
October	1979	IT'S A DISCO NIGHT	T Neck
April	1980	DON'T SAY GOODNIGHT	T Neck
April	1981	HURRY UP AND WAIT	T Neck

IVAN

Real Name: Jerry Allison
Hometown: Lubbock, Texas

Drummer Jerry Allison of Buddy Holly's Crickets decided to do a vocal during the summer of 1958. With Buddy Holly playing lead guitar, Jerry on drums, and Joe Mauldin on bass, he recorded "Real Wild Child," which became a moderately popular hit that fall.

September 1958	REAL WILD CHILD	Coral

BURL IVES

Real Name: Burl Icle Ivanhoe Ives
Born: June 14, 1909
Hometown: Hunt City, Illinois

Burl Ives is something of a Renaissance man. He has studied at three colleges; he's a serious collector and anthologizer of American folk songs (he's memorized some five hundred of them); he's done radio, TV, concert tours, summer stock, and more. His film credits include: *East of Eden, Cat on a Hot Tin Roof*, and an Academy Award for his performance in *The Big Country*. He's also an author with a half dozen books to his credit. His most successful single record was a top-ten number back in 1961 called "A Little Bitty Tear."

April	1949	RIDERS IN THE SKY	Columbia
February	1957	MARIANNE	Decca

December	1961	A LITTLE BITTY TEAR	Decca
March	1962	FUNNY WAY OF LAUGHIN'	Decca
July	1962	CALL ME MR. IN-BETWEEN	Decca
October	1962	MARY ANN REGRETS	Decca
January	1963	THE SAME OLD HURT	Decca
July	1963	THIS IS ALL I ASK	Decca
December	1963	TRUE LOVE GOES ON AND ON	Decca
September	1964	PEARLY SHELLS	Decca

THE IVY THREE

Members:
>   Charlie Cane (Koppelman)—lead
>   Artie Berk (Berkowitz)
>   Don Rubin
Hometown: New York, New York

The trio started singing together as students at Adelphi College in Garden City, Long Island, in late 1959. They decided to call themselves "The Ivy Three" because the school was ivy-covered.

In 1960, they signed a recording contract with Shell records and recorded a song that Charlie had written along with producers Lou Stallman and Sid Jacobson based on a TV character on the Huckleberry Hound show. By July 1960, the song "Yogi" became a national hit.

Today Don is an independent record producer, Artie is in the insurance business, and Charlie is president of his own record production company called The Entertainment Company, producing albums for stars like Barbra Streisand, Diana Ross and Dolly Parton.

| July | 1960 | YOGI | Shell |

J

THE JACKS

Members:
    Aaron Collins—lead
    George Hollis—second tenor
    Will "Dub" Jones—bass
    Ted Taylor
Hometown: Los Angeles, California

See entry for The Cadets.

October   1955   WHY DON'T YOU WRITE ME   RPM

BULLMOOSE JACKSON

Real Name: Benjamin Jackson
Hometown: Cleveland, Ohio

Bullmoose was discovered by bandleader Lucky Millinder in the forties when Jackson was singing with the Harlem Hotshots. Jackson joined Millinder's group, known as the Buffalo Bearcats. Jackson sang with them until the late forties when he went on his own and recorded for King records.

His first five records sold a million records each on the R & B charts in the late forties. He hit the pop music charts very briefly in the fall of 1961 with "I Love You, Yes I Do."

September 1961   I LOVE YOU, YES I DO   Seven Arts

CHUCK JACKSON

Real Name: Charles Jackson
Born: July 22, 1937
Hometown: Latta, South Carolina—moved to Pittsburgh, Pennsylvania

While a student at South Carolina State College in the late fifties, Chuck decided to leave school and return to Pittsburgh. Chuck then auditioned for Joe Averback, who was managing the Del Vikings, who had a major hit with "Come Go With Me." Dave Lerchey, the group's baritone, was leaving the group. Chuck replaced him from 1957 until 1959. He sang lead.

In 1959, he left the group and signed a contract with Clock records. After four or five bad recordings, Chuck left the label and went on tour with his good friend Jackie Wilson. At the Apollo theater in New York Chuck met Luther Dixon, a writer and producer for Scepter records. Luther liked Chuck's style and had him signed to Scepter's subsidiary, Wand records.

In late 1960, Chuck and Luther collaborated on "I Don't Want To

CHUCK JACKSON

Cry," in January 1961 which became Chuck's first major hit for the label. Burt Bacharach wrote a song called "Any Day Now" that he wanted Chuck to record. Scepter president Florence Greenberg had Tommy Hunt record the song. Burt, however, refused to let them release it. After a year, Scepter let Chuck record it and it became his biggest all-time seller.

Today, Chuck lives with his family in New Jersey, while still traveling and performing all over the country.

February	1961	I DON'T WANT TO CRY	Wand
April	1961	IT NEVER HAPPENS IN REAL LIFE	Wand
August	1961	I WAKE UP CRYING	Wand
April	1962	ANY DAY NOW	Wand
August	1962	I KEEP FORGETTIN'	Wand
November	1962	GETTING READY FOR THE HEARTBREAK	Wand
January	1963	TELL HIM I'M NOT HOME	Wand
October	1963	ANY OTHER WAY	Wand
March	1964	HAND IT OVER	Wand
May	1964	BEG ME	Wand
November	1964	SINCE I DON'T HAVE YOU	Wand
April	1965	I NEED YOU	Wand
August	1965	IF I DIDN'T LOVE YOU	Wand
October	1967	SHAME ON ME	Wand
March	1968	YOU CAN'T LET THE BOY OVERPOWER THE MAN IN YOU	Motown

STONEWALL JACKSON

Born: November 6, 1932
Hometown: Tabor City, North Carolina

STONEWALL JACKSON

Stonewall decided to make Country music his career after getting out of the Navy in 1954. The following year he headed for Nashville in his pickup to try to crack the big time. Wess Rose, whose father had given Hank Williams his start, was instrumental in getting Stonewall Grand Ole Opry and Columbia records contracts. Stonewall's records have always done well on the Country charts. His biggest pop number was the million seller "Waterloo" back in 1959.

May	1959	WATERLOO	Columbia
October	1959	IGMOO	Columbia
January	1960	MARY DON'T YOU WEEP	Columbia
March	1960	WHY I'M WALKIN'	Columbia

WANDA JACKSON

Born: October 20, 1937
Hometown: Oklahoma City, Oklahoma

Wanda's father taught her guitar, piano, and how to read music. An appearance in a talent contest while still in high school led to a spot singing with Hank Thompson's band. After graduating from high school, she toured with Thompson and Elvis Presley. Her records have always done well on the Country charts. She's had moderate success on the pop side with such early sixties numbers as "Right or Wrong" and "In the Middle of a Heartache." One of the few Country performers who's done well in Las Vegas, Wanda still resides in Oklahoma City.

August	1960	LET'S HAVE A PARTY	Capitol
June	1961	RIGHT OR WRONG	Capitol
October	1961	IN THE MIDDLE OF A HEARTACHE	Capitol
January	1962	A LITTLE BITTY TEAR	Capitol
April	1962	IF I CRIED EVERY TIME YOU HURT ME	Capitol

DICK JACOBS

Dick was a musical arranger and conductor for Coral and Brunswick records in the fifties. In the mid-fifties he had several hits of his own on Coral, the first of which was "Main Title and Molly-O" in early 1956.

February	1956	MAIN TITLE AND MOLLY-O	Coral
June	1956	TE AMO	Coral
September	1956	EAST OF EDEN	Coral
October	1956	PETTICOATS OF PORTUGAL	Coral
February	1957	TOWER'S TROT	Coral
August	1957	FASCINATION	Coral

ETTA JAMES

Real Name: Etta James Hawkins
Born: 1938
Hometown: Los Angeles, California

Etta was discovered by songwriter-bandleader Johnny Otis on the West Coast in the mid-fifties. Johnny liked her style and decided to write a tune for her that was an answer-song to Hank Ballard's hits with the Midnighters like "Work with Me Annie" and "Annie Had a Baby." The song was originally called "Roll with Me Henry." After the song was released on Modern records, the company felt the title was too risqué so it was changed to "The Wallflower." Later the title was changed again to "Dance with Me Henry," which is how the tune is known today.

After beating her drug problem, she is now doing selected night club appearances.

January	1955	THE WALLFLOWER	Modern
October	1955	GOOD ROCKIN' DADDY	Modern
April	1960	ALL I COULD DO WAS CRY	Argo
September	1960	MY DEAREST DARLING	Argo
January	1961	AT LAST	Argo
March	1961	TRUST IN ME	Argo
June	1961	FOOL THAT I AM	Argo
July	1961	DON'T CRY BABY	Argo
October	1961	IT'S TOO SOON TO KNOW	Argo
February	1962	SOMETHING'S GOT A HOLD ON ME	Argo
July	1962	STOP THE WEDDING	Argo
October	1962	NEXT DOOR TO THE BLUES	Argo
January	1963	WOULD IT MAKE ANY DIFFERENCE TO YOU	Argo
April	1963	PUSHOVER	Argo
July	1963	PAY BACK	Argo
October	1963	TWO SIDES TO EVERY STORY	Argo
January	1964	BABY WHAT YOU WANT ME TO DO	Argo
April	1964	LOVING YOU MORE EVERY DAY	Argo
October	1967	TELL MAMA	Cadet
March	1968	SECURITY	Cadet
May	1968	I GOT YOU BABE	Cadet
January	1969	ALMOST PERSUADED	Cadet
October	1970	LOSERS WEEPERS—PART 1	Cadet

JONI JAMES

Real Name: Joan Carmella Babbo
Born: September 22, 1930
Hometown: Chicago, Illinois

Joni grew up in an extremely poor neighborhood, and became a dancer until an emergency appendectomy interrupted her career. While sidelined, a friend who was getting married asked her to fill in singing in a night club. Just two years later Joni was a major television, movie, and recording star. In the summer of 1954 she became the first pop singer ever to appear with the Cleveland Symphony Orchestra. Her first hit, back in 1952, "Why Don't You Believe Me," was a number one song.

Today, her only regret is that she never did get back to that dancing career.

October	1952	WHY DON'T YOU BELIEVE ME	MGM
December	1952	HAVE YOU HEARD	MGM
February	1953	YOUR CHEATIN' HEART	MGM
April	1953	IS IT ANY WONDER	MGM
August	1953	MY LOVE, MY LOVE	MGM
January	1955	HOW IMPORTANT CAN IT BE?	MGM
May	1955	YOU ARE MY LOVE	MGM
October	1955	MY BELIEVING HEART	MGM
February	1956	DON'T TELL ME NOT TO LOVE YOU	MGM
March	1956	I WOKE UP CRYING	MGM
July	1956	GIVE US THIS DAY	MGM
June	1957	SUMMER LOVE	MGM
September	1958	THERE GOES MY HEART	MGM
January	1959	THERE MUST BE A WAY	MGM
April	1959	I STILL GET A THRILL	MGM
July	1959	I STILL GET JEALOUS	MGM
January	1960	LITTLE THINGS MEAN A LOT	MGM
April	1960	I NEED YOU NOW	MGM
December	1960	MY LAST DATE WITH YOU	MGM

SONNY JAMES

Real Name: James Loden
Born: March 1, 1929
Hometown: Hackleburg, Alabama

At the age of four, Sonny made his first appearance on a radio show with his mother, father, and older sister. After high school Sonny went into the National Guard and spent fifteen months in Korea. When he got out of the service, he went to see his old friend Chet Atkins in Nashville, who introduced him to Ken Nelson of Capitol records. Ken signed Sonny to the label and changed his name from James Loden to Sonny James.

In November 1956, Bill Lowery, a friend of Sonny's, brought him a tune written by Ric Cartey and Carole Joyner, a young couple from Atlanta, Georgia, who were dating each other at the time. Sonny went into the studio and recorded "Young Love," which became his first and biggest all-time seller.

In 1972, Sonny joined Columbia records, for whom he continues to record country hits. He has a ranch in Hackleburg, where he raises Black Angus cattle.

December	1956	YOUNG LOVE	Capitol
March	1957	FIRST DATE, FIRST KISS, FIRST LOVE	Capitol

December	1957	UH-HUH-MM	Capitol
September	1958	YOU GOT THAT TOUCH	Capitol
May	1959	TALK OF THE SCHOOL	Capitol
January	1960	I FORGOT MORE THAN YOU'LL EVER KNOW	Capitol
April	1960	JENNY LOU	NRC
March	1961	APACHE	RCA
August	1963	THE MINUTE YOU'RE GONE	Capitol
November	1964	YOU'RE THE ONLY WORLD I KNOW	Capitol
July	1967	I'LL NEVER FIND ANOTHER YOU	Capitol
November	1968	BORN TO BE WITH YOU	Capitol
February	1969	ONLY THE LONELY	Capitol
May	1969	RUNNING BEAR	Capitol
September	1969	SINCE I MET YOU, BABY	Capitol
January	1970	IT'S JUST A MATTER OF TIME	Capitol
April	1971	EMPTY ARMS	Capitol
July	1971	BRIGHT LIGHTS, BIG CITY	Capitol

THE JAMIES

Members:
    Tom Jameson
    Serena Jameson
    Jeannie Roy
    Arthur Blair—bass
Hometown: Dorchester, Massachusetts

The group started singing together in the church choir of the First Baptist church in Dorchester, Massachusetts. Sherm Feller of Boston's WEZE radio heard a dub recording of the group. He arranged a recording contract with Epic records, and the group recorded a song that Tom had written called "Summertime, Summertime," which became a hit for them in August 1958.

The Jamesons are brother and sister.

August	1958	SUMMERTIME, SUMMERTIME	Epic

JAN AND ARNIE

Real Names:
    Jan Berry—born: April 3, 1941
    Arnie Ginsberg
Hometown: Los Angeles, California

Jan and Arnie recorded a song called "Jenny Lee" in Jan's garage on a couple of home recorders. It became a hit on Arwin records in April 1958.

April	1958	JENNIE LEE	Arwin
August	1958	GAS MONEY	Arwin

JAN & DEAN

Jan Berry (left) and
Dean Torrence (right)

JAN AND DEAN

Real Names:
> Jan Berry—born: April 3, 1941
> Dean Torrence—born: March 10, 1941

Hometown: Los Angeles, California

Jan and Dean met at Emerson Junior High School in West Los Angeles, where they formed a singing group known as The Barons. Their first hit was inspired by a burlesque dancer in Los Angeles. They recorded "Jennie Lee (The Bazoom Girl)" in Jan's garage on a couple of home re-corders. The rough recording was sold to Arwin records and released in April 1958. "Jennie Lee" became the first hit for Jan and buddy Arnie Ginsberg (Dean had to leave the group to serve six months' active duty in the Army). After Dean came out of the army he joined Jan, since Arnie had decided to give up singing.

In 1959, Jan and Dean recorded a song their friend Lou Adler had given them. Herb Alpert, an unknown at the time, worked on the song's arrangement. They took the rough song into a recording studio, added a rhythm section, and presto, they had a top ten tune called "Baby Talk."

Jan and Dean's biggest hit was written by their good friend Brian Wilson of the Beach Boys. The song, "Surf City," became number one and sold over a million copies during the summer of 1963.

In late 1965, Jan Berry was involved in a serious auto crash in which three persons were killed. He suffered brain damage and was hospitalized for a very long time. Today they both live in Los Angeles and have been traveling around the country as Jan and Dean, performing their hits of the sixties to capacity crowds.

August	1959	BABY TALK	Dore
October	1959	THERE'S A GIRL	Dore
February	1960	CLEMENTINE	Dore
July	1960	WE GO TOGETHER	Dore
November	1960	GEE	Dore
June	1961	HEART AND SOUL	Challenge
January	1962	A SUNDAY KIND OF LOVE	Liberty
May	1962	TENNESSEE	Liberty
February	1963	LINDA	Liberty
June	1963	SURF CITY	Liberty
September	1963	HONOLULU LULU	Liberty
November	1963	DRAG CITY	Liberty
February	1964	DEAD MAN'S CURVE	Liberty
March	1964	THE NEW GIRL IN SCHOOL	Liberty
June	1964	THE LITTLE OLD LADY (FROM PASADENA)	Liberty
September	1964	RIDE THE WILD SURF	Liberty
October	1964	SIDEWALK SURFIN'	Liberty
February	1965	FROM ALL OVER THE WORLD	Liberty
May	1965	YOU REALLY KNOW HOW TO HURT A GUY	Liberty
October	1965	I FOUND A GIRL	Liberty
January	1966	BATMAN	Liberty
May	1966	POPSICLE	Liberty
August	1966	FIDDLE AROUND	Liberty

THE JARMELS

Members:
>   Nathaniel Ruff—1939
>   Ray Smith—1941
>   Paul Burnett—1942
>   Earl Christian—1940
>   Tom Eldridge—1941

Hometown: Richmond, Virginia

The fellows chose the name of the group after a street in Harlem. They all belonged to the same church choir and had sung together for many years. Eventually they signed with Laurie records in 1961 and recorded

"Little Lonely One," which was not too successful. In the summer of 1961, they had their only major hit with "A Little Bit of Soap."

July   1961   A LITTLE BIT OF SOAP   Laurie

JAY AND THE AMERICANS

Members:
   Jay Traynor—lead—replaced by Jay Black (November 2, 1938) in
      1962
   Sandy Yaguda—January 31, 1940
   Kenny Vance—December 8, 1943
   Marty Sanders—February 28, 1940
   Howie Kane—1940
Hometown: New York, New York

In late 1959, Kenny, Sandy, and Howie got together with John "Jay" Traynor, who had been singing with the Mystics, and formed a group

JAY AND THE AMERICANS

Clockwise from top: Sandy
Yaguda, Jay Black, Marty
Sanders, Kenny Vance

called the Harbor-Lites. In 1961, the group auditioned for record producers Jerry Leiber and Mike Stoller. The group was signed by United Artists. They wanted to call the group Binky Jones and the Americans, a
name the fellows didn't like. They compromised with Jay and the Americans.

In the fall of 1961, they recorded their first song, "Tonight," from
West Side Story. They recorded "Dawning" and "She Cried" in January
1962. "Dawning" was to be the "A" side, but "She Cried" developed as the
hit on the West Coast. During the recording of "She Cried," guitarist
Marty Sanders was asked to sing and remained with the group as a vocalist.

After the song "This Is It" in the summer of 1962, Jay Traynor left
the group. Marty sought out his good friend David Black to audition for
the lead spot. David auditioned and won the spot. He then changed his
name to Jay to accommodate the group. A few months later, they were in
the offices of Leiber and Stoller and heard a song the Drifters had just
recorded, "Only In America." The group felt this would be a great song
for them. Ironically, Leiber and Stoller were informed by Atlantic records
that they were not going to release the record, because it was not right
for a black group to be singing about becoming President when this was
not how many people in this country felt. Leiber and Stoller then made
an arrangement with Atlantic to purchase the master tape and had Jay
and The Americans record over the original musical track. The result that
summer was the group's first major hit with Jay Black as lead.

Jay made a chart single in 1980, as Jay Black, which placed on the
national charts for a few weeks. He, along with new members, performs as
Jay Black And The Americans at many local New York shows.

February	1962	SHE CRIED	United Artists
August	1963	ONLY IN AMERICA	United Artists
November	1963	COME DANCE WITH ME	United Artists
September	1964	COME A LITTLE BIT CLOSER	United Artists
December	1964	LET'S LOCK THE DOOR	United Artists
March	1965	THINK OF THE GOOD TIMES	United Artists
May	1965	CARA, MIA	United Artists
August	1965	SOME ENCHANTED EVENING	United Artists
November	1965	SUNDAY AND ME	United Artists
February	1966	WHY CAN'T YOU BRING ME HOME	United Artists
May	1966	CRYING	United Artists
July	1966	LIVIN' ABOVE YOUR HEAD	United Artists
November	1966	HE'S RAINING IN MY SUNSHINE	United Artists
December	1968	THIS MAGIC MOMENT	United Artists
March	1969	WHEN YOU DANCE	United Artists
May	1969	HUSHABYE	United Artists
November	1969	WALKIN' IN THE RAIN	United Artists
March	1970	CAPTURE THE MOMENT	United Artists
JAY BLACK			
September	1980	THE PART OF ME THAT NEEDS YOU MOST	Midsong

THE JAYHAWKS

Members:

James Johnson—first tenor
Carl Fisher—second tenor
Dave Govan—baritone
Carver Bunkum—bass—replaced by Don Bradley
Richard Owens—tenor

Hometown: Los Angeles, California

James, Carl, Dave, and Carver formed the group in high school in 1956. They called themselves the Jayhawks and recorded a song that James had written called "Stranded In The Jungle," which was taken to the Flash Record Store in Los Angeles. The owners felt it had potential and released it on their own label during the summer of 1956. It became a national hit. The group then joined Aladdin records, at which time Carver left the group and was replaced by Don Bradley.

Because of the nature of "Stranded In The Jungle," the Jayhawks were typed as a novelty group. Consequently, when they left Aladdin records, they changed their name to the Vibrations.

In March 1961 they had a national hit called "The Watusi" for Checker records. At the same time they decided to do a little moonlighting and recorded the song "Peanut Butter" as the Marathons for Arvee records during the summer of 1961.

When Checker found out, a lawsuit followed. Checker obtained the rights to "Peanut Butter" and released it on their subsidiary label, Argo records.

June   1956   STRANDED IN THE JUNGLE   Flash

THE JAYNETTS

Members:

Ada Ray—1944
Mary Sue Wells—1946
Ethel Davis—1944
Yvonne Bushnell—1945
Johnnie Louise Richardson—1945

Hometown: Bronx, New York

Abner Spector, an A & R man from Chicago, came to New York in June 1963 in search of a female singing group. He asked Zell Sanders, a composer and publisher, to help him. Zell got two girls from her J & S label,

Ethel Davis and Yvonne Bushnell, who had been single acts. She then added Ada Ray and a fourth member, Mary Sue Wells, by advertising for a girl singer in the New York *Post*.

The girls recorded a song that Zelma Sanders had written called "Sally, Go 'Round The Roses" and it was released on Tuff records during the summer of 1963. It became the group's only national hit.

After the recording, Johnnie Louise Richardson, Zell's daughter, was added to the group. Johnnie had previously been one half of the duo of Johnnie and Joe of "Over The Mountain" fame.

| August | 1963 | SALLY, GO 'ROUND THE ROSES | | Tuff |

KRIS JENSEN

Born: April 4, 1942
Hometown: New Haven, Connecticut

Kris became interested in music through his father's collection of Burl Ives and Chet Atkins records. After graduation from high school in June 1960, he went on a family vacation in Tennessee, where he met country and western great Wesley Rose. Rose contacted Kapp records and Kris was then signed to a two-year contract.

In 1962, after his contract expired, he signed with the Nashville-based Hickory records and had his only hit with "Torture" in the fall.

| August | 1962 | TORTURE | | Hickory |

THE JESTERS

Members:
  Lennie McKay—lead—died: 1971
  Adam Jackson—first tenor—born: March 10, 1938
  Jimmy Smith—second tenor
  Melvin Lewis—baritone
  Donald Lewis—bass
Hometown: New York, New York

The group was formed in Harlem. In late 1956, they signed with Winley records, when owner Paul Winley chanced to hear them.

In January 1957, the group recorded their first song for the label, "Love No One But You," which became a big New York "doo wop" (R & B group vocal) hit. The flip side of the song, "So Strange," became a national chart record in June 1957.

Their biggest national hit was their version of a Chantels hit called "The Plea." Today the group members still live in New York. They appear as the Jesters at various rock shows.

January	1957	LOVE NO ONE BUT YOU	Winley
June	1957	SO STRANGE	Winley
October	1957	THE PLEA	Winley
February	1958	THE WIND	Winley
April	1958	OH BABY	Winley
July	1958	I LAUGHED	Cyclone

THE JEWELS

Hometown: Los Angeles, California

The Jewels were a R & B group who, in the mid-fifties, first recorded "Hearts of Stone." The song later became a hit for both the Charms and the Fontane Sisters in 1954.

August	1954	HEARTS OF STONE	Imperial

JOSE JIMENEZ

Real Name: Bill Dana
Born: October 5, 1924
Hometown: Quincy, Massachusetts

Bill created a character named Jose Jimenez which he used in his night club routine in the fifties. The character became so popular because of his TV appearances that he signed with Kapp records to do a comedy album. "The Astronaut" became a hit during the summer of 1961.

July	1961	THE ASTRONAUT	Kapp

THE JIVE BOMBERS

The Jive Bombers signed with Herman Lubinsky's Savoy records in the mid-fifties and began singing in the New Jersey area. In late 1956, the group recorded a song Lil Armstrong had written called "Bad Boy" which was a hit for Savoy in early 1957. The song featured Clarence Palmer's unique style of singing a melodic line with a "Yahd, yahd, yahd, yahd, yahd," being chanted in the background. That catchy gimmick that helped to sell the record.

January	1957	BAD BOY	Savoy

THE JIVE FIVE

Members:
Eugene Pitt—lead—November 6, 1937
Jerome Hanna—first tenor—replaced by Webster Harris
Billy Prophet—second tenor—replaced by Casey Spencer
Richard Harris—baritone
Norman Johnson—bass
Hometown: Brooklyn, New York

Eugene formed the group at Public School 54 in Brooklyn back in 1959. They were looking for a name for the group when they threw various names in a hat and the name the Jive Five was selected.

The group then met Oscar Waltzer, who began to manage them. Oscar took them to see his old friend Joe Rene, the A & R chief of Beltone records, and he signed them to a contract. In late 1960, the group recorded a song Eugene and Oscar had written, "My True Story," which became the group's first hit.

After a couple of years with Beltone, the group signed with United Artists and recorded a song that group member Casey Spencer had written, called "I'm A Happy Man," which became a hit for the group in July 1965. By 1969, with only four members in the group—Gene, Webster, Casey, and Richard—the name Jive Five no longer was appropriate, so they changed the spelling to the Jyve Fyve.

Today Eugene keeps the group active in the New York area by performing at many local shows.

June	1961	MY TRUE STORY	Beltone
October	1961	NEVER, NEVER	Beltone
September	1962	WHAT TIME IS IT	Beltone
July	1965	I'M A HAPPY MAN	United Artists

DAMITA JO

Real Name: Damita Jo DuBlanc
Born: August 5, 1940
Hometown: Austin, Texas

In 1951, she was featured as a singer with Steve Gibson and his Red Caps. She went out as a single in 1958.

In 1960, she signed with Mercury and had her first major hit that fall with the song "I'll Save The Last Dance For You," an answer to the Drifters' big hit.

DAMITA JO

August	1959	BREAKING UP IS HARD TO DO	Mercury
October	1960	I'LL SAVE THE LAST DANCE FOR YOU	Mercury
February	1961	KEEP YOUR HANDS OFF OF HIM	Mercury
June	1961	I'LL BE THERE	Mercury
December	1967	IF YOU GO AWAY	Epic

THE JODIMARS

Members:
  Bob Simpson—piano
  Jim Buffington—drums
  Charles Hess—guitar
  Joe Ambrose—tenor sax
  Dick Richards—vocals
  Marshall Lytell—vocals and bass

The group name Jodimars came from combining the names of JOey, DIck, and MARshall. They signed with Capitol and had a hit with "Well Now Dig This" in 1956.

| January | 1956 | WELL NOW DIG THIS | Capitol |

JOHNNIE AND JOE

Johnnie Richardson (top) & Joe Rivers (bottom)

JOHNNIE AND JOE

Members:

Johnnie Richardson—hometown: Montgomery, Alabama—born: June 29, 1945

Joe Rivers—hometown: Charleston, South Carolina—born: March 20, 1937

In the spring of 1957, while living in the Bronx, Joe heard a song that his neighbor Rex Garvin had written and liked the song very much. Joe took Rex over to Zell Sanders' house to rehearse the song. Zell liked the song but felt that someone should sing background on it. Zell had her daughter Johnnie rehearse the song with Joe and they finally recorded it. The recording was sold to Chess records and in April 1957, "Over The Mountain, Across The Sea" became a national hit.

Although the duo went their separate ways during the sixties, today they both still live in the Bronx and are still singing at local clubs as Johnnie and Joe.

April   1957   OVER THE MOUNTAIN, ACROSS THE SEA   Chess

JOHNNY AND THE HURRICANES

Members:

Johnny Paris—sax—1941

Paul Tesluk—organ—1941

Dave Yorko—lead guitar—1941

Lionel "Butch" Mattice—bass guitar—1941
Tony Kaye—drums—1941
Hometown: Toledo, Ohio

The group was formed in Toledo and played Pearson Park and then many local clubs.

In early 1959, they signed with Warwick records, which released their first hit, "Crossfire," in April of that year. A few months later came their biggest hit with "Red River Rock."

April	1959	CROSSFIIRE	Warwick
July	1959	RED RIVER ROCK	Warwick
October	1959	REVEILLE ROCK	Warwick
February	1960	BEATNIK FLY	Warwick
May	1960	DOWN YONDER	Big Top
September	1960	ROCKING GOOSE	Big Top
December	1960	YOU ARE MY SUNSHINE	Big Top
March	1961	JA-DA	Big Top

BETTY JOHNSON

Born: March 16, 1932
Hometown: Possom Walk, North Carolina

Betty began singing in the late forties with her parents (The Johnson Family) in the Charlotte, North Carolina, area. In the early fifties Betty went to New York, where she did a couple of radio commercials and began singing at some small clubs. Around this time she met Charlie Grean, who became her manager and later her husband.

Betty went to Chicago to do Don McNeil's Breakfast Club for a year. After her return to New York, she cut a couple of songs for RCA Victor. In 1955, she married Charlie and a year later he wrote her a hit song called "I Dreamed" which was released by Bally records. The record reached the top ten on the chart.

In the late fifties Betty became a regular on the Jack Parr show and her popularity grew. She signed with Atlantic records in 1957, and in February 1958 had her biggest hit with the song "The Little Blue Man," written by Fred Ebb, author of "Cabaret" and other hits for Liza Minnelli.

Today Betty lives with her family in Connecticut.

February	1956	I'LL WAIT	Bally
July	1956	CLAY IDOL	Bally
October	1956	I DREAMED	Bally
April	1957	LITTLE WHITE LIES	Bally
February	1958	THE LITTLE BLUE MAN	Atlantic
June	1958	DREAM	Atlantic
October	1958	HOOPLA HOOLA	Atlantic
January	1959	YOU CAN'T GET TO HEAVEN ON ROLLER SKATES	Atlantic

BUBBER JOHNSON

Bubber, who looked like Fats Domino, was a ballad singer and piano player who had one major hit on the charts, "Come Home," in the summer of 1955. Since rock was romping at the time, most of his releases did not sell as well as those by rocking piano players like Fats Domino and Little Richard.

July	1955	COME HOME	King

BUDDY JOHNSON

Born: January 10, 1912

Buddy was a popular bandleader in the late thirties and forties who recorded for Decca. He was also a very talented songwriter with many hits, including the classic "Since I Fell for You."

After Buddy signed with Mercury, he recorded many songs with his sister Ella singing the vocal parts, such as "I Don't Want Nobody" and "It's Obdacious." Singer Arthur Prysock got his start as a vocalist with Buddy's band.

Buddy's band was very popular with teens in the mid-fifties because of its combination swing and rock style.

August	1949	DID YOU SEE JACKIE ROBINSON HIT THE BALL?	Decca
February	1950	BECAUSE	Decca
June	1953	HITTIN' ON ME	Mercury
January	1954	I'M JUST YOUR FOOL	Mercury
January	1955	(GOTTA GO) UPSIDE YOUR HEAD (Ella Johnson)	Mercury
August	1955	IT'S OBDACIOUS	Mercury
February	1956	I DON'T WANT NOBODY (Ella Johnson)	Mercury

MARV JOHNSON

Born: October 15, 1938
Hometown: Detroit, Michigan

Marv performed briefly with a local group called the Serenaders. While working in a record store in Detroit, he met Berry Gordy, Jr., a young songwriter. Berry wrote a tune for him that was recorded in early 1959. The master recording was sold to United Artists records, and he had his first hit, "Come To Me." In November of the same year he had another major hit with "You Got What It Takes."

March	1959	COME TO ME	United Artists
July	1959	I'M COMIN' HOME	United Artists

MARV JOHNSON

November	1959	YOU GOT WHAT IT TAKES	United Artists
February	1960	I LOVE THE WAY YOU LOVE	United Artists
May	1960	AIN'T GONNA BE THAT WAY	United Artists
May	1960	ALL THE LOVE I GOT	United Artists
September	1960	MOVE TWO MOUNTAINS	United Artists
November	1960	HAPPY DAYS	United Artists
March	1961	MERRY-GO-ROUND	United Artists

THE JOINER, ARKANSAS, JUNIOR HIGH SCHOOL BAND

This group had only one major hit, but due to the exposure they received on Dick Clark's "American Bandstand," it was a national hit. They used the marching band sound (complete with whistle) and recorded the instrumental hit "National City" for Liberty records in the summer of 1960.

May	1960	NATIONAL CITY	Liberty

JACK JONES

Born: January 14, 1938
Hometown: Los Angeles, California

Jack's father, Allan Jones, recorded the classic "Donkey Serenade." His mother, actress Irene Hervey, started Jack as a performer. He signed with

JACK JONES

Kapp records in early 1962, and had his first major hit for the label in March of that year with "Lollipops and Roses," which won him the Grammy Award for the Best Single Record of 1962.

Today Jack continues to travel and perform both on TV and at night clubs.

March	1962	LOLLIPOPS AND ROSES	Kapp
April	1963	CALL ME IRRESPONSIBLE	Kapp
October	1963	WIVES AND LOVERS	Kapp
February	1964	LOVE WITH THE PROPER STRANGER	Kapp
May	1964	THE FIRST NIGHT OF THE FULL MOON	Kapp
August	1964	WHERE LOVE HAS GONE	Kapp
November	1964	DEAR HEART	Kapp
February	1965	THE RACE IS ON	Kapp
May	1965	SEEIN' THE RIGHT LOVE GO WRONG	Kapp
October	1965	JUST YESTERDAY	Kapp
December	1965	LOVE BUG	Kapp
June	1966	THE IMPOSSIBLE DREAM	Kapp
October	1966	A DAY IN THE LIFE OF A FOOL	Kapp
January	1967	LADY	Kapp
April	1967	I'M INDESTRUCTIBLE	Kapp
June	1967	NOW I KNOW	Kapp
September	1967	OUR SONG	Kapp
December	1967	LIVE FOR LIFE	RCA
February	1968	IF YOU EVER LEAVE ME	RCA

JIMMY JONES

Born: June 2, 1937
Hometown: Birmingham, Alabama

Jimmy moved to New York City in his teens and became interested in singing when he was at George Washington High. In late 1959 he was heard singing a demo of an Otis Blackwell song called "Handy Man." Cub records, a subsidiary of MGM, liked Jimmy's rendition of the song, and decided to release it. (Jimmy's emendations to the song also earned him a credit as coauthor.) The result was a top ten hit for him and the label in January 1960.

Today Jimmy lives and makes many appearances at clubs and concerts in the New York area.

January	1960	HANDY MAN	Cub
April	1960	GOOD TIMIN'	Cub
July	1960	THAT'S WHEN I CRIED	Cub
March	1961	I TOLD YOU SO	Cub

JOE JONES

Born: August 12, 1926
Hometown: New Orleans, Louisiana

Joe was a bandleader for fifteen years. He recorded songs like "You Done Me Wrong" for Herald records and "A Tisket A Tasket" for Roulette in the fifties.

JIMMY JONES

In September 1960, he had his only major hit, a song he had written called "You Talk Too Much," on Ric records, which was then sold to Roulette.

| September 1960 | YOU TALK TOO MUCH | Roulette |
| March 1961 | CALIFORNIA SUN | Roulette |

DON JULIAN & THE MEADOWLARKS

Members:
        Don Julian—lead
        Ronald Barrett
        Glenn Reagan
        Earl Jones
Hometown: Los Angeles, California

Don and his group's soft ballad sound gained moderate acceptance in the Los Angeles area in the mid-fifties. Dootsie Williams, the president of Dootone records, had recently lost his group the Penguins ("Earth Angel") to Mercury records. He signed the group, and their one major hit with the label was "Heaven and Paradise" in 1955.

| June 1955 | HEAVEN AND PARADISE | Dootone |

BILL JUSTIS

Born: October 14, 1926
Hometown: Birmingham, Alabama

Bill was a studio musician and staff producer for Sun records in Memphis in the mid-fifties. In October 1967, he wrote and recorded a song called "Raunchy." It became a national hit just a few weeks after it was released. Bill played alto sax on the session and his co-writer, Sid Manker, played guitar. The title "Raunchy" became a teenage expression for "sloppy" at the time.

| October 1957 | RAUNCHY | Phillips |
| February 1958 | COLLEGE MAN | Phillips |

BERT KAEMPFERT

Hometown: Hamburg, Germany

The well-known European composer, conductor, and arranger made his musical debut with Hans Busch's orchestra in Danzig. After World War II, he formed his own band. In November 1960, Bert had a number one song in the United States on Decca records when his band recorded "Wonderland By Night."

November	1960	WONDERLAND BY NIGHT	Decca
January	1961	CERVEZA	Decca
March	1961	TENDERLY	Decca
July	1961	NOW AND FOREVER	Decca
January	1962	AFRIKAAN BEAT	Decca
May	1962	THAT HAPPY FEELING	Decca
January	1965	RED ROSES FOR A BLUE LADY	Decca
April	1965	THREE O'CLOCK IN THE MORNING	Decca
June	1965	MOON OVER NAPLES	Decca
January	1965	BYE BYE BLUES	Decca

THE KALIN TWINS

Members:
Herbie Kalin—born: February 16, 1939
Harold Kalin—born: February 16, 1939

The twin brothers got their big break when songwriter Clint Ballard, Jr., heard a demo record of theirs and took it to Decca records. This led to a recording contract in 1958.

In May of that year they recorded "When" written by Paul Evans (who had recorded "Seven Little Girls Sitting in the Back Seat" and "Happy-Go-Lucky Me.") It became their biggest hit.

May	1958	WHEN	Decca
October	1958	FORGET ME NOT	Decca
January	1959	IT'S ONLY THE BEGINNING	Decca
July	1959	SWEET SUGAR LIPS	Decca

KITTY KALLEN

Born: May 25, 1923

Hometown: South Philadelphia, Pennsylvania

Kitty was a band singer with Jack Teagarden, Jimmy Dorsey, and Harry James. In the early fifties she signed with Decca records. In March 1954, she had a number one song with "Little Things Mean a Lot."

She retired in 1957 and lived quietly in Englewood, New Jersey, with her husband, TV producer Budd Granoff. In 1959, she had a change of heart and signed with Columbia records. She had a hit in October of that year with "If I Give My Heart to You."

Kitty retired from show business in 1967.

March	1954	LITTLE THINGS MEAN A LOT	Decca
July	1954	IN THE CHAPEL IN THE MOONLIGHT	Decca
November	1954	I WANT YOU ALL TO MYSELF	Decca
December	1955	GO ON WITH THE WEDDING	Decca
September	1959	IF I GIVE MY HEART TO YOU	Columbia
February	1960	THAT OLD FEELING	Columbia
December	1962	MY COLORING BOOK	RCA

KITTY KALLEN

BOB KAYLI

Real Name: Robert Gordy
Hometown: Detroit, Michigan

The brother of Berry Gordy, Jr., the founder of Motown records, Bob recorded under the name of Bob Kayli in late 1958 on Carlton and had one hit record called "Everyone Was There." The song was about a beach party in which many of the popular song figures like Jennie Lee, Patricia and Peggy Sue were having a ball.

Today Bob is the head of Motown's music publishing firm, Jobete Music (named after Berry's three daughters Joann, Betty, and Terry). He also appeared in the movie *Lady Sings the Blues* in which he played the dope hustler.

November 1958	EVERYONE WAS THERE	Carlton

ERNIE K-DOE

Real Name: Ernest Kador, Jr.
Hometown: New Orleans, Louisiana

Ernie was the ninth of eleven children born to the Reverend Ernest Kador, Sr., a Baptist minister. At age seven, he began singing in his father's choir. At age fifteen, he entered and won a local talent show. A year later he began his professional career in night clubs. During this time he finished high school, where he starred in football, basketball, and track. After graduation he began traveling around the country and singing at various supper clubs. It was during this time he began to record some of the songs he had written.

In 1961, he signed with Minit records and recorded a song called "Mother-In-Law," which became a number one song in April of that year.

April	1961	MOTHER-IN-LAW	Minit
June	1961	TE-TA-TE-TA-TA	Minit
November	1961	I CRIED MY LAST TEAR	Minit

JERRY KELLER

Born: June 20, 1937
Hometown: Fort Smith, Arkansas

Jerry's family moved to Tulsa, Oklahoma, when he was seven and he lived there until 1956. At age thirteen, he became a member of a religious chorale group, "The Tulsa Boy Singers." In high school he organized a quartet, the Lads of Note. The group had a daily fifteen-minute TV show on a Tulsa station.

In 1959 Jerry went to New York and appeared on the Ted Steele and Joe Franklin shows. This eventually led to a recording contract with Kapp records. In June 1959, Jerry recorded a song that he wrote called "Here Comes Summer," which became his only hit for the label.

June	1959	HERE COMES SUMMER	Kapp

MONTY KELLY

Born: 1919
Hometown: Oakland, California

As a youngster Monty began playing the piano, but soon switched to the trumpet. By the time he was seventeen, he had toured Australia playing his trumpet.

In 1941, he was hired as trumpet player for Paul Whiteman, with whom he remained until he entered the service. In the Army he met bandleader Skinnay Ennis and the two of them became close friends. After his discharge, Monte joined Skinnay's band on Bob Hope's radio show.

After this Monte headed for New York, where he wrote arrangements for a new star named Al Martino. In early 1960, he had a top-forty hit with the instrumental "Summer Set" on the Carlton label.

February	1960	SUMMER SET	Carlton

CHRIS KENNER

Died: January 25, 1976, of a heart attack

Chris was a popular songwriter who worked out of New Orleans in the fifties. In New Orleans Chris met Joe Banashak of Instant records. Joe liked Chris's style and asked him to record for his label.

In early 1961, Chris recorded a song he wrote called "I Like It Like That," which became a national smash. Two years later he had another chart record with "Land of 1,000 Dances," which he also wrote. The song was only mildly popular for him but it was a big seller for both Cannibal & The Headhunters and Wilson Pickett later on in the sixties.

May	1961	I LIKE IT LIKE THAT	Instant
June	1963	LAND OF 1,000 DANCES	Instant

ADRIAN KIMBERLY

Most high school and college graduates are familiar with the processional called "Pomp and Circumstance." Adrian Kimberly gave it a new arrangement in June 1961, and it became a national hit. Many stations continue to play the song regularly at graduation time each year.

June   1961   POMP AND CIRCUMSTANCE   Calliope

B. B. KING

Real Name: Riley B. King
Born: 1925
Hometown: Indianola, Mississippi

B.B. King, the world's greatest blues singer had—like a lot of soul people —some hard times. He lived with his mother (his parents were separated) until he was nine. When his mother died, he lived alone, taking care of himself by doing farm chores for the people who had employed his mother.

B. B. KING

B. B. began his recording career in 1949 with a company called Bullet, but that was after he had perfected the unique style that has since become justifiably famous. His style didn't just happen either; there was a reason for it. "My coordination wasn't very good," he says, "So trying to sing and play at the same time didn't get to me. ... When I'm entertaining, while I'm trying to get my breath, or think of a new line to tell you, then the guitar takes over. ..."

It was only recently that B.B.—maybe it all began to happen in 1968—became a star outside the R & B audience circuit. "I was working for eighteen years, and I had two articles done about me, one in *Ebony* and one in *Jet*. Then it changed, and I still don't believe it ... it may take me twenty years to believe it."

It was the kids, the young rock players who had learned the most from B.B., who brought him to the attention of the white audiences. For most of their 1969 tour, The Rolling Stones insisted on having B.B. King with them. And it was in that same year that B.B. was finally rated among the top R & B singles artists by *Billboard*.

December	1951	3 O'CLOCK BLUES	RPM
September	1952	YOU KNOW I LOVE YOU	RPM
December	1952	STORY FROM MY HEART AND SOUL	RPM
March	1953	WOKE UP THIS MORNING	RPM
June	1953	PLEASE LOVE ME	RPM
October	1953	PLEASE HURRY HOME	RPM
October	1954	YOU UPSET ME BABY	RPM
November	1954	WHOLE LOTTA' LOVE	RPM
January	1955	EVERY DAY I HAVE THE BLUES	RPM
January	1955	SNEAKIN' AROUND	RPM
September	1955	TEN LONG YEARS	RPM
January	1956	CRYING WON'T HELP YOU	RPM
August	1956	BAD LUCK/SWEET LITTLE ANGEL	RPM
November	1956	ON MY WORD OF HONOR	RPM
May	1957	TROUBLES, TROUBLES TROUBLES/ I WANT TO GET MARRIED	RPM
November	1958	YOU'VE BEEN AN ANGEL	Kent
November	1958	PLEASE ACCEPT MY LOVE	Kent
January	1960	SWEET SIXTEEN	Kent
June	1960	GOT A RIGHT TO LOVE MY BABY	Kent
July	1960	PARTIN' TIME	Kent
October	1960	WALKING DR. BILL	Kent
June	1961	SOMEDAY	Kent
June	1961	PEACE OF MIND	Kent
February	1962	MY SOMETIMES BABY	Kent
May	1962	GONNA MISS YOU AROUND HERE	Kent
June	1965	BLUE SHADOWS	Kent
February	1966	EYESIGHT TO THE BLIND	Kent
September	1966	I STAY IN THE MOOD	Kent
January	1967	IT'S A MEAN WORLD	Kent
March	1967	THE JUNGLE	Kent
August	1968	THE WOMAN I LOVE	Kent

October	1966	DON'T ANSWER THE DOOR	ABC
April	1968	PAYING THE COST TO BE THE BOSS	Bluesway
August	1968	I'M GONNA DO WHAT THEY DO TO ME	Bluesway
October	1968	YOU PUT IT ON ME	Bluesway
May	1969	WHY I SING THE BLUES	Bluesway
August	1969	I WANT YOU SO BAD	Bluesway
August	1969	GET OFF MY BACK WOMAN	Bluesway
November	1969	JUST A LITTLE LOVE	Bluesway
January	1970	THE THRILL IS GONE	Bluesway
April	1970	SO EXCITED	Bluesway
August	1970	HUMMINGBIRD	ABC
November	1970	CHAINS AND THINGS	ABC
February	1971	ASK ME NO QUESTIONS	ABC
August	1970	WORRIED LIFE	Kent
March	1971	THAT EVIL CHILD	Kent
June	1971	HELP THE POOR	ABC
September	1971	GHETTO WOMAN	ABC
November	1971	AIN'T NOBODY HOME	ABC
May	1972	I GOT SOME HELP I DON'T NEED	ABC
August	1972	GUESS WHO	ABC
August	1973	TO KNOW YOU IS TO LOVE YOU	ABC
December	1973	I LIKE TO LIVE THE LOVE	ABC
June	1974	WHO ARE YOU	ABC
November	1974	PHILADELPHIA	ABC

BEN E. KING

Real Name: Benjamin Nelson
Born: September 28, 1938
Hometown: Henderson, North Carolina

Ben began his singing career while working in his father's luncheonette in New York City. He sang with a group called the Crowns, which in 1959 became the nucleus for the Drifters. While with the Drifters, Ben sang lead on such songs as "There Goes My Baby," "Dance With Me," "This Magic Moment," "Lonely Winds," and the Drifters' only number one record, "Save The Last Dance For Me."

He left the Drifters in May 1960 to go out as a single. In January 1961, he had his first major hit with a Jerry Leiber–Phil Spector song called "Spanish Harlem." In May of the same year, he had a hit with a song he wrote along with Jerry Leiber and Mike Stoller called "Stand By Me."

Today Ben lives with his family in Teaneck, New Jersey, and entertains as a solo performer around the New York area.

January	1961	SPANISH HARLEM	Atco
May	1961	STAND BY ME	Atco
July	1961	AMOR	Atco
October	1961	YOUNG BOY BLUES	Atco
February	1962	ECSTASY	Atco
April	1962	DON'T PLAY THAT SONG	Atco

BEN E. KING

August	1962	TOO BAD	Atco
March	1963	HOW CAN I FORGET	Atco
June	1963	I (WHO HAVE NOTHING)	Atco
October	1963	I COULD HAVE DANCED ALL NIGHT	Atco
March	1964	THAT'S WHEN IT HURTS	Atco
September	1964	IT'S ALL OVER	Atco
December	1964	SEVEN LETTERS	Atco
April	1965	THE RECORD	Atco
January	1966	GOODNIGHT MY LOVE	Acto
May	1966	SO MUCH LOVE	Atco
April	1967	TEARS, TEARS, TEARS	Atco
February	1975	SUPERNATURAL THING PART 1	Atlantic
June	1975	DO IT IN THE NAME OF LOVE	Atlantic

CAROLE KING

Real Name: Carole Klein
Born: February 9, 1941
Hometown: Brooklyn, New York

Carole began singing at age four. At fourteen she formed a vocal group called the Cosines. Her professional career started at seventeen, when she met Don Kirshner and Al Nevins, who signed her as a writer. At the same time she married a young lyric-writer and record-producer named Gerry Goffin. Together they wrote hits like "Will You Still Love Me Tomorrow," "Take Good Care of My Baby," "Her Royal Majesty," "Loco-Motion," and dozens of others. In August 1962, she began a recording career on Dimension records with the song "It Might As Well Rain until September."

Carole was also the inspiration for Neil Sedaka's hit "Oh! Carol" in October 1959, since she was a close friend of Neil's and they grew up in the same neighborhood.

Carole has become, over the years, one of the most successful hit-songwriters and performers of all time. Her LP *Tapestry* in 1971 was one of the most popular albums ever recorded.

August	1962	IT MIGHT AS WELL RAIN UNTIL SEPTEMBER	Dimension
April	1963	HE'S A BAD BOY	Dimension
May	1971	IT'S TOO LATE	Ode
June	1971	I FEEL THE EARTH MOVE	Ode
August	1971	SO FAR AWAY	Ode
September	1971	SMACKWATER JACK	Ode
January	1972	SWEET SEASONS	Ode
November	1972	BEEN TO CANAAN	Ode
July	1973	YOU LIGHT UP MY LIFE	Ode
October	1973	CORAZON	Ode
August	1974	JAZZMAN	Ode
January	1975	NIGHTINGALE	Ode
February	1976	ONLY LOVE IS REAL	Ode
May	1976	HIGH OUT OF TIME	Ode
July	1977	HARD ROCK CAFE	Capitol
May	1980	ONE FINE DAY	Capitol

CAROLE KING

CLAUDE KING

CLAUDE KING

Born: February 5, 1933
Hometown: Shreveport, Louisiana

Claude bought his first guitar from a farmer when he was twelve for fifty cents. Later he attended the University of Idaho and went to business college in Shreveport.

In 1961, he signed with Columbia records and recorded "Big River, Big Man." In May 1962, he recorded a song that he had written along with Merle Kilgore called "Wolverton Mountain," which became his biggest hit.

July	1961	BIG RIVER, BIG MAN	Columbia
October	1961	THE COMANCHEROS	Columbia
May	1962	WOLVERTON MOUNTAIN	Columbia
September	1962	THE BURNING OF ATLANTA	Columbia

FREDDY KING

Born: September 3, 1934, Gilmer, Texas
Died: December 28, 1976, of ulcers, Dallas, Texas

Guitarist Freddy King developed his swinging blues style of playing while recording for the Cincinnati-based Federal records. His biggest hit, in the spring of 1961, was the instrumental "Hide Away."

January	1961	YOU'VE GOT TO LOVE HER WITH A FEELING	Federal
March	1961	HIDE AWAY	Federal
May	1961	LONESOME WHISTLE BLUES	Federal
August	1961	SAN-HO-ZAY	Federal

THE KINGSMEN

See entry for Bill Haley & The Comets.

In 1958, Bill Haley's Comets, minus Bill Haley, recorded a song they wrote called "Week End." They took the song to their label, Decca, which

FREDDY KING

turned it down. Decca told the group, however, that if they could make a deal to release the song on another label (providing they did not use the name The Comets) Decca would have no objection. So the group walked across the street to Atlantic records and made a deal for the song to be released on Atlantic's subsidiary East-West in the summer of 1958. The song was released for the Comets under the name of The Kingsmen, and the group had two hits on the national charts at the same time, "Week End" as the Kingsmen and "Lean Jean" as Bill Haley & The Comets.

August   1958   WEEK END   East-West

THE KINGSMEN

Members:
  Lynn Easton
  Gary Abbott
  Don Gallucci
  Mike Mitchell
  Norm Sundholm
Hometown: Portland, Oregon

Lynn first organized the group when he entered Portland's David Douglas High School. From 1957 until 1963, they worked fairs, fashion shows, and local dances. In late 1962, they became the house band for Portland's teen-age night spot, The Chase.

One of their evening performances, in 1963, was recorded at the club by producer Jerry Dennon. He made the show into an album and sold it to Wand records. In November of 1963, one of the cuts from the album was released as a single. The result was their first hit, "Louie Louie." Another cut from the album, "Money," was a hit in early 1964.

November	1963	LOUIE LOUIE	Wand
February	1964	MONEY	Wand
July	1964	LITTLE LATIN LUPE LU	Wand
September	1964	DEATH OF AN ANGEL	Wand
January	1965	THE JOLLY GREEN GIANT	Wand
May	1965	THE CLIMB	Wand
August	1965	ANNIE FANNY	Wand
April	1966	KILLER JOE	Wand

THE KINGSTON TRIO

Members:

Bob Shane—born: February 1, 1934—Hawaii

Nick Reynolds—born: July 27, 1933—Coronado, California

Dave Guard—born: October 19, 1934—San Francisco, California—replaced by John Stewart in May 1961.

The group was first formed in the spring of 1957. At the time Dave, a graduate student at Stanford, joined forces with Menlo College pals Bob and Nick. They played in coffeehouses and basement clubs around San Francisco. While performing at the Cracker Pat in Palo Alto, publicist Frank Werber heard them and signed them on the spot to a contract written on a table napkin.

They polished their act for a month and then began trekking across the country becoming more popular as they traveled. Their first release, "Scarlet Ribbons," for Capitol was in April 1958. In October 1958, they recorded "Tom Dooley," which became the group's only number one recording.

In 1961, Dave Guard left the group and was replaced by John Stewart, who at one time sang with The Cumberland Three. John had a solo hit in 1979 with "Gold," for RSO Records. Bob Shane, with two new members, still performs as The Kingston Trio.

October	1958	TOM DOOLEY	Capitol
January	1959	RASPBERRIES, STRAWBERRIES	Capitol
March	1959	THE TIJUANA JAIL	Capitol
June	1959	M.T.A.	Capitol
September	1959	A WORRIED MAN	Capitol
February	1960	EL MATADOR	Capitol
June	1960	BAD MAN BLUNDER	Capitol
October	1960	EVERGLADES	Capitol

THE KINGSTON TRIO

Clockwise from top:
John Stewart, Bob Shane,
Nick Reynolds

January	1962	WHERE HAVE ALL THE FLOWERS GONE	Capitol
April	1962	SCOTCH AND SODA	Capitol
October	1962	ONE MORE TOWN	Capitol
January	1963	GREENBACK DOLLAR	Capitol
March	1963	REVEREND MR. BLACK	Capitol
August	1963	DESERT PETE	Capitol
November	1963	ALLY, ALLY OXEN FREE	Capitol

THE KIRBY STONE FOUR

Members:
   Kirby Stone
   Eddie Hall
   Larry Foster
   Michael Gardner
Hometown: New York, New York

The fellows got together in the mid-fifties. They began playing a lot of smaller clubs in the New York area and guesting a number of local TV

THE KIRBY STONE FOUR

shows. Their big break came in 1958 when they appeared on "The Ed Sullivan Show." This appearance ultimately led to a recording contract with Columbia records.

In May 1958, they recorded "Baubles, Bangles and Beads" from the Broadway show *Kismet*. Their swinging version of the song became a top-forty hit that summer.

July	1958	BAUBLES, BANGLES AND BEADS	Columbia

EARTHA KITT

Born: January 26, 1928
Hometown: Columbia, South Carolina

When Eartha was seven her family moved from South Carolina to Brooklyn. Eartha, who highlighted many local entertainment bills as a child, left school at fifteen and worked as a sewing machine operator. A friend introduced her to famed dancer Katherine Dunham, who added Eartha to her troupe. Eartha toured Europe, Mexico, and Scandinavia; a year later she was headlining many of the top clubs in Europe with her spirited dancing and singing. She appeared as Helen of Troy in Orson Welles's production of *Faust*.

Returning to the United States after making three successful French films, Eartha was booked into several New York night spots, including La Vie en Rose and the Village Vanguard. She was held over twelve weeks. In her West Coast debut at Mocambo she broke all that club's attendance records.

Eartha's biggest hit was her sultry recording of "Santa Baby" on RCA in 1953.

June	1953	C'EST SI BON	RCA Victor
November	1953	SANTA BABY	RCA Victor
February	1959	SOMEBODY BAD STOLE DE WEDDING BELL	RCA Victor

GLADYS KNIGHT AND THE PIPS

Members:
  Gladys Knight—lead—May 28, 1944
  Merald Knight—her older brother—September 4, 1942
  William Guest—her cousin—June 2, 1941
  Edward Patten—her cousin—August 2, 1939
Hometown: Atlanta, Georgia

They began singing together around 1952, at a family party. It was at this time that they decided to pursue a professional career. Another cousin, James Woods, began to manage the group and get them engagements around Atlanta. They needed a group name and decided to call themselves the Pips, which was James's nickname.

In early 1961, the group recorded "Every Beat of My Heart" in Atlanta, for Huntom records. The record began to get air play in Atlanta and started to create some excitement. Marshall Sehorn scouted in Atlanta for Fury and told a disc jockey in Atlanta to send a record to Bobby Robinson in New York, the owner of Fury records. Bobby liked the song immediately and had the group fly to New York, where they rerecorded the song exactly like the original and did it in two takes. The song was released in April 1961, with the group simply known as Gladys Knight and The Pips. It became their first major hit for Fury records.

At the same time, Vee Jay records released the same song by the Pips because the fellow in Atlanta who owned Huntom records pressed the record without signing the group. Consequently, he had the record, but did not have the act. Nevertheless, he sold the record to Vee Jay and they released it. Fury records then sued Vee Jay and Vee Jay had to give up their rights to the group.

GLADYS KNIGHT AND THE PIPS

Left to right: William Guest, Merald Knight,
Edward Patten, Gladys Knight

After Fury went out of business, the group had to survive in New York on their own for a while, since Gladys was pregnant and had returned to Atlanta with her husband. About a year later, Gladys returned to New York, and they began to practice some more.

In 1966 they signed with Soul records, a division of Motown records. In October 1967 they recorded their first gold record with "I Heard It through the Grapevine." The group remained with Soul records until 1973, whereupon they switched to Buddah records.

They have become one of the few groups to have hit records on three separate labels. It is also one of the most successful and lasting family acts in the business.

May	1961	EVERY BEAT OF MY HEART	Fury
November	1961	LETTER FULL OF TEARS	Fury
April	1962	OPERATOR	Fury
May	1964	GIVING UP	Maxx
August	1964	LOVERS ALWAYS FORGIVE	Maxx
April	1967	TAKE ME IN YOUR ARMS AND LOVE ME	Soul
July	1967	EVERYBODY NEEDS LOVE	Soul
October	1967	I HEARD IT THROUGH THE GRAPEVINE	Soul
February	1968	THE END OF OUR ROAD	Soul
May	1968	IT SHOULD HAVE BEEN ME	Soul
August	1968	I WISH IT WOULD RAIN	Soul
February	1969	DIDN'T YOU KNOW	Soul
July	1969	THE NITTY GRITTY	Soul
October	1969	FRIENDSHIP TRAIN	Soul
March	1970	YOU NEED LOVE LIKE I DO (DON'T YOU)	Soul
November	1970	IF I WERE YOUR WOMAN	Soul
June	1971	I DON'T WANT TO DO WRONG	Soul
December	1971	MAKE ME THE WOMAN THAT YOU GO HOME TO	Soul

March	1972	HELP ME MAKE IT THROUGH THE NIGHT	Soul
January	1973	NEITHER ONE OF US	Soul
April	1973	DADDY COULD SWEAR I DECLARE	Motown
June	1973	WHERE PEACEFUL WATERS FLOW	Buddah
August	1973	ALL I NEED IS TIME	Soul
September	1973	MIDNIGHT TRAIN TO GEORGIA	Buddah
November	1973	I'VE GOT TO USE MY IMAGINATION	Buddah
February	1974	BEST THING THAT EVER HAPPENED TO ME	Buddah
April	1974	ON AND ON	Buddah
June	1974	BETWEEN HER GOODBYE AND MY HELLO	Soul
October	1974	I FEEL A SONG IN MY HEART	Buddah
February	1975	LOVE FINDS ITS OWN WAY	Buddah
April	1975	TRY TO REMEMBER / THE WAY WE WERE	Buddah
August	1975	MONEY	Buddah
November	1975	PART TIME LOVE	Buddah
October	1976	SO SAD THE SONG	Buddah
June	1977	BABY DON'T CHANGE YOUR MIND	Buddah
June	1980	LANDLORD	Columbia

SONNY KNIGHT

Sonny began singing around the Los Angeles area in the mid-fifties and was discovered by Hite Morgan, who became his manager. In 1956, Hite's wife, Dorinda, wrote a song for Sonny called "Confidential." Sonny recorded it along with a song called "Jailbird." The songs were sold to Vita records in Los Angeles, and "Jailbird" was chosen as the "A" side.

Hite took the record to Art Laboe of station KPOP (KGBS today) and Art began playing it. Requests were more numerous for the flip side, "Confidential." Dot records then purchased the song from Vita and released it in the fall of 1956. The song became a big, big hit.

Today, Sonny performs regularly in Hawaii.

October	1956	CONFIDENTIAL	Dot

THE KNOCKOUTS

Members:

> Bob D'Andrea—lead—hometown: North Bergen, New Jersey
> Eddie Parente—guitar—hometown: North Bergen, New Jersey
> Harry Venuta—drums—hometown: Bayonne, New Jersey
> Bob Collada—piano—hometown: Bayonne, New Jersey

The group played at local clubs in Lyndhurst, New Jersey, in the late fifties. In January 1960, they released "Darling Lorraine," which became the group's only major hit.

January	1960	DARLING LORRAINE	Shad

BUDDY KNOX

BUDDY KNOX

Born: April 14, 1933
Hometown: Happy, Texas

In 1954, Buddy's family moved to Canyon, Texas, where Buddy enrolled at West Texas State College. There he met bass guitarist Jimmy Bowen, guitarist Don Lanier, and drummer Dave Alldred, all members of the college glee club called the Serenaders. The four of them formed a group called the Rhythm Orchids.

After graduation, a song that Buddy had written along with Jimmy Bowen came to the attention of music publisher Phil Kahl. The boys flew to New York, and recorded the song for Roulette records. "Party Doll" was released in February 1957 and became an instant smash.

Group member Jimmy Bowen recorded his "I'm Stickin' with You" at the same time. It was also released on Roulette and became a hit.

Today Buddy works as a staff producer for Jimmy Bowen's Amos Productions in Los Angeles. He also owns a string of night clubs in Canada.

| February | 1957 | PARTY DOLL | Roulette |
| May | 1957 | ROCK YOUR LITTLE BABY TO SLEEP | Roulette |

August	1957	HULA LOVE	Roulette
January	1958	SWINGIN' DADDY	Roulette
July	1958	SOMEBODY TOUCHED ME	Roulette
January	1959	TEASABLE PLEASABLE YOU	Roulette
April	1959	I THINK I'M GONNA KILL MYSELF	Roulette
December	1960	LOVEY DOVEY	Liberty
February	1961	LING-TING-TONG	Liberty

THE MOE KOFFMAN QUARTETTE

Members:

Moe Koffman—flute—born: December 28, 1948—Toronto, Canada
Ed Bickert—guitar
Hugh Currie—bass
Ron Rully—drums

Moe Koffman, one of Canada's leading flute players, recorded a couple of moderately popular jazz-inspired cuts in 1958. His biggest was "The Swingin' Shepherd Blues."

| January | 1958 | THE SWINGIN' SHEPHERD BLUES | Jubilee |
| June | 1958 | LITTLE PIXIE | Jubilee |

KOKOMO

In early 1961, Kokomo raced up the charts with a jumping piano-oriented instrumental called "Asia Minor." It was his only hit for Felsted records.

| February | 1961 | ASIA MINOR | Felsted |

THE KUF-LINX

In early 1958, both the Kuf-Linx on Challenge records and the Casuals on Back Beat records recorded versions of the song "So Tough." The Casuals wound up with the more popular version. The title "So Tough" was a teen expression at the time, describing something as being great or the best. The song described how "tough" a certain girl was, and that's why this guy loved her.

| February | 1958 | SO TOUGH | Challenge |

L

FRANKIE LAINE

PATTI LaBELLE & THE BLUE BELLES

Members:
    Patti LaBelle—Philadelphia, Pennsylvania
    Sarah Dash—Philadelphia, Pennsylvania
    Cindy Birdsong—Trenton, New Jersey
    Nona Hendryx—Trenton, New Jersey

The girls first recorded for Newtown as the Blue Belles with "I Sold My Heart to the Junkman" in the spring of 1962. On this song Sarah sang lead. After some minor hits they changed their name to Patti LaBelle & The Blue Belles and recorded "Down the Aisle" for Newtown in the fall of 1963, a top-forty record on which Patti sang lead. Shortly after that, they switched over to Philadelphia-based Parkway records and in early 1964 they had another top-forty record with "You'll Never Walk Alone."

Cindy Birdsong became a member of the Supremes in the late sixties.

In 1975, Sarah, Cindy and Nona were simply known as LaBelle, having several hits for Epic records. Today, they are all pursuing individual careers. (See also *Rock On: The Modern Years*.)

September	1963	DOWN THE AISLE	Newtown
January	1964	YOU'LL NEVER WALK ALONE	Parkway
December	1964	DANNY BOY	Parkway
November	1965	ALL OR NOTHING	Atlantic
December	1966	TAKE ME FOR A LITTLE WHILE	Atlantic

THE LAFAYETTES

The group was formed in 1962 and began working many New York area clubs until they attained the sound they were looking for. Although they were all white, they were able to attain the black-oriented sound of the fifties rock singers.

In the summer of 1962, on RCA, they had their only national chart record with "Life's Too Short."

July	1962	LIFE'S TOO SHORT	RCA

FRANKIE LAINE

Real Name: Frank LoVecchio
Born: March 30, 1913
Hometown: Chicago, Illinois

Frankie became interested in singing while he was a youngster in Chicago. In the early forties he went to Cleveland, Ohio, to pursue his career, but did not have too much luck. He went on to Los Angeles, where he got a few jobs singing at small clubs. While he was at one of these clubs he was spotted by songwriter Hoagy Carmichael. Hoagy liked Frankie's big booming voice and felt that he had great potential, so he got him a job at a larger club. After a while Frankie came to the attention of Mercury records and signed a recording contract with them in 1946. Later that year he recorded "That's My Desire." The song was released by Mercury in June 1947 and went on to become Frankie's first big hit for the label.

He stayed with Mercury until 1951, when Mitch Miller lured him over to Columbia records, where he premiered with "Jezebel" in April 1951.

During the late forties and early fifties, Frankie was one of the most popular male vocalists in the country, with a voice that was powerful enough to fill an auditorium without the use of a microphone.

Today Frankie lives on the West Coast and travels around the country singing on TV shows and concerts.

June	1947	THAT'S MY DESIRE	Mercury
February	1948	SHINE	Mercury
August	1948	AH BUT IT HAPPENS	Mercury
December	1948	YOU'RE ALL I WANT FOR CHRISTMAS	Mercury
August	1949	THAT LUCKY OLD SUN	Mercury
September	1949	NOW THAT I NEED YOU	Mercury
October	1949	MULE TRAIN	Mercury
January	1950	THE CRY OF THE WILD GOOSE	Mercury
March	1950	SWAMP GIRL	Mercury
May	1950	STARS AND STRIPES FOREVER	Mercury

August	1950	MUSIC, MAESTRO, PLEASE	Mercury
March	1951	METRO POLKA	Mercury
April	1951	JEZEBEL	Columbia
May	1951	ROSE, ROSE, I LOVE YOU	Columbia
August	1951	THE GIRL IN THE WOOD	Columbia
November	1951	JEALOUSY (JALOUSIE)	Columbia
March	1952	THE GANDY DANCERS' BALL	Columbia
July	1952	HIGH NOON	Columbia
September	1952	THE MERMAID	Columbia
February	1953	I BELIEVE	Columbia
March	1953	TELL ME A STORY (Jimmy Boyd)	Columbia
August	1953	HEY JOE!	Columbia
June	1954	SOME DAY	Columbia
October	1954	RAIN, RAIN, RAIN (Four Lads)	Columbia
July	1955	A WOMAN IN LOVE	Columbia
June	1956	DON'T CRY	Columbia
November	1956	MOONLIGHT GAMBLER	Columbia
March	1957	LOVE IS A GOLDEN RING	Columbia
April	1963	DON'T MAKE MY BABY BLUE	Columbia
January	1967	I'LL TAKE CARE OF YOUR CARES	ABC
March	1967	MAKING MEMORIES	ABC
June	1967	YOU WANTED SOMEONE TO PLAY WITH	ABC
August	1967	LAURA, WHAT'S HE GOT THAT I AIN'T GOT	ABC
October	1967	YOU, NO ONE BUT YOU	ABC
January	1968	TO EACH HIS OWN	ABC
February	1969	YOU GAVE ME A MOUNTAIN	ABC
June	1969	DAMMIT ISN'T GOD'S NAME	ABC

MAJOR LANCE

Born: 1941
Hometown: Chicago, Illinois

Major Lance turned from a career as a boxer to one as a performer. He later turned to singing, joining a gospel group called the Five Harmonaires. After the group broke up in 1959, he met disc jockey Jim Lounsbury, who took him to Mercury records. He recorded songs like "I Got a Girl" and "Delilah."

In 1963, Major Lance signed with Okeh records and in the summer of that year recorded a song written by Curtis Mayfield of the Impressions called "The Monkey Time," which became his first hit.

June	1963	THE MONKEY TIME	Okeh
October	1963	HEY LITTLE GIRL	Okeh
January	1964	UM, UM, UM, UM, UM, UM	Okeh
March	1964	THE MATADOR	Okeh
June	1964	IT AIN'T NO USE	Okeh
June	1964	GIRLS	Okeh
August	1964	RHYTHM	Okeh
November	1964	SOMETIMES I WONDER	Okeh
February	1965	COME SEE	Okeh
June	1965	AIN'T IT A SHAME	Okeh
August	1965	TOO HOT TO HOLD	Okeh
August	1970	STAY AWAY FROM ME (I LOVE YOU TOO MUCH)	Curtom

MAJOR LANCE

SNOOKY LANSON

Snooky's two hits were "The Old Master Painter" in 1949 for London records and "It's Almost Tomorrow" for the Dot label in 1955.

Snooky, one-time star of the popular TV show "Your Hit Parade" along with Russell Arms, Dorothy Collins, and Gisele MacKenzie in the early fifties, today sells automobiles in Nashville, Tennessee.

December	1949	THE OLD MASTER PAINTER	London
July	1955	IT'S ALMOST TOMORROW	Dot

MARIO LANZA

Real Name: Alfred Arnold Cocozza
Born: January 31, 1921
Died: October 7, 1959
Hometown: Philadelphia, Pennsylvania

Lanza started singing as a teen-ager while in his high school choir. In 1942 Serge Koussevitzky, of the Boston Symphony Orchestra, heard Mario sing and suggested he pursue a professional career. Later that same year Mario went into the military where he remained until 1945. It was during 1945 that he married Betty Hicks (the sister of his former sergeant) and returned to Philadelphia. Mario was called Freddy by his friends, but decided to change his professional name from Alfred Cocozza to a masculinized version of his mother's maiden name: Mario Lanza.

In 1947, he toured the United States with Frances Yeend and George London as the Bel Canto Trio, then in 1948 made his operatic debut in New Orleans in *Madama Butterfly*.

A few years earlier, in 1945, RCA Victor had signed him to a ten-year recording contract.

In 1949, he made his motion picture debut for M-G-M with the film *That Midnight Kiss* and one year later was a success in the film *The Toast of New Orleans*, in which the song "Be My Love" was featured. The song became a number one national hit in early 1951 and was able to introduce operatic singing to millions and make it popular to the masses.

In 1951, he reached his greatest personal triumph when he portrayed his idol Enrico Caruso in the film *The Great Caruso*.

In 1957, he went to Rome to embark on a new career. It was while in this city, on October 7, 1959, that he died of a heart attack at the age of thirty-eight, at the Guila Clinic. Doctors felt it was due to the tremendous strain his heart had suffered over the years in Mario's bouts with rapid weight losses and gains.

November	1950	BE MY LOVE	RCA Victor
February	1951	VESTI LA GIUBBA	RCA Victor
April	1951	THE LOVELIEST NIGHT OF THE YEAR	RCA Victor
June	1951	BECAUSE	RCA Victor
August	1952	BECAUSE YOU'RE MINE	RCA Victor
August	1956	EARTHBOUND	RCA
May	1958	ARRIVEDERCI ROMA	RCA

THE LARKS

In the mid-fifties, Don Julian had a group called the Meadowlarks, which recorded for Dootone records in Los Angeles. Their biggest song called "Heaven and Paradise," was recorded in 1955.

In the early sixties he decided to form another group which he called simply the Larks, and he had them record several things for Sheryl records. In the fall of 1964, the Larks recorded a song Don had written called "The Jerk," which became a top-ten national hit.

July	1951	EYESIGHT TO THE BLIND	Apollo
September	1951	LITTLE SIDE CAR	Apollo
March	1961	IT'S UNBELIEVABLE	Sheryl
October	1964	THE JERK	Money

JULIUS LaROSA

Born: January 2, 1930
Hometown: Brooklyn, New York

JULIUS LA ROSA

Julius, a recording artist, was at one time a star on the Arthur Godfrey TV show until he was fired by Godfrey on the air on October 19, 1953.

In 1977, Julius left radio station WNEW in New York City to pursue singing once again. He is very active on local TV and in New York night clubs.

January	1953	ANYWHERE I WANDER	Cadence
August	1953	EH CUMPARI	Cadence
July	1955	DOMANI	Cadence
October	1955	SUDDENLY THERE'S A VALLEY	Cadence
January	1956	LIPSTICK & CANDY & RUBBER SOLE SHOES	RCA
June	1956	I'VE GOT LOVE	RCA
July	1956	GET ME TO THE CHURCH ON TIME	RCA
April	1957	MAMA GUITAR	RCA

ROD LAUREN

Born: March 26, 1940

In the late fifties, while Elvis was in the Army, RCA was looking for a young artist to rival the likes of Paul Anka, Rick Nelson, and Frankie Avalon. They put an exhaustive promotional campaign behind West Coast singer Rod Lauren. The result of all this hype was one moderately popular chart record in late 1959 called "If I Had a Girl." Not too much was heard from Rod after that.

December	1959	IF I HAD A GIRL	RCA

ANNIE LAURIE

In the late forties Annie recorded for Regal records, a subsidiary of Savoy records. After singing with the Paul Gayten band and recording for Okeh records, she signed with DeLuxe and had her biggest hit in early 1957 with "It Hurts to Be in Love."

February	1957	IT HURTS TO BE IN LOVE	De Luxe
July	1960	IF YOU'RE LONELY	De Luxe

EDDIE LAWRENCE

Eddie was a night club comedian who, in the mid-fifties, enjoyed temporary success as a recording artist when he recorded a comedy single called "The Old Philosopher" for Coral records. The recording featured one of his night club characters who tried to offer people advice when they were feeling low. This gimmick record made the national charts in the summer of 1956, and became Eddie's only hit.

Today Eddie is an artist and holds art shows in New York.

July	1956	THE OLD PHILOSOPHER	Coral

STEVE LAWRENCE

Real Name: Steven Leibowitz
Born: July 8, 1935
Hometown: Brooklyn, New York

Steve's big break was becoming a member of the "Tonight" show cast in 1954. He remained on the show four years and near the end of his tenure married fellow cast member and singer Eydie Gorme. He and Eydie starred in their own television show in 1959 and Steve had his own show in 1965. He made his stage debut in *What Makes Sammy Run* in 1964 and later starred with Eydie in *Golden Rainbow*.

Steve spent much of the fifties battling the great rock artists for space on the charts and then had to turn around and take on the Beatle-influenced music of the sixties and seventies. He's done quite well. He had a half dozen top-forty hits in both the fifties and the sixties. His biggest hit came in 1962 with the lushly romantic "Go Away Little Girl." It was a number one record.

Today, he and Eydie make frequent TV guest appearances and are very big in Las Vegas.

May	1952	POINCIANA	King
January	1957	THE BANANA BOAT SONG	Coral
February	1957	PARTY DOLL	Coral
May	1957	CAN'T WAIT FOR SUMMER	Coral

STEVE LAWRENCE

October	1957	FRAULEIN	Coral
February	1958	UH-HUH, OH YEAH	Coral
September	1958	MANY A TIME	Coral
May	1959	ONLY LOVE ME	ABC
November	1959	PRETTY BLUE EYES	ABC
February	1960	FOOTSTEPS	ABC
March	1961	PORTRAIT OF MY LOVE	United Artists
July	1961	MY CLAIRE DE LUNE	United Artists
August	1961	IN TIME	United Artists
October	1961	SOMEWHERE ALONG THE WAY	United Artists
November	1962	GO AWAY LITTLE GIRL	Columbia
February	1963	DON'T BE AFRAID LITTLE DARLIN'	Columbia
May	1963	POOR LITTLE RICH GIRL	Columbia
October	1963	WALKING PROUD	Columbia
May	1964	EVERYBODY KNOWS	Columbia
August	1964	YET . . . I KNOW	Columbia

BRENDA LEE

Real Name: Brenda Mae Tarpley
Born: December 11, 1944
Hometown: Atlanta, Georgia

Brenda started singing at age four. Two years later she won top honors in a local TV children's talent contest which got her a regular TV show in Atlanta.

When her family moved to Augusta, she performed on a local radio show there. One day while Red Foley was in Augusta, doing a country & western show, a local disc jockey took Brenda to meet him. Brenda appeared with Red and was a smash! She subsequently appeared on his network TV show called "Ozark Jubilee." A short time later, in 1956, she signed a long-term pact with Decca records.

BRENDA LEE

Shortly thereafter, she changed her last name from Tarpley to Lee by just keeping the last part of Tarpley, easier to pronounce and remember. She had her first hit for Decca in November 1956 with "One Step at a Time," which was followed by "Dynamite" some six months later. The song "Dynamite" was responsible for her nickname "Little Miss Dynamite," which characterized her big voice and explosive stage presence.

In September 1959, she had her first major hit with the Ronnie Self song "Sweet Nothin's." In May 1960, "I'm Sorry" became a national number one song. Her follow-up in the fall, "I Want to Be Wanted," also became a number one song.

Her biggest year was 1960, for not only did she record several number one hits, but she recorded a Christmas classic, "Rockin' Around the Christmas Tree," which was written by Johnny Marks, the same man who wrote "Rudolph the Red-Nosed Reindeer."

Today Brenda lives with her husband Ronnie and her children in Nashville.

February	1957	ONE STEP AT A TIME	Decca
July	1957	DYNAMITE	Decca
December	1959	SWEET NOTHIN'S	Decca
June	1960	I'M SORRY	Decca
June	1960	THAT'S ALL YOU GOTTA DO	Decca
September	1960	I WANT TO BE WANTED	Decca
October	1960	JUST A LITTLE	Decca
December	1960	ROCKIN' AROUND THE CHRISTMAS TREE	Decca
December	1961	ROCKIN' AROUND THE CHRISTMAS TREE	Decca
December	1962	ROCKIN' AROUND THE CHRISTMAS TREE	Decca
January	1961	EMOTIONS	Decca
February	1961	I'M LEARNING ABOUT LOVE	Decca
April	1961	YOU CAN DEPEND ON ME	Decca
June	1961	DUM DUM	Decca

July	1961	EVENTUALLY	Decca
October	1961	FOOL #1	Decca
October	1961	ANYBODY BUT ME	Decca
January	1962	BREAK IT TO ME GENTLY	Decca
January	1962	SO DEEP	Decca
April	1962	EVERYBODY LOVES ME BUT YOU	Decca
April	1962	HERE COMES THAT FEELIN'	Decca
June	1962	IT STARTED ALL OVER AGAIN	Decca
July	1962	HEART IN HAND	Decca
September	1962	SAVE ALL YOUR LOVIN' FOR ME	Decca
September	1962	ALL ALONE AM I	Decca
January	1963	YOUR USED TO BE	Decca
January	1963	SHE'LL NEVER KNOW	Decca
April	1963	LOSING YOU	Decca
April	1963	HE'S SO HEAVENLY	Decca
July	1963	MY WHOLE WORLD IS FALLING DOWN	Decca
July	1963	I WONDER	Decca
September	1963	THE GRASS IS GREENER	Decca
September	1963	SWEET IMPOSSIBLE YOU	Decca
December	1963	AS USUAL	Decca
March	1964	THINK	Decca
June	1964	MY DREAMS	Decca
June	1964	ALONE WITH YOU	Decca
August	1964	WHEN YOU LOVED ME	Decca
October	1964	IS IT TRUE	Decca
January	1965	THE CRYING GAME	Decca
January	1965	THANKS A LOT	Decca
April	1965	TRULY, TRULY, TRUE	Decca
May	1965	TOO MANY RIVERS	Decca
May	1965	NO ONE	Decca
October	1965	RUSTY BELLS	Decca
July	1966	AIN'T GONNA CRY NO MORE	Decca
January	1966	COMING ON STRONG	Decca
January	1967	RIDE, RIDE, RIDE	Decca
February	1969	JOHNNY ONE TIME	Decca
May	1969	YOU DON'T NEED ME FOR ANYTHING ANYMORE	Decca
May	1970	I THINK I LOVE YOU AGAIN	Decca
March	1973	NOBODY WINS	MCA

CURTIS LEE

Born: October 28, 1941
Hometown: Yuma, Arizona

Singer Ray Peterson and his manager Stan Shulman saw Curtis performing at a club in Tucson. They were impressed with his act, and convinced him to go to New York and record for Dunes records, the same label Ray was recording for. He debuted on the label with "Pledge of Love." The record went nowhere. However, during the summer of 1961, he recorded a song that he had written along with Tommy Boyce, "Pretty Little Angel Eyes." It became his biggest hit. The background singers on that hit were the Halos, who had a big hit with "Nag."

June	1961	PRETTY LITTLE ANGEL EYES	Dunes
October	1961	UNDER THE MOON OF LOVE	Dunes

DICKEY LEE

DICKEY LEE

Born: September 21, 1940
Hometown: Memphis, Tennessee

Dickey was a boxer as a teen-ager and a good all-around athlete. He was also an excellent artist and majored in art in college. He used his hobby—singing—to help pay for his tuition. Bill Hall heard Dickey sing and landed him a contract with Smash records. Dickey's two biggest hits were about forlorn girls who died—"Patches" (in 1962) and "Laurie" (early 1965).

March	1961	OH MEIN PAPA	Blue Bell
August	1962	PATCHES	Smash
November	1962	I SAW LINDA YESTERDAY	Smash
March	1963	DON'T WANNA THINK ABOUT PAULA	Smash
May	1965	LAURIE	TCF Hall
August	1965	THE GIRL FROM PEYTON PLACE	TCF Hall
November	1976	9,999,999 TEARS	RCA

JACKIE LEE

The important thing about Jackie Lee's career was that when he was with Mirwood records in 1965 his song "The Duck" was produced by his manager Barry White (the same Barry White who today is a top artist as a solo and with Love Unlimited). Barry's talent at that time enabled Jackie to sing his way up the charts into the top ten in late 1965.

November	1965	THE DUCK	Mirwood
April	1968	AFRICAN BOO-GA-LOO	Keyman
August	1970	THE CHICKEN	Uni

PEGGY LEE

Real Name: Norma Delores Egstrom
Born: May 6, 1920
Hometown: Jamestown, North Dakota

In the early forties, Peggy auditioned for a job as a singer at a Fargo, North Dakota, radio station, WDAY. Ken Kennedy, the program director, liked her and gave her a contract. He was not too taken with her real name, Norma. Someone at the station ventured: "You know she kind of looks like a Peggy," so Peggy it was. Someone else asked, "And what goes with Peggy?" Came the retort: "Something simple, like Lee."

Peggy's career is well known. She's a spectacular stage presence who brings an audience to its feet. She's had many hits over the years, most notably "Manana" (a number one record in 1948), her big hit "Fever" (1958), and most recently "Is That All There Is" (1969). She makes her home in Los Angeles and records for Atlantic records.

November	1945	WAITIN' FOR THE TRAIN TO COME IN	Capitol
November	1947	GOLDEN EARRINGS	Capitol
January	1948	MANANA	Capitol
June	1949	BALI HA'I	Capitol
May	1952	LOVER (Gordon Jenkins)	Decca
February	1956	MR. WONDERFUL	Decca
April	1956	JOEY, JOEY, JOEY	Decca
June	1958	FEVER	Capitol
November	1958	LIGHT OF LOVE	Capitol
January	1959	ALRIGHT, OKAY, YOU WIN	Capitol
May	1959	HALLELUJAH, I LOVE HIM SO	Capitol
January	1963	I'M A WOMAN	Capitol
February	1965	PASS ME BY	Capitol
September	1969	IS THAT ALL THERE IS	Capitol

THE LENNON SISTERS

The four sisters became popular in the 1950s due to their exposure on the Lawrence Welk TV show. They signed with Coral records and in the summer of 1956 did a version of Patience & Prudence's big hit "Tonight

You Belong to Me." The song became a top-ten record for the Lennon Sisters as well. In 1961, they repeated the pattern with Sue Thompson's hit "Sad Movies Make Me Cry."

August	1956	TONIGHT YOU BELONG TO ME	Coral
October	1961	SAD MOVIES MAKE ME CRY	Dot

KETTY LESTER

Hometown: Hope, Arkansas

Ketty was studying to be a nurse at City College in San Francisco when the director of the school's choral group asked her to join. She became so interested in singing that she enrolled at San Francisco State College to study music. She auditioned for a job at San Francisco's Purple Onion and got it. After fourteen months there, Cab Calloway added her to his troupe which was about to tour South America.

On her return in late 1961, she signed with Era records. In the early part of 1962, she premiered for the label with "Love Letters," which became her biggest hit.

February	1962	LOVE LETTERS	Era
June	1962	BUT NOT FOR ME	Era
October	1962	YOU CAN'T LIE TO A LIAR	Era
November	1962	THIS LAND IS YOUR LAND	Era

KETTY LESTER

THE LETTERMEN

Members:

Bob Engemann—born: February 19, 1936—hometown: Highland Park, Michigan

Tony Butala—born: November 20, 1940—hometown: Sharon, Pennsylvania

Jim Pike—born: November 6, 1938—hometown: St. Louis, Missouri

Bob was a missionary for two years and an elder in the Mormon church. Tony was a veteran night club singer, while Jim was a letterman in high school football. Bob and Jim met in Brigham Young University in Utah, where they sang at local clubs. In 1960, they met Tony in Los Angeles, and sang as a trio. After an unsuccessful stint with Warner Brothers, they went over to Capitol. In September 1961, they had their first major hit with their new label with the song "The Way You Look Tonight."

Tony, with two new members, keeps the name The Lettermen alive by actively singing and entertaining all over the country.

September	1961	THE WAY YOU LOOK TONIGHT	Capitol
November	1961	WHEN I FALL IN LOVE	Capitol
January	1962	COME BACK SILLY GIRL	Capitol
May	1962	HOW IS JULIE	Capitol
August	1962	SILLY BOY	Capitol
December	1963	WHERE OR WHEN	Capitol
June	1965	THEME FROM A SUMMER PLACE	Capitol
September	1965	SECRETLY	Capitol
June	1966	I ONLY HAVE EYES FOR YOU	Capitol
January	1967	OUR WINTER LOVE	Capitol
December	1967	GOIN' OUT OF MY HEAD/CAN'T TAKE MY EYES OFF YOU	Capitol
March	1968	SHERRY DON'T GO	Capitol
January	1968	PUT YOUR HEAD ON MY SHOULDER	Capitol
May	1969	HURT SO BAD	Capitol
October	1969	SHANGRI-LA	Capitol
December	1969	TRACES/MEMORIES MEDLEY	Capitol
March	1970	HANG ON SLOOPY	Capitol
June	1970	SHE CRIED	Capitol
January	1971	EVERYTHING IS GOOD ABOUT YOU	Capitol
October	1971	LOVE	Capitol

BARBARA LEWIS

Born: February 9, 1944
Hometown: Detroit, Michigan

Barbara comes from a family of musicians and began writing songs at an early age. In the early sixties she took her tunes to Ollie Mclaughlin, hoping that he could use them. He liked her tunes as well as her voice and decided to manage her.

In early 1963, he got her a contract with Atlantic records, and in April of that year she recorded one of her tunes, "Hello Stranger," which became her first hit for the label.

May	1963	HELLO STRANGER	Atlantic
August	1963	STRAIGHTEN UP YOUR HEART	Atlantic
January	1964	PUPPY LOVE	Atlantic
June	1965	BABY, I'M YOURS	Atlantic
August	1965	MAKE ME YOUR BABY	Atlantic
January	1966	DON'T FORGET ABOUT ME	Atlantic
July	1966	MAKE ME BELONG TO YOU	Atlantic
October	1966	BABY WHAT YOU WANT ME TO DO	Atlantic
April	1967	I'LL MAKE HIM LOVE ME	Atlantic

BOBBY LEWIS

Born: February 17, 1933
Hometown: Indianapolis, Indiana

Bobby's early career was varied: selling pots for a traveling Indian, singing in a road show called "Bimbo's," and working for Soupy Sales.

Bobby went to Chicago and cut his first record on the Parrot label. He then signed with Spotlight records and had "Mumbles Blues" in 1956. Bobby had "Oh! Mr. Somebody" on Mercury in March 1958. Later that year Jackie Wilson asked Bobby to leave Detroit and join him in New York. After a couple of years of knocking around New York, Bobby

BOBBY LEWIS

wound up with a recording contract with Beltone records in early 1961. In March Bobby recorded a song that was written by Ritchie Adams, former lead singer of the Fireflies (of "You Were Mine" fame), that became a number one song. In fact, "Tossin' and Turnin'" wound up as the number one song for the entire year.

Today Bobby resides in New York City and works many clubs and area rock concerts.

March	1961	TOSSIN' AND TURNIN'	Beltone
August	1961	ONE TRACK MIND	Beltone
November	1961	WHAT A WALK	Beltone
July	1962	I'M TOSSIN' AND TURNIN' AGAIN	Beltone

JERRY LEWIS

Born: March 16, 1926
Hometown: Irvington, New Jersey

Gadzooks! Jerry Lewis a recording star? Yes, sports fans, the irrepressible comic, movie star, and producer-director had a top-ten song with "Rock-A-Bye Your Baby with a Dixie Melody" for Decca in 1956.

| October | 1956 | ROCK-A-BYE YOUR BABY WITH A DIXIE MELODY | Decca |
| April | 1957 | IT ALL DEPENDS ON YOU | Decca |

JERRY LEE LEWIS

Born: September 29, 1935
Hometown: Ferriday, Louisiana

Jerry made his first public appearance at age fourteen in Natchez, Louisiana, at an auto show showing 1949 Fords. Jerry sang "Hadacol Boogie" and earned nine dollars. As a youngster, Jerry was influenced by blues singers like B. B. King.

In January 1957, Jerry's father took him to Sun records in Memphis and had him meet and audition for owner Sam Phillips and his brother Jud Phillips. This led to a recording contract and his first release "Crazy Arms." In May 1957, he recorded a song called "Whole Lotta Shakin' Goin' On" that really launched his career on a successful note. Even though Jerry came very close to becoming a minister by studying at the Bible Institute at Wauxhatchie, Texas, his records were banned on many radio stations throughout the country in 1958 when he married his thirteen-year-old cousin, Myra Brown. In 1971, Jerry and Myra got a divorce and Jerry continued with his singing career.

JERRY LEE LEWIS

Although he was a popular rock singer in the fifties on Sun records, today he is more popular with country and western music audiences. Jerry lives in Memphis, and records for Mercury records and continues to travel over the country appearing in his own revue show, with an occasional rock revival show now and then. The man with the "pumpin' piano" and the frantic way of playing on stage with his elbows and his feet has become a classic performer and one of the most dynamic stage performers of rock and roll.

Jerry almost lost his life during the summer of 1981, due to complications resulting from stomach surgery, but he is on the road to a recording comeback.

June	1957	WHOLE LOT OF SHAKIN' GOING ON	Sun
November	1957	GREAT BALLS OF FIRE	Sun
February	1958	YOU WIN AGAIN	Sun
February	1958	BREATHLESS	Sun
May	1958	HIGH SCHOOL CONFIDENTIAL	Sun
September	1958	I'LL MAKE IT ALL UP TO YOU	Sun
September	1958	BREAK-UP	Sun
January	1959	I'LL SAIL MY SHIP ALONE	Sun
April	1961	WHAT'D I SAY	Sun
September	1962	SWEET LITTLE SIXTEEN	Sun
April	1964	I'M ON FIRE	Smash
November	1964	HIGH HEEL SNEAKERS	Smash
March	1968	ANOTHER PLACE, ANOTHER TIME	Smash
July	1968	WHAT'S MADE MILWAUKEE FAMOUS	Smash
November	1971	ME AND BOBBY MCGEE	Mercury
March	1972	CHANTILLY LACE	Mercury
July	1972	TURN ON YOUR LOVE LIGHT	Mercury
April	1973	DRINKING WINE SPO-DEE O'DEE	Mercury

SMILEY LEWIS

Real Name: Overton Lemon
Homestate: Texas

Smiley became well known recording for Imperial records in the early
fifties. His main claim to fame is that other artists later recorded and were
more successful with his material. For example, in 1955 Smiley recorded
the Dave Bartholomew song "I Hear You Knocking." It became an even
bigger hit for both Fats Domino and Gale Storm. The same thing happened to the songs "Blue Monday" (another of Fats's big hits) and "One
Night," which was a big hit for Elvis Presley.

| August | 1952 | THE BELLS ARE RINGING | Imperial |
| August | 1955 | I HEAR YOU KNOCKING | Imperial |

THE LIMELIGHTERS

Members:
    Lou Gottlieb—bass fiddle—1923, Los Angeles, California
    Glenn Yarborough—classical guitar and lyric tenor—January 12, 1930,
        Milwaukee, Wisconsin
    Alex Hassilev—guitar and banjo—July 11, 1932, Paris, France

THE LIMELIGHTERS

Left to right: Alex Hassilev,
Lou Gottlieb, Glenn
Yarborough

The trio was formed in Los Angeles in 1959 and took its name from a club in Aspen, Colorado, called The Limelight. Their biggest hit with RCA was "A Dollar Down" in April 1961. Glenn Yarborough left the group in November 1963. He later went on to a very successful career as a single artist.

April	1961	A DOLLAR DOWN	RCA

KATHY LINDEN

The soft sweet sound of little Kathy Linden enabled her to reach stardom in the late fifties when she recorded for Felsted records. "Billy," her first hit, and "Goodbye, Jimmy, Goodbye," her most popular song, created a short-lived vogue for songs that incorporated boys' names in their titles.

February	1958	BILLY	Felsted
May	1958	YOU'D BE SURPRISED	Felsted
April	1959	GOODBYE JIMMY, GOODBYE	Felsted
July	1959	YOU DON'T KNOW GIRLS	Felsted

LITTLE ANTHONY AND THE IMPERIALS

Members:

> Anthony Gourdine—lead—January 8, 1940
> Tracy Lord—first tenor—later replaced by Sam Strain—December 9, 1940
> Ernie Wright—second tenor—August 24, 1939
> Clarence Collins—bass—March 17, 1939
> Glouster Rogers—baritone—1940

Hometown: Brooklyn, New York

Anthony was originally a member of a group called the Duponts. After high school he left them to join the Chesters, in which Ernie and Clarence were members.

In early 1958, Richard Barrett, an A & R man for End records, spotted the group and signed them to a contract. Anthony, Tracy, Ernie, Clarence, and Glouster named the group the Imperials and in the summer of 1958 they recorded "Tears on My Pillow," which launched their career. The late Alan Freed, at the time a disc jockey on WINS radio in New York, called the group Little Anthony and The Imperials because Anthony was so small. The nickname stuck.

In 1960, the group left End records and began to look for a new label. Some four years later, a long time admirer of theirs, Teddy Ran-

**LITTLE ANTHONY
AND THE IMPERIALS**

Top: Little Anthony Gourdine
Left to right: Glouster Rogers,
Tracy Lord, Clarence Collins,
Ernest Wright

dazzo (one-time member of the singing group the Three Chuckles) brought the group to the attention of Don Costa and his DCP records. This led to a recording contract in the summer of 1964, and a brand new career with their first release for DCP records with "I'm on the Outside Looking In."

Sam Strain of the group has, for the past few years, been performing as one of The O'Jays.

August	1958	TEARS ON MY PILLOW / TWO PEOPLE IN THE WORLD	End
October	1958	TRAVELLING STRANGER	End
December	1958	SO MUCH	End
March	1959	WISHFUL THINKING	End
June	1959	A PRAYER AND A JUKE BOX	End
November	1959	SHIMMY, SHIMMY, KO-KO-BOP	End
April	1960	MY EMPTY ROOM	End
August	1964	I'M ON THE OUTSIDE (LOOKING IN)	DCP
October	1964	GOIN' OUT OF MY HEAD	DCP
January	1965	HURT SO BAD	DCP
June	1965	TAKE ME BACK	DCP
October	1965	I MISS YOU SO	DCP
January	1966	HURT	DCP
April	1966	BETTER USE YOUR HEAD	Veep
October	1966	IT'S NOT THE SAME	Veep
July	1969	OUT OF SIGHT, OUT OF MIND	United Artists
October	1969	THE TEN COMMANDMENTS OF LOVE	United Artists
November	1970	HELP ME FIND A WAY (TO SAY I LOVE YOU)	United Artists
June	1974	I'M FALLING IN LOVE WITH YOU	Avco

LITTLE CAESAR AND THE ROMANS

Members:

    Carl Burnett (Little Caesar)—lead—hometown: Dallas, Texas—1944
    Johnny Simmons—hometown: Los Angeles, California—1943
    Early Harris—hometown: Los Angeles, California—1943
    David Johnson—hometown: Los Angeles, California—1942
    Leroy Sanders—hometown: Los Angeles, California—1943

While living in Los Angeles, Carl met Johnny, Early, David, and Leroy, who were members of singing groups like the Jewels, the Kuf-Linx, and the Cubans. The five were known as the Up-Fronts for a while.

In early 1961, they changed the name of the group to the Romans and Carl became known as Little Caesar. That same year they signed with Robert Keene's Del Fi records and in April of that year recorded their biggest hit, "Those Oldies But Goodies."

April	1961	THOSE OLDIES BUT GOODIES	Del Fi
July	1961	HULLY GULLY AGAIN	Del Fi
August	1965	MY GIRL SLOOPY (& THE CONSULS)	Mala

THE LITTLE DIPPERS

The Anita Kerr singers recorded the song "Forever" in late 1959 and released it under the name the Little Dippers on University records in January 1960.

| January | 1960 | FOREVER | University |

LITTLE ESTHER PHILLIPS

Born: December 23, 1935
Hometown: Houston, Texas

At the age of thirteen, she went to Johnny Otis's night club, entered an amateur contest, and won. Johnny then signed her to record and sing with his band, the Johnny Otis Revue.

Record executives Bob Gans and Lelan Rogers heard her performing in Houston, Texas, at a club in 1962 and signed her to Lenox records.

In September 1962, she recorded her first hit, "Release Me," which oddly enough became Engelbert Humperdinck's first success some five years later.

In 1975, she was known simply as Esther Phillips, and had a big disco hit with "What A Difference A Day Makes."

| May | 1950 | CUPID'S BOOGIE | Savoy |
| February | 1952 | RING-A-DING-DOO | Federal |

LITTLE ESTHER PHILLIPS

October	1962	RELEASE ME	Lenox
April	1965	AND I LOVE HIM	Atlantic
May	1966	WHEN A WOMAN LOVES A MAN	Atlantic
March	1969	TOO LATE TO WORRY, TOO BLUE TO CRY	Roulette
August	1970	SET ME FREE	Atlantic
August	1975	WHAT A DIFFERENCE A DAY MAKES	Kudu

LITTLE EVA

Real Name: Eva Narcissus Boyd
Born: 1944
Hometown: Belhaven, North Carolina

Eva wanted to be either a nurse or a singer. Eventually she left her home in North Carolina and came to New York. She got a job as a baby-sitter for songwriters Carole King and her husband Gerry Goffin. Because Eva liked to sing while she was in the house, Carole and Gerry had Eva try a song they had written. They liked what they heard so well that they took her into the studio and had her record it.

In the summer of 1962, the song was released on Dimension records as "The Loco-Motion" and became a number one hit. At the time of the recording, three unknown singers were used as background singers on the record. A few months later, these three unknown singers became the Cookies and had their own hit with "Chains."

Today Eva lives in New York and makes occasional appearances at rock concerts.

June	1962	THE LOCO-MOTION	Dimension
October	1962	KEEP YOUR HANDS OFF MY BABY	Dimension
February	1963	LET'S TURKEY TROT	Dimension
May	1963	OLD SMOKEY LOCOMOTION	Dimension

LITTLE JOE AND THE THRILLERS

Members:

Joe Cook—lead
Harry Pascle
Farris Hill
Donald Burnett
Richard Frazier

Hometown: Philadelphia, Pennsylvania

In late 1957, Joe got his group to record a song he had written called "Peanuts," which was then sold to Okeh records in New York. The song was released in September 1957 and became the group's only national hit.

September 1957	PEANUTS	Okeh

LITTLE JOEY AND THE FLIPS

Members:

Joseph Hall (Little Joey)—lead—hometown: Philadelphia, Pennsylvania—1943
James Meagher—hometown: Upper Darby, Pennsylvania—1946
John Smith—hometown: Upper Darby, Pennsylvania—1946
Jeff Leonard—hometown: Upper Darby, Pennsylvania—1946
Fred Gerace—hometown: Upper Darby, Pennsylvania—1947

The boys met while they were in high school. Their managers, Marc Levin and Barry Rich, set up an audition with Joy records in 1962, and they auditioned with a song they wrote called "Bongo Stomp." The song was released that summer and became the group's only hit.

June	1962	BONGO STOMP	Joy

LITTLE JUNIOR PARKER

Junior was discovered by Sam Phillips of Sun records in the early fifties. (In fact, Sam had Junior record "Mystery Train" on Sun records before

Elvis Presley.) Elvis recorded "Mystery Train" on Sun in 1955. It was one of his early hits on the label. Junior, who played the harmonica, stayed with Sam for a while and then was signed by the Texas-based Duke records. In early 1957, he had his first major hit for the label with "The Next Time You See Me."

February	1957	NEXT TIME YOU SEE ME	Duke
January	1958	THAT'S ALRIGHT	Duke
December	1958	SWEET HOME CHICAGO	Duke
April	1959	FIVE LONG YEARS	Duke
January	1961	STAND BY ME	Duke
May	1961	DRIVING WHEEL	Duke
October	1961	IN THE DARK	Duke
March	1962	ANNIE GET YOUR YO-YO	Duke
January	1963	SOMEONE SOMEWHERE	Duke
June	1965	CRYING FOR MY BABY	Duke
December	1966	MAN OR MOUSE	Duke
August	1967	I CAN'T PUT MY FINGER ON IT	Mercury
April	1969	AIN'T GON' BE NO CUTTING ALOOSE	Blue Rock
December	1969	WORRIED LIFE BLUES	Minit
January	1971	DROWNING ON DRY LAND	Capitol

LITTLE PEGGY MARCH

Born: March 8, 1948
Hometown: Philadelphia, Pennsylvania

She began singing at the age of five and won a talent contest. Later she auditioned for the Rex Trailer TV show in Philadelphia and became a regular on the show. She then sang with local bands.

LITTLE PEGGY MARCH

In 1963, while singing at a cousin's wedding, someone heard her and informed the people at RCA records. This resulted in a recording contract. While only fifteen, and still a student at Lansdale, a Philadelphia Catholic high school, she recorded a song, "I Will Follow Him," that became a number one song shortly after its release in March 1963.

After being a hit in Germany for the past few years, she is now making a U.S. comeback as Peggy March in places like Atlantic City, New Jersey.

March	1963	I WILL FOLLOW HIM	RCA
May	1963	I WISH I WERE A PRINCESS	RCA
August	1963	HELLO HEARTACHE, GOODBYE LOVE	RCA
November	1963	THE IMPOSSIBLE HAPPENED	RCA
February	1964	EVERY LITTLE MOVE YOU MAKE	RCA

LITTLE RICHARD

Real Name: Richard Penniman
Born: December 5, 1932
Hometown: Macon, Georgia

Richard was the third child of fourteen. At the age of seven he sang for nickels and dimes in the streets of Macon. He was the lead singer in the church choir when he was fourteen years old.

In 1951, he won a talent show in Atlanta, which resulted in a recording contract with RCA records, for whom he recorded songs like "Get Rich Quick" and "Taxi Blues." From there he went on to record for Peacock records in Houston.

In 1955, while working at the Greyhound bus station in Macon washing dishes, Richard sent Art Rupe of Specialty records in Los Angeles a tape of a song he had recorded. Art then purchased Richard's contract from Peacock and sent Bumps Blackwell, an A & R man, to meet Richard at the Cosmo studios in New Orleans. They cut nine tracks instead of the originally scheduled eight. The ninth was Richard's audition demo of a song called "Tutti-Frutti." The original song was a little too risqué at the time so Bumps had Dorothy LaBostrie tone it down. The song was released on Specialty in late 1955, and became the first in a long list of hits by Little Richard.

His next release, "Long Tall Sally," was rerecorded in Los Angeles, with Lee Allen on the sax solo.

Joe Lutcher, an artist on Specialty, told Richard that pop music was evil. When *Sputnik* went up in 1957, Joe told Richard that this was a sign from heaven to quit. Little Richard gave up singing for several years to join the ministry.

Today, Richard has, once again, given up show business to return to the ministry.

LITTLE RICHARD

December	1955	TUTTI-FRUITTI	Specialty
March	1956	LONG TALL SALLY	Specialty
March	1956	SLIPPIN' AND SLIDIN'	Specialty
June	1956	RIP IT UP	Specialty
June	1956	READY TEDDY	Specialty
January	1957	THE GIRL CAN'T HELP IT	Specialty
March	1957	LUCILLE	Specialty
March	1957	SEND ME SOME LOVIN'	Specialty
June	1957	JENNY, JENNY	Specialty
June	1957	MISS ANN	Specialty
September	1957	KEEP A KNOCKIN'	Specialty
January	1958	GOOD GOLLY, MISS MOLLY	Specialty
May	1958	OOH! MY SOUL	Specialty
June	1958	TRUE, FINE MAMA	Specialty
September	1958	BABY FACE	Specialty
May	1959	KANSAS CITY	Specialty
July	1964	BAMA LAMA BAMA LOO	Specialty
November	1965	I DON'T KNOW WHAT YOU'VE GOT BUT IT'S GOT ME	Vee Jay
August	1966	POOR DOG (WHO CAN'T WAG HIS OWN TAIL)	Okeh
May	1970	FREEDOM BLUES	Reprise
September	1970	GREENWOOD MISSISSIPPI	Reprise

LITTLE WILLIE JOHN

Real Name: William J. Woods
Born: November 15, 1937
Died: May 26, 1968
Hometown: Camden, Arkansas

Born in Camden, Willie eventually moved to Detroit, where he spent most of his life. Everyone called him Little Willie, because he was just over five feet tall.

LITTLE WILLIE JOHN

In the early fifties, Willie sang with the Paul Williams Orchestra and the Duke Ellington and Count Basie bands. By 1955, he had signed with King records out of Cincinnati and recorded "All Around the World" as his first song that year. One year later, during the summer of 1956, he recorded his first major hit with a song he had cowritten with Eddie Cooley, called "Fever." The song also was a hit for Peggy Lee in 1958.

After several moderately popular songs he recorded his next major hit in March 1958, entitled "Talk to Me, Talk to Me." This also became a hit for Sunny and the Sunglows in 1963.

His biggest chart record was "Sleep" in September 1960, which oddly enough was considered by Willie to be his worst recording. He was the master of the blues ballad.

In May 1966, Willie was sent to Washington State Penitentiary in Walla Walla for stabbing a man to death during a brawl in a Seattle cafe. He died of pneumonia in prison on May 26, 1968.

September	1955	ALL AROUND THE WORLD	King
January	1956	NEED YOUR LOVE SO BAD	King
June	1956	FEVER	King
March	1958	TALK TO ME, TALK TO ME	King
July	1958	YOU'RE A SWEETHEART	King
July	1959	LEAVE MY KITTEN ALONE	King
February	1960	LET THEM TALK	King
May	1960	COTTAGE FOR SALE	King
June	1960	HEARTBREAK (IT'S HURTIN' ME)	King
September	1960	SLEEP	King
November	1960	WALK SLOW	King
January	1961	LEAVE MY KITTEN ALONE	King

March	1961	THE VERY THOUGHT OF YOU	King
May	1961	(I'VE GOT) SPRING FEVER	King
July	1961	NOW YOU KNOW	King
September	1961	TAKE MY LOVE (I WANT TO GIVE IT ALL TO YOU)	King

HANK LOCKLIN

Born: February 15, 1918
Hometown: McLellan, Florida

Hank is a very big country and western star who is credited with bringing American C & W music to Ireland. One of his country numbers cut a swath through the popular charts in 1960, a little tune called "Please Help Me, I'm Falling."

December	1957	GEISHA GIRL	RCA
May	1958	SEND ME THE PILLOW YOU DREAM ON	RCA
May	1960	PLEASE HELP ME, I'M FALLING	RCA

LOLITA

Real Name: Lolita Ditta
Hometown: Vienna, Austria

Lolita was a former kindergarten teacher who decided to pursue a singing career. In fall of 1960, she recorded a German song called "Sailor," which became a hit in Europe. The record was sent to Kapp records in the United States and president Dave Kapp decided to release it on his label. Although Lolita sang the song in German, it still became a top-ten hit in the United States.

| October | 1960 | SAILOR | Kapp |
| January | 1961 | COWBOY JIMMY JOE | Kapp |

JULIE LONDON

Julie, the ex-wife of actor Jack Webb, had her only major hit in 1955, with a song on Liberty called "Cry Me A River."

| August | 1955 | CRY ME A RIVER | Liberty |

LAURIE LONDON

Hometown: London, England

In late 1957, thirteen-year-old Laurie recorded a classic called "He's Got the Whole World (in His Hands)," which became a big hit in London,

JULIE LONDON

and throughout Europe as well. A copy of the record got to Capitol records in the United States and they decided to release the song here. In early 1958, the song went up the pop charts, going as high as position number two. It never made it to the number one spot because of two other songs that alternated for it at that time: Elvis Presley's "Don't" and The Champs' "Tequila."

Today Laurie still resides in London.

February 1958 HE'S GOT THE WHOLE WORLD (IN HIS HANDS) Capitol

TRINI LOPEZ

Real Name: Trinidad Lopez, III
Born: May 15, 1937
Hometown: Dallas, Texas

At age fifteen Trini played guitar in Latin clubs in Dallas. Next he formed a five-piece combo and toured the Southwest. After high school he toured the United States with a group for four years. Then Trini played Los Angeles. His first appearance was at Ye Little Club with Joanie Sommers. It was planned as a two-week engagement, but lasted a year instead.

While at P.J.'s in Hollywood, in 1963, Don Costa saw Trini perform and brought him to Reprise records. In the summer of 1963, he released "If I Had a Hammer," a song Peter, Paul and Mary had a hit with one year earlier, and it was a hit for him.

July	1963	IF I HAD A HAMMER	Reprise
October	1963	KANSAS CITY	Reprise
March	1964	JAILER BRING ME WATER	Reprise
April	1964	WHAT HAVE I GOT OF MY OWN	Reprise
August	1964	MICHAEL	Reprise
January	1965	LEMON TREE	Reprise
April	1965	SAD TOMORROWS	Reprise
June	1965	ARE YOU SINCERE	Reprise
October	1965	SINNER MAN	Reprise
March	1966	I'M COMIN' HOME CINDY	Reprise
June	1966	LA BAMBA	Reprise
February	1967	GONNA GET ALONG WITHOUT YA' NOW	Reprise
March	1968	SALLY WAS A GOOD OLD GIRL	Reprise

LOS INDIOS TABAJARAS

Members:
    Natalicio Moreyra Lima
    Antenor Moreyra Lima
Hometown: Ceara, Brazil

Born in the jungles of Brazil, they found a guitar in the jungle left by a party of white men exploring the area. They taught themselves to play

TRINI LOPEZ

and went to Rio de Janiero to make their debut playing the guitar as accompaniment to tribal folk songs.

An agent heard them and arranged for formal instruction in Mexico. After that they toured South America and Europe. In 1963 they signed with RCA. In September of that year they recorded "Maria Elena," which became their biggest hit.

| September 1963 | MARIA ELENA | RCA |
| February 1964 | ALWAYS IN MY HEART | RCA |

BONNIE LOU

In the 1955 motion picture *Blackboard Jungle* Glenn Ford portrayed a teacher called "Daddy-O" by his pupils. It was only a question of time before someone came up with a song utilizing that name. In the summer of 1955, Bonnie Lou recorded a song about a guy all the girls were crazy about called "Daddy-O," which became a national hit on King records.

| July | 1955 | DADDY-O | King |

JOHN D. LOUDERMILK

Born: March, 31, 1934
Hometown: Durham, North Carolina

JOHN D. LOUDERMILK

John inherited his musical ability from his mother, who played the guitar and taught John to play the ukulele at the age of eight. At age ten, he played and sang on a local radio show. In high school he got four of his friends to form a band called the Pine Toppers. After high school the band broke up and John began to travel.

In 1954, he appeared on TV and played in a small combo. At this time he began writing songs like "A Rose and a Baby Ruth," "Sittin' in the Balcony," "Norman," "Abilene," and "Torture." In 1961, he signed with RCA as a singer and recorded "Language Of Love" in October of that year.

October	1961	LANGUAGE OF LOVE	RCA
March	1962	THOU SHALT NOT STEAL	RCA
July	1962	CALLIN' DOCTOR CASEY	RCA
December	1962	ROAD HOG	RCA

DARLENE LOVE

Hometown: Los Angeles, California

Darlene Love was discovered in 1962 by record producer Phil Spector while she was singing with a group called the Blossoms. Phil used Darlene to sing lead with his group, the Crystals, on a song written by singer Gene Pitney called "He's A Rebel." The song became the Crystals' only number one song after it was released in the fall of 1962.

Phil then asked Darlene, along with her girl friend Fanita James, to leave the Blossoms to join Bobby Sheen and form a new group called Bob B. Soxx and the Blue Jeans. The trio was then signed to Spector's Philles records and recorded a song called "Zip-A-Dee-Doo-Dah" which became their first national hit in October 1962.

In April 1963, Darlene launched a solo career on Philles records with "Today I Met the Boy I'm Gonna Marry." Since that time she has been singing all over the country. Today, she travels with Dionne Warwick as one of Dionne's background singers.

April	1963	TODAY I MET THE BOY I'M GONNA MARRY	Philles
July	1963	WAIT 'TIL MY BOBBY GETS HOME	Philles
October	1963	A FINE FINE BOY	Philles

JIM LOWE
Born: May 7, 1927
Hometown: Springfield, Missouri

Jim followed his years in the Army from 1942 to 1945 with a college education at the University of Missouri, returning after graduation to

Springfield to begin a long career as a disc jockey. From there he moved to Indianapolis, and by 1950 was working in Chicago.

In 1953 he wrote "Gambler's Guitar" which became a hit as Rusty Draper's recording. A year later Jim was a disc jockey for WCBS in New York.

Bob Davie and Marvin Moore presented Jim with a song they had written in 1956. Jim recorded it in Bob Davie's Greenwich Village apartment, Davie himself supplying the piano accompaniment. The tapes were sold to Dot records and "The Green Door" became a number one national hit that same year.

Jim continues to work as a disc jockey, currently for WNEW in New York.

August	1956	THE GREEN DOOR	Dot
December	1956	BY YOU, BY YOU, BY YOU	Dot
April	1957	FOUR WALLS	Dot
April	1957	TALKIN' TO THE BLUES	Dot

ROBIN LUKE

Born: March 19, 1942
Hometown: Honolulu, Hawaii

Robin has been writing and singing since he was eight years old. In 1958, he wrote a song about his five-year-old sister that he recorded in Hawaii, for International records. The song was sold to Dot records on the mainland and released in August of that year. "Susie Darlin' " became his only hit.

Today he is a college professor in Norfolk, Virginia.

| August | 1958 | SUSIE DARLIN' | Dot |

BOB LUMAN

Born: April 15, 1938
Died: December 27, 1978, Nashville, Tennessee
Hometown: Nacogdoches, Texas

During his high school days in Kilgore, Texas, Bob concentrated on sports and almost pursued a professional baseball career. He appeared on the "Louisiana Hayride" and the "Town Hall Party." In 1960, he signed with Warner Brothers records and recorded a Boudleaux Bryant song in August of that year called "Let's Think About Living," which became his only hit.

| August | 1960 | LET'S THINK ABOUT LIVING | Warner Bros. |

THE LY-DELLS

In the summer of 1961, this group recorded a song that was a takeoff on the Wizard of Oz theme, in which they would take you to see "The Wizard of Love." In fact it began "We're off to see the Wizard, the wonderful Wizard of love." The bouncy melody and lyrics made it a national chart hit for Master records.

August	1961	WIZARD OF LOVE	Master

ARTHUR LYMAN

Arthur was a very popular musical arranger in the late fifties and early sixties. After some moderately popular recordings, he recorded a song called "Yellow Bird" on the Hi-Fi label in the summer of 1961. This instrumental had an island flavor, somewhat reminiscent of Martin Denny's hit, "Quiet Village," several years before.

June	1959	TABOO	Hi-Fi
May	1961	YELLOW BIRD	Hi-Fi
February	1963	LOVE FOR SALE	Hi-Fi

FRANKIE LYMON AND THE TEENAGERS

Members:

    Frankie Lymon—lead—born: September 30, 1942; died: February 28, 1968

    Herman Santiago—first tenor—born: February 18, 1941

    Jimmy Merchant—second tenor—born: February 10, 1940

    Joe Negroni—baritone—born: September 9, 1940; died: September 5, 1978

    Sherman Garnes—bass—born: June 8, 1940; died: February 26, 1977

Hometown: New York, New York

The Teenagers were formed by Joe Negroni. All the members were in their teens except Frankie, who was only twelve at the time. Richard Barrett, who sang with the Valentines on Rama records and was also A & R director for that label, liked the group's sound and rehearsed them in a junior high school music room until he felt they were ready to record.

    Their maiden effort was a song called "Why Do Fools Fall in Love" which Frankie and Herman had written. Richard wanted Herman to sing lead on the song, but on the day the group was to record Herman had a bad throat, so Frankie sang lead instead. The song was an instant hit, the first of many for the group.

    In 1957 Frankie left the group to go out as a single. His first record,

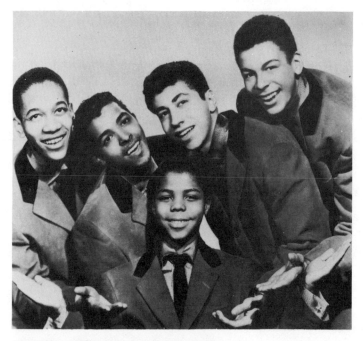

FRANKIE LYMON AND THE TEENAGERS

Left to right: Jimmy Merchant, Herman Santiago, Joe Negroni,
Sherman Garnes   Bottom center: Frankie Lymon

"Goody Goody," did quite well. Ten years later Frankie was arrested on drug charges; a few months later an article in a national magazine reported how he had kicked the habit. In 1968, he died of a reported overdose in a friend's apartment. Sherman died in 1977, during open heart surgery in New York, while Joe died the following year of an aneurysm of the brain.

Today, Jimmy, Herman and Pearl McKinnon, a woman who sounds remarkably like the late Frankie Lymon, perform as Frankie Lymon's Teenagers. In fact, they appeared at Radio City Music Hall in September of 1981 with The Manhattan Transfer.

In late 1981, Diana Ross turned their 1956 hit "Why Do Fools Fall In Love" into a major hit all over again.

January	1956	WHY DO FOOLS FALL IN LOVE	Gee
April	1956	I WANT YOU TO BE MY GIRL / I'M NOT A KNOW IT ALL	Gee
July	1956	I PROMISE TO REMEMBER	Gee
October	1956	ABC'S OF LOVE	Gee
December	1956	I'M NOT A JUVENILE DELINQUENT	Gee
February	1957	TEENAGE LOVE	Gee
May	1957	OUT IN THE COLD AGAIN	Gee
July	1957	GOODY GOODY	Gee
August	1960	LITTLE BITTY PRETTY ONE	Roulette

BARBARA LYNN

Real Name: Barbara Lynn Ozone
Born: 1942
Hometown: Beaumont, Texas

A rocky romance in real life led Barbara to write a song that she recorded in New Orleans, under the supervision of her personal manager Huey P. Meaux, in 1962. The song, "You'll Lose A Good Thing," was sold to Jamie records in Philadelphia and released as her first hit that summer.

May	1962	YOU'LL LOSE A GOOD THING	Jamie
September	1962	SECOND FIDDLE GIRL	Jamie
December	1962	YOU'RE GONNA NEED ME	Jamie
February	1963	DON'T BE CRUEL	Jamie
July	1963	I CRIED AT LAURA'S WEDDING	Jamie
June	1964	OH! BABY	Jamie
January	1965	IT'S BETTER TO HAVE IT	Jamie
October	1966	YOU LEFT THE WATER RUNNING	Tribe
February	1968	THIS IS THE THANKS I GET	Atlantic
July	1971	(UNTIL THEN) I'LL SUFFER	Atlantic

VERA LYNN

Hometown: London, England

Vera had a big, melodious voice. She always tackled a song straightforwardly, hitting all the pitches squarely and staying with the beat. During the forties she was Britain's top female vocalist. In 1952 she had a number one record in the United States—"Auf Wiederseh'n Sweetheart."

May	1948	YOU CAN'T BE TRUE DEAR	London
January	1949	AGAIN	London
May	1952	AUF WIEDERSEH'N SWEETHEART	London
October	1952	YOURS	London
May	1954	IF YOU LOVE ME (REALLY LOVE ME)	London
February	1956	SUCH A DAY	London
April	1957	DON'T CRY MY LOVE	London

GLORIA LYNNE

Gloria was exclusively a jazz singer until her songs began to reach the pop music charts in 1961. Her biggest hit was in early 1964 with "I Wish You Love," a recording that emphasized her sultry ballad style.

September	1961	IMPOSSIBLE	Everest
December	1961	YOU DON'T HAVE TO BE A TOWER OF STRENGTH	Everest
January	1964	I WISH YOU LOVE	Everest
March	1964	I SHOULD CARE	Everest
July	1964	DON'T TAKE YOUR LOVE FROM ME	Everest
June	1965	WATERMELON MAN	Fontana

M

GENE McDANIELS

JIMMY McCRACKLIN

The blues-singing piano player got his start performing in the Bay area of San Francisco during the fifties. In early 1958, Jimmy recorded a song he wrote called "The Walk," which was released on Checker records. The dance the song described was appropriated by the dance-crazed contingent on "American Bandstand" and within a few weeks the song became a top-ten national hit.

February	1958	THE WALK	Checker
October	1961	JUST GOT TO KNOW	Art-Tone
February	1962	SHAME, SHAME, SHAME	Art-Tone
April	1965	EVERY NIGHT, EVERY DAY	Imperial

GENE McDANIELS

Real Name: Eugene B. McDaniels
Born: February 12, 1935
Hometown: Kansas City, Missouri

The son of the Reverend B. T. McDaniels, Gene joined a professional gospel group at age thirteen. He played the sax in his high school orchestra and later formed his own vocal quartet.

In late 1960, he signed with Liberty records and recorded songs like "Green Door" and "In Times Like These." In March 1961, he had his first major hit with "A Hundred Pounds of Clay."

Today he still performs as a singer under the name Eugene McDaniels.

March	1961	A HUNDRED POUNDS OF CLAY	Liberty
June	1961	A TEAR	Liberty
October	1961	TOWER OF STRENGTH	Liberty
January	1962	CHIP CHIP	Liberty

July	1962	POINT OF NO RETURN	Liberty
October	1962	SPANISH LACE	Liberty
August	1963	IT'S A LONELY TOWN	Liberty

THE McGUIRE SISTERS

Members:
Chris—born: July 30, 1929
Dotty—born: February 13, 1930
Phyllis—born: February 14, 1931
Hometown: Middletown, Ohio

The sisters got their big break when they appeared on the Arthur Godfrey talent scout show and won. In 1954, they signed with Coral records and recorded "Goodnight, Sweetheart, Goodnight," their first major hit, in May of that year. In November 1954, they recorded their all-time biggest seller, "Sincerely," which became a number one hit nationwide. The song was a cover version of the Moonglows' R & B hit, written by Harvey Fuqua of the group and their manager, disc jockey Alan Freed.

Today Phyllis McGuire performs regularly as a solo in Las Vegas.

June	1954	GOODNIGHT, SWEETHEART, GOODNIGHT	Coral
October	1954	MUSKRAT RAMBLE	Coral
December	1954	SINCERELY	Coral
March	1955	IT MAY SOUND SILLY	Coral
May	1955	SOMETHING'S GOTTA GIVE	Coral
July	1955	GIVE ME LOVE	Coral
October	1955	HE	Coral
February	1956	MISSING	Coral
April	1956	PICNIC	Coral
July	1956	WEARY BLUES	Coral
September	1956	EV'RE DAY OF MY LIFE	Coral
November	1956	GOODNIGHT MY LOVE	Coral
August	1957	AROUND THE WORLD	Coral
December	1957	SUGARTIME	Coral
May	1958	DING DONG	Coral
August	1958	VOLARE	Coral
January	1959	MAY YOU ALWAYS	Coral
May	1959	SUMMER DREAMS	Coral
January	1960	LIVIN' DANGEROUSLY	Coral
August	1960	THE LAST DANCE	Coral
March	1961	JUST FOR OLD TIME'S SAKE	Coral
July	1961	TEARS ON MY PILLOW	Coral
November	1961	JUST BECAUSE	Coral

LONNIE MACK

Real Name: Lonnie McIntosh
Born: July 18, 1941
Hometown: Aurora, Indiana

At age four Lonnie got his first guitar, a $9.95 Lone Ranger model. Two years later he began to sing country and western music with his brother and sister. He switched to the electric guitar at thirteen and began working clubs with his brother Alvin. They always performed Chuck Berry's song "Memphis" as a vocal. One night their singer was absent, so Lonnie played the song as an instrumental. It was well received. Carl Edmondson took Lonnie to Harry Carlson, the president of Fraternity records, in 1963. Harry liked the song and released it as a single. In the summer of 1963 "Memphis" became Lonnie's biggest hit.

May	1963	MEMPHIS	Fraternity
August	1963	WHAMI	Fraternity
November	1963	BABY, WHAT'S WRONG	Fraternity
October	1965	HONKY TONK '65	Fraternity

GISELE MacKENZIE

Born: January 10, 1927
Hometown: Winnipeg, Canada

As a young girl Gisele learned to play the piano and violin. Her first professional job was as pianist for the Bob Shuttleworth Band which was playing at the Glenmouth Hotel in Canada. Shuttleworth later became her manager. During the late forties Gisele had her own daily radio show on the CBC. In the United States, she sang on two popular television

GISELE MacKENZIE

BIG JAY McNEELY

shows, "Club 15" and "Your Hit Parade." A contract with "X" records and a couple of middle-size hits followed.

May	1955	HARD TO GET	"X"
September	1955	PEPPER-HOT BABY	"X"
October	1956	THE STAR YOU WISHED UPON LAST NIGHT	Vik

PHIL McLEAN

Hometown: Detroit, Michigan

Phil moved to Cleveland, Ohio, in the early 1950s and started working at radio station WERE as a disc jockey. His show became very popular and he remained one of the country's top air personalities.

He cut a parody of Jimmy Dean's hit "Big Bad John," called "Small Sad Sam." The song was released in November 1961 and became a national hit on Versatile records.

| November | 1961 | SMALL SAD SAM | Versatile |

BIG JAY McNEELY

Born: April 29, 1928

Saxophone-playing Jay was a dynamic fifties stage presence who always broke up the show with his frantic playing. All the house lights would be extinguished and then Jay's big band would begin to play, fluoresent lights reflecting off their shirts, while Jay lay down on the stage and played.

In the early part of 1959, he wrote a song called "There Is Something on Your Mind," which became his only national pop hit. (He had many R & B hits in the fifties on King records.) Jay's song became an even bigger hit for Bobby Marchan on Fire records in the summer of 1960.

May   1959   THERE IS SOMETHING ON YOUR MIND   Swingin

CLYDE McPHATTER

Born: 1931
Died: June 13, 1972
Hometown: Durham, North Carolina

Clyde was a choir boy at Mt. Calvary Baptist Church in Durham. At age twelve, he moved to New York and continued singing in churches. In 1950, he met Billy Ward and joined the singing group the Dominoes, recording songs with them like "Do Something For Me" and "Sixty Minute Man" in 1951, "Have Mercy Baby" and "I'd Be Satisfied" in 1952, and "The Bells" and "These Foolish Things" in 1953, all on Federal records.

Clyde left the Dominoes in September 1953, to form his own group, the Drifters. In October 1953, they released the first of many hits for Atlantic records, "Money Honey."

In 1954, Clyde was drafted. On leave from the Army, he recorded his first solo hit in late 1955, "Seven Days." On his return to civilian life in 1956, he had a smash hit with the song "Treasure of Love."

CLYDE McPHATTER

Clyde met an untimely death in June 1972, when he died of a heart attack at the age of forty-one, at his home in Teaneck, New Jersey.

November	1955	SEVEN DAYS	Atlantic
April	1956	TREASURE OF LOVE	Atlantic
January	1957	WITHOUT LOVE (THERE IS NOTHING)	Atlantic
April	1957	JUST TO HOLD MY HAND	Atlantic
August	1957	LONG LONELY NIGHTS	Atlantic
May	1958	COME WHAT MAY	Atlantic
October	1958	A LOVER'S QUESTION	Atlantic
April	1959	LOVEY DOVEY	Atlantic
June	1959	SINCE YOU'VE BEEN GONE	Atlantic
November	1959	YOU WENT BACK ON YOUR WORD	Atlantic
April	1959	I TOLD MYSELF A LIE	MGM
December	1959	LET'S TRY IT AGAIN	MGM
April	1960	THINK ME A KISS	MGM
July	1960	TA TA	Mercury
July	1961	I NEVER KNEW	Mercury
February	1962	LOVER PLEASE	Mercury
June	1962	LITTLE BITTY PRETTY ONE	Mercury
January	1964	DEEP IN THE HEART OF HARLEM	Mercury
April	1965	CRYING WON'T HELP YOU NOW	Mercury

GORDON MacRAE

Born: March 12, 1931
Hometown: East Orange, New Jersey

As a child actor and singer, Gordon appeared with the Ray Bolger Revue. He's appeared in many movies, including *Tea for Two, Desert Song, Oklahoma,* and *Carousel.* His biggest chart record, a top-ten tune, "Hair of Gold, Eyes of Blue," was released in the summer of 1948. Gordon was formerly married to the entertainer Sheila MacRae. Their daughters, Meredith and Heather, are successful actresses in their own right.

July	1948	IT'S MAGIC	Capitol
August	1948	HAIR OF GOLD, EYES OF BLUE	Capitol
October	1948	RAMBLING ROSE	Capitol
February	1949	SO IN LOVE	Capitol
April	1956	I'VE GROWN ACCUSTOMED TO HER FACE	Capitol
September	1958	THE SECRET	Capitol

JOHNNY MADDOX

Born: 1929
Hometown: Gallatin, Tennessee

A precocious piano player, Johnny learned how to play at four and was giving concerts at five. In the early fifties he worked at Randy Wood's record shop in Gallatin and played with an orchestra in his spare time.

Randy thought that Johnny should record and took him to a local radio station and had him cut a few songs. Randy decided to release the songs on a new label he was starting called Dot records (shortly thereafter the home of artists like The Hilltoppers, Billy Vaughn, Pat Boone, The Fontane Sisters, and Gale Storm). Dot records also became one of the big "cover" labels of the fifties.

Johnny worked as a piano player for Randy's label and had some chart records in the early fifties, his first big one being "The Crazy Otto" in early 1955.

January	1955	THE CRAZY OTTO (MEDLEY)	Dot
September	1956	HEART AND SOUL	Dot
January	1958	YELLOW DOG BLUES	Dot

THE MAGNIFICENTS

In 1956, Nathaniel Montague came to Chicago and got a job at radio station WAAF as a disc jockey. In just a short time he began calling himself "Magnificent Montague" and became one of the most popular black disc jockeys in the city.

That same year he formed a singing group consisting of four guys and one girl which sang at different hops in Chicago. He called them the Magnificents, after his own nickname. He then wrote a song for the group called "Up on a Mountain," and took them to meet the president of Vee Jay records, Ewart Abner. Ewart liked the song and the group, and had them record the tune. It was released during the summer of 1956 on Vee Jay and became a national hit, the group's only successful record.

| July | 1956 | UP ON THE MOUNTAIN | Vee Jay |

THE MAJORS

Members:
   Ricky Cordo—lead—Baltimore, Maryland—1939
   Frank Trout—Philadelphia, Pennsylvania—1940
   Ronald Gathers—Philadelphia, Pennsylvania—1941
   Eugene Glass—Philadelphia, Pennsylvania—1939
   Idella Morris—Philadelphia, Pennsylvania—1943

The group was formed in 1961; with manager Bill Fox, they worked on creating a distinctive sound. In early 1962, they recorded a song that Lew Chudd, the president of Imperial records, had heard and decided to release on his label. In August of 1962, "A Wonderful Dream" became the first and biggest hit on the label.

The high lead voice on the song is not that of Idella Morris, but actually that of Ricky Cordo, an unusually high tenor.

| August | 1962 | A WONDERFUL DREAM | Imperial |
| October | 1962 | A LITTLE BIT NOW | Imperial |

RICHARD MALTBY

Born: June 26, 1914
Hometown: Chicago, Illinois

Arranger-conductor-trumpeteer Richard Maltby worked for "X" records in the fifties and helped on sessions for many of the label's artists. A subsidiary of RCA, "X" afforded Maltby the opportunity to become a chart artist after he recorded the instrumental hit "St. Louis Blues Mambo" in the fall of 1954.

| September | 1954 | ST. LOUIS BLUES MAMBO | "X" |
| February | 1956 | THEMES FROM THE MAN WITH THE GOLDEN ARM | Vik |

HENRY MANCINI

Born: April 16, 1924
Hometown: Cleveland, Ohio

In the late fifties, Henry worked composing songs for TV shows like "Mr. Lucky" and did a few film scores. He signed with RCA records and in 1961 collaborated with lyricist Johnny Mercer to write the score for the

HENRY MANCINI

motion picture *Breakfast at Tiffany's.* One of the songs, "Moon River," won an Oscar as the best song of 1961. This feat was duplicated in 1962, with "Days Of Wine And Roses" from the film of the same name.

Henry has won more Oscars and Grammys (the record industry's award) than any other artist. He continues to write great songs for movies and TV from his home in Los Angeles.

March	1960	MR. LUCKY	RCA
April	1961	THEME FROM THE GREAT IMPOSTER	RCA
October	1961	MOON RIVER	RCA
April	1962	MOON RIVER	RCA
July	1962	THEME FROM HATARI	RCA
January	1963	DAYS OF WINE AND ROSES	RCA
June	1963	BANZAI PIPELINE	RCA
December	1963	CHARADE	RCA
April	1964	PINK PANTHER THEME	RCA
December	1964	DEAR HEART	RCA
May	1969	LOVE THEME FROM ROMEO & JULIET	RCA
September	1969	MOONLIGHT SONATA	RCA
January	1971	THEME FROM LOVE STORY	RCA
March	1977	THEME FROM "CHARLIE'S ANGELS"	RCA

THE MANHATTAN BROTHERS

The group consisted of four black singers who had a very white-oriented sound. In early 1956 their pretty ballad "Lovely Lies" became their only major hit.

January	1956	LOVELY LIES	London

BARRY MANN

Real Name: Barry Iberman
Born: February 9, 1939
Hometown: Brooklyn, New York

After high school Barry originally wanted to study architecture at Pratt Institute, but decided on a musical career instead. In 1960, he started writing songs like "Footsteps," "The Way Of A Clown," and "Time Machine," which turned out to be hits for Steve Lawrence, Teddy Randazzo, and Dante & the Evergreens, respectively.

Al Nevins and Don Kirshner, for whom Barry was working as a song writer, discovered his singing talent and decided to try him as a recording artist, signing him for ABC records. In July 1961, he recorded a song that he had written with Gerry Goffin, "Who Put The Bomp," which became an instant hit that summer. It was his only major hit for ABC.

In 1977, he co-wrote the hit "Sometimes When We Touch" with Canadian singer Dan Hill.

July	1961	WHO PUT THE BOMP	ABC
August	1976	THE PRINCESS & THE PUNK	Arista

GLORIA MANN

Gloria launched her career on Sound records in early 1955, with her version of the Penguins' big hit called "Earth Angel." The record did fairly well and gave her national exposure.

Later that summer, she recorded a ballad song called "Teen-Age Prayer," in which her youthful voice sang about the fellow who was the love of her life and the answer to her teen-age prayer.

January	1955	EARTH ANGEL	Sound
August	1955	TEEN-AGE PRAYER	Sound
February	1956	WHY DO FOOLS FALL IN LOVE	Decca

MANTOVANI

Real Name: Annunzio Paulo Mantovani
Born: November 15, 1905, Venice, Italy
Died: March 29, 1980, London, England
Hometown: London, England

Mantovani studied the violin and piano as a youngster. At seventeen, he was leading the orchestra at the largest hotel in Birmingham, England. Other engagements in bigger hotels and clubs in London followed. During the forties Mantovani recognized the public's preference for sweet and danceable songs. He put together his own orchestra and soon became known as one of Britain's best makers of pop music. His big hits on the national charts in the United States have included "The Moulin Rouge Theme" (1953), "Around the World" (1957), and the theme from the motion picture *Exodus* (1961).

October	1951	CHARMAINE	London
May	1953	THE MOULIN ROUGE THEME	London
June	1957	AROUND THE WORLD	London
November	1961	MAIN THEME FROM EXODUS	London

THE MARATHONS

Members:
    James Johnson—lead
    Richard Owens—first tenor
    Carl Fisher—second tenor
    David Govan—baritone
    Don Bradley—bass
Hometown: Los Angeles, California

See entry for the Vibrations.

April	1961	PEANUT BUTTER	Arvee

THE MARCELS

Members:
    Cornelius Harp—lead
    Ronald "Bingo" Mundy—first tenor
    Gene Bricker—second tenor
    Dick Knauss—baritone
    Fred Johnson—bass
Hometown: Pittsburgh, Pennsylvania

When Dick Knauss auditioned for a local singing group in Pittsburgh called the Dynamics, manager Jules Kuspir offered Dick the job. Instead of taking it, however, Dick told him about a group he had just found. Jules became interested in hearing them, so an audition was arranged. He was so impressed with the group that he signed them up. The group decided to call itself the Marcels after a hair style that one of the members wore at the time.

They cut an audition tape that Jules sent to Colpix records. Colpix arranger Stu Phillips liked Fred's bass voice on one of the songs and decided to use it as a gimmick on the 1934 Rodgers and Hart classic "Blue Moon." The song was recorded and released in February 1961. In a short time it became a number one national hit.

Later that same year, Dick and Gene left the group to be replaced by Allen Johnson, Fred's brother, and Walt Maddox. That September, the group had its only other major hit with "Heartaches." Right after that, Ron Mundy left the group.

February	1961	BLUE MOON	Colpix
May	1961	SUMMERTIME	Colpix
October	1961	HEARTACHES	Colpix

BOBBY MARCHAN

Born: April 30, 1930
Hometown: Youngstown, Ohio

Bobby attended East High School in Youngstown and received early training in the church choir. In 1955, he sang as a solo performer and recorded the song "Chick-A-Wa-Wa." He joined Huey Smith on Ace records in 1958, becoming part of Huey's singing group, the Clowns. They recorded "Don't You Just Know It" and "Don't You Know Yockomo."

In early 1959, he left the group and formed another, called the Tick Tocks. He signed as a solo performer on Fire records in early 1960, and in June of that year had a hit with "There's Something On Your Mind."

| June | 1960 | THERE'S SOMETHING ON YOUR MIND | Fire |

ERNIE MARESCA

Born: April 21, 1939
Hometown: Bronx, New York

Ernie wrote many songs for Dion DiMucci of the Belmonts. He used the sound of the record "Quarter to Three" to write "Runaround Sue" with Dion. Ernie wrote "The Wanderer" around the hit "Kansas City."

In early 1962, Danny Kessler of Seville records suggested that Ernie try singing a song he had written called "Shout! Shout! (Knock Yourself Out)." Marv Holtzman and Murray Spahn, also of Seville records, encouraged Ernie to try it to see what would happen. Ernie got together with the Del Satins, the group that backed Dion up on all his hits without the Belmonts, and in March 1962 "Shout! Shout!" became a top-ten hit.

Today Ernie works for Laurie records in New York as a staff writer and producer and as the head of their publishing branch.

March	1962	SHOUT! SHOUT! (KNOCK YOURSELF OUT)	Seville

THE MARK IV

This group had two major hits during the late fifties. "The Shake," on the Cosmic label, was a dance song, and "I Got a Wife," for Mercury, was a novelty song, a husband singing about the trials and tribulations of matrimony. "I Got a Wife," the more successful of the pair, was a top-forty record.

February	1958	THE SHAKE	Cosmic
January	1959	I GOT A WIFE	Mercury

THE MARKETTS

The Marketts were a West Coast group who had some instrumental hits in the early sixties on Liberty records, the first of which was "Surfer's Stomp." Surfing became a very popular sport in 1962, due to the popularity of another West Coast group called the Beach Boys. In 1963, the Marketts signed with Warner Brothers and had a top-ten hit with a Michael Gordon song called "Out of Limits." This instrumental was their biggest hit.

January	1962	SURFER'S STOMP	Liberty
April	1962	BALBOA BLUE	Liberty
November	1963	OUT OF LIMITS	Warner Bros.
March	1964	VANISHING POINT	Warner Bros.
February	1966	BATMAN THEME	Warner Bros.

THE MAR-KEYS

Members:
Terry Johnson—drums
Steve Cropper—guitar
Donald "Duck" Dunn—bass guitar
Charles Axton—tenor sax
Don Nix—baritone sax
Wayne Jackson—trumpet
Jerry Lee "Smoochee" Smith—piano and organ
Hometown: Memphis, Tennessee

The group first started playing together in 1958, in Memphis, as a four-piece combo, but added brass and an organ in 1960. They played local dances in Memphis and later became staff musicians for Satellite records in Memphis.

In 1961, Charles and Jerry of the group, along with A & R man Chips Moman, wrote a song called "Last Night" that became a top hit for the group on Satellite records. Later that year, Steve and Don left the group to join forces with drummer Al Jackson and organist Booker T. Jones, forming Booker T. and the MG's (Memphis Group), and had their first hit on Stax records with "Green Onions" in August 1962.

June	1961	LAST NIGHT	Satellite
October	1961	MORNING AFTER	Stax
March	1962	POP-EYE STROLL	Stax
March	1966	PHILLY DOG	Stax

RALPH MARTERIE

Hometown: Chicago, Illinois

Ralph wanted to be a musician like his father, who was with the Civic Opera Orchestra in Chicago, so he took up the trumpet. By the time he was seventeen, he was playing with many big orchestras in Chicago. He later did some network radio work for NBC in Chicago, playing with the Paul Whiteman and Percy Faith bands.

In the early forties Ralph joined the Navy and organized a service band. After his discharge he got a job with ABC, doing his own radio show. Shortly after that he was signed by Mercury records and was billed as "The Caruso of the Trumpet." In January 1953, he had one of his first pop hits, the song "Pretend."

January	1953	PRETEND	Mercury
March	1953	CARAVAN	Mercury

August	1954	SKOKIAAN	Mercury
April	1956	THEME FROM PICNIC	Mercury
February	1957	TRICKY	Mercury
April	1957	SHISH-KEBAB	Mercury

MARTHA AND THE VANDELLAS

Members:
Martha Reeves—lead
Roslyn Ashford
Annette Beard
Hometown: Detroit, Michigan

Martha got a job at Motown records in 1962, working as a secretary in the office assisting some of the Motown writers. In her job she was called upon occasionally to sing background on some of the recordings of artists like Marvin Gaye and Mary Wells. In early 1963, she was given an opportunity to get together with several of her high school friends and record a song of their own. They called themselves Martha and the Vandellas and recorded "Come And Get These Memories," which became their first hit

**MARTHA AND
THE VANDELLAS**

in March 1963. In the summer of 1964, they recorded a song Marvin Gaye had written, "Dancing In The Street," which became the group's biggest hit.

Around 1965, the group changed their name to Martha Reeves and the Vandellas. In December 1971, Martha made her last appearance with the group, at Cobo Hall in Detroit. Shortly after that she signed with MCA records. Today she lives in Los Angeles and is establishing a new career as a solo artist.

March	1963	COME AND GET THESE MEMORIES	Gordy
July	1963	HEAT WAVE	Gordy
November	1963	QUICKSAND	Gordy
January	1964	LIVE WIRE	Gordy
April	1964	IN MY LONELY ROOM	Gordy
August	1964	DANCING IN THE STREET	Gordy
December	1964	WILD ONE	Gordy
February	1965	NOWHERE TO RUN	Gordy
August	1965	YOU'VE BEEN IN LOVE TOO LONG	Gordy
January	1966	MY BABY LOVES ME	Gordy
May	1966	WHAT AM I GOING TO DO WITHOUT YOUR LOVE	Gordy
October	1966	I'M READY FOR LOVE	Gordy
February	1967	JIMMY MACK	Gordy
August	1967	LOVE BUG LEAVE MY HEART ALONE	Gordy
November	1967	HONEY CHILE	Gordy
April	1968	I PROMISE TO WAIT MY LOVE	Gordy
July	1968	I CAN'T DANCE TO THE MUSIC YOU'RE PLAYIN'	Gordy
November	1968	SWEET DARLIN'	Gordy
April	1969	WE'VE GOT HONEY LOVE	Gordy
November	1970	I GOTTA LET YOU GO	Gordy
October	1971	BLESS YOU	Gordy

DEAN MARTIN

Real Name: Dino Crocetti
Born: June 7, 1917
Hometown: Steubenville, Ohio

One of six children, Dean worked as a coal miner, boxer, gas station attendant, and mill hand. By the time he was twenty-seven, he decided he wanted to become a singer, even though he had no previous experience. In 1946, while he was in Atlantic City, the owner of the 500 Club needed an act and asked Dean to team with a young comedian named Jerry Lewis. They agreed, and the rest is history.

By 1950, Dean had signed a recording contract with Capitol records, which released his "I'll Always Love You" that summer. He had his first national number one song with "Memories Are Made Of This" in 1955.

In 1956, Jerry and Dean decided to split up and pursue separate careers.

Dean left Capitol records at the end of 1959, and in 1962 signed with Reprise records. In June 1964, he recorded his next number one song, "Everybody Loves Somebody," which has since become his theme song.

August	1950	I'LL ALWAYS LOVE YOU	Capitol
January	1951	IF	Capitol
August	1952	YOU BELONG TO ME	Capitol
November	1953	THAT'S AMORE	Capitol
July	1954	SWAY	Capitol
July	1955	MEMORIES ARE MADE OF THIS	Capitol
February	1956	INNAMORATA	Capitol
May	1956	STANDING ON THE CORNER	Capitol
March	1958	RETURN TO ME	Capitol
June	1958	ANGEL, BABY	Capitol
August	1958	VOLARE	Capitol
July	1959	ON AN EVENING IN ROMA	Capitol
December	1962	FROM THE BOTTOM OF MY HEART	Reprise
June	1964	EVERYBODY LOVES SOMEBODY	Reprise
September	1964	THE DOOR IS STILL OPEN TO MY HEART	Reprise
December	1964	YOU'RE NOBODY TILL SOMEBODY LOVES YOU	Reprise
February	1965	SEND ME THE PILLOW YOU DREAM ON	Reprise
May	1965	REMEMBER ME I'M THE ONE WHO LOVES YOU	Reprise
August	1965	HOUSTON	Reprise
October	1965	I WILL	Reprise
January	1966	SOMEWHERE THERE'S A SOMEONE	Reprise
May	1966	COME RUNNING BACK	Reprise
July	1966	A MILLION AND ONE	Reprise
October	1966	NOBODY'S BABY AGAIN	Reprise
December	1966	LET THE GOOD TIMES IN	Reprise
April	1967	LAY SOME HAPPINESS ON ME	Reprise
July	1967	IN THE CHAPEL IN THE MOONLIGHT	Reprise
August	1967	LITTLE OLD WINE DRINKER ME	Reprise
December	1967	IN THE MISTY MOONLIGHT	Reprise
March	1968	YOU'VE STILL GOT A PLACE IN MY HEART	Reprise
November	1968	NOT ENOUGH INDIANS	Reprise
August	1969	I TAKE A LOT OF PRIDE IN WHAT I AM	Reprise

TONY MARTIN

Real Name: Alvin Morris, Jr.
Born: December 25, 1913
Hometown: San Francisco, California

Tony started his career as a saxophonist. Subsequently he became an actor and recording star. His film credits include *Sing, Baby, Sing, Follow the Fleet, Till the Clouds Roll By, Easy to Love,* and *Let's Be Happy.* His recording career hit its peak during the late forties and early fifties. His first three chart records all made the top ten as did "There's No Tomorrow," "I Said My Pajamas," "La Vie en Rose," "I Get Ideas," and "Kiss of

Fire."

Tony served with the Air Force during World War II and was awarded the bronze star. He married the very lovely Cyd Charisse in 1948, and since that time they have lived in Hollywood. They appear together in night clubs and on TV.

October	1941	TONIGHT WE LOVE	Decca
August	1946	TO EACH HIS OWN	Mercury
October	1946	RUMORS ARE FLYING	Mercury
May	1948	FOR EVERY MAN THERE'S A WOMAN	RCA Victor
July	1948	IT'S MAGIC	RCA Victor
November	1949	THERE'S NO TOMORROW	RCA Victor
January	1950	I SAID MY PAJAMAS (AND PUT ON MY PRAYERS) (Fran Warren)	RCA Victor
May	1950	VALENCIA	RCA Victor
June	1950	LA VIE EN ROSE	RCA Victor
February	1951	WOULD I LOVE YOU (LOVE YOU, LOVE YOU)	RCA Victor
May	1951	I GET IDEAS	RCA Victor
October	1951	OVER A BOTTLE OF WINE	RCA Victor
October	1951	DOMINO	RCA Victor
April	1952	KISS OF FIRE	RCA Victor
October	1952	DANCE OF DESTINY	RCA Victor
December	1953	STRANGER IN PARADISE	RCA Victor
March	1954	HERE	RCA Victor
March	1956	WALK HAND IN HAND	RCA
August	1956	IT'S BETTER IN THE DARK	RCA
April	1957	DO I LOVE YOU	RCA

VINCE MARTIN AND THE TARRIERS

Members:
   Vince Martin—lead vocalist
   Alan Arkin—baritone
   Bob Carey—bass voice and guitar
   Erik Darling—tenor
Hometown: New York, New York

The fellows got together in the New York area and began singing Calypso-influenced music. They were signed to Glory records in 1956, and Alan, Bob, and Erik backed up Vince Martin with their instruments on the popular "Cindy, Oh Cindy" that fall.

Later that year, they recorded as the Tarriers a song that Alan, Bob, and Erik had written called "Banana Boat Song," which became a top-ten hit. Harry Belafonte then recorded a similar version called "Banana Boat" ("Day-O") which was a top-ten hit for him in early 1957.

Alan Arkin is today a very successful movie and television actor. Erik formed the Rooftop Singers in 1962, who recorded the number one song "Walk Right In."

| September | 1956 | CINDY, OH CINDY | Glory |
| November | 1956 | THE BANANA BOAT SONG | Glory |

WINK MARTINDALE

Real Name: Winston Conrad
Born: 1934
Hometown: Bells, Tennessee

At sixteen Wink worked as an announcer for WPIL in Jackson, Tennessee. In 1953, he joined WHBQ in Memphis, where he did the morning radio show, as well as some early TV work. In March 1959, he went to KHJ-TV in Los Angeles and hosted the "Dance Party" show on Saturday nights. He signed with Dot records in August 1959, and narrated a song called "Deck Of Cards" that became a national hit that fall.

Today Wink, who is known as Win Martindale, is a very popular game-show host on TV.

| November | 1959 | DECK OF CARDS | Dot |

AL MARTINO

Real Name: Alfred Cini
Born: October 7, 1927
Hometown: Philadelphia, Pennsylvania

Al was a bricklayer in South Philadelphia when, in 1950, a fellow Philadelphian, Mario Lanza, encouraged him to pursue a recording career. In 1952, he signed with Capitol and had a hit in May of that year with "Here In My Heart," which went to number one.

After an important role in the film "The Godfather," Al's career took an upward swing again. He is a very popular night club entertainer around the country.

May	1952	HERE IN MY HEART	BBS
June	1952	TAKE MY HEART	Capitol
May	1959	I CAN'T GET YOU OUT OF MY HEART	20th Fox
October	1959	DARLING, I LOVE YOU	20th Fox
July	1961	HERE IN MY HEART	Capitol
March	1963	I LOVE YOU BECAUSE	Capitol
July	1963	PAINTED, TAINTED ROSE	Capitol
October	1963	LIVING A LIE	Capitol
January	1964	I LOVE YOU MORE & MORE EVERY DAY	Capitol

May	1964	TEARS AND ROSES	Capitol
August	1964	ALWAYS TOGETHER	Capitol
January	1965	MY HEART WOULD KNOW	Capitol
March	1965	SOMEBODY ELSE IS TAKING MY PLACE	Capitol
June	1965	MY CHERIE	Capitol
October	1965	FORGIVE ME	Capitol
December	1965	SPANISH EYES	Capitol
February	1966	THINK I'LL GO SOMEWHERE AND CRY MYSELF TO SLEEP	Capitol
May	1966	WIEDERSEH'N	Capitol
August	1966	JUST YESTERDAY	Capitol
October	1966	THE WHEEL OF HURT	Capitol
January	1967	DADDY'S LITTLE GIRL	Capitol
May	1967	MARY IN THE MORNING	Capitol
September	1967	MORE THAN THE EYE CAN SEE	Capitol
December	1967	A VOICE IN THE CHOIR	Capitol
February	1968	LOVE IS BLUE	Capitol
April	1968	LILI MARLENE	Capitol
May	1969	SAUSALITO	Capitol
December	1969	I STARTED LOVING YOU AGAIN	Capitol
February	1970	CAN'T HELP FALLING IN LOVE	Capitol
April	1972	LOVE THEME FROM "THE GODFATHER"	Capitol
December	1974	TO THE DOOR OF THE SUN	Capitol
November	1975	VOLARE	Capitol
December	1977	THE NEXT HUNDRED YEARS	Capitol

THE MARVELETTES

Members:

    Gladys Horton—lead—1944

    Katherine Anderson—1944

    Georgeanna Tillman—1944; died: January 6, 1980

    Juanita Cowart—1944

    Wanda Young—1944

Hometown: Detroit, Michigan

In 1961, when the girls were at Inkster High in Detroit, Berry Gordy, Jr., the president of Motown records, saw them perform at a talent show. He was so impressed that he signed them to his Tamla label. In September 1961, their first national hit, "Please Mr. Postman," became number one—their only record to reach the top spot on the charts.

    Georgeanna died in 1980 of lupus disease and sickle cell anemia.

September	1961	PLEASE MR. POSTMAN	Tamla
January	1962	TWISTIN' POSTMAN	Tamla
April	1962	PLAYBOY	Tamla
August	1962	BEECHWOOD 4-5789	Tamla
November	1962	STRANGE I KNOW	Tamla
March	1963	LOCKING UP MY HEART	Tamla
July	1963	MY DADDY KNOWS BEST	Tamla
October	1963	AS LONG AS I KNOW HE'S MINE	Tamla

THE MARVELETTES

February	1964	HE'S A GOOD GUY	Tamla
June	1964	YOU'RE MY REMEDY	Tamla
November	1964	TOO MANY FISH IN THE SEA	Tamla
May	1965	I'LL KEEP HOLDING ON	Tamla
August	1965	DANGER HEARTBREAK DEAD AHEAD	Tamla
January	1966	DON'T MESS WITH BILL	Tamla
April	1966	YOU'RE THE ONE	Tamla
January	1967	THE HUNTER GETS CAPTURED BY THE GAME	Tamla
April	1967	WHEN YOU'RE YOUNG AND IN LOVE	Tamla
December	1967	MY BABY MUST BE A MAGICIAN	Tamla
June	1968	HERE I AM BABY	Tamla
October	1968	DESTINATION: ANYWHERE	Tamla

MARVIN & JOHNNY

Members:

Marvin Phillips

Joe Josea

In 1953, Marvin Phillips began singing with Jesse Belvin in the Los Angeles area. They were billed as Jesse and Marvin. In a short time they signed with Specialty records and recorded a song they had written called "Dream Girl," which became an R & B hit in 1953.

Later that year the duo split up. Jesse went on as a single to record "Goodnight My Love" and "Guess Who." Marvin got together with Joe Josea and they became known as Marvin and Johnny. The duo auditioned for Saul and Jules Bihari of Modern records and were signed to a contract.

In 1954, they recorded their classic "Cherry Pie," which they had both written. (The song was a hit for Skip & Flip in 1960.) Later that year came another Marvin & Johnny classic called "Tick Tock."

| April | 1954 | CHERRY PIE | Modern |
| August | 1954 | TICK TOCK | Modern |

JOHNNY MAESTRO

Real Name: Johnny Mastrangelo

Johnny Maestro, after singing as the lead voice for the Crests on "Sixteen Candles" and many other hits, decided to leave that group and go on his own in late 1960. He was not as successful as a single as he had been with the Crests; however, he had several moderately popular hits.

In 1968, Johnny formed the Brooklyn Bridge and recorded the smash "The Worst that Could Happen."

January	1961	MODEL GIRL	Coed
April	1961	WHAT A SURPRISE	Coed
July	1961	MR. HAPPINESS	Coed

JOHNNY MATHIS

Born: September 30, 1935
Hometown: San Francisco, California

Johnny's father noticed his talent when he was a youngster and encouraged him to pursue a singing career. There was a time in the early fifties that Johnny considered a career as an English teacher or an athletic coach. In fact, Johnny was so outstanding in track and field at San Francisco State College that he was invited to try out for the 1956 Olympics. However, just prior to this, during the summer of 1955, Columbia records executive George Avakian, vacationing in San Francisco, had gone to Ann's 440 Club and heard Johnny for the first time. He was so impressed with Johnny's voice that he signed him to the label.

When Johnny first recorded for Columbia, it had him work with some jazz arrangers. The results were not too successful. However, with Mitch Miller, who was Columbia's A & R head at the time, it became a different story. Mitch rechanneled Johnny's efforts into the soft-ballad sound.

In late 1956, Mitch had Johnny record four songs. "Warm and

JOHNNY MATHIS

Tender," "Wonderful! Wonderful!," "When Sunny Gets Blue," and "It's Not For Me To Say" were the first with that special "Mathis Magic." Of the four, "Wonderful! Wonderful!" was chosen as Johnny's single release. By January 1957, it had become a national hit, the first in a long series. Later that year "Chances Are" was released, the song Johnny considers to technically represent some of the best singing he has ever done.

In late 1957, Johnny's schedule interfered with the planned recording of a new album. Consequently, Mitch put together Johnny's first five recordings with some others and released "Johnny Mathis' Greatest Hits." The album remained on *Billboard* magazine's pop album charts for over four hundred straight weeks. This set not only a record, but the precedent for all other "Best Of" albums.

Johnny is the master of the love ballad and for almost twenty years has presented his "Mathis Magic" (which he describes as "a highly personal sound that seems to float a few inches off the ground, never landing with a thud") to a world of people falling in love. He is still the master of the tender and poignant lyric and gets better as he gets older. A Los Angeles resident, he continues to record for Columbia records and entertain millions all over the world.

Johnny's teaming up with Deniece Williams in 1978 resulted in his first ever number one single "Too Much, Too Little, Too Late."

January	1957	WONDERFUL! WONDERFUL!	Columbia
April	1957	IT'S NOT FOR ME TO SAY	Columbia
August	1957	CHANCES ARE	Columbia
August	1957	THE TWELFTH OF NEVER	Columbia
December	1957	WILD IS THE WIND	Columbia
December	1957	NO LOVE (BUT YOUR LOVE)	Columbia
February	1958	COME TO ME	Columbia

March	1958	ALL THE TIME	Columbia
March	1958	TEACHER, TEACHER	Columbia
June	1958	A CERTAIN SMILE	Columbia
October	1958	CALL ME	Columbia
January	1959	YOU ARE BEAUTIFUL	Columbia
January	1959	LET'S LOVE	Columbia
March	1959	SOMEONE	Columbia
June	1959	SMALL WORLD	Columbia
October	1959	MISTY	Columbia
November	1959	THE BEST OF EVERYTHING	Columbia
February	1960	STARBRIGHT	Columbia
June	1960	MARIA	Columbia
August	1960	MY LOVE FOR YOU	Columbia
January	1961	HOW TO HANDLE A WOMAN	Columbia
October	1961	WASN'T THE SUMMER SHORT	Columbia
March	1962	SWEET THURSDAY	Columbia
June	1962	MARIANNA	Columbia
September	1962	GINA	Columbia
January	1963	WHAT WILL MARY SAY	Columbia
May	1963	EVERY STEP OF THE WAY	Columbia
August	1963	SOONER OR LATER	Columbia
December	1963	I'LL SEARCH MY HEART	Columbia
October	1963	YOUR TEEN-AGE DREAMS	Mercury
October	1963	COME BACK	Mercury
January	1964	BYE BYE BARBARA	Mercury
June	1964	TASTE OF TEARS	Mercury
October	1964	LISTEN LONELY GIRL	Mercury
December	1965	ON A CLEAR DAY YOU CAN SEE FOREVER	Mercury
September	1973	I'M COMING HOME	Columbia
December	1973	LIFE IS A SONG WORTH SINGING	Columbia
WITH DENIECE WILLIAMS			
April	1978	TOO MUCH, TOO LITTLE, TOO LATE	Columbia
July	1978	YOU'RE ALL I NEED TO GET BY	Columbia

THE MATYS BROTHERS

This group's major hit was a novelty song that centered on a Polish delicacy called Keeshka. The record decried the fact that someone purloined the beloved Keeshka. After this one record for Select in January 1963, neither the Keeshka nor the Matys Brothers were heard from again.

January	1963	WHO STOLE THE KEESHKA	Select

BILLY MAY

Billy, a staff conductor with Capitol, was very instrumental in the success of Frank Sinatra's hit albums like "Come Dance with Me." In early 1956, he recorded the theme from the motion picture *Man with the Golden Arm*, which starred Sinatra. It became a top-forty hit for Billy on Capitol.

February	1956	MAN WITH THE GOLDEN ARM	Capitol

NATHANIEL MAYER

Fortune records, a small Detroit operation, had moderate success in the motor city before the dominance of the Motown operation in the early sixties. The early success of Fortune was due to the song "The Wind" by Nolan Strong and the Diablos in the mid-fifties.

In the spring of 1962, the company enjoyed more success with Nathaniel Mayer's composition "Village of Love," which highlighted his deep raspy voice and had a driving brass section. The song became a national hit and Nathaniel's only chart record.

| April | 1962 | VILLAGE OF LOVE | Fortune |

THE MEDALLIONS

Members:
 Vernon Green—lead
 Randolph Bryant
 Willie Graham
 Ira Foley
Hometown: Los Angeles, California

The Medallions came to the attention of Dootsie Williams, the president of Dootone records, who signed them up. They first scored in 1954 with the ballad "The Letter," then later that same year had a hit with "Buick 59." The reason it was called Buick 59 instead of Buick 54 was that they hoped it would be a hit in '54, and then reissued as a hit in '59.

| April | 1954 | THE LETTER | Dootone |
| July | 1954 | BUICK 59 | Dootone |

THE MEGATRONS

"Velvet Waters" was recorded by a group of studio musicians in early 1959. The demo was taken to Gene Schwartz of Laurie records who liked the song and decided to release it on one of Laurie's subsidiary labels. At this point the studio musicians were christened the Megatrons.

Gene took the record to New York's top disc jockey at the time, Peter Tripp of WMGM radio. Peter did not like the song, but decided to air it and get a listener reaction. The song became a hit shortly thereafter.

| May | 1959 | VELVET WATERS | Acousticon |

THE MELLO-KINGS

Members:
> Bob Scholl—lead—born: July 14, 1938; died: August 27, 1975
> Jerry Scholl—first tenor—born: November 12, 1941
> Eddie Quinn—second tenor—1940
> Neil Arama—baritone—1940
> Larry Esposito—bass—1940
> Dick Levister—musical arranger

Hometown: Mount Vernon, New York

The group began in early 1957, when Bob and his younger brother Jerry got together with three other friends and formed the Mello-Tones. They came to New York from their homes in Mount Vernon and auditioned for Al Silver, the president of Herald records, with a song called "Tonight

THE MELLO-KINGS

Left to right: Bob Scholl, Larry Esposito, Neil Arama,
Eddie Quinn, Jerry Scholl
Bottom center: Dick Levister

Tonight." Al liked the song and they recorded it for Herald as the Mello-Tones. They had to change their name to the Mello-Kings when they found out that there was another group called the Mello-Tones who were recording for Gee records at the time, with "Rosie Lee."

When the song was first released in July 1957, many people thought the group was black, due to the style their arranger Dick Levister had developed. In a short time the song was a hit and has become a classic ballad in rock and roll.

Bob died as a result of a boating accident in 1975. Today, his brother Jerry keeps the name Mello-Kings active with all new members, while still residing in Mount Vernon, New York. Eddie is a hotel manager in Las Vegas, Neil is an insurance salesman, while Larry is in the construction business.

July	1957	TONIGHT TONIGHT	Herald
September	1957	SASSAFRAS	Herald
January	1958	BABY TELL ME	Herald
April	1958	VALERIE	Herald

THE MELLO-TONES

The group signed with George Goldner's Gee records in 1957. (The same label had Frankie Lymon and the Cleftones.) The Mello-Tones had only one national chart record, a song about a girl named "Rosie Lee."

| April | 1957 | ROSIE LEE | Gee |

MICKEY AND SYLVIA

Members:

Mickey "Guitar" Baker—October 15, 1925—Louisville, Kentucky

Sylvia (Vanderpool) Robinson—May 6, 1936—New York, New York

Both Mickey and Sylvia are accomplished guitar players. Sylvia, during her teens, recorded under the name of "Little Sylvia." In 1956, they signed with Groove records and recorded "Walkin' in the Rain" in September of that year as their first release. A few months later, Mickey and Sylvia recorded a song called "Love Is Strange," which became a hit in November 1956.

Sylvia left Mickey a few years later but rejoined him in July 1960, upon the insistence of producers Hugo & Luigi, to sign with RCA.

Sylvia Vanderpool married Joe Robinson in the fifties. They had their first child, Joe, Jr., in June 1962.

In March 1973, Sylvia came back on the hit trail with a song she wrote and recorded, "Pillow Talk," which became a national hit on her

MICKEY & SYLVIA

Mickey Baker and
Sylvia Robinson

own label, Vibration records.

Sylvia is very active running her own record company and has worked with many groups over the years such as The Moments, who today record as Ray, Goodman and Brown. Mickey Baker now resides in New York doing some studio recording.

November	1956	LOVE IS STRANGE	Groove
March	1957	THERE OUGHTA BE A LAW	Vik
May	1958	BEWILDERED	Vik
January	1961	WHAT WOULD I DO	RCA

THE MIDNIGHTERS

Members:
    Hank Ballard—lead—November 18, 1936
    Lawson Smith—baritone—1936
    Norman Thrasher—bass—1936—replaced by Charles Sutton
    Billy Davis—guitar—1936—replaced by Arthur Porter
    Henry Booth—tenor—deceased—1935—replaced by Sonny Woods
Hometown: Detroit, Michigan

The Midnighters were first formed as the Royals in 1952, and signed with Federal records in Cincinnati. Their first hit was a Johnny Otis song called "Every Beat Of My Heart" (also a hit for Gladys Knight and the Pips in 1961), which launched their sound in 1952. Hank was discovered by Johnny Otis, of the Little Esther Revue, and was signed to sing with the Royals around 1953.

In 1953, the group changed their name from the Royals to the Midnighters because the parent label, King records, had just signed a group called the "5" Royales. It was at this time that the group recorded a song with sexually oriented lyrics called "Get It." Many radio stations refrained from playing the song because it was a "dirty" record.

In 1954, Hank Ballard wrote a song called "Work With Me Annie" which was drawn from "Get It." It became the first in a series of "Annie" records, songs that used "Annie" in the title. Etta James's "Wallflower" ("Roll With Me Henry") was an answer to Hank's "Annie" song. Also in 1954, came "Sexy Ways" and "Annie Had A Baby," which became very successful.

Hank sang lead with the Midnighters on Federal until late 1958, when he went out on his own on the parent label, King records. In early 1959, he wrote and recorded "The Twist," which became popular for him. One year later, this same song would be recorded by Chubby Checker and not only become Chubby's biggest hit and the most popular song of

THE MIDNIGHTERS

Clockwise from center: Sonny Woods, Lawson Smith,
Hank Ballard, Arthur Porter, Charles Sutton

the sixties, but set the pace for the dance trend songs of the early part of that decade.

Hank went on to write and record "Finger Poppin' Time" and his favorite, "Let's Go, Let's Go, Let's Go."

April	1954	WORK WITH ME ANNIE	Federal
June	1954	SEXY WAYS	Federal
August	1954	ANNIE HAD A BABY	Federal
December	1954	ANNIE'S AUNT FANNY	Federal
May	1955	HENRY'S GOT FLAT FEET	Federal
August	1955	IT'S LOVE, BABY	Federal
November	1955	GIVE IT UP	Federal
January	1956	THAT HOUSE ON THE HILL	Federal
March	1956	OPEN UP THE BACK DOOR	Federal
June	1956	TORE UP OVER YOU	Federal

AMOS MILBURN

Born: April 1, 1927, Houston, Texas
Died: January 3, 1980, Houston, Texas

Amos was a piano-playing blues singer who was one of the early pioneers of R & B back in the late forties. Some of the songs he recorded like "Chicken Shack Boogie" directly influenced young artists like Fats Domino to become entertainers.

April	1949	HOLD ME BABY	Aladdin
June	1949	IN THE MIDDLE OF THE NIGHT	Aladdin
September	1949	ROOMING HOUSE BOOGIE	Aladdin
September	1949	EMPTY ARM BLUES	Aladdin
November	1949	LET'S MAKE CHRISTMAS MERRY, BABY	Aladdin
December	1949	REAL PRETTY MAMA	Aladdin
April	1950	WALKIN' BLUES	Aladdin
November	1950	BAD, BAD WHISKEY	Aladdin
April	1951	TEARS, TEARS, TEARS	Aladdin
February	1953	LET ME GO HOME, WHISKEY	Aladdin
September	1953	ONE SCOTCH, ONE BOURBON, ONE BEER	Aladdin

GARRY MILES

Real Name: James (Buzz) Cason
Hometown: Nashville, Tennessee

Garry's only major hit, "Look for a Star," came from the motion picture *Circus of Horrors*. Dean Hawley recorded the same song for Dore records; however, Garry's was the bigger of the two. Garry also sang as Buzz Cason with the group The Statues (of "Blue Velvet" fame) on Liberty.

May	1960	LOOK FOR A STAR	Liberty

CHUCK MILLER

Chuck was a country artist whose "The House of Blue Lights" crossed over to the pop charts in 1955. The song was a very catchy tune in the be-bop vein, the kind of tune The Andrews Sisters might have recorded in the forties. Its catchy lyrics and melody made it a top-ten hit in the summer of 1955.

| May | 1955 | THE HOUSE OF BLUE LIGHTS | Mercury |
| November | 1956 | THE AUCTIONEER | Mercury |

MITCH MILLER

Real Name: Mitchell William Miller
Born: July 4, 1911
Hometown: Rochester, New York

Mitch graduated from the Eastman School of Music in 1932. In the early thirties he was an oboist with the Rochester Philharmonic Orchestra. From 1935 to 1947 he was oboe soloist with the CBS Symphony, also playing on occasion with the Saidenberg Little Symphony and the Budapest String Quartet. One of Mitch's most successful enterprises was his television sing-along show which featured all the old favorites. Mitch had

MITCH MILLER

a number of chart hits, old-fashioned presentations that muscled aside more contemporary rock and roll numbers of the fifties. His "The Yellow Rose of Texas" was a top-ten tune in 1955.

Today he lives by himself in New York City in semiretirement.

June	1950	TZENA, TZENA, TZENA	Columbia
May	1955	THE YELLOW ROSE OF TEXAS	Columbia
August	1955	BONNIE BLUE GAL	Columbia
October	1955	AUTUMN LEAVES	Columbia
January	1956	LISBON ANTIGUA	Columbia
February	1956	MADEIRA	Columbia
July	1956	SONG FOR A SUMMER NIGHT	Columbia
November	1956	SONG OF THE SPARROW	Columbia
February	1957	A VERY SPECIAL LOVE	Columbia
January	1958	MARCH FROM THE RIVER KWAI & COLONEL BOGEY	Columbia
January	1959	THE CHILDREN'S MARCHING SONG	Columbia
December	1959	DO-RE-MI	Columbia
March	1961	TUNES OF GLORY	Columbia

NED MILLER

Ned was a country singer who got his big chance in 1962 when he signed with Fabor records and recorded a song he wrote called "From a Jack to a King." The song became a top-ten national hit.

December	1962	FROM A JACK TO A KING	Fabor
December	1964	DO WHAT YOU DO WELL	Fabor

HAYLEY MILLS

Born: April 18, 1946
Hometown: London, England

Hayley, who came from a very talented acting family, was signed as a teen-ager to appear in Walt Disney spectacles like *The Parent Trap*. The Disney people decided to capitalize on her popularity by having her record on their own Vista label. In the summer of 1961, she recorded "Let's Get Together," which became a top-ten national hit.

Today Hayley and her husband, sixty-year-old motion picture director Roy Boulting, live with their young son, Chrispian, in Los Angeles. She still makes movies, but no longer sings.

August	1961	LET'S GET TOGETHER	Vista
March	1962	JOHNNY JINGO	Vista

THE MILLS BROTHERS

THE MILLS BROTHERS

Members:
> John Mills—born: February 11, 1889—died: 1935
> Herbert Mills—born: April 2, 1912
> Harry Mills—born: August 9, 1913
> Donald Mills—born: April 29, 1915

Hometown: Piqua, Ohio

The brothers have had a long and varied career. They've been recording stars during the big band era, the rocking fifties, and the sophisticated sixties. The group began singing on radio station WSAI in Cincinnati. They became popular almost immediately, headlining New York's Palace for fourteen weeks, and then playing a variety of radio and club dates. They had back-to-back hit records in 1943 and 1944 with "Paper Doll" (a million seller) and "You Always Hurt the One You Love." They had top-ten hits in the fifties with "Daddy's Little Girl" and "Glow Worm." Their last top-forty record was "Cab Driver" in 1968.

| July | 1943 | PAPER DOLL | Decca |
| June | 1944 | YOU ALWAYS HURT THE ONE YOU LOVE | Decca |

September	1944	TILL THEN	Decca
July	1945	I WISH	Decca
May	1947	ACROSS THE ALLEY FROM THE ALAMO	Decca
November	1948	GLORIA	Decca
February	1949	I LOVE YOU SO MUCH IT HURTS	Decca
February	1949	I'VE GOT MY LOVE TO KEEP ME WARM	Decca
August	1949	SOMEDAY (YOU'LL WANT ME TO WANT YOU)	Decca
February	1950	DADDY'S LITTLE GIRL	Decca
October	1950	NEVERTHELESS	Decca
January	1952	BE MY LIFE'S COMPANION	Decca
September	1952	GLOW WORM	Decca
January	1954	THE JONES BOY	Decca
May	1955	SUDDENLY THERE'S A VALLEY	Decca
January	1956	ALL THE WAY AROUND THE WORLD	Decca
April	1956	STANDING ON THE CORNER	Decca
May	1957	QUEEN OF THE SENIOR PROM	Decca
January	1959	YELLOW BIRD	Dot
January	1968	CAB DRIVER	Dot
May	1968	MY SHY VIOLET	Dot
November	1968	THE OL' RACE TRACK	Dot

GARNET MIMMS AND THE ENCHANTERS

Members:

Garnet Mimms—lead—West Virginia
Zola Pearnell—Philadelphia, Pennsylvania
Sam Bell—Philadelphia, Pennsylvania
Charles Boyer—North Carolina

They all had a great deal of experience as individual singers before form-ing a group. Zola sang in Europe with the Paul Roberts choir, Charles sang with the Spiritual Group Ambassadors, Sam was a songwriter, and Garnet was a piano player.

In 1963, the group signed with United Artists records and in August of that year had their first and biggest hit with the Bert Russell song "Cry Baby."

August	1963	CRY BABY	United Artists
January	1963	BABY DON'T YOU WEEP	United Artists
November	1963	FOR YOUR PRECIOUS LOVE	United Artists
February	1964	TELL ME BABY	United Artists
May	1964	ONE GIRL	United Artists
October	1964	LOOK AWAY	United Artists
March	1966	I'LL TAKE GOOD CARE OF YOU	United Artists

SAL MINEO

Born: January 10, 1939
Died: February 13, 1976
Hometown: Bronx, New York

SAL MINEO

Sal's career as an actor overshadows his modest success as a recording artist. He appeared on Broadway in *The Rose Tatoo, The King and I,* and *Something About a Soldier.* Among his many film credits: *Rebel Without a Cause, Rock Pretty Baby, Dino, Exodus,* and *Cheyenne Autumn.* In April 1957 he had his most successful record, a top-ten chart record called "Start Movin'."

Sal was stabbed to death in early 1976 on his way home to his Los Angeles, California, apartment.

April	1957	START MOVIN'	Epic
August	1957	LASTING LOVE	Epic
November	1957	PARTY TIME	Epic
January	1958	LITTLE PIGEON	Epic

THE MIRACLES

Members:
William "Smokey" Robinson—lead—February 19, 1940
Claudette (Rodgers) Robinson—1942
Ronald White—1939
Robert Rodgers—1940
Warren "Pete" Moore—1939
Hometown: Detroit, Michigan

The five of them formed their group in 1957 and began singing small local engagements for the exposure. After some months they ran across

**SMOKEY ROBINSON
& THE MIRACLES**

Clockwise from top:
Bobby Rogers, Ronnie
White, Smokey
Robinson, Warren
"Pete" Moore

songwriter and record producer Berry Gordy, Jr. who was working at the time with a young singer named Jackie Wilson. Berry became very much interested in the Miracles and wanted to record them.

In early 1958, Berry, Smokey, and Tyronne Carlo (Jackie Wilson's cousin) wrote a song called "Got A Job," which was an answer to one number one song at the time, by the Silhouettes, called "Get A Job." The song became the first recording for the Miracles.

Not much happened after that song, and it wasn't until March 1959 that the group released another recording. At that time the group recorded another song that Berry and Smokey had cowritten, "Bad Girl." Because Berry was not then set up for national distribution, they leased the song to Chess records, whereupon it became the Miracles' first national release.

At this time Berry decided to try his hand at national distribution with his own Tamla label and released the Miracles' next song, "Way Over There," in the spring of 1960. This became the first Tamla hit for the Miracles. Later that year, Smokey and Berry had cowritten another song, "Shop Around," which they were going to offer to another Berry Gordy, Jr., artist, Barrett Strong, who had a hit earlier that year with a song called "Money." They had some difficulties getting Barrett to record the song, so Smokey felt the Miracles should give it a try. The song was recorded and released in October 1960, going on to become a million seller and a number one national hit. It was the song that got Tamla records (a division of Motown records) and Berry Gordy's musical empire off the ground.

Smokey (a nickname his uncle gave him) has written almost all the hits for the Miracles and numerous hits for other Motown artists, like "My Guy" for Mary Wells, "My Girl" for the Temptations, and "Ain't That Peculiar" for Marvin Gaye, to name a few. The name of Smokey Robinson has become synonymous with hit music over the past fourteen years, while artists like Bob Dylan have referred to him as "the world's greatest living poet."

The group changed their name to Smokey Robinson and the Miracles in 1967, in recognition of Smokey's unique voice and talent.

Smokey left the group in 1972, to go into management full time with Motown. He was replaced by Bill Griffin, who not only looked but sounded almost like Smokey.

Today The Miracles continue to travel and record, while Smokey is very popular as a solo artist.

Month	Year	Title	Label
March	1958	GOT A JOB	End
March	1959	BAD GIRL	Chess
April	1960	WAY OVER THERE	Tamla
July	1959	BAD GIRL	Chess
November	1960	SHOP AROUND	Tamla
April	1961	AIN'T IT, BABY	Tamla
July	1961	MIGHTY GOOD LOVIN'	Tamla
November	1961	EVERYBODY'S GOTTA PAY SOME DUES	Tamla
January	1962	WHAT'S SO GOOD ABOUT GOOD-BYE	Tamla
May	1962	I'll TRY SOMETHING NEW	Tamla
December	1962	YOU'VE REALLY GOT A HOLD ON ME	Tamla
April	1963	A LOVE SHE CAN COUNT ON	Tamla
August	1963	MICKEY'S MONKEY	Tamla
November	1963	I GOTTA DANCE TO KEEP FROM CRYING	Tamla
February	1964	YOU CAN'T LET THE BOY OVER-POWER THE MAN IN YOU	Tamla
June	1964	I LIKE IT LIKE THAT	Tamla
September	1964	THAT'S WHAT LOVE IS MADE OF	Tamla
December	1964	COME ON DO THE JERK	Tamla
April	1965	OOO BABY BABY	Tamla
July	1965	THE TRACKS OF MY TEARS	Tamla
December	1965	MY GIRL HAS GONE	Tamla
January	1966	GOING TO A GO-GO	Tamla
June	1966	WHOLE LOT OF SHAKIN' IN MY HEART	Tamla
November	1966	(COME 'ROUND HERE) I'M THE ONE YOU NEED	Tamla
March	1967	THE LOVE I SAW IN YOU WAS JUST A MIRAGE	Tamla
June	1967	MORE LOVE	Tamla
November	1967	I SECOND THAT EMOTION	Tamla
February	1968	IF YOU CAN WANT	Tamla

June	1968	YESTER LOVE	Tamla
August	1968	SPECIAL OCCASION	Tamla
January	1969	BABY, BABY DON'T CRY	Tamla
June	1969	DOGGONE RIGHT	Tamla
July	1969	ABRAHAM, MARTIN & JOHN	Tamla
December	1969	POINT IT OUT	Tamla
June	1970	WHO'S GONNA TAKE THE BLAME	Tamla
December	1970	THE TEARS OF A CLOWN	Tamla
March	1971	I DON'T BLAME YOU AT ALL	Tamla
July	1971	CRAZY ABOUT THE LA LA LA	Tamla
November	1971	SATISFACTION	Tamla
July	1972	WE'VE COME TOO FAR TO END IT NOW	Tamla
December	1972	I CAN'T STAND TO SEE YOU CRY	Tamla
July	1973	SWEET HARMONY	Tamla
November	1973	BABY COME CLOSE	Tamla
August	1974	DO IT BABY	Tamla
December	1974	DON'T CHA LOVE IT	Tamla
October	1975	LOVE MACHINE PT. 1	Tamla

CHAD MITCHELL TRIO

Members:
    Chad Mitchell—1939
    Mike Kobluk—1939
    Joe Frazier—1939
Hometown: Spokane, Washington

Chad Mitchell formed his trio in the early sixties and they began recording folk songs. In late 1961, they signed with Kapp records and recorded several chart records with their biggest being "Lizzie Borden."

    After the group went to Mercury, Chad left the group and they became known as The Mitchell Trio with Michael Kobluk, Joseph Frazier, and an unknown named John Denver (today a big, big star on RCA). They had several hit albums for Mercury in the mid-sixties.

January	1962	LIZZIE BORDEN	Kapp
November	1963	THE MARVELOUS TOY	Mercury

GUY MITCHELL

Real Name: Al Cernik
Born: February 27, 1927
Hometown: Detroit, Michigan

Yugoslavian-born Guy went to school in San Francisco and joined the Navy in 1945. Upon his discharge, he began a singing career. Mitch Miller heard him in 1950 and signed him on Columbia records. His first hit for the label was in December 1950, with "My Heart Cries For You." He followed with many more top hits until 1960.

GUY MITCHELL

December	1950	MY HEART CRIES FOR YOU	Columbia
December	1950	THE ROVING KIND	Columbia
February	1951	SPARROW IN THE TREE TOP	Columbia
April	1951	UNLESS	Columbia
May	1951	MY TRULY, TRULY FAIR	Columbia
July	1951	BELLE, BELLE, MY LIBERTY BELLE	Columbia
February	1952	PITTSBURGH, PENNSYLVANIA	Columbia
August	1952	FEET UP (PAT HIM ON THE PO-PO)	Columbia
October	1952	'CAUSE I LOVE YOU THAT'S A-WHY (Mindy Carson)	Columbia
January	1956	NINETY NINE YEARS	Columbia
October	1956	SINGING THE BLUES	Columbia
January	1957	KNEE DEEP IN THE BLUES	Columbia
March	1957	ROCK-A-BILLY	Columbia
May	1957	SWEET STUFF	Columbia
October	1959	HEARTACHES BY THE NUMBER	Columbia
March	1960	THE SAME OLD ME	Columbia
July	1960	MY SHOES KEEP WALKING BACK TO YOU	Columbia

ROBERT MITCHUM

Born: 1917
Hometown: Bridgeport, Connecticut

Everyone knows Robert Mitchum, the tough-guy film actor. Among his film credits: *Not as a Stranger, The Longest Day, Heaven Knows, Mr. Allison, Home from the Hill,* and *Ryan's Daughter.* Few people remember or have need to remember Mitchum's forgettable recording career. His most popular song was "The Ballad of Thunder Road," which just edged onto the pop charts in August 1958.

| August | 1958 | THE BALLAD OF THUNDER ROAD | Capitol |
| July | 1967 | LITTLE OLD WINE DRINKER ME | Monument |

DOMENICO MODUGNO

Born: 1929
Hometown: Sicily, Italy

In 1954, Erberto Landi caught a Milan show featuring the famous Italian comedian Walter Chiari. On the same bill was Domenico, a guitarist and singer of Sicilian songs. Landi signed him up and began to manage him. In 1955, he signed him to a tour of the United States and Canada, playing clubs like the Blue Angel in New York. Later returning to Italy, he wrote the song "Lazzarella," which won second place in the festival of Naples.

In 1958, he wrote a song called "Volare" which took first prize in the San Remo festival in Italy. The song was sold to Decca records in the United States and released in July 1958, becoming a number one song in a short time. In fact, it wound up as the number one song for the entire year.

| July | 1958 | NEL BLU DIPINTO DI BLU (VOLARE) | Decca |

THE MONOTONES

Members:
    Charles Patrick—lead—born: September 11, 1938
    Warren Davis—first tenor—born: March 1, 1939
    George Malone—second tenor—born: January 5, 1940
    Warren Ryanes—baritone—born: December 14, 1937
    John Smith—bass—born: May 13, 1938
    John Ryanes—bass—born: November 16, 1940—died: May 30, 1972
Hometown: Newark, New Jersey

The fellows lived in the same housing project called Baxter Terrace, in Newark. In 1954, while in high school, they decided to form a singing group. They were very content just playing local functions and really didn't consider a recording career. They were looking for a group name when they heard of another group in Newark called the Monotones, who were not really making use of the name. Consequently, they decided to borrow the name for themselves, since they felt "one sound" described their style.

In 1957, Charles Patrick was listening to the radio one day when he had an idea for a song. It seems that while he was looking at some sheet music entitled "Book Of Love," a song written by Al Stillman for the Four Lads, Charles heard the Pepsodent commercial for toothpaste with the line "wonder where the yellow went." From there he used the line "I wonder, wonder, wonder who! who wrote the book of love" as an idea for a song. He went home and got together with George Malone and Warren Davis of the group and they finished the song.

Although they had the song, they never thought of recording it themselves. When another singing group from Newark, the Kodaks, wanted to record "The Book of Love," the Monotones decided to do it themselves. They recorded the song in January 1958 and sold the tape to Argo records, which released it. A few months later it went on to become a pop chart hit and a rock and roll classic.

Today all the fellows still live in New Jersey, and sing together as the Monotones on occasion with the exception of John Ryanes, one of the two original bass singers, who died in May 1972.

| February | 1958 | BOOK OF LOVE | Argo |
| June | 1958 | THE LEGEND OF SLEEPY HOLLOW | Argo |

THE MONOTONES

Top row: Warren Davis, John Smith, John Ryanes
Bottom row: Warren Ryanes, Charles Patrick, George Malone

MATT MONRO

Hometown: London, England

Matt, a one-time truck and bus driver made his first professional appearance in 1954, with little initial success. He did not perform again until 1956, when he appeared in local clubs in England. In 1961, he recorded a song that was released on Warwick records in June of the same year in the United States. The song, "My Kind Of Girl," became his biggest hit.

| June | 1961 | MY KIND OF GIRL | Warwick |
| November | 1964 | WALK AWAY | Liberty |

VAUGHN MONROE

Born: October 7, 1911
Died: May 22, 1973
Hometown: Akron, Ohio

At fourteen, he won the Wisconsin state trumpet-playing championship. He started his own band in 1940, and recorded songs like "There I Go" on Bluebird records. His biggest hits like "Ballerina," "Ghost Riders in The Sky," and "Mule Train" came in the late forties on RCA Victor records.

December	1940	THERE I GO	Bluebird
August	1942	MY DEVOTION	Victor
October	1942	WHEN THE LIGHTS GO ON AGAIN	Victor
June	1943	LET'S GET LOST	Victor
December	1944	THE TROLLEY SONG	Victor
February	1945	RUM AND COCA-COLA	Victor
April	1945	THERE! I'VE SAID IT AGAIN	Victor
December	1945	LET IT SNOW! LET IT SNOW! LET IT SNOW!	Victor
August	1947	I WISH I DIDN'T LOVE YOU SO	RCA Victor
October	1947	KOKOMO, INDIANA	RCA Victor
October	1947	YOU DO	RCA Victor
October	1947	BALLERINA	RCA Victor
November	1947	HOW SOON? (WILL I BE SEEING YOU)	RCA Victor
June	1948	THE MAHARAJAH OF MAGADOR	RCA Victor
June	1948	COOL WATER (Sons of the Pioneers)	RCA Victor
July	1948	EVERYDAY I LOVE YOU	RCA Victor
January	1949	RED ROSES FOR A BLUE LADY	RCA Victor
April	1949	RIDERS IN THE SKY	RCA Victor
July	1949	SOMEDAY	RCA Victor
September	1949	THAT LUCKY OLD SUN	RCA Victor
October	1949	MULE TRAIN	RCA Victor
January	1950	BAMBOO	RCA Victor
April	1951	SOUND OFF	RCA Victor
April	1951	ON TOP OF OLD SMOKY	RCA Victor
May	1951	OLD SOLDIERS NEVER DIE	RCA Victor
July	1954	THEY WERE DOIN' THE MAMBO	RCA Victor

September	1955	BLACK DENIM TROUSERS	RCA
January	1956	DON'T GO TO STRANGERS	RCA
August	1956	IN THE MIDDLE OF THE HOUSE	RCA
May	1959	THE BATTLE OF NEW ORLEANS	RCA

LOU MONTE

Born: April 2, 1917
Hometown: Lyndhurst, New Jersey

Lou has been playing the guitar and singing since he was a child. His first break came when he had a radio show in Newark, New Jersey. Lou spent fifteen years in the musical minor leagues before he had his first hit for RCA, "At the Darktown Strutters' Ball," in 1954.

January	1954	AT THE DARKTOWN STRUTTERS' BALL	RCA Victor
February	1958	LAZY MARY	RCA
June	1958	SHEIK OF ARABY	RCA
December	1962	PEPINO THE ITALIAN MOUSE	Reprise
February	1963	PEPINO'S FRIEND PASQUAL	Reprise

LOU MONTE

CHRIS MONTEZ

Born: January 17, 1944
Hometown: Los Angeles, California

Chris's brothers taught him to play the guitar. At age fifteen, he began to write and follow in the vocal stylings of his idol Ritchie Valens. After high school graduation in 1961, Chris met Jim Lee, a young man who had started Monogram records. He signed with Jim's new label and recorded a song he wrote called "All You Had To Do Was Tell Me," which was a hit only on the West Coast.

In July 1962, he recorded a song that Jim Lee had written, "Let's Dance," which became a national hit.

Herb Alpert convinced him to join his label A & M records in late 1965, and he recorded his first hit at that time: "Call Me."

July	1962	LET'S DANCE	Monogram
December	1962	SOME KINDA FUN	Monogram
January	1966	CALL ME	A & M
April	1966	THE MORE I SEE YOU	A & M
July	1966	THERE WILL NEVER BE ANOTHER YOU	A & M
October	1966	TIME AFTER TIME	A & M

ART MOONEY

Art began to play the saxophone as a youngster. In the forties he formed his own dance band in Detroit.

After service in World War II he went to New York and worked the Edison Hotel. Soon, he had many other bookings and eventually signed with MGM records in 1947.

Toward the end of 1947, Art was presented with a novelty song to record called "I'm Looking Over a Four Leaf Clover," which he didn't care for. He recorded it, never figuring it would do anything. The song was a million seller in early 1948, and became the first in a long series of hits Art recorded for MGM.

January	1948	I'M LOOKING OVER A FOUR LEAF CLOVER	MGM
March	1948	BABY FACE	MGM
June	1948	BLUE BIRD OF HAPPINESS	MGM
February	1949	BEAUTIFUL EYES	MGM
May	1949	MERRY-GO-ROUND WALTZ	MGM
July	1949	TWENTY-FOUR HOURS OF SUNSHINE	MGM
July	1949	AGAIN	MGM
September	1949	HOP-SCOTCH POLKA	MGM
October	1949	TOOT, TOOT, TOOTSIE (GOOD-BYE)	MGM
December	1949	I NEVER SEE MAGGIE ALONE	MGM
March	1955	HONEY-BABE	MGM

June	1956	DAY DREAMS	MGM
October	1956	GIANT	MGM
January	1958	MARCH FROM THE RIVER KWAI & COLONEL BOGEY	MGM

THE MOONGLOWS

Members:

Harvey Fuqua—lead—1924
Bobby Lester—first tenor—January 13, 1930; died: October 15, 1980
Pete Graves—second tenor—April 17, 1936
Prentiss Barnes—bass—1921
Billy Johnson—guitar—1924

Hometown: Louisville, Kentucky

Bobby first organized the group in 1951, in Louisville. Their big break came when they went to Cleveland, Ohio, and met disc jockey Alan Freed, who was working at radio station WJW, doing the "Moondog Show." Alan suggested they call themselves something that came close to the name of his show, so they chose "Moonglows." He got them a record-

THE MOONGLOWS

Left to right: Prentiss Barnes, Bobby Lester,
Alexander "Pete" Graves, Harvey Fuqua
Bottom center: Billy Johnson

ing contract with Chance records, and they had a couple of hits with "Ooh, Rockin' Daddy" and "Secret Love."

In 1954, they recorded "Sincerely," a song that Harvey Fuqua had written with Alan Freed for Chess records. This song established the Moonglows' sound. In June 1958, they recorded the classic "Ten Commandments of Love."

Harvey left the group in 1959, and began working with other groups like The Spinners (today they are the same group recording for Atlantic).

Bobby Lester died in October of 1980, of cancer at his home in Louisville, Kentucky. The name of The Moonglows is kept active by four new members, none of whom is an original.

June	1953	BABY PLEASE	Chance
November	1953	JUST A LONELY CHRISTMAS	Chance
April	1954	SECRET LOVE	Chance
June	1954	OOH ROCKING DADDY	Chance
November	1954	SINCERELY	Chess
April	1955	MOST OF ALL	Chess
June	1955	FOOLISH ME	Chess
November	1955	IN MY DIARY	Chess
June	1956	WE GO TOGETHER	Chess
September	1956	SEE SAW / WHEN I'M WITH YOU	Chess
November	1956	OVER AND OVER AGAIN	Chess
May	1957	PLEASE SEND ME SOMEONE TO LOVE	Chess
June	1958	TEN COMMANDMENTS OF LOVE	Chess

BOB MOORE

Born: November 30, 1932
Hometown: Nashville, Tennessee

Bob's instrumental record "Mexico" became a top-ten hit. Possibly his "Mexican" sound was a little premature, for a year later Herb Alpert launched his career with the very successful "The Lonely Bull."

August	1961	MEXICO	Monument

JANE MORGAN

Jane was a very popular artist of the forties who, in the fifties, found new success with Dave Kapp's label. Her first major chart hit for the label was a 1956 song she did with another Kapp star Roger Williams called "Two Different Worlds." Jane had her biggest hit during the summer of 1957 with the ballad "Fascination," which inched its way up the charts, pushing aside the rock hits that dominated the charts of the time.

October	1956	TWO DIFFERENT WORLDS (& Roger Williams)	Kapp
July	1957	FASCINATION	Kapp

JAYE P. MORGAN

September	1958	THE DAY THE RAINS CAME	Kapp
August	1959	WITH OPEN ARMS	Kapp
November	1959	HAPPY ANNIVERSARY	Kapp

JAYE P. MORGAN

Real Name: Mary Morgan
Born: 1932
Hometown: Mancos, Colorado

Jaye was born in a log cabin in a small town outside of Denver, Colorado. As a child, she toured with the family act: the Morgan Family Variety Troupe. When Jaye was thirteen her father died and the act was discontinued. At eighteen she won a job singing with the Frank DeVol orchestra. Later, in New York, she auditioned and won a slot on the "Robert Q. Lewis Show." She appeared on Lewis's show for the next two years as well as on the popular show "Stop the Music."

Jaye's low, husky voice enables her to really get behind a song. Her first hit was her biggest, a top-ten disc in 1954 called "That's All I Want From You."

Today, Jaye is still singing and is a frequent guest on television talk and variety shows.

November	1954	THAT'S ALL I WANT FROM YOU	RCA Victor
March	1955	DANGER! HEARTBREAK AHEAD	RCA Victor

August	1955	THE LONGEST WALK	RCA Victor
July	1955	PEPPER-HOT BABY	RCA
November	1955	NOT ONE GOODBYE	RCA
March	1956	SWEET LIPS	RCA
March	1956	GET UP, GET UP	RCA
April	1956	LOST IN THE SHUFFLE	RCA
July	1956	JOHNNY CASANOVA	RCA
February	1959	ARE YOU LONESOME TONIGHT	MGM
February	1959	MISS YOU	MGM
September	1960	I WALK THE LINE	MGM

JOHNNIE MORISETTE

The late Sam Cooke and his friend Bumps Blackwell had their own label called Sar records, on which Sam released the records of many of his friends trying to make the crossover from gospel to pop. Sam signed his good friend Johnnie to the label and Johnnie had one national chart record with "Meet Me at the Twistin' Place" in early 1962. The song leaned heavily on the dance of the same name for its inspiration.

March	1962	MEET ME AT THE TWISTIN' PLACE	Sar

MICKEY MOZART QUINTET

This was another one of those impromptu backup groups that recorded their song during the waning moments of a studio session. "Little Dipper" was their only hit.

April	1959	LITTLE DIPPER	Roulette

JERRY MURAD'S HARMONICATS

Members:
    Jerry Murad
    Don Les
    Al Fiore

All three members of the group were harmonica nuts. Jerry and Al met at a Chicago harmonica club before World War II. Jerry later, while he was in the service, met Don, who was entertaining with the Rascals. The group had only one semisuccessful hit, a harmonica version of "Cherry Pink and Apple Blossom White."

December	1960	CHERRY PINK & APPLE BLOSSOM WHITE	Columbia

THE MURMAIDS

Members:
    Carol Fischer—1948
    Terry Fischer—1946
    Sally Gordon—1946
Hometown: Los Angeles, California

The Fischer girls are the daughters of the late Carl Fischer, noted musical arranger and director for Frankie Laine. Sally Gordon was a long-time friend and neighbor. Mrs. Fischer brought the group to the attention of Ruth Conte, the president of Chattahoochee records. At the time, Kim Fowley, the recording director for the label, had just acquired a tune written by neighbor David Gates (later to form the group Bread), which they felt was suitable for the girls.

In October 1963, the girls recorded "Popsicles And Icicles" while they were all in college. It turned out to be a national hit and the only one they ever had.

November 1963   POPSICLES AND ICICLES   Chattahoochee

BILLY MYLES

Billy was a successful songwriter in New York. Among his hits was "Tonight Tonight" for the Mello-Kings in 1957. He wrote the song "The Joker" and wanted the Mello-Kings to record it, but they demurred. Billy decided to record the song himself and it was released on Ember in the fall of 1957. Billy had the last laugh as the song became a top-forty record.

October   1957   THE JOKER   Ember

THE MYSTICS

Members:
    Phil Cracolici—lead—September 17, 1937
    Albee Cracolici—baritone—April 29, 1936
    Bob Ferrante—first tenor—1936
    George Galfo—second tenor—1940
    Allie Contrera—bass—January 8, 1940
Hometown: Brooklyn, New York

The fellows began singing together in the late fifties on the street corners of Brooklyn. They were looking for a name for the group and put several names in a hat. Mystics popped out.

Jim Gribble heard a demo record that the fellows had recorded and asked them if they would like to audition for Bob and Gene Schwartz of Laurie records. A recording contract followed.

The group was to record a song that Doc Pomus and Mort Shuman had written, "Teenager In Love," but instead the song was given to another group that recorded for Laurie, Dion and the Belmonts. The Schwartz brothers then told Doc and Morty to write another song in the style of the big hit for the Elegants in 1958, called "Little Star." The result was "Hushabye," which the Mystics recorded in May 1959 and which went on to become a national hit.

While they were with Laurie records they recorded a song called "All Through the Night," in which they utilized the singing talents of a young man named Jerry (of Tom and Jerry "Hey School Girl" fame in 1957 on Big records). His real name was Paul Simon, later of Simon and Garfunkel.

Today Phil and his brother Albee are in engineering in New York City, Allie is in sales, Bob lives in Staten Island, and is also an engineer, and George lives in Florida. Phil, Albee, and Allie sing with two new members as the Mystics and perform in the New York area.

May	1959	HUSHABYE	Laurie
October	1959	DON'T TAKE THE STARS	Laurie
February	1960	ALL THROUGH THE NIGHT	Laurie
April	1960	WHITE CLIFFS OF DOVER	Laurie

THE MYSTICS

Left to right: Bob Ferrante, George Galfo, Phil Cracolici, Allie Contrera, Albee Cracolici

NAPOLEON XIV

Real Name: Jerry Samuels

Jerry, a recording engineer at Associated recording studios in New York, had an idea for a crazy song. He recorded it during the summer of 1966 as a joke. "They're Coming To Take Me Away" was sold to Warner Brothers and became a national smash. Jerry also wrote the "Shelter Of Your Arms" for Sammy Davis, Jr.

July   1966   THEY'RE COMING TO TAKE ME AWAY, HA-HAAA   Warner Bros.

JOHNNY NASH

Born: August 19, 1940
Hometown: Houston, Texas

Johnny began singing in a choir at the age of six. At thirteen, he became a regular on the show "Matinee" on KPRC-TV in Houston. After winning the Arthur Godfrey Talent Scouts show, he appeared on Godfrey's radio and TV show.

In 1957, Johnny signed with ABC Paramount and recorded a few moderately popular chart records during the two years he was with the label.

Johnny writes songs as well. In the summer of 1962 Joey Dee recorded one of his songs called "What Kind of Love Is This."

Johnny signed with Jad records in 1968 and that summer he wrote and recorded the top-ten hit "Hold Me Tight." Today he records for Epic.

December	1957	A VERY SPECIAL LOVE	ABC
October	1958	ALMOST IN YOUR ARMS	ABC
February	1959	AS TIME GOES BY	ABC
September	1965	LET'S MOVE AND GROOVE TOGETHER	Joda
May	1966	SOMEWHERE	Joda
August	1968	HOLD ME TIGHT	Jad
November	1969	CUPID	Jad
September	1972	I CAN SEE CLEARLY NOW	Epic
February	1973	STIR IT UP	Epic
June	1973	MY MERRY-GO-ROUND	Epic

RICK NELSON

Real Name: Eric Hilliard Nelson
Born: May 8, 1940, New Jersey
Hometown: Los Angeles, California

Rick debuted on the family radio show "Ozzie and Harriet" in 1949. The success of the radio and subsequent TV show set the stage for his recording career. In April 1957, on Verve records, he recorded Fats Domino's "I'm Walkin'." Surprisingly it became a national hit. (He cut a total of three songs for Verve—"I'm Walkin'," "A Teenager's Romance," and "You're My One and Only Love.")

In August 1957, Lew Chudd, the president of Imperial records, got Rick to sign with his label. His first release came that September, "Be-Bop Baby." Rick got guitarist James Burton, bass guitarist Joe Osborne, piano player Ray Johnson, and drummer Richie Frost to back him on his recordings in the sessions and on the TV show.

In June 1958, he had his first number one song with a composition by Sharon Sheeley (Eddie Cochran's girl friend), "Poor Little Fool." His biggest all-time seller came in April 1961, "Travellin' Man," written by Jerry Fuller (who later wrote hits for Gary Puckett & The Union Gap). The song was originally sent to Sam Cooke, who turned it down. The flip side, "Hello Mary Lou," was written by Gene Pitney, who originally recorded the song with little success.

Rick and Elvis Presley have the distinction of being the only two major rock stars never to have appeared on "American Bandstand." Today Rick continues to record with his group, the Stone Canyon Band. While performing in Madison Square Garden at a rock and roll revival show in 1972, he got the idea to write the song "Garden Party," which went on to become a big hit that summer.

RICK NELSON

Rick still lives in Los Angeles and continues to perform around the country.

May	1957	I'M WALKING	Verve
May	1957	A TEENAGER'S ROMANCE	Verve
August	1957	YOU'RE MY ONE AND ONLY LOVE	Verve
September	1957	BE-BOP BABY	Imperial
September	1957	HAVE I TOLD YOU LATELY THAT I LOVE YOU	Imperial
December	1957	STOOD UP	Imperial
December	1957	WAITIN' IN SCHOOL	Imperial
March	1958	MY BUCKET'S GOT A HOLE IN IT	Imperial
March	1958	BELIEVE WHAT YOU SAY	Imperial
June	1958	POOR LITTLE FOOL	Imperial
October	1958	I GOT A FEELING	Imperial
October	1958	LONESOME TOWN	Imperial
March	1959	NEVER BE ANYONE ELSE BUT YOU	Imperial
February	1959	IT'S LATE	Imperial
July	1959	JUST A LITTLE TOO MUCH	Imperial
July	1959	SWEETER THAN YOU	Imperial
December	1959	I WANNA BE LOVED	Imperial
December	1959	MIGHTY GOOD	Imperial
May	1960	YOUNG EMOTIONS	Imperial
August	1960	I'M NOT AFRAID	Imperial
August	1960	YES SIR, THAT'S MY BABY	Imperial
January	1961	YOU ARE THE ONLY ONE	Imperial
April	1961	TRAVELIN' MAN	Imperial
May	1961	HELLO MARY LOU	Imperial
September	1961	A WONDER LIKE YOU	Imperial
September	1961	EVERLOVIN'	Imperial
February	1962	YOUNG WORLD	Imperial

July	1962	TEEN AGE IDOL	Imperial
December	1962	IT'S UP TO YOU	Imperial
February	1963	THAT'S ALL	Imperial
April	1963	OLD ENOUGH TO LOVE	Imperial
November	1963	TODAY'S TEARDROPS	Imperial
March	1964	CONGRATULATIONS	Imperial
March	1963	YOU DON'T LOVE ME ANYMORE	Decca
March	1963	I GOT A WOMAN	Decca
May	1963	STRING ALONG	Decca
September	1963	FOOLS RUSH IN	Decca
December	1963	FOR YOU	Decca
April	1964	THE VERY THOUGHT OF YOU	Decca
August	1964	THERE'S NOTHING I CAN SAY	Decca
November	1964	A HAPPY GUY	Decca
March	1965	MEAN OLD WORLD	Decca
October	1969	SHE BELONGS TO ME	Decca
March	1970	EASY TO BE FREE	Decca
July	1972	GARDEN PARTY	Decca
February	1973	PALACE GUARD	MCA

SANDY NELSON

Born: 1942

Hometown: Los Angeles, California

Sandy played drums with local bands and on recording sessions in Hollywood studios. In September 1959 he had his first major hit on Original Sound records with "Teen Beat."

September	1959	TEEN BEAT	Original Sound
October	1961	LET THERE BE DRUMS	Imperial
January	1962	DRUMS ARE MY BEAT	Imperial
April	1962	DRUMMIN' UP A STORM	Imperial
July	1962	ALL NIGHT LONG	Imperial
September	1962	AND THEN THERE WERE DRUMS	Imperial
September	1964	TEEN BEAT '65	Imperial

THE NEW CHRISTY MINSTRELS

During the 1800s, Edwin P. Christy took his American minstrel group throughout the South and West and popularized songs like "Oh, Susanna," "Old Folks at Home," and "Camptown Races." In the early 1960s folk songs became very popular again due in part to artists like the Kingston Trio, the Brothers Four, and the Highwaymen. In 1962, a young folk singer named Randy Sparks assembled a group of singers and musicians and called them The New Christy Minstrels.

They began performing folksy, sing-along material and that same year were signed by Columbia. After a number of moderately popular songs, Randy, along with lead singer Barry McGuire (Barry had a

THE NEW CHRISTY MINSTRELS

number one song in the summer of 1965 called "Eve of Destruction"),
wrote a song called "Green, Green," which was released in the summer of
1963 and became the group's biggest hit.

November	1962	THIS LAND IS YOUR LAND	Columbia
June	1963	GREEN GREEN	Columbia
October	1963	SATURDAY NIGHT	Columbia
March	1964	TODAY	Columbia
July	1964	SILLY OL' SUMMERTIME	Columbia
April	1965	CHIM, CHIM, CHEREE	Columbia

WAYNE NEWTON

Born: April 3, 1942
Hometown: Roanoke, Virginia

Wayne first got interested in singing as a youngster when he was taken to
see the Grand Ole Opry in Roanoke. After that there could be only one

career for Wayne. After much practice and small engagements, his first major break came in the early sixties, when he was asked to appear on the Jackie Gleason TV show. He was such a hit that he made about twelve appearances during the next two years.

In early 1963, he was signed on Capitol records and recorded the song "Heart" as his first release. A few months later, while appearing in Las Vegas, Bobby Darin, Wayne's producer at the time, was shown a song by German composer Bert Kaempfert called "Danke Schoen," which he wanted Bobby to record. Instead, Bobby felt that this was the right song for Wayne and had him record it. It was released during the summer of 1963 and became Wayne's first major hit.

After about five years with Capitol, Wayne left the label and concentrated on his night club act. In 1972, Buzz Wilburn, who worked for Wayne at the time, found a dub recording of a song he thought was just right for him. Wayne listened to it when he was in Los Angeles and liked it so much that he took the song back with him to Las Vegas. He then had his arranger adapt the song and presented it on stage opening night. The response to the song was so great that Wayne decided to record it. The result was that "Daddy Don't You Walk So Fast" became Wayne's biggest all-time hit.

Today Wayne Newton is a superstar, who is considered by many as the nation's richest show business personality, owning the $80 million Aladdin Hotel and pulling down $1 million a month when he headlines in Las Vegas.

April	1963	HEART	Capitol
June	1963	DANKE SCHOEN	Capitol
October	1963	SHIRL GIRL	Capitol
January	1965	COMING ON TOO STRONG	Capitol
February	1965	RED ROSES FOR A BLUE LADY	Capitol
May	1965	APPLE BLOSSOM TIME	Capitol
July	1965	SUMMER WIND	Capitol
October	1965	REMEMBER WHEN	Capitol
October	1966	GAMES THAT LOVERS PLAY	Capitol
June	1968	DREAMS OF THE EVERYDAY HOUSEWIFE	MGM
May	1972	DADDY DON'T YOU WALK SO FAST	Chelsea
January	1973	ANTHEM	Chelsea
May	1976	HUNGRY YEARS	Chelsea
September	1979	YOU STEPPED INTO MY LIFE	Aires II
February	1980	YEARS	Aires II

NINO AND THE EBB TIDES

Members:

Antonio "Nino" Aiello—lead—June 29, 1937

Tony DiBari—second tenor—November 16, 1939

Tony Imbimbo—baritone—May 26, 1936
Vinnie Drago—bass—September 3, 1936
Hometown: Bronx, New York

Around 1955, Nino, Vinnie, Tony DeLesio, and another friend formed a
singing group called the Ebb Tides, singing around the neighborhood and
at local functions for about a year. In 1956, they changed their name to
Nino and the Ebb Tides and recorded a song called "Franny Franny,"
which Nino and Vinnie had written for Acme records. The song became a
hit in the New York area and launched the group's career. Soon after that
Ralph Bracco joined the group and Tony DeLesio was replaced by Tony
Imbimbo.

The group then signed with Recorte records and launched another
hit with the song "Puppy Love" (not the same song as Paul Anka's). In
1960, Ralph Bracco was replaced by Tony DiBari and the group signed
with Marco records. One year later the group signed with Madison
records and recorded their first major national hit, "Those Oldies But
Goodies," in which Tony DiBari sang lead. Later that same year they
recorded their biggest hit with "Juke Box Saturday Night."

In 1962, Madison records went bankrupt and the group had to find
another label. Although they found another label, they never found
another major hit.

Today Nino, Vinnie, Tony DeBari, and Tony Imbimbo still sing on
occasion as Nino and the Ebb Tides around New York. When they are
not singing, Nino works as a record distributor in New York; Vinnie operates a radio & TV sales and service outlet in Crestwood, New York; Tony
DiBari lives in New Jersey and is a district manager for American
Express; and Tony Imbimbo is a New York City policeman.

June	1956	FRANNY FRANNY	Acme
April	1961	THOSE OLDIES BUT GOODIES	Madison
August	1961	JUKE BOX SATURDAY NIGHT	Madison

JACK NITZSCHE

Jack was a West Coast arranger who worked with the talented Phil Spector when Phil went to the West Coast to record "He's a Rebel" with his
group, the Crystals, in the summer of 1962. From that point on, Jack did
most of the arranging for Phil on his Philles records.

In the summer of 1963, Jack recorded an instrumental he had
arranged called "The Lonely Surfer" which became a national hit on
Reprise records.

| July | 1963 | THE LONELY SURFER | Reprise |

NERVOUS NORVUS

Real Name: Jimmy Drake

In early 1956, Jimmy Drake wrote a song called "Transfusion," a gimmick number about a guy who drove his auto recklessly, finally getting into an auto crash and crying, "I'm never, never, never going to speed again; shoot the juice to me Bruce." Mid-fifties teens went wild over the song. Jimmy recorded the song under the name of Nervous Norvus and it became a top-ten hit during the summer of 1956. He had several other novelty songs, "Ape" and "Fang" among them later on.

May	1956	TRANSFUSION	Dot
June	1956	APE CALL	Dot
September	1956	FANG	Dot

THE NUTMEGS

Members:

    Leroy Griffin—lead—deceased
    James "Sonny" Griffin—first tenor
    James "Coco" Tyson—second tenor
    Billy Emery—baritone—replaced by Sonny Washburn
    Leroy MacNiel—bass

Hometown: New Haven, Connecticut

In 1954, Leroy and his brother Sonny got together with Coco, Billy, and Leroy and formed a group called the Lyres. They began singing on corners and for any local function they could.

In early 1955, the group went into New York, to audition for various record companies. They wound up at Al Silver's Herald records, where they were awarded a recording contract.

It was at this time that Silver suggested that they change the name of the group. They chose the name the Nutmegs, in honor of Connecticut, the Nutmeg State.

In April of 1955, they recorded a song that Leroy Griffin had written, called "Story Untold." This became the group's first release for Herald that year and their biggest hit. It was followed a few months later by "Ship of Love."

Today Sonny Griffin (brother of the late Leroy), James Tyson, Sonny Washburn, and Leroy MacNeil all reside in New Haven, and they still do occasional shows at rock concerts in New York.

| May | 1955 | STORY UNTOLD | Herald |
| August | 1955 | SHIP OF LOVE | Herald |

THE NU TORNADOS

Dick Clark's popular TV show "American Bandstand" was responsible for hypoing the careers of many artists during the fifties. Many became major stars, while others only had one major hit. In late 1958, several one-record groups emerged like The Playboys, The Quaker City Boys, and The Nu Tornados.

The Nu Tornados recorded the song "Philadelphia, U.S.A." for Carlton records in late 1958, in which they spotlighted America's most notable city at the time. It was a one-record group who have not been heard from since.

November 1958   PHILADELPHIA, U.S.A.   Carlton

THE NUTTY SQUIRRELS

Members:
    Sascha Burland
    Don Elliot
Hometown: New York, New York

Sascha and Don recorded a song they had written which utilized a chipmunk-type sound. (They recorded a human voice at one speed and then speeded up the tape.) The same technique was used successfully by David Seville and his Chipmunks. Sascha and Don called their voices the Nutty Squirrels. Their song called "Uh! Oh!" became a hit during the 1959 Christmas season.

November 1959   UH! OH! Part 2   Hanover

THE OLYMPICS

THE OLYMPICS

Members:
  Walter Ward—lead—Jackson, Mississippi—1940
  Eddie Lewis—tenor—Houston, Texas—1937
  Charles Fizer—second tenor—Shreveport, Louisiana—1940
  Melvin King—bass—Shreveport, Louisiana—1940

Hometown: Los Angeles, California

Walter Ward got the group together while they were attending high school in Los Angeles. In 1958, they signed with Demon records and recorded their first major hit with "Western Movies." In 1959, they signed with Arvee records and had a hit with "Big Boy Pete" in May of that year.

| June | 1958 | WESTERN MOVIES | Demon |
| December | 1958 | DANCE WITH THE TEACHER | Demon |

September	1959	PRIVATE EYE	Arvee
May	1960	BIG BOY PETE	Arvee
September	1960	SHIMMY LIKE KATE	Arvee
December	1960	DANCE BY THE LIGHT OF THE MOON	Arvee
March	1961	LITTLE PEDRO	Arvee
June	1961	DOOLEY	Arvee
April	1963	THE BOUNCE	Tri Disc
July	1963	DANCIN' HOLIDAY	Tri Disc
April	1965	GOOD LOVIN'	Loma
October	1966	BABY DO THE PHILLY DOG	Mirwood

ROY ORBISON

Born: April 23, 1936
Hometown: Wink, Texas

Born in Vernon, Texas, Roy has played the guitar and harmonica since childhood.

Roy signed first with Sun records after college friend Pat Boone encouraged him and had his first major hit in June 1956, with "Ooby Dooby." In late 1959, he signed with Monument records and premiered with "Uptown" in January 1960. Next came his first major hit, with one of his own compositions, "Only the Lonely," in the summer of 1960.

In twenty-nine chart records, Roy only had two number one national hits. The first was "Running Scared" in March 1961, and the other was "Oh, Pretty Woman" in August 1964.

Roy continues to travel and entertain all over the country. His songs have become big hits all over again for performers such as Linda Ronstadt and Don McLean.

June	1956	OOBY DOOBY	Sun
January	1960	UPTOWN	Monument
May	1960	ONLY THE LONELY	Monument
September	1960	BLUE ANGEL	Monument
December	1960	I'M HURTIN'	Monument
March	1961	RUNNING SCARED	Monument
August	1961	CRYING	Monument
August	1961	CANDY MAN	Monument
February	1962	DREAM BABY	Monument
May	1962	THE CROWD	Monument
September	1962	WORKIN' FOR THE MAN	Monument
October	1962	LEAH	Monument
February	1963	IN DREAMS	Monument
June	1963	FALLING	Monument
September	1963	MEAN WOMAN BLUES	Monument
September	1963	BLUE BAYOU	Monument
December	1963	PRETTY PAPER	Monument
April	1964	IT'S OVER	Monument
August	1964	OH, PRETTY WOMAN	Monument
January	1965	GOODNIGHT	Monument
July	1965	SAY YOU'RE MY GIRL	Monument

ROY ORBISON

November	1965	LET THE GOOD TIMES ROLL	Monument
August	1965	RIDE AWAY	MGM
November	1965	CRAWLING BACK	MGM
January	1966	BREAKIN' UP IS BREAKIN' MY HEART	MGM
April	1966	TWINKLE TOES	MGM
July	1966	TOO SOON TO KNOW	MGM
December	1966	COMMUNICATION BREAKDOWN	MGM
July	1967	CRY SOFTLY LONELY ONE	MGM
WITH EMMY LOU HARRIS			
June	1980	THAT LOVIN' YOU FEELIN' AGAIN	Warner Bros.

THE ORIOLES

Members:

> Sonny Til—lead—real name: Earlington Tilghman—born: August 18, 1928; died: December 9, 1981, of a heart attack, Baltimore.
>
> George Nelson—second tenor—replaced by Gregory Carrol in 1953
>
> Alexander Sharp—tenor
>
> Johnny Reed—bass
>
> Tommy Gaither—guitarist—killed in auto accident in 1950

Hometown: Baltimore, Maryland

They were discovered by Deborah Chessler in Baltimore in 1947 when the group was known as the Vibranairs. In 1948 they changed their name to the Orioles, the state bird, and auditioned for ex-bandleader Jerry Blaine, who owned Jubilee records. Receiving a contract, they recorded their first song, "It's Too Soon To Know," in 1949. Next came "Tell Me So" in the spring of 1949. In 1953, they recorded their classic "Crying In The Chapel."

The Orioles were one of the first R & B groups to receive national publicity, and their songs have become classics over the years. From 1949 to 1953, they were probably the most popular recording group in the R & B field.

Sonny still sings today as Sonny Til and the Orioles with several new members. He lives in New York and does occasional rock concerts.

January	1949	IT'S TOO SOON TO KNOW	National
April	1949	TELL ME SO	Jubilee
August	1949	A KISS AND A ROSE	Jubilee
November	1949	FORGIVE AND FORGET	Jubilee
December	1949	WHAT ARE YOU DOING NEW YEAR'S EVE	Jubilee
December	1949	(IT'S GONNA BE A) LONELY CHRISTMAS	Jubilee
January	1952	BABY, PLEASE DON'T GO	Jubilee
July	1953	CRYING IN THE CHAPEL	Jubilee

TONY ORLANDO

Real Name: Michael Anthony Orlando
Born: April 3, 1944
Hometown: New York, New York

At age fifteen, while studying mechanics at Aviation High School in Queens, Tony was discovered by Don Kirshner and hired as a staff song-writer for Aldon Music Company, which was owned by Kirshner and Al Nevins. In April 1961, they had Tony cut "Halfway to Paradise," which was sold to Epic records and became his first national hit.

After a short recording career, Tony began working as a promotion man in the record industry. In May 1970, he was asked to sing a demo record with two girls named Thelma Hopkins and Joyce Vincent. After much persuasion, he agreed to record "Candida." Bell records liked the

TONY ORLANDO

song and decided to release it, having no information on the members of the group other than the name Dawn on the record.

Tony continued in his job and forgot all about the song he had recorded, but by August 1970, the song had become a national hit, which sent Bell records looking for the group. When Tony and the girls were contacted to sign with Bell as a recording group, he was hesitant. He thought the record was a fluke and considered his current job more secure. Finally he signed, and they recorded "Knock Three Times," which became a number one national hit. After about seven hit records they changed the name of the group to Tony Orlando and Dawn. In 1973, he recorded "Tie a Yellow Ribbon," which reached number one and became the number one song for the entire year. They created a new sound called "rag rock." (For subsequent career information see DAWN, *Rock On: The Modern Years.*)

May	1961	HALFWAY TO PARADISE	Epic
August	1961	BLESS YOU	Epic
December	1961	HAPPY TIMES ARE HERE TO STAY	Epic
July	1970	CANDIDA	Bell
November	1970	KNOCK THREE TIMES	Bell
March	1971	I PLAY AND SING	Bell
June	1971	SUMMER SAND	Bell
October	1971	WHAT ARE YOU DOING SUNDAY	Bell
November	1972	YOU'RE A LADY	Bell
February	1973	TIE A YELLOW RIBBON	Bell
July	1973	SAY HAS ANYBODY SEEN MY SWEET GYPSIE ROSE	Bell
November	1973	WHO'S IN THE STRAWBERRY PATCH WITH SALLY	Bell

THE ORLONS

Members:
> Shirley Brickley—lead—December 9, 1944
> Rosetta Hightower—June 23, 1944
> Marlena Davis—October 4, 1944
> Steve Caldwell—bass—November 22, 1942

Hometown: Philadelphia, Pennsylvania

Formed in junior high school, the group consisted originally of Shirley, Rosetta, Marlena, and Shirley's two sisters, Jean and Audrey. They performed together for a few years, and then the group broke up. Some time later, Steve and Shirley decided to re-form the group, recruiting Rosetta and Marlena from the original five, and began singing together. They began appearing with a group called the Cashmeres (who later became the Dovells of "Bristol Stomp" fame) and decided to call themselves the Orlons so the names would be similar.

After about a year, Len Barry, the lead singer of the Dovells, set up an audition with Cameo records, the label he recorded on. The audition led to a contract and their first recording in 1960, "I'll Be True."

THE ORLONS

Left to right: Steve Caldwell, Marlena Davis,
Shirley Brickley, Rosetta Hightower

After several others, they cut their biggest all-time seller in the summer of 1962, with a song Kal Mann and Dave Appell had written, "The Wah Watusi," which was their first national hit as well.

Today, Steve lives in Philadelphia and manages a singing group, while Marlena is a housewife in the same city. Rosetta is a singer in London, England, where she lives with her husband Ian Green. Lead singer Shirley Brickley also lives in Philadelphia and sings with Jimmy Lewis and Ella Webster as the Orlons.

May	1962	THE WAH WATUSI	Cameo
October	1962	DON'T HANG UP	Cameo
February	1963	SOUTH STREET	Cameo
May	1963	NOT ME	Cameo
September	1963	CROSS FIRE!	Cameo
December	1963	BON-DOO-WAH	Cameo
January	1964	SHIMMY SHIMMY	Cameo
May	1964	RULES OF LOVE	Cameo
August	1964	KNOCK KNOCK (WHO'S THERE)	Cameo

JOHNNY OTIS

JOHNNY OTIS

Born: December 28, 1924

Johnny was a bandleader and songwriter who in the early fifties was responsible for the success of artists like Little Esther Phillips and Hank Ballard. Johnny wrote many songs including "So Fine" for the Sheiks and "Double Crossing Blues" for Little Esther, "Wallflower (Dance With Me Henry)" and "Every Beat of My Heart" for the Pips.

He also recorded as a solo artist for Savoy records in the early fifties. In the summer of 1958, he had a top-ten pop music hit when he wrote and recorded "Willie and the Hand Jive" for Capitol.

Today Johnny still resides on the West Coast, but travels a lot with his mobile R & B Museum, which he takes from city to city displaying the memorabilia of the early R & B period.

January	1950	DOUBLE CROSSING BLUES (Little Esther & The Robins)	Savoy
March	1950	MISTRUSTIN' BLUES (Little Esther, Mel Walker & The Robins)	Savoy
August	1950	DECEIVIN' BLUES (Little Esther, Mel Walker & The Robins)	Savoy
September	1950	DREAMIN' BLUES (Mel Walker)	Regent
October	1950	WEDDING BOOGIE (Little Esther & The Robins)	Savoy
December	1950	FAR AWAY CHRISTMAS BLUES (Little Esther & Mel Walker)	Savoy
December	1950	ROCKIN' BLUES (Mel Walker)	Savoy
March	1951	MAMBO BOOGIE	Savoy
April	1951	GEE BABY (Mel Walker)	Savoy
August	1951	ALL NITE LONG	Savoy
January	1952	SUNSET TO DAWN (Mel Walker)	Savoy

June	1958	WILLIE AND THE HAND JIVE	Capitol
November	1958	CRAZY COUNTRY HOP	Capitol
May	1959	CASTIN' MY SPELL	Capitol
February	1960	MUMBLIN' MOSIE	Capitol
March	1969	COUNTRY GIRL	Kent

DONNIE OWENS

Born: October 30, 1938

Donnie's country-flavored style was a cross between Elvis and Conway Twitty. His only major hit, "Need You," might have been a bigger hit had not Conway Twitty's number one record "It's Only Make Believe" been on the charts at the same time.

| September 1958 | NEED YOU | Guyden |

REG OWEN

Born: February 1928

In 1958, European orchestra leader Reg Owen recorded a song written by Billy Maxted (author of "Satin Doll") called "Manhattan Spiritual," which was sold to Palette records. The instrumental hit was released in late 1958 and became a top-ten smash with its blaring brass and swinging sound.

| November 1958 | MANHATTAN SPIRITUAL | Palette |

REG OWEN

PATTI PAGE

PATTI PAGE

Real Name: Clara Ann Fowler
Born: November 8, 1927
Hometown: Claremore, Oklahoma

One of eleven children, Patti began singing in a Tulsa church choir with her seven sisters. In 1946, when Patti was nineteen, she got a job at radio station KTUL in Tulsa, as a staff singer. When one of the featured vocalists suddenly got laryngitis, Patti filled in and won the job. It was at this time that she decided to change her name. Since one of the sponsors on the program was the Page Milk Company, she chose Page as her professional name.

At this time bandleader Jack Rael heard Patti and signed her to a contract. He was so impressed with her sound that he decided to give up his band in order to manage her full time. By 1948, she had signed a recording contract with Mercury records and released her first hit, "Confess," which was a unique recording since she dubbed in the harmony part, making herself sound like a duo. In 1949, she had "With My Eyes Wide Open I'm Dreaming" and in late 1950, her first number one national hit with "Tennessee Waltz."

The 5'3" blonde became one of the top vocalists of her time with all her hits in the early fifties.

Patti, who is divorced, lives in west Los Angeles, with her two adopted children. She makes occasional appearances today.

June	1948	CONFESS	Mercury
February	1949	SO IN LOVE	Mercury
December	1949	WITH MY EYES WIDE OPEN I'M DREAMING	Mercury
August	1950	ALL MY LOVE	Mercury
October	1950	THE TENNESSEE WALTZ	Mercury
January	1951	WOULD I LOVE YOU (LOVE YOU)	Mercury
February	1951	MOCKIN' BIRD HILL	Mercury
May	1951	MISTER AND MISSISSIPPI	Mercury
July	1951	DETOUR	Mercury
September	1951	AND SO TO SLEEP AGAIN	Mercury
February	1952	COME WHAT MAY	Mercury
March	1952	WHISPERING WINDS	Mercury
June	1952	ONCE IN AWHILE	Mercury
August	1952	I WENT TO YOUR WEDDING	Mercury
August	1952	YOU BELONG TO ME	Mercury
November	1952	WHY DON'T YOU BELIEVE ME	Mercury
January	1953	THE DOGGIE IN THE WINDOW	Mercury
July	1953	BUTTERFLIES	Mercury
November	1953	CHANGING PARTNERS	Mercury
February	1954	CROSS OVER THE BRIDGE	Mercury
May	1954	STEAM HEAT	Mercury
July	1954	WHAT A DREAM	Mercury
November	1954	I CRIED	Mercury
October	1954	THE MAMA DOLL SONG	Mercury
December	1954	LET ME GO, LOVER!	Mercury
July	1955	CROCE DI ORO	Mercury
December	1955	GO ON WITH THE WEDDING	Mercury
April	1956	TOO YOUNG TO GO STEADY	Mercury
June	1956	ALLEGHENY MOON	Mercury
October	1956	MAMA FROM THE TRAIN	Mercury
January	1957	REPEAT AFTER ME	Mercury
February	1957	A POOR MAN'S ROSES	Mercury
May	1957	OLD CAPE COD	Mercury
October	1957	I'LL REMEMBER TODAY	Mercury
January	1958	BELONGING TO SOMEONE	Mercury
April	1958	ANOTHER TIME, ANOTHER PLACE	Mercury
June	1958	LEFT RIGHT OUT OF YOUR HEART	Mercury
September	1958	FIBBIN'	Mercury
January	1959	TRUST IN ME	Mercury
April	1959	THE WALLS HAVE EARS	Mercury
June	1959	WITH MY EYES WIDE OPEN I'M DREAMING	Mercury
October	1959	GOODBYE CHARLIE	Mercury
January	1960	THE SOUND OF MUSIC	Mercury
April	1960	TWO THOUSAND, TWO HUNDRED TWENTY-THREE MILES	Mercury
June	1960	ONE OF US (WILL WEEP TONIGHT)	Mercury
October	1960	I WISH I'D NEVER BEEN BORN	Mercury
January	1961	DON'T READ THE LETTER	Mercury
April	1961	A CITY GIRL STOLE MY COUNTRY BOY	Mercury
July	1961	YOU'LL ANSWER TO ME	Mercury
October	1961	A BROKEN HEART & A PILLOW FILLED WITH TEARS	Mercury
December	1960	GO ON HOME	Mercury
April	1962	MOST PEOPLE GET MARRIED	Mercury

August	1962	BOY'S NIGHT OUT	Mercury
March	1963	PRETTY BOY LONELY	Columbia
June	1963	SAY WONDERFUL THINGS	Columbia
April	1965	HUSH, HUSH, SWEET CHARLOTTE	Columbia
September	1965	YOU CAN'T BE TRUE DEAR	Columbia
January	1968	GENTLE ON MY MIND	Columbia
July	1968	LITTLE GREEN APPLES	Columbia

THE PARADONS

Members:
> Chuck Weldon
> William Powers
> West Tyler
> Billy Myers

Hometown: Bakersfield, California

They formed the group in high school, and in 1960, signed with Milestone records. Their only hit came in August of that year with "Diamonds and Pearls."

| August | 1960 | DIAMONDS AND PEARLS | Milestone |

THE PARAGONS

Hometown: Brooklyn, New York

The Paragons practiced on street corners and in hallways until they achieved the sound they wanted. In the late fifties they went to Harold Winley of Winley records to audition. He liked the group, especially the unique voice of lead singer Julian McMichael. Winley signed the group to his label and they began recording many songs that became New York hits like the ballad "Florence" (which Julian and Harold wrote together).

The group's biggest popularity came when Winley records released "The Paragons Meet the Jesters" (another Winley group). The record was, in essence, a sing-off between two of the best-known New York "doo wop" (R & B street-corner harmony) groups.

May	1957	FLORENCE	Winley
August	1957	THE VOWS OF LOVE	Winley
October	1957	LET'S START ALL OVER AGAIN	Winley
December	1957	TWILIGHT	Winley
July	1961	IF	Tap

THE PARIS SISTERS

Members:
> Pricilla Paris—lead
> Albeth Paris
> Sherrell Paris

Hometown: San Francisco, California

THE PARIS SISTERS

The sisters began performing at ages nine, thirteen, and eleven respectively, at a U.S.O. show. Years later, while they were performing at various clubs, Lester Sill of Gregmark records caught their act and signed them to a contract. Their initial release in April 1961, "Be My Boy," was moderately popular, but their follow-up in September of that year, the Barry Mann song "I Love How You Love Me," became their biggest hit.

April	1961	BE MY BOY	Gregmark
September	1961	I LOVE HOW YOU LOVE ME	Gregmark
January	1962	HE KNOWS I LOVE HIM TOO MUCH	Gregmark
April	1962	LET ME BE THE ONE	Gregmark
May	1964	DREAM LOVER	MGM

FESS PARKER

Born: August 16, 1927
Hometown: Fort Worth, Texas

Fess was an actor who, in 1955, signed with Walt Disney to portray the legendary character Davy Crockett on television. The show became a big hit and its title song was recorded by Bill Hayes for Cadence records in early 1955. In fact, it became a number one national hit. To capitalize on the popularity of the song, Fess Parker recorded a version for Columbia, which went on to become a top-ten hit for him.

FESS PARKER

In 1957, Fess dueled Bill Hayes again. They both recorded another Walt Disney TV song called "Wringle Wrangle" and Fess had the bigger of the two hits this time.

Today Fess and his wife, Marchella, live with their two children in Santa Barbara, California, where he is heavily involved in real estate.

| February | 1955 | BALLAD OF DAVY CROCKETT | Columbia |
| January | 1957 | WRINGLE WRANGLE | Disneyland |

BILL PARSONS

Born: September 8, 1934
Hometown: Crossville, Tennessee

Bill was taught to play the guitar at the age of eight, by his brother. He spent nineteen months in the Army in Germany, touring with Special Services. After his discharge he moved to Wellston, Ohio.

In 1958, singer Bobby Bare recorded "The All American Boy" and a flip side called "Rubber Dolly" for Harry Carlson's Fraternity records in Cincinnati, Ohio. A short while later, Harry decided to release the single, because of the interest generated by Elvis's induction into the Army. Since Bobby was not around to go on tour and promote the record, Harry used Bobby's song, but had the label read Bill Parsons. Bill went on tour and made appearances around the country lip-synching Bobby's hit. It wasn't until 1960 that it was discovered that, in fact, Bobby Bare and not Bill Parsons recorded "The All American Boy." Nevertheless, to this day,

Bill Parsons is still listed as the artist for the December 1958 hit on Fraternity.

Bill did get to record on his own for Starday records in December 1960, with "Guitar Blues" and "Hot Rod Volkswagen."

December 1958	THE ALL AMERICAN BOY	Fraternity

THE PASSIONS

Members:
Jimmy Gallagher—lead—1940
Tony Armato—first tenor—1940
Albee Galione—second tenor—November 11, 1939
Vinnie Acierno (1939)—baritone—replaced by Lou Rotondo
Hometown: Brooklyn, New York

The group was formed in 1959 as the Sinceres and began performing in the Bensonhurst section of Brooklyn. After about six months together, they met another neighborhood group called the Mystics (of "Hushabye" fame) who introduced them to their manager Jim Gribble. Jim had them change their name to the Passions and presented them with a demo song called "Just To Be With You" by the Cousins. (The Cousins were Carole King and Paul Simon, unknowns at the time, who recorded demo records for other singers.) The group recorded the song, which was then sold to Audicon records and was released in September 1959, becoming a national hit.

Today Jimmy lives in Florida, and Albee, Lou, and Tony in Brooklyn. Albee and Lou still sing, but with a group called the Classics (the same group that recorded "Till Then"). Tony sings with the Mystics.

September 1959	JUST TO BE WITH YOU	Audicon
January 1960	I ONLY WANT YOU	Audicon
March 1960	GLORIA	Audicon
May 1960	THIS IS MY LOVE	Audicon

THE PASTELS

Members:
"Big" Dee Irwin—lead
J. B. Willingham
Tony Thomas
Richard Travis

The guys formed the group while they were stationed in the Air Force in Greenland, in the late fifties. They called themselves the Pastels and

THE PASTELS

Left to right: Tony Thomas, J. B. Willingham, Richard Travis, Dee Irwin

began working on a song that Dee and J. B. had written, called "Been So Long."

When they came back to the States in late 1957, they went to New York, and auditioned for Mascot records. They recorded the song, and it was released in December 1957. By January 1958, the song had been sold to Argo records and was on its way to becoming a hit. The fellows were discharged from the Air Force in January 1958 and recorded their follow-up song, "So Far Away," which was released that spring.

Today Dee lives on the West Coast and works in the record business. He makes an occasional trip to New York, to appear with the Pastels on a rock revival show.

| January | 1958 | BEEN SO LONG | Argo |
| April | 1958 | SO FAR AWAY | Argo |

THE PASTEL 6

Members:
>   Bob Toten
>   Tony Stealman
>   Rick Rodreguez
>   Erick Fickert
>   Lynn Hamm
>   Bill Myers
>   Dave Cadison

Hometown: North Hollywood, California

They first organized their group in 1958. In 1962, they named a dance after a club they had headlined at in North Hollywood, California, called the Cinnamon Cinder. They made a recording of the dance and sold it to Zen records. In December 1962, "The Cinnamon Cinder" became a national hit.

December 1962   THE CINNAMON CINDER   Zen

PAT & THE SATELLITES

The group had only one hit for Atco, an instrumental called "Jupiter-C," which featured a wailing sax and driving guitar. Great song for jitterbugging. I'd give it an 80; you could really dance to it.

January   1959   JUPITER-C   Atco

PATIENCE & PRUDENCE

Members:
>   Patience McIntyre
>   Prudence McIntyre

Hometown: Los Angeles, California

In 1956, songwriter Mark McIntyre heard his two daughters singing an old standard called "Tonight You Belong to Me," which was written by Lee David and Billy Rose. Mark liked the way the girls sounded and took them to his friend Ross Bagdasarian (David Seville) who was then a songwriter. Ross suggested that Mark record the girls, who were eleven and fourteen at the time.

Mark took his daughters to Liberty records where they recorded the song and it became a top-ten national hit that summer. Their follow-up,

PATIENCE & PRUDENCE

"Gonna Get Along Without You Now," which was written by good friend Milt Kellem, became a national hit that fall.

July	1956	TONIGHT YOU BELONG TO ME	Liberty
October	1956	GONNA GET ALONG WITHOUT YA NOW	Liberty

LES PAUL AND MARY FORD

Real Names:
    Lester Polfus—June 9, 1923
    Colleen Summer—born: July 7, 1924; died: September 30, 1977
Hometown: Waukesha, Wisconsin

Les met Mary in the late forties. They were married in 1948, eventually moving to Long Island, New York.

Though Les could not read music, he had a knack for the guitar and was able to develop a technique called "overdubbing." This involved recording on tape more than one sound in such a manner that there was almost a reverberation and echo. This was an early technique that would be utilized by many in years to come.

In 1950, they signed with Capitol records and released "Nola" as their first song in June of that year. After several big hits they had a number one national hit with "How High the Moon" in March 1951. The duo were the singing sensations of the early fifties with a steady stream of hits.

In May of 1963, Les and Mary split up after fifteen years of marriage. In September of 1977, Mary died of diabetes in Los Angeles.

June	1950	NOLA	Capitol
September	1950	GOOFUS	Capitol
December	1950	TENNESSEE WALTZ	Capitol
February	1951	MOCKIN' BIRD HILL	Capitol
March	1951	HOW HIGH THE MOON	Capitol
July	1951	THE WORLD IS WAITING FOR THE SUNRISE	Capitol
December	1951	JUST ONE MORE CHANCE	Capitol
May	1952	I'M CONFESSIN'	Capitol
June	1952	SMOKE RINGS	Capitol
August	1952	TAKE ME IN YOUR ARMS AND HOLD ME	Capitol
December	1952	MY BABY'S COMING HOME	Capitol
December	1952	BYE BYE BLUES	Capitol
March	1953	I'M SITTING ON TOP OF THE WORLD	Capitol
June	1953	VAYA CON DIOS	Capitol
April	1954	I REALLY DON'T WANT TO KNOW	Capitol
July	1954	I'M A FOOL TO CARE	Capitol
October	1954	WHITHER THOU GOEST	Capitol
July	1955	HUMMINGBIRD	Capitol

**LES PAUL &
MARY FORD**

January	1956	TEXAS LADY	Capitol
February	1956	MORITAT (THEME FROM THREE PENNY OPERA)	Capitol
January	1957	CINCO ROBLES	Capitol
August	1958	PUT A RING ON MY FINGER	Columbia
April	1961	JURA	Columbia

PAUL AND PAULA

Members:

> Paul—real name: Ray Hildebrand—born: December 21, 1940—hometown: Joshua, Texas

> Paula—real name: Jill Jackson—born: May 20, 1942—hometown: McCaney, Texas

While attending Howard Payne College in Texas, Ray decided to form a duo to sing for a charity drive radio program. He took Jill to Fort Worth to audition a song that he had written for record producer Major Bill Smith. This led to a recording contract with Philips records. They changed their names to Paul and Paula and in November 1962 recorded "Hey Paula," which became a number one song.

Today Paul lives in Kansas City, Missouri. Paula is now a solo act in Texas.

November	1962	HEY PAULA	Philips
February	1963	YOUNG LOVERS	Philips
June	1963	FIRST QUARREL	Philips
August	1963	SOMETHING OLD, SOMETHING NEW	Philips
October	1963	FIRST DAY BACK AT SCHOOL	Philips

PAUL AND PAULA

THE PENGUINS

Left to right: Curtis Williams, Cleve Duncan,
Dexter Tisby, Bruce Tate

MIKE PEDICIN

Mike recorded a reprise of Faye Adams's big hit called "Shake a Hand." The song did fairly well because of the exposure Mike received on "American Bandstand."

| February | 1956 | LARGE LARGE HOUSE | RCA |
| January | 1958 | SHAKE A HAND | Cameo |

THE PENGUINS

Members:
    Cleveland Duncan—lead—July 23, 1935
    Dexter Tisby—second tenor—1936
    Curtis Williams (1935)—replaced by Randy Jones
    Bruce Tate (1935)—replaced by Teddy Harper
Hometown: Los Angeles, California

In 1954, Cleve Duncan, from Freemont High in Los Angeles, decided to form a singing group. A short time later Cleve met Curtis Williams, a friend from grammar school whom Cleve had not seen for some time, at a local club. Curtis told him about a song he had written for his girl friend, called "Earth Angel." Cleve thought it would be a good song to practice with, so he brought in Dexter, while Curtis got his friend Bruce Tate, and they formed a group. They called themselves the Penguins after Willie the Penguin on the Kools cigarette pack.

The four of them practiced the song in a backyard garage from June to September of that year. They then contacted Dootsie Williams, the owner of Dootone records, to listen to the group. He liked their sound and decided to sign them to his label.

They recorded "Earth Angel" and "Hey Senorita" and released the two songs in November 1954, with "Hey Senorita" picked as the hit side. However, several disc jockeys in Los Angeles, including Johnny Otis, started playing "Earth Angel" with tremendous success. The result was one of the first R & B hit records to make it on the pop music charts on a national level. The song has been an all-time rock and roll classic ever since and has also become one of the most-played and biggest-selling records ever.

Today Cleve still lives in Los Angeles, and sings with several new members at local clubs as the Penguins. He does make an occasional trip to New York, to appear on some major rock shows.

November	1954	EARTH ANGEL / HEY SENORITA	Dootone
January	1955	OOKEY OOK	Dootone
April	1955	BE MINE OR BE A FOOL	Mercury

THE PENTAGONS

Members:
    Ken Goodlie
    Ted Goodlie
    Odis Munsen
    Joe Munsen
    Carl McGinnis
Hometown: San Bernadino, California

The fellows joined forces in the early sixties and began to sing locally at high school functions. A song that group member Ken Goodlie had written, called "To Be Loved (Forever)," always got a great response whenever they did it. In late 1960, they recorded the song, and the recording eventually came to the attention of one of the A & R men at Donna records. (This was the same label Ron Holden had his big hit "Love You So" on in the spring of 1960.) Executives at the label liked the song and released it in early 1961. It went on to become a top-forty hit.

| February | 1961 | TO BE LOVED (FOREVER) | Donna |
| October | 1961 | I WONDER | Jamie |

EMILIO PERICOLI

Born: 1928
Hometown: Cesenatico, Italy

Emilio, star of Italian radio and TV, had a hit in Italy in 1962 that also won at the San Remo song festival. Warner Brothers bought the recording and released it in the United States in April 1962, making "Al Di La" a national hit.

April   1962   AL DI LA   Warner Bros.

CARL PERKINS

Born: April 9, 1932
Hometown: Jackson, Tennessee

Living in Tennessee, Carl was very much influenced by country and western music as a youngster. He began to play the guitar and sing songs around the neighborhood at an early age. Because he came from a poor family, simple things were very important to him. That is why he felt that articles of clothing like shoes were very important to a youngster. He felt that a good pair of shoes was his most important possession. Conse-

CARL PERKINS

quently, in late 1955, he wrote a song about "Blue Suede Shoes" that he took to the Sun studios in Memphis to record. Owner Sam Phillips liked the song and decided to release it on his label. Sam felt young Carl was in the style of another younger singer, Elvis Presley, whose contract he had just sold to RCA records.

In January 1956, "Blue Suede Shoes" was released and went on to be his biggest hit. A few months later the song wound up as a hit for Elvis as well.

On March 21, 1956, on his way to New York, Carl was involved in an auto crash in Wilmington, Delaware, that almost claimed his life. After several months in the hospital he was released to resume his career, but the records that followed were never the hits his first one had been.

Today Carl travels with Johnny Cash's show as a featured guitarist.

January	1956	BLUE SUEDE SHOES	Sun
June	1956	BOPPIN' THE BLUES	Sun
March	1957	YOUR TRUE LOVE	Sun
April	1958	PINK PEDAL PUSHERS	Columbia
June	1959	POINTED TOE SHOES	Columbia

PETER, PAUL AND MARY

Members:

Peter Yarrow—hometown: New York City—May 31, 1938

Noel "Paul" Stookey—hometown: Birmingham, Michigan—November 30, 1937

Mary Ellin Travers—hometown: Louisville, Kentucky—November 7, 1937

They met in Greenwich Village, where they were all working in the early sixties. Peter was appearing as a single after a successful tour that included the Newport Folk Festival. Paul was doing a standup comic routine in the Village, while helping Mary get back on her feet as a singer after her work in a Broadway flop, "The Next President."

They worked together for seven months on eighteen songs. With the help of Milton Okun, they polished their arrangements and were set to open at the Village's Bitter End. The engagement was a success, which led to a recording contract in 1962 with Warner Brothers. In April of that year, they released their first song "Lemon Tree," which became their first national hit. But of all the songs they recorded only the John Denver tune "Leaving on a Jet Plane" ever became number one.

After many years apart, the trio have finally gotten together once again and are performing to capacity crowds all over the country.

| April | 1962 | LEMON TREE | Warner Bros. |

PETER, PAUL AND MARY

Clockwise from top: Peter
Yarrow, Mary Travers, Paul
Stookey

August	1962	IF I HAD A HAMMER	Warner Bros.
January	1963	SETTLE DOWN	Warner Bros.
March	1963	PUFF THE MAGIC DRAGON	Warner Bros.
June	1963	BLOWIN' IN THE WIND	Warner Bros.
September	1963	DON'T THINK TWICE, IT'S ALL RIGHT	Warner Bros.
November	1963	STEWBALL	Warner Bros.
February	1964	TELL IT ON THE MOUNTAIN	Warner Bros.
June	1964	OH, ROCK MY SOUL	Warner Bros.
January	1965	FOR LOVIN' ME	Warner Bros.
April	1965	WHEN THE SHIP COMES IN	Warner Bros.
October	1965	EARLY MORNING RAIN	Warner Bros.
April	1966	THE CRUEL WAR	Warner Bros.
August	1967	I DIG ROCK AND ROLL MUSIC	Warner Bros.
November	1967	TOO MUCH OF NOTHING	Warner Bros.
April	1969	DAY IS DONE	Warner Bros.
October	1969	LEAVING ON A JET PLANE	Warner Bros.

PAUL PETERSON

Born: September 23, 1945
Hometown: Glendale, California

Paul got his start in show business as a Mouseketeer, then performed on
the "Lux Video Theater," "General Electric Theater," and "Playhouse 90."
In the early sixties he played Donna Reed's son on "The Donna Reed
Show."

RAY PETERSON

In 1962 he signed with Colpix records and had his first hit for the label in March of that year with "She Can't Find Her Keys."

February	1962	SHE CAN'T FIND HER KEYS	Colpix
May	1962	KEEP YOUR LOVE LOCKED	Colpix
August	1962	LOLLIPOPS AND ROSES	Colpix
October	1962	MY DAD	Colpix
March	1963	AMY	Colpix
November	1963	THE CHEER LEADER	Colpix

RAY PETERSON

Born: April 23, 1939
Hometown: Denton, Texas

Ray started singing while he was a polio patient in Warm Springs Foundation Hospital in Texas, to amuse the other patients.

Ray, who has a four and one half-octave range, began singing in small clubs and later moved to Los Angeles. It was while he was singing at a small club there that he was discovered by Stan Shulman, who became his manager and got him a contract with RCA records in 1958. His first release for the label was in February 1958, with "Let's Try Romance," followed by "Tail Light" a few months later. It wasn't until May 1959 that he had his first major hit with "The Wonder of You."

May	1959	THE WONDER OF YOU	RCA
November	1959	GOODNIGHT MY LOVE	RCA

June	1960	TELL LAURA I LOVE HER	RCA
November	1960	CORINNA, CORINNA	Dunes
July	1961	MISSING YOU	Dunes
December	1961	I COULD HAVE LOVED YOU SO WELL	Dunes
June	1963	GIVE US YOUR BLESSING	Dunes

THE PETS

The only notable thing about the Pets, who had one major hit on Arwin records during the summer of 1958, was that group member Richard Podolor became a top independent producer working with Three Dog Night and Steppenwolf. A far cry from his hit called "Cha-Hua-Hua" in 1958.

| May | 1958 | CHA-HUA-HUA | Arwin |

PHIL PHILLIPS

Real Name: John Phillip Baptiste
Born: March 14, 1931
Hometown: Lake Charles, Louisiana

Phil, a Navy veteran and one-time bellhop, began his career as a member of the Gateway Quartet. In 1959, he wrote a song with his friend George Khoury, owner of a record store in Lake Charles, to show his girl friend just how much he loved her. The song was sold to Mercury records in June of 1959, and "Sea Of Love" became a national hit.

Today he works as a radio station time salesman in Jennings, Louisiana.

| June | 1959 | SEA OF LOVE | Mercury |

BOBBY "BORIS" PICKETT

Born: February 11, 1940
Hometown: Somerville, Massachusetts

After three years in the Signal Corps in Korea, Bobby took up residency in Hollywood and began appearing as a comedian. In 1961, after attempts to become a TV and film actor, he joined a singing group called the Cordials. It was while he was with the group that he along with Leonard Capizzi, the leader of the Cordials, wrote a song called "Monster Mash." Since the group was signed to Gary Paxton (Flip of Skip and Flip fame), they took the song to him. Gary liked the song and decided to release it on his label, Garpax records. By September 1962, the song was on its way to number one.

The song came back as a hit all over again in May 1973 and brought Bobby back on to the music scene once more.

September	1962	MONSTER MASH	Garpax
November	1962	MONSTERS' HOLIDAY	Garpax
August	1970	MONSTER MASH	Parrot
May	1973	MONSTER MASH	Parrot

WILSON PICKETT

Born: March 18, 1941

Hometown: Detroit, Michigan

In 1962 Wilson, who had sung rhythm and blues since he was a young-ster, joined a Detroit group called the Falcons (who three years earlier had had a hit with "You're So Fine"). They recorded "I Found A Love" for LuPine records. It became a moderate hit in March of that year.

Producer Robert Bateman convinced Wilson to go out as a single and he signed with Double-L records, premiering in March 1963, with "If You Need Me."

In 1965, he signed with Atlantic records and in June of that year, had the first of many hits when "In the Midnight Hour" was released.

Today, Wilson, along with Joe Tex, Solomon Burke and Don Covay, performs as The Soul Clan at certain New York shows.

May	1963	IF YOU NEED ME	Double-L
August	1963	IT'S TOO LATE	Double-L
June	1965	IN THE MIDNIGHT HOUR	Atlantic
November	1965	DON'T FIGHT IT	Atlantic
February	1966	634-5789	Atlantic
May	1966	NINETY-NINE AND A HALF	Atlantic
August	1966	LAND OF 1000 DANCES	Atlantic
December	1966	MUSTANG SALLY	Atlantic
January	1967	EVERYBODY NEEDS SOMEBODY TO LOVE	Atlantic
March	1967	I FOUND A LOVE	Atlantic
June	1967	SOUL DANCE NUMBER THREE	Atlantic
August	1967	FUNKY BROADWAY	Atlantic
October	1967	STAG-O-LEE	Atlantic
December	1967	I'M IN LOVE	Atlantic
February	1968	JEALOUS LOVE	Atlantic
April	1968	SHE'S LOOKIN' GOOD	Atlantic
July	1968	I'M A MIDNIGHT MOVER	Atlantic
September	1968	I FOUND A TRUE LOVE	Atlantic
November	1968	A MAN AND A HALF	Atlantic
January	1969	HEY JUDE	Atlantic
April	1969	MINI-SKIRT MINNIE	Atlantic
May	1969	BORN TO BE WILD	Atlantic
December	1969	YOU KEEP ME HANGING ON	Atlantic
April	1970	SUGAR SUGAR/COLE, COOKE & REDDING	Atlantic
August	1970	SHE SAID YES	Atlantic

WILSON PICKETT

October	1970	ENGINE NUMBER 9	Atlantic
January	1971	DON'T LET THE GREEN GRASS FOOL YOU	Atlantic
May	1971	DON'T KNOCK MY LOVE	Atlantic
August	1971	CALL MY NAME, I'LL BE THERE	Atlantic
May	1972	FUNK FACTORY	Atlantic
November	1972	MAMA TOLD ME NOT TO COME	Atlantic
April	1973	MR. MAGIC MAN	RCA
September	1973	TAKE A CLOSER LOOK AT THE WOMAN YOU'RE WITH	RCA

WEBB PIERCE

Born: August 8, 1926
Hometown: West Monroe, Louisiana

Webb got his big break when he landed a feature role on the radio show "Louisiana Hayride." Shortly thereafter he launched his own show over KWKH. Webb has been very successful as a country artist and a few of his songs (most of which he writes himself) have crossed over to the pop charts, most notably a 1959 tune "I Ain't Never," which became a top-forty record. Webb was also instrumental in the careers of Faron Young and Goldie Hill by giving them slots on his radio show.

May	1957	BYE BYE LOVE	Decca
July	1959	I AIN'T NEVER	Decca
January	1960	NO LOVE HAVE I	Decca
May	1960	IS IT WRONG FOR LOVING YOU	Decca

GENE PITNEY

Born: February 17, 1941
Hometown: Rockville, Connecticut

Electronics was Gene's hobby and he often experimented with his hi-fi system, electronically creating voice duplication by rerecording over various tapes. He created as many as seven voices on a recording.

In early 1961, he did a song called "(I Wanna) Love My Life Away," which became his first hit on Musicor records.

Gene has written many songs including "He's A Rebel" for The Crystals and "Hello Mary Lou" for Rick Nelson. Today Gene is somewhat of a recluse living in Connecticut.

January	1961	(I WANNA) LOVE MY LIFE AWAY	Musicor
July	1961	EVERY BREATH I TAKE	Musicor
October	1961	TOWN WITHOUT PITY	Musicor
April	1962	(THE MAN WHO SHOT) LIBERTY VALANCE	Musicor
September	1962	ONLY LOVE CAN BREAK A HEART	Musicor
December	1962	HALF HEAVEN-HALF HEARTACHE	Musicor
March	1963	MECCA	Musicor
June	1963	TRUE LOVE NEVER RUNS SMOOTH	Musicor
October	1963	TWENTY FOUR HOURS FROM TULSA	Musicor
January	1964	THAT GIRL BELONGS TO YESTERDAY	Musicor
May	1964	YESTERDAY'S HERO	Musicor
June	1964	IT HURTS TO BE IN LOVE	Musicor
October	1964	I'M GONNA BE STRONG	Musicor
February	1965	I MUST BE SEEING THINGS	Musicor
May	1965	LAST CHANCE TO TURN AROUND	Musicor
July	1965	LOOKING THROUGH THE EYES OF LOVE	Musicor
November	1965	PRINCESS IN RAGS	Musicor
April	1966	BACKSTAGE	Musicor
December	1966	JUST ONE SMILE	Musicor
May	1968	SHE'S A HEARTBREAKER	Musicor
November	1968	BILLY, YOU'RE MY FRIEND	Musicor
December	1969	SHE LETS HER HAIR DOWN	Musicor

EDDIE PLATT

Eddie was a saxophone player in Cleveland, Ohio. In the fifties he formed a band which played a lot of the local clubs and teen dances in the area. In early 1958 Eddie's band recorded a version of the song "Tequila" which began to get air play on station WERE in Cleveland. ABC purchased the master recording, released the song and it became a moderately popular national hit.

| February | 1958 | TEQUILA | ABC |
| May | 1958 | CHA-HUA-HUA | Gone |

THE PLATTERS

Top left to right: Dave Lynch, Paul Robi
Top to bottom middle: Tony Williams, Herb Reed, Zola Taylor

THE PLATTERS

Members:
> Tony Williams—lead—hometown: Elizabeth, New Jersey—born: April 5, 1928
> Zola Taylor—hometown: Los Angeles, California
> David Lynch—second tenor—hometown: St. Louis, Missouri—born: 1929; died: January 2, 1981
> Paul Robi—baritone—hometown: New Orleans, Louisiana—replaced Alex Hodge
> Herb Reed—bass—hometown: Kansas City, Missouri

Tony, David, Herb, and Alex Hodge formed the Platters in Los Angeles, in 1953. Shortly thereafter, Tony had the group audition for songwriter Buck Ram, who liked their sound. Buck worked with the group for a while and got them a recording contract with Federal records in Cincinnati, Ohio. After a couple of records, Buck recruited a fifteen-year-old singer named Zola Taylor to add a little different sound to the group. Zola left a group called Shirley Gunter and the Queens to join the Platters. At this time Alex Hodge left and was replaced by Paul Robi.

In 1955, Buck had the group record a song he had written called "Only You," which was rather poorly done. Sales on the song were only moderate; consequently, Federal became disenchanted with the group.

Buck began looking for a major label to take on the Platters because he felt a large company would be able to promote his new group more effectively. Since Buck was ready to make a recording deal with Mercury for another group he managed, the Penguins (who had had a major hit with "Earth Angel" on Dootone records in 1954), Buck told Mercury that the only way they would be able to sign the Penguins was to sign the Platters as well. After long negotiations, Mercury finally gave in.

In the summer of 1955, the group rerecorded "Only You" for Mercury. Disc jockey Bob Salter in Seattle, Washington, began giving the record a great deal of air play, which resulted in its becoming the group's first national hit. Later that same year, the group recorded another Buck Ram song, called "The Great Pretender," which became a number one song and the group's biggest all-time seller.

From 1955 until 1960, with Tony Williams as the lead voice, the group had four number one songs and sixteen gold records. They became the most popular vocal group of the fifties.

Tony left the group on June 6, 1960, to become a solo performer. Tony introduced his replacement at the Copa Club in Newport, Kentucky on that day. His replacement, a twenty-one-year-old Clevelander named Sonny Turner, premiered on June 16, 1960, at the Lotus Club in Washington.

Tony lives with his wife, Helen, in New York City, and occasionally sings with their son and two other members locally. Zola Taylor lives in Los Angeles, as does Paul Robi. Herb Reed lives in Atlanta, Georgia, and has a singing group that he travels with. David Lynch died of cancer in Long Beach, California, in early 1981.

August	1954	TELL THE WORLD	Federal
July	1955	ONLY YOU	Mercury
October	1955	THE GREAT PRETENDER	Mercury
February	1956	THE MAGIC TOUCH	Mercury
June	1956	MY PRAYER	Mercury
June	1956	HEAVEN ON EARTH	Mercury
September	1956	YOU'LL NEVER NEVER KNOW	Mercury
September	1956	IT ISN'T RIGHT	Mercury
December	1956	ONE IN A MILLION	Mercury
December	1956	ON MY WORD OF HONOR	Mercury
February	1957	I'M SORRY	Mercury
February	1957	HE'S MINE	Mercury
May	1957	MY DREAM	Mercury

October	1957	ONLY BECAUSE	Mercury
January	1958	HELPLESS	Mercury
March	1958	TWILIGHT TIME	Mercury
June	1958	YOU'RE MAKING A MISTAKE	Mercury
September	1958	I WISH	Mercury
November	1958	SMOKE GETS IN YOUR EYES	Mercury
March	1959	ENCHANTED	Mercury
June	1959	REMEMBER WHEN	Mercury
August	1959	WHERE	Mercury
January	1960	HARBOR LIGHTS	Mercury
May	1960	EBB TIDE	Mercury
July	1960	RED SAILS IN THE SUNSET	Mercury
October	1960	TO EACH HIS OWN	Mercury
January	1961	IF I DIDN'T CARE	Mercury
April	1961	TREES	Mercury
August	1961	I'LL NEVER SMILE AGAIN	Mercury
February	1962	IT'S MAGIC	Mercury
April	1966	I LOVE YOU 1000 TIMES	Musicor
December	1966	I'LL BE HOME	Musicor
February	1967	WITH THIS RING	Musicor
July	1967	WASHED ASHORE	Musicor
October	1967	SWEET, SWEET LOVIN'	Musicor

THE PLAYBOYS

Due to the popularity of "American Bandstand" on TV in the fifties, many of the artists on the Philadelphia-based Cameo Parkway records were frequently spotlighted. The Playboys (in reality a studio recording group) had one national hit on Cameo in the summer of 1958, a swinging vocal called "Over the Weekend."

August	1958	OVER THE WEEKEND	Cameo

THE PLAYMATES

Members:
    Donny Conn—born: March 29, 1930
    Morey Carr—born: July 31, 1932
    Chic Hetti—born: February 26, 1930
Hometown: Waterbury, Connecticut

While at the University of Connecticut, they began to mold their act. In 1952, they made tours of the United States and Canada, primarily as a comedy act. They later changed their emphasis to singing. In 1956, their name, the Nitwits, was dropped in favor of the Playmates.

They signed, in 1957, with Roulette records and recorded "Darling," which was followed by "It's Wonderful." In late 1957, they recorded "Jo-Ann," which became their first major hit for the label in early 1958.

THE PLAYMATES

January	1958	JO-ANN	Roulette
April	1958	LET'S BE LOVERS	Roulette
May	1958	DON'T GO HOME	Roulette
October	1958	BEEP BEEP	Roulette
April	1959	STAR LOVE	Roulette
June	1959	WHAT IS LOVE	Roulette
October	1960	WAIT FOR ME	Roulette
March	1961	LITTLE MISS STUCKUP	Roulette

THE PONI-TAILS

Members:
    Toni Cistone—lead
    LaVerne Novak
    Patti McCabe
Hometown: Cleveland, Ohio

The Poni-Tails began singing at Brush High in Lyndhurst, Ohio, a suburb of Cleveland. They wrote a song called "Que La" which they sang at a benefit, where Cleveland attorney John R. Jewitt heard and liked them. He introduced himself to the girls and then had them meet a music publisher, Tom Illius. Tom became their manager and took one of their recordings to Don Costa in New York. This led to a recording contract with ABC records. They premiered with the song "Just My Luck to Be Fifteen" which was not very successful. However, in June 1958 they had their biggest hit with "Born Too Late."

Today the women are housewives and still live in the greater Cleve-

THE PONI-TAILS

land area. They do no singing as a group together any more, though they have been approached to do so.

June	1958	BORN TOO LATE	ABC
December	1958	SEVEN MINUTES IN HEAVEN	ABC

FRANK POURCEL

Born: January 1, 1928

Frank Pourcel, a musical arranger and conductor, took the Platters' big hit of 1955 called "Only You" and created his own version of the song, utilizing the lush sounds of strings. The result was an instrumental hit in the spring of 1959.

March	1959	ONLY YOU	.	Capitol

JOEY POWERS

Born: 1939
Hometown: Little Washington, Pennsylvania

Joey was born in the same town as Perry Como—Canonsburg, Pennsylvania—and was later brought to New York by Perry in 1959, to produce the John Hills exercise show on NBC-TV. He later taught wrestling at Ohio State University, where he began to do some songwriting.

In early 1963, he teamed with Artie Wayne to record Artie's song

"Midnight Mary," which was then sold to Amy records and released in November of that year. The song was Joey's only hit.

November 1963   MIDNIGHT MARY   Amy

PEREZ PRADO

Born: 1922
Hometown: Mantanzas, Cuba

Perez began his musical career by playing the piano and organ. He is called "El Rey del Mambo," the Mambo King. Most of his hits were released on RCA's international label but a few made the United States charts, including a pair of number one records, "Cherry Pink and Apple Blossom White" (1955) and "Patricia" (1958).

February	1955	CHERRY PINK AND APPLE BLOSSOM WHITE	RCA Victor
May	1958	PATRICIA	RCA
October	1958	GUAGLIONE	RCA
March	1962	PATRICIA TWIST	RCA

PEREZ PRADO

ELVIS PRESLEY

ELVIS PRESLEY

Born: January 8, 1935
Died: August 16, 1977, Memphis, Tennessee
Hometown: Tupelo, Mississippi

Elvis had a twin brother who died at birth. He began singing when he was only a few years old at a church in Tupelo. At age thirteen, his family moved to Memphis, where he later got a job as an usher at the Loew's State Theater. After high school he drove a truck for an electric company.

One day he decided to make a record for his mother, so he went to Sun records and paid four dollars to record the song "That's All Right Mamma." Sam Phillips, the president of Sun, saw the potential in this unknown singer.

Bob Neal became Elvis's first manager (later followed by Colonel Tom Parker) as he toured the South billed as the "hillbilly cat." While singing at a record convention of country and western disc jockeys, Steve Shoales of RCA records decided he wanted to sign him. He paid Sun records $35,000 for his contract plus five unrealized master discs.

In January 1956, Elvis premiered with his first major hit, "Heartbreak Hotel," which became a number one song. In 1956, he also appeared in his first motion picture, Hal Wallis' "Love Me Tender."

Elvis went into the Army in May 1958, amid a great deal of publicity.

He married Priscilla Beaulieu on May 1, 1967. On February 1, 1968, their only child, Lisa Marie, was born.

Undoubtedly, Elvis was the "King of Rock 'N' Roll," a form of music he single-handedly gave the impetus it needed in the mid-fifties to make it popular with teen-agers. He has sold more records (over 500 million), had more top ten hits (39), more gold albums (28), and had 18 number-one hits, second to The Beatles who had 20, than any other recording artist.

Elvis died of heart failure at his Graceland Mansion in Memphis on August 16, 1977.

The King is dead, but his movies and music live on forever.

February	1956	HEARTBREAK HOTEL	RCA
February	1956	I WAS THE ONE	RCA
March	1956	BLUE SUEDE SHOES	RCA
May	1956	MONEY HONEY	RCA
May	1956	I WANT YOU, I NEED YOU, I LOVE YOU	RCA
May	1956	MY BABY LEFT ME	RCA
July	1956	HOUND DOG	RCA
July	1956	DON'T BE CRUEL	RCA
September	1956	BLUE MOON	RCA
September	1956	I DON'T CARE IF THE SUN DON'T SHINE	RCA
October	1956	LOVE ME TENDER	RCA
October	1956	ANYWAY YOU WANT ME	RCA
November	1956	LOVE ME	RCA
November	1956	WHEN MY BLUE MOON TURNS TO GOLD AGAIN	RCA
December	1956	PARALYZED	RCA
December	1956	OLD SHEP	RCA
December	1956	POOR BOY	RCA
January	1957	TOO MUCH	RCA
January	1957	PLAYING FOR KEEPS	RCA
March	1957	PEACE IN THE VALLEY	RCA
March	1957	ALL SHOOK UP	RCA
March	1957	THAT'S WHEN YOUR HEARTACHES BEGIN	RCA
June	1957	LET ME BE YOUR TEDDY BEAR	RCA
June	1957	LOVING YOU	RCA
October	1957	JAILHOUSE ROCK	RCA
October	1957	TREAT ME NICE	RCA
January	1958	DON'T	RCA
January	1958	I BEG OF YOU	RCA
April	1958	WEAR MY RING AROUND YOUR NECK	RCA
April	1958	DONCHA' THINK IT'S TIME	RCA
June	1958	HARD HEADED WOMAN	RCA
June	1958	DON'T ASK ME WHY	RCA
November	1958	I GOT STUNG	RCA
November	1958	ONE NIGHT	RCA
March	1959	A FOOL SUCH AS I	RCA
April	1959	I NEED YOUR LOVE TONIGHT	RCA
July	1959	A BIG HUNK O' LOVE	RCA
July	1959	MY WISH CAME TRUE	RCA
April	1960	STUCK ON YOU	RCA
April	1960	FAME AND FORTUNE	RCA
July	1960	IT'S NOW OR NEVER	RCA

July	1960	A MESS OF BLUES	RCA
November	1960	ARE YOU LONESOME TONIGHT	RCA
November	1960	I GOTTA KNOW	RCA
February	1961	SURRENDER	RCA
March	1961	LONELY MAN	RCA
April	1961	FLAMING STAR	RCA
May	1961	I FEEL SO BAD	RCA
June	1961	WILD IN THE COUNTRY	RCA
August	1961	LITTLE SISTER	RCA
September	1961	MARIE'S THE NAME HIS LATEST FLAME	RCA
December	1961	CAN'T HELP FALLING IN LOVE	RCA
December	1961	ROCK-A-HULA BABY	RCA
March	1962	GOOD LUCK CHARM	RCA
March	1962	ANYTHING THAT'S PART OF YOU	RCA
May	1962	FOLLOW THAT DREAM	RCA
August	1962	SHE'S NOT YOU	RCA
August	1962	JUST TELL HER JIM SAID HELLO	RCA
September	1962	KING OF THE WHOLE WIDE WORLD	RCA
October	1962	RETURN TO SENDER	RCA
February	1963	ONE BROKEN HEART FOR SALE	RCA
June	1963	(YOU'RE THE) DEVIL IN DISGUISE	RCA
October	1963	BOSSA NOVA BABY	RCA
October	1963	WITCHCRAFT	RCA
February	1964	KISSIN' COUSINS	RCA
February	1964	IT HURTS ME	RCA
May	1964	KISS ME QUICK	RCA
May	1964	VIVA LAS VEGAS	RCA
May	1964	WHAT'D I SAY	RCA
July	1964	SUCH A NIGHT	RCA
October	1964	AIN'T THAT LOVING YOU BABY	RCA
October	1964	ASK ME	RCA
February	1965	DO THE CLAM	RCA
April	1965	CRYING IN THE CHAPEL	RCA
June	1965	(SUCH AN) EASY QUESTION	RCA
August	1965	I'M YOURS	RCA
November	1965	PUPPET ON A STRING	RCA
January	1966	TELL ME WHY	RCA
March	1966	FRANKIE AND JOHNNY	RCA
March	1966	PLEASE DON'T STOP LOVING ME	RCA
July	1966	LOVE LETTERS	RCA
October	1966	SPINOUT	RCA
October	1966	ALL THAT I AM	RCA
January	1967	INDESCRIBABLY BLUE	RCA
May	1967	LONG LEGGED GIRL	RCA
August	1967	THERE'S ALWAYS ME	RCA
October	1967	BIG BOSS MAN	RCA
October	1967	YOU DON'T KNOW ME	RCA
January	1968	GUITAR MAN	RCA
March	1968	U.S. MALE	RCA
March	1968	STAY AWAY	RCA
June	1968	LET YOURSELF GO	RCA
October	1968	A LITTLE LESS CONVERSATION	RCA
November	1968	IF I CAN DREAM	RCA
March	1969	MEMORIES	RCA
May	1969	IN THE GHETTO	RCA
July	1969	CLEAN UP YOUR OWN BACK YARD	RCA
September	1969	SUSPICIOUS MINDS	RCA

November	1969	DON'T CRY DADDY/RUBBERNECKIN'	RCA
February	1970	KENTUCKY RAIN	RCA
May	1970	THE WONDER OF YOU	RCA
August	1970	I'VE LOST YOU/THE NEXT STEP IS LOVE	RCA
October	1970	YOU DON'T HAVE TO SAY YOU LOVE ME/PATCH IT UP	RCA
December	1970	I REALLY DON'T WANT TO KNOW/ THERE GOES MY EVERYTHING	RCA
March	1971	WHERE DID THEY GO, LORD/RAGS TO RICHES	RCA
May	1971	LIFE	RCA
July	1971	I'M LEAVIN'	RCA
October	1971	IT'S ONLY LOVE	RCA
May	1972	AN AMERICAN TRILOGY	RCA
August	1972	BURNING LOVE	RCA
December	1972	SEPARATE WAYS	RCA
April	1973	STEAMROLLER BLUES	RCA
April	1973	FOOL	RCA
September	1973	RAISED ON ROCK	RCA
September	1973	FOR OL' TIMES SAKE	RCA
February	1974	I'VE GOT A THING ABOUT YOU BABY	RCA
June	1974	IF YOU TALK IN YOUR SLEEP	RCA
October	1974	PROMISED LAND	RCA
January	1975	MY BOY	RCA
May	1975	T-R-O-U-B-L-E	RCA
October	1975	BRINGING IT BACK	RCA
March	1976	HURT	RCA
December	1976	MOODY BLUE	RCA
February	1977	SHE THINKS I STILL CARE	RCA
June	1977	WAY DOWN	RCA
November	1977	MY WAY	RCA
January	1981	GUITAR MAN	RCA

JOHNNY PRESTON

Real Name: John Courville
Born: August 18, 1939
Hometown: Port Arthur, Texas

Johnny started entertaining in high school with a band he formed, the Shades. In the late fifties he met a disc jockey in Beaumont, Texas, Jape Richardson (J. P. Richardson or the Big Bopper of "Chantilly Lace" fame), who wanted to help guide Johnny's career. He guided Johnny to sign with Mercury records, a label the Bopper had recorded for. J. P. wrote a song inspired by a commercial about Dove soap, "Running Bear," which he had Johnny record. On the recording, the voice in the background making the Indian oom-pah-pah sounds was none other than J. P. Richardson.

It wasn't until J. P.'s untimely death with Buddy Holly and Ritchie

LLOYD PRICE

Valens on February 2, 1959, that Johnny's record became a hit. It was released in September 1959, and in a short time became a number one song.

October	1959	RUNNING BEAR	Mercury
April	1960	CRADLE OF LOVE	Mercury
June	1960	FEEL SO FINE	Mercury
February	1961	LEAVE MY KITTEN ALONE	Mercury
December	1961	FREE ME	Mercury

LLOYD PRICE

Born: March 9, 1933
Hometown: New Orleans, Louisiana

Lloyd had ten brothers and sisters. His father taught him to play the guitar and his mother taught him to play the piano. Lloyd became interested in singing while a member of the church choir.

In the early fifties, Lloyd wrote a song called "Lawdy Miss Clawdy" which was to be used as a radio station commercial in New Orleans. The piano player on the record was Fats Domino. In early 1952, Art Rupe, the president of Specialty records, while in New Orleans to audition new talent, heard the tune and decided to sign Lloyd to the label. The song was released in May 1952 and became a hit.

From 1954 until 1956 Lloyd was in the service stationed in Korea.

After his discharge he went to Washington, D.C., and formed his own company, KRC records (Kent Record Company). In late 1956, he recorded a song he wrote, "Just Because," which was later released on KRC. In a short time the song was sold to Am-Par records and released by ABC Paramount in January 1957. Later that year Lloyd signed with Atlantic records but continued to release his material on KRC. Atlantic would then distribute the records.

In late 1958, he wrote a song with his manager, Harold Logan, that was released on ABC, since he had rejoined the label. The song, "Stagger Lee," became a number one national hit in November 1958, the only one he was ever to have.

After operating a New York night club called the Turn Table in the late sixties, Lloyd moved to Philadelphia, where he writes new material and appears on many rock shows around the country.

May	1952	LAWDY MISS CLAWDY	Specialty
October	1952	OOOH-OOOH-OOOH	Specialty
January	1953	AIN'T IT A SHAME	Specialty
February	1957	JUST BECAUSE	KRC
September	1957	LONELY CHAIR	KRC
December	1958	STAGGER LEE	ABC
March	1959	WHERE WERE YOU (ON OUR WEDDING DAY)	ABC
April	1959	PERSONALITY	ABC
August	1959	I'M GONNA GET MARRIED	ABC
November	1959	COME INTO MY HEART	ABC
February	1960	LADY LUCK	ABC
April	1960	NO IF'S—NO AND'S	ABC
July	1960	QUESTION	ABC
December	1960	YOU BETTER KNOW WHAT YOU'RE DOING	ABC
October	1963	MISTY	Double-L
January	1964	BILLIE BABY	Double-L
October	1969	BAD CONDITIONS	Turntable

RAY PRICE

Born: January 12, 1926
Hometown: Dallas, Texas

Ray had studied veterinary medicine at North Texas Agricultural College for three and a half years before chucking it and deciding to become a professional singer. His singing career was sidetracked by a stint with the Marines during World War II and a stint as a rodeo cowboy after his discharge. Finally, in January 1952 Ray was signed to WSM's "Grand Ole Opry" program.

He had many country hits for Columbia in the years that followed. Occasionally his records would make their way onto the pop charts but, oddly enough, even though Ray had several pop hits in the fifties and sixties, it wasn't until 1970 that he really struck pop gold with a top-ten record called "For the Good Times."

October	1957	MY SHOES KEEP WALKING BACK TO YOU	Columbia
August	1958	CITY LIGHTS	Columbia
March	1967	DANNY BOY	Columbia
August	1970	FOR THE GOOD TIMES	Columbia
March	1971	I WON'T MENTION IT AGAIN	Columbia
August	1971	I'D RATHER BE SORRY	Columbia

LOUIS PRIMA

Born: December 7, 1912
Hometown: New Orleans, Louisiana

As a youngster Louis was influenced by the sound of King Oliver, and he switched from playing the violin to the trumpet. He started playing with Red Nichols and his Pennies but soon thereafter started his own band. After playing many New Orleans clubs, Louis went on the road and did engagements in New York, Las Vegas, and Lake Tahoe.

In addition to his recording career, he has been a successful songwriter, producing the notable "Sunday Kind of Love," among other songs. His biggest hit came in 1958 when he and Keely Smith recorded "That Old Black Magic"; the song became a top-ten hit for them.

June	1945	BELL-BOTTOM TROUSERS	Majestic
October	1947	CIVILIZATION	RCA Victor
November	1950	OH, BABE!	Robin Hood
November	1958	THAT OLD BLACK MAGIC	Capitol
March	1959	I'VE GOT YOU UNDER MY SKIN	Capitol
July	1959	BEI MIR BIST DU SCHOEN	Dot
November	1960	WONDERLAND BY NIGHT	Dot

RED PRYSOCK

In 1948, while in the Army in Germany, Red bought a secondhand sax and in six months' time joined the Army band. After his discharge he eventually got a contract with Mercury records. In 1955, he had hits like "Finger Tips" and "Hand Clappin'," and in 1956, "Rock and Roll Party."

September	1955	FINGER TIPS	Mercury
November	1955	HAND CLAPPIN'	Mercury
February	1956	ROCK N' ROLL PARTY	Mercury

BILL PURSELL

Hometown: Tulare, California

Bill began playing the piano as a youngster and learned how to read music by the age of five. After high school graduation, he received a scholarship to the Peabody Conservatory of Music in Baltimore, Maryland, and studied there for several years until he entered the Air Force. After his discharge he attended the Eastman School of Music in Rochester, New York.

In 1962, Columbia signed him to a recording contract. Late that year he was sent to Nashville to record an album for the label. Arranger Bill Justis (of "Raunchy" fame in 1957) helped select a country-sounding repertoire. Among the album cuts: "Bye Bye Love," "Four Walls," "Born to Lose," and "Our Winter Love." The last was released as a single in early 1963 and became a top-ten hit.

January   1963   OUR WINTER LOVE   Columbia

BILL PURSELL

THE QUAKER CITY BOYS

"American Bandstand" helped make this local group popular momentarily. The Quaker City Boys signed with Philadelphia-based Swan records and had an instrumental hit with "Teasin' " in late 1958.

December 1958   TEASIN   Swan

THE QUIN-TONES

Hometown: Philadelphia, Pennsylvania

The group, which consisted of four girls and a guy, began singing around Philadelphia in the late fifties. In 1958, they wrote a song called "Down the Aisle of Love," which they recorded. They took the recording to Hunt records, which released it that summer. Soon thereafter it became a national hit. It had a unique beginning with the organ playing the wedding march as though someone were ready to walk down the aisle.

August   1958   DOWN THE AISLE OF LOVE   Hunt

THE QUOTATIONS

Members:
> Larry Kaye—real name: Larry Kassman—lead—born: March 12, 1942
> Richard Schwartz—first tenor—born: May 17, 1944
> Lew Arno—second tenor—1943
> Harvey Hershkowitz—baritone—February 7, 1943

Hometown: Brooklyn, New York

The fellows, who came from the Kings Highway area in Brooklyn, got together in 1959. Two years later they met Helen Miller of MGM records, who liked their sound. She wanted them to record the standard "Imagination" in an essentially gimmicky manner (as the Marcels had done with the song "Blue Moon" earlier that year). "Imagination" was recorded in that Marcels manner and released on Verve records in November 1961. It became the group's only major hit.

Today Larry (who runs a delivery service) and Richard (who's vice-president of a painting company) still live in Brooklyn. Lew and Harvey live in Freehold, New Jersey. Lew operates a patio furniture firm, while Harvey is art director for *Teen World* magazine.

November 1961　IMAGINATION　　　　　　　　　　Verve

THE RAINBOWS

Members:
    John Berry—lead
    Sonny Spencer
    Don Covay
    Billy Stewart
    Marvin Gaye
    Chester Simmons—bass
Hometown: Washington, D.C.

The group was first formed in Washington, in 1955, by Don and John. They met Jay Perry, who went on to become their manager. Jay took them to New York to meet Bobby Robinson of Red Robin records. This resulted in a contract and a hit that summer with the song "Mary Lee."

In the group, Marvin Gaye, along with Billy Stewart and Don Covay, went on to become big stars on their own years later.

June   1955   MARY LEE   Red Robin

THE RAINDROPS

Members:
    Jeff Barry—April 3, 1938
    Ellie Greenwich—October 23, 1940
Hometown: New York, New York

Jeff Barry and his wife Ellie Greenwich wrote many top hits in the early sixties, like "Da Doo Ron Ron," "Be My Baby," "Then He Kissed Me," "Chapel of Love," "I Wanna Love Him So Bad," "The Leader of the Pack," and "Maybe I Know."

In 1963, they decided to record some of their own material. Their first effort: "What a Guy." By taping their voices several times over, they sounded like an entire singing group. They christened themselves the Raindrops and had their first release on Jubilee records that spring. Later that summer their "The Kind of Boy You Can't Forget" became their biggest hit.

Today Ellie has been writing and singing national commercials while doing background singing for Blondie, ELO and Jim Stafford. Jeff has written theme songs for popular TV shows while scoring the film *The Idolmaker*.

April	1963	WHAT A GUY	Jubilee
July	1963	THE KIND OF BOY YOU CAN'T FORGET	Jubilee
November	1963	THAT BOY JOHN	Jubilee
March	1964	BOOK OF LOVE	Jubilee

MARVIN RAINWATER

Born: July 2, 1925
Hometown: Wichita, Kansas

Marvin, an American Indian, became very much interested in singing pop music in the 1950s, and in 1957 was discovered by a record executive from MGM, after appearing on Arthur Godfrey's talent scout show. That spring, he had his first national hit for the label, "Gonna Find Me a Bluebird," which was also his biggest seller.

Marvin appeared in Indian dress whenever he performed on stage, and is today still performing throughout the Southwest.

April	1957	GONNA FIND ME A BLUEBIRD	MGM
March	1958	WHOLE LOTTA WOMAN	MGM
August	1959	HALF-BREED	MGM

THE RAMRODS

In late 1949, Vaughn Monroe had a big hit on RCA Victor called "Riders in the Sky." In early 1961, the Ramrods recorded an instrumental of this song complete with cowboy cattle calls and special effects, which became a national hit for them on New York–based Amy records. It was their only major hit.

January	1961	(GHOST RIDERS) IN THE SKY	Amy

TEDDY RANDAZZO

Born: May 20, 1937
Hometown: New York, New York

Teddy's grandfather encouraged him to follow a musical career. At age twelve he played the accordion very well. He began his singing career with Tom Romano and Russ Giliberto as the Three Chuckles. Teddy played the accordion, Tom the guitar, and Russ the string bass. Teddy went out on his own in May 1957, on Vik records, with "Next Stop Paradise." A year later, in July 1958, he had a hit with "Little Serenade."

He signed with ABC in 1960 and had "The Way of a Clown" in April that year. Around 1964, he worked with Little Anthony and the Imperials when they signed with DCP records and wrote some of their biggest hits, like "Goin' Out of My Head." In the mid-fifties he starred in the Alan Freed movie "Rock, Rock, Rock."

May	1958	LITTLE SERENADE	Vik
April	1960	THE WAY OF A CLOWN	ABC
January	1963	BIG WIDE WORLD	Colpix

BOOTS RANDOLPH

Boots worked as a staff musician in Nashville, playing the sax on many major recording dates in the late fifties. Finally, in early 1963, he had a hit of his own called "Yakety Sax" on Monument records.

January	1963	YAKETY SAX	Monument
April	1964	HEY, MR. SAX MAN	Monument
December	1966	THE SHADOW OF YOUR SMILE	Monument
July	1967	TEMPTATION	Monument

RANDY AND THE RAINBOWS

Members:
    Dominick "Randy" Safuto—lead—born: April 19, 1947
    Mike Zero—first tenor—born: April 4, 1947
    Sal Zero—second tenor—born: October 30, 1942—replaced in 1974
        by Vinnie Carella—born: April 8, 1947
    Frank Safuto—baritone—born: September 26, 1938
    Ken Arcipowski—bass—born: May 26, 1945
Hometown: Maspeth, New York

They first got together in 1961, in Maspeth, where they sang under the name of the Dialtones. Dominick and his brother Frank, along with Mike and his brother Sal and their friend Ken, felt they had a good group, and needed only the right guidance. The father of one of the group members knew songwriter Neil Levenson, who met with the group and gave them a song he had written called "Denise." Neil also suggested that they change their name to Randy and the Rainbows.

The group practiced the song and went to see Neil's friends the Tokens (of "The Lion Sleeps Tonight" fame), who in turn wound up producing the record. They took the disc to Bob Schwartz of Laurie records, who released it on his subsidiary Rust records in the spring of 1963.

Today, Randy, Mike, Frank and Vinnie keep the group active by performing in shows throughout the eastern part of the country.

| May | 1963 | DENISE | Rust |
| December | 1963 | WHY DO KIDS GROW UP | Rust |

THE RAVENS

Members:
  Maithe Marshall—lead
  Len Puzey—second tenor
  Warren Scuttles—baritone
  Jimmy Ricks—bass—replaced by Tommy Evans
Hometown: New York, New York

The group was the first of the real rhythm and blues singers, even though their sound was closer to that of the Mills Brothers. They laid the groundwork for the black singing groups that would follow in the years to come. The group first got together in 1946 and decided to call themselves the Ravens, since everyone was "raving" about their sound. Most of their recordings featured the deep bass voice of Jimmy Ricks, which made their sound unique.

They first signed with King records in 1946 and recorded "Bye Bye Baby Blues." From there they went to Hub records in 1947, then wound up with National records, where they had their first big smash with "Ol' Man River." In 1948, they recorded the classic "White Christmas," which was the first R & B version of this song.

Today the group gets together for rare appearances on certain rock shows in New York. When they do, they show exactly why they are considered the pioneer group. They never sounded better.

May	1946	BYE BYE BABY BLUES	King
March	1947	OL' MAN RIVER	National
June	1948	SEPTEMBER SONG	National
December	1948	WHITE CHRISTMAS	National
January	1949	ALWAYS	National
March	1949	DEEP PURPLE	National
January	1950	I DON'T HAVE TO RIDE NO MORE	National

DIANE RAY

Born: September 1, 1942
Hometown: Gastonia, North Carolina

Diane started singing with local bands in 1961 and worked with a local group called the Continentals. She entered a talent contest on WAYS radio in Charlotte, North Carolina, and won. On the panel was Shelby Singleton, who signed her to Mercury records.

In July 1963, she had her only hit for the label with "Please Don't Talk to the Lifeguard."

July	1963	PLEASE DON'T TALK TO THE LIFEGUARD	Mercury

JAMES RAY

Real Name: James Raymond Ray
Born: 1941
Hometown: Washington, District of Columbia

Rudy Clark, who was a mailman in New York, went into a club one night and heard a singer named James Ray. Rudy liked his voice and told him he had written a song called "If You Gotta Make a Fool of Somebody" and wanted Ray to record it. Since Ray's career was going nowhere at the time, he felt he had nothing to lose.

Rudy took off from his mail route to go knocking on doors to find someone interested in this new singer and his song. On his rounds he met Neil Galligan, who had Ray record the song for Caprice. It became a national hit in November 1961.

Rudy left his mail job and became a staff writer for Good Songs, Inc., while James Ray continued his career on Caprice.

November	1961	IF YOU GOTTA MAKE A FOOL OF SOMEBODY	Caprice
March	1962	ITTY BITTY PIECES	Caprice

JOHNNIE RAY

Real Name: John Alvin Ray
Born: January 10, 1927
Hometown: Dallas, Oregon

Although Johnnie began to go deaf as a youngster, it did not diminish his interest in becoming a singer. He enjoyed country and western and spiritual music and began his early singing in a church choir.

JOHNNIE RAY

In the late forties Johnnie left Oregon for Detroit, to begin a career as a singer. It was while he was in Detroit that he met La Vern Baker at the Flame show bar. He became interested in her singing style and eventually got to meet her manager, Al Green. Al liked Johnnie and got him a job playing several local clubs. It was while playing one of these clubs that local disc jockey Robin Seymour heard Johnnie and went on to contact one of his friends from Okeh records, which eventually led to Johnnie signing with the label.

In early 1951 Johnnie recorded "Whiskey and Gin," for Okeh records, which began to break in Cleveland, Ohio. Later that year, Johnnie went to New York and recorded a song for Mitch Miller and Columbia records (the parent company of Okeh) called "Cry" that really established the shrieking Johnnie Ray style. On that session, the background singers were four unknowns called the Four Lads, who would go on to record many big hits for Columbia a few years later, like "Moments to Remember." The song was released in October 1951 and went right into 1952, winding up as the number one song for all of 1952.

From 1951 until around 1956 Johnnie, "The Prince of Wails," was one of the most played and most popular vocalists on the charts. His emotional style became his trade mark as a singer. Today he makes occasional appearances in Las Vegas and some TV shows. He has considered recording full time again.

October	1951	CRY	Okeh
October	1951	THE LITTLE WHITE CLOUD THAT CRIED	Okeh
January	1952	PLEASE, MR. SUN	Columbia
March	1952	WHAT'S THE USE?	Columbia
May	1952	WALKIN' MY BABY BACK HOME	Columbia
July	1952	ALL OF ME	Columbia
September	1952	LOVE ME (BABY CAN'T YOU LOVE ME)	Columbia
April	1953	SOMEBODY STOLE MY GAL	Columbia
June	1954	HERNANDO'S HIDEAWAY	Columbia
August	1956	JUST WALKING IN THE RAIN	Columbia
January	1957	YOU DON'T OWE ME A THING	Columbia
January	1957	LOOK HOMEWARD, ANGEL	Columbia
March	1957	YES TONIGHT, JOSEPHINE	Columbia
July	1957	BUILD YOUR LOVE	Columbia
August	1958	UP UNTIL NOW	Columbia
September	1959	I'LL NEVER FALL IN LOVE AGAIN	Columbia

MARGIE RAYBURN

Margie sang in a group called the Sunnysiders, where she met her husband, Norman Malkin. Norman then wrote a big song that the group recorded, called "Hey! Mr. Banjo."

In 1957, Norman found a song that Dave Burgess of The Champs had written, "I'm Available," which he had Margie record. She overdubbed her voice to sound as though there were three of her, and the finished master was sold to Liberty. The label released it in the fall of 1957. It became her only major hit.

Today she lives with her husband in Los Angeles.

| October | 1957 | I'M AVAILABLE | Liberty |

THE RAYS

Members:
>   Harold "Hal" Miller—lead—born: January 17, 1931
>   Walter Ford—tenor—September 5, 1931
>   Davey Jones—second tenor—1931
>   Harry James—baritone—1932
Hometown: New York, New York

In 1955, Hal and Davey sang with a group called the Four Fellows ("Soldier Boy" on Glory records) and then decided to leave the group. They

THE RAYS

Top: Davey Jones, Harry James, Walt Ford
Bottom: Hal Miller

got together with Walter and Harry and formed a new group, calling themselves the Rays on the recommendation of their vocal arranger, Jimmy Duggan.

They went with Chess records and recorded "Tippity Top," which was mildly popular. At this same time they met songwriters Bob Crewe and Frank Slay, Jr., who signed them to their label, XYZ records.

In May 1957, while Bob was riding a train through Pennsylvania, it stopped at a town where he saw two people silhouetted on a shade. This gave him an idea for a song. He took it to Frank Slay, and they wrote "Silhouettes," which they had the group record. Bob gave the record to Hy Lit, a disc jockey at WFIL in Philadelphia, who took it home to listen to with a dozen others. He put them on his record player and proceeded to take a nap while the records played. "Silhouettes" was the last record on the stack and wound up being played a half-dozen times before Hy got up to shut the machine off. He was so taken by the song that he took it with him to play on his show the next day. The rest is history. The song was leased on Cameo records in Philadelphia, and by September 1957, it was a national hit. The flip side, "Daddy Cool," was sung with Walter Ford as lead.

Today Hal lives in Brooklyn. Walt and Harry own real estate agencies, while Davey operates a bar in Brooklyn. The group gets together for a rare appearance with only Hal and Walter of the original members.

September	1957	SILHOUETTES/DADDY COOL	Cameo
February	1958	ELEVATOR OPERATOR	XYZ
January	1960	MEDITERRANEAN MOON	XYZ
August	1961	MAGIC MOON	XYZ

OTIS REDDING

Born: September 9, 1941
Died: December 10, 1967
Hometown: Macon, Georgia

Otis grew up in the same area of Georgia that Little Richard and James Brown hailed from. He became interested in singing in church choirs and began singing regularly.

OTIS REDDING

In the late fifties he became an avid admirer of Sam Cooke, and wanted to imitate Sam's style. He signed with the Memphis-based Volt records in May 1963 and recorded "These Arms of Mine" as his first release. After that, Otis became a great star in his own right, with a long list of hit records.

In December 1967, while on tour with another Volt group, the Bar-Kays (of "Soul Finger" fame), Otis chartered a plane from Cleveland, Ohio, to their next engagement. The plane crashed on route ending his career. It is ironic that Otis died during the month of December, only a few days away from the anniversary of the death of his idol Sam Cooke.

In December 1967, shortly after his death, Volt records released a song that Otis had written with Steve Cropper (guitar player with Booker T. & the M.G.'s), called "Sittin' on the Dock of the Bay," which went on to become a number one national hit in early 1968.

Otis recorded a few hits with Carla Thomas (see OTIS & CARLA, *Rock On: The Modern Years*).

May	1963	THESE ARMS OF MINE	Volt
October	1963	THAT'S WHAT MY HEART NEEDS	Volt
November	1963	PAIN IN MY HEART	Volt
March	1964	COME TO ME	Volt
October	1964	CHAINED AND BOUND	Volt
February	1965	MR. PITIFUL	Volt
April	1965	I'VE BEEN LOVING YOU TOO LONG	Volt
September	1965	RESPECT	Volt
December	1965	JUST ONE MORE DAY	Volt
February	1966	SATISFACTION	Volt
June	1966	MY LOVER'S PRAYER	Volt
October	1966	FA-FA-FA-FA-FA	Volt
December	1966	TRY A LITTLE TENDERNESS	Volt
March	1967	I LOVE YOU MORE THAN WORDS CAN SAY	Volt
May	1967	SHAKE	Volt
July	1967	GLORY OF LOVE	Volt
January	1968	(SITTIN' ON) THE DOCK OF THE BAY	Volt
April	1968	THE HAPPY SONG (DUM DUM)	Volt
June	1968	AMEN	Atco
September	1968	I'VE GOT DREAMS TO REMEMBER	Atco
November	1968	PAPA'S GOT A BRAND NEW BAG	Atco
February	1969	A LOVER'S QUESTION	Atco
May	1969	LOVE MAN	Atco
August	1969	FREE ME	Atco

JERRY REED

Real Name: Jerry Reed Hubbard
Born: March 20, 1937
Hometown: Atlanta, Georgia

Guitar-playing Jerry Reed signed with Columbia records in early 1962, and had a couple of average hits with the label. It wasn't until he signed

JERRY REED

with RCA however, that he had real success with the songs he wrote and recorded, like "Amos Moses" in late 1970.

Today Jerry is also getting more involved with moviemaking after appearing with Burt Reynolds in *Smokey and the Bandit*.

June	1962	GOODNIGHT, IRENE	Columbia
October	1962	HULLY GULLY GUITARS	Columbia
June	1966	KNOCKIN' AT YOUR DOOR	Exodus
October	1970	AMOS MOSES	RCA
May	1971	WHEN YOU'RE HOT, YOU'RE HOT	RCA
September	1971	KO-KO JOE	RCA

JIMMY REED

Born: 1926
Died: August 29, 1976, in San Francisco, California
Hometown: Leland, Mississippi

Before turning pro, Jimmy spent several years in Gary, Indiana, in a steel foundry, where he sang and picked a guitar during his lunch hour. He first signed with Vee Jay records in December 1953, and had his first major hit in early 1955, with "You Don't Have to Go."

He is still active today performing around the country.

February	1955	YOU DON'T HAVE TO GO	Vee Jay
January	1956	AIN'T THAT LOVIN' YOU BABY	Vee Jay

JIMMY REED

December	1956	YOU'VE GOT ME DIZZY	Vee Jay
June	1957	THE SUN IS SHINING	Vee Jay
October	1957	HONEST I DO	Vee Jay
October	1958	I'M GONNA GET MY BABY	Vee Jay
January	1959	I TOLD YOU BABY	Vee Jay
February	1960	BABY, WHAT YOU WANT ME TO DO	Vee Jay
June	1960	FOUND LOVE	Vee Jay
October	1960	HUSH-HUSH	Vee Jay
January	1961	CLOSE TOGETHER	Vee Jay
April	1961	BIG BOSS MAN	Vee Jay
September	1961	BRIGHT LIGHTS BIG CITY	Vee Jay
February	1960	BABY WHAT YOU WANT ME TO DO	Vee Jay
May	1960	FOUND LOVE	Vee Jay
October	1960	HUSH HUSH	Vee Jay
January	1961	CLOSE TOGETHER	Vee Jay
May	1961	BIG BOSS MAN	Vee Jay
September	1961	BRIGHT LIGHTS, BIG CITY	Vee Jay
June	1962	GOOD LOVER	Vee Jay
April	1963	SHAME, SHAME, SHAME	Vee Jay

DELLA REESE

Born: July 6, 1932
Hometown: Detroit, Michigan

Della was a gospel singer with Mahalia Jackson and then the Clara Ward singers. Her big pop music break came when she signed a managerial agreement with Lee Magid, who got her a job with the Erskine Hawkins orchestra. She was awarded a contract with Jubilee records in 1957 and recorded "And That Reminds Me" for the label that summer.

In 1959, she signed with RCA and had her biggest hit with the song "Don't You Know" in September of that year.

July	1957	AND THAT REMINDS ME	Jubilee
January	1958	SERMONETTE	Jubilee
September	1959	DON'T YOU KNOW	RCA
December	1959	NOT ONE MINUTE MORE	RCA
March	1960	SOMEDAY	RCA
September	1960	AND NOW	RCA
February	1961	THE MOST BEAUTIFUL WORDS	RCA
April	1961	BILL BAILEY	RCA
July	1965	AFTER LOVING YOU	ABC

JIM REEVES

Born: August 20, 1924
Died: July 31, 1964, in a plane crash
Hometown: Panola County, Texas

Jim attended the University of Texas, where he earned his tuition by playing the guitar. His major ambition was to be a professional baseball

DELLA REESE

JIM REEVES

player. He did play for the St. Louis Cardinals, until a leg injury ended his career. Then he started playing the guitar again and later became a disc jockey.

He recorded "Mexican Joe" and joined the "Louisiana Hayride" in Shreveport. Shortly afterwards he had a hit with the song "Bimbo."

In 1955, he joined the Grand Ole Opry. In April 1957, "Four Walls" became his first major pop hit. He had his biggest all-time seller in January 1960 with "He'll Have to Go."

April	1957	FOUR WALLS	RCA
January	1958	ANNA MARIE	RCA
July	1958	BLUE BOY	RCA
December	1958	BILLY BAYOU	RCA
January	1960	HE'LL HAVE TO GO	RCA
June	1960	I'M GETTIN' BETTER	RCA
October	1960	AM I LOSING YOU	RCA
March	1961	THE BLIZZARD	RCA
June	1961	WHAT WOULD YOU DO	RCA
November	1961	LOSING YOUR LOVE	RCA
April	1962	ADIOS AMIGO	RCA
October	1962	I'M GONNA CHANGE EVERYTHING	RCA
August	1964	I GUESS I'M CRAZY	RCA
November	1964	I WON'T FORGET YOU	RCA
February	1965	THIS IS IT	RCA
August	1965	IS IT REALLY OVER	RCA
January	1966	SNOW FLAKE	RCA
April	1966	DISTANT DRUMS	RCA
August	1966	BLUE SIDE OF LONESOME	RCA

THE REGENTS

Members:
> Guy Villari—lead—born: August 11, 1942
> Sal Cuomo—first tenor—born: August 10, 1939
> Charles Fassert—second tenor—1939
> Don Jacobucci—baritone—born: August 8, 1938
> Tony Gravagna—bass—1939

Hometown: Bronx, New York

The group first got together in 1959 and began singing on street corners in the Bronx. They called themselves the Regents, because lead singer Guy Villari was smoking Regent cigarettes at the time and the group did some recording at Regent Sound studios.

In 1959, the group recorded a song that Charles Fassert's brother Fred had written, "Barbara-Ann." The group would sing the song whenever they appeared at local functions, and it became a favorite with their fans. Several years later they took the recording to Lou Cicchetti, who owned a record shop named Cousins records. Lou liked the song and called a friend of his, Morris Diamond, to listen to the recording. Morris agreed and they decided to release it on their own label, Cousins records, named after the store.

The song was released in April 1961 and began to sell rapidly throughout the New York area. The master recording was then sold to Morris Levy and was released on his Gee records label. The song went on to become a national hit that summer.

Their follow-up, "Runaround," written by Ernie Maresca, who wrote many hits for Dion, like "Runaround Sue" and "The Wanderer," was also a national hit during the summer of 1961. Their last major hit for Gee records was a song called "Liar."

In 1962, the group changed their name to the Runarounds and recorded songs like "Unbelievable" and "Let Them Talk," which were only mildly popular, on K-C records (Nat King Cole's label).

Today Guy lives on Long Island and works as a record distributor in Long Island City. Don is a businessman in Florida, while Chuck is with Sussex records in California. Guy still sings on weekends with Ronnie Lapinsky and Bob Falcone as the Regents in the New York area.

April	1961	BARBARA-ANN	Gee
July	1961	RUNAROUND	Gee
October	1961	LIAR	Gee
February	1962	UNBELIEVABLE	K-C
May	1962	LET THEM TALK	K-C

JOE REISMAN

Born: September 16, 1924
Hometown: Dallas, Texas

Joe began playing the sax as a youngster. In the forties he played with dance orchestras like Bob Crosby's and Louis Prima's. From 1948 through 1955 he was Patti Page's arranger, from 1955 to 1959 he did the same for Perry Como, June Valli, and the Ames Brothers while at RCA.

In late 1956, while musical conductor at RCA, he had a pop hit with "Armen's Theme."

| November | 1956 | ARMEN'S THEME | RCA |
| February | 1957 | PAMELA THROWS A PARTY | RCA |

GOOGIE RENE COMBO

Owner Leon Rene of Class records did some piano and organ playing under the name of Googie Rene. In the fifties he had some R & B hits; in early 1966 he enjoyed his only national pop hit with the song "Smokey Joe's La La" on his own label.

| February | 1966 | SMOKEY JOE'S LA LA | Class |

THE REVELS

Right in time for Halloween in 1959, Bill Jackson wrote a song called "The Midnight Stroll" that the Revels recorded for Norgolde records. It was an eerie song, complete with tower bells sounding and goblins screaming. This novelty number was a top-forty record.

| October | 1959 | MIDNIGHT STROLL | Norgolde |

PAUL REVERE & THE RAIDERS

Members:
   Paul Revere—piano
   Mark Lindsay—lead singer
   Drake Levin—lead guitar—replaced by Jim Valley—replaced by Freddy Weller
   Phil Volk—rhythm guitar—replaced by Charlie Coe—replaced by Keith Allison
   Mike Smith—drums—replaced temporarily by Joe Correro, Jr.
Hometown: Caldwell, Idaho

PAUL REVERE & THE RAIDERS

Left to right: Drake Levin, Mike Smith
Mark Lindsay, Paul Revere, Phil Volk

The group first got together in the early sixties and recorded a song called "Like Long Hair," an instrumental. The song was sold to Gardena records and released in April 1961, becoming a national hit.

In 1963, the group was signed by Columbia records—the first rock group signed by the label. They were unique, for they all wore Revolutionary War uniforms and Mark wore his hair in a pony tail. It was at this time that Dick Clark signed them to appear on his Los Angeles–based "Where The Action Is" show. They achieved a tremendous amount of popularity because of the network TV exposure.

In the fall of 1965, they had their first major hit for Columbia records with "Steppin' Out." A short time later they became known as simply the Raiders.

April	1961	LIKE LONG HAIR	Gardena
September	1965	STEPPIN' OUT	Columbia
December	1965	JUST LIKE ME	Columbia
March	1966	KICKS	Columbia
May	1966	HUNGRY	Columbia
October	1966	THE GREAT AIRPLANE STRIKE	Columbia
November	1966	GOOD THING	Columbia

February	1967	UPS AND DOWNS	Columbia
April	1967	HIM OR ME—WHAT'S IT GONNA BE	Columbia
August	1967	I HAD A DREAM	Columbia
November	1967	PEACE OF MIND	Columbia
January	1968	TOO MUCH TALK	Columbia
June	1968	DON'T TAKE IT SO HARD	Columbia
October	1968	CINDERELLA SUNSHINE	Columbia
January	1969	MR. SUN, MR. MOON	Columbia
May	1969	LET ME	Columbia
September	1969	WE GOTTA ALL GET TOGETHER	Columbia
February	1970	JUST SEVENTEEN	Columbia
April	1971	INDIAN RESERVATION	Columbia
September	1971	BIRDS OF A FEATHER	Columbia

DEBBIE REYNOLDS

Real Name: Mary Frances Reynolds
Born: April 1, 1932
Hometown: El Paso, Texas

When Debbie was eight, her father, a carpenter for the Southern Pacific railroad, was transferred to Southern California, where they settled in Burbank. In 1948, she entered the Miss Burbank contest, doing an imitation of Betty Hutton, and won a prize. A talent scout saw her and got her a movie contract.

In July 1957, a song she recorded from one of her movies, *Tammy and the Bachelor*—the title song simply called "Tammy"—became a number one song on Coral records, pushing aside a number of successful rock tunes including "Diana" by Paul Anka and "That'll Be the Day" by Buddy Holly and the Crickets.

Debbie married Eddie Fisher on September 26, 1955; three years later they were divorced. Their daughter, Carrie Fisher, has become a big star, appearing in the *Star Wars* films.

July	1957	TAMMY	Coral
January	1958	A VERY SPECIAL LOVE	Coral
January	1960	AM I THAT EASY TO FORGET	Dot
April	1960	CITY LIGHTS	Dot

JODY REYNOLDS

Jody began his career by playing around the Los Angeles area with the Storms. They worked many local clubs and became quite popular.

In early 1958, he auditioned for Demon records in Los Angeles, playing a song he had written called "Endless Sleep." They liked the song and had him record it with his band. The song was released in the spring of

1958, and Jody had a top-ten national hit. The combination of his rumbling guitar and his emotional singing was responsible for the song's success.

Today Jody lives in Palm Springs, California, where he appears at local clubs. Until recently, he owned a guitar shop there.

April	1958	ENDLESS SLEEP	Demor
August	1958	FIRE OF LOVE	Demon

CHARLIE RICH

Born: December 12, 1932
Hometown: Colt, Arkansas

After his discharge from the Air Force in the mid-fifties, Charlie went into the fields picking cotton in order to support his family. He then moved from Arkansas to Memphis in order to pursue a singing career. It was there that he cut an audition tape at the Sun recording studios. Sun president Sam Phillips and A & R man Bill Justis heard Charlie and liked him enough to sign him to the label.

After several years of unsuccessful recordings, he wrote and recorded a song in early 1960, released on the Phillips label, called "Lonely Weekends." This became his only major hit for Phillips.

In 1965, after he signed with Smash records, he had his only other pop hit with "Mohair Sam" during the summer of 1965. After another long period of time, Charlie (now a country and western singer) signed with Epic records and in late 1973 came up with a number one national pop hit, "The Most Beautiful Girl." Today he has found new popularity with country and western fans as well as the pop audience.

CHARLIE RICH

March	1960	LONELY WEEKENDS	Phillips
August	1965	MOHAIR SAM	Smash
March	1970	JULY 12, 1939	Epic
April	1973	BEHIND CLOSED DOORS	Epic
October	1973	THE MOST BEAUTIFUL GIRL	Epic
January	1974	THERE WON'T BE ANYMORE	RCA
February	1974	A VERY SPECIAL LOVE SONG	Epic
May	1974	I DON'T SEE ME IN YOUR EYES ANYMORE	RCA
August	1974	I LOVE MY FRIEND	Epic
September	1974	SHE CALLED ME BABY	RCA
February	1975	MY ELUSIVE DREAMS	Epic
May	1975	EVERY TIME YOU TOUCH ME (I GET HIGH)	Epic
January	1976	SINCE I FELL FOR YOU	Epic

RICK AND THE KEENS

In late 1957, Joe Cook wrote a song called "Peanuts," which he recorded with his group Little Joe and the Thrillers for Okeh. In the summer of 1961, Rick and the Keens recorded the same song for Mercury records. Their version did not do quite as well as the original.

June	1961	PEANUTS	Smash

NELSON RIDDLE

Born: June 1, 1921
Hometown: Oradell, New Jersey

Nelson has been a very important musical arranger and staff producer for Capitol records for many years. He has been responsible for most of Frank Sinatra's hit songs for Capitol.

Today he is a staff arranger and producer for Reprise records on the West Coast.

September	1955	LISBON ANTIGUA	Capitol
March	1956	PORT AU PRINCE	Capitol
July	1956	THEME FROM THE PROUD ONES	Capitol
May	1962	ROUTE 66 THEME	Capitol

THE RIGHTEOUS BROTHERS

Members:

Bill Medley—born: September 19, 1940—hometown: Santa Ana, California

Bobby Hatfield—born: August 10, 1940—hometown: Anaheim, California

In 1962, Bobby and Bill started rehearsing an act together and were signed by Ray Maxwell of Moonglow records. They were first known as the Paramours, but Ray had them change their names to the Righteous Brothers when black fans called their music "Blue-eyed Soul" and their sound "Righteous."

Their first release on Moonglow was in April 1963, with "Little Latin Lupe Lu" a song that Bill had written. In 1964, they left Moonglow and went to Phil Spector's label, Philles records. That fall, they became part of ABC-TV's popular music show, "Shindig," where they were featured each week.

They recorded a song in October that Phil Spector had written with Barry Mann and Cynthia Weil, called "You've Lost That Lovin' Feelin'." They sang the song on the TV show and in a short time it went on to become a number one national hit.

They left Philles records in 1965 and signed with Verve records. In February 1966, their first release for their new label was another Barry Mann and Cynthia Weil tune called "(You're My) Soul and Inspiration," which became another number one national hit for the duo.

In 1968, Bobby and Billy split up to pursue solo careers. Bill signed with MGM records, while Bobby got another fellow and continued to perform as the Righteous Brothers.

After a few hits together in 1974, they have gone back to pursuing solo careers. They did, however, reunite on Dick Clark's thirtieth anniversary special salute to "American Bandstand" on October 30, 1981.

May	1963	LITTLE LATIN LUPE LU	Moonglow
August	1963	MY BABE	Moonglow
January	1965	BRING YOUR LOVE TO ME	Moonglow
May	1965	YOU CAN HAVE HER	Moonglow
July	1965	JUSTINE	Moonglow
February	1966	GEORGIA ON MY MIND	Moonglow
November	1964	YOU'VE LOST THAT LOVIN' FEELIN'	Philles
March	1965	JUST ONCE IN MY LIFE	Philles
July	1965	UNCHAINED MELODY	Philles
November	1965	EBB TIDE	Philles
February	1966	(YOU'RE MY) SOUL AND INSPIRATION	Verve
June	1966	HE	Verve
August	1966	GO AHEAD AND CRY	Verve
October	1966	ON THIS SIDE OF GOODBYE	Verve
April	1967	MELANCHOLY MUSIC MAN	Verve
September	1967	STRANDED IN THE MIDDLE OF NO PLACE	Verve
May	1974	ROCK 'N' ROLL HEAVEN	Haven
September	1974	GIVE IT TO THE PEOPLE	Haven
November	1974	DREAM ON	Haven

THE RINKY-DINKS

In 1958 Bobby Darin was afraid Atco records was going to drop him, for up to that point he had not had a hit record. In order to protect himself, he recorded a song he wrote called "Early in the Morning" under the name the Rinky-Dinks. He sold the recording to Brunswick records, so that if he were dropped by Atco, he might have another label to go to.

In June 1958, his song "Splish Splash" became a hit for Atco and the company became very much interested in retaining Bobby. However, "Early in the Morning" was released on Brunswick and started moving up the charts. Atco then made a deal for the recording and decided to release it, still under the name the Rinky-Dinks. The song went on to be a top-twenty hit that summer.

| July | 1958 | EARLY IN THE MORNING | Atco |

THE RIP CHORDS

Members:
   Phil Stewart
   Arnie Marcus
   Rich Rotkin
   Bernie Bringas

These four young men from Southern California got together in 1961 and began playing local clubs in their area. In early 1963, they were spotted by Columbia records and signed to a contract. Later that year they recorded a song called "Hey Little Cobra" which went on to be a top-ten national hit. It was a song about hot-rodding, a theme that was popular at the time in the wake of the Beach Boys' "409" and Jan and Dean's "Drag City."

March	1963	HERE I STAND	Columbia
August	1963	GONE	Columbia
November	1963	HEY LITTLE COBRA	Columbia
April	1964	THREE WINDOW COUPE	Columbia

TEX RITTER

Real Name: Woodward Maurice Ritter
Born: January 12, 1906
Died: January 3, 1974
Hometown: Panola, Texas

Tex began studying law at the University of Texas and Northwestern University, but gave it up for a career in show business. He went first to

New York, then to Hollywood, where he became a western hero, appearing in some eighty movies with his horse Whiteflash. He was not only an actor, but a singer and songwriter as well. In 1952, while recording for Capitol records, he had his first big hit with the song "High Noon." He had hits also with "Boll Weevil," "The Wayward Wind," and in 1961, "I Dreamed of a Hill-Billy Heaven," which was about going to heaven to see all the big country recording stars.

Later in life, Tex gravitated toward politics. He ran unsuccessfully for the United States Senate and the governorship of Tennessee. On January 3, 1974, while visiting the Nashville jail, he was stricken with a heart attack. He died later that evening at Baptist Hospital.

August	1952	HIGH NOON	Capitol
June	1956	THE WAYWARD WIND	Capitol
June	1961	I DREAMED OF A HILL-BILLY HEAVEN	Capitol

THE RIVIERAS

The Rivieras hailed from the New York City area. In the summer of 1958, the group made an appointment to see George Paxton of Coed records (home label of the Crests and the Duprees) and auditioned a ballad called "Count Every Star." George liked what he heard and decided to release the tune on his label. By August 1958, their ballad started climbing the national charts.

August	1958	COUNT EVERY STAR	Coed
February	1959	MOONLIGHT SERENADE	Coed
January	1960	SINCE I MADE YOU CRY	Coed

THE RIVINGTONS

Members:
    Carl White—lead—born: 1932, Dallas, Texas; died: January 7, 1980
    Sonny Harris—Texas
    Al Frazier—California
    Rocky Wilson, Jr.—bass—Pensacola, Florida

The Rivingtons met accidentally at a hotel in downtown Los Angeles, and began singing together. In 1961, West Coast producers Jack L. Levy and Adam Ross heard the group and began working with them.

Jack and Adam decided to call the group the Rivingtons after the street on New York's Lower East Side where they both grew up.

THE RIVINGTONS
Left to right: Carl White, Al Frazier,
Rocky Wilson, Jr., Sonny Harris

In 1962, the group signed with Liberty records and in June of that year launched their careers with "Papa-Oom-Mow-Mow."

June	1962	PAPA-OOM-MOW-MOW	Liberty
September	1962	MAMA-OOM-MOW-MOW	Liberty
March	1963	THE BIRD'S THE WORD	Liberty

MARTY ROBBINS

Real Name: Martin D. Robinson
Born: September 26, 1925
Hometown: Glendale, Arizona

After serving in the Navy, Marty got a job singing at KTYL radio in Mesa, Arizona, where he formed a band called K-Bar Cowboys. In 1953, he joined WSM radio's Grand Ole Opry and signed with Columbia records.

One of his first country hits to go pop was his version of Guy Mitchell's "Singing The Blues" in late 1956. In March 1957, he had a smash hit with a song he wrote, "A White Sport Coat." He had his biggest hit in October 1959, "El Paso," which went to number one.

Today he lives in Nashville with his wife and son, while he records for MCA records.

October	1956	SINGING THE BLUES	Columbia
March	1957	A WHITE SPORT COAT	Columbia
October	1957	THE STORY OF MY LIFE	Columbia
March	1958	JUST MARRIED	Columbia
August	1958	SHE WAS ONLY SEVENTEEN	Columbia
February	1959	THE HANGING TREE	Columbia
June	1959	CAP AND GOWN	Columbia
October	1959	EL PASO	Columbia
March	1960	BIG IRON	Columbia
June	1960	IS THERE ANY CHANCE	Columbia
October	1960	BALLAD OF THE ALAMO	Columbia
January	1961	DON'T WORRY	Columbia
June	1961	JIMMY MARTINEZ	Columbia
September	1961	IT'S YOUR WORLD	Columbia
December	1961	I TOLD THE BROOK	Columbia
April	1962	LOVE CAN'T WAIT	Columbia
July	1962	DEVIL WOMAN	Columbia
November	1962	RUBY ANN	Columbia
November	1963	BEGGING TO YOU	Columbia
October	1968	I WALK ALONE	Columbia
March	1970	MY WOMAN MY WOMAN, MY WIFE	Columbia

ROBERT AND JOHNNY

Members:
 Robert Carr
 Johnny Mitchell
Hometown: Bronx, New York

Both fellows lived on the same block in the Bronx and started singing together in school. In 1956, they auditioned for Hy Weiss of Old Town records and were awarded a recording contract.

Robert first wrote "I Believe," which was recorded in June 1956. Next came "You're Mine" in November 1956. In February 1958, they collaborated on a song which became their biggest hit: "We Belong Together."

February	1958	WE BELONG TOGETHER	Old Town
July	1958	I BELIEVE IN YOU	Old Town

DON ROBERTSON

Born: December 5, 1922
Hometown: Chicago, Illinois

Don was born in Peking, China, and came to the United States when he was five. He began to play the piano and eventually enrolled at the University of Chicago, majoring in music. After further study at Chicago's Musical College, he began to work as a pianist in the local area.

In the spring of 1956, his instrumental composition "The Happy Whistler" was a top-ten hit for Capitol records.

Some of the big songs he wrote for other artists include "I Really Don't Want To Know," "Please Help Me, I'm Falling" and "I Love You More and More Every Day."

March	1956	THE HAPPY WHISTLER	Capitol

IVO ROBIC

Real Name: Eevo Robish
Born: 1931
Hometown: Zagreb, Yugoslavia

Ivo wanted to be a music teacher, but wound up as a pop singer when he auditioned for Zagreb radio's dance orchestra. He cut his first records in 1948. By 1959, he had made over one hundred records and was Yugoslavia's top performer, able to speak and sing in German, French, Italian, Spanish, and English.

In 1959, he recorded a German song called "Morgen" ("Morning"). The song became a hit in Hamburg, on Polydor records. It was released in the U.S. on Laurie records in July 1959 and became a national hit.

July	1959	MORGEN	Laurie
January	1960	THE HAPPY MULETEER	Laurie

THE ROBINS

Members:
    Carl Gardner—lead
    Ty Terrell—tenor
    Grady Chapman—tenor
    Billy Richards
    Roy Richards
    Bobby Nunn—bass
Hometown: Los Angeles, California

The group was formed on the West Coast and had a hit for Jerry Leiber and Mike Stoller's Spark records in 1955 with "Smokey Joe's Cafe." When the master was sold to Atco records, Carl and Bobby left the group to organize the Coasters and record for Atco. The remaining members stayed on with Whippit records and recorded "Cherry Lips" in 1956.

| July | 1955 | SMOKEY JOE'S CAFE | Atco |
| December | 1955 | CHERRY LIPS | Whippet |

FLOYD ROBINSON

Floyd's interest in singing began when he was a youngster growing up in the Nashville area. As he grew older he began to sing at local functions and at parties. After high school he seriously considered a professional career in singing. In 1959, he was spotted by an RCA executive, who signed him to the label.

During the summer of 1959, while still in his teens, he recorded his only major hit, "Makin' Love."

| July | 1959 | MAKIN' LOVE | RCA |

ROCHELL AND THE CANDLES

In the early sixties, Hunter Hancock, a onetime popular disc jockey from Los Angeles, decided to start a record label of his own. He got together with Roger Davenport and formed Swingin' records.

In late 1960 they met a young man named Johnny Wyatt, who had written a song called "Once upon a Time," which he sang with a group called Rochell and the Candles. Davenport and Hancock like the ballad and decided to release it on their label, and in early 1961, the song became a national hit.

| January | 1961 | ONCE UPON A TIME | Swingin' |

THE ROCK-A-TEENS

Members:
   Vic Mizell
   Bill Cook
   Bill Smith
   Paul Evans
   Boo Walker
   Eddie Robinson
Hometown: New York, New York

The six fellows went to Morris Levy's Roulette records in 1959, with a unique song that George McGraw had written called "Woo-Hoo." The only lyric in the song was "Woo-Hoo," which was chanted through the entire recording over the driving beat of drums and guitars. Roulette felt the song was catchy and released it that fall. It went on to become the group's only hit.

September 1959	WOO-HOO	Roulette

THE ROCKIN' REBELS

Members:
Lee Carrol—Pittsburgh, Pennsylvania
Kenny Mills—Pittsburgh, Pennsylvania
Tony DiMaria—Stuebenville, Ohio
Eddy Jay—New York, New York

The group was formed in 1960. In 1962, they signed a contract with Swan records and recorded "Wild Weekend" in November of that year for their first and biggest hit on the label.

November	1962	WILD WEEKEND	Swan
April	1963	ROCKIN' CRICKETS	Swan

THE ROCKY FELLERS

Members:
Eddie—1955
Albert—1953
Tony—1947
Junior—1945
Pop—1924
Hometown: Shanghai, China, and Manila, The Philippines

The Rocky Fellers was a family act that went on the road in 1959. The boys also had five sisters at home in Manila, who were not in the act. In early 1963, they signed with Scepter records and had their first hit called "Killer Joe."

March	1963	KILLER JOE	Scepter
June	1963	LIKE THE BIG GUYS DO	Scepter

EILEEN RODGERS

Born: 1933
Hometown: Pittsburgh, Pennsylvania

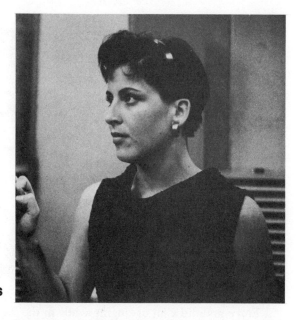

EILEEN RODGERS

While attending Pittsburgh's Cathedral High School for Girls in the late forties, Eileen became active in the glee club and sang in various school shows. After graduation, she took an office job, but quickly became bored. One night, while out on a date at a local Pittsburgh club she sang a few songs with the band. The owner was so impressed that he invited her back to sing on a regular basis.

From Pittsburgh she moved to Chicago, in the early fifties, where she did TV and night clubs. Bandleader Charlie Spivak spotted her and asked her to join his band. She stayed with Charlie until 1956, when she left to work in New York, where she made an audition record that Mitch Miller heard and liked. He signed her to a Columbia records contract. By the summer of 1956 she had her first hit, "Miracle of Love."

July	1956	MIRACLE OF LOVE	Columbia
November	1956	GIVE ME	Columbia
March	1957	THE WALL	Columbia
May	1957	DON'T CALL ME SWEETIE	Columbia
September	1957	THIRD FINGER LEFT HAND	Columbia
August	1958	TREASURE OF YOUR LOVE	Columbia

JIMMIE RODGERS

Born: September 18, 1933
Hometown: Camas, Washington

As a youngster, Jimmie went to Seattle to try his hand at singing and worked in the area for a while. During the Korean War, he enlisted in the

JIMMIE RODGERS

Air Force and did a lot of singing while in the service. After his discharge, he pursued a professional career.

In early 1957, he auditioned for Hugo and Luigi at Roulette records with a song called "Honeycomb." They liked the song, had Jimmie record it and, in July 1957, saw it zoom to the top of the charts—the only number one hit he ever had. In 1961, after a long string of "rockabilly" hits for Roulette, Jimmie signed with Dot records.

In a rock and roll age which emphasized a heavy beat and group harmonies, Jimmie's art was unique. His folk sound proved to be a very successful blend.

In Los Angeles on December 2, 1967, Jimmie was found in his car with a fractured skull—a mysterious incident which almost claimed his life. Today he makes few public appearances.

July	1957	HONEYCOMB	Roulette
October	1957	KISSES SWEETER THAN WINE	Roulette
January	1958	OH-OH, I'M FALLING IN LOVE AGAIN	Roulette
April	1958	SECRETLY	Roulette
July	1958	ARE YOU REALLY MINE	Roulette
July	1958	THE WIZARD	Roulette
November	1958	BIMBOMBEY	Roulette
February	1959	I'M NEVER GONNA TELL	Roulette
June	1959	RING-A-LING-A-LARIO	Roulette
June	1959	WONDERFUL YOU	Roulette
September	1959	TUCUMCARI	Roulette
January	1960	T.L.C. TENDER LOVE AND CARE	Roulette
January	1960	WALTZING MATILDA	Roulette
April	1960	JUST A CLOSER WALK WITH THEE	Roulette
July	1960	THE WRECK OF THE "JOHN B"	Roulette
September	1961	A LITTLE DOG CRIED	Roulette

September 1962	NO ONE WILL EVER KNOW	Dot
November 1962	RAINBOW AT MIDNIGHT	Dot
May 1964	THE WORLD I USED TO KNOW	Dot
May 1966	IT'S OVER	Dot
September 1967	CHILD OF CLAY	A&M

TOMMY ROE

Real Name: Thomas David Roe
Born: May 9, 1943
Hometown: Atlanta, Georgia

After graduation from high school in 1960, Tommy formed his own band and began traveling throughout the Southwest. In 1962, he signed with ABC records and, in June of that year, released his first original hit, "Sheila," which went to number one. He continued to write many other hits for himself including "Everybody," "Sweet Pea," "Hooray for Hazel" and "Dizzy."

Today Tommy records for MGM while he travels around the country as Tommy Roe and His Trio.

June	1962	SHEILA	ABC
September	1962	SUSIE DARLIN'	ABC
May	1963	THE FOLK SINGER	ABC
October	1963	EVERYBODY	ABC
January	1964	COME ON	ABC
April	1964	CAROL	ABC
May	1966	SWEET PEA	ABC
September	1966	HOORAY FOR HAZEL	ABC
December	1966	IT'S NOW WINTER'S DAY	ABC
June	1967	LITTLE MISS SUNSHINE	ABC
January	1969	DIZZY	ABC
April	1969	HEATHER HONEY	ABC
July	1969	JACK AND JILL	ABC
November	1969	JAM UP JELLY TIGHT	ABC
February	1970	STIR IT UP AND SERVE IT	ABC
June	1970	PEARL	ABC
September	1970	WE CAN MAKE MUSIC	ABC
August	1971	STAGGER LEE	ABC
September	1972	MEAN LITTLE WOMAN, ROSALIE	MGM
May	1973	WORKING CLASS HERO	MGM

TIMMIE ROGERS

Timmie for many years was a popular vaudeville comedian and worked theaters like the Apollo in New York. His trade mark was the familiar yell "Oh yeah."

In the fall of 1957, he recorded a swinging narrative about the feelings of kids going back to school, called "Back to School Again." The song

TIMMIE RODGERS

was released on Bernie Lowe's Cameo records, out of Philadelphia. Because of its "American Bandstand" exposure, it went on to be a national hit.

September 1957	BACK TO SCHOOL AGAIN		Cameo

DON RONDO

Don's big baritone won him many fans in the mid-fifties, when he was singing at local clubs around New York. Jubilee records signed Don to the label. In late 1956, he recorded "Two Different Worlds," which went on to become a national hit for him. In the summer of 1957, he had his biggest hit with the swinging tune "White Silver Sands."

October	1956	TWO DIFFERENT WORLDS	Jubilee
June	1957	WHITE SILVER SANDS	Jubilee
October	1957	THERE'S ONLY YOU	Jubilee

THE RONETTES

Members:
    Ronnie (Bennett) Spector—lead—August 10, 1947
    Estelle Bennett—July 22, 1946
    Nedra Talley—January 27, 1947
Hometown: New York, New York

Ronnie and her older sister Estelle, along with their first cousin Nedra, started the group in 1959. Their first opportunity to perform professionally came with the opening of the Peppermint Lounge in New York City, where they appeared in the Joey Dee revue.

In 1963, Phil Spector heard the girls and signed them to record for his label, Philles (Phil Spector and Lester Sil) records. In August of that year they had their first hit, "Be My Baby," a song that Phil had written along with Ellie Greenwich and Jeff Barry. Eventually Ronnie and Phil were married in 1968, and divorced in 1974.

Today Ronnie still lives in New York, while traveling around the country as a solo performer.

August	1963	BE MY BABY	Philles
December	1963	BABY I LOVE YOU	Philles
March	1964	THE BEST PART OF BREAKIN' UP	Philles
June	1964	DO I LOVE YOU	Philles
October	1964	WALKING IN THE RAIN	Philles
January	1965	BORN TO BE TOGETHER	Philles
May	1965	IS THIS WHAT I GET FOR LOVING YOU	Philles

THE RONETTES

From top: Estelle Bennett, Nedra Talley,
Ronnie Bennett Spector

RONNIE AND THE HI-LITES

Members:
>
> Ronnie Goodson—lead—1947; died: November 4, 1980, of a brain
> tumor in Jersey City, New Jersey
> Sonny Caldwell—first tenor—1943
> John Whitney—second tenor—1944
> Stanley Brown—baritone—1944
> Ken Overby—bass—1944

Hometown: Jersey City, New Jersey

The group met in 1961, at a church choir rehearsal. They practiced for a while and in 1962, signed with Joy records.

In March of that year, fourteen-year-old Ronnie sang lead and recorded the group's only hit with "I Wish That We Were Married."

March	1962	I WISH THAT WE WERE MARRIED	Joy

THE ROOFTOP SINGERS

Members:
>
> Erik Darling—lead
> Lynne Taylor
> Bill Svanoe

In 1956, banjo player Erik organized a quartet that later became known as the Tarriers. (Another member was actor Alan Arkin.)

Lynne, one-time vocalist with Bennie Goodman, got together with Erik and Bill, a solo guitar player, and formed the Rooftop Singers in late 1962. They signed with Vanguard records and in December 1962 recorded a song by Erik and Bill called "Walk Right In" which became a number one hit.

January	1963	WALK RIGHT IN	Vanguard
February	1963	TOM CAT	Vanguard
July	1963	MAMA DON'T ALLOW	Vanguard

THE ROOMATES

This group from Long Island, New York, backed up a young singer named Cathy Jean (Cathy Jean and the Roomates) on a song called "Please Love Me Forever" on Valmor in March 1961. After the success of that song, they decided to record one on their own as simply the Roomates. The result was "Glory of Love." Both songs were national chart hits at the same time, with "Please Love Me Forever" the bigger of the two.

March	1961	GLORY OF LOVE	Valmor

DAVID ROSE

Born: June 15, 1910
Hometown: Chicago, Illinois

Born in London, England, Dave and his family moved to Chicago when he was three years old. There he began to study music and play the piano. After high school he got jobs with several big bands, going on to become the musical arranger on several Hollywood films. He then took a job as musical director at KHJ radio in Hollywood, where he did coast-to-coast broadcasts.

After a stint in the Army in the forties, he returned to civilian life and formed his own band. Shortly afterwards he signed with MGM records and launched a successful recording career.

In the spring of 1962, Dave's orchestra recorded a song he had written called "The Stripper," which went on to become a number one national hit.

October	1955	LOVE IS A MANY-SPLENDORED THING	MGM
January	1957	HOLIDAY FOR TROMBONES	MGM
March	1957	CALYPSO MELODY	MGM
February	1958	SWINGIN' SHEPHERD BLUES	MGM
April	1962	THE STRIPPER	MGM

ROSIE & THE ORIGINALS

Rosie Hamlin grew up in Alaska and later moved to San Diego. She taught herself to play the piano and began writing tunes.

In late 1960, she met a group called the Originals who needed a singer. Rosie joined the group, and in November of that year, recorded a song she had written called "Angel Baby," which sold to Highland records. It became a major hit for the group in early 1961.

Later that year Jackie Wilson saw her and introduced her to his manager Nat Tarnapool. He got her a contract on Brunswick records and in February 1961 "Lonely Blue Nights" was recorded.

| November | 1960 | ANGEL BABY | Highland |
| March | 1961 | LONELY BLUE NIGHTS | Brunswick |

SPENCER ROSS

In late 1959, Spencer Ross recorded several songs utilizing the superb sax of Jimmy Abato, an instructor at the Juilliard School of Music. One of the songs, a soft instrumental called "Tracy's Theme," became a national hit in early 1960.

| January | 1960 | TRACY'S THEME | Columbia |

THE ROUTERS

Joe Saraceno, Sid Sharp, Mike Gordon, and two other friends formed their group in 1962, and began playing at high school dances and local functions. During this time the dance craze was sweeping the country, so they decided to record a song to dance the Pony to. "Let's Go" was recorded complete with hand-clapping and the rhythmic shouting of the words "Let's Go" throughout. Warner Brothers liked the song and decided to release it on their label. In the fall of 1962, it became a national hit for the group.

| October | 1962 | LET'S GO | Warner Bros |
| April | 1963 | STING RAY | Warner Bros. |

THE ROVER BOYS

The Rover Boys were a vocal group from Canada who came to New York in 1956 and auditioned for Don Costa of ABC Paramount records. He liked their ballad style and signed them to the label.

In the spring of 1956, they recorded the classic "Graduation Day." Even though other groups, like the Four Freshmen, recorded the same song at the same time, the Rover Boys had one of the biggest versions of the song.

This same group was instrumental in getting Paul Anka to record for ABC Paramount, in 1957.

| April | 1956 | GRADUATION DAY | ABC |
| August | 1956 | FROM A SCHOOL RING TO A WEDDING RING | ABC |

THE ROYAL TEENS

Members:
Joe Villa—vocals—Brooklyn, New York
Bob Gaudio—piano—Fort Lee, New Jersey
Tom Austin—drums—Fort Lee, New Jersey
Bill Crandall—sax—Fort Lee, New Jersey—replaced by
   Larry Qualaino
Billy Dalton—bass—replaced by Al Kooper

The five fellows got together in 1957 and formed an instrumental combo known as the Royal Tones. They then decided to change it to the Royal Teens, since all the members were in their teens at the time.

In late 1957, Bob, Tom, and both Billys collaborated on a song called "Short Shorts" which they recorded and sold to ABC-Paramount. The

THE ROYAL TEENS

Left to right: Tom Austin, Larry Qualaino,
Bob Gaudio, Joe Villa, Billy Dalton

song was released in January 1958 and became a national hit almost over-
night.

After several other recordings like "Harvey's Got a Girl Friend" and
"Big Name Button," the group left ABC and signed with Capitol records.
Their biggest hit for Capitol came in late 1959, with "Believe Me," written
by Joe and Tom.

Although the group only had about four hit records as the Royal
Teens, it contained three famous artists. Joe had sung with the Three
Friends in 1956, and recorded a national hit with "Blanche." Bob Gaudio
went on to form the Four Seasons in the early sixties and wrote most of
the Seasons' biggest hits. And of course Al Kooper went on to be a big
star in his own right in the late sixties.

Today Bob Gaudio is a very successful West Coast writer and record
producer performing songs with The Four Seasons, among others.

January	1958	SHORT SHORTS	ABC
April	1958	BIG NAME BUTTON	ABC
August	1958	HARVEY'S GOT A GIRL FRIEND	ABC
October	1959	BELIEVE ME	Capitol

THE ROYALTONES

Members:
  George Kaye—real name: George Katsakis—sax
  Karl Kay—guitar
  Greg Popoff—drums
  Mike Popoff—piano
Hometown: Detroit, Michigan

The group got together in Detroit in the late fifties and played many of the local dances. As their popularity grew, they were finally spotted by an executive from Jubilee records. In the fall of 1958, they recorded an instrumental which featured a "honking" sax, and "Poor Boy" went on to be a national hit.

Two years later, in late 1960, they recorded another driving instrumental that George, Greg, and Mike had written—"Flamingo Express"—which was sold to George Goldner's Goldisc records in New York. This song became another national hit for the group in early 1961.

| October | 1958 | POOR BOY | Jubilee |
| January | 1961 | FLAMINGO EXPRESS | Goldisc |

RUBY AND THE ROMANTICS

Members:
  Ruby Nash—lead
  Edward Roberts
  Robert Mosley
  Leroy Fann
  George Lee
Hometown: Akron, Ohio

The four fellows sang under the name of the Supremes in Akron, before Ruby joined them. Although Ruby had never sung professionally before, the guys would let her sing with the group now and then. Allen Stanten, the pop A & R director of Kapp records, heard the group and suggested Ruby join the group permanently. He changed their name to Ruby and the Romantics and signed them to Kapp in late 1962.

In January 1963, the group recorded "Our Day Will Come," which became a number one song.

January	1963	OUR DAY WILL COME	Kapp
April	1963	MY SUMMER LOVE	Kapp
August	1963	HEY THERE LONELY BOY	Kapp
October	1963	YOUNG WINGS CAN FLY	Kapp

March	1964	OUR EVERLASTING LOVE	Kapp
July	1964	BABY COME HOME	Kapp
October	1964	WHEN YOU'RE YOUNG AND IN LOVE	Kapp

CHARLIE RYAN

Charlie had an interesting song out in the spring of 1960. It was about racing around in a souped-up car. His version of "Hot Rod Lincoln," which he recorded for 4 Star records, was the first release of the song. Johnny Bond had a slightly bigger hit with the same song on Republic records a few months later.

| April | 1960 | HOT ROD LINCOLN | 4 Star |
| October | 1960 | SIDE CAR CYCLE | 4 Star |

BOBBY RYDELL

Real Name: Robert Lewis Ridarelli
Born: April 26, 1942
Hometown: Philadelphia, Pennsylvania

At four or five years old, Bobby used to sit in front of the TV set trying to impersonate performers like Louis Prima, Milton Berle, or Johnny Ray.

BOBBY RYDELL

Bobby's father noticed his talent and encouraged him to pursue a show business career. At age six, Bobby began playing drums because he admired Gene Krupa. By age seven, he had begun to work night clubs in Philadelphia as a child star.

Two years later, he entered bandleader Paul Whiteman's amateur show, broadcast from Philadelphia, and won first place. He then became a regular on the show for the next three years. It was during this time that Paul Whiteman changed Bobby's last name to Rydell, because he had trouble pronouncing Ridarelli.

At around sixteen, Bobby started playing drums with various local groups, eventually winding up with Rocco and the Saints, the group Frankie Avalon used to play trumpet in. While playing with the group at Somers Point, New Jersey, Bobby met Frankie Day, the man who was to become Bobby's manager for so many years. Frankie took Bobby to a small independent record company in Philadelphia called Cameo Parkway records, where Bernie Lowe signed Bobby.

Bobby did about four songs that went nowhere, but in the summer of 1959, he recorded "Kissin' Time," which launched his career. In 1961, he appeared at the Copacabana in New York, and was a hit. In 1963, he starred in the movie "Bye Bye Birdie."

Today Bobby lives with his wife Camille and their two children in Penn Valley, Pennsylvania, outside of Philadelphia.

Bobby is active as a performer traveling all over the country.

April	1959	KISSIN' TIME	Cameo
October	1959	WE GOT LOVE	Cameo
October	1958	I DIG GIRLS	Cameo
January	1960	WILD ONE	Cameo
January	1960	LITTLE BITTY GIRL	Cameo
May	1960	SWINGIN' SCHOOL	Cameo
May	1960	DING-A-LING	Cameo
July	1960	VOLARE	Cameo
November	1960	SWAY	Cameo
January	1961	GOOD TIME BABY	Cameo
April	1961	THAT OLD BLACK MAGIC	Cameo
July	1961	THE FISH	Cameo
October	1961	I WANNA THANK YOU	Cameo
December	1961	JINGLE BELL ROCK (& CHUBBY CHECKER)	Cameo
January	1962	I'VE GOT BONNIE	Cameo
June	1962	I'LL NEVER DANCE AGAIN	Cameo
October	1962	THE CHA-CHA-CHA	Cameo
February	1963	BUTTERFLY BABY	Cameo
May	1963	WILDWOOD DAYS	Cameo
November	1963	FORGET HIM	Cameo
March	1964	MAKE ME FORGET	Cameo
May	1964	A WORLD WITHOUT LOVE	Cameo
December	1964	I JUST CAN'T SAY GOODBYE	Capitol
February	1965	DIANA	Capitol

S

THE SAFARIS

Members:
    Jim Stephens—lead singer and piano—1940
    Richard Lee Clasky—guitar—1942
    Marvin Rosenberg—1942
    Shelley Briar—1943
Hometown: Los Angeles, California

The group was formed in Los Angeles, in 1959, and appeared in local clubs. In early 1960, Richard and Marvin wrote and recorded a song called "Image Of A Girl." It was sold to Eldo records, and became a national hit that summer. The sound of the clock was accomplished by backup musician Bobby Rey striking a wood block with a drum stick.

| May | 1960 | IMAGE OF A GIRL | Eldo |
| October | 1960 | GIRL WITH THE STORY IN HER EYES | Eldo |

KYU SAKAMOTO

Born: 1941
Hometown: Kawasaki, Japan

Kyu (pronounced "Q") had been a star in Japan since 1959, with eight hit albums and fifteen hit singles. In early 1963, a Washington State disc jockey named Rich Osborne, of KORD radio, played a cut called "Ue O Mui Te Aruko" from a Japanese album by Kyu on Toshiba records. There was such a response to the song that Capitol records, the U.S. associate of Toshiba, decided to release it in this country. They changed the name to "Sukiyaki" and by June 1963, it had become a number one hit.

| May | 1963 | SUKIYAKI | Capitol |
| August | 1963 | CHINA NIGHTS | Capitol |

JODIE SANDS

Bob Marcucci and Pete De Angelis formed Chancellor records in the late fifties in Philadelphia. Their big recording artists included Frankie Avalon and Fabian.

Bob discovered little Jodie Sands in early 1957 and had her record the song "With All My Heart." It became one of Chancellor's first big hits.

| May | 1957 | WITH ALL MY HEART | Chancellor |
| October | 1958 | SOMEDAY | Chancellor |

TOMMY SANDS

Born: August 27, 1937
Hometown: Chicago, Illinois

His father was a piano player, so Tommy started singing at age nine. He then learned to play the guitar. At age twelve, he became a disc jockey in Houston, Texas, until graduation from high school. As a teenager in Houston, he was awarded for being the best actor in 1952.

He was later introduced to Ted Lewis and Tennessee Ernie Ford, and appeared on their shows several times. In January 1957, he played the part of a singing sensation on NBC's Kraft television theater's play called "The Singing Idol." In the show he sang two songs called "Hep Dee Hootie" and "Teenage Crush." The latter became his first hit for Capitol records in February 1957.

January	1957	TEEN-AGE CRUSH	Capitol
April	1957	RING-A-DING-A-DING	Capitol
April	1957	GOIN' STEADY	Capitol
January	1958	SING BOY SING	Capitol
August	1958	BLUE RIBBON BABY	Capitol
January	1959	THE WORRYIN' KIND	Capitol
October	1959	I'LL BE SEEING YOU	Capitol
August	1960	THE OLD OAKEN BUCKET	Capitol

MONGO SANTAMARIA

MONGO SANTAMARIA

Jazz-oriented Mongo Santamaria created a new sound in the early sixties, a combination of jazz and Latin music. This was popularized with the tune "Watermelon Man," which became a top-ten hit in early 1963. After that his funky, rhythmic sound became very big and sold many albums for Columbia records.

February	1963	WATERMELON MAN	Battle
June	1963	YEH-YEH	Battle
March	1965	EL PUSSY CAT	Columbia
February	1969	CLOUD NINE	Columbia

SANTO AND JOHNNY

Members:
    Santo Farina—steel guitar—born: October 24, 1937
    Johnny Farina—rhythm guitar—born: April 30, 1941
Hometown: Brooklyn, New York

Santo took up the steel guitar at age nine, and Johnny the regular guitar at age twelve. The two brothers wrote "Sleep Walk" in 1959, and recorded it at Trinity music in New York. The disc was leased to Canadian American records, and in August 1959, became their first hit, and a number one song at that.

August	1959	SLEEP WALK	Canadian American
November	1959	TEAR DROP	Canadian American
March	1960	CARAVAN	Canadian American
December	1960	TWISTIN' BELLS	Canadian American
April	1961	HOP SCOTCH	Canadian American
January	1964	I'LL REMEMBER (IN THE STILL OF THE NIGHT)	Canadian American

SAVERIO SARIDIS

Born: June 16, 1933
Hometown: Brooklyn, New York

Saverio performed in the U.S. Army as a singer. After his discharge in 1955, he began taking voice lessons. Joining the New York Police Department, he was assigned to the Eighteenth Precinct in Manhattan. While walking his beat he learned six operas and fifty arias. He then made a ten dollar recording while singing over an André Kostelanetz record.

Leonard Ashbach, who owned a record store, heard this recording and suggested that it be sent to Warner Brothers. This resulted in a recording contract and in January 1962, the song "Love Is the Sweetest Thing" became a national hit for him. This eventually led to a five-week engagement to star at the Persian Room of the Plaza Hotel, located in his old Eighteenth Precinct.

| January | 1962 | LOVE IS THE SWEETEST THING | Warner Bros. |

THE SCHOOLBOYS

Members:
    Harold Atley—lead—replaced by Leslie Martin
    James Edwards—first tenor
    Roger Hayes—second tenor
    James McKay—baritone
    Renaldo Gamble—bass
Hometown: New York City

The group got together in Harlem, in 1955, and won first prize on the "Ted Mack Amateur Hour." At the time they were called the Scobians. They met New York disc jockey Tommy Smalls, who changed their name to the Schoolboys.

THE SCHOOLBOYS

In 1956, they signed a recording contract with Okeh records and recorded "Please Say You Want Me" and later "Carol." "Shirley," their only national chart record, appeared in January 1957. That was also the year in which the group disbanded.

August	1956	PLEASE SAY YOU WANT ME	Okeh
October	1956	CAROL	Okeh
January	1957	SHIRLEY	Okeh

BOBBY SCOTT

Born: January 29, 1937
Hometown: Bronx, New York

At fourteen he started playing the piano with Louis Prima, after which he went to the Metropole Club in New York, where he played piano. In 1955, he met some executives from ABC-Paramount and told them he could sing and would like to record for the company. Later that year he got his chance when he recorded "Chain Gang" (not the same as Sam Cooke's later hit). After that he turned exclusively to writing. Among his credits: "Taste of Honey."

Today he lives in New Jersey and continues to write for other artists.

December 1955	CHAIN GANG		ABC

FREDDY SCOTT

Born: April 24, 1933
Hometown: Providence, Rhode Island

Both Freddy's mother and his grandmother were singers. He graduated from Cooper High School in New York City and started writing songs, among them "It Only Lasts for a Little While" for Paul Anka and "From Day to Day" for Gene Chandler.

While working as a writer for Columbia music in 1963, Freddy recorded a Carole King–Gerry Goffin composition called "Hey Girl" that came out so well, the company decided to release it on their label Colpix records. It became his first national hit that summer.

July	1963	HEY GIRL	Colpix
October	1963	I GOT A WOMAN	Colpix
March	1964	WHERE DOES LOVE GO	Colpix
December	1966	ARE YOU LONELY FOR ME	Shout
March	1967	CRY TO ME	Shout
May	1967	AM I GROOVING YOU	Shout
August	1968	(YOU) GOT WHAT I NEED	Shout
June	1970	I SHALL BE RELEASED	Probe

JACK SCOTT

Real Name: Jack Scafone, Jr.
Born: January 24, 1936
Hometown: Windsor, Ontario, Canada

Jack's father was a great guitarist who gave Jack a guitar at age eight. The family left Canada when Jack was ten and moved to Hazel Park, Michigan, near Detroit. At this point Jack, who was one of seven children, started singing on a local radio show.

He first signed with ABC-Paramount records and recorded "Two-Timin' Woman" in October 1957. In 1958, he signed with Carlton records and "Leroy," a song he had written, was released in April of that year. It was a moderate hit, and a few months later, the record was flipped over and the other side, "My True Love," became a top national hit.

JACK SCOTT

May	1958	LEROY	Carlton
June	1958	MY TRUE LOVE	Carlton
October	1958	WITH YOUR LOVE	Carlton
December	1958	GOODBYE BABY	Carlton
March	1959	I NEVER FELT LIKE THIS	Carlton
July	1959	THE WAY I WALK	Carlton
October	1959	THERE COMES A TIME	Carlton
January	1960	WHAT IN THE WORLD'S COME OVER YOU	Top Rank
April	1960	BURNING BRIDGES	Top Rank
May	1960	OH, LITTLE ONE	Top Rank
July	1960	IT ONLY HAPPENED YESTERDAY	Top Rank
October	1960	PATSY	Top Rank
January	1961	IS THERE SOMETHING ON YOUR MIND	Top Rank
June	1961	A LITTLE FEELING	Capitol
September	1961	MY DREAM COME TRUE	Capitol
November	1961	STEPS 1 AND 2	Capitol

LINDA SCOTT

Real Name: Linda Joy Sampson
Born: June 1, 1945
Hometown: Queens, New York

Linda began singing at age four. In 1956, her family moved to New Jersey, where she continued to pursue a recording career. In early 1961, as a sophomore in high school, she recorded "I've Told Every Little Star," which became a national hit record.

March	1961	I'VE TOLD EVERY LITTLE STAR	Canadian American
July	1961	DON'T BET MONEY HONEY	Canadian American
July	1961	STARLIGHT, STARBRIGHT	Canadian American
November	1961	I DON'T KNOW WHY	Canadian American
February	1962	BERMUDA	Canadian American
March	1962	COUNT EVERY STAR	Canadian American
February	1962	YESSIREE	Congress
June	1962	NEVER IN A MILLION YEARS	Congress
September	1962	I LEFT MY HEART IN THE BALCONY	Congress

THE SECRETS

Members:
    Kragen Gray
    Jacie Allen
    Carole Raymont
    Pat Miller
Hometown: Cleveland, Ohio

The girls met as freshmen in high school and performed at home parties and school functions. Shortly afterwards they met personal manager Redda Robbins, who had established other Cleveland groups like the Bobbi Pins and the Visions. Mrs. Robbins worked with them and booked them into local clubs. At one of these clubs, an executive from Philips records heard the group and decided to sign them to a contract.

In October 1963, they had their only hit for the label with "The Boy Next Door."

October	1963	THE BOY NEXT DOOR	Philips

NEIL SEDAKA

Born: March 13, 1939
Hometown: Brooklyn, New York

By the time he was thirteen, Neil had begun writing songs. A few years later, around 1954, he formed a singing group from his math class at Abraham Lincoln High School, which he called the Tokens. This was the same group that went on to record "Tonight I Fell In Love" and "The Lion Sleeps Tonight" years later.

In 1956, the great Artur Rubinstein selected Neil to play on New York's classical music station WQXR. The result was a two-year piano

NEIL SEDAKA

scholarship at Juilliard. At eighteen, he had his first professionally recorded song, "Passing Time," which was done by the Cookies on Atlantic records.

At this time he also became interested in a singing career and, in 1958, recorded "Ring-A-Rockin'" for Guyden records. That same year Neil, along with a classmate of his, lyricist Howard Greenfield, wrote two songs "Stupid Cupid" and "Fallin'," which Al Nevins of the Three Suns took to Steve Sholes of RCA. Steve liked what he heard and signed Neil to the label as a vocalist. Ironically, the songs "Stupid Cupid" and "Fallin'" became hits for Connie Francis in 1958.

In November 1958, at the age of nineteen, Neil began his recording career for RCA with a ballad he had written, "The Diary." Almost one year later, in October 1959, Neil recorded "Oh! Carol," about a young friend of his named Carol Klein, who went to Madison High in Brooklyn. She was an early admirer of Neil's group the Tokens and used to follow them all over Brooklyn. Years later Carol Klein became Carole King, vocalist and songwriter extraordinaire.

Neil's biggest hit came in June of 1962, when he recorded a number one national hit, "Breaking Up Is Hard to Do."

Today Neil, with his wife and two children, lives in New York, where he writes for other artists and continues to work on his own new material. He has written songs like "Puppet Man" for Tom Jones, "Workin' on A Groovy Thing" for the Fifth Dimension, "Don't Hide Your Love" for Cher, and "Solitaire" for Andy Williams.

Today Neil still records and performs in Las Vegas and around the country.

November	1958	THE DIARY	RCA
March	1959	I GO APE	RCA
October	1959	OH! CAROL	RCA
March	1960	STAIRWAY TO HEAVEN	RCA
August	1960	YOU MEAN EVERYTHING TO ME	RCA

August	1960	RUN SAMSON RUN	RCA
December	1960	CALENDAR GIRL	RCA
May	1961	LITTLE DEVIL	RCA
August	1961	SWEET LITTLE YOU	RCA
November	1961	HAPPY BIRTHDAY, SWEET SIXTEEN	RCA
March	1962	KING OF CLOWNS	RCA
June	1962	BREAKING UP IS HARD TO DO	RCA
October	1962	NEXT DOOR TO AN ANGEL	RCA
January	1963	ALICE IN WONDERLAND	RCA
April	1963	LET'S GO STEADY AGAIN	RCA
July	1963	THE DREAMER	RCA
November	1963	BAD GIRL	RCA
July	1964	SUNNY	RCA
August	1965	THE WORLD THROUGH A TEAR	RCA
January	1966	THE ANSWER TO MY PRAYER	RCA
October	1974	LAUGHTER IN THE RAIN	Rocket
March	1975	THE IMMIGRANT	Rocket
June	1975	THAT'S WHEN THE MUSIC TAKES ME	Rocket
September	1975	BAD BLOOD	Rocket
December	1975	BREAKING UP IS HARD TO DO	Rocket
April	1976	LOVE IN THE SHADOWS	Rocket
June	1976	STEPPIN' OUT	Rocket
September	1976	YOU GOTTA MAKE YOUR OWN SUNSHINE	Rocket
May	1977	AMARILLO	Rocket
March	1980	SHOULD'VE NEVER LET YOU GO (with Dara Sedaka)	Elektra

THE SENSATIONS

Members:
  Yvonne Baker—lead
  Richard Curtain—tenor
  Sam Armstrong—baritone
  Alphonso Howell—bass
Hometown: Philadelphia, Pennsylvania

In 1954, Alphonso and Yvonne formed the Sensations with several other members, and with Yvonne as lead, recorded "Yes Sir, That's My Baby" and "Please Mr. D.J." for Atco records in 1956. Later Yvonne left the group to get married and raise a family.

In March 1961, Alphonso persuaded Yvonne to come out of retirement, adding Sam and Richard to re-form the group. They signed with Argo records and in July of that year released their first hit, "Music, Music, Music."

In January 1962, they had their biggest all-time seller when they recorded a song Yvonne had written called "Let Me In."

January	1956	YES SIR, THAT'S MY BABY	Atco
August	1961	MUSIC, MUSIC, MUSIC	Argo
January	1962	LET ME IN	Argo
April	1962	THAT'S MY DESIRE	Argo

DAVID SEVILLE

Real Name: Ross Bagdasarian
Born: January 27, 1919
Died: January 16, 1972
Hometown: Fresno, California

David began writing songs at an early age. In 1951, he and his cousin, William Saroyan, wrote a number one hit for Rosemary Clooney called "Come On-a My House."

David signed with Liberty records as an artist in 1956 and recorded "Armen's Theme." In 1958, he came up with the novel idea of recording the human voice on tape at one speed, then playing the tape back at a faster speed to mimic the voices of tiny animals. He created characters for the voices. The first time he did this, in March 1958, the novelty song "Witch Doctor" became a number one hit. Later that year, he gave the voices he created the name of the Chipmunks—Alvin, Theodore, and Simon—and came up with a Christmas classic called "The Chipmunk Song."

November	1956	ARMEN'S THEME	Liberty
August	1957	GOTTA GET TO YOUR HOUSE	Liberty
March	1958	WITCH DOCTOR	Liberty
June	1958	THE BIRD ON MY HEAD	Liberty
August	1958	THE LITTLE BRASS BAND	Liberty
May	1959	JUDY	Liberty

THE SEVILLES

In the fifties there were many songs titled with girl's names: "Diana," "Peggy Sue," "Lucille," and "Jennie Lee."

In early 1961, the Sevilles came up with a rather exotic variation on this popular theme with their song "Charlena." The result was a national hit for the group and JC records.

January	1961	CHARLENA	JC

DEL SHANNON

Real Name: Charles Westover
Born: December 30, 1939
Hometown: Grand Rapids, Michigan

Del started playing the guitar at age fourteen. After high school graduation in 1957, he entered the service and later appeared in the Seventh

DEL SHANNON

Army's musical productions. After his discharge, he appeared in local clubs in Michigan, where disc jockey Ollie McLaughlin of station WHRV, in Ann Arbor, had Del audition for Harry Balk and Irving Micahnik of Embee productions in Detroit. A recording session was set up in early 1961, and "Runaway" emerged. It was sold to Big Top records and became a number one hit.

Today Del lives in Canyon County, California, and has recorded an LP on Network records that was produced by Tom Petty.

February	1961	RUNAWAY	Big Top
May	1961	HATS OFF TO LARRY	Big Top
September	1961	SO LONG BABY	Big Top
December	1961	HEY LITTLE GIRL	Big Top
September	1962	THE SWISS MAID	Big Top
December	1962	LITTLE TOWN FLIRT	Big Top
April	1963	TWO KINDS OF TEARDROPS	Big Top
June	1963	FROM ME TO YOU	Big Top
July	1964	HANDY MAN	Amy
September	1964	DO YOU WANT TO DANCE	Amy
November	1964	KEEP SEARCHIN'	Amy
February	1965	STRANGER IN TOWN	Amy
May	1965	BREAK UP	Amy
May	1966	THE BIG HURT	Liberty
December	1981	SEA OF LOVE	Network

DEE DEE SHARP

Real Name: Dione LaRue
Born: September 9, 1945
Hometown: Philadelphia, Pennsylvania

Dee Dee sang at an early age in her grandfather's church choir and learned to play the piano. In 1961, she answered Cameo records' ad in a Philadelphia paper for a girl who could read music, play the piano, and sing. She was hired and sang background on several songs, including Chubby Checker's hit "Slow Twistin'." In February 1962, she recorded her first single, "Mashed Potato Time," which became her biggest hit.

Today Dee Dee still lives in Philadelphia and records new material for her husband, record producer Kenny Gamble.

February	1962	MASHED POTATO TIME	Cameo
June	1962	GRAVY	Cameo
October	1962	RIDE!	Cameo
February	1963	DO THE BIRD	Cameo
June	1963	ROCK ME IN THE CRADLE OF LOVE	Cameo
July	1963	WILD	Cameo
February	1964	WHERE DID I GO WRONG	Cameo
November	1965	I REALLY LOVE YOU	Cameo

RAY SHARPE

Born: February 8, 1938

In 1959, producers Lester Sill and Lee Hazlewood, of Jamie records in Philadelphia, saw Texan Ray Sharpe in Las Vegas, where he was a blackjack dealer. They found out that he liked to sing. At the time, Lester and Lee were writing for and producing Duane Eddy out of their hometown of Phoenix, Arizona. They set up a recording session in which Ray recorded a song he had written called "Linda Lu." They sent the demo to president Harold Lipsius of Jamie records, who liked the song and decided to release it on his label. The song became a national hit during the summer of 1959.

July	1959	LINDA LU	Jamie

THE SHELLS

Members:
    Nate Bouknight—lead
    Bobby Nurse—first tenor
    Randy Alston—second tenor
    Gus Geter—baritone
    Danny Small—bass
Hometown: Brooklyn, New York

The group got together in 1960, when Nate became acquainted with Hiram Johnson, brother of band leader Buddy Johnson and president of Johnson records. In November 1960, they had their biggest hit with "Baby, Oh Baby."

November 1960   BABY OH BABY   Johnson

SHEP AND THE LIMELITES

Members:

    James "Shep" Sheppard—lead—died: January 24, 1970

    Clarence Bassett

    Charles Baskerville

Hometown: Jamaica, New York

After singing lead with the Heartbeats from 1956 until around 1958, Shep decided to form another group in 1961. This group had a unique sound as they did not have a bass singer but relied instead on two-part harmony and the blending of their voices.

    Shep, who authored almost all the songs for both groups, wrote "Daddy's Home" as an answer to his hit of a few years earlier with the Heartbeats, "A Thousand Miles Away." The new song was recorded and

SHEP AND THE LIMELITES

From top: Charles Baskerville, Clarence Bassett, James "Shep" Sheppard released on Hull records in March 1961, and in a short time "Daddy's Home" became a top-ten national hit.

Years later, on January 24, 1970, Shep was found dead in his automobile on the Long Island expressway, after having been beaten and robbed —a tragic end to such a great artist.

March	1961	DADDY'S HOME	Hull
July	1961	READY FOR YOUR LOVE	Hull
October	1961	THREE STEPS TO THE ALTAR	Hull
February	1962	OUR ANNIVERSARY	Hull

THE SHEPHERD SISTERS

The three bouncy blondes were a very popular New York stage act in the mid-fifties. In the summer of 1957, they recorded a happy-sounding tune called "Alone," which was their first national hit on Lance records. They were not heard from much after that. The McGuire Sisters had the sister-act spot locked up at the time.

September 1957	ALONE	Lance

ALLAN SHERMAN

Born: November 30, 1924
Died: November 21, 1973
Hometown: Chicago, Illinois

After college, Allan became a comedy writer for Jackie Gleason, Joe E. Lewis, and Jerry Lester, among others. He helped to create the TV show "I've Got a Secret," which he produced for six years, and also wrote and produced other shows, such as "Broadway Open House," "Steve Allen Show," and a Phil Silvers special.

In 1963, Allan recorded a comedy song he had written called "Hello Mudduh, Hello Fadduh!" which was released by Warner Brothers that summer. The song went as high as the number two spot on the national charts.

After a number of other successful comedy albums and scripts, Allan moved to the West Coast. It was there that he died at the age of forty-nine.

July	1963	HULLO MUDDUH, HELLO FADDUH!	Warner Bros.
March	1965	CRAZY DOWNTOWN	Warner Bros.
December	1965	THE DRINKING MAN'S DIET	Warner Bros.

THE SHERRYS

Hometown: Philadelphia, Pennsylvania

Joe Cook, one-time lead singer of Little Joe and the Thrillers (of "Peanuts" fame on Okeh in 1957), formed a singing group consisting of his two daughters and two of their friends.

The four girls were called the Sherrys, and he had them record "Pop Pop Pop-Pie," which he took to Harold Lipsius of Jamie/Guyden records in Philadelphia. Harold liked the song and decided to release it on his Guyden label in the fall of 1962. Due to the big dance craze that was sweeping the nation at the time, the song went on to be a national hit.

September 1962	POP POP POP-PIE	Guyden
January 1963	SLOP TIME	Guyden

THE SHIELDS

Members:
  Frankie Ervin—lead
  Jesse Belvin
  Johnny "Guitar" Watson
  Charles Wright
Hometown: Los Angeles, California

In the summer of 1958, George Motola, owner of Tender records in Los Angeles, got a call from a friend of his in Dallas telling him about a big local song called "You Cheated" by the Slades. He told him that many labels were bidding for the song and that George should make an offer. George requested that a copy of the record be sent to him. The record reached him on a Saturday. He had the Shields record the song the same day. Fifty thousand records were pressed and shipped by the end of the week.

Although the Slades were already on the charts with "You Cheated" on Domino records, the Shields' version eventually got more air play and became a bigger hit. After the song started selling on the Tender label, Dot records bought the master and released the song nationally.

In the group, Jesse Belvin became a big star in his own right, while Charles Wright became a star with The Watts 103rd Street Rhythm Band.

September 1958	YOU CHEATED	Dot

THE SHIRELLES

Left to right: Doris Kenner, Beverly Lee,
Micky Harris, Shirley Alston

THE SHIRELLES

Members:
 Shirley Alston (Owens)—lead—June 10, 1941
 Beverly Lee—August 3, 1941
 Addie "Micky" Harris—January 22, 1940
 Doris Kenner (Coley)—August 2, 1941
Hometown: Passaic, New Jersey

The Shirelles' name came from wanting something feminine-sounding like the Chantels, who were popular at the time, so lead singer Shirley's name was used to form the word Shir-elles.

The four girls went to school with Florence Greenberg's daughter Mary Jane. Mary Jane asked them to sing for her mother, which resulted in Mrs. Greenberg's managing the girls. At the time Mrs. Greenberg owned a small record company called Tiara records, which later became Scepter records.

In 1958, the girls wrote a song called "I Met Him on a Sunday," which was released on Tiara. Because the label was so small, the recording was sold to Decca and released in March 1958.

The group's first hit for Scepter was "Dedicated to the One I Love" in 1959, which featured Doris as lead. They decided to record the song because they liked the way the "5" Royales used to sing it. Shortly after that, Shirley cowrote, with Luther Dixon, the song "Tonight's the Night." where she became the group's new lead. She then went on to sing lead on all the group's hits.

In late 1960, the group recorded a Carole King and Gerry Goffin classic, "Will You Still Love Me Tomorrow," which became their first number one hit, and a top hit in early 1961.

Today Doris, Beverly and Micky still live in New Jersey and continue to sing as The Shirelles at many concerts and shows around the country. Former lead singer Shirley Alston is pursuing a solo career.

March	1958	I MET HIM ON A SUNDAY	Decca
July	1959	DEDICATED TO THE ONE I LOVE	Scepter
September	1960	TONIGHTS THE NIGHT	Scepter
November	1960	WILL YOU LOVE ME TOMORROW	Scepter
January	1961	DEDICATED TO THE ONE I LOVE	Scepter
April	1961	MAMA SAID	Scepter
July	1961	A THING OF THE PAST	Scepter
July	1961	WHAT A SWEET THING THAT WAS	Scepter
October	1961	BIG JOHN	Scepter
December	1961	BABY IT'S YOU	Scepter
March	1962	SOLDIER BOY	Scepter
June	1962	WELCOME HOME BABY	Scepter
August	1962	STOP THE MUSIC	Scepter
November	1962	EVERYBODY LOVES A LOVER	Scepter
March	1963	FOOLISH LITTLE GIRL	Scepter
May	1963	DON'T SAY GOODNIGHT AND MEAN GOODBYE	Scepter
September	1963	WHAT DOES A GIRL DO	Scepter
October	1963	IT'S A MAD, MAD, MAD, MAD WORLD	Scepter
January	1964	TONIGHT YOU'RE GONNA FALL IN LOVE WITH ME	Scepter
March	1964	SHA-LA-LA	Scepter
July	1964	THANK YOU BABY	Scepter
October	1964	MAYBE TONIGHT	Scepter
August	1967	LAST MINUTE MIRACLE	Scepter

SHIRLEY AND LEE

Members:
> Shirley Pixley—born: June 19, 1936
> Leonard Lee—June 29, 1935
Hometown: New Orleans, Louisiana

Known as the "Sweethearts of the Blues," they started together in their hometown of New Orleans, in the early fifties. In 1952, they received a contract from Aladdin records and recorded "I'm Gone."

After a series of minor hits, they had their first major one with a song Leonard had written called "Feel So Good," which went to the top in July 1955. In July 1956, they recorded their biggest all-time seller, "Let The

Good Times Roll," also written by Leonard. Their last major hit for Aladdin was in November 1956, with "I Feel Good."

In 1960, they signed with Warwick records and did "I've Never Been Loved Before" in June 1960.

They were called the "Sweethearts of the Blues" by Eddie Mesner of Aladdin records, because they were the youngest blues singers on the label, they were a duo, and many people might think they were in love. However, they were never more than just good friends. Today, Shirley lives in Los Angeles with her son, under the name Shirley Goodman. Leonard lives in New Orleans and works with the poverty program. They occasionally see each other, and on rare instances, for an occasional revival rock show, get together to sing as a duo again.

December	1952	I'M GONE	Aladdin
August	1955	FEEL SO GOOD	Aladdin
July	1956	LET THE GOOD TIMES ROLL	Aladdin
November	1956	I FEEL GOOD	Aladdin
June	1960	I'VE BEEN LOVED BEFORE	Warwick
September	1960	LET THE GOOD TIMES ROLL	Warwick
July	1961	WELL-A, WELL-A	Warwick

TROY SHONDELL

Born: May 14, 1944
Hometown: Fort Wayne, Indiana

Troy, who plays organ, guitar, trumpet, sax, and drums, attended Valparaiso University in Valparaiso, Indiana, where he majored in music. In the summer of 1961, he recorded and produced a song called "This Time" in a small Fort Wayne recording studio. He released the song on his own label, Gold Crest records. Chicago disc jockeys Stan Major and Jim Lounsbury liked the song and brought it to the attention of Liberty records, who in turn, bought the master and released it on their label. This became Troy's biggest hit.

Today he lives in Nashville, and records for Bright Star records.

| September | 1961 | THIS TIME | Liberty |
| December | 1961 | TEARS FROM AN ANGEL | Liberty |

DINAH SHORE

Real Name: Frances Rose Shore
Born: March 1, 1917
Hometown: Winchester, Tennessee

When Dinah was six, her family moved to Nashville, where she made her public debut four years later singing for her mother's Ladies' Aid Society.

DINAH SHORE

When she had worked as a vocalist for a while at radio station WSM in Nashville, she left for New York in 1937 to further her career. After many letdowns and small singing jobs, Dinah did some local radio work and eventually became Diva of the Blues with the Chamber Music Society of Lower Basin Street. She later joined Eddie Cantor's troupe, appearing on many radio programs in the early forties.

After originally signing with Bluebird records, her hits began to make the charts on Victor, Columbia, and RCA Victor during the forties and fifties.

She married actor George Montgomery in 1943, which lasted until 1962. After a successful TV show in the late seventies, Dinah now makes occasional guest TV appearances.

January	1941	YES, MY DARLING DAUGHTER	Bluebird
March	1941	I HEAR A RHAPSODY	Bluebird
October	1941	"JIM"	Bluebird
February	1942	BLUES IN THE NIGHT	Bluebird
February	1942	MISS YOU	Bluebird
June	1942	ONE DOZEN ROSES	Victor
December	1942	DEARLY BELOVED	Victor
January	1943	WHY DON'T YOU FALL IN LOVE WITH ME?	Victor
February	1943	YOU'D BE SO NICE TO COME HOME TO	Victor
April	1943	"MURDER", HE SAYS	Victor
August	1944	I'LL WALK ALONE	Victor
April	1945	CANDY	Victor

September	1945	ALONG THE NAVAJO TRAIL	Victor
April	1946	SHOO-FLY PIE AND APPLE PAN DOWDY	Columbia
March	1946	LAUGHING ON THE OUTSIDE (CRYING ON THE INSIDE)	Columbia
May	1946	THE GYPSY	Columbia
June	1946	DOIN' WHAT COMES NATUR'LLY	Columbia
January	1947	(I LOVE YOU) FOR SENTIMENTAL REASONS	Columbia
February	1947	ANNIVERSARY SONG	Columbia
October	1947	I WISH I DIDN'T LOVE YOU SO	Columbia
November	1947	YOU DO	Columbia
December	1947	HOW SOON (WILL I BE SEEING YOU)	Columbia
September	1948	BUTTONS AND BOWS	Columbia
December	1948	LAVENDER BLUE	Columbia
February	1949	SO IN LOVE	Columbia
May	1949	BABY, IT'S COLD OUTSIDE	Columbia
November	1949	DEAR HEARTS AND GENTLE PEOPLE	Columbia
February	1950	IT'S SO NICE TO HAVE A MAN AROUND THE HOUSE	Columbia
December	1950	MY HEART CRIES FOR YOU	RCA Victor
January	1951	A PENNY A KISS (Tony Martin)	RCA Victor
June	1951	SWEET VIOLETS	RCA Victor
October	1952	BLUES IN ADVANCE	RCA Victor
June	1955	WHATEVER LOLA WANTS	RCA Victor
November	1955	LOVE AND MARRIAGE	RCA
February	1956	STOLEN LOVE	RCA
April	1956	I COULD HAVE DANCED ALL NIGHT	RCA
January	1957	CHANTEZ-CHANTEZ	RCA
June	1957	CATTLE CALL	RCA

THE SHOWMEN

After enjoying one hit on Minit, "It Will Stand," lead singer Norman Johnson eventually left the group. In late 1969, he formed another group called Chairmen of the Board, with whom he also sang lead. The group then signed with Invictus records and "Give Me Just a Little More Time" became a hit for them in January 1970.

November	1961	IT WILL STAND	Minit

THE SILHOUETTES

Members:
    Billy Horton—lead—born: December 25, 1929
    Richard Lewis—tenor—born: September 2, 1933
    Earl Beal—baritone—born: July 18, 1924
    Raymond Edwards—bass—born: September 27, 1922
Hometown: Philadelphia, Pennsylvania

The group was first formed in 1955, as a gospel group, the Gospel Tornados. After a while they started to sing "blues" numbers as the Thunderbirds.

THE SILHOUETTES

Left to right: Richard Lewis, Ray Edwards, Earl Beal
Bottom center: Billy Horton

In 1957, the fellows met Philadelphia disc jockey Kae Williams of station WDAS. Kae liked the group and decided to manage them. He thought they should change their name, and Earl Beal suggested the Silhouettes. Several months later, Richard Lewis, who had just joined the group, suggested an idea he had had for a song while in the Army. The fellows liked the song and presented it to arranger Howard Biggs, who came up with the catchy lyric lines like "Sha na na na, sha na na na na," and "yip yip yip yip yip yip yip, boom boom boom boom." The result was "Get A Job." The line of this song also became the inspiration for the name of the group Sha Na Na today.

They recorded the song in Philadelphia, in late 1957, and released it on Kae's label Junior records. After the song began to sell, the tape was sold to Al Silver of Ember records in New York, and by January 1958, it had reached the national charts and wound up as a number one national hit. The song was the only one the group had that made the national charts.

Today, all the fellows still reside and work in Philadelphia. They got together in the fall of 1980 for a rock show in New York, and have done occasional shows since then.

| January | 1958 | GET A JOB | Ember |
| April | 1958 | HEADING FOR THE POOR HOUSE | Ember |

THE HARRY SIMEONE CHORALE

Born: May 9, 1914
Hometown: Newark, New Jersey

Harry graduated from the Juilliard School of Music and went to CBS as a staff arranger. In 1939, he joined Fred Waring's staff. He then went to Paramount in Hollywood and worked with Victor Young on some Bing Crosby and Bob Hope road pictures.

In 1945, he rejoined the Waring staff and was made the editor of Waring's Shawnee Press. He became the chorale arranger and conductor for the "Firestone Hour" on TV in 1952.

In late 1958, he recorded a Christmas album called "Sing We Now of Christmas" for 20th Century-Fox records. One of the selections, "The Little Drummer Boy," went on to become a Christmas classic.

December 1958	THE LITTLE DRUMMER BOY	20th Fox

NINA SIMONE

As a jazz singer, Nina was very popular in the fifties. In the summer of 1959, her jazz-flavored "I Loves You, Porgy," from the show *Porgy and Bess*, became a national pop hit on Bethlehem records. It was her first major pop hit and the biggest of her career.

July	1959	I LOVES YOU, PORGY	Bethlehem
October	1968	DO WHAT YOU GOTTA DO	RCA
December	1969	TO BE YOUNG, GIFTED & BLACK	RCA

THE SIMS TWINS

The Sims Twins were brothers from Los Angeles who began their musical career as gospel singers. In the early sixties, when singing star Sam Cooke founded Sar records, he had the brothers signed to the label. In late 1961, they had their only pop chart hit with "Soothe Me."

October	1961	SOOTHE ME	Sar

FRANK SINATRA

Real Name: Francis Albert Sinatra
Born: December 12, 1915
Hometown: Hoboken, New Jersey

Frank got his first break in the late thirties when he became a regular on the Major Bowes talent show. From there he signed with the Harry James band and then sang with the Tommy Dorsey orchestra. It was while sing-ing with Tommy that Frank learned his breathing technique which has produced his perfect singing style and interpretation of lyrics.

In 1943, Frank signed with Columbia records and recorded one of his favorites from the Harry James days, called "All or Nothing at All," which had many girls swooning for the young crooner. When appearing at the Paramount in New York, he would bring hysteria upon his bobby-soxed admirers.

In the late forties, after a rift with Mitch Miller, because he felt Mitch spent more time cultivating the career of another Frankie (Frankie Laine), Sinatra left the label. In 1952, he signed with Capitol and began a new career. His career took an upswing after he won an Oscar for his performance in the film *From Here to Eternity,* in 1953.

His recording career skyrocketed, too, after working with great Capi-tol arrangers like Nelson Riddle, Gordon Jenkins, and Billy May. The hits started to flow: "Young At Heart," "Learnin' the Blues," "Love and Mar-riage," and "Hey! Jealous Lover." In 1960, he left Capitol to form his own label, Reprise records.

Finally, in May 1966, he had a number one song with a Bert Kaemp-fert tune called "Strangers in the Night."

In 1971, he retired from show business to devote more time to his personal life, but in November 1973, he came back with a TV special for NBC called "Ole Blue Eyes Is Back." He appeared in Las Vegas in Janu-ary 1974, and began a cross-country tour a few months later.

Sinatra truly is a legend and *the* giant name in show business, who has influenced more singers than anyone else.

June	1943	ALL OR NOTHING AT ALL (Harry James)	Columbia
July	1943	YOU'LL NEVER KNOW	Columbia
September	1943	SUNDAY, MONDAY OR ALWAYS	Columbia
September	1943	PEOPLE WILL SAY WE'RE IN LOVE	Columbia
February	1944	I COULDN'T SLEEP A WINK LAST NIGHT	Columbia
December	1944	WHITE CHRISTMAS	Columbia
January	1945	I DREAM OF YOU	Columbia
February	1945	SATURDAY NIGHT (IS THE LONELIEST NIGHT IN THE WEEK)	Columbia
May	1945	DREAM	Columbia
November	1945	NANCY	Columbia
February	1946	OH! WHAT IT SEEMED TO BE	Columbia
June	1946	THEY SAY IT'S WONDERFUL	Columbia
August	1946	FIVE MINUTES MORE	Columbia
October	1946	THE COFFEE SONG	Columbia
December	1946	WHITE CHRISTMAS	Columbia
May	1947	MAM'SELLE	Columbia
May	1948	NATURE BOY	Columbia
April	1949	SUNFLOWER	Columbia
June	1949	THE HUCKLE BUCK	Columbia
June	1949	SOME ENCHANTED EVENING	Columbia

October	1949	LET HER GO, LET HER GO, LET	
		HER GO (DON'T CRY, JOE)	Columbia
December	1949	THE OLD MASTER PAINTER	Columbia
March	1950	CHATTANOOGIE SHOE SHINE BOY	Columbia
July	1950	GOODNIGHT IRENE	Columbia
September	1951	CASTLE ROCK (Harry James)	Columbia
February	1954	YOUNG-AT-HEART	Capitol
May	1954	DON'T WORRY 'BOUT ME	Capitol
May	1954	THREE COINS IN THE FOUNTAIN	Capitol
February	1955	LEARNIN' THE BLUES	Capitol
November	1955	SAME OLD SATURDAY NIGHT	Capitol
August	1955	LOVE AND MARRIAGE	Capitol
September	1955	THE TENDER TRAP	Capitol
February	1956	FLOWERS MEAN FORGIVENESS	Capitol
May	1956	HOW LITTLE WE KNOW	Capitol
July	1956	YOU'RE SENSATIONAL	Capitol
October	1956	HEY! JEALOUS LOVER	Capitol
January	1957	CAN I STEAL A LITTLE LOVE	Capitol
April	1957	CRAZY LOVE	Capitol
October	1957	CHICAGO	Capitol
October	1957	ALL THE WAY	Capitol
January	1958	WITCHCRAFT	Capitol
May	1958	HOW ARE YA' FIXED FOR LOVE	Capitol
November	1958	MR. SUCCESS	Capitol
April	1959	FRENCH FOREIGN LEGION	Capitol
June	1959	HIGH HOPES	Capitol
October	1959	TALK TO ME	Capitol
June	1960	RIVER STAY 'WAY FROM MY DOOR	Capitol
September	1960	NICE 'N' EASY	Capitol
November	1960	OL' MacDONALD	Capitol
March	1962	THE MOON WAS YELLOW	Capitol
March	1961	THE SECOND TIME AROUND	Reprise
July	1961	GRANADA	Reprise
October	1961	I'LL BE SEEING YOU	Reprise
December	1961	POCKETFUL OF MIRACLES	Reprise
March	1962	STARDUST	Reprise
April	1962	EV'RYBODY'S TWISTIN'	Reprise
April	1963	CALL ME IRRESPONSIBLE	Reprise
January	1964	STAY WITH ME	Reprise
September	1964	SOFTLY, AS I LEAVE YOU	Reprise
December	1964	SOMEWHERE IN YOUR HEART	Reprise
March	1965	ANYTIME AT ALL	Reprise
May	1965	TELL HER (YOU LOVE HER EVERY DAY)	Reprise
June	1965	FORGET DOMANI	Reprise
December	1965	IT WAS A VERY GOOD YEAR	Reprise
May	1966	STRANGERS IN THE NIGHT	Reprise
September	1966	SUMMER WIND	Reprise
November	1966	THAT'S LIFE	Reprise
August	1967	THE WORLD WE KNEW	Reprise
October	1967	THIS TOWN	Reprise
April	1968	I CAN'T BELIEVE I'M LOSING YOU	Reprise
August	1968	MY WAY OF LIFE	Reprise
October	1968	CYCLES	Reprise
January	1969	RAIN IN MY HEART	Reprise
March	1969	MY WAY	Reprise
September	1969	LOVE'S BEEN GOOD TO ME	Reprise

November	1969	GOIN' OUT OF MY HEAD/FORGET	Reprise
March	1970	I WOULD BE IN LOVE ANYWAY	Reprise
November	1973	LET ME TRY AGAIN (LAISSE MOI LE TEMPS)	Reprise
April	1974	BAD, BAD LEROY BROWN	Reprise
August	1974	YOU TURNED MY WORLD AROUND	Reprise
April	1975	ANYTIME (I'LL BE THERE)	Reprise
August	1975	I BELIEVE I'M GONNA LOVE YOU	Reprise
May	1980	THEME FROM NEW YORK, NEW YORK	Reprise

NANCY & FRANK SINATRA

| March | 1967 | SOMETHIN' STUPID | Reprise |

THE SINGING NUN

Real Name: Janine Deckers

Janine Deckers, a Belgian nun known as Soeur Sourire (French for "Sister Smile"), in 1963 wrote a song called "Dominique," which she sang around the convent, accompanying herself on the guitar. The other nuns persuaded her to record the song and radio stations in Europe began to play it. Shortly thereafter it became a number one hit, and she became the "singing nun." Unfortunately, a career as a recording artist did not work out and today she is a lay worker with handicapped children in Belgium.

| October | 1963 | DOMINIQUE | Philips |

THE SIX TEENS

Members:
    Trudy Williams—lead
    Louise Williams
    Beverly Pecot
    Darryl Lewis
    Kenneth Sinclair
    Ed Wells
Hometown: Los Angeles, California

The group was organized by Ed Wells in early 1956. They called themselves the Six Teens, because all of them were in their teens, with Ed the oldest and lead singer Trudy, sister of Louise, the youngest.

In May 1956, they recorded a song Ed had written, called "A Casual Look," which they sold to a California record company, Flip records. The song became a national hit a few months later.

| June | 1956 | A CASUAL LOOK | Flip |
| July | 1957 | ARROW OF LOVE | Flip |

SKIP AND FLIP

Members:

Skip—real name: Clyde Battin—hometown: Galipolis, Ohio

Flip—real name: Gary Paxton—hometown: Mesa, Arizona

Skip and Flip attended the University of Arizona in the late fifties and formed a band called the Pledges. While Skip was working as a disc jockey at KMOP in Tucson, he recorded with Flip, in May 1959, a song called "It Was I." The song was sold to Brent records and went on to become a national hit.

After several other recordings, including the 1960 hit "Cherry Pie," they went their separate ways. Gary joined a group called the Hollywood Argyles and sang lead on their number one hit "Alley Oop" in 1960.

A few years later, Gary formed his own record label, Garpax records (GARy PAXton), which had the number one hit in 1962, "Monster Mash," by Bobby "Boris" Pickett.

Clyde now plays with The New Riders Of The Purple Sage.

June	1959	IT WAS I	Brent
November	1959	FANCY NANCY	Brent
March	1960	CHERRY PIE	Brent

THE SKYLINERS

Members:

Jimmy Beaumont—lead—born: October 21, 1940

Janet Vogel (Rapp)—first tenor—born: June 10, 1942—died: February 21, 1980

Wally Lester—second tenor—born: October 5, 1941

Joe Verscharen—baritone—1940

Jack Taylor—bass—1941

Hometown: Pittsburgh, Pennsylvania

The Skyliners were first formed in Pittsburgh, from two different groups. Jimmy, Wally, and Jack had a group called The Crescents with three other fellows. After the group broke up, they had Joe and Janet join them, after both had left a group called the El Rios. They still called themselves the Crescents until their manager, Joe Rock, decided to change their name to the Skyliners, from the song "Skyliner," a hit by Charlie Barnett.

In late 1958 the group, along with Joe Rock, wrote a song that they all liked, called "Since I Don't Have You" and wanted to record it. They auditioned the song for Calico records in Pittsburgh, and the company decided to record the group. This was also the first time a rock song had a full complement of strings and brass. The song was released in January 1959, and became the group's biggest all-time seller.

THE SKYLINERS

Clockwise from center: Janet Vogel, Wally Lester,
Joe Verscharen, Jack Taylor, Jimmy Beaumont

Janet Rapp, a housewife and mother of two, took her own life in a carbon monoxide poisoning in Pittsburgh. Jimmy keeps the group active with two new members, while Wally and Joe both have regular jobs, in Pittsburgh. The whereabouts of Jack Taylor are unknown.

January	1959	SINCE I DON'T HAVE YOU	Calico
May	1959	THIS I SWEAR	Calico
October	1959	IT HAPPENED TODAY	Calico
May	1960	PENNIES FROM HEAVEN	Calico
March	1975	WHERE HAVE THEY GONE	Capitol

THE SLADES

Members:
    Don Burch—lead
    Tommy Kasper
    Jimmy Williams
    Jimmy Goeke
Hometown: Austin, Texas

The group met at McCallum High in Austin, where they began singing in 1957. They decided to record a song that Don had written, called "You Cheated." They took it to a good friend of theirs named Jane Bowers, who in turn took it to Domino records in Austin. The label liked the song and released it in the summer of 1958, where in just a short time it began to make the national charts. Unfortunately for the Slades, Los Angeles record-company owner George Motola put together a group called the Shields to record the song for his Tender label. The Shields' version became the bigger hit.

July	1958	YOU CHEATED	Domino

HUEY "PIANO" SMITH

Born: October 10, 1924
Hometown: New Orleans, Louisiana

Huey went to McDowell High and Xavier College in New Orleans. In 1957, he became the pianist for Earl King's band. It was while he was performing with the band that the president of New Orleans's Ace records, Ray Vincent, heard him and signed him to his label.

In July 1957, Huey recorded an instrumental called "Rocking Pneumonia and the Boogie Woogie Flu" and decided to do the same song on the flip side, but this time with lyrics. He wrote and recorded the song and it went on to become his first hit, in the summer of 1957.

In March 1958 came his biggest hit, "Don't You Just Know It." In 1959, he wrote "Sea Cruise" for a protégé of his named Frankie Ford. Huey's band played on the record and it became a big hit that spring.

July	1957	ROCKING PNEUMONIA & THE BOOGIE WOOGIE FLU	Ace
March	1958	DON'T YOU JUST KNOW IT	Ace
December	1958	DON'T YOU KNOW YOCKOMO	Ace
February	1962	POP-EYE	Ace

JIMMY SMITH

Organist Jimmy Smith was primarily a jazz musician who moved over into the pop vein in the early sixties. After several hits on Blue Note records, he switched to Verve records. "Walk On The Wild Side," from the motion picture of the same name, was his first hit for the label, in the summer of 1962.

February	1962	MIDNIGHT SPECIAL	Blue Note
March	1962	BACK AT THE CHICKEN SHACK	Blue Note
May	1962	WALK ON THE WILD SIDE	Verve

May	1963	HOBO FLATS (Part 1)	Verve
April	1964	WHO'S AFRAID OF VIRGINIA WOOLF	Verve
September	1964	THE CAT	Verve
October	1965	THE ORGAN GRINDER'S SWING	Verve
April	1966	GOT MY MOJO WORKING	Verve
August	1966	I'M YOUR HOOCHIE COOCHE MAN	Verve

O. C. SMITH

Real Name: Ocie Smith
Born: June 21, 1932
Hometown: Mansfield, Louisiana

While in the Air Force, from 1951 until 1955, Ocie traveled with the Air Force variety show throughout the world. In 1953, he joined Horace Heidt's show and toured bases for a while. He also represented the Air Force at the Waldorf-Astoria in shows with performers like Red Buttons and Ed Sullivan.

After his discharge, he joined Sy Olivers' band as a vocalist. He then appeared on "Arthur Godfrey's Talent Scouts" and became a hit. Next he was awarded a contract with Cadence records. He recorded the vocal version of the Sil Austin instrumental hit, "Slow Walk," in December 1956.

In the sixties Ocie changed his name to O. C. and started a new and successful career on Columbia records.

February	1968	THE SON OF HICKORY HOLLER'S TRAMP	Columbia
August	1968	LITTLE GREEN APPLES	Columbia
December	1968	ISN'T IT LONELY TOGETHER	Columbia
February	1969	HONEY	Columbia
May	1969	FRIEND, LOVER, WOMAN, WIFE	Columbia
August	1969	DADDY'S LITTLE MAN	Columbia

RAY SMITH

Born: October 31, 1938
Died: November 29, 1979, of self-inflicted gunshot wounds
Hometown: Paducah, Kentucky

Ray began his career while in the Army. After his discharge, he formed a band and had weekly TV shows in Paducah and in Evansville, Indiana. While touring the country, Charlie Terrell heard Ray and asked to become his manager. This led to a recording contract with Judd records in late 1959, and his first hit for the label, in early 1960, called "Rockin' Little Angel."

January	1960	ROCKIN' LITTLE ANGEL	Judd

SOMETHIN' SMITH AND THE REDHEADS

SOMETHIN' SMITH AND THE REDHEADS

Members:
 Somethin' Smith—lead
 Saul Striks
 Major Short
Hometown: Los Angeles, California

As a youth, Smith started playing the banjo in Norfolk, Virginia. During the early forties he was in the Navy, where he picked up the guitar as well.

In 1946, he was a winner on the "Arthur Godfrey Talent Scouts" show. Shortly thereafter, while attending the University of California at Los Angeles, he met piano player Saul Striks and violin player Major Short. They decided to form a trio. They played the L.A. area and their fame began to spread. In the mid-fifties they were signed to Columbia records; in the spring of 1955, they had their first national hit with "It's a Sin To Tell a Lie."

March	1955	IT'S A SIN TO TELL A LIE	Epic
May	1956	IN A SHANTY IN OLD SHANTY TOWN	Epic
August	1956	HEARTACHES	Epic

JOANIE SOMMERS

JOANIE SOMMERS

Born: 1942
Hometown: Buffalo, New York

Joanie began her career at age ten, on a local TV show in Buffalo. Later her family moved to Venice, California, where she won top honors, becoming a vocalist with the Venice high school dance band and the Santa Monica City College Band. Band leader Tommy Oliver heard her and had her audition for Warner Brothers records in 1960, which resulted in a recording contract. In June 1960, she debuted on the label with "One Boy" from the show "Bye Bye Birdie."

June	1960	ONE BOY	Warner Bros.
May	1962	JOHNNY GET ANGRY	Warner Bros.
October	1962	WHEN THE BOYS GET TOGETHER	Warner Bros.

JIMMY SOUL

Real Name: James McCleese
Born: 1942
Hometown: Portsmouth, Virginia

Back in 1962, Frank Guida, song writer and record producer of such local Norfolk artists as Tommy Facenda (of "High School U.S.A." fame) and Gary "U.S." Bonds (of "New Orleans" and "Quarter to Three" fame) decided to combine the Latin and soul sounds. Frank had been to Trinidad in the mid-forties and he enjoyed the calypso beat. In 1945, he had brought back a song called "Matilda," which Harry Belafonte had a hit with in the fifties.

In 1962, Frank took the same basic sound, changed the tempo, and released it as "Twistin' Matilda" at the height of the Twist craze. He asked a local singer named James McCleese to record the song. Frank felt he had to change the young man's name. "Soul" was a new concept at that time, so James McCleese became Jimmy Soul. "Twistin' Matilda" became a national hit by the summer of 1962.

In the spring of 1963, Jimmy recorded a song that Frank, his wife Carmela, and their friend Joseph Royster had written, "If You Wanna Be Happy," which was a spinoff of the calypso standard "Ugly Woman." The song became a number one national hit. After that song, Jimmy went into the Army and never had another hit.

| August | 1962 | TWISTIN' MATILDA | SPQR |
| March | 1963 | IF YOU WANNA BE HAPPY | SPQR |

JOE SOUTH

Born: February 28, 1940
Hometown: Atlanta, Georgia

Joe wanted to be an entertainer as a youngster. One day he went to radio station WGST in Atlanta to see disc jockey Bill Lowery, telling him he wanted to be on the radio. Bill admired his courage and put him on a 6:00 A.M. Saturday show. Later Joe got a job as a guitar player with Pete Drake's band, where he stayed until he went to Southern Technical for electronics and communications. When Bill Lowery formed his own label in Atlanta, he signed Joe to record for him.

In the sixties, Joe worked as a staff musician for artists like Dylan and Simon and Garfunkel. In 1968, Joe returned to singing his own material and signed with Capitol records. His recording of "Games People Play" earned him two Grammies, becoming one of the top songs of 1969 after its release early that year.

July	1958	THE PURPLE PEOPLE EATER MEETS THE WITCH DOCTOR	NRC
August	1961	YOU'RE THE REASON	Fairlane
January	1969	GAMES PEOPLE PLAY	Capitol
June	1969	BIRDS OF A FEATHER	Capitol
August	1969	DON'T IT MAKE YOU WANT TO GO HOME	Capitol
January	1970	WALK A MILE IN MY SHOES	Capitol
March	1970	CHILDREN	Capitol
November	1971	FOOL ME	Capitol

THE SPACEMEN

The Spacemen were a group of musicians who had only one national chart single called "The Clouds," which was a swinging jazz-flavored instrumental. This contagious blues number was much more sparkling than the flip side, which was called "Lonely Jet Pilot."

October	1959	THE CLOUDS	Alton

THE SPANIELS

Members:
> James "Pookie" Hudson—lead—born: June 11, 1934
> Ernest Warren—1st tenor—replaced by James Cochran
> Willis C. Jackson—second tenor—replaced by Donald Porter
> Opal Cortney Jr.—baritone—replaced by Carl Rainge
> Gerald Gregory—bass—replaced by Lester Williams

Hometown: Gary, Indiana

The fellows started singing together at Roosevelt High in Gary, Indiana, in the early fifties. They called themselves the Spaniels to be different, since there were so many groups at the time named after various birds, like the Orioles, the Wrens, the Ravens, and the Crows.

They continued singing together in the high school glee club. Just before graduation, they were singing at a school dance when disc jockey Vivian Carter heard them. She liked the group so well that when she went to Chicago to form Vee Jay records with her husband James Bracken (Vivian, "Vee"; Jimmy, "Jay") in 1953, the Spaniels were the first artists she signed.

Their first hit for the label was "Baby It's You," followed in 1954 by their biggest seller, "Goodnite Sweetheart, Goodnite," written by Pookie and Calvin Carter. Around 1955, Ernest, Willis, Opal, and Gerald were replaced by James, Donald, Carl, and Lester.

Today Pookie lives and works in South Bend, Indiana, and does occasional rock shows in New York, with new members.

August	1953	BABY IT'S YOU	Chance
April	1954	GOODNITE SWEETHEART, GOODNITE	Vee Jay
October	1955	YOU PAINTED PICTURES	Vee Jay
December	1956	YOU GAVE ME PEACE OF MIND	Vee Jay
June	1957	EVERYONE'S LAUGHING	Vee Jay
April	1958	STORMY WEATHER	Vee Jay
July	1960	I KNOW	Vee Jay
September	1970	FAIRY TALES	Calla

THE SPARKLETONES

Members:
Joe Bennet—lead vocalist and guitar
Howard Childress—guitar
Wayne Arthur—bass guitar
Irving Denton—drums
Hometown: Spartanburg, South Carolina

The group's manager, Bob Cox, got them a contract with Am Par records in 1957, and they first recorded "Bopin' Rock Boogie." It wasn't until they did "Black Slacks," in July 1957, however, that they became nationally known. At the time of their hits, the group members ranged in ages from fourteen to seventeen.

| May | 1957 | BOPIN' ROCK BOOGIE | Am Par |
| July | 1957 | BLACK SLACKS | Am Par |

THE SPIDERS

The New Orleans–based Spiders, featuring Chuck Carbo's lead voice, had an unusual R & B sound in the mid-fifties: down-tempo blues. This was evident in their first release for Imperial records in early 1954, with the double-sided hit "I Didn't Want To Do It" and "You're the One."

Imperial records president Lew Chudd felt this group had a very marketable way with blues ballads. His belief in them was justified, for while with Imperial records, from 1954 to 1957, they had a number of R & B hits, including their biggest, the swinging "Witchcraft," in late 1955.

January	1954	I DIDN'T WANT TO DO IT	Imperial
March	1954	YOU'RE THE ONE	Imperial
November	1955	WITCHCRAFT	Imperial

THE SPINNERS

Members:
Robert Smith—born: April 10, 1936
Philippe Wynn—born: April 3, 1938—replaced in 1977 by John Edwards—born: December 25, 1944
Billy Henderson—born: August 9, 1939
Henry Fambrough—born: May 10, 1938
Pervis Jackson—born: May 17, 1938

The Spinners originated in Detroit, where three of them were in the same high school graduating class. Their big break came when Gwen Gordy and Harvey Fuqua, who became the group's personal manager, had them record "That's What Girls Are Made Of" for Tri-Phi records in June 1961. It became their first hit.

This group has been turning out hit records for over twenty years with the same members except for one replacement in 1977, when Philippe Wynn left the group.

June	1961	THAT'S WHAT GIRLS ARE MADE FOR	Tri-Phi
July	1965	I'LL ALWAYS LOVE YOU	Motown
May	1966	TRULY YOURS	Motown
July	1970	IT'S A SHAME	V.I.P.
January	1971	WE'LL HAVE IT MADE	V.I.P.
August	1972	HOW COULD I LET YOU GET AWAY	Atlantic
September	1972	I'LL BE AROUND	Atlantic
December	1972	COULD IT BE I'M FALLING IN LOVE	Atlantic
April	1973	ONE OF A KIND (LOVE AFFAIR)	Atlantic
May	1973	TOGETHER WE CAN MAKE SUCH SWEET MUSIC	Motown
August	1973	GHETTO CHILD	Atlantic
January	1974	MIGHTY LOVE PT. 1	Atlantic
May	1974	I'M COMING HOME	Atlantic
August	1974	LOVE DON'T LOVE NOBODY	Atlantic
November	1974	THEN CAME YOU (with Dionne Warwick)	Atlantic
March	1975	LIVING A LITTLE, LAUGHING A LITTLE	Atlantic
May	1975	SADIE	Atlantic
August	1975	(THEY JUST CAN'T STOP IT) THE GAMES PEOPLE PLAY	Atlantic
December	1975	LOVE OR LEAVE	Atlantic
July	1976	WAKE UP SUSAN	Atlantic
September	1976	THE RUBBERBAND MAN	Atlantic
March	1977	YOU'RE THROWING A GOOD LOVE AWAY	Atlantic
October	1977	HEAVEN ON EARTH	Atlantic
July	1978	IF YOU WANNA' DO A DANCE ALL NIGHT	Atlantic
December	1979	WORKING MY WAY BACK TO YOU	Atlantic
May	1980	CUPID	Atlantic
February	1981	YESTERDAY ONCE MORE	Atlantic

THE SPRINGFIELDS

Members:

> Tom Springfield—hometown: West Hampstead, England
> Dusty Springfield—hometown: West Hampstead, England
> Tim Field (replaced by Mike Pickworth)

In 1960, Tom was singing in a London club when his partner fell ill. Tom got Tim to join him for a short while. Later, Tom's younger sister, Dusty, joined the group, and they called themselves the Springfields. They sang a repertoire of songs in nine languages which zoomed them to the top of British show business. In 1961, they were voted the top English vocal group by the *New Musical Express*, their leading magazine.

In the summer of 1962, one of their songs, "Silver Threads and Golden Needles," became very big in the United States on Philips records. In November 1962, Tim left the group to be replaced by Mike Pickworth. The whole group split up in October 1963.

Dusty continued to record for Philips as a solo artist and premiered in January 1964 with "I Only Want to Be with You."

July	1962	SILVER THREADS & GOLDEN NEEDLES	Philips
October	1962	DEAR HEARTS AND GENTLE PEOPLE	Philips

JO STAFFORD

Born: November 12, 1920
Hometown: Coalinga, California

As a youngster, Jo developed an interest in the folk music of the Tennessee hills. She made her public singing debut at the age of twelve in Long Beach, California. In 1935, she and her two sisters, Pauline and Betty Jane, organized a trio called the Stafford Sisters. They sang on several radio shows together until one of the girls married, at which time Jo joined Tommy Dorsey's band. She was a featured soloist with the famous Pied Pipers, where she had the chance to work with Frank Sinatra.

In 1944, she performed on the Johnny Mercer radio show and ultimately landed a recording contract with Capitol records.

In 1951, she signed with Columbia, where she enjoyed top hits like "Shrimp Boats" and number one hits like "You Belong To Me" and "Make Love To Me."

April	1944	I LOVE YOU	Capitol
April	1944	LONG AGO (AND FAR AWAY)	Capitol
September	1944	IT COULD HAPPEN TO YOU	Capitol
November	1945	THAT'S FOR ME	Capitol
January	1946	SYMPHONY	Capitol
October	1947	FEUDIN' AND FIGHTIN'	Capitol
December	1947	SERENADE OF THE BELLS	Capitol
October	1948	EVERYDAY I LOVE YOU	Capitol
May	1949	SOME ENCHANTED EVENING	Capitol
June	1950	PLAY A SIMPLE MELODY	Capitol
August	1950	NO OTHER LOVE	Capitol
August	1950	SOMETIME	Capitol
September	1950	GOODNIGHT IRENE	Capitol
January	1951	TENNESSEE WALTZ	Columbia

November	1951	SHRIMP BOATS	Columbia
March	1952	A-ROUND THE CORNER	Columbia
July	1952	YOU BELONG TO ME	Columbia
August	1952	JAMBALAYA	Columbia
November	1952	KEEP IT A SECRET	Columbia
January	1954	MAKE LOVE TO ME!	Columbia
June	1954	THANK YOU FOR CALLING	Columbia
November	1954	TEACH ME TONIGHT	Columbia
July	1955	SUDDENLY THERE'S A VALLEY	Columbia
October	1955	IT'S ALMOST TOMORROW	Columbia
July	1956	WITH A LITTLE BIT OF LUCK	Columbia
November	1956	LOVE ME GOOD	Columbia
November	1956	ON LONDON BRIDGE	Columbia
March	1957	WIND IN THE WILLOW	Columbia

CYRIL STAPLETON

Cyril was a British orchestra leader who was very popular in England during the forties and fifties. In 1956, he recorded a song for London records called "The Italian Theme," which was then released in the United States and became a hit. Several years later he recorded the classic "The Children's Marching Song." The song became his biggest hit in this country in early 1959.

| August | 1956 | THE ITALIAN THEME | London |
| January | 1959 | THE CHILDREN'S MARCHING SONG | London |

KAY STARR

Real Name: Kay Stark
Born: July 21, 1922
Hometown: Dougherty, Oklahoma

Kay began as a hillbilly singer in Dallas and Memphis. Later she sang with bands like Bob Crosby and Charlie Barnett. She then went out as a solo artist on Capitol records in 1948, recording songs like "You Were Only Foolin'," "Hoop-Dee-Doo," "Wheel Of Fortune," and "Side By Side."

In 1955, she signed with RCA and had a hit later that year with "Rock and Roll Waltz."

December	1948	YOU WERE ONLY FOOLIN'	Capitol
February	1949	SO TIRED	Capitol
May	1950	HOOP-DEE-DOO	Capitol
June	1950	BONAPARTE'S RETREAT	Capitol
August	1950	I'LL NEVER BE FREE (Tennessee Ernie Ford)	Capitol
November	1950	OH, BABE	Capitol
July	1951	COME ON-A MY HOUSE	Capitol

KAY STARR

January	1952	WHEEL OF FORTUNE	Capitol
May	1952	I WAITED A LITTLE TOO LONG	Capitol
August	1952	FOOL, FOOL, FOOL	Capitol
January	1953	SIDE BY SIDE	Capitol
June	1953	HALF A PHOTOGRAPH	Capitol
June	1953	ALLEZ-VOUS-EN	Capitol
December	1953	CHANGING PARTNERS	Capitol
April	1954	MAN UPSTAIRS	Capitol
April	1954	IF YOU LOVE ME (REALLY LOVE ME)	Capitol
December	1955	ROCK AND ROLL WALTZ	RCA
May	1956	SECOND FIDDLE	RCA
August	1956	GOOD BOOK	RCA
April	1957	JAMIE BOY	RCA
August	1957	MY HEART REMINDS ME	RCA
March	1961	FOOLIN' AROUND	Capitol
June	1961	I'LL NEVER BE FREE	Capitol
October	1962	FOUR WALLS	Capitol

RANDY STARR

Born: July 2, 1930
Hometown: New York, New York

After graduating from dental school in 1954, Randy entered the Air Force, where he remained for two years as a dentist. After his discharge, he returned to New York to begin his practice. It was in 1957 that he began writing songs as a hobby. In the early part of the year he wrote a song with a friend Frank Metis called "After School." The two of them recorded a demo which bandleader Sammy Kaye heard and decided to release it on his own label, Dale records. The song became a top-forty record.

In late 1959, Randy wrote another song with his friend called "The Enchanted Island" and went into the studio with a group of musicians to record it. Randy played guitar and whistled on the record. After the session, Randy named the "group" the Islanders and got the song released on Mayflower records. It went on to become a very big national hit. He continued writing songs that became hits for other artists like "Early Morning," for The Kingston Trio, "Empty Chapel" for Connie Francis, and "Kissin' Cousins" for Elvis Presley.

In 1970, he stopped writing to devote full time to his dental practice.

March   1957   AFTER SCHOOL   Dale

THE STATUES

Members:
    James "Buzz" Cason—lead
    Richard Williams
    Hugh Jarrett—bass
Hometown: Nashville, Tennessee

Hugh organized the group in 1959, to work as background singers in Nashville. Liberty president Al Bennett signed the group to his label in 1960 and sent Snuff Garrett to Nashville that summer to record them. The result was "Blue Velvet" which was their only hit.

That same summer, James Cason, singing under the name of Garry Miles, had a solo hit on Liberty, "Look For A Star."

Hugh Jarrett was once a member of the famous Jordanaires.

July   1960   BLUE VELVET   Liberty

THE STEREOS

This five-man group from Steubenville, Ohio, had only one major hit, "I Really Love You." They recorded the song in their hometown and offered the recording to several companies. Cub records in New York (a division of MGM records) liked the song's good hand-clapping beat. They released it in late 1961 and it became a top-forty record.

September 1961   I REALLY LOVE YOU   Cub

STEVE & EYDIE

STEVE AND EYDIE

Although Eydie Gormé had had many chart hits on ABC and Columbia records during her career, and husband Steve Lawrence had had many on Coral, ABC, United Artists, and Columbia, they never had a chart hit together until the summer of 1963, when they recorded a Carole King song called "I Want To Stay Here." Later that year they had another winner with the up-tempo "I Can't Stop Talking about You."

July	1963	I WANT TO STAY HERE	Columbia
December	1963	I CAN'T STOP TALKING ABOUT YOU	Columbia
September	1972	WE CAN MAKE IT TOGETHER	MGM

CONNIE STEVENS

Real Name: Concetta Ann Ingolia
Born: April 8, 1938
Hometown: Brooklyn, New York

The star of TV's "Hawaiian Eye" began her recording career with Warner Brothers in 1959, singing with Ed "Kookie" Byrnes on the recording

CONNIE STEVENS

"Kookie, Kookie, Lend Me Your Comb." "Sixteen Reasons," her first solo release was in January 1960.

January	1960	SIXTEEN REASONS	Warner Bros.
May	1962	WHY'D YOU WANNA MAKE ME CRY	Warner Bros.
July	1962	MR. SONGWRITER	Warner Bros.
April	1965	NOW THAT YOU'VE GONE	Warner Bros.

DODIE STEVENS

Real Name: Geraldine Ann Pasquale
Born: February 17, 1947
Hometown: Temple City, California

Dodie was born in Chicago and moved with her family to California when she was about three. From 1951 to 1959, she did U.S.O. shows and performed at Army and Navy hospitals.

In 1959, at the age of thirteen, she had her first and biggest hit with "Pink Shoe Laces" on Crystalette records.

February	1959	PINK SHOE LACES	Crystalette
May	1959	YES-SIR-EE	Crystalette
August	1960	NO	Dot

RAY STEVENS

Born: January 24, 1941
Hometown: Clarkdale, Georgia

Ray became a disc jockey at fifteen, and had his own show at sixteen. In 1957, he recorded "Silver Bracelet" and "Five More Steps," for Prep records.

He signed with Capitol and had a small hit with "Chickie-Chickie Wah Wah" in 1958. In the summer of 1961, he cut a record that became his first hit on Mercury: the song with the longest title ever, "Jeremiah Peabody's Poly Unsaturated Quick Dissolving Fast Acting Pleasant Tasting Green And Purple Pills."

August	1961	JEREMIAH PEABODY'S POLY UNSATURATED QUICK DISSOLVING FAST ACTION PLEASANT TASTING GREEN AND PURPLE PILLS	Mercury
June	1962	AHAB, THE ARAB	Mercury
November	1962	SANTA CLAUS IS WATCHING YOU	Mercury
March	1963	FUNNY MAN	Mercury
June	1963	HARRY THE HAIRY APE	Mercury
October	1963	SPEED BALL	Mercury
April	1968	UNWIND	Monument
July	1968	MR. BUSINESSMAN	Monument
March	1969	GITARZAN	Monument
June	1969	ALONG CAME JONES	Monument
October	1969	SUNDAY MORNIN' COMIN' DOWN	Monument
April	1970	EVERYTHING IS BEAUTIFUL	Barnaby
July	1970	AMERICA, COMMUNICATE WITH ME	Barnaby
November	1970	SUNSET STRIP	Barnaby
December	1970	BRIDGET THE MIDGET (THE QUEEN OF THE BLUES)	Barnaby
May	1971	A MAMA AND A PAPA	Barnaby
August	1971	ALL MY TRIALS	Barnaby
November	1971	TURN YOUR RADIO ON	Barnaby
April	1974	THE STREAK	Barnaby
July	1974	MOONLIGHT SPECIAL	Barnaby
April	1975	MISTY	Barnaby
October	1975	INDIAN LOVE CALL	Barnaby
July	1976	YOUNG LOVE	Barnaby
March	1979	I NEED YOUR HELP BARRY MANILOW	Warner Bros.

BILLY STEWART

Died: January 17, 1970
Hometown: Washington, D.C.

Billy started out in Washington as a singer with the Rainbows, who had one hit for Red Robin records called "Mary Lee" in June 1955. He then went to Chess records and had his first solo hit, "Billy's Blues." He was killed in an auto crash in 1970.

July	1956	BILLY BLUES Pr. 1 & 2	Chess
July	1962	REAP WHAT YOU SOW	Chess
September	1963	STRANGE FEELING	Chess
March	1965	I DO LOVE YOU	Chess

BILLY STEWART

February	1969	I DO LOVE YOU	Chess
June	1965	SITTING IN THE PARK	Chess
January	1966	BECAUSE I LOVE YOU	Chess
June	1966	SUMMERTIME	Chess
October	1966	SECRET LOVE	Chess
February	1967	EVERYDAY I HAVE THE BLUES	Chess
December	1967	CROSS MY HEART	Chess

SANDY STEWART

Real Name: Sandra Ester Galitz
Born: July 10, 1937
Hometown: Philadelphia, Pennsylvania

Sandy started singing at the age of ten in Philadelphia, on local radio and TV shows. At age sixteen she went to New York, where she auditioned for the Ernie Kovacs TV show, on which she appeared regularly thereafter. She also appeared on the Eddie Fisher TV show. In the early sixties she was a regular on the Perry Como show.

In late 1962, Sandy's good friend Kay Ballard was given a song called "My Coloring Book." Kay felt the song was not right for her and suggested that Sandy sing it instead. On Como's October 31, 1962 show, Sandy sang the song for the first time and the response was overwhelming. Sandy's beau Moose Charlap called his friend Don Costa the next day and said they should record the song. They did, and "My Coloring Book" became a national hit on Colpix by December of that year.

Today she is a widow who lives with her two children in New York.

| December | 1962 | MY COLORING BOOK | Colpix |

GARY STITES

Born: July 23, 1940
Hometown: Denver, Colorado

Gary began his career as a magician at thirteen. He started singing a year later, when he was confined to bed with rheumatic fever. He taught himself to play the guitar and started a band called the Satellites.

In March 1959, his group backed him up on his first hit, for Carlton records, called "Lonely For You."

March	1959	LONELY FOR YOU	Carlton
November	1959	STARRY EYED	Carlton
February	1960	LAWDY MISS CLAWDY	Carlton

MORRIS STOLOFF

Born: August 1, 1898
Died: April 16, 1980
Hometown: Philadelphia, Pennsylvania

Morris's early career included stints as violinist with the Los Angeles Philharmonic, the Paramount Studio Orchestra, and his own string quartet. He became the general music director of Columbia Pictures in 1936. Among the films he scored were *Cover Girl, The Jolson Story, The Eddy Duchin Story,* and *Song Without End.*

In March 1956, he had a chart hit on Decca records with the theme from the film *Picnic,* called "Moonglow and the Theme from Picnic," which became a number two national hit. Although it was on the charts for twenty-seven weeks, it never made it to the number one spot, playing second fiddle to "Heartbreak Hotel" by Elvis Presley and, later, "Wayward Wind" by Gogi Grant.

| March | 1956 | MOONGLOW & THEME FROM PICNIC | Decca |

BILLY STORM

Born: June 29, 1938

Billy was originally the lead singer for the Valiants, who had "This Is the Night" on Keen records in 1957. He left the group to go on as a solo performer and had one national hit for Columbia in 1959 with "I've Come of Age."

| March | 1959 | I'VE COME OF AGE | Columbia |

GALE STORM

GALE STORM

Real Name: Josephine Cottle
Born: 1922
Homestate: Texas

Gale went to Hollywood in 1940, as the winner of the "Gateway to Hollywood" contest, from her home in Texas. In a short time she started making movies for Universal and RKO, where she appeared in a number of westerns with Roy Rogers. She was offered a role in the TV series "My Little Margie" in 1952, which was her big break. After the show grew in popularity, she moved into another area she dearly loved: singing.

In 1955, she signed with Randy Wood's Dot records and recorded a cover version of Smiley Lewis's and Fats Domino's song "I Hear You Knocking." By the summer of 1955, it became a number two national hit.

Gale had a very successful career on Dot, making many cover records during the fifties.

Today she does some local theatre work, while she resides with her husband, Lee Bonnell, in the San Fernando Valley.

| June | 1955 | I HEAR YOU KNOCKING | Dot |
| December | 1955 | TEENAGE PRAYER | Dot |

November	1955	MEMORIES ARE MADE OF THIS	Dot
February	1956	WHY DO FOOLS FALL IN LOVE	Dot
April	1956	IVORY TOWER	Dot
June	1956	TELL ME WHY	Dot
September	1956	NOW IS THE HOUR	Dot
March	1957	ON TREASURE ISLAND	Dot
March	1957	DARK MOON	Dot

THE STRING-A-LONGS

Members:

Keith McCormack—vocal and rhythm guitar
Jimmy Torres—lead guitar
Richard Stephens—guitar
Aubrey Lee DeCordova—bass guitar
Don Allen—drums

Hometown: Clovis, New Mexico

The group first started playing together in high school. In the fall of 1960, they auditioned for Norman Petty, the same man who discovered Buddy Holly. He liked the group and had them record an instrumental he had written, "Wheels," which he sold to Warwick records. It came out in early 1961 and became a national hit.

January	1961	WHEELS	Warwick
April	1961	BRASS BUTTONS	Warwick
June	1961	SHOULD I	Warwick

BARRETT STRONG

Born: February 5, 1941
Hometown: Detroit, Michigan

As a youngster, Barrett moved with his family from Mississippi to Detroit, where his cousin Nolan Strong (lead voice of the Diablos) was living. Barrett began singing at local clubs, where he met a young songwriter named Berry Gordy, Jr. Berry asked Barrett if he would like to record a song that Berry had written with Janie Bradford called "Money." Barrett said yes, and they recorded the song for Berry's Anna records (named after Berry's sister). The song became one of the first major hits for Berry Gordy, Jr., who built Motown records into an empire in the sixties.

Later Barrett became a writer for Motown, writing many of the Temptations' hits, like "I Wish It Would Rain" and "Papa Was a Rolling Stone."

| January | 1960 | MONEY | Anna |

SUNNY AND THE SUNGLOWS

Members:
    Sunny Ozuna—lead
    Jesse Villanueva
    Oscar Villanueva
    Ray Villanueva
    Tony Tostado
    Gilbert Fernandez
    Alfred Luna
Hometown: San Antonio, Texas

The Sunglows started out in 1959, while attending Burbank Vocational High in San Antonio. They approached independent record producer Huey P. Meaux at a night club in Galveston, Texas, and asked him to manage them. Under his guidance they became a hot local item. They had minor hits with "Golly Gee" and "Just A Moment," but it wasn't until August 1963, when they recorded the old Little Willie John classic "Talk To Me," that things began to happen for them. It became a hit on Tear Drop records and launched the group's sound. Shortly after that they changed their name to Sunny and the Sunliners.

August	1963	TALK TO ME	Tear Drop
November	1963	RAGS TO RICHES	Tear Drop
February	1964	OUT OF SIGHT-OUT OF MIND	Tear Drop

THE SUPREMES

Members:
    Diana Ross (March 26, 1944)—replaced by Jean Terrell—replaced
        by Shari Payne—November 14, 1944
    Florence Ballard—replaced by Cindy Birdsong—December 15, 1939
    Mary Wilson—March 4, 1944
Hometown: Detroit, Michigan

Diana, who went to Cass Technical High, and Mary and Florence, who both went to Northwestern High in Detroit, began singing as a trio in 1960, as the Primettes. The girls sang together at a high school talent show and won first prize. At this time they came to the attention of Berry Gordy, Jr., the president of Motown records, who liked the girls but told them to come back to him after they finished high school. After graduation, Florence suggested they change the name of the group to the Supremes, which they did. They went to see Gordy, who signed them to his label as background singers.

THE SUPREMES

Clockwise from left: Diana Ross,
Cindy Birdsong, Mary Wilson

In the summer of 1962, they had their first chart record with "Your Heart Belongs to Me." Five chart records later, they hit big in the summer of 1964 with their first number one national hit, "Where Did Our Love Go," written by Eddie and Brian Holland and Lamont Dozier. The names Holland, Dozier, and Holland would become synonymous with hit records for the Supremes, for their next four releases became number one national hits as well.

In 1967, after twenty chart hits, ten of which were number one hits, Florence left the group and was replaced by Cindy Birdsong, a former member of Patti La Belle and the Bluebells. It was at this point that the billing became Diana Ross and the Supremes.

Throughout the rest of 1967 and even 1968, the hits were far too infrequent. The group lost some of its popularity when Holland, Dozier, and Holland left Motown to go on their own. In 1969, Diana Ross decided to go out as a single and was replaced by Jean Terrell (heavyweight fighter Ernie Terrell's sister). Diana left the group in a blaze of glory, for in November of 1969, their "Someday We'll Be Together" was a number one hit—their last top record. With Diana as lead, the group had twelve number one national hits, an unbelievable figure. Only the Beatles (twenty) and Elvis (eighteen) had more number one hits. Today Diana Ross is a major superstar both in films and in making records.

August	1962	YOUR HEART BELONGS TO ME	Motown
December	1962	LET ME GO THE RIGHT WAY	Motown
July	1963	A BREATH TAKING GUY	Motown
November	1963	WHEN THE LOVELIGHT STARTS SHINING THROUGH HIS EYES	Motown
March	1964	RUN, RUN, RUN	Motown
July	1964	WHERE DID OUR LOVE GO	Motown
October	1964	BABY LOVE	Motown
November	1964	COME SEE ABOUT ME	Motown
February	1965	STOP! IN THE NAME OF LOVE!	Motown
May	1965	BACK IN MY ARMS AGAIN	Motown
July	1965	NOTHING BUT HEARTACHES	Motown
October	1965	I HEAR A SYMPHONY	Motown
January	1966	MY WORLD IS EMPTY WITHOUT YOU	Motown
April	1966	LOVE IS LIKE AN ITCHING IN MY HEART	Motown
August	1966	YOU CAN'T HURRY LOVE	Motown
October	1966	YOU KEEP ME HANGIN' ON	Motown
January	1967	LOVE IS HERE AND NOW YOU'RE GONE	Motown
April	1967	THE HAPPENING	Motown
August	1967	REFLECTIONS	Motown
November	1967	IN AND OUT OF LOVE	Motown
March	1968	FOREVER CAME TODAY	Motown
June	1968	SOME THINGS YOU NEVER GET USED TO	Motown
October	1968	LOVE CHILD	Motown
January	1969	I'M LIVIN' IN SHAME	Motown
April	1969	THE COMPOSER	Motown
May	1969	NO MATTER WHAT SIGN YOU ARE	Motown
August	1969	THE YOUNG FOLKS	
November	1969	SOMEDAY WE'LL BE TOGETHER	Motown
March	1970	UP THE LADDER TO THE ROOF	Motown
July	1970	EVERYBODY'S GOT THE RIGHT TO LOVE	Motown
November	1970	STONED LOVE	Motown
May	1971	NATHAN JONES	Motown
October	1971	TOUCH	Motown
May	1972	AUTOMATICALLY SUNSHINE	Motown
July	1972	YOUR WONDERFUL SWEET, SWEET LOVE	Motown
October	1972	I GUESS I'LL MISS THE MAN	Motown
June	1973	BAD WEATHER	Motown
May	1976	I'M GONNA LET MY HEART DO THE WALKING	Motown
December	1976	YOU'RE MY DRIVING WHEEL	Motown

THE SURFARIS

Members:
Jim Pash—1949
Jim Fuller—1947
Bob Berryhill—1947
Pat Connolly—1947

Ron Wilson—1945
Hometown: Glendora, California

In 1963, the group was a big local favorite in Glendora. During that year, the group wrote and recorded an instrumental which featured the infectious laugh of their manager, Dale Smallins, at the beginning of the song. "Wipe Out" was sold to Dot records and became a summertime smash.

June	1963	WIPE OUT	Dot
August	1963	SURFER JOE	Dot
September	1963	POINT PANIC	Decca

THE SWALLOWS

This R & B group from the Baltimore area had several hits in the early fifties, which featured the lead voice of Herman "Junior" Denby. In the fall of 1958, they had their only successful pop record with their version of Bobby Hendricks' hit "Itchy Twitchy Feeling."

August	1951	WILL YOU BE MINE	King
July	1952	BESIDE YOU	King
September	1958	ITCHY TWITCHY FEELING	Federal

SYLVIA SYMS

Sylvia was a night club entertainer, much like Mabel Mercer, and included a lot of standard tunes in her repertoire. She came to the attention of Decca records in the mid-fifties and had a few chart records over the next couple of years. Her biggest chart entry came in the spring of 1956, with "I Could Have Danced All Night" from the popular Broadway show *My Fair Lady*.

April	1956	I COULD HAVE DANCED ALL NIGHT	Decca
July	1956	ENGLISH MUFFINS & IRISH STEW	Decca
December	1956	DANCING CHANDELIER	Decca

T

THE TAMS

Members:

Charles Pope—born: August 7, 1936
Joseph Pope—born: November 6, 1933
Robert Smith—born: March 18, 1936
Floyd Ashton—born: August 15, 1933
Horace Key—born: April 13, 1934

Hometown: Atlanta, Georgia

The Tams began singing in the Southeast in 1959. In 1962, they went to Lowery Music in Atlanta to see Bill Lowery. He signed them to Harry Finfer's Arlen records, and they recorded "Untie Me" as their first hit in late 1962. The group was signed to ABC records in 1963 and in November recorded their biggest all-time seller with "What Kind of Fool (Do You Think I Am)." Charles and Joseph's brother Otis, became the group's road manager.

October	1962	UNTIE ME	Arlen
November	1963	WHAT KIND OF FOOL (DO YOU THINK I AM)	ABC
March	1964	YOU LIED TO YOUR DADDY	ABC
June	1964	HEY GIRL, DON'T BOTHER ME	ABC
November	1964	SILLY LITTLE GIRL	ABC
June	1968	BE YOUNG, BE FOOLISH, BE HAPPY	ABC

THE TARRIERS

Members:

Erik Darling
Bob Carey
Alan Arkin

The group had a nice Calypso sound which was shown to advantage on "The Banana Boat Song." Unfortunately for them, Harry Belafonte's version was the bigger hit. In 1963, Erik Darling formed another trio called the Rooftop Singers and had a number one song, with "Walk Right In." Alan Arkin went on to become a popular film star.

| January | 1957 | THE BANANA BOAT SONG | Glory |

JOHNNIE TAYLOR

Born: May 5, 1937
Hometown: West Memphis, Arkansas

In the mid-fifties, when Sam Cooke left the gospel group the Soul Stirrers, Johnnie replaced him. Later Johnnie also left the group and traveled with Sam as a singer for about eight years.

In 1967, while Johnnie was visiting his grandmother in West Memphis, he took a twenty-minute ride to Memphis, Tennessee, the home of Stax records. He auditioned for them and wound up with a recording contract. In October 1968, he had his first gold record, "Who's Making Love," which became a top-ten national hit.

November	1967	SOMEBODY'S SLEEPING IN MY BED	Stax
October	1968	WHO'S MAKING LOVE	Stax
January	1969	TAKE CARE OF YOUR HOMEWORK	Stax
May	1969	I WANNA TESTIFY	Stax
August	1969	I COULD NEVER BE PRESIDENT	Stax
December	1969	LOVE BONES	Stax
June	1973	I BELIEVE IN YOU (YOU BELIEVE IN ME)	Stax
October	1973	CHEAPER TO KEEP HER	Stax
January	1974	WE'RE GETTING CARELESS WITH OUR LOVE	Stax
June	1974	I'VE BEEN BORN AGAIN	Stax
April	1976	DISCO LADY	Stax
June	1976	SOMEBODY'S GETTIN' IT	Stax
February	1977	LOVE IS BETTER IN THE A.M.	Stax
October	1977	DISCO 9000	Stax

THE TEDDY BEARS

Members
    Annette Kleinbard—lead—1940
    Marshall Lieb—January 26, 1939
    Phil Spector—December 26, 1939
Hometown: Los Angeles, California

The three met at Fairfax High School in Los Angeles, in 1958, and began singing together as a trio. In August 1958, the group recorded a song that Phil had written, "To Know Him Is to Love Him," which was then sold to Dore records in Los Angeles. The song went on to become a number one national hit and was an early start for the young genius Phil Spector, who, a few years later, would go on to produce and write for such talents as the Crystals, the Ronettes, and the Righteous Brothers.

| August | 1958 | TO KNOW HIM, IS TO LOVE HIM | Dore |
| March | 1959 | OH WHY | Imperial |

THE TEEN QUEENS

Members:
    Betty Collins
    Rosie Collins
Hometown: Los Angeles, California

Betty and her sister Rosie began singing together in 1955. Late that year they dubbed themselves the Teen Queens and recorded a song their brother Aaron had written with his friend Maxwell Davis, called "Eddie My Love," which was sold to RPM records in Los Angeles. The song became their biggest all-time seller when it was released in early 1956.

| January | 1956 | EDDIE MY LOVE | RPM |

THE TEEN QUEENS

Betty Collins (left)
and Rosie Collins (right)

**NINO TEMPO &
APRIL STEVENS**

NINO TEMPO AND APRIL STEVENS

Members:
    Nino—born: January 6, 1937
    April—born: April 29, 1936
Hometown: Niagara Falls, New York

This brother and sister act had worked successfully as single performers for many years. Nino had been performing since age three. At seven, he was singing with Benny Goodman's orchestra and later joined Glenn Miller's band.

April, a solo vocalist, joined her brother in the early sixties. In 1963, they signed with Atco records and premiered with "Sweet and Lovely." In September of the same year they had a number one song with "Deep Purple."

Today they both record as soloists, with Nino recording for A & M records. On occasion they work as a duo.

July	1962	SWEET AND LOVELY	Atco
September	1963	DEEP PURPLE	Atco
December	1963	WHISPERING	Atco
February	1964	STARDUST	Atco
May	1964	TEA FOR TWO	Atco
August	1966	ALL STRUNG OUT	White Whale

THE TEMPOS

Members:
   Mike Lazo—lead
   Gene Schachter
   Jim Drake
   Tom Monito
Hometown: Pittsburgh, Pennsylvania

Mike and Gene were in the Army together in Korea, where they did some entertaining. After their discharge, they returned to Pittsburgh, where they formed a group by adding Jim and Tom, music majors at Duquesne University.

In 1959, they signed with Climax records and in June of the same year recorded their only major hit, "See You In September."

June   1959   SEE YOU IN SEPTEMBER   Climax

THE TEMPTATIONS

This group, not to be confused with Motown's Temptations, was a typical New York group, a bunch of clean-cut all-American boys who were good-looking and sang love ballads, like Dion and the Belmonts, the Elegants, the Passions, the Regents, and the Mystics.

The Temptations were signed to George Goldner's Goldisc records in early 1960. Their one major hit was "Barbara," a moderate tempo ballad.

April   1960   BARBARA   Goldisc

CARLA THOMAS

Born: 1947
Hometown: Memphis, Tennessee

The daughter of the "Memphis Queen of Soul" got her introduction to music from her father Rufus (who later had a couple of hits himself on Stax in 1963, with "The Dog" and "Walking the Dog"), a disc jockey on WDAI in Memphis. Rufus persuaded his daughter to cut a demo of a song she had written called "Gee Whiz (Look at His Eyes)," which she did in late 1960. Atlantic records heard the song and signed Carla to the label. In early 1961, "Gee Whiz (Look at His Eyes)" became a national hit.

In 1965, she switched from the Atlantic label to Stax records in Memphis (which is one of the labels Atlantic distributes). In the summer of 1966, she recorded another song Isaac Hayes wrote, "B-A-B-Y," which was her biggest hit for Stax.

January	1961	GEE WHIZ (LOOK AT HIS EYES)	Atlantic
May	1961	A LOVE OF MY OWN	Atlantic
October	1962	I'LL BRING IT ON HOME TO YOU	Atlantic
August	1964	I'VE GOT NO TIME TO LOSE	Atlantic
November	1964	A WOMAN'S LOVE	Atlantic
April	1966	LET ME BE GOOD TO YOU	Stax
August	1966	B-A-B-Y	Stax
January	1967	SOMETHING GOOD	Stax
June	1967	I'LL ALWAYS HAVE FAITH IN YOU	Stax
December	1967	PICK UP THE PIECES	Stax
February	1969	I LIKE WHAT YOU'RE DOING (TO ME)	Stax

RUFUS THOMAS

Hometown: Memphis, Tennessee

A onetime disc jockey for WDIA radio in Memphis, Rufus decided to pursue a recording career in late 1962. He signed with Stax records and recorded "The Dog" in January 1963. Later that year, he had his biggest all-time seller with one of his own compositions, "Walking The Dog."

His daughter is singer Carla Thomas of "Gee Whiz" fame.

January	1963	THE DOG	Stax
September	1963	WALKING THE DOG	Stax
February	1964	CAN YOUR MONKEY DO THE DOG	Stax
October	1964	JUMP BACK	Stax

SUE THOMPSON

Real Name: Eva Sue McKee
Born: July 19, 1926
Hometown: Sheridan, California

Born on a farm in Nevada, Missouri, Sue began singing and playing the guitar at age seven. When her family moved to California, she entered a vaudeville show and won a two-week engagement. She also appeared on local radio shows and began recording for Mercury records. She later married Art Penny and settled in Las Vegas.

Sue signed with Decca, Columbia, and finally settled with Hickory records in 1961. In August 1961, she recorded a John D. Loudermilk song, "Sad Movies (Make Me Cry)," which became her first major hit. A few

SUE THOMPSON

months later she had a second big hit with another John D. Loudermilk song called "Norman."

August	1961	SAD MOVIES (MAKE ME CRY)	Hickory
November	1961	NORMAN	Hickory
February	1962	TWO OF A KIND	Hickory
June	1962	HAVE A GOOD TIME	Hickory
September	1962	JAMES (HOLD THE LADDER STEADY)	Hickory
January	1965	PAPER TIGER	Hickory

WILLIE MAE THORNTON

Born: December 11, 1926
Hometown: Montgomery, Alabama

Blues singer Willie Mae Thornton, whose nickname was "Big Mama," signed with Don Robey's Peacock records in 1951. Although her forte was R & B, her best-remembered tune was a song Jerry Leiber and Mike Stoller had written, called "Hound Dog." She recorded the song with Johnny Otis's band, and it went on to be a national R & B hit in the spring of 1953. Three years later it became a million seller for Elvis Presley.

| March | 1953 | HOUND DOG | Peacock |

THE THREE FRIENDS

Members:
    Frank Starpoli—lead
    Joe Francavilla—harmony
    Tony Grochowski—first tenor
Hometown: Brooklyn, New York

The trio got together in the mid-fifties and called themselves simply the Three Friends. In 1956, the three wrote a song called "Blanche" which they recorded and released that year. Although the song was not big nationally, it was a major hit in the New York City area.

In 1958, Joe changed his name to Joe Villa and joined a group called the Royal Teens, which went on to have a big national hit that year with "Short Shorts."

June	1956	BLANCHE	Lido

JOHNNY THUNDER

Born: 1941
Hometown: Leesburg, Florida

As a youngster, Johnny sang in the church choir with his family. Record producer Teddy Vann heard Johnny sing and asked him to record a song Teddy had written. They took the finished song to Diamond record executive Phil Kahl, who liked it and decided to release it on his label. The song, "Loop De Loop," became a solid smash in early 1963.

December	1962	LOOP DE LOOP	Diamond
November	1965	EVERYBODY DO THE SLOOPY	Diamond

TICO AND THE TRIUMPHS

Paul Simon, after recording with Art Garfunkel in 1957 on Big records with "Hey! Schoolgirl" as Tom and Jerry, went on his own for a while. In late 1961, he recorded a song called "Motorcycle" with two other fellows. The song had one week on the national charts on Amy records.

December	1961	MOTORCYCLE	Amy

JOHNNY TILLOTSON

Born: April 20, 1939
Hometown: Jacksonville, Florida

Johnny's first professional appearance was a guest spot on Toby Dowdy's TV show. His big break came when Lee Rosenberg, owner of Southern Bell music, heard him on a Pet Milk talent show in Nashville and arranged for an audition with Archie Bleyer, the president of Cadence records. This resulted in a recording contract and his first release in late 1958, called "Well, I'm Your Man," followed a few months later by "Dreamy Eyes," the flip side of the record.

His biggest all-time seller was "Poetry in Motion," in September 1960.

October	1958	WELL, I'M YOUR MAN	Cadence
November	1958	DREAMY EYES	Cadence
August	1959	TRUE TRUE HAPPINESS	Cadence
January	1960	WHY DO I LOVE YOU SO	Cadence
April	1960	EARTH ANGEL	Cadence
July	1960	POETRY IN MOTION	Cadence
January	1961	JIMMY'S GIRL	Cadence
July	1961	WITHOUT YOU	Cadence
December	1961	DREAMY EYES	Cadence
May	1962	IT KEEPS RIGHT ON A-HURTIN'	Cadence
August	1962	SEND ME THE PILLOW YOU DREAM ON	Cadence
October	1962	I CAN'T HELP IT	Cadence
February	1963	OUT OF MY MIND	Cadence
August	1963	YOU CAN NEVER STOP ME LOVING YOU	Cadence
October	1963	FUNNY HOW TIME SLIPS AWAY	Cadence
November	1963	TALK BACK TREMBLING LIPS	MGM
February	1964	WORRIED GUY	MGM
May	1964	I RISE, I FALL	MGM
July	1964	WORRY	MGM
October	1964	SHE UNDERSTANDS ME	MGM
February	1965	ANGEL	MGM
August	1965	HEARTACHES BY THE NUMBER	MGM
November	1965	OUR WORLD	MGM

THE TIME-TONES

New York record-store owner Irving "Slim" Rose, of Times Square records, ran a contest on the small radio station he was working at the time to find the best singing group in the New York area. Five young men (two of them white and three black) won the contest and Slim decided to call them the Time-Tones after his Times Square record company and store. They had one national hit, "In My Heart," in the spring of 1961.

April	1961	IN MY HEART	Times Square

ART & DOTTY TODD

Art and Dotty met in Providence, Rhode Island, in 1941, and shortly thereafter were married. They began singing as a duo and by the early fifties had signed a recording contract with RCA Victor. After several hits that were popular in Europe, but not in the United States, they left RCA.

In 1958, Art found a song written by Wayne Shanklin called "Chanson d'Amour," which they recorded. He took the finished song to various record companies and Era finally took it on. In the spring of 1958, it became their only big hit.

Today Art & Dotty are a top lounge act in Las Vegas.

March   1958   CHANSON D'AMOUR   Era

NICK TODD

Real Name: Nick Boone
Hometown: Nashville, Tennessee

Nick is Pat Boone's younger brother. Pat introduced him to Randy Wood, the president of Dot, and Randy decided to give him a chance. However, Randy didn't want Nick to use the same last name as his brother, so they chose the name Todd, which is Dot records spelled backwards.

In the fall of 1957, Nick sang his way up the charts with a catchy tune called "Plaything," which became a top-forty record.

September 1957   PLAYTHING   Dot
December 1957   AT THE HOP   Dot

THE TOKENS

Members:
    Jay Siegal—lead singer—guitar—October 20, 1939
    Mitchell Margo—first tenor—piano and drums—May 25, 1947
    Philip Margo—baritone—piano, drums and guitar—April 1, 1942
    Henry Medress—second tenor—piano and bass—November 19, 1938
Hometown: Brooklyn, New York

The fellows first started singing in the fifties with Neil Sedaka as their vocalist. After Neil left the group, they remained together, thirteen-year-old Mitchell going to school as an eighth grader and brother Phil, along with Jay and Hank, attending Brooklyn College. Their manager, Seymour Barash, arranged for them to go to Warwick records in early 1961, where they recorded their only major hit for the label, "Tonight I Fell in Love."

THE TOKENS
Top row: Jay Siegal, Hank Medress. Front row: Mitch Margo, Phil Margo

In late 1961, they signed with RCA and recorded "The Lion Sleeps Tonight," which became a number one song.

On October 3, 1981, all four original members were reunited at the Royal New York Doo Wopp Show at New York's Radio City Music Hall.

February	1961	TONIGHT I FELL IN LOVE	Warwick
October	1961	THE LION SLEEPS TONIGHT	RCA
February	1962	B'WA NINA	RCA
June	1962	LA BOMBA	RCA
August	1964	HE'S IN TOWN	B.T. Puppy
March	1966	I HEAR THE TRUMPETS BLOW	B.T. Puppy
March	1967	PORTRAIT OF MY LOVE	Warner Bros.
July	1967	IT'S A HAPPENING WORLD	Warner Bros.
December	1969	SHE LETS HER HAIR DOWN	Buddah
March	1970	DON'T WORRY BABY	Buddah
August	1973	IN THE MIDNIGHT HOUR	Atco

TOM AND JERRY

Members:

Tom—real name: Art Garfunkel—October 13, 1942—hometown: New York, New York

Jerry—real name: Paul Simon—November 5, 1942—hometown: Newark, New Jersey

This unknown duo of 1957, who recorded one hit for Big records called "Hey! Schoolgirl," went on to become superstars for Columbia records in the mid-sixties. Their long list of hits as Simon and Garfunkel includes, "Sounds of Silence," "Homeward Bound," "Bridge Over Troubled Water," and "Cecilia."

November 1957   HEY! SCHOOLGIRL   Big

MEL TORME

Real Name: Melvin Howard
Born: September 13, 1925
Hometown: Chicago, Illinois

Mel's first public appearance was at the age of four in Chicago's Black-hawk Restaurant. He was out to dinner with his parents and asked to sing a tune with the band. The band obliged, and another star was born. As a teen-ager he learned how to play the piano and drums and also did a bit of songwriting.

He became a drummer with Chico Marx's band and traveled with them to Hollywood. When the band broke up he organized his own group, the Mel-Tones. The group became popular and even appeared in several movies.

MEL TORME

After getting out of the service in the late forties, Mel went out as a single. His biggest hits were "Careless Hands" and "Again" for Capitol in 1949.

A prolific songwriter, he wrote—among many other tunes—the classic "Christmas Song" for Nat King Cole.

February	1949	CARELESS HANDS	Capitol
March	1949	AGAIN	Capitol
June	1949	FOUR WINDS AND SEVEN SEAS	Capitol
October	1962	COMIN' HOME BABY	Atlantic

THE TORNADOES

Members:
> Clem Cattini—drums—1938
> George Bellamy—guitar—1940
> Heinz Burt—guitar—1942
> Allan Caddy—guitar—1940
> Roger LaVern—piano and organ—1938

Hometown: London, England

The fellows got together as a studio group doing backup at recording sessions. Their first song as the Tornadoes, "Telstar," was written by recording engineer Joe Meek and recorded off the cuff in the studio. The song was released on Decca records in England and became a hit in 1962. Later that year, the song was released in the United States on London records and also became a number one song over here.

| October | 1962 | TELSTAR | London |
| January | 1963 | RIDIN' THE WIND | London |

MITCHELL TOROK

Mitchell began as a Texas country singer. In the mid-fifties, he appeared on the "Louisiana Hayride" and became a star. In 1957, he signed with Decca and had a national hit with "Pledge of Love" that spring. Several years later he had another hit, this time on Guyden records, called "Caribbean."

March	1957	PLEDGE OF LOVE	Decca
July	1959	CARIBBEAN	Guyden
May	1960	PINK CHIFFON	Guyden

ED TOWNSEND

ED TOWNSEND

Born: April 16, 1929
Hometown: Fayetteville, Tennessee

At twenty-two Ed joined the Marines and went to Korea. It was there that Horace Heidt heard him sing and asked him to join his troupe touring the Far East. After leaving Heidt, he had his own TV show in Los Angeles and also formed a music publishing business.

In 1958, while with Capitol records, he wrote and recorded "For Your Love," which became a national hit in April of that year. It was his biggest all-time seller.

| March | 1958 | FOR YOUR LOVE | Capitol |
| September | 1958 | WHEN I GROW TOO OLD TO DREAM | Capitol |

THE TRASHMEN

Members:
    Tony Andreason
    Dal Winslow
    Bob Reed
    Steve Wahres
Hometown: Minneapolis, Minnesota

In late 1962 the group was playing locally in Minneapolis. A year later they recorded a wild novelty song for Garrett records called "Surfin' Bird," which became a national hit in December 1963.

| December | 1963 | SURFIN' BIRD | Garrett |
| February | 1964 | BIRD DANCE BEAT | Garrett |

TRAVIS AND BOB

Real Names:
    Travis Pritchett—March 18, 1939
    Bob Weaver—1939
Hometown: Mobile, Alabama

This banjo-playing duo started singing together throughout the South in the late fifties. They had a kind of neo–Everly Brothers sound. In early 1959, they recorded a song Travis had written called "Tell Him No" and took the song to Sandy records in Mobile. The company liked the song and decided to release it. It went on to become a top-ten national hit in the spring of that year and the only major hit for the duo.

| March | 1959 | TELL HIM NO | Sandy |

DORIS TROY

Born: January 6, 1937
Hometown: New York, New York

Doris's father was a preacher, and his choir constituted her first introduction to singing. While working as an usher at New York's Apollo Theater, she began to consider singing professionally.

She first teamed with a trio called The Halos and then sang with Jay and Dee. Doris also did some background singing for Solomon Burke and Chuck Jackson, and dabbled in songwriting with "How 'Bout That" for Dee Clark.

In 1963, she signed with Atlantic records and recorded a song called "Just One Look," which became her only major hit in May of that year.

Doris was a background singer on the highly successful Pink Floyd LP *Dark Side Of The Moon* in 1973.

| May | 1963 | JUST ONE LOOK | Atlantic |

THE TUNE ROCKERS

In the summer of 1958, the Tune Rockers had a driving instrumental hit on United Artists that featured a unique guitar sound, which was supposed to simulate the sound of a mosquito in flight. This gimmick sound, along with the good dance beat, enabled the song to become a national hit that summer.

August   1958   THE GREEN MOSQUITO   United Artists

THE TUNE WEAVERS

Members:
> Margo J. Sylvia—lead—born: April 4, 1936
> John Sylvia—born: September 8, 1935
> Charlotte Davis—born: November 12, 1936
> Gilbert J. Lopez—born: July 4, 1934

Hometown: Boston, Massachusetts

When Gilbert Lopez got out of the service in the mid-fifties, he asked his sister Margo to join him as a duo and begin singing around Boston.

THE TUNE WEAVERS

Clockwise from left:
Charlotte Davis, Margo
Sylvia, Gilbert Lopez,
Johnny Sylvia

Although Margo liked the idea, her husband John did not want her traveling without him. Gilbert suggested that John join the group. Cousin Charlotte was added and the group was born. They first called themselves the Tone Weavers, but when a disc jockey emceeing a local dance called them the Tune Weavers by mistake, they decided to let the name stick.

After rehearsing the hits of other groups, Gilbert suggested that they record some original material. They rehearsed a song Margo had written some five years earlier called "Happy, Happy Birthday Baby" and decided to use it in their stage show.

While appearing at a night club, they did the song and Frank Paul heard it. He had them record it and then decided to manage the group. They had copies of the song made and distributed to Boston radio stations, but with no response. Some eight months later, Paul sent several copies to Philadelphia, where a disc jockey played the song by accident one night and was deluged with enthusiastic phone calls. The disc jockey ·called his friends at Chess records in Chicago and told them about the song. They got in touch with Paul and a deal was made to release it on their Checker label. In August of 1957, the song became a national hit.

After the one hit, the group left Checker records, never to have another national smash.

Today Margo is divorced and works as a solo performer in Boston, Her former husband John is a therapist at Boston State College. Brother John manages an electric plant on the Cape, while cousin Charlotte is a housewife in Boston.

August   1957   HAPPY, HAPPY BIRTHDAY BABY   Checker

THE TURBANS

Members:
    Al Banks—lead—born: July 26, 1937
    Matthew Platt—tenor
    Charlie Williams—baritone
    Andrew Jones—bass
Hometown: Philadelphia, Pennsylvania

The fellows got together in the mid-fifties in the Philadelphia area and began playing at local functions. In early 1955, they were discovered by Herman Gillespie. He took them to Al Silver, the president of Herald records, and they were awarded a recording contract.

In July 1955, they recorded a song bass singer Andrew Jones had written called "When You Dance," which became their first and biggest hit.

THE TURBANS
Left to right: Charlie Williams, Andrew Jones,
Matthew Platt, Al Banks

Today Al still lives in Philadelphia but now sings with the Original
Drifters, consisting of Charlie Thomas, Doc Green, and Berry Hobbs. The
other members of the Turbans still live in Philly also, but no longer sing
together.

July	1955	WHEN YOU DANCE	Herald
February	1956	SISTER SOOKEY	Herald
May	1956	B-I-N-G-O	Herald
August	1956	IT WAS A NITE LIKE THIS	Herald
January	1957	VALLEY OF LOVE	Herald
December	1957	THE WADDA-DO	Herald

IKE & TINA TURNER

Ike Turner—born: November, 1934—hometown: Clarksdale, Mississippi
Tina Turner—born: November 25, 1941—hometown: Nashville, Tennessee

Ike taught himself to play the piano as a youngster. After high school he
formed a group called the Kings of Rhythm, who played in the Clarks-

dale area. Ike took the group on the road in 1956, settling in St. Louis where they became big local stars.

At this time a sixteen-year-old named Annie Mae Bullock came to see Ike play his wild piano at a St. Louis club. She wanted to sing with him, but Ike was not interested in her at the time. She persisted and he let her join the group. Shortly thereafter he married her.

They recorded a song called "A Fool in Love" during the summer of 1960, which became a national hit on Sue records. In the summer of 1961, they recorded their biggest hit for Sue, "It's Gonna Work Out Fine."

Ike and Tina Turner, along with their backup group, the Ikettes (who had their own hit "I'm Blue" on Atco records in 1962), became big favorites all over the country with their dynamic stage show.

Today Tina is divorced from Ike and has become a major solo rock performer.

August	1960	A FOOL IN LOVE	Sue
December	1960	I IDOLIZE YOU	Sue
July	1961	IT'S GONNA WORK OUT FINE	Sue
December	1961	POOR FOOL	Sue
March	1962	TRA LA LA LA LA	Sue
June	1962	YOU SHOULD'A TREATED ME RIGHT	Sue
May	1966	RIVER DEEP-MOUNTAIN HIGH	Philles
April	1969	I'VE BEEN LOVING YOU TOO LONG	Blue Thumb
July	1969	THE HUNTER	Blue Thumb
December	1969	BOLD SOUL SISTER	Blue Thumb
March	1970	COME TOGETHER	Minit
May	1970	I WANT TO TAKE YOU HIGHER	Liberty
January	1971	PROUD MARY	Liberty
May	1971	OOH POO PAH DOO	United Artists
February	1972	UP IN HEAH	United Artists
September	1973	NUTBUSH CITY LIMITS	United Artists
December	1974	SEXY IDA	United Artists
June	1975	BABY GET IT ON	United Artists

JOE TURNER

Born: May 18, 1911
Hometown: Kansas City, Missouri

Joe, nicknamed "The Boss of the Blues," began his career at fourteen, appearing at various local clubs in the 1920s. On Christmas Eve, 1938, he appeared at Carnegie Hall in New York, in the "Spirituals To Swing" show with Benny Goodman, Hazel Scott, Count Basie, and Billie Holliday. It was Joe's first major break.

In early 1951, Ahmet Ertegun, one of the owners of Atlantic records, heard Joe at New York's Apollo theater in Harlem. This led to a recording contract and "Chains of Love" came out later that summer. A few years later, he had "Honey Hush," and in early 1954, a solid smash with "Shake,

JOE TURNER

Rattle And Roll," which also became a hit later on for Bill Haley and the Comets.

Exactly two years later, in 1956, he recorded his biggest hit, "Corrine Corrina," which was a popular tune from the twenties. The same song also became a hit for Ray Peterson in 1960.

Joe was also known as "Big Joe" because he was 6'2" and weighed 250 lbs.

February	1950	STILL IN THE DARK	Freedom
June	1951	CHAINS OF LOVE (Van "Piano Man" Walls)	Atlantic
April	1952	SWEET SIXTEEN (Van "Piano Man" Walls)	Atlantic
September	1953	HONEY HUSH	Atlantic
January	1954	TV MAMA	Atlantic
April	1954	SHAKE, RATTLE AND ROLL	Atlantic
February	1955	FLIP FLOP AND FLY	Atlantic
August	1955	HIDE AND SEEK	Atlantic
January	1956	THE CHICKEN AND THE HAWK/	
		MORNING, NOON AND NIGHT	Atlantic
April	1956	CORRINE CORRINA	Atlantic
August	1956	ROCK A WHILE/LIPSTICK, POWDER AND PAINT	Atlantic

SAMMY TURNER

Born: June 2, 1932
Hometown: Patterson, New Jersey

Sammy started composing songs in high school. His career was interrupted by the Korean War, when he served six months as a paratrooper.

SAMMY TURNER

In 1959, he signed with Big Top records and recorded "Sweet Annie Laurie" in early 1959. Later that year, he had his biggest all-time seller with the standard "Lavender Blue," which became a hit that summer.

Today Sammy resides in New York City.

March	1959	SWEET ANNIE LAURIE	Big Top
June	1959	LAVENDER BLUE	Big Top
October	1959	ALWAYS	Big Top
February	1960	PARADISE	Big Top

TITUS TURNER

In 1960, Al Gallico, general manager of Shapiro-Bernstein Music, found a song that had been popular in the military after World War II: "Sound Off." Al liked the song and got R & B singer Titus Turner, a young man from Georgia, to do it. They recorded it late that year and released it on Philadelphia-based Jamie records. By early 1961, it had become a national hit, and Titus's biggest.

January	1961	SOUND OFF	Jamie

CONWAY TWITTY

Real Name: Harold Lloyd Jenkins
Born: September 1, 1935
Hometown: Friars Point, Mississippi

At age ten, Conway sang his first songs on station KFFA in Helena, Arkansas. When he was in his teens, his family moved to Alabama, where he formed his own band, the Phillips Country Ramblers.

While stationed with the Army in Japan, he joined a USO group called the Cimarrons. One of the members told him to contact manager Don Seat, when he returned to the United States. After his discharge he returned to Arkansas, where he was heard by Tabby West of the Ozark Jubilee, and signed to the show.

Later, he contacted Don Seat, who met Conway in Pittsburgh. It was at this time that Don decided that Harold Jenkins would not do as a professional name. They got out several road maps and saw Conway, Arkansas, and Twitty, Texas, and came up with the name Conway Twitty.

He first recorded "I Need Your Lovin' " in 1957, but it was in the fall of 1958 that Conway wrote and recorded his biggest hit. The song, "It's Only Make Believe," reached number one.

Today Conway is a very popular country and western artist recording for MCA records.

May	1957	I NEED YOUR LOVIN'	Mercury
September	1958	IT'S ONLY MAKE BELIEVE	MGM
January	1959	THE STORY OF MY LOVE	MGM
May	1959	HEY! LITTLE LUCY	MGM

CONWAY TWITTY

July	1959	MONA LISA	MGM
September	1959	DANNY BOY	MGM
January	1960	LONELY BLUE BOY	MGM
March	1960	WHAT AM I LIVING FOR	MGM
June	1960	IS A BLUE BIRD BLUE	MGM
November	1960	A WHOLE LOT OF SHAKIN' GOIN' ON	MGM
January	1961	C'EST SI BON	MGM
April	1961	THE NEXT KISS	MGM
July	1970	HELLO DARLIN'	Decca
October	1970	FIFTEEN YEARS AGO	Decca
August	1973	YOU'VE NEVER BEEN THIS FAR BEFORE	MCA
February	1975	LINDA ON MY MIND	MCA
December	1975	DON'T CRY JONI	MCA

THE TYMES

Members:
　　Donald Banks
　　Al Berry—drums
　　Norman Burnett—guitar
　　George Hilliard—piano
　　George Williams, Jr.—trumpet
Hometown: Philadelphia, Pennsylvania

THE TYMES

At summer camp in 1956, Norman and George Hilliard met and began singing together. A few months later they teamed up with Don, Al, and George Williams. They began singing at record hops and local clubs in Philadelphia.

In April 1963, they appeared in Philly on a WDAS talent show. An executive from Parkway records heard the group and signed them to the label. One month later, they recorded a song George Williams had written with Roy Straigis, "So Much In Love," which went on to become a number one national hit.

May	1963	SO MUCH IN LOVE	Parkway
August	1963	WONDERFUL! WONDERFUL!	Parkway
December	1963	SOMEWHERE	Parkway
February	1964	TO EACH HIS OWN	Parkway
November	1964	HERE SHE COMES	Parkway
October	1968	PEOPLE	Columbia
August	1974	YOU LITTLE TRUSTMAKER	RCA
December	1974	MS. GRACE	RCA
May	1976	IT'S COOL	RCA

U

PHILIP UPCHURCH COMBO

Phil Upchurch, who played bass guitar, was a studio musician before forming his own group in 1961. He wrote a song called "You Can't Sit Down" which was recorded on Texas-based Boyd records. The song was so long that it was released in two parts. In the summer of 1961, Part 2 began to get airplay and soon became a national hit. The driving instrumental became the group's only major success.

In the spring of 1963, Kal Mann, a writer for Cameo Parkway records in Philadelphia, added lyrics to the song, and the Dovells recorded it. It became one of their biggest hits. Today Phil still does studio work as a bass guitarist in Chicago.

June   1961   YOU CAN'T SIT DOWN-Part 2   Boyd

JERRY VALE

JERRY VALE

Real Name: Genaro Louis Vitaliano
Born: July 8, 1932
Hometown: Bronx, New York

Jerry's mother encouraged him to be a singer. As an elementary school student, Jerry worked as a shoeshine boy outside a barbershop. The barber directed Jerry to a pianist with whom he could practice. After high school, Jerry got a job making transformers for fluorescent lights, while he continued singing on a part-time basis.

Jerry entered a talent contest at the Club del Rio, and won a weekend engagement. He became so popular that he remained at the club for a year and a half. It was at this time that he changed his name to Jerry Vale. While working at the Enchanted Room in Yonkers, New York, Columbia artist Guy Mitchell heard Jerry. He was so impressed that he set up an audition with Mitch Miller of Columbia, which resulted in a contract. In early 1956, Jerry had his first major hit with "Innamorata."

February	1956	INNAMORATA	Columbia
June	1956	YOU DON'T KNOW ME	Columbia
October	1957	PRETEND YOU DON'T SEE HER	Columbia
October	1958	GO CHASE A MOONBEAM	Columbia
December	1964	HAVE YOU LOOKED INTO YOUR HEART	Columbia
February	1965	FOR MAMA	Columbia
May	1965	TEARS KEEP ON FALLING	Columbia
October	1966	DOMMAGE, DOMMAGE	Columbia

RITCHIE VALENS

RITCHIE VALENS

Real Name: Ritchie Valenzuela
Born: May 13, 1941
Died: February 3, 1959
Hometown: Los Angeles, California

Ritchie's recording career was launched in 1958, when he recorded "Come On, Let's Go" for Bob Keene's Del-Fi records in Los Angeles. In late 1958, he wrote a song for his high school sweetheart, Donna Ludwig. The song, "Donna," became his biggest all-time hit. Ritchie met an untimely death, along with Buddy Holly and the Big Bopper, when their plane crashed in a cornfield in Clear Lake, Iowa, on February 3, 1959. They had been traveling to Fargo, North Dakota, with a rock and roll show.

September	1958	COME ON, LET'S GO	Del-Fi
November	1958	DONNA	Del-Fi
January	1959	LA BAMBA	Del-Fi
March	1959	THAT'S MY LITTLE SUSIE	Del-Fi
July	1959	LITTLE GIRL	Del-Fi

THE VALENTINES

Members:
    Richard Barrett—lead
    Mickey Francis—first tenor
    Eddy Edgehill—second tenor
    Ray Briggs—tenor
    Ronnie Bright—bass
Hometown: New York, New York

In 1952, Carl Hogan joined a group called the Dreamers which consisted of Mickey Francis, Ray Briggs, and Ronnie Bright. They sang for a while on the streetcorners of Harlem, trying to develop their own style. A young singer from Philadelphia by the name of Richard Barrett was asked to join the group and became the group's new lead voice in 1953.

In 1954, the group decided to change their name and decided on the Valentines. It was at this time that Carl left the group. Soon after, the group signed with Old Town records and recorded "Tonight Kathleen."

In 1955, they signed with Rama records and recorded their first major hit, "Lilly MaeBelle." Ray Briggs was replaced by a young singer named David Clowney who had just left a Detroit group called the Pearls. David would go on to become a star a few years later under the name of Dave "Baby" Cortez with the "Happy Organ."

Carl Hogan returned to the group in 1957, replacing Eddy Edgehill, and they recorded their last hit for Rama, "Don't Say Goodnight." The group finally broke up in 1958.

February	1955	LILY MAEBELLE	Rama
March	1955	WOO WOO TRAIN	Rama
June	1957	DON'T SAY GOODNIGHT	Rama

MARK VALENTINO

Real Name: Anthony Busillo
Born: March 12, 1942
Hometown: Philadelphia, Pennsylvania

Mark sang with a group in high school, but went out on his own in 1962 and signed with Bob Marcucci (Frankie Avalon's old manager) and Swan records. In October 1962, he had his only hit with the label, "The Push and Kick."

October	1962	THE PUSH AND KICK	Swan

THE VALENTINOS

When Sam Cooke started his Sar records he asked the Womack Brothers of Cleveland, a group with a gospel sound, to record for him. He renamed them the Valentinos. Their only popular record was "Lookin' for a Love" in 1962. Two years later the group disbanded.

Today, Bobby Womack is a top solo artist. His brother Cecil is married to singing star Mary Wells. The other three Womack brothers reside in Cleveland and occasionally sing locally.

July   1962   LOOKIN' FOR A LOVE   Sar

THE VALIANTS

In 1957, lead singer Billy Storm and three of his friends formed a group called the Valiants and began appearing in the Los Angeles area. They sought out Bumps Blackwell of Keen records (Bumps arranged many of Little Richard's hits on Specialty and at the time was managing and representing a new artist on his Keen records named Sam Cooke) and auditioned for him. Bumps liked their sound—especially Billy's unique high voice. He decided to record them and had them cut a song they had written called "This Is The Night." The ballad became a national hit. Shortly afterwards, the group disbanded.

November 1957   THIS IS THE NIGHT   Keen

VALJEAN

"Ben Casey," starring Vince Edwards, was a very popular doctor show during the early sixties. Arranger-conductor Valjean managed a top-forty record by recording the show's theme in the spring of 1962.

April   1962   THEME FROM BEN CASEY   Carlton

FRANKIE VALLI

Real Name: Frank Castelluccio
Born: May 3, 1937
Hometown: Newark, New Jersey

Frankie began his career with the Four Lovers in the mid-fifties and went on to become immensely successful as the lead voice of the Four Seasons (see Seasons biography). The record company wanted to capitalize on his unique voice by having him record as a solo performer as well. This would enable them to have two hit records on the charts at the same time. Thus, in the early summer of 1967, Frankie recorded "Can't Take

My Eyes Off You," which became a top-ten hit for him as a soloist. At the same time "C'mon Marianne" was in the top ten for the Four Seasons. In fact, "Can't Take My Eyes Off You" went as high as number two on the national charts and nearly succeeded in displacing "Groovin'" by the Young Rascals and "Windy" by the Association for the number one spot.

Frankie still records and performs with The Four Seasons, where he is the only remaining member of the original group.

January	1966	YOU'RE GONNA HURT YOURSELF	Smash
October	1966	THE PROUD ONE	Philips
May	1967	CAN'T TAKE MY EYES OFF YOU	Philips
August	1967	I MAKE A FOOL OF MYSELF	Philips
December	1967	TO GIVE (THE REASON I LIVE)	Philips
November	1974	MY EYES ADORED YOU	Private Stock
May	1975	SWEARIN' TO GOD	Private Stock
October	1975	OUR DAY WILL COME	Private Stock
April	1976	FALLIN' ANGEL	Private Stock
August	1976	WE'RE ALL ALONE	Private Stock
October	1976	BOOMERANG	Private Stock
May	1978	GREASE	RSO
January	1979	FANCY DANCER	Warner/Curb
July	1980	WHERE DID WE GO WRONG	MCA/Curb

JUNE VALLI

Born: June 30, 1930
Hometown: Bronx, New York

June's first chance to sing professionally came when her mother could not perform at a wedding and so asked June to take her place. One of the guests at the wedding was so impressed with her voice that he made arrangements for her to appear on Arthur Godfrey's "Talent Scouts" program. She went on the show and won first prize.

In 1953, she was signed to RCA Victor where in the summer of that year, she had her biggest hit with the ballad "Crying in the Chapel," which became a top-ten national hit. In 1954, she married Chicago disc jockey Howard Miller.

July	1953	CRYING IN THE CHAPEL	RCA Victor
May	1954	I UNDERSTAND	RCA Victor
April	1955	UNCHAINED MELODY	RCA Victor
November	1958	THE WEDDING	Mercury
March	1960	APPLE GREEN	Mercury

LEROY VAN DYKE

Born: October 4, 1929
Hometown: Spring Fork, Mississippi

Leroy started singing and playing the guitar in the Army while stationed in Korea. After two years in the service, he was discharged and began a career as a livestock auctioneer, which gave him the idea for a song called "The Auctioneer," which he recorded in late 1956. The song was sold to Dot records and became a national hit. It was his only major one for Dot.

In late 1961, he recorded his biggest hit for Mercury records, "Walk On By."

October	1956	AUCTIONEER	Dot
October	1961	WALK ON BY	Mercury
February	1962	IF A WOMAN ANSWERS	Mercury

SARAH VAUGHAN

Born. March 27, 1924
Hometown: Newark, New Jersey

Sarah began her career singing in a church choir and later entered a talent show in the early forties at the Apollo Theatre in Harlem, where she won first prize. Consequently, Earl "Fatha" Hines hired her to sing with his band along with another new vocalist named Billy Eckstine. When Billy left Hines's band to form his own, he took Sarah with him. She worked with Billy for a while, then decided to go out as a solo performer.

By the late forties her reputation as a singer had begun to spread, and she was being booked into many of the top clubs in the country. She did some recordings for Musicraft and Columbia and had several chart records. It wasn't until she went to Mercury in 1954, however, that she got the big pop hits, beginning with her great ballad "Make Yourself Comfortable" in late 1954.

Her biggest hit on Mercury came in the summer of 1959, a song called "Broken-Hearted Melody," the lyrics of which were written by a then-unknown lyricist named Hal David, who later would become part of the Bacharach and David songwriting team.

August	1948	IT'S MAGIC	Musicraft
June	1951	THESE THINGS I OFFER YOU	Columbia
November	1954	MAKE YOURSELF COMFORTABLE	Mercury
February	1955	HOW IMPORTANT CAN IT BE?	Mercury
March	1955	WHATEVER LOLA WANTS	Mercury
November	1955	C'EST LA VIE	Mercury
January	1956	MR. WONDERFUL	Mercury
June	1956	FABULOUS CHARACTER	Mercury
September	1956	IT HAPPENED AGAIN	Mercury
December	1956	THE BANANA BOAT SONG	Mercury
July	1957	PASSING STRANGERS (& BILLY ECKSTINE)	Mercury
July	1959	BROKEN-HEARTED MELODY	Mercury

SARAH VAUGHAN

November	1959	SMOOTH OPERATOR	Mercury
February	1960	ETERNALLY	Mercury
April	1966	**A LOVER'S CONCERTO**	Mercury

BILLY VAUGHN

Born: April 12, 1931
Hometown: Glasgow, Kentucky

Billy, a one-time member of the singing group the Hilltoppers (of "Til Then" and "P.S. I Love You" fame), left the group in the mid-fifties to become the head of A & R at Dot records, where he has remained.

December	1954	MELODY OF LOVE	Dot
August	1955	THE SHIFTING WHISPERING SANDS	Dot
January	1956	**A THEME FROM THE THREE PENNY OPERA**	Dot
August	1956	WHEN THE WHITE LILACS BLOOM AGAIN	Dot

December	1956	PETTICOATS OF PORTUGAL	Dot
March	1957	THE SHIP THAT NEVER SAILED	Dot
November	1957	RAUNCHY	Dot
November	1957	SAIL ALONG SILVERY MOON	Dot
March	1958	TUMBLING TUMBLEWEEDS	Dot
June	1958	SINGING HILLS	Dot
July	1958	LA PALOMA	Dot
October	1958	CIMARRON	Dot
January	1959	BLUE HAWAII	Dot
May	1959	YOUR CHEATIN' HEART	Dot
June	1960	LOOK FOR A STAR	Dot
October	1960	THE SUNDOWNERS	Dot
February	1961	WHEELS	Dot
June	1961	BLUE TOMORROW	Dot
September	1961	BERLIN MELODY	Dot
March	1962	CHAPEL BY THE SEA	Dot
July	1962	A SWINGIN' SAFARI	Dot
January	1966	MICHELLE	Dot

BOBBY VEE

Real Name: Robert Thomas Velline
Born: April 30, 1943
Hometown: Fargo, North Dakota

Bobby came from a musical family. His father Sidney played the violin and piano, his uncle played sax, and his two older brothers, Bill and Sidney, Jr., both played guitar. Bobby learned to play the guitar in high school. He played for a while in a group called the Shadows with his brother Bill and friends Jim Stillman and Bob Korum.

On February 3, 1959, when Buddy Holly, the Big Bopper, and Ritchie Valens were killed in a plane crash, the Shadows were asked to fill in on the scheduled show in Fargo, North Dakota. Bobby was asked to sing with the group because he knew the lyrics of six of Buddy Holly's songs. The audience loved his performance so much that an executive from Liberty records contacted Bobby to sign with the label. Later that year, he had his first release on the label, "Suzy Baby."

His first major hit was a song the Clovers had made popular in 1956, called "Devil Or Angel" which became a hit for Bobby during the summer of 1960. In July of 1961, he recorded his only number one national hit with the Carole King and Gerry Goffin tune "Take Good Care Of My Baby."

September	1959	SUZY BABY	Liberty
March	1960	WHAT DO YOU WANT	Liberty
July	1960	DEVIL OR ANGEL	Liberty
November	1960	RUBBER BALL	Liberty

BOBBY VEE

February	1961	STAYIN' IN	Liberty
May	1961	HOW MANY TEARS	Liberty
July	1961	TAKE GOOD CARE OF MY BABY	Liberty
November	1961	RUN TO HIM	Liberty
February	1962	PLEASE DON'T ASK ABOUT BARBARA	Liberty
May	1962	SHARING YOU	Liberty
September	1962	PUNISH HER	Liberty
November	1962	THE NIGHT HAS A THOUSAND EYES	Liberty
March	1963	CHARMS	Liberty
June	1962	BE TRUE TO YOURSELF	Liberty
October	1963	YESTERDAY AND YOU	Liberty
January	1964	STRANGER IN YOUR ARMS	Liberty
February	1964	I'LL MAKE YOU MINE	Liberty
May	1964	HICKORY, DICK AND DOC	Liberty
December	1964	EV'RY LITTLE BIT HURTS	Liberty
May	1965	KEEP ON TRYING	Liberty
June	1966	LOOK AT ME GIRL	Liberty
July	1967	COME BACK WHEN YOU GROW UP	Liberty
November	1967	BEAUTIFUL PEOPLE	Liberty
February	1968	MAYBE JUST TODAY	Liberty
April	1968	MEDLEY: MY GIRL, HEY GIRL	Liberty
August	1968	DO WHAT YOU GOTTA DO	Liberty
December	1968	SOMEONE TO LOVE ME	Liberty
August	1969	LET'S CALL IT A DAY GIRL	Liberty
November	1970	SWEET SWEETHEART	Liberty

THE VELOURS

Members:
  Jerome Ramos—lead
  John Cheetum
  Don Haywood
  John Pearson
  Charles Moffett—bass
Hometown: Brooklyn, New York

The group was first formed in Brooklyn, in 1956, and sang on neighborhood corners. In the summer of 1957, they recorded their biggest hit, for Onyx records, "Can I Come Over Tonight."

June   1957   CAN I COME OVER TONIGHT   Onyx

THE VELVETS

Members:
  Virgil Johnson—lead—December 29, 1935
  Clarence Rigsby—tenor lead—1947
  Robert Thursby—first tenor—1947
  William Solomon—baritone—1947
  Mark Prince—bass—1947
Hometown: Odessa, Texas

In 1960, while Virgil was an eighth-grade English teacher at Blackshear Junior High in Odessa, he began writing songs and doing some singing. He formed a group with Clarence, Robert, William, and Mark, who were students of his in his English class. They did some singing around the area and eventually came to the attention of singing star Roy Orbison, from Wink, Texas, a short distance from Odessa. Roy, who was recording for Monument records, liked Virgil's group and asked them if they would like to record. He then set up a recording date with Monument records in Nashville, Tennessee, where the group flew to record in early 1961.

When they got there, the people from Monument changed the group's name to the Velvets and had them record several songs, the first of which was "That Lucky Old Sun." At the same session they recorded a song Virgil had written called "Tonight (Could Be the Night)," which became a big hit in May 1961. The group was not able to travel around promoting the record, so, their recording career was short-lived.

Today, Virgil lives in Lubbock, Texas. He teaches and coaches at Struggs Junior High. The rest of the fellows live in Odessa.

May   1961   TONIGHT (COULD BE THE NIGHT)   Monument

THE VENTURES

Members:

Nokie Edwards—lead guitar—May 9, 1939
Don Wilson—guitar—February 10, 1937
Bob Bogle—guitar—January 16, 1937
Howie Johnson—drums—1938—replaced by Jowe Barili—replaced
    by Mel Taylor

Hometown: Tacoma, Washington

Don and Bob started taking guitar lessons in 1959, and began playing around the area shortly thereafter.

In early 1960, they added Nokie and Howie and recorded a song called "Walk Don't Run" on a home recorder and took it to Bob Reisdorff, the manager of The Fleetwoods. Bob did not like the song, at the time, so he turned the fellows down. The fellows decided to go into a professional studio and record the song themselves. They recorded the song, then they changed their name from The Versatones to The Ventures (because they were beginning a new "venture") and took the song to their good friend Pat O'Day of KJR radio in Seattle, who began playing the song after each newscast. Bob Reisdorff heard the song on the air, called Pat to find out who the group was, and to his surprise, it was The Ventures.

Bob then signed them to Dolton records and by June of 1960, the song became a national hit.

Today Nokie, Don, Bob and new member Mel are busier than ever playing Europe and Japan, while also playing the New Wave club circuit in the U.S.

June	1960	WALK DON'T RUN	Dolton
October	1960	PERFIDIA	Dolton
January	1961	RAM-BUNK-SHUSH	Dolton
April	1961	LULLABY OF THE LEAVES	Dolton
September	1961	THEME FROM SILVER CITY	Dolton
October	1961	BLUE MOON	Dolton
July	1962	LOLITA YA-YA	Dolton
July	1964	WALK-DON'T RUN '64	Dolton
October	1964	SLAUGHTER ON TENTH AVENUE	Dolton
February	1966	SECRET AGENT MAN	Dolton
March	1969	HAWAII FIVE-O	Liberty
June	1969	THEME FROM A SUMMER PLACE	Liberty

LARRY VERNE

Born: February 8, 1936
Hometown: Minneapolis, Minnesota

Larry originally played the piano as a youngster, but later switched to the guitar. In August 1960, he recorded a novelty song about Custer's last

THE VIBRATIONS

stand, which Al DeLory and Fred Darian had written, called "Mr. Custer." It became a number one song on Era records.

August	1960	MR. CUSTER	Era
December	1960	MR. LIVINGSTON	Era

THE VIBRATIONS

Members:
    James Johnson—lead—1940
    Richard Owens—first tenor—1940
    Carl Fisher—second tenor—1940
    Dave Govan—baritone—1940
    Don Bradley—bass—1937
Hometown: Los Angeles, California

The fellows first got together in Los Angeles, in 1956, and called themselves the Jayhawks. They had a national hit on Flash records in the summer of 1956, with "Stranded In The Jungle."

A few years later they changed their name to the Vibrations when they signed with Bet records. Shortly thereafter they joined Checker records and had their biggest hit with the label in the spring of 1961, with "The Watusi." It was at this time that they decided to do a little moonlighting and recorded a song called "Peanut Butter" as the Marathons for Arvee records during the summer of 1961. When Checker found out, there was a lawsuit which resulted in Checker's obtaining the recording, which they released on their subsidiary label Argo records.

February	1961	THE WATUSI	Checker
March	1964	MY GIRL SLOOPY	Atlantic
October	1965	MISTY	Okeh

THE VILLAGE STOMPERS

Members:
Frank Hubbell
Joe Muranyi
Dick Brady
Don Coates
Mitchell May
Al McManus
Ralph Casale
Lenny Pogan

THE VILLAGE STOMPERS

Their easy-swinging Dixieland sound caught on while they were playing together in Greenwich Village, in New York City, in 1963, at places like Basin Street East. They recorded a song in August 1963 called "Washington Square." The song was sold to Epic records and became a national hit that year.

September 1963	WASHINGTON SQUARE	Epic
April 1964	FROM RUSSIA WITH LOVE	Epic

GENE VINCENT

Real Name: Vincent Eugene Craddock
Born: February 11, 1935
Died: October 12, 1971
Hometown: Norfolk, Virginia

THE BLUE CAPS

> Gene Vincent—lead vocal and guitar
> Galloping Cliff Gallup—lead guitar
> Wee Willie Williams—rhythm guitar
> Jumpin' Jack Neal—bass
> Be-Bop Harrell—drums

Gene began singing in church as a youngster and later learned to play the guitar. While stationed in Korea with the Navy, he badly injured his left leg. The injury was so severe that the doctors wanted to amputate the leg, but Gene chose to live with the pain and a limp for the rest of his life.

After the Navy, he returned to Norfolk, where he formed his own singing group. He called them the Blue Caps (they actually wore blue caps) after the hat that the then President Eisenhower always wore on the golf course. The group played in the Norfolk area until Gene heard of a talent contest that Capital records was conducting on the West Coast to find an Elvis-type singer.

In April 1956 he went to Los Angeles, with a song he and his friend Sheriff Tex Davis had written called "Be-Bop-a-Lula" (inspired by the comic strip character Little Lulu) and won first prize in the talent contest. He received a recording contract with Capitol and his group went on to cut the record, which became a top-ten national hit and million seller during the summer of 1956.

From 1960 until 1967 Gene lived in London, England, attempting a comeback. Times were tough for him in the late sixties and resulted in acute depression which led to bleeding ulcers. He died on October 12, 1971, in Newhall, California.

**GENE VINCENT AND
HIS BLUE CAPS**

Clockwise from top:
Jumpin' Jack Neal,
Be-Bop Harrell, Gene
Vincent, Wee Willie
Williams, Galloping
Cliff Gallup

May	1956	BE-BOP-A-LULA	Capitol
October	1956	RACE WITH THE DEVIL	Capitol
July	1957	LOTTA LOVIN'	Capitol
November	1957	DANCE TO THE BOP	Capitol

BOBBY VINTON

Real Name: Stanley Bobby Vinton
Born: April 16, 1941
Hometown: Canonsburg, Pennsylvania

As a youngster, Bobby played the clarinet and became interested in the "Big Band" sound of artists like Les Brown and Stan Kenton. His father had his own band in the Pittsburgh area, and also greatly influenced Bobby. He formed his own band while in high school in the late fifties, and began to play at nearby Duquesne University.

In 1960, Bobby signed with Epic and recorded two albums of band

BOBBY VINTON

music called "Dancing at the Hop" and "Bobby Vinton Plays for Li'l Dar-lin's." Neither album did very well. Epic was about to drop Bobby from the label when he noticed that his contract called for two more songs. He told Epic that he wanted to try singing them. At first they were reluctant, but they were finally persuaded to let him do the songs. At the session Bobby recorded "Mr. Lonely" and "Roses Are Red." Epic released "Roses Are Red" in May 1962, and it went on to become a number one national hit. Other hits followed, and Bobby decided to leave the band and go out on his own as a solo artist.

He had several other number one songs, like "Blue Velvet," "There! I've Said It Again," and finally "Mr. Lonely" (Bobby's favorite recording). He described his sound as "sentimental and sincere"; his love songs were much welcomed during the heavy rock of the early sixties.

Bobby moved to Los Angeles in 1971 with his wife and four children.

He established Polish pride with his big hit "My Melody Of Love" in 1974, and was crowned "The Polish Prince" by his fans.

May	1962	ROSES ARE RED	Epic
August	1962	RAIN RAIN GO AWAY	Epic
December	1962	LET'S KISS AND MAKE UP	Epic
December	1962	TROUBLE IS MY MIDDLE NAME	Epic
February	1963	OVER THE MOUNTAIN (ACROSS THE SEA)	Epic
May	1963	BLUE ON BLUE	Epic
July	1963	BLUE VELVET	Epic
November	1963	THERE! I'VE SAID IT AGAIN	Epic
February	1964	MY HEART BELONGS TO ONLY YOU	Epic
May	1964	TELL MY WHY	Epic
July	1964	CLINGING VINE	Epic
October	1964	MR. LONELY	Epic
March	1965	LONG LONELY NIGHTS	Epic

May	1965	L-O-N-E-L-Y	Epic
June	1965	THEME FROM "HARLOW"	Epic
September	1965	WHAT COLOR IS A MAN	Epic
December	1965	SATIN PILLOWS	Epic
February	1966	TEARS	Epic
April	1966	DUM-DE-DA	Epic
October	1966	COMING HOME SOLDIER	Epic
March	1967	FOR HE'S A JOLLY GOOD FELLOW	Epic
September	1967	PLEASE LOVE ME FOREVER	Epic
December	1967	JUST AS MUCH AS EVER	Epic
March	1968	TAKE GOOD CARE OF MY BABY	Epic
July	1968	HALFWAY TO PARADISE	Epic
November	1968	I LOVE HOW YOU LOVE ME	Epic
March	1969	TO KNOW YOU IS TO LOVE YOU	Epic
June	1969	THE DAYS OF SAND AND SHOVELS	Epic
February	1970	MY ELUSIVE DREAMS	Epic
July	1970	NO ARMS CAN EVER HOLD YOU	Epic
January	1972	EVERY DAY OF MY LIFE	Epic
June	1972	SEALED WITH A KISS	Epic
December	1972	BUT I DO	Epic
September	1974	MY MELODY OF LOVE	ABC
March	1975	BEER BARREL POLKA	ABC
June	1975	WOODEN HEART	ABC
May	1976	MOONLIGHT SERENADE	ABC
May	1976	SAVE YOUR KISSES FOR ME	ABC
June	1977	ONLY LOVE CAN BREAK A HEART	ABC
January	1980	MAKE BELIEVE IT'S YOUR FIRST TIME	Tapestry

THE VIRTUES

Members:
    Frank Virtue—lead guitar—born: January 29, 1933
    Jimmy Bruno—guitar
    Ralph Frederico—piano
    Barry Smith—drums
Hometown: Philadelphia, Pennsylvania

Frank formed the group around 1947, and they began playing in the Philadelphia area as the Virtues, named after their leader. They started making many radio appearances, and by the mid-fifties began getting on TV as well.

In late 1958, they began playing a song one of Frank's old Navy buddies, Arthur Smith, had written, called "Guitar Boogie." They changed the song somewhat and recorded it as "Guitar Boogie Shuffle." Dick Clark heard the song being played locally in Philadelphia and got Hunt records to buy it. By early 1959, the song became a top-ten national hit.

Today, Frank resides in Philadelphia, and is the proprietor of Virtue Recording Studios. The other fellows work as musicians in the area.

February	1959	GUITAR BOOGIE SHUFFLE	Hunt

THE VISCOUNTS

Members:
Bobby Spievak—lead guitar
Joe Spievak—bass guitar
Harry Haller—sax
Larry Vecchio—organ
Clark Smith—drums
Homestate: New Jersey

Bobby and his brother Joe formed the group with some friends to sing in the New Jersey area. In late 1959, they recorded the instrumental "Harlem Nocturne," which they took to New York and offered to Madison records, which released the song in early 1960. It became their first national hit.

January	1960	HARLEM NOCTURNE	Madison
July	1960	NIGHT TRAIN	Madison
November	1960	WABASH BLUES	Madison
October	1965	HARLEM NOCTURNE	Amy

VITO AND THE SALUTATIONS

Members:
Vito Balsamo—lead and baritone—April 28, 1946
Randy Silverman—lead and first tenor—August 24, 1945
Shelly Buchansky—first and second tenor—April 17, 1942
Frankie Fox—baritone—replaced by Frank Hidalgo—September 15, 1945
Lenny Citrin—bass—February 19, 1942
Hometown: Brooklyn, New York

The group was formed around 1961, while the guys were in high school. While they were singing together one night record producer Dave Rick heard the group and offered to manage them. They agreed, and Dave got them a contract with Rayna records.

They came up with the name of the group after listening to New York disc jockey "Jocko" Henderson begin his show with the line "Greetings and Salutations," which they adapted to Vito and the Salutations.

In early 1962, they recorded a popular New York song called "Gloria," which had been a hit for many groups including the Cadillacs and the Passions. It became the group's first big hit. Although the song was only an East Coast hit, it got the group started.

After a few more releases for Rayna, the group left and eventually signed with Herald records.

In late 1963, they recorded the popular ballad "Unchained Melody." The group decided to use a new arrangement featuring their high falsetto tenors and unique bass sound. The song became a national hit and established the sound of Vito and the Salutations.

Today the group still performs around the New York area.

February	1962	GLORIA	Rayna
October	1963	UNCHAINED MELODY	Herald

VITO AND THE SALUTATIONS

THE VOLUMES

Members:
    Ed Union—lead
    Elijah Davis—first tenor
    Larry Wright—second tenor
    Joe Travillion—baritone
    Ernest Newsom—bass
Hometown: Detroit, Michigan

Joe, Elijah, Ernest, and Ed all went to Central High in Detroit, while Larry had attended Chadsey High. In late 1961, while the group was appearing across the river in Windsor, Canada, Willie Ewing happened to hear them sing. He signed them to a recording contract and began to manage them.

Willie and bass singer Ernest collaborated on a song called "I Love You," which the group recorded in early 1962. Willie sold the song to Chex Records, and by spring of that year, it was a national hit.

Today the fellows still live in the Detroit area and do sing occasionally. Willie has become a minister in Detroit.

| April | 1962 | I LOVE YOU | Chex |

THE VOXPOPPERS

In the mid-fifties Mercury records was very successful with singing groups like the Gaylords, the Platters, the Diamonds and the Crew Cuts were able to sell millions of records with their primarily ballad sound. In 1958, they signed a group called the Voxpoppers, which had one major hit that year, the ballad "Wishing for Your Love." Unfortunately, it proved to be the group's only popular recording.

| March | 1958 | WISHING FOR YOUR LOVE | Mercury |

ADAM WADE

ADAM WADE

Born: March 17, 1937
Hometown: Pittsburgh, Pennsylvania

Adam worked at one time with Dr. Jonas Salk on the polio research team. He wanted to pursue a recording career and signed with Coed records in late 1959. At that time he did his first song, "Tell Her For Me." In early 1960, he had his first major hit with "Ruby," which had a Johnny Mathis–type sound.

January	1960	TELL HER FOR ME	Coed
March	1960	RUBY	Coed
June	1960	I CAN'T HELP IT	Coed
November	1960	GLORIA'S THEME	Coed
February	1961	TAKE GOOD CARE OF HER	Coed
May	1961	THE WRITING ON THE WALL	Coed
July	1961	AS IF I DIDN'T KNOW	Coed
September	1961	TONIGHT I WON'T BE THERE	Coed

THE WAILERS

Members:
  John Greek—lead guitar
  Richard Dangel—guitar
  Mark Marush—sax
  Mike Burk—drums
  Kent Morrill—piano
Hometown: Tacoma, Washington

The group met at a jam session and began practicing together. They made their first public appearance in October 1958, at a high school dance.

In 1959, they signed with Golden Crest records and in April of that year recorded an instrumental called "Tall Cool One," which went on to become a national hit.

May	1959	TALL COOL ONE	Golden Crest
August	1959	MAU-MAU	Golden Crest

JERRY WALLACE

Born: December 15, 1938
Hometown: Kansas City, Missouri

Jerry's mother was a former torch singer. His father ran a grocery business. Jerry got a guitar on his fourteenth birthday and began singing.

In 1958, he signed with Challenge records and in the summer of that year had his first hit for the label, "How the Time Flies." His biggest hit for the label came the following summer when he recorded "Primrose Lane."

Today Jerry records for MCA records.

August	1958	HOW THE TIME FLIES	Challenge
November	1958	DIAMOND RING	Challenge
August	1959	PRIMROSE LANE	Challenge
January	1960	LITTLE COCO PALM	Challenge
January	1961	THERE SHE GOES	Challenge
May	1961	LIFE'S A HOLIDAY	Challenge
October	1962	SHUTTERS AND BOARDS	Challenge
July	1964	IN THE MISTY MOONLIGHT	Challenge
August	1964	IT'S A COTTON CANDY WORLD	Mercury
March	1972	TO GET TO YOU	Decca
August	1972	IF YOU LEAVE ME TONIGHT I'LL CRY	Decca

BILLY WARD AND THE DOMINOES

Though Billy Ward's name was used in the billing of the group, he sang lead with them only a couple of times. He was a piano player and arranger who formed the Dominoes in 1950 and found lead singers like Clyde McPhatter and Jackie Wilson to sing with the group. (See Dominoes biography.)

When Clyde left the group in 1953, Jackie replaced him as lead until 1957. He then left to go on as a solo performer.

After having R & B hits for Federal, King, Jubilee, and Decca

JERRY WALLACE

records, in 1957 the group switched to Liberty, where they had a big pop hit that summer with the Hoagy Carmichael classic "Stardust."

December	1952	I'D BE SATISFIED	Federal
January	1953	THE BELLS	Federal
May	1953	THESE FOOLISH THINGS REMIND ME OF YOU	Federal
November	1953	RAGS TO RICHES	King
July	1956	ST. THERESE OF THE ROSES	Decca
June	1957	STAR DUST	Liberty
September	1957	DEEP PURPLE	Liberty

ROBIN WARD

Real Name: Jackie Ward
Homestate: Nebraska

After singing as a youngster in Nebraska, Jackie moved to Los Angeles, where she eventually got married and began to raise a family. In 1963, she changed her name to Robin (after one of her daughters) and recorded a song that she'd found, written by Perry Botkin, Jr., and Gil Garfield, called "Wonderful Summer." The recording was sold to Dot records, and it became a national hit by the fall of 1963.

Today Robin still lives in Los Angeles and does a lot of commercials for radio and TV.

October	1963	WONDERFUL SUMMER	Dot

DIONNE WARWICK

Born: December 12, 1940
Hometown: East Orange, New Jersey

Dionne started singing at the age of six in church choirs and with local gospel groups. In the early sixties, she was singing demo records in New York. At this time a young, unknown songwriter named Burt Bacharach heard her sing and was captivated by her voice. He took her to see a good friend of his, Florence Greenberg, the president of Scepter records, and Florence signed Dionne to a contract.

In late 1962, Dionne recorded a song Burt had written with lyricist Hal David, called "Don't Make Me Over," which was to launch the Bacharach sound and a very successful relationship for the three of them for many years to come.

A few years ago, she added the letter "e" to her last name for luck. After hosting the syndicated music show "Solid Gold" for a year, Dionne is now back to her recording career.

December	1962	DON'T MAKE ME OVER	Scepter
March	1963	THIS EMPTY PLACE	Scepter
July	1963	MAKE THE MUSIC PLAY	Scepter
December	1963	ANYONE WHO HAD A HEART	Scepter
April	1964	WALK ON BY	Scepter
July	1964	A HOUSE IS NOT A HOME	Scepter
July	1964	YOU'LL NEVER GET TO HEAVEN	Scepter
October	1964	REACH OUT FOR ME	Scepter
February	1965	WHO CAN I TURN TO	Scepter
March	1965	YOU CAN HAVE HIM	Scepter
July	1965	HERE I AM	Scepter
October	1965	LOOKING WITH MY EYES	Scepter
December	1965	ARE YOU THERE	Scepter
April	1966	MESSAGE TO MICHAEL	Scepter
June	1966	TRAINS AND BOATS AND PLANES	Scepter
October	1965	I JUST DON'T KNOW WHAT TO DO WITH MYSELF	Scepter
December	1966	ANOTHER NIGHT	Scepter
April	1967	ALFIE	Scepter
July	1967	THE WINDOWS OF THE WORLD	Scepter
October	1967	I SAY A LITTLE PRAYER	Scepter
January	1968	(THEME FROM) VALLEY OF THE DOLLS	Scepter
April	1968	DO YOU KNOW THE WAY TO SAN JOSE	Scepter
August	1968	WHO IS GONNA LOVE ME	Scepter
August	1968	ALWAYS SOMETHING THERE TO REMIND ME	Scepter
October	1968	PROMISES, PROMISES	Scepter
February	1969	THIS GIRL'S IN LOVE WITH YOU	Scepter
October	1969	THE APRIL FOOLS	Scepter
October	1969	YOU'VE LOST THAT LOVIN' FEELING	Scepter
January	1970	I'LL NEVER FALL IN LOVE AGAIN	Scepter
May	1970	LET ME GO TO HIM	Scepter
October	1970	MAKE IT EASY ON YOURSELF	Scepter
April	1971	WHO GETS THE GUY	Scepter

BABY WASHINGTON

August	1971	AMANDA	Scepter
March	1972	IF WE ONLY HAVE LOVE	Scepter
November	1974	THEN CAME YOU (with Spinners)	Atlantic
January	1976	ONCE YOU HIT THE ROAD	Warner Bros.
June	1979	I'LL NEVER LOVE THIS WAY AGAIN	Arista
November	1979	DEJA VU	Arista
March	1980	AFTER YOU	Arista
July	1980	NO NIGHT SO LONG	Arista
November	1980	EASY LOVE	Arista
June	1981	SOME CHANGES ARE FOR GOOD	Arista

BABY WASHINGTON

Baby sang in the mid-fifties with a group called the Hearts, who recorded for Baton. For a few years after that, she sang on the Hearts' manager Zell Sanders's new label J & S as a solo performer.

After a lot of local exposure in New York, and some regional hits, she signed with New Jersey–based Neptune records and recorded "The Time," which became a top hit on the R & B charts in early 1959. In 1963, she went to Sue records and had her first major hit on the pop charts with "That's How Heartaches Are Made."

January	1959	THE TIME	Neptune
June	1959	THE BELLS	Neptune
April	1961	NOBODY CARES	Neptune
March	1963	THAT'S HOW HEARTACHES ARE MADE	Sue
July	1963	LEAVE ME ALONE	Sue
March	1964	I CAN'T WAIT UNTIL I SEE MY BABY	Sue
July	1965	ONLY THOSE IN LOVE	Sue

DINAH WASHINGTON

Real Name: Ruth Jones
Born: August 29, 1924
Died: December 14, 1963
Hometown: Chicago, Illinois

Born in Tuscaloosa, Alabama, Dinah began singing the blues as a youngster. When her family moved to Chicago, in the mid-thirties, she began

DINAH WASHINGTON

playing the piano in a Baptist church. By age fifteen, she won an amateur contest and got to play in many Chicago clubs.

In 1942, she changed her name to Dinah Washington and met Joe Glaser, who got her a job with Lionel Hampton's band until 1946. At that point she began a career as a solo jazz singer.

In early 1959, while recording for Mercury, she had her biggest pop hit when she recorded "What A Difference A Day Makes." For the next couple of years, she had many big hits for Mercury, including several with Brook Benton in 1960. In July of 1963, she married Detroit Lions' football star Dick "Night Train" Lane, which was Dinah's seventh marriage.

On December 14, 1963, she was found dead in her Detroit home from an accidental overdose of sleeping pills.

July	1949	BABY, GET LOST	Mercury
August	1949	LONG JOHN BLUES	Mercury
November	1949	GOOD DADDY BLUES	Mercury
March	1950	I ONLY KNOW	Mercury
March	1950	IT ISN'T FAIR	Mercury
June	1950	I WANNA BE LOVED	Mercury
September	1950	I'LL NEVER BE FREE	Mercury
May	1951	I WON'T CRY ANYMORE	Mercury
November	1951	COLD, COLD HEART	Mercury
February	1952	WHEEL OF FORTUNE	Mercury
March	1952	TROUBLE IN MIND	Mercury
October	1953	TV IS THE THING (THIS YEAR)	Mercury

October	1954	I DON'T HURT ANYMORE	Mercury
December	1954	TEACH ME TONIGHT	Mercury
January	1955	THAT'S ALL I WANT FROM YOU	Mercury
May	1955	IF IT'S THE LAST THING I DO/I DIDDIE	Mercury
October	1955	I CONCENTRATE ON YOU	Mercury
October	1955	I'M LOST WITHOUT YOU TONIGHT/	
		YOU MIGHT HAVE TOLD ME	Mercury
September	1956	SOFT WINDS	Mercury
December	1958	MAKE ME A PRESENT OF YOU	Mercury
May	1959	WHAT A DIFF'RENCE A DAY MAKES	Mercury
October	1959	UNFORGETTABLE	Mercury
April	1960	IT COULD HAPPEN TO YOU	Mercury
June	1960	THIS BITTER EARTH	Mercury
October	1960	LOVE WALKED IN	Mercury
January	1961	WE HAVE LOVE	Mercury
April	1961	OUR LOVE IS HERE TO STAY	Mercury
October	1961	SEPTEMBER IN THE RAIN	Mercury
January	1962	TEARS AND LAUGHTER	Mercury
August	1962	I WANNA BE LOVED	Mercury
May	1962	WHERE ARE YOU	Roulette
May	1962	YOU'RE NOBODY 'TIL SOMEBODY LOVES YOU	Roulette
August	1962	FOR ALL WE KNOW	Roulette
May	1963	SOULVILLE	Roulette

MUDDY WATERS

Real Name: McKinley Morganfield
Born: April 4, 1915
Hometown: Rolling Fork, Mississippi

Muddy Waters was the first of the Delta bluesmen to mate big city sounds to simple country blues. One of Muddy's earliest tunes, "Rollin' Stone," became the title of the super-successful British rock group and later an underground periodical published in San Francisco.

Muddy made his first recording for Plant records in 1941. A few years later he moved to Chicago and recorded for Aristocrat records, which later became Chess.

In the fifties Muddy had a dozen top-ten hits on the R & B charts. In 1955 it was Muddy who guided and advised a young guitar player from St. Louis named Chuck Berry to sing with Chess.

January	1951	LOUISIANA BLUES	Chess
April	1951	LONG DISTANCE CALL	Chess
November	1953	MAD LOVE	Chess
March	1954	I'M YOUR HOOTCHIE COOCHE MAN	Chess
May	1954	JUST MAKE LOVE TO ME	Chess
October	1954	I'M READY	Chess
July	1955	MANISH BOY	Chess
April	1956	FORTY DAYS & FORTY NIGHTS	Chess
October	1958	CLOSE TO YOU	Chess

NOBLE "THIN MAN" WATTS

In 1957, sax player Noble Watts, nicknamed "Thin Man," recorded an instrumental hit for Baton records in New York, called "Hard Times (The Slop)." It was a real blues-type instrumental that wailed with a honking sax sound and was recorded for a popular teen-age dance called "the Slop." The song came out in late 1957 and became a national hit.

November 1957	HARD TIMES (THE SLOP)	Baton

THOMAS WAYNE

Born: July 22, 1941
Died: 1975, in an auto accident
Hometown: Memphis, Tennessee

Thomas graduated from Humes High in Memphis, which was also Elvis Presley's alma mater. Wayne's brother, who played guitar for Johnny Cash, set up an audition for him with Elvis's old guitar player Scotty Moore. Scotty got him a contract with Fernwood records. In January 1959, Thomas recorded his biggest hit, "Tragedy."

January 1959	TRAGEDY	Fernwood

THE WEAVERS

Members:
    Lee Hays
    Ronnie Gilbert
    Fred Hellerman
    Pete Seeger—May 3, 1919
Hometown: New York, New York

The group was formed in New York around 1948 and began singing folk songs and material by Woody Guthrie. In the early fifties they signed with Decca and recorded classics like "Goodnight Irene" and "On Top of Old Smoky." They were the forerunners of many folk groups.

    Pete Seeger became a very popular folk artist and writer of folk music in the sixties, writing tunes like "If I Had a Hammer" for Peter, Paul and Mary, which became a major hit for them in the sixties. Pete also had a national pop hit of his own in early 1964, for Columbia records with "Little Boxes."

January	1951	THE ROVING KIND	Decca
March	1951	ON TOP OF OLD SMOKY	Decca
July	1951	KISSES SWEETER THAN WINE	Decca
February	1952	WIMOWEH (Gordon Jenkins)	Decca

JOAN WEBER

JOAN WEBER

Born: 1936
Died: May 13, 1981, Winslow Township, New Jersey
Hometown: Paulsboro, New Jersey

In October of 1954, an eighteen-year-old housewife named Joan Weber was making the rounds in New York, trying to get some work as a singer. Being pregnant at the time made it difficult for her to find work.

Mitch Miller of Columbia records had her cut a demo record entitled "Let Me Go, Devil" and thought about releasing the song. The title was changed to "Let Me Go, Lover" and the song was released that month. After only moderate sales, Joan returned to New Jersey, to have her baby and forget about show business. On Monday evening November 15, 1954, Joan's song was used as background music for a drama on CBS-TV's "Studio One" and was played many times during the show. The next day the response was overwhelming, for everyone wanted to get the record. Joan's newborn daughter, Terry Lyn, came one week later, and by January 22, 1955, her song became a number one national hit. The song was her only hit.

October   1954   LET ME GO LOVER   Columbia

FRANK WEIR

Frank, a saxophone player in England, recorded a great sing-along tune in 1954, "The Happy Wanderer." The recording was sold to London records and released in the United States in the spring of 1954. This European song was recorded with English lyrics, translated from the original German, and became a top-ten national hit in this country. It was Weir's only hit in the United States.

April	1954	THE HAPPY WANDERER	London

LENNY WELCH

Born: May 15, 1938
Hometown: Asbury Park, New Jersey

Lenny began his professional career in Asbury Park, in 1958. Later that same year, he went to New York, and met lawyer Shelly Kravitz and disc jockey Gordie Baker, who signed him to a personal management contract. By late 1959, Lenny had cut several demo records. Archie Bleyer, the president of Cadence records, liked what he heard and signed Lenny to his label.

His first release came in February 1960, with "You Don't Know Me." His biggest seller for the label, in September 1963, was "Since I Fell for You."

February	1960	YOU DON'T KNOW ME	Cadence
September	1963	SINCE I FELL FOR YOU	Cadence
March	1964	EBB TIDE	Cadence
June	1965	DARLING TAKE ME BACK	Kapp
August	1965	TWO DIFFERENT WORLDS	Kapp
November	1965	RUN TO MY LOVIN' ARMS	Kapp
January	1970	BREAKING UP IS HARD TO DO	Commonwealth
August	1972	A SUNDAY KIND OF LOVE	Atco

LAWRENCE WELK

Born: March 11, 1903
Hometown: Strasburg, North Dakota

Lawrence's family left their native Alsace-Lorraine in the late nineteenth century and settled in North Dakota, where they earned their living as wheat farmers. Each member of the family played a musical instrument; Lawrence's specialties were piano and accordion.

After a while he formed a band with three other musicians, and they set out to tour the country. They were quite successful. Slowly Welk

MARY WELLS

increased the size of his group. He called his music "the Champagne Sound" because it had a smooth yet bubbling quality to it.

Welk's TV show was an enormous help to his recording career. He's had many hit records, including a number one tune, "Calcutta," in 1960, which shouldered aside the Shirelles' "Will You Love Me Tomorrow?"

April	1944	DON'T SWEETHEART ME	Decca
January	1953	OH, HAPPY DAY	Coral
February	1956	MORITAT (A THEME FROM THE THREE PENNY OPERA)	Coral
March	1956	THE POOR PEOPLE OF PARIS	Coral
September	1956	WHEN THE WHITE LILACS BLOOM AGAIN	Coral
November	1957	LIECHTENSTEINER POLKA	Coral
October	1960	LAST DATE	Dot
November	1960	CALCUTTA	Dot
March	1961	THEME FROM MY THREE SONS	Dot
June	1961	YELLOW BIRD	Dot
October	1961	RIDERS IN THE SKY	Dot
April	1962	RUNAWAY	Dot
June	1962	BABY ELEPHANT WALK	Dot
June	1963	SCARLETT O'HARA	Dot
April	1965	APPLES AND BANANAS	Dot

MARY WELLS

Born: May 13, 1943
Hometown: Detroit, Michigan

Mary always wanted to be a singer. In late 1960, she got her chance. She went to Motown records and auditioned for Berry Gordy, Jr. with a song she had written called "Bye Bye Baby." Berry liked her voice and signed her to a contract. At that time the only major act he had recording for his label were the Miracles. Mary recorded the song and in January 1961, it became a national hit.

In March 1964, Mary recorded a Smokey Robinson song called "My Guy," which went on to become her only number one national song.

Today Mary lives with her husband Cecil Womack (brother of singer Bobby Womack) in Los Angeles.

January	1961	BYE BYE BABY	Motown
July	1961	I DON'T WANT TO TAKE A CHANCE	Motown
March	1962	THE ONE WHO REALLY LOVES YOU	Motown
July	1962	YOU BEAT ME TO THE PUNCH	Motown
November	1962	TWO LOVERS	Motown
February	1963	LAUGHING BOY	Motown
May	1963	YOUR OLD STAND BY	Motown
September	1963	YOU LOST THE SWEETEST BOY	Motown
September	1963	WHAT'S EASY FOR TWO IS SO HARD FOR ONE	Motown
March	1964	MY GUY	Motown
October	1964	AIN'T IT THE TRUTH	20th Fox
January	1965	USE YOUR HEAD	20th Fox
March	1965	NEVER, NEVER LEAVE ME	20th Fox
June	1965	HE'S A LOVER	20th Fox
January	1966	CAN'T YOU SEE	Atco
January	1966	DEAR LOVER	Atco
May	1968	THE DOCTOR	Jubilee

KIM WESTON

Kim sang around the Detroit area as a youngster, where she eventually came to the attention of Berry Gordy, Jr., the president of Motown records. Berry liked her style and had her signed to his Tamla label in 1963. By the summer of that year she had her first national hit with "Love Me All the Way."

In 1964, she did some singing with Marvin Gaye on a couple of records which did fairly well on the national charts. In the fall of 1965, she had her biggest hit with the song "Take Me in Your Arms," on Motown's Gordy records.

July	1963	LOVE ME ALL THE WAY	Tamla
October	1965	TAKE ME IN YOUR ARMS	Gordy
March	1966	HELPLESS	Gordy

DAVID WHITFIELD

A one-time truck driver, David decided to pursue a career in singing. In 1954 he went to London records, in England, and recorded Tulio Trapani and Lee Lange's composition, "Cara Mia." The song did very well in England and was released in the United States in the summer of 1954. In a short time it became a top-ten national hit. The same song also became a top-ten hit for Jay and the Americans in the summer of 1965.

David had a couple of other hits for London before his popularity began to wane in 1957.

July	1954	CARA MIA	London
December	1954	SANTO NATALE	London
January	1956	WHEN YOU LOSE THE ONE YOU LOVE	London

MARGARET WHITING

Born: July 22, 1924
Hometown: Detroit, Michigan

Margaret, the eldest daughter of composer Richard Whiting, became interested in music as a youngster. When her family moved to the West Coast in the late twenties, Margaret began to study voice and piano with her father. Although he died when she was in her teens, family friend Johnny Mercer encouraged her to keep on with her musical studies. Her big break came when Mercer gave her a solo guest spot on his radio show.

When Johnny helped form Capitol records in the forties, he insisted she be signed to the label. She was, and she repaid him with many hits during the late forties.

March	1947	GUILTY	Capitol
October	1947	YOU DO	Capitol
February	1948	NOW IS THE HOUR	Capitol
July	1948	A TREE IN THE MEADOW	Capitol
December	1948	FAR AWAY PLACES	Capitol
April	1949	FOREVER AND EVER	Capitol
April	1949	A WONDERFUL GUY	Capitol
May	1949	BABY, IT'S COLD OUTSIDE (Johnny Mercer)	Capitol
June	1950	BLIND DATE (Bob Hope)	Capitol
November	1956	THE MONEY TREE	Capitol
October	1966	THE WHEEL OF HURT	London

ANDRE WILLIAMS

Andre began singing in his hometown of Detroit. By the mid-fifties he was working many of the local clubs. He was signed by Epic records in 1956 and recorded a moderate-tempo number called "Bacon Fat," which did well on the R & B charts in early 1957. After a few songs including the clever "Greasy Chicken" in 1958, he finally made the pop charts in a big way in early 1956, with "Rib Tips" for Avin records. Today Andre lives in Chicago, where he is a record producer.

January	1957	BACON FAT	Epic
September	1958	CADILLAC JACK	Checker
January	1966	RIB TIPS	Avin

ANDY WILLIAMS

Born: December 3, 1927
Hometown: Wall Lake, Iowa

Andy started singing in his father Jay Williams's church choir in Wall Lake. When the family moved to Des Moines, the Williams Brothers got their own radio show on WHO. From there they went to WLS radio in Chicago, and then to WLW radio in Cincinnati.

In 1952, the Williams Brothers disbanded after the three oldest members got married. This left young Andy to begin a career as a solo artist. He went to New York, and was signed as a vocalist on Steve Allen's "Tonight" show, where he remained for almost three years.

In 1956, he signed with Cadence records and recorded "Walk Hand in Hand" as his first major hit. Next came "Canadian Sunset" during the summer of 1956. In 1959, he did a one-hour television show as a summer replacement, which was continued for the next two summers.

In 1961, he left Cadence and signed with Columbia where he still records today.

March	1956	WALK HAND IN HAND	Cadence
August	1956	CANADIAN SUNSET	Cadence
November	1956	BABY DOLL	Cadence
January	1957	BUTTERFLY	Cadence
May	1957	I LIKE YOUR KIND OF LOVE	Cadence
September	1957	LIPS OF WINE	Cadence
February	1958	ARE YOU SINCERE	Cadence
August	1958	PROMISE ME, LOVE	Cadence
January	1959	THE HAWAIIAN WEDDING SONG	Cadence
September	1959	LONELY STREET	Cadence
December	1959	THE VILLAGE OF ST. BERNADETTE	Cadence
March	1960	WAKE ME WHEN IT'S OVER	Cadence
July	1960	DO YOU MIND	Cadence
December	1960	YOU DON'T WANT MY LOVE	Cadence
April	1961	THE BILBAO SONG	Cadence
December	1962	TWILIGHT TIME	Cadence
October	1961	DANNY BOY	Columbia
June	1962	STRANGER ON THE SHORE	Columbia
September	1962	DON'T YOU BELIEVE IT	Columbia
February	1963	CAN'T GET USED TO LOSING YOU	Columbia
February	1963	DAYS OF WINE AND ROSES	Columbia
June	1963	HOPELESS	Columbia

ANDY WILLIAMS

January	1964	A FOOL NEVER LEARNS	Columbia
April	1964	WRONG FOR EACH OTHER	Columbia
September	1964	ON THE STREET WHERE YOU LIVE	Columbia
October	1964	ALMOST THERE	Columbia
October	1964	DEAR HEART	Columbia
April	1965	AND ROSES AND ROSES	Columbia
September	1965	AIN'T IT TRUE	Columbia
August	1965	IN THE ARMS OF LOVE	Columbia
March	1967	MUSIC TO WATCH GIRLS BY	Columbia
July	1967	MORE AND MORE	Columbia
June	1968	SWEET MEMORIES	Columbia
October	1968	BATTLE HYMN OF THE REPUBLIC	Columbia
April	1969	HAPPY HEART	Columbia
February	1970	CAN'T HELP FALLING IN LOVE	Columbia
June	1970	ONE DAY OF YOUR LIFE	Columbia
February	1971	(WHERE DO I BEGIN) LOVE STORY	Columbia
August	1971	A SONG FOR YOU	Columbia
April	1972	LOVE THEME FROM "THE GODFATHER"	Columbia
January	1976	TELL IT LIKE IT IS	Columbia

BILLY WILLIAMS

Born: December 28, 1916
Died: October 17, 1972
Hometown: Waco, Texas

The son of a Methodist minister, Billy began studying for the ministry himself, until he met three other fellows in college and formed the Charioteers. They began to perform locally at Wilberforce College in Ohio, and

656

BILLY WILLIAMS

won a regular spot on radio station WLW in Cincinnati. They then went to New York and worked on WOR radio for a while. Around 1940 they went to the West Coast to work on Bing Crosby's radio show.

In 1949, Billy left the Charioteers and formed the Billy Williams Quartet, which became a very hot act on TV. They had a long run on Sid Caesar's "Show of Shows." Around 1954, the group signed with Coral records, where they enjoyed their biggest hits, including a top-ten smash in 1957 called "I'm Gonna Sit Right Down and Write Myself a Letter." Billy died in 1972 in Chicago, where he had been employed as a social worker.

March	1956	A CRAZY LITTLE PALACE	Coral
February	1957	THE PIED PIPER	Coral
May	1957	I'M GONNA SIT RIGHT DOWN AND WRITE MYSELF A LETTER	Coral
November	1957	GOT A DATE WITH AN ANGEL	Coral
March	1958	BABY, BABY	Coral
January	1959	NOLA	Coral

LARRY WILLIAMS

Real Name: Lawrence E. Williams
Born: May 10, 1935
Died: January 2, 1980, of self-inflicted gunshot wounds
Hometown: New Orleans, Louisiana

Larry started out as Lloyd Price's valet while Lloyd was recording for Specialty records in the early fifties. When Lloyd left the label, Art Rupe, the president, persuaded Larry to record Lloyd's hit "Just Because." This became Larry's first hit. In the summer of 1957, he recorded "Short Fat Fannie," a song he wrote that became a national hit.

June	1957	SHORT FAT FANNIE	Specialty
October	1957	BONY MORONIE	Specialty
October	1957	YOU BUG ME, BABY	Specialty
March	1958	DIZZY, MISS LIZZY	Specialty

LARRY WILLIAMS

MAURICE WILLIAMS AND THE ZODIACS

Members:
    Maurice Williams
    Henry Gasten
    Willie Bennet
    Charles Thomas
Hometown: Lancaster, South Carolina

The group won a talent show in 1955, at Barr Street High in Lancaster, as the Royal Charms. In 1957, as the Gladiolas, they recorded a song Maurice had written called "Little Darlin'," which became a hit on Excello records. However, the Diamonds did a cover version of the song and wound up with a much bigger hit.

In 1958, they became the Excellos and in 1959 finally settled on the Zodiacs. In September 1960, they recorded another song by Maurice, called "Stay," which became a number one song all around the country on Herald records.

September 1960	STAY	Herald
January 1961	I REMEMBER	Herald
April 1961	COME ALONG	Herald

OTIS WILLIAMS AND HIS NEW GROUP

Born: June 2, 1936
Hometown: Cincinnati, Ohio

Otis Williams, the lead singer of popular Cincinnati group called the Charms, (see biography of the Charms) had the name changed to Otis Williams and His New Group when they started to gain popularity in 1956. Their first major hit under this new billing came in early 1956, with the swinging, R & B-flavored "That's Your Mistake," which became a national hit.

Their follow-up, "Ivory Tower" (also recorded on another Cincinnati label, Fraternity records, by Cathy Carr, who had the bigger hit of the two), became the group's biggest pop disc.

January 1956	THAT'S YOUR MISTAKE	DeLuxe
February 1956	IVORY TOWER	DeLuxe
March 1961	LITTLE TURTLE DOVE	King

ROGER WILLIAMS

Hometown: Omaha, Nebraska

The son of a music teacher, Roger had mastered a number of instruments

ROGER WILLIAMS

by age twelve. In 1951, he went to New York, enrolled at Juilliard, and won on Arthur Godfrey's "Talent Scouts." Dave Kapp, the president of Kapp records, heard Roger play and signed him to his label.

His first successful disc was "Autumn Leaves" in late 1955.

Today he records for MCA records.

July	1955	AUTUMN LEAVES	Kapp
October	1955	WANTING YOU	Kapp
February	1956	BEYOND THE SEA	Kapp
May	1956	HI LILI HI LO	Kapp
August	1956	TUMBLING TUMBLEWEEDS	Kapp
February	1957	ALMOST PARADISE	Kapp
October	1957	TILL	Kapp
March	1958	ARRIVEDERCI ROMA	Kapp
August	1958	NEAR YOU	Kapp
October	1960	TEMPTATION	Kapp
December	1961	MARIA	Kapp
February	1962	AMOR	Kapp
June	1966	LARA'S THEME FROM "DR. ZHIVAGO"	Kapp
August	1966	BORN FREE	Kapp
January	1967	SUNRISE, SUNSET	Kapp
April	1967	LOVE ME FOREVER	Kapp
June	1968	THE IMPOSSIBLE DREAM	Kapp

CHUCK WILLIS

CHUCK WILLIS

Born: February 1928
Died: April 10, 1958
Hometown: Atlanta, Georgia

Chuck was discovered by disc jockey Daddy Sears of WAOK radio, and started as a vocalist with Red McAllister's band, working around Atlanta. He was heard by a scout from Columbia records and signed to their subsidiary label Okeh records in 1952.

By April 1956, Chuck had a contract with Atlantic records. He began turning out hits like "It's Too Late" in August 1956, and then "Juanita" later that year. Chuck was crowned "King of the Stroll" when, in early 1957, he recorded his biggest hit "C. C. Rider"—the perfect Stroll record. He also wrote songs for many other artists, including "Oh, What a Dream" for Patti Page, "Close Your Eyes" for the Five Keys, "Let Me Explain" for the Cadillacs, "From the Bottom of My Heart" for the Clovers, and "The Door Is Still Open" for Dean Martin. His songs were based on true incidents in his life. He liked to compare his style to that of Johnny Ace.

It was ironic that his last two hits, recorded in February 1958, should be entitled "What Am I Living For" and the flip side "Hang Up My Rock and Roll Shoes." He died at the Hugh Spalding Hospital in Atlanta, on April 10, 1958, after a serious operation.

October	1952	MY STORY	Okeh
May	1953	GOING TO THE RIVER	Okeh

July	1953	DON'T DECEIVE ME	Okeh
January	1954	YOU'RE STILL MY BABY	Okeh
June	1956	IT'S TOO LATE	Atlantic
March	1957	C.C. RIDER	Atlantic
January	1958	BETTY AND DUPREE	Atlantic
April	1958	WHAT AM I LIVING FOR/HANG UP MY	
		ROCK AND ROLL SHOES	Atlantic
August	1958	MY LIFE	Atlantic
November	1958	KEEP A-DRIVING	Atlantic

THE WILLOWS

Members:
 Tony Middleton—lead
 Richie Davis—first tenor
 Ralph Martin—second tenor
 Joe Martin—baritone
 John Steele—bass
Hometown: New York, New York

In 1952, the fellows formed the Five Willows and began harmonizing on street corners in Harlem. After much practicing, they signed with Allen

THE WILLOWS

Clockwise from top left: John Thomas Steele, Ralph Martin, Richie Davis, Joe Martin, Tony Middleton

records in 1953. They remained with the label for several years until it went bankrupt in 1955. At this point they signed with Herald records and recorded a couple of songs.

Later that year they signed with Morty Craft's Melba records. They then changed the name of the group from the Five Willows to simply the Willows.

In early 1956, Tony's wife came up with an idea for a song about church bells ringing. The group wrote "Church Bells May Ring," on which Morty Craft decided to dub in chimes. Interestingly enough, the person who played the chimes on the recording was an unknown singer named Neil Sedaka. The song was released that spring and became a million-seller and the group's only major hit.

| March | 1956 | CHURCH BELLS MAY RING | Melba |

JACKIE WILSON

Born: June 9, 1934
Hometown: Detroit, Michigan

As a teen-ager in Detroit, Jackie won the Golden Gloves at the age of sixteen. He even thought of becoming a professional fighter, but was persuaded to pursue a somewhat more stable career: singing.

One of the groups he admired at the time was the Dominoes, and particularly Clyde McPhatter. When they were passing through Detroit in 1953, Jackie went to audition for the group, as he had heard Clyde was going to leave. Clyde did indeed leave the Dominoes that year to form a new group called the Drifters, and Jackie's dream was realized when he became the Dominoes' new lead voice. In 1957, Jackie left the Dominoes to go out as a solo artist. He was managed first by Al Green, and after Al's death, by Nat Tarnapool.

In September 1957, Jackie's career was launched with "Reet Petite," a song by a young unknown writer from Detroit, Berry Gordy, Jr. (who, a few years later, would become head of the recording giant Motown Records). In March 1958, Jackie had his first gold record with another Berry Gordy ballad called "To Be Loved." He recorded his biggest seller in early 1960, the double-sided hit "Doggin' Around" and "Night."

Jackie's career almost came to a premature end in 1961. He was shot in the stomach by a female fan while trying to prevent her from shooting herself. In fact, he still carries the bullet in his body today.

Jackie suffered a heart attack while performing at The Latin Casino in Cherry Hill, New Jersey, in September 1975, and has been in a coma ever since in a hospital in New Jersey.

JACKIE WILSON

October	1957	REET PETITE	Brunswick
March	1958	TO BE LOVED	Brunswick
September	1958	WE HAVE LOVE	Brunswick
November	1958	LONELY TEARDROPS	Brunswick
March	1959	THAT'S WHY	Brunswick
June	1959	I'LL BE SATISFIED	Brunswick
September	1959	YOU BETTER KNOW IT	Brunswick
November	1959	TALK THAT TALK	Brunswick
March	1960	NIGHT	Brunswick
March	1960	DOGGIN' AROUND	Brunswick
June	1960	ALL MY LOVE	Brunswick
June	1960	A WOMAN, A LOVER, A FRIEND	Brunswick
October	1960	ALONE AT LAST	Brunswick
October	1960	AM I THE MAN	Brunswick
January	1961	MY EMPTY ARMS	Brunswick
March	1961	PLEASE TELL ME WHY	Brunswick
June	1961	I'M COMIN' ON BACK TO YOU	Brunswick
August	1961	YEARS FROM NOW	Brunswick
October	1961	THE WAY I AM	Brunswick
January	1962	THE GREATEST HURT	Brunswick
March	1962	HEARTS	Brunswick
July	1962	I JUST CAN'T HELP IT	Brunswick
March	1963	BABY WORKOUT	Brunswick
July	1963	SHAKE, SHAKE, SHAKE	Brunswick
September	1963	BABY GET IT	Brunswick
August	1964	SQUEEZE HER-TEASE HER	Brunswick
February	1965	DANNY BOY	Brunswick
June	1965	NO PITY (IN THE NAKED CITY)	Brunswick
May	1970	LET THIS BE A LETTER (TO MY BABY)	Brunswick
December	1970	THIS LOVE IS REAL	Brunswick
November	1971	LOVE IS FUNNY THAT WAY	Brunswick
March	1972	YOU GOT ME WALKING	Brunswick

October	1966	WHISPERS	Brunswick
March	1967	I DON'T WANT TO LOSE YOU	Brunswick
April	1967	I'VE LOST YOU	Brunswick
August	1967	(YOUR LOVE KEEPS LIFTING ME) HIGHER AND HIGHER	Brunswick
November	1967	SINCE YOU SHOWED ME HOW TO BE HAPPY	Brunswick
July	1968	I GET THE SWEETEST FEELING	Brunswick
November	1968	FOR ONCE IN MY LIFE	Brunswick
November	1971	LOVE IS FUNNY THAT WAY	Brunswick
May	1970	LET THIS BE A LETTER (TO MY BABY)	Brunswick
December	1970	THIS LOVE IS REAL	Brunswick

NANCY WILSON

Born: February 20, 1940
Hometown: Chillicothe, Ohio

By the early sixties Nancy was working in Columbus, performing on local TV stations. At this time Cannonball Adderley was appearing with his group in Columbus, and Nancy went to see him. While watching him perform, she got up and began singing with his group. He was so impressed with her voice that he told her to look him up if she ever got to New York.

She did just that in 1962, and he introduced her to some of his friends from Capitol. The result was a recording contract and her first hit record in the summer of 1963.

She continues to record for Capitol today.

August	1963	TELL ME THE TRUTH	Capitol
June	1964	(YOU DON'T KNOW) HOW GLAD I AM	Capitol
July	1964	I WANNA BE WITH YOU	Capitol
January	1965	DON'T COME RUNNING BACK TO ME	Capitol
May	1968	FACE IT GIRL, IT'S OVER	Capitol
September	1968	PEACE OF MIND	Capitol
November	1969	CAN'T TAKE MY EYES OFF YOU	Capitol

KAI WINDING

Born: March 18, 1929

Kai played trombone with J. J. Johnson as a popular jazz group known as J & K for many years. In 1963, due to the success of the motion picture *Mondo Cane*, many people recorded the title song "More." Kai did an instrumental version for Verve records which became a top-ten hit that summer.

June	1963	MORE	Verve

KAI WINDING

HUGO WINTERHALTER

Born: August 15, 1910
Died: September 17, 1973
Hometown: Wilkes-Barre, Pennsylvania

At the age of six, Hugo began his musical career by playing the violin. Later on, in high school, he studied reed instruments; in college, he led the campus orchestra. After college he got a job playing saxophone with a local band. Subsequently, he took a job as a music teacher at a high school.

In the early thirties, he left his teaching position to go to New York, where he got a job working as a saxophonist in a couple of club bands. In 1938, he joined Larry Clinton for several years, after which he went on to do arranging for Billy Eckstine, Claude Thornhill, Vaughn Monroe, and Kate Smith.

In the early fifties, he was appointed chief musical director for RCA Victor, where he not only arranged dates for RCA's artists but became a label artist himself, beginning with "Count Every Star" in early 1950. His biggest hit was the instrumental "Canadian Sunset," which was on the charts for eight months in 1956.

| May | 1950 | COUNT EVERY STAR | RCA Victor |
| June | 1950 | I WANNA BE LOVED (Fontane Sisters) | RCA Victor |

March	1951	ACROSS THE WIDE MISSOURI	RCA Victor
February	1952	A KISS TO BUILD A DREAM ON	RCA Victor
February	1952	BLUE TANGO	RCA Victor
July	1952	VANESSA	RCA Victor
November	1952	BLUE VIOLINS	RCA Victor
October	1953	THE VELVET GLOVE (Henri Rene)	RCA Victor
July	1954	THE LITTLE SHOEMAKER	RCA Victor
July	1954	THE MAGIC TANGO	RCA Victor
December	1954	SONG OF THE BAREFOOT CONTESSA	RCA Victor
January	1956	MEMORIES OF YOU	RCA
February	1956	LITTLE MUSICIANS	RCA
May	1956	CANADIAN SUNSET	RCA

HOWLIN' WOLF

Real Name: Chester Burnett
Born: June 10, 1910
Hometown: Aberdeen, Mississippi

Harmonica-playing blues singer Howlin' Wolf had his first formal recording session in Memphis back in 1948. In the early fifties he signed with Chess records and began recording many R & B blues hits. He was an influence on many other blues singers of the fifties.

November	1951	HOW MANY MORE YEARS	Chess
February	1956	SMOKE STACK LIGHTNING	Chess

STEVIE WONDER

Real Name: Steveland Morris Hardaway
Born: May 13, 1950
Hometown: Detroit, Michigan

Though born blind, his handicap never presented much of a problem for Stevie, and he was as active as most of the kids his age. His first musical instrument was a simple four-hole harmonica, which he practiced on constantly.

In the early sixties, Stevie began to spend a lot of time at the home of Ronnie White of the Miracles, playing with Ronnie's kid brother. Ronnie heard Stevie sing and play the harmonica and offered to take him over to Motown records. The company was so impressed that they signed him to the label. They changed his name to Little Stevie Wonder and he began to record songs like "I Call It Pretty Music" and "Contract on Love."

In 1963, during a live performance, he recorded a song called "Fingertips–Pt. 2," which Tamla released that summer. The song became not only Stevie's first national hit, but a number one smash as well.

STEVIE WONDER

Stevie married a young lady named Syreeta, who worked at Motown, in 1971. He moved to New York and decided to change his musical style. He wanted a strong departure from the typical Motown sound. In the summer of 1972, Stevie went on tour with the Rolling Stones. It was on this tour that he introduced the "new" Stevie Wonder and his album "Talking Book," which resulted in three chart singles: "Super Woman," "Superstition," and "You Are the Sunshine of My Life." This young genius of the pop and soul scene is able to absorb the life around him and transform it into meaningful and successful records. He has had over fourteen hit albums and several dozen hit singles.

He continues to record and perform today as one of pop music's true superstars.

June	1963	FINGERTIPS—PT. 2	Tamla
October	1963	WORKOUT STEVIE, WORKOUT	Tamla
February	1964	CASTLES IN THE SAND	Tamla
June	1964	HEY HARMONICA MAN	Tamla
August	1965	HIGH HEEL SNEAKERS	Tamla
December	1965	UP TIGHT (EVERYTHING'S ALRIGHT)	Tamla
April	1966	NOTHING'S TOO GOOD FOR MY BABY	Tamla
July	1966	BLOWIN' IN THE WIND	Tamla
November	1966	A PLACE IN THE SUN	Tamla
March	1967	TRAVELIN' MAN	Tamla
April	1967	HEY LOVE	Tamla
June	1967	I WAS MADE TO LOVER HER	Tamla
October	1967	I'M WONDERING	Tamla
April	1968	SHOO-BE-DOO-BE-DOO-DA-DAY	Tamla
July	1968	YOU MET YOUR MATCH	Tamla
November	1968	FOR ONCE IN MY LIFE	Tamla
February	1969	I DON'T KNOW WHY	Tamla
May	1969	MY CHERIE AMOUR	Tamla

October	1969	YESTER-ME, YESTER-YOU, YESTERDAY	Tamla
February	1970	NEVER HAD A DREAM COME TRUE	Tamla
July	1970	SIGNED, SEALED, DELIVERED I'M YOURS	Tamla
October	1970	HEAVEN HELP US ALL	Tamla
March	1971	WE CAN WORK IT OUT	Tamla
August	1971	IF YOU REALLY LOVE ME	Tamla
February	1970	NEVER HAD A DREAM COME TRUE	Tamla
June	1970	SIGNED, SEALED, DELIVERED I'M YOURS	Tamla
October	1970	HEAVEN HELP US ALL	Tamla
March	1971	WE CAN WORK IT OUT	Tamla
June	1971	NEVER DREAMED YOU'D LEAVE IN SUMMER	Tamla
August	1971	IF YOU REALLY LOVE ME	Tamla
May	1972	SUPER WOMAN	Tamla
September	1972	KEEP ON RUNNING	Tamla
November	1972	SUPERSTITION	Tamla
March	1973	YOU ARE THE SUNSHINE OF MY LIFE	Tamla
August	1973	HIGHER GROUND	Tamla
November	1973	LIVING FOR THE CITY	Tamla
April	1974	DON'T YOU WORRY 'BOUT A THING	Tamla
August	1974	YOU HAVEN'T DONE NOTHIN'	Tamla
November	1974	BOOGIE ON REGGAE WOMAN	Tamla
December	1976	I WISH	Tamla
April	1977	SIR DUKE	Tamla
August	1977	ANOTHER STAR	Tamla
November	1977	AS	Tamla
January	1979	POPS, WE LOVE YOU	Motown
November	1979	SEND ONE YOUR LOVE	Tamla
March	1980	OUTSIDE MY WINDOW	Tamla
September	1980	MASTER BLASTER	Tamla
December	1980	I AIN'T GONNA STAND FOR IT	Tamla
April	1981	LATELY	Tamla

SHEB WOOLEY

Real Name: Ben Colder (Shelby Wooley)
Born: April 10, 1921
Hometown: Erick, Oklahoma

Sheb grew up on his father's farm and was a rodeo rider as a young man. He was also interested in music; he began playing the guitar at the age of eleven and sang western tunes at various rodeos in Texas and Oklahoma.

By 1946, he formed his own western band and toured the country. In 1948 he signed a recording contract with MGM records. He went to California in 1951 for a screen test which led to a featured role in the Errol Flynn film *Rocky Mountain*. He appeared in other films: *Boy From Oklahoma, Little Big Horn, Hellgate* and *Distant Drums*. He also had a good role as the drinking heavy at the railroad station in *High Noon* with Gary Cooper.

After writing and recording many songs for MGM, he scored his greatest triumph in the summer of 1958 when he wrote and recorded the novelty song "Purple People Eater," which became a number one national hit.

Today Sheb enjoys working on his ranch in the San Fernando Valley, while he continues to record for MGM.

May	1958	THE PURPLE PEOPLE EATER	MGM
June	1959	SWEET CHILE	MGM
January	1962	THAT'S MY PA	MGM

LINK WRAY AND THE WRAY MEN

Born: May 2, 1935
Hometown: Dunn, North Carolina

Link's parents were preachers and he launched his career singing in the choir with his family. While in the Army, he entertained for the Armed Forces radio network, playing both the drums and bass guitar.

Link and his two brothers formed the Wray Men and, in March 1958, recorded an instrumental smash for Cadence records called "Rumble," which became their biggest hit.

April	1958	RUMBLE	Cadence
January	1959	RAW-HIDE	Epic

LINK WRAY

Y

FARON YOUNG

Born: February 25, 1932
Hometown: Shreveport, Louisiana

Faron learned to play the guitar as a youngster. In high school he formed his own singing group and played local functions. After a while he became very popular in the Louisiana area and eventually got to appear on the popular radio show "Louisiana Hayride," where he impressed the show's star, Webb Pierce.

In 1951, Capitol signed Faron and he began his recording career, but the Korean War interrupted his career for several years. After his discharge from the Army, he joined the Grand Ole Opry and started having many country hits again.

In the spring of 1961, he had his biggest pop hit for Capitol when he recorded Willie Nelson's tune, "Hello Walls."

Today Faron lives with his family in Nashville, where he owns a recording studio with Billy Grammer.

July	1958	ALONE WITH YOU	Capitol
January	1960	RIVERBOAT	Capitol
March	1961	HELLO WALLS	Capitol
October	1961	BACKTRACK	Capitol

KATHY YOUNG AND THE INNOCENTS

Born: October 21, 1945
Hometown: Long Beach, California

Kathy sang at high school dances. She asked Los Angeles disc jockey Wink Martindale, at one of his TV dance party shows, how to go about making a record. He suggested Indigo records. She went for an audition and wound up recording "A Thousand Stars," which was written and recorded by Gene Pearson when he sang lead with the Rivileers in the mid-fifties. Kathy had the Innocents back her on the song (the Innocents also had a hit on their own called "Honest I Do") and it became a hit in the fall of 1960.

| October | 1960 | A THOUSAND STARS | Indigo |
| February | 1961 | HAPPY BIRTHDAY BLUES | Indigo |

VICTOR YOUNG

Born: August 8, 1900
Died: November 11, 1956
Hometown: Chicago, Illinois

At the age of ten Victor went to Warsaw, Poland, where he studied at the Warsaw Conservatory as a concert violinist. He made various concert tours as a youngster in Europe and eventually returned to the United States to make his concert debut in Chicago.

In the late forties he signed with Decca records and by the 1950s had several big chart hits. "The High and the Mighty" from the film of the same name was his biggest hit for Decca, during the summer of 1954.

June	1950	LA VIE EN ROSE	Decca
June	1950	MONA LISA	Decca
February	1951	MY HEART CRIES FOR YOU	Decca
May	1953	RUBY	Decca
July	1954	THE HIGH AND THE MIGHTY	Decca
September	1955	AUTUMN LEAVES	Decca
May	1957	AROUND THE WORLD	Decca

TIMI YURO

Real Name: Rosemarie Yuro
Born: August 4, 1941
Hometown: Chicago, Illinois

In 1952, Timi's family moved to Los Angeles, where she began singing in her mother's Italian restaurant. About eight years later, Liberty records president, Al Bennett signed her to his label, but was not pleased with the initial results. Bennett gave it some more thought, and decided to have her work with veteran writer and producer Clyde Otis, who had just joined Liberty.

The outcome of their first session together was her biggest hit, "Hurt," in the summer of 1961.

July	1961	HURT	Liberty
November	1961	SMILE	Liberty
February	1962	LET ME CALL YOU SWEETHEART	Liberty
June	1962	WHAT'S A MATTER BABY	Liberty
December	1962	THE LOVE OF A BOY	Liberty
July	1963	MAKE THE WORLD GO AWAY	Liberty
October	1963	GOTTA TRAVEL ON	Liberty

HELMUT ZACHARIAS

In 1956, popular German artist Helmut Zacharias had a big instrumental hit in Europe called "When the White Lilacs Bloom Again." A representative from Decca brought a copy of the song back to the United States and played it for Milt Gabler, the A & R head, who felt it could be a hit over here as well.

The song, released that summer, went on to become a big national hit—Helmut's only United States top-seller.

August   1956   WHEN THE WHITE LILACS BLOOM AGAIN   Decca

JOHN ZACHERLE

Born: September 26, 1918
Hometown: Philadelphia, Pennsylvania

During the late fifties, Zacherle was the host of horror movies on WCAU-TV in Philadelphia, where he was known as Roland. He had a tremendous following because of the crazy things he would do on the air. The children of Bernie Lowe, who was the president of Philadelphia-based Cameo/Parkway records, told their father how much they enjoyed the program. Bernie had Zacherle come to their studios, where Bernie decided to record him doing his crazy character over a driving music track.

The song was first played on a Philadelphia radio station, after which

SI ZENTNER

Zacherle was invited to appear on "American Bandstand." That national exposure helped make his song a top-ten national hit.

February   1958   DINNER WITH DRAC   Cameo

SI ZENTNER

Trombonist Si Zentner worked as a studio musician for a long time, learning styles and techniques from many top people. Eventually he formed his own group and, in 1961, did some big-band arrangements with a swinging new sound for Liberty records. One of the songs was released as a single in the fall of 1961. The old standard "Up a Lazy River," with Si's great new arrangement, became a national hit for him that year.

October   1961   UP A LAZY RIVER   Liberty

Index of Song Titles

"A"—You're Adorable, 136
ABC's Of Love, 400
Abigail Beecher, 88
Abilene, 289
About This Thing Called Love, 229
Above The Stars, 46
Abraham, Martin And John, 188, 438
Across The Alley From The Alamo, 434
Across The Wide Missouri, 666
Action, 88
Add Some Music To Your Day, 31
Adios, 239
Adios Amigo, 518
Adorable, 135
Adorable/Steamboat, 207
African Boo-Ga-Loo, 377
Afrikaan Beat, 347
After Loving You, 517
After New Year's Eve, 298
After School, 584
After The Dance, 269
After The Lights Go Down Low, 302
After You, 645
Again, 160, 170, 401, 444, 608
Age For Love, The, 102
Ah But It Happens, 367
Ahab, The Arab, 587
Ain't Doing Too Bad, 49
Ain't Gon' Be No Cutting Aloose, 389
Ain't Gonna Be That Way, 343
Ain't Gonna Cry No More, 375
Ain't Gonna Tell Nobody, 275
Ain't Got No Home, 301
Ain't Got Time, 319
Ain't It A Shame, 193, 500
Ain't It, Baby, 437
Ain't It Funky Now, 67
Ain't It The Truth, 652
Ain't It True, 655
Ain't No Love In The Heart Of The City, 50
Ain't No Mountain High Enough, 269
Ain't No Telling, 49
Ain't No Way, 262
Ain't Nobody Home, 353
Ain't Nothing Like The Real Thing, 262, 269
Ain't Nothing You Can Do, 49

Ain't That A Groove, 66
Ain't That A Shame, 58, 256, 368
Ain't That Just Like A Woman, 194
Ain't That Love, 103
Ain't That Loving You Baby, 497, 515
Ain't That Peculiar, 268
Al Di La, 481
Alabam, 59
Aladdin, 158
Alfie, 644
Alice In Wonderland, 554
Alimony, 247
All, 166
All Alone Am I, 375
All American Boy, The, 473
All Around The World, 392
All At Once You Love Her, 137
All By Myself, 193
All Grown Up, 156
All I Could Do Was Cry, 328
All I Have To Do Is Dream, 96, 226
All I Need Is Time, 363
All In My Mind, 68
All My Love, 232, 469, 663
All My Trials, 184, 587
All Night Long, 74, 454, 466
All Of A Sudden My Heart Sings, 12, 91
All Of Everything, 20
All Of Me, 511
All Or Nothing, 366
All Or Nothing At All, 568
All Over Again/What Do I Care, 93
All Over The World, 134
All Shook Up, 496
All Strung Out, 599
All That I Am, 497
All The King's Horses, 262
All The Love I Got, 343
All The Time, 424
All The Way Around The World, 434
All The Way, 569
All Through The Night, 450
Allegheny Moon, 469
Alley Cat, 229
Alley-Oop, 163, 309
Allez-Vous-En, 583

Alligator Wine, 296
Ally, Ally Oxen Free, 359
Almost Grown, 44
Almost In Your Arms, 452
Almost Paradise, 659
Almost Persuaded, 328
Almost There, 655
Alone, 256, 559
Alone At Last, 663
Alone With You, 375, 670
Along Came Jones, 129, 587
Along The Navajo Trail, 565
Alright, Okay, You Win, 377
Alvin For President, 110
Alvin Twist, The, 110
Alvin's Harmonica, 110
Alvin's Orchestra, 110
Always, 508, 616
Always In My Heart, 396
Always Something There To Remind Me, 644
Always Together, 176, 420
Am I Grooving You, 550
Am I Losing You, 518
Am I That Easy To Forget, 522
Am I The Man, 663
Amanda, 645
Amarillo, 554
Amen, 319, 514
America, Communicate With Me, 587
America Is My Home, 66
American Music, 4
Among My Souvenirs, 260
Amor, 353, 659
Amos Moses, 515
Amy, 484
An Affair To Remember, 160
An American Trilogy, 498
Anastasia, 58
And I Love Him, 387
And I Love You So, 137, 277
And Now, 517
And Roses And Roses, 655
And So To Sleep Again, 469
And That Reminds Me, 257, 517
And Then There Were Drums, 454
Anema E Core, 238
Angel, 262, 604
Angel Baby, 417, 539
Angel Face, 166
Angel On My Shoulder, 246
Angel Smile, 134
Angela Jones, 234
Angels In The Sky, 152
Angels Listened In, The, 150
Anna, 4, 320
Anna Marie, 518
Annie Fanny, 358
Annie Get Your Yo-Yo, 389
Annie Had A Baby, 430
Annie's Aunt Fanny, 430
Anniversary Song, 565
Ann-Marie, 35
Another Cup Of Coffee, 41
Another Night, 644
Another Place, Another Time, 382
Another Saturday Night, 141
Another Sleepless Night, 115

Another Star, 668
Another Time, Another Place, 469
Answer Me, My Love, 134
Answer To My Prayer, The, 554
Anthem, 456
Anthony & Cleopatra Theme, 234
Anthony Boy, 44
Any Day Now, 326
Any Other Way, 326
Any Time, 237
Anybody But Me, 375
Anymore, 2, 63
Anyone Who Had A Heart, 644
Anything That's Part Of You, 497
Anytime At All, 569
Anytime (I'll Be There), 12, 570
Anyway The Wind Blows, 171
Anyway You Want Me, 496
Anywhere I Wander, 371
Apache, 320, 330
Ape Call, 458
Apple Blossom Time, 313, 456
Apple Green, 625
Apples And Bananas, 651
April Fools, The, 644
April In Portugal, 29, 160, 297
April Love, 58
Are You Getting Any Sunshine, 114
Are You Happy, 80
Are You Lonely For Me, 550
Are You Lonesome Tonight, 448, 496
Are You Really Mine, 534
Are You Sincere, 395, 654
Are You There, 644
Armen's Theme, 520, 555
Around The Corner, 210, 582
Around The World, 403, 411, 671
Arrivederci Roma, 370, 659
Arrow Of Love, 570
Artificial Flowers, 164
As, 668
As If I Didn't Know, 641
As Long As I Know He's Mine, 420
As Long As I'm Moving/I Can See Everybody's
    Baby, 70
As Long As She Needs Me, 167
As Time Goes By, 452
As Usual, 375
Asia Minor, 365
Ask Me, 68, 134, 259, 497
Ask Me No Questions, 353
Astronaut, The, 337
At Last, 14, 328
At My Front Door, 58, 117, 218
At The Club, 207
At The Darktown Strutters' Ball, 443
At The Hop, 605
At The Hop/Sometimes When I'm All Alone,
    162
Auctioneer, The, 431, 626
Auf Wiederseh'n Sweetheart, 401
Automatically Sunshine, 594
Autumn Leaves, 432, 659, 671
Autumn Of My Life, 277
Autumn Waltz, The, 39
Ave Maria, 136

B-A-B-Y, 601
Baby, Baby, 656
Baby, Baby Don't Cry, 438
Baby Blue, 213
Baby Come Close, 438
Baby Come Home, 543
Baby Come On Home, 76
Baby Do The Philly Dog, 461
Baby Doll, 155, 654
Baby Don't Change Your Mind, 363
Baby, Don't Do It, 241, 268
Baby Don't You Cry, 104
Baby Don't You Weep, 434
Baby Elephant Walk, 651
Baby Face, 164, 391, 444
Baby Get It, 663
Baby Get It On, 614
Baby, Get Lost, 646
Baby I Love You, 262, 537
Baby, I'm Yours, 380
Baby It's Cold Outside, 104, 565, 653
Baby It's You, 562, 578
Baby Let Me Hold Your Hand, 103
Baby Love, 594
Baby Oh Baby, 558
Baby Please, 446
Baby, Please Don't Go, 463
Baby Scratch My Back, 291
Baby Talk, 332
Baby Tell Me, 427
(Baby) Turn On To Me, 319
Baby What I Mean, 207
Baby What You Want Me To Do, 328, 380, 516
Baby, What's Wrong, 404
Baby Workout, 663
Baby You're Driving Me Crazy, 174
Baby, You're Right, 66
Baby (You've Got What It Takes), 41
Back At The Chicken Shack, 573
Back Door Man, 158
Back In My Arms Again, 594
Back In The U.S.A., 44
Back In The U.S.S.R., 107
Back Street, 74
Back To School Again, 536
Back To The Hop, 162
Backstage, 488
Backtrack, 670
Bacon Fat, 654
Bad, Bad Leroy Brown, 570
Bad, Bad Whiskey, 430
Bad Blood, 554
Bad Boy, 337
Bad Conditions, 500
Bad Girl, 437, 554
Bad Luck, 52
Bad Luck/Sweet Little Angel, 352
Bad Man Blunder, 358
Bad Weather, 594
Bahama Mama, 249
Balboa Blue, 413
Bali Ha'i, 136, 377
Ballad Of A Teenage Queen, 93
Ballad Of Davy Crockett, The, 248, 297, 472
Ballad Of Irving, The, 267
Ballad Of Paladin, The, 214
Ballad Of The Alamo, 75, 529

Ballad Of Thunder Road, The, 440
Ballerina, 134, 442
Bama Lama Bama Loo, 391
Bamboo, 442
Banana Boat Song, The, 247, 372, 419, 597, 626
Banana Boat, 32, 263
Band Of Gold, 90, 91, 109
Banda, A, 6
Bandit Of My Dreams, 306
Banzai Pipeline, 410
Barbara, 600
Barbara Ann, 31, 519
Batman, 332
Batman & His Grandmother, 277
Batman Theme, 413
Battle Hymn Of The Republic, 655
Battle Of New Orleans, The, 311, 443
Baubles, Bangles And Beads, 360
(Bazoom) I Need Your Lovin', 108
Be Anything But Be Mine, 260
Be Careful Of Stones That You Throw, 188
Be Mad Little Girl, 165
Be Mine Or Be A Fool, 480
Be My Baby, 184, 537
Be My Boy, 471
Be My Guest, 193
Be My Life's Companion, 124, 434
Be My Love, 370
Be Sure My Love, 209
Be True To Your School, 31
Be True To Yourself, 629
Be Young, Be Foolish, Be Happy, 596
Beach Boys Medley, The, 31
Beach Girl, 59
Beach Party, 157
Beachcomber, 164
Beatnik Fly, 341
Beautiful Brown Eyes, 124
Beautiful Delilah, 44
Beautiful Eyes, 444
Beautiful People, 629
Be-Bop Baby, 453
Be-Bop-A-Lula, 635
Because, 136, 342, 370
Because I Love You, 588
Because Of You, 29, 38
Because They're Young, 214
Because You're Mine, 134, 370
Beechwood 4-5789, 420
Been So Long, 474
Been To Canaan, 355
Beep Beep, 492
Beer Barrel Polka, 637
Beg Me, 326
Beggin', 257
Begging To You, 529
Behind Closed Doors, 524
Bei Mir Bist Du Schoen, 501
Believe Me, 541
Believe What You Say, 453
Bell Bottom Blues, 62
Bell-Bottom Trousers, 501
Belle, Belle, My Liberty Belle, 439
Bells Are Ringing, The, 383
Bells, Bells, Bells, 47
Bells, The, 66, 643, 645

Belonging To Someone, 469
Ben Crazy, 277
Berlin Melody, 628
Bermuda, 552
Bernardine, 58
Besame Mucho, 129
Beside My Love, 209
Beside You, 595
Best Of Everthing, The, 424
Best Part Of Breakin' Up, The, 537
Best Thing That Ever Happened To Me, 363
Better To Give Than To Receive, 305
Better Use Your Head, 385
Betty And Dupree, 661
Betty In Bermudas, 201
Betty Lou Got A New Pair Of Shoes, 264
Betty, My Angel, 265
Between Her Goodbye And My Hello, 363
Bewildered, 66, 428
Bewitched, 170
Beyond, 6
Beyond The Blue Horizon, 114
Beyond The Sea, 164, 659
Beyond The Sunset, 58
Bibbidi-Bobbidi-Boo (Fontaine Sisters), 136
Bible Tells Me So, The, 144
Big Bad John, 172
Big Beat, The, 193
Big Big World, 78
Big Bopper's Wedding, 45
Big Boss Man, 497, 516
Big Boy Pete, 461
Big Cold Wind, 59
Big Daddy, 144
Big Draft, The, 256
Big Girls Don't Cry, 256
Big Hunk O' Love, A, 496
Big Hurt, The, 238, 556
Big Iron, 529
Big John, 562
Big Love, 300
Big Man, 256
Big Man In Town, 257
Big Name Button, 541
Big River, Big Man, 356
Big Time, 114
Big Wide World, 507
Bilbao Song, The, 654
Bill Bailey, 517
Billie Baby, 500
Billy, 384
Billy Bayou, 518
Billy Blues Pr. 1 & 2, 587
Billy Goat, 287
Billy, You're My Friend, 488
Bim Bam Boom, 218
Bimbombey, 534
B-I-N-G-O, 613
Bip Bam, 207
Bird Dance Beat, 610
Bird Dog, 226
Bird Man, The, 304
Bird On My Head, The, 555
Birdland, 107
Birds Of A Feather, 522, 577
Birds Of Britain, 152
Bird's The Word, The, 528

Birth Of The Boogie, 287
Birthday Party, 19
Black Berries, 322
Black Denim Trousers, 108, 443
Black Slacks, 37, 579
Blackjack / Greenbacks, 103
Blame It On The Bossa Nova, 280
Blanche, 603
Bless Our Love, 97
Bless You, 416, 464
Blind Date, 653
Blind Man, 49
Blip Blop, 191
Blistered / See Ruby Fall, 94
Blizzard, The, 518
Blob, The, 238
Blossom Fell, A, / If I May, 134
Blowin' In The Wind, 483, 668
Blue Angel, 461
Blue Autumn, 277
Blue Bayou, 461
Blue Bird Of Happiness, 444
Blue Blue Day, 273
Blue Boy, 518
Blue Christmas, 70
Blue Guitar, 96
Blue Hawaii, 628
Blue Monday, 193
Blue Moon, 412, 496, 631
Blue On Blue, 636
Blue Ribbon Baby, 546
Blue Room, 136
Blue Shadows, 352
Blue Side of Lonesome, 518
Blue Suede Shoes, 36, 482, 496
Blue Tango, 29, 48, 666
Blue Tomorrow, 628
Blue Velvet, 38, 126, 584, 636
Blue Violins, 666
Blue Water Line, 65
Blue Winter, 260
Blueberry Hill, 17, 193
Bluebird On Your Windowsill, 170
Bluebird, The Buzzard And The Oriole, The,
    169
Bluebirds Over The Mountain, 31, 303
Blues In Advance, 565
Blues In The Night, 124, 564
Blues Stay Away From Me, 86
Bo Diddley / I'm A Man, 186
Bo Weevil, 63, 193
Bobby Sox To Stockings, 20
Bobby's Girl, 50
Body Heat, 67
Bold Soul Sister, 614
Boll Weevil Song, The, 40
Bonanza, 84, 93
Bonaparte's Retreat, 282, 582
Bon-Doo-Wah, 465
Bongo, Bongo, Bongo, 222
Bongo Rock, 222
Bongo Stomp, 388
Bonnie Blue Gal, 432
Bonnie Came Back, 214
Bony Moronie, 657
Boogaloo Party, The, 244
Boogie Bear, 36

Boogie On Reggae Woman, 668
Boogie Woogie, 29
Book Of Love, 441, 506
Boom Boom, 310
Boom Boom Boomerang, 172
Boomerang, 625
Boot-Leg, 57
Boppin' Rock Boogie, 579
Boppin' The Blues, 482
Bop-Ting-A-Ling/That's All I Need, 22
Border Song, 262
Born Free, 659
Born To Be Loved, 49
Born To Be Together, 537
Born To Be Wild, 486
Born To Be With You, 111, 330
Born To Lose, 104
Born Too Late, 493
Borrowed Dreams, 300
Boss Guitar, 214
Bossa Nova Baby, 497
Bossa Nova U.S.A., 72
Botch-A-Me, 124
Both Sides Now, 188
Bottle Of Wine, 236
Bounce, The, 461
Bowling Green, 227
Boy Named Sue, A, 93
Boy Next Door, The, 552
Boy Without A Girl, A, 20
Boy's Night Out, 470
Brand New Me, 262
Brass Buttons, 591
Break Away, 31
Break It To Me Gently, 262, 375
Break Up, 556
Breakin' In A Brand New Broken Heart, 260
Breakin' Up Is Breakin' My Heart, 462
Breaking Up Is Hard To Do, 339, 554, 650
Break-up, 382
Breath Taking Guy, A, 594
Breathless, 382
Bridge Of Love, 201
Bridge Over Troubled Water, 262
Bridget The Midget (The Queen Of The Blues),
    587
Brigade Of Broken Hearts, 225
Bright Lights, Big City, 330, 516
Brighton Hill, 181
Bring A Little Sunshine, 161
Bring Back The Thrill, 237
Bring It On Home To Me, 141
Bring It Up, 66
Bring Your Love To Me, 525
Bringing It Back, 498
Brink Of Disaster, 279
Bristol Stomp, 201
Bristol Twistin' Annie, 201
Broken Heart & A Pillow Filled With Tears, A,
    469
Broken Heart, 235
Broken-Hearted Melody, 626
Broomstick Cowboy, 277
Brother Rapp (Part 1), 67
Buchanan & Goodman On Trial, 74
Buffalo Soldier, 244
Buick 59, 425

Build Your Love, 511
Bulldog, 236
Bumble Bee, 22
Bumble Boogie, 29
Bunny Hop, 15
Burn That Candle, 287
Burning Bridges, 551
Burning Love, 498
Burning Of Atlanta, The, 356
Bus Stop Song, The, 254
Bushel And A Peck, A, 137, 170
Busted, 104
But I Do, 637
But Not For Me, 378
Butterflies, 469
Butterfly, 282, 654
Butterfly Baby, 544
Buttons And Bows, 565
Buzz Buzz A-Diddle-It, 87
Buzz-Buzz-Buzz, 309
B'Wa Nina, 606
By The Light Of The Silvery Moon, 60
By The Time I Get To Phoenix, 84
By You, By You, By You, 398
Bye Bye Baby Blues, 508
Bye Bye Baby, 98, 257, 652
Bye Bye Barbara, 424
Bye Bye Blues, 347, 477
Bye, Bye Love, 226, 487

Ca C'est L'amour, 39
Cab Driver, 434
Cabaret, 6
Cadillac Jack, 654
Cajun Queen, The, 172
Calcutta, 256, 651
Calendar Girl, 554
California Girls, 31
California Nights, 279
California Saga, 31
California Sun, 346
Call Me, 262, 424, 444
Call Me Irresponsible, 344, 569
Call Me Mr. In-Between, 323
Call My Name, I'll Be There, 487
Call On Me, 49
Calla Calla, 160
Callin' Doctor Casey, 397
Calypso Melody, 539
Can Anyone Explain?, 6, 14
Can I Come Over Tonight, 630
Can I Get A Witness, 268
Can I Steal A Little Love, 569
Can You Do It, 140
Can You Feel It, 277
Can You Find It In Your Heart, 39
Can You Fool, 85
Can You Jerk Like Me, 140
Can Your Monkey Do The Dog, 601
Canadian Capers, 170
Canadian Sunset, 654, 666
Candida, 464
Candy, 564
Candy And Cake, 91
Candy Apple Red, 285
Candy Girl, 256
Candy Man, 167, 461

Candy Sweet, 58
Candy To Me, 307
Cannonball, 214
Can't Get Over (The Bossa Nova), 280
Can't Get Used To Losing You, 654
Can't Help Falling In Love, 420, 497, 655
Can't I, 134
Can't Nobody Love You, 75
Can't Satisfy, 319
Can't Take My Eyes Off You, 625, 664
Can't Wait For Summer, 372
Can't We Be Sweethearts, 120
Can't You Just See Me, 262
Can't You See, 652
Cap And Gown, 529
Capture The Moment, 334
Cara, Mia, 334, 653
Caravan, 414, 548
Careless Hands, 608
Caribbean, 608
Carmen, 6
Carol, 44, 535, 549
Casino Royale, 6
Cast Your Fate To The Wind, 4, 246, 285
Castin' My Spell, 467
Castle Rock, 569
Castles In The Sand, 667
Casual Look, A, 570
Cat, The, 574
Catch A Falling Star/Magic Moments, 137
Caterina, 137
Cathy's Clown, 226
Cattle Call, 565
'Cause I Love You That's A-Why, 439
Cause You're Mine, 270
C.C. Rider, 661
Certain Smile, A, 424
Cerveza, 347
C'est La Vie, 175, 626
C'est Si Bon, 361, 618
Cha-Cha-Cha, The, 544
Cha-Hua-Hua, 485, 488
Chain Gang, 141, 550
Chain Of Fools, 262
Chained, 268
Chained And Bound, 514
Chains, 142
Chains And Things, 353
Chains Of Love, 50, 58, 207, 615
Chances Are, 423
Change Is Gonna Come, A, 142
Changing Partners, 469, 583
Chanson D'Amour, 247, 605
Chantez-Chantez, 565
Chantilly Lace, 45, 382
Chapel By The Sea, 628
Chapel Of Dreams, 209
Charade, 410
Chariot Rock, 96
Charlena, 555
Charleston, The, 234
Charlie Brown, 129
Charmaine, 253, 411
Charms, 629
Chattanooga Choo Choo, 149, 234
Chattanooga Shoe Shine Boy, 87, 569
Cheaper To Keep Her, 597

Cheat, The, 117
Check Out Your Mind, 319
Cheer Leader, The, 484
Cherie, I Love You, 58
Cherry Lips, 531
Cherry Pie, 422, 571
Cherry Pink & Apple Blossom White, 448, 494
Chi-Baba Chi-Baba, 136
Chicago, 569
Chicken, 108
Chicken And The Hawk, The/Morning, Noon
   And Night, 615
Chicken Feed, 229
Chicken, The, 377
Child Of Clay, 535
Child Of God, 164
Children, 577
Children's Marching Song, The, 432, 582
Chim, Chim, Cheree, 455
China Doll, 7
China Nights, 546
Chinese Checkers, 57
Chip Chip, 402
Chip Off The Old Block, 18
Chipmunk Song, The, 110
Choice Of Colors, 319
Choo'n Gum, 62
Christmas Auld Lang Syne, 164
Christmas Dragnet, 263
Christmas Dream, 137
Christmas Song, The, 134
Church Bells May Ring, 183, 662
Cimarron, 628
Cinco Robles, 16, 478
Cinderella, 12, 256
Cinderella Sunshine, 522
Cindy, Oh Cindy, 238, 419
Cindy's Birthday, 149
Cindy's Gonna Cry, 149
Cinnamon, 158
Cinnamon Cinder, The, 475
Cinnamon Sinner, 39
City Girl Stole My Country Boy, A, 469
City Lights, 501, 522
City Lights, 501
Clap Your Hands, 32
Clapping Song, The, 222
Class, The, 107
Claudette, 226
Clay Idol, 341
Clean Up Your Own Back Yard, 497
Clementine, 164, 332
Click-Clack, 198
Climb Ev'ry Mountain, 39
Climb, The, 358
Clinging Vine, 637
Clock, The, 2
Close To Cathy, 122
Close To You, 80, 647
Close Together, 516
Close Your Eyes, 241
Closer You Are, The, 98
Cloud Nine, 547
Clouds, The, 578
C'mon And Swim, 264
C'mon Everybody, 131
C'mon Marianne, 257

Cocoanut Woman, 32
Coffee Song, The, 568
Cold, Cold Heart, 38, 646
Cold Sweat, 66
College Man, 346
Comancheros, The, 356
Come A Little Bit Closer, 334
Come Along, 658
Come And Get Me, 181
Come And Get These Memories, 416
Come Back, 115, 424
Come Back Home, 277
Come Back Silly Girl, 379
Come Back When You Grow Up, 629
Come Closer To Me, 134
Come Dance With Me, 334
Come Get To This, 269
Come Go With Me, 31, 179, 188
Come Home, 342
Come Into My Heart, 500
Come Live With Me, 105
Come On, 535
Come On And Get Me, 229
Come On Baby, 98
Come On Do The Jerk, 437
Come On, Let's Go, 622
Come On Little Angel, 35
Come On Over To My Place, 207
Come On, React, 236
Come On-A My House, 124, 582
Come Rain Or Come Shine, 104
(Come 'Round Here) I'm The One You Need,
    437
Come Running Back, 417
Come See, 368
Come See About Me, 594
Come Softly To Me, 246
Come To Me, 262, 342, 424, 514
Come Together, 614
Come What May, 407, 469
Comin' Home Baby, 608
Comin' On, 48
Coming Back To You, 68
Coming Home Solider, 637
Coming On Strong, 375
Coming On Too Strong, 456
Communication Breakdown, 462
Composer, The, 594
Coney Island Baby / You Baby You, 227
Confess, 170, 469
Confidential, 363
Congratulations, 454
Conscience, 166
Continental Walk, The, 24
Cool Shake, 179
Cool Water (Sons of the Pioneers), 442
Copy Cat, 54
Corazon, 355
Corinna, Corinna, 485
Corrine Corrina, 615
Cottage For Sale, 392
Cottonfields, 86, 304
Could It Be I'm Falling In Love, 580
Could This Be Magic, 209
Count Down, 146
Count Every Star, 14, 527, 552, 665
Count Your Blessings, 238

Country Boy, 85, 193
Country Girl, 467
Cousin Of Mine, 142
Cowboy Boots, 209
Cowboy Jimmy Joe, 393
Crackin Up, 186
Cradle Of Love, 499
Crawlin', 126
Crawling Back, 462
Crawling King Snake Blues, 310
Crazy, 122
Crazy About The La La La, 438
Crazy Arms, 32
Crazy 'Bout You, Baby, 152
Crazy Country Hop, 467
Crazy, Crazy, Crazy, 242
Crazy Downtown, 559
Crazy For You, 298
Crazy Little Palace, A, 656
Crazy Love, 12, 569
Crazy Man, Crazy, 287
Crazy Otto (Medley), The, 408
Croce Di Oro, 469
Cross Fire!, 465
Cross My Heart, 2, 588
Cross Over The Bridge, 469
Crossfire, 341
Crossfire Time, 117
Crowd, The, 461
Cruel War, The, 483
Cry, 104, 511
Cry Baby, 55, 434
Cry Baby Cry, 10
Cry, Cry, Cry, 49
Cry Like I Cried, 292
Cry Me A River, 393
Cry Of The Wild Goose, The, 248, 367
Cry Softly Lonely One, 462
Cry To Me, 75, 550
Crying, 334, 461
Crying For My Baby, 389
Crying Game, The, 375
Crying In The Chapel, 463, 497, 625
Crying In The Rain, 227
Crying Time, 104
Crying Won't Help You Now, 407
Crying Won't Help You, 352
Crystal Chandelier, 161
Cupid, 141, 452, 580
Cupid's Boogie, 386
Curly, 115
Cycles, 569

Da Doo Ron Ron, 156
Daddy Could Swear I Declare, 363
Daddy Daddy, 70
Daddy Don't You Walk So Fast, 456
Daddy Sang Bass, 93
Daddy-O, 396
Daddy-O / Adorable, 247
Daddy's Home, 559
Daddy's Little Girl, 420, 434
Daddy's Little Man, 574
Daisy Petal Pickin', 275
Dammit Isn't God's Name, 368
Dance By The Light Of The Moon, 461
Dance, Dance, Dance, 31, 174

Dance, Everybody, Dance, 166
Dance Girl, 105
Dance Of Destiny, 418
Dance On Little Girl, 12
Dance The Mess Around, 107
Dance To The Bop, 635
Dance With Me Georgie, 52
Dance With Me Henry, 272
Dance With Me, 207
Dance With The Guitar Man, 214
Dance With The Teacher, 460
Dancin', 137
Dancin' Holiday, 461
Dancin' Party, 107
Dancing Chandelier, 595
Dancing In The Street, 416
Dancing With My Shadow, 258
Danger, 161
Danger Heartbreak Dead Ahead, 421
Danger! Heartbreak Ahead, 447
Danke Schoen, 456
Danny Boy, 19, 366, 501, 618, 654, 663
Dark Moon, 285, 591
Darkest Street In Town, 115
Darlin', 31
Darling Be Home Soon, 165
Darling How Long, 298
Darling, I Love You, 419
Darling Je Vous Aime Beaucoup, 134
Darling Lorraine, 363
Darling Take Me Back, 650
Dawn, 257
Day By Day, 253
Day Dreams, 445
Day In The Life Of A Fool, A, 344
Day Is Done, 483
Day The Rains Came, The, 447
Daydreaming, 262
Daydreams, 149
Days Of Sand And Shovels, The, 637
Days Of Wine And Roses, 410, 654
Dead Man's Curve, 332
Dear Abby, 299
Dear Dad, 44
Dear Heart, 344, 410, 655
Dear Hearts And Gentle People, 565, 580
Dear Ivan, 172
Dear John, 59
Dear Lady Twist, 54
Dear Lonely Hearts, 134
Dear Lover, 652
Dear One, 235
Dearly Beloved, 564
Death Of An Angel, 358
Deceivin' Blues, 466
December, 63 (Oh, What A Night), 257
Deck Of Cards, 419
Dede Dinah, 20
Dedicated To The One I Love, 242, 562
Dedication Song, The, 88
Deep Blue Sea, 172
Deep In The Heart Of Texas, 214
Deep In The Heat of Harlem, 407
Deep Purple, 508, 599, 643
Deja Vu, 645
Delaware, 137
Delia Gone, 58

Delicado, 232
Denise, 508
Desafinado, 271
Desert Pete, 359
Deserie, 105
Desire Me, 141
Destination: Anywhere, 421
Detour, 469
Detroit City, 25
Devil Or Angel, 629
Devil Or Angel/Hey, Doll Baby, 126
Devil Woman, 529
Devoted To You, 226
Diamond Ring, 642
Diamonds and Pearls, 470
Diana, 12, 544
Diane, 291
Diary, The, 554
Did You Ever See A Dream Walking, 194
Did You Have A Happy Birthday, 12
Did You See Jackie Robinson Hit The Ball?, 342
Diddle-De-Dum, 35
Diddley Daddy, 186
Didn't You Know, 363
Dig You Later (A Hubba-Hubba-Hubba), 135
Dim, Dim The Lights, 287
Ding Dong, 403
Ding-A-Ling, 544
Dinner With Drac, 674
Disco Lady, 597
Disco 9000, 597
Distant Drums, 518
Distant Love, A, 176
Distant Lover, 269
Dizzy, 535
Dizzy, Miss Lizzy, 657
Do I Love You, 12, 160, 418, 537
Do It Again, 31
Do It Baby, 438
Do It In The Name Of Love, 354
Do It Right, 41
Do It-Rat Now, 48
Do Something For Me, 196
Do The Bird, 557
Do The Clam, 497
Do The Freddie, 107
Do The Monkey, 157
Do The New Continental, 201
Do What You Did, 293
Do What You Do Well, 432
Do What You Gotta Do, 567, 629
Do You Know How To Twist, 24
Do You Know The Way To San Jose, 644
Do You Love Me, 140
Do You Mind, 654
Do You Wanna Dance, 31
Do You Want To Dance, 264, 556
Do Your Own Thing, 41
Doctor, The, 652
Does Anybody Know I'm Here, 176
Does He Mean That Much To You, 18
Does Your Chewing Gum Lose Its Flavor, 197
Dog, The, 601
Doggie In The Window, The, 469
Doggin' Around, 663
Doggone Right, 438

Doin' The Continental Walk, 162
Doin' What Comes Natur'lly, 565
Doll House, 64
Dollar Down, A, 384
Domani, 371
Dominique, 570
Domino, 418
Dommage, Dommage, 621
Doncha' Think It's Time, 496
Donna, 622
Donna The Prima Donna, 188
Don't, 496
Don't Answer The Door, 353
Don't Ask Me To Be Friends, 227
Don't Ask Me To Be Lonely, 209
Don't Ask Me Why, 496
Don't Be A Drop-Out, 66
Don't Be Afraid Little Darlin', 373
Don't Be Angry, 68
Don't Be Angry/Chop Chop Boom, 152
Don't Be Cruel, 48, 401, 496
Don't Bet Money Honey, 552
Don't Blame Me, 227
Don't Blame The Children, 167
Don't Break The Heart That Loves You, 260
Don't Call Me Sweetie, 533
Don't Cha Love It, 438
Don't Change On Me, 104
Don't Come Knockin', 193
Don't Come Running Back To Me, 664
Don't Cry, 368
Don't Cry Baby, 262, 328
Don't Cry Daddy/Rubberneckin', 497
Don't Cry Joni, 618
Don't Cry My Love, 319, 401
Don't Cry No More, 49
Don't Deceive Me, 70, 661
Don't Ever Leave Me, 260
Don't Ever Love Me, 32
Don't Fence Me In, 218
Don't Fight It, 486
Don't Forbid Me, 58
Don't Forget About Me, 380
Don't Get Around Much Anymore, 35
Don't Go Home, 492
Don't Go Near The Indians, 5
Don't Go To Strangers, 443
Don't Hang Up, 465
Don't It Make You Want To Go Home, 41, 577
Don't Knock My Love, 487
Don't Knock On My Door, 269
Don't Let Go, 290
Don't Let Her Be Your Baby, 140
Don't Let Love Hang You Up, 80
Don't Let The Flame Burn Out, 181
Don't Let The Green Grass Fool You, 487
Don't Let The Stars Get In Your Eyes, 137
Don't Make Me Over, 644
Don't Make My Baby Blue, 368
Don't Mess With Bill, 421
Don't Pity Me, 189
Don't Play That Song, 262, 353
Don't Pull Your Love/Then You Can Tell Me
    Goodbye, 85
Don't Read The Letter, 469
Don't Say Goodnight And Mean Goodbye, 562
Don't Say Goodnight, 322, 629

Don't Say Nothin' Bad, 142
Don't Set Me Free, 104
Don't Sweetheart Me, 651
Don't Take It So Hard, 522
Don't Take The Stars, 450
Don't Take Your Guns To Town, 93
Don't Take Your Love From Me, 401
Don't Tell Me Not To Love You, 329
Don't Tell Me Your Troubles, 273
Don't Think Twice, It's All Right, 483
Don't Throw Away All Those Teardrops, 20
Don't Try To Fight It Baby, 280
Don't Wait Too Long, 39
Don't Wanna Think About Paula, 376
Don't Worry, 529
Don't Worry 'Bout Me, 569
Don't Worry Baby, 31, 606
Don't You Believe It, 654
Don't You Just Know It, 573
Don't You Know I Love You, 126
Don't You Know Yockomo, 573
Don't You Know, 103, 193, 517
Don't You Worry, 267
Don't You Worry 'Bout A Thing, 668
Dooley, 461
Door Is Still Open To My Heart, The, 417
Do-Re-Mi, 199
Do-Re-Mi, 432
Dottie, 162
Double Crossing Blues, 466
Do-Wah-Diddy, 227
Down And Out In New York City, 67
Down At Papa Joe's, 190
Down By The Station, 256
Down In Mexico, 129
Down In The Alley, 295
Down In The Valley, 75
Down On My Knees, 298
Down The Aisle Of Love, 503
Down The Aisle, 366
Down The Hall, 257
Down The Street To 301, 93
Down Yonder, 89, 341
Downhearted, 237
Drag City, 332
Dragnet, 14
Dream, 341, 568
Dream Baby, 461
Dream Baby (How Long Must I Dream), 85
Dream Boy, 13
Dream Lover, 164, 471
Dream On, 525
Dream On Little Dreamer, 137
Dreamer, The, 554
Dreamer's Holiday, A, 136
Dreamin', 78
Dreamin' Blues, 466
Dreams Of The Everyday Housewife, 84, 456
Dreamy Eyes, 255, 604
Driftin' Blues, 49
Drinking Man's Diet, The, 559
Drinking Wine Spo-dee O'dee, 382
Drip Drop, 188, 207
Drive In Show, 131
Drivin' Home, 214
Driving Wheel, 389
Drown In My Own Tears, 103

Drownin' My Sorrows, 260
Drowning On Dry Land, 389
Drummin' Up A Storm, 454
Drums Are My Beat, 454
Duck, The, 377
Duke Of Earl, 97
Dum Dum, 374
Dum Dum Dee Dum, 158
Dum-De-Da, 637
Dumplin's, 21, 264
Dungaree Doll, 238
Dutchman's Gold, 62
Dynamite, 374

Early In The Morning, 309, 526
Early Morning Rain, 483
Earth Angel, 152, 411, 480, 604
Earthbound, 167, 370
Easier Said Than Done, 223
East Of Eden, 327
Easy Love, 645
Easy To Be Free, 454
Ebb Tide, 264, 290, 491, 525, 650
Ebony Eyes, 226
Ecstasy, 353
Eddie My Love, 111, 247, 598
Eh Cumpari, 371
18 Yellow Roses, 164
El Matador, 358
El Paso, 529
El Pussy Cat, 547
El Rancho Rock, 96
El Watusi, 27
Eleanor Rigby, 104, 262
Electric Stories, 257
Electronic Magnetism, The, (That's Heavy, Baby), 76
Elevator Operator, 513
11th Hour Melody, 302
Emotions, 374
Empty Arm Blues, 430
Empty Arms, 63, 330
Empty Arms/Love's A Hurting Game, 313
Enchanted, 491
Enchanted Island, 254
Enchanted Sea, The, 180
End Of Our Road, The, 269, 363
End Of The World, The, 169
End, The, 283
Endless Sleep, 523
Endlessly, 40
Energy Crisis, 74, 277
Engine Number 9, 486
English Muffins & Irish Stew, 595
Escape-ism, 67
Eso Beso, 12
Eternally, 627
Even Now, 237
Evening Rain, 283
Eventually, 375
Everglades, 358
Everlovin', 453
Ever-Lovin' Fingers, 60
Every Beat Of My Heart, 66, 362
Every Breath I Take, 488
Every Day I Have The Blues, 352
Every Day I Have To Cry, 4

Every Day Of My Life, 637
Every Little Move You Make, 390
Every Little Thing I Do, 189
Every Night About This Time, 193
Every Night, 12, 101
Every Night, Every Day, 402
Every Step Of The Way, 424
Every Time You Touch Me (I Get High), 524
Everybody, 535
Everybody Do The Sloopy, 603
Everybody Go Home, 280
Everybody Knows, 373
Everybody Like To Cha Cha Cha, 141
Everybody Loves A Lover, 171, 562
Everybody Loves A Nut, 93
Everybody Loves Me But You, 375
Everybody Loves Somebody, 417
Everybody Monkey, 88
Everybody Needs Love, 362
Everybody Needs Somebody To Love, 75, 486
Everybody Ought To Be In Love, 12
Everybody's Got A Home But Me, 290
Everybody's Got The Right To Love, 594
Everybody's Gotta Pay Some Dues, 437
Everybody's Somebody's Fool, 260, 298
Everyday I Have The Blues, 588
Everybody I Have To Cry Some, 4
Everyday I Love You, 442, 581
Everyone Was There, 349
Everyone's Laughing, 578
Everything A Man Could Ever Need, 85
Everything Is Beautiful, 587
Everything Is Good About You, 379
Ev're Day Of My Life, 403
Ev'ry Little Bit Hurts, 629
Ev'rybody's Twistin', 569
Exclusively Yours, 190
Exodus, 234, 292
Exodus Song, The, 59
Eyes, 212
Eyesight To The Blind, 352, 370

Fabulous, 282
Fabulous Character, 626
Face It Girl, It's Over, 664
Faded Love, 123, 180
Fa-Fa-Fa-Fa-Fa, 514
Fairy Tales, 578
Faith Can Move Mountains, 134
Fallen Star, A, 305, 314
Fallin', 260
Fallin' Angel, 625
Falling, 461
Fame And Fortune, 496
Fancy Dancer, 625
Fancy Nancy, 571
Fang, 458
Fannie Mae, 65
Far Away Christmas Blues, 466
Far Away Places, 136, 653
Far, Far Away, 273
Farther Up The Road, 49
Fascination, 90, 327, 446
Fat Man, The, 193
Father Of Girls, 137
Feel It, 141, 142
Feel So Bad, 104

Feel So Fine, 499
Feel So Good, 563
Feeling Is Gone, The, 49
Feet Up (Pat Him On The Po-Po), 439
Fell In Love On Monday, 194
Ferris Wheel, The, 227
Feudin' And Fightin', 581
Fever, 377, 392
Fibbin', 469
Fiddle Around, 332
Fifteen Years Ago, 618
Fight For The Power Pt 1, 322
Find Another Girl, 79
Fine Fine Boy, A, 397
Finger Poppin' Time, 24
Finger Tips, 501
Fingertips—Pt. 2, 667
Finally Got Myself Together, 319
Fire Of Love, 523
Firefly, 39
First Anniversary, 89
First Born, 248
First Date, First Kiss, First Love, 329
First Day Back At School, 478
First I Look At The Purse, 140
First Name Initial, 13
First Night Of The Full Moon, The, 344
First Quarrel, 478
First Thing Ev'ry Morning, The, 172
Fish, The, 544
500 Miles Away From Home, 26
Five Long Years, 389
Five Minutes More, 568
5-10-15 Hours, 70
Flaming Star, 496
Flamingo, 6, 59, 393
Flamingo Express, 542
Flamingo L'Amore, 270
Flesh And Blood, 94
Flip Flop And Fly, 615
Flip, Flop And Bop, 149
Flip Top Box, 198
Float, The, 24
Florence, 470
Flowers Mean Forgiveness, 569
Flowers Of Love, 150
Fly Me To The Moon, 22, 39
Fly Me To The Moon Bossa Nova, 291
Fly, The, 107
Flying Saucer The 2nd, 74
Flying Saucer, The, 74
Folk Singer, The, 535
Follow Me, 207
Follow That Dream, 497
Follow The Boys, 260
Folsom Prison Blues, 93
Fool #1, 375
Fool, 498
Fool And The Angel, The, 300
Fool, Fool, Fool, 126, 583
Fool For You, 319
Fool For You, A/This Little Girl Of Mine, 103
Fool In Love, A, 614
Fool Me, 577
Fool Never Learns, A, 655
Fool Such As I, A, 496
Fool That I Am, 328

Fool, The, 117, 266
Foolin' Around, 583
Foolish Little Girl, 562
Foolish Me, 446
Fools Fall In Love, 207
Fool's Hall Of Fame, The, 58
Fools Rush In, 40, 454
Foot Stomping—Part 1, 245
Footsteps, 373
For A Penny, 58
For All We Know, 647
For Every Man There's A Woman, 418
For He's A Jolly Good Fellow, 637
For Lovin' Me, 483
For Mama, 261, 621
For Me And My Gal, 87
For My Baby, 40
For My Good Fortune, 58
For Ol' Times Sake, 498
For Once In My Life, 39, 664, 668
For The Good Times, 501
For The Love Of You (Part 1 & 2), 322
For What It's Worth, 157
For You, 454
For Your Love, 609
For Your Precious Love, 79, 434
For Your Sweet Love, 92
Forever, 386
Forever And Ever, 136, 653
Forever Came Today, 594
Forever Darling, 7
Forget Domani, 261, 569
Forget Him, 544
Forget Me Not, 348
Forgive And Forget, 463
Forgive Me, 237, 420
Forgive My Heart, 134
Fortune Teller, 158
Forty Cups Of Coffee, 287
Forty Days, 295
Forty Days & Forty Nights, 647
Forty Miles Of Bad Road, 214
49 Shades Of Green, 7
Found Love, 516
Fountain Of Youth, 254
Four Little Heels, 314
409, 31
Four Strong Winds, 26
Four Walls, 398, 518, 583
Four Winds And Seven Seas, 608
Fox Hunt, 6
Frankie, 260
Frankie And Johnny, 40, 142, 497
Frankie's Man, Johnny, 93
Franny Franny, 457
Fraulein, 300, 373
Free Me, 499, 514
Freedom, 322
Freedom Blues, 391
Freight Train, 202
French Foreign Legion, 569
Fried Eggs, 320
Friend, Lover, Woman, Wife, 574
Friendly Persuasion, 58, 249
Friends, 31
Friendship Train, 363
Frogg, 65

From A Jack To A King, 432
From A School Ring To A Wedding Ring, 540
From All Over The World, 332
From Me To You, 556
From Russia With Love, 634
From The Bottom Of My Heart, 126, 417
From The Candy Store On The Corner To The
　　Chapel On The Hill, 39
From The Vine Came The Grape, 270, 305
Fun, Fun, Fun, 31
Funk Factory, 487
Funky Broadway, 486
Funky Drummer (Part 1), 67
Funky President (People It's Bad), 67
Funny, 36, 68, 305
Funny How Time Slips Away, 220, 604
Funny Man, 587
Funny Way Of Laughin', 323

Galveston, 84
Gambler's Guitar, 202
Games People Play, 577
Games That Lovers Play, 238, 456
Gandy Dancers' Ball, The, 368
Gang That Sang Heart Of My Heart, The, 249
Garden In The Rain, A, 161, 249
Garden Party, 454
Gas Money, 330
Gee, 154, 289, 332
Gee Baby, 466
Gee, But It's Lonely, 58
Gee Whittakers!, 58
Gee Whiz, 320
Gee Whiz (Look At His Eyes), 601
Geisha Girl, 393
Gentle On My Mind, 84, 470
Georgia On My Mind, 104, 525
Georgia Rose, 39
Get A Job, 566
Get Down, 97
Get Him, 227
Get Into Something, 322
Get It Together, 66
Get Me To The Church On Time, 371
Get Off My Back Woman, 353
Get Out Of My Life, Woman, 199
Get Rhythm, 93
Get The Message, 315
Get Up, Get Into It, Get Involved, 67
Get Up, Get Up, 448
Get Up I Feel Like Being A Sex Machine, 67
Get Up Offa That Thang, 67
Getting Ready For The Heartbreak, 326
Ghetto Child, 580
Ghetto Woman, 353
(Ghost Riders) In The Sky, 506
Ghost Town, 109
Giant, 29, 445
Gidget, 166
Gigi, 160
Gina, 424
Ginger Bread, 20
Ginnie Bell, 187
Ginny Come Lately, 314
Girl, A Girl, A, 238
Girl Can't Help It, The, 391
Girl Come Running, 257

Girl Don't Care, 97
Girl From Peyton Place, The, 376
Girl Has To Know, A, 270
Girl In My Dreams, 88
Girl In The Wood, The, 368
Girl Of My Best Friend, 198
Girl Of My Dreams, 123
Girl On Page 44, The, 254
Girl That Stood Beside Me, The, 165
Girl With The Golden Braids, The, 137
Girl With The Story In Her Eyes, 545
Girls, 368
(Girls, Girls, Girls) Made To Love, 306
Girls, Girls, Girls, 129
Girls Grow Up Faster Than Boys, 142
Girls Will Be Girls, Boys Will Be Boys, 322
Girl's Work Is Never Done, A, 111
Gitarzan, 587
Give It To The People, 525
Give It Up, 430
Give It Up Or Turnit A Loose, 67
Give Me, 533
Give Me Love, 403
Give Me Your Hand, 136
Give Myself A Party, 273
Give Us This Day, 329
Give Us Your Blessing, 485
Give Your Baby A Standing Ovation, 177
Giving Up, 362
Giving Up On Love, 79
Glad Rags, 248
Glad She's A Woman, 277
Gleam In Your Eye, The, 98
Glendora, 137
Gloria, 434, 473, 639
Gloria/I Wonder Why, 83
Gloria's Theme, 641
Glory Of Love, The, 177, 241, 267, 514, 538
Glow Worm, 434
Go Ahead and Cry, 525
Go Away Little Girl, 373
Go Chase A Moonbeam, 621
Go, Jimmy, Go, 115
Go On Home, 469
Go On With The Wedding, 348, 469
God, Country And My Baby, 78
God Only Knows, 31
Go-Go Girl, 199
Goin' Away, 236
Goin' Down Slow, 50
Goin' Home, 193
Goin' On, 31
Goin' Out Of My Head, 385
Goin' Out Of My Head/Forget, 570
Goin' Out Of My Head/Can't Take My Eyes Off
　　You, 379
Goin' Steady, 546
Going Back To Louisiana, 98
Going Going Gone, 41
Going To A Go-Go, 437
Going To The River, 660
Golden Earrings, 377
Golden Teardrops, 244
Gone, 314, 526
Gone, Gone Gone, 227
Gone With The Wind, 210
Gonna Find Me A Bluebird, 18, 506

Gonna Get Along Without Ya' Now, 169, 395, 476
Gonna Miss You Around Here, 352
Gonna Raise A Ruckus Tonight, 172
Gonzo, 55
Good Book, 583
Good Daddy Blues, 646
Good Foot, 67
Good Golly, Missy Molly, 391
Good Life, The, 39
Good Lover, 516
Good Lovin', 126, 461
Good Lovin' Ain't Easy To Come By, 269
Good Luck Charm, 497
Good News, 142
Good Rockin' Daddy, 328
Good Rockin' Tonight, 58
Good Thing, 521
Good Time Baby, 544
Good Time Charlie, 49
Good Times, 79, 97, 142
Good Timin', 31, 345
Good Vibrations, 31
Goodby My Love, 67
Goodbye Baby (Baby Goodbye), 75
Goodbye Baby, 551
Goodbye Charlie, 469
Goodbye Cruel World, 166
Goodbye Jimmy, Goodbye, 384
Goodbye To Rome, 272
Goodnight, 220, 461
Goodnight, Irene, 515, 569, 581
Goodnight My Love, 12, 36, 246, 354, 403, 484
Goodnight, Sweetheart, Goodnight, 403, 578
Goody Goody, 400
Goofus, 477
Got A Date With An Angel, 656
Got A Girl, 256
Got A Job, 437
Got A Match, 267
Got A Right To Love My Baby, 352
Got My Mojo Working, 574
Got The Feeling, 229
Got To Get You Off My Mind, 76
Got To Give It Up Pt 1, 269
Got To Have You Back, 322
Got To See If I Can't Get Mommy (To Come Back Home), 80
Gotta Get To Know You, 50
Gotta Get To Your House, 555
(Gotta Go) Upside Your Head, 342
Gotta Have Rain, 280
Gotta Lotta Love, 4
Gotta Travel On, 282, 672
Graduation Day, 253, 540
Graduation's Here, 246
Granada, 569
Grass Is Greener, The, 375
Gravy, 557
Grease, 625
Great Airplane Strike, The, 521
Great Balls Of Fire, 382
Great Pretender, The, 490
Greatest Hurt, The, 663
Green Christmas, 263
Green Door, The, 398

Green Green, 455
Green Leaves Of Summer, The, 23, 65
Green Mosquito, The, 611
Green Onions, 57
Greenback Dollar, 359
Greenfields, 65
Greenwood Mississippi, 391
Groovin', 57
Groovy Situation, 97
Ground Hog, 70
Grow Closer Together, 318
Guaglione, 494
Guess Things Happen That Way, 93
Guess Who, 36, 312, 353
Guilty, 653
Guilty Of Loving You, 265
Guitar Boogie Shuffle, 637
Guitar Man, 497, 498
Gum Drop, 152
Guy Is A Guy, A, 170
Gypsy Cried, The, 114
Gypsy, The, 565
Gypsy Woman, 315, 318

Hail To The Conquering Hero, 166
Hair of Gold, Eyes of Blue, 407
Hajji Baba, 134
Half A Photograph, 583
Half As Much, 124
Half Heaven-Half Heartache, 488
Half-Breed, 506
Halfway To Paradise, 464, 637
Hallelujah I Love Her So, 103
Hallelujah, I Love Him So, 377
Hand Clappin', 501
Hand It Over, 326
Handy Man, 345, 556
Hang 'Em High, 57
Hang On Sloopy, 379
Hanging Tree, The, 529
Happening, The, 6, 594
Happier, 12
Happiness, 47
Happiness Street, 39, 272
Happy, 12, 165
Happy Anniversary, 254, 447
Happy Birthday Blues, 671
Happy Birthday, Sweet Sixteen, 554
Happy Days, 343
Happy Guy, A, 454
Happy, Happy Birthday Baby, 612
Happy Heart, 655
Happy Muleteer, The, 530
Happy Organ, The, 145
Happy Shades Of Blue, 87
Happy Song (Dum Dum), The, 514
Happy Times Are Here To Stay, 464
Happy Wanderer, The, 650
Happy Weekend, 146
Happy Whistler, The, 530
Happy-Go-Lucky-Me, 225
Harbor Lights, 14, 491
Hard Headed Woman, 496
Hard Times (The Slop), 648
Hard To Get, 405
Harlem Nocturne, 638
Harmony, 49

Harper Valley P.T.A., 157
Harry The Hairy Ape, 587
Harvest For The World, 322
Harvey's Got A Girl Friend, 541
Hats Off To Larry, 556
Have A Good Time, 38, 602
Have I Stayed Away Too Long, 26
Have I Told You Lately That I Love You, 453
Have Mercy Baby, 52, 196
Have You Ever Been Lonely, 63, 89
Have You Heard, 210, 329
Have You Looked Into Your Heart, 621
Havin' Fun, 187
Having A Party, 141
Hawaii Five-O, 631
Hawaiian War Chant, 6
Hawaiian Wedding Song, The, 654
He, 302, 403, 525
He Knows I Love Him Too Much, 471
He Says The Same Thing To Me, 169
He Will Break Your Heart, 79
Heading For The Poor House, 566
Heart, 238, 249, 456
Heart And Soul, 120, 249, 332, 408
Heart Hideaway, 89
Heart In Hand, 375
Heart Of My Heart, 144
Heartaches, 123, 412, 575
Heartaches By The Number, 439, 604
Heartbeat, 309
Heartbreak Hill, 194
Heartbreak Hotel, 263, 496
Heartbreak (It's Hurtin' Me), 392
Heartbreaker, 154
Hearts, 663
Hearts Of Stone, 48, 105, 247, 337
Heat Wave, 416
Heather Honey, 535
Heaven And Paradise, 346
Heaven Help Us All, 668
Heaven On Earth, 490, 580
Heavenly Lover, 63
Held For Questioning, 202
He'll Have To Go, 75, 518
He'll Have to Stay, 48
Hello Darlin', 618
Hello, Dolly!, 17, 165
Hello Heartache, Goodbye Love, 390
Hello Jim, 12
Hello Mary Lou, 453
Hello Stranger, 380
Hello Walls, 670
Hello Young Lovers, 12
Help Me Find A Way (To Say I Love You), 385
Help Me Make It Through The Night, 363
Help Me Rhonda, 31
Help Me Somebody, 241
Help The Poor, 353
Helpless, 491, 652
Henrietta, 173
Henry's Got Flat Feet, 430
Her Royal Majesty, 166
Here, 418
Here Comes Heaven, 18
Here Comes Summer, 350
Here Comes That Feelin', 375
Here Comes The Night, 31

Here Comes The Rain, Baby, 18
Here I Am, 644
Here I Am Baby, 421
Here I Stand, 526
Here In My Heart, 38, 419
Here She Comes, 619
Here We Go Again, 104
Hernando's Hideaway, 50, 511
Heroes And Villains, 31
He's A Bad Boy, 355
He's A Good Guy, 420
He's A Lover, 652
He's A Rebel, 156
He's Gone, 101
He's Got The Power, 227
He's Got The Whole World (In His Hands), 394
He's In Town, 606
He's Mine, 490
He's My Dreamboat, 260
He's Raining In My Sunshine, 334
He's So Fine, 109
He's So Heavenly, 375
He's Sure The Boy I Love, 156
He's The Great Imposter, 246
Hey! Baby, 98
Hey Bobba Needle, 107
Hey Girl, 550
Hey Girl, Don't Bother Me, 596
Hey Harmonica Man, 667
Hey! Jealous Lover, 569
Hey Jean, Hey Dean, 172
Hey Joe!, 368
Hey Jude, 486
Hey, Let's Twist, 173
Hey Little Cobra, 526
Hey Little Girl, 117, 368, 556
Hey! Little Lucy, 617
Hey Little One, 77, 84
Hey Love, 668
Hey, Miss Fannie, 126
Hey, Mr. Sax Man, 507
Hey Now, 279
Hey Paula, 478
Hey! School Girl, 607
Hey Seniorita, 480
Hey There, 124, 167
Hey There Lonely Boy, 542
Hey, Western Union Man, 80
Hey You Little Boo-ga-Loo, 107
Hi Diddle Diddle, 259
Hi Lili Hi Lo, 315, 659
Hickory, Dick And Doc, 629
Hide And Seek, 615
Hide Away, 356
Hide 'Nor Hair, 104
Hideaway, 251
High And The Mighty, The, 29, 310, 671
High Heel Sneakers, 382, 668
High Hopes, 569
High Noon, 368, 527
High Out Of Time, 355
High School Confidential, 382
High School Romance, 289
High School U.S.A., 230
High Sign, 183
Higher Ground, 668
Hi-Lili, Hi-Lo, 96

Him Or Me—What's It Gonna Be, 522
Hip Hug-Her, 57
Hit And Run Affair, 137
Hit Record, 41
Hit The Road Jack, 104
Hitch Hike, 268
Hittin' On Me, 342
Ho Ho Song, The, 80
Hobo Blues, 310
Hobo Flats (Part 1), 574
Hold 'Em Joe, 32
Hold It, 191
Hold Me Baby, 430
Hold Me, Thrill Me, Kiss Me, 91
Hold Me Tight, 452
Hold My Hand, 144
Holiday For Trombones, 539
Holy Cow, 199
Home For The Holidays, 137
Home Of The Blues, 92
Honest I Do, 320, 516
Honey, 277, 574
Honey Chile, 416
Honey Come Back, 85
Honey Hush, 615
Honey Love, 207
Honey-Babe, 444
Honeycomb, 534
Honky Tonk '65, 404
Honky Tonk, 67, 190
Honky Tonk (Part 2), 191
Honolulu Lulu, 332
Hoochie Coochie Coo, The, 24
Hooka Tooka, 107
Hoop-Dee Doo, 137, 170, 582
Hoopla Hoola, 341
Hooray For Hazel, 535
Hootenanny, 276
Hootenanny Saturday Night, 65
Hop Scotch, 548
Hope That We Can Be Together Soon, 52
Hopeless, 654
Hop-Scotch Polka, 444
Hot Cakes (1st Serving), 146
Hot Diggity, 137
Hot Dog Buddy Buddy, 287
Hot Fudge, 74
Hot Pants (She Got To Use What She Got To
   Get What She Wants, 67
Hot Pastrami, 166
Hot Pastrami With Mashed Potatoes, 174
Hot Pepper, 149
Hot Rod Lincoln, 53, 543
Hotel Happiness, 41
Houdini, 62
Hound Dog, 496, 602
Hound Dog Man, 229
House, A Car And A Wedding Ring, A, 294
House Is Not A Home, A, 41, 644
House Of Bamboo, 283
House of Blue Lights, The, 431
House That Jack Built, The, 262
House With Love In It, A, 254
Houston, 417
Houston (I'm Coming To See You), 85
How About That, 117
How Are Ya' Fixed For Love, 569

How Can I Forget, 354
How Can I Forget/Gonna Give Her All The
   Love I've Got, 268
How Could I Let You Get Away, 580
How Deep Is The Ocean, 238
How Did We Lose It Baby, 80
How High The Moon, 477
How Important Can It Be?, 329, 626
How Is Julie, 379
How Little We Know, 569
How Long, 193
How Many More Years, 666
How Many Teardrops, 114
How Many Tears, 629
How Soon? (Will I Be Seeing You), 442, 565
How Sweet It Is To Be Loved By You, 268
How The Time Flies, 642
How To Handle A Woman, 424
Hucklebuck, The, 107, 568
Hula Hoop Song, The, 63, 272
Hula Love, 365
Hullo Mudduh, Hello Fadduh!, 559
Hully Gully Again, 386
Hully Gully Baby, 201
Hully Gully Guitars, 515
Humdinger, 87
Hummingbird, 353, 477
Humpty Dumpty Heart, 22
Hunch, The, 270
Hundred Pounds of Clay, A, 402
Hung Up In Your Eyes, 314
Hungry, 521
Hungry Years, 456
Hunter Gets Captured By The Game, The, 421
Hunter, The, 614
Hurry Up And Wait, 322
Hurt, 290, 385, 498, 672
Hurt By Love, 259
Hurt So Bad, 379, 385
Hurts Me To My Heart, 2
Hush, Hush, Sweet Charlotte, 470
Hushabye, 334, 450
Hush-Hush, 516
Hypnotized, 207

I, 144
I Adore Him, 10
I Ain't Gonna Stand For It, 668
I Ain't Never, 256, 487
I Almost Lost My Mind, 58, 312
I Am, 39
I Am With You, 196
I Beg Of You, 496
I Believe, 212, 368
I Believe I'm Gonna Love You, 570
I Believe In You, 529
I Believe In You (You Believe In Me), 597
I Believe There's Nothing Stronger . . ., 12
I Can Hear Music, 31
I Can Make It Through The Day, 105
I Can Make It With You, 181
I Can See Clearly Now, 452
I Can Sing A Rainbow/Love Is Blue, 177
I Can't Believe I'm Losing You, 569
I Can't Dance To The Music You're Playin',
   416
I Can't Do Enough, 177

I Can't Do It By Myself, 73
I Can't Get You Out Of My Heart, 419
(I Can't Help You) I'm Falling Too, 168
I Can't Help It, 604, 641
I Can't Love You Enough, 22
I Can't Put My Finger On It, 389
I Can't Say Goodbye, 236
I Can't See Myself Leaving You, 262
I Can't Stand Myself, 66
I Can't Stand To See You Cry, 438
I Can't Stay Away From You, 319
I Can't Stay Mad At You, 169
I Can't Stop Loving You, 104
I Can't Stop Talking About You, 585
I Can't Wait Until I See My Baby, 645
I Chose To Sing The Blues, 104
I Concentrate On You, 647
I Could Have Danced All Night, 124, 354, 565,
  595
I Could Have Loved You So Well, 485
I Could Never Be President, 597
I Could Write A Book, 80
I Couldn't Sleep A Wink Last Night, 568
I Count The Tears, 207
I Cried, 67, 469
I Cried A Tear, 22
I Cried At Laura's Wedding, 401
I Cried Like A Baby, 68
I Cried My Last Tear, 349
I Cross My Fingers, 137
I Cross My Fingers, 232
I Didn't Slip—I Wasn't Pushed—I Fell, 170
I Didn't Want To Do It, 579
I Dig Girls, 544
I Dig Rock and Roll Music, 483
I Dig You Baby, 79
I Do Love You, 587, 588
(I Do The) Shimmy-Shimmy, 264
I Don't Blame You At All, 438
I Don't Care If The Sun Don't Shine, 496
I Don't Have To Ride No More, 508
I Don't Hurt Anymore, 647
I Don't Know What It Is, 51
I Don't Know What You've Got But It's Got Me,
  391
I Don't Know Why, 552, 668
I Don't Know Why, But I Do, 301
I Don't Know, 70
I Don't Like It Like That, 52
I Don't Like To Sleep Alone, 12
I Don't Mind, 66
I Don't Need You Anymore, 181
I Don't See Me In Your Eyes Anymore, 136,
  524
I Don't Wanna Be A Loser, 279
I Don't Want Nobody, 342
I Don't Want Nobody To Give Me Nothing, 67
I Don't Want To Be Hurt Any More, 134
I Don't Want To Cry, 326
I Don't Want To Do Wrong, 363
I Don't Want To Know Your Name, 85
I Don't Want To Lose You, 664
I Don't Want To See Tomorrow, 134
I Don't Want To Take A Chance, 652
I Dream Of You, 135, 568
I Dreamed, 341
I Dreamed Of A Hill-Billy Heaven, 527

I Fall To Pieces, 122
I Feel A Sin Coming On, 76
I Feel A Song In My Heart, 363
I Feel Good, 563
I Feel So Bad, 496
I Feel The Earth Move, 355
I Fooled You This Time, 97
I Forgot More Than You'll Ever Know, 330
I Found A Girl, 332
I Found A Love, 232, 486
I Found A New Baby, 164
I Found A True Love, 486
I Get Around, 31
I Get Ideas, 17, 418
I Get So Lonely, 253
I Get The Sweetest Feeling, 664
I Go Ape, 554
I Got A Bag Of My Own, 67
I Got A Feeling, 453
I Got A Wife, 413
I Got A Woman, 454, 550
I Got Ants In My Pants, 67
I Got Some Help I Don't Need, 353
I Got Stripes, 93
I Got Stung, 496
I Got The Feelin', 66
I Got What I Wanted, 41
I Got You Babe, 328
I Got You (I Feel Good), 66
I Gotta Dance To Keep From Crying, 437
I Gotta Get Myself A Woman, 207
I Gotta Know, 496
I Gotta Let You Go, 416
I Gotta Woman, 104
I Guess I'll Always Love You, 322
I Guess I'll Have To Cry, Cry, Cry, 66
I Guess I'll Miss The Man, 594
I Guess I'm Crazy, 518
I Had A dream, 522
I Have A Boyfriend, 109
I Have But One Heart, 160
I Hear A Rhapsody, 564
I Hear A Symphony, 594
I Hear The Trumpets Blow, 606
I Hear You Knocking, 194, 383, 590
I Heard It Through The Grapevine, 157, 268,
  363
I Idolize You, 614
I Just Can't Help It, 663
I Just Can't Say Goodbye, 544
I Just Don't Know What To Do With Myself,
  644
I Just Don't Know, 254
I Just Don't Understand, 14
I Keep Forgettin', 326
I Knew Jesus (Before He Was A Star), 85
I Know, 70, 137, 271, 578
I Know Where I'm Goin', 289
I Know You Better Than That, 277
I Laughed, 337
I Left My Heart In San Francisco, 39
I Left My Heart In The Balcony, 552
I Like It Like That, 350, 437
I Like To Live The Love, 353
I Like What You're Doing (To Me), 601
I Like Your Kind Of Love, 654
I Lost My Baby, 174

I Love How You Love Me, 471, 637
I Love Mickey, 63
I Love My Baby, 144
I Love My Friend, 524
I Love My Truck, 85
I Love The Way You Love, 343
I Love You 1000 Times, 491
I Love You, 581, 640
I Love You Baby, 12
I Love You Because, 419
I Love You Don't You Forget It, 137
I Love You Drops, 161
(I Love You) For Sentimental Reasons, 120,
   133, 141, 565
I Love You Honey, 310
I Love You In The Same Old Way, 12
I Love You Madly/Maybe, 250
I Love You More & More Every Day, 419
I Love You More Than Words Can Say, 514
I Love You So Much It Hurts, 282, 434
I Love You So, 101
I Love You, Yes I Do, 324
I Loved And I Lost, 319
I Loves You, Porgy, 567
I Make A Fool Of Myself, 625
I May Not Live To See Tomorrow, 314
I Met Him On A Sunday, 562
I Miss You, 52, 177
I Miss You So, 12, 139, 385
I Must Be Seeing Things, 488
I Need Someone, 35
I Need You, 319, 326
I Need You Barry Manilow, 587
I Need You Now, 238, 329
I Need You So, 313
I Need Your Love Tonight, 496
I Need Your Loving, 267, 290, 617
I Never Felt Like This, 551
I Never Knew, 407
I Never Loved A Man (The Way I Love You),
   262
I Never See Maggie Alone, 444
I.O.U., 172
I Only Have Eyes For You, 244, 379
I Only Know I Love You, 249
I Only Know, 646
I Only Want You, 473
I Pity The Fool, 49
I Play And Sing, 464
I Played The Fool, 126
I Promise To Remember, 400
I Promise To Wait My Love, 416
I Put A Spell On You, 296
I Quit My Pretty Mama, 312
I Really Don't Want To Know, 75, 218, 477
I Really Don't Want To Know/There Goes My
   Everything, 497
I Really Love You, 557, 584
I Remember, 239, 658
I Remember You, 316
I Rise, I Fall, 604
I Said My Pajamas (And Put On My Prayers),
   170, 418
I Saw Esau, 7
I Saw Linda Yesterday, 376
I Say A Little Prayer, 262, 644
I Second That Emotion, 437

I Shall Be Released, 550
I Shot Mr. Lee, 52
I Should Care, 401
I Sold My Heart To The Junkman, 51
I Stand Accused, 79
I Started Loving You Again, 420
I Stay In The Mood, 352
I Still Feel The Same About You, 272
I Still Get A Thrill, 329
I Still Get Jealous, 17, 329
I Still Love You, 193
I Surrender Dear, 262
I Take A Lot Of Pride In What I Am, 417
I Think I Love You Again, 375
I Think I'm Gonna Kill Myself, 365
I Think Of You, 137
I Told Myself A Lie, 407
I Told The Brook, 529
I Told You Baby, 516
I Told You So, 345
I Turned You On, 322
I Understand Just How You Feel, 258, 270
I Understand, 625
I Waited A Little Too Long, 583
I Waited Too Long, 22
I Wake Up Crying, 326
I Walk Alone, 529
I Walk The Line, 92, 448
I Wanna Be Around, 39
I Wanna Be Loved, 172, 453, 646, 647, 665
I Wanna Be With You, 664
I Wanna Do It To You, 80
I Wanna Go Home, 136
I Wanna Live, 84
(I Wanna) Love My Life Away, 488
I Wanna Love You, 7
I Wanna Testify, 597
I Wanna Thank You, 544
I Want To Be Happy Cha Cha, 200
I Want To Be Wanted, 374
I Want To Go With You, 18
I Want To Stay Here, 585
I Want To Take You Higher, 614
I Want To Talk About You, 104
I Want To Walk You Home, 193
I Want You, 269
I Want You All To Myself, 348
I Want You, I Need You, I Love You, 496
I Want You So Bad, 66, 353
I Want You To Be My Boy, 227
I Want You To Be My Baby, 272
I Want You To Be My Girl/I'm Not A Know It
   All, 400
I Want You To Know, 193
I Want You To Meet My Baby, 280
(I Was) Born To Cry, 188
I Was Checkin' Out, She Was Checkin' In, 147
I Was Made To Love Her, 157, 668
I Was Such A Fool, 260
I Was The One, 496
I Went To Your Wedding, 469
I (Who Have Nothing), 354
I Will, 161, 417
I Will Follow Him, 390
I Will Live My Life For You, 39
I Will Love You, 96
I Wish, 434, 491, 668

I Wish I Didn't Love You So, 442, 565
I Wish I Knew, 76
I Wish I Were A Princess, 390
I Wish I'd Never Been Born, 469
I Wish It Was Me You Loved, 177
I Wish It Would Rain, 363
I Wish That We Were Married, 538
I Wish You Love, 401
I Woke Up Crying, 329
I Wonder, 375, 480
I Wonder What She's Doing Tonight, 27
I Wonder Who's Kissing Her Now, 136, 165
I Wonder Why, 189
I Won't Cry Anymore, 38, 646
I Won't Forget You, 518
I Won't Love You Anymore, 279
I Won't Mention it Again, 501
I Would Be In Love Anyway, 570
I Wouldn't Treat A Dog (The Way You Treated Me), 50
I'd Be Satisfied, 643
I'd Rather Be Here In Your Arms, 210
I'd Rather Be Sorry, 501
Idaho, 257
Idol With The Golden Head, 129
If, 137, 417, 470
If A Man Answers, 164
If A Woman Answers, 626
If Dreams Came True, 58
If I Can Dream, 497
If I Could Build My Whole World Around You, 269
If I Could Do It Over Again, 212
If I Cried Every Time You Hurt Me, 327
If I Didn't Care, 260, 491
If I Didn't Love You, 326
If I Give My Heart To You, 170, 348
If I Had A Girl, 371
If I Had A Hammer, 395, 482
If I Knew, 134
If I Knew You Were Comin' I'd've Baked A Cake, 28, 272
If I Loved You, 135, 290
If I Never Knew Your Name, 161
If I Ruled The World, 39
If I Should Lose You, 203
If I Were A Carpenter, 165
If I Were Your Woman, 363
If It's Real What I Feel, 80
If It's The Last Thing I Do/I Diddie, 647
If Mary's There, 314
If My Pillow Could Talk, 260
If Teardrops Were Pennies, 124
If This World Were Mine, 269
If We Only Have Love, 645
If You Can Dream, 249
If You Can Want, 437
If You Don't Know Me By Now, 52
If You Don't Want My Lovin' 190
If You Ever Leave Me, 344
If You Go Away, 339
If You Gotta Make A Fool Of Somebody, 68, 509
If You Leave Me Tonight I'll Cry, 642
If You Love Me (Really Love Me), 401, 583
If You Need Me, 75, 486
If You Really Love Me, 668

If You Talk In Your Sleep, 498
If You Wanna Be Happy, 577
If You Wanna Do A Dance All Night, 580
If You Were A Rock & Roll Record, 87
If You Were Mine, 104
If You're Lonely, 372
If You've Got A Heart, 50, 277
Igmoo, 327
I'll Always Have Faith In You, 601
I'll Always Love You, 417, 580
I'll Be Around, 580
I'll Be Doggone, 268
I'll Be Forever Loving You, 218
I'll Be Home, 58, 244, 491
I'll Be Satisfied, 663
I'll Be Seeing You, 243, 546, 569
I'll Be There, 339
I'll Be True, 2
I'll Bring It On Home To You, 601
I'll Go Crazy, 66
I'll Hold You In My Heart, 237
I'll Keep Holding On, 420
I'll Know, 167
I'll Make Him Love Me, 380
I'll Make It All Up To You, 382
I'll Make You Mine, 629
I'll Never Be Free, 582, 583, 646
I'll Never Dance Again, 544
I'll Never Fall In Love Again, 511, 644
I'll Never Find Another You, 330
I'll Never Know, 254
I'll Never Love This Way Again, 645
I'll Never Smile Again, 491
I'll Never Stop Loving You, 170
I'll Never Stop Wanting You, 314
I'll Remember (In The Still Of The Night), 548
I'll Remember Today, 469
I'll Remember Tonight, 58
I'll Sail My Ship Alone, 382
I'll Save The Last Dance For You, 339
I'll Search My Heart, 424
I'll See You In My Dreams, 59
I'll Take Care Of You, 49
I'll Take Care Of Your Cares, 368
I'll Take Good Care Of You, 434
I'll Take Romance, 280
I'll Take You Home, 145, 207
I'll Take You Where The Music's Playing, 207
I'll Try Something New, 437
I'll Wait, 341
I'll Wait For You, 20, 70
I'll Walk Alone, 144, 564
I'll Walk The Line, 146
I'm Wondering, 668
I'm A Drifter, 277
I'm A Fool To Care, 27, 104, 477
I'm A Greedy Man, 67
I'm A Happy Man, 338
I'm A Hog For You, 129
I'm A Man, 229
I'm A Midnight Mover, 486
I'm A Woman, 377
I'm Afraid To Go Home, 314
I'm Always Chasing Rainbows, 135
I'm A-Telling You, 79
I'm Available, 511
I'm Blue, 317

I'm Comin' Home Cindy, 395
I'm Comin' On Back To You, 663
I'm Coming Home, 342, 424, 580
I'm Confessin', 316, 477
I'm Falling In Love With You, 385
I'm Gettin' Better, 518
I'm Going Back To School, 117
I'm Gone, 563
I'm Gonna Be A Wheel Some Day, 193
I'm Gonna Be Strong, 488
I'm Gonna Be Warm This Winter, 260
I'm Gonna Change Everythng, 518
I'm Gonna Do What They Do To Me, 353
I'm Gonna Get Married, 500
I'm Gonna Get My Baby, 516
I'm Gonna Knock On Your Door, 306
I'm Gonna Let My Heart Do The Walking, 594
I'm Gonna Love That Gal, 135
I'm Gonna Make You Mine, 114
I'm Gonna Sit Right Down And Write Myself A
   Letter, 656
I'm Here To Get My Baby Out Of Jail, 226
I'm Hurtin', 461
I'm In Love, 262, 486
I'm In Love Again, 193, 247
I'm In The Mood For Love, 110
I'm In The Mood, 310
I'm Indestructible, 344
I'm Just A Fool For You, 97
I'm Just Your Fool, 342
I'm Learning About Love, 374
I'm Leavin', 498
I'm Leaving It Up To You, 159
I'm Livin' In Shame, 594
I'm Looking Over A Four Leaf Clover, 444
I'm Lost Without You Tonight/You Might Have
   Told Me, 647
I'm Movin' On, 104
I'm Never Gonna Tell, 534
I'm Not A Juvenile Delinquent, 400
I'm Not Afraid, 453
I'm On Fire, 382
I'm On My Way, 304
I'm On The Outside (Looking In), 385
I'm Over You, 61
I'm Ready, 193, 647
I'm Ready For Love, 416
I'm Saving My Love, 169
I'm Serious, 305
I'm Sitting On Top Of The World, 477
I'm So Proud, 319
I'm So Thankful, 317
I'm Sorry, 50, 186, 374, 490
I'm Sorry I Made You Cry, 260
I'm Stickin' With You, 60, 247
I'm The Girl From Wolverton Mountain, 86
I'm The One Who Loves You, 319
I'm Too Far Gone (To Turn Around), 49
I'm Tossin' And Turnin' Again, 381
I'm Waiting Just For You, 58
I'm Walking, 193, 453
I'm Walking Behind You, 237
I'm Walking The Floor Over You, 272
I'm Your Hoochie Cooche Man, 574, 647
I'm Yours, 144, 237, 249, 497
Image Of A Girl, 545
Imagination, 504

Immigrant, The, 554
Impossible, 401
Impossible Dream, The, 344, 659
Impossible Happened, The, 390
In A Shanty In Old Shanty Town, 575
In And Out Of Love, 594
In Dreams, 461
In My Diary, 446
In My Heart, 604
In My Little Corner Of The World, 73
In My Lonely Room, 416
In My Room, 31
In The Arms Of Love, 655
In The Chapel In The Moonlight, 348, 417
In The Dark, 389
In The Ghetto, 497
In The Heat Of The Night, 104
In The Middle Of A Heartache, 327
In The Middle Of An Island, 39, 248
In The Middle Of The House, 202, 443
In The Middle Of The Night, 430
In The Midnight Hour, 486, 606
In The Misty Moonlight, 417, 642
In The Mood, 234
In The Still Of The Night, 12, 189
In The Still Of The Night/The Jones Girl, 243
In The Summer Of His Years, 260
In Time, 373
Indescribably Blue, 497
Indian Love Call, 264, 587
Indian Reservation, 522
Innamorata, 417, 621
Inner City Blues (Make Me Wanna Holler), 269
Into The Night, 203
Invisible Tears, 139
Irresistible You, 164
Is A Blue Bird Blue, 618
Is It Any Wonder, 329
Is It Really Over, 518
Is It True, 375
Is It Wrong For Loving You, 487
Is That All There Is, 377
Is There Any Chance, 529
Is There Something On Your Mind, 551
Is This What I Get For Loving You, 537
Is You Is Or Is You Ain't My Baby, 65
Island In The Sun, 32
Isle Of Capri, 270, 377
Isn't It Amazing, 150
Isn't It Lonely Together, 574
Istanbul, 254
It Ain't Me Babe, 93
It Ain't No Use, 368
It All Depends On You, 381
It Could Happen To You, 581, 647
It Does Me So Good, 14
It Doesn't Matter Anymore, 309
It Don't Hurt No More, 68
It Happened Again, 626
It Happened Today, 572
It Hurts Me, 277, 497
It Hurts To Be In Love, 372, 488
It Hurts To Be Sixteen, 90
It Isn't Fair, 646
It Isn't Right, 490
It Keeps On Rainin', 194
It Keeps Right On A-Hurtin', 604

It May Sound Silly, 403
It Might As Well Rain Until September, 355
It Never Happens In Real Life, 326
It Only Happened Yesterday, 551
It Only Hurts For A Little While, 7
It Should Have Been Me, 103, 363
It Started All Over Again, 375
It Takes Two, 269
It Was A Nite Like This, 613
It Was A Very Good Year, 569
It Was I, 571
It Will Stand, 565
Italian Theme, The, 582
Itchy Twitchy Feeling, 300, 595
It's A Blue World, 253
It's A Cotton Candy World, 642
It's A Disco Night, 322
It's A Happening World, 606
It's A Lonely Town, 403
Its A Mad, Mad, Mad, Mad World, 562
It's A Man's Man's Man's World, 66
It's A Mean World, 352
It's A New Day, 67
It's A Shame, 580
It's A Sin To Tell A Lie, 39, 575
It's A Woman's World, 249
It's All In The Game, 218
It's All Over, 354
It's All Right, 319
It's Almost Tomorrow, 90, 203, 369, 582
It's Beginning To Look Like Christmas (Fon-
    taine Sisters), 137
It's Better In The Dark, 418
It's Better To Have It, 401
It's Cool, 619
(It's Gonna Be A) Lonely Christmas, 463
It's Gonna Be Alright, 68
It's Gonna Work Out Fine, 614
It's Got The Whole World Shakin', 142
It's Impossible, 137
It's Just A House Without You, 40
It's Just A Matter Of Time, 40, 330
It's Just About Time, 93
It's Late, 453
It's Love, Baby, 70, 430
It's Magic, 170, 407, 418, 491, 626
It's My Party, 278
It's No Sin, 210, 253
It's Not For Me To Say, 423
It's Not The End Of Everything, 218
It's Not The Same, 385
It's Now Or Never, 496
It's Now Winter's Day, 535
It's Obdacious, 342
It's O.K., 31
It's Only Love, 498
It's Only Make Believe, 85, 617
It's Only The Beginning, 348
It's Over, 18, 461, 535
It's So Easy, 154
It's So Hard Being A Loser, 140
It's So Nice To Have A Man Around The House,
    565
It's So Nice, 181
It's Time To Cry, 12
It's Too Late, 277, 355, 486, 661
It's Too Soon To Know, 58, 328, 463

It's Unbelievable, 370
It's Up To You, 454
It's You I Love, 193
It's Your Thing, 322
It's Your World, 529
It's Yours, 172
Itsy Bitsy Teenie Weenie Yellow Polka Dot Bi-
    kini, 314
Itty Bitty Pieces, 509
I've Been Around, 193
I've Been Born Again, 597
I've Been Loved Before, 563
I've Been Loving You Too Long, 514, 614
I've Been There, 218
I've Been Waiting For You All My Life, 12
I've Got A Thing About You Baby, 498
I've Come Of Age, 589
I've Got A Woman / Come Back, 103
I've Got Bonnie, 544
I've Got Dreams To Remember, 514
I've Got Love, 371
I've Got My Eyes On You, 126
I've Got My Love To Keep Me Warm, 434
I've Got News For You, 104
I've Got No Time To Lose, 601
I've Got Sand In My Shoes, 207
(I've Got) Spring Fever, 393
I've Got To Use My Imagination, 363
I've Got You Under My Skin, 257, 263, 501
I've Gotta Be Me, 167
I've Grown Accustomed To Her Face, 407
I've Grown Accustomed To Your Face, 124
I've Had It, 33
I've Lost You, 664
I've Lost You / The Next Step Is Love, 497
I've Told Every Little Star, 552
Ivory Tower, 89, 591, 658
Ivy Rose, 137

Jack And Jill, 535
Jack O' Diamonds, 70
Jacqueline, 300
Ja-Da, 341
Jailer Bring Me Water, 395
Jailhouse Rock, 496
Jam, The, 285
Jam Up Jelly Tight, 535
Jamaica Farewell, 32
Jambalaya, 138, 194, 582
James (Hold The Ladder Steady), 602
Jamie, 307
Jamie Boy, 583
Java, 149
Jay Walker, 83
Jazzman, 355
Jealous Heart, 247, 261, 313
Jealous Love, 486
Jealous Of You, 260
Jealousy (Jalousie), 368
Jeannie, Jeannie, Jeannie, 131
Jeepers Creepers, 176
Jelly Bread, 57
Jennie Lee, 330
Jenny, Jenny, 391
Jenny Lou, 330
Jeremiah Peabody's Poly Unsaturated Quick
    Dissolving Fast Action Pleasant Tasting
    Green And Purple Pills, 587

Jerk, The, 370
Jerusalem, 6
Jet, 134
Jezebel, 368
Jilted, 62
"Jim," 564
Jim Dandy, 22
Jim Dandy Got Married, 22
Jimmy Mack, 416
Jimmy Martinez, 529
Jimmy's Girl, 604
Jingle Bell Rock, 300, 544
Jingle Bells, 137
Jitterbug, The, 201
Jo-Ann, 492
Joey, Joey, Joey, 377
Joey's Song, 287
John And Marsha, 263
Johnny Angel, 228
Johnny B. Goode, 44, 188
Johnny Casanova, 448
Johnny Freedom, 311
Johnny Get Angry, 576
Johnny Jingo, 432
Johnny Loves Me, 228
Johnny One Time, 375
Johnny Reb, 311
Johnny Will, 59
Johnny's House Party, 299
Jo-Jo The Dog-Faced Boy, 13
Joker, The, 305, 449
Joker Went Wild, The, 314
Jole Blon, 54
Jolly Green Giant, The, 358
Jones Boy, The, 434
Josephine, 48
Journey Of Love, 150
Jubilation, 12
Judy, 555
Judy Loves Me, 149
Judy's Turn To Cry, 278
Juke Box Baby, 137
Juke Box Saturday Night, 457
July 12, 1939, 524
Jump, 262
Jump Back, 157, 601
Jump Over, 87
June Night, 199
Jungle, The, 352
Jupiter-C, 475
Jura, 478
Just A Closer Walk With Thee, 534
Just A Dream, 115
Just A Little Love, 353
Just A Little Misunderstanding, 140
Just A Little Too Much, 453
Just A Little, 374
Just A Lonely Christmas, 446
Just Ain't Enough Love, 307
Just As Much As Ever, 32, 637
Just Ask Your Heart, 20
Just Be True, 97
Just Because, 403, 500
Just Between You And Me, 111
Just Born, 137
Just Come Home, 312
Just For Old Time's Sake, 403

Just Got To Know, 402
Just In Time, 39
Just Keep It Up, 117
Just Like Me, 521
Just Make Love To Me, 647
Just Married, 529
Just Once In My Life, 525
Just One Kiss From You, 319
Just One Look, 610
Just One More Chance, 477
Just One More Day, 514
Just One Smile, 488
Just One Time, 273
Just One Way To Say I Love You, 136
Just Out Of Reach, 75
Just Say I Love Her, 160
Just Seventeen, 522
Just Tell Her Jim Said Hello, 497
Just To Be With You, 473
Just To Hold My Hand, 407
Just Walking In The Rain, 511
Just Yesterday, 344, 420
Just Young, 12
Justine, 196, 525

Ka-Ding-Dong, 183, 270, 305
Kansas City, 24, 66, 294, 391, 395
Kathy-O, 183
Katy Too, 93
Keep A Knockin', 391
Keep A Light In The Window Till I Come Home,
    76
Keep A-Driving, 661
Keep It A Secret, 582
Keep On Dancing, 24
Keep On Doin', 322
Keep On Lovin' Me, Honey, 269
Keep On Loving Me (You'll See The Change),
    50
Keep On Pushing, 319
Keep On Running, 668
Keep On Trying, 629
Keep Searchin', 556
Keep Your Hands Off My Baby, 388
Keep Your Hands Off Of Him, 339
Keep Your Love Locked, 484
Kentuckian Song, The, 305
Kentucky Rain, 497
Kewpie Doll, 137
Kicks, 521
Kiddio, 40
Killer Joe, 358, 532
Kind Of Boy You Can't Forget, The, 506
King Of Clowns, 554
King Of The Whole Wide World, 497
Kiss And A Rose, A, 463
Kiss From Your Lips, A, 244
Kiss Me Another, 272
Kiss Me Baby, 103
Kiss Me Quick, 497
Kiss Of Fire, 16, 272, 418
Kiss To Build A Dream On, A, 17, 666
Kisses Sweeter Than Wine, 534, 648
Kissin' And Twistin', 229
Kissin' Cousins, 497
Kissin' Game, 187
Kissin' On The Phone, 12

Kissin' Time, 544
Kissin'/Cry Cry Cry, 212
Knee Deep In The Blues, 439
Knock Knock (Who's There), 465
Knock Three Times, 464
Knockin' At Your Door, 515
Ko Ko Mo, 137, 152, 271
Ko-Ko Joe, 515
Kokomo, Indiana, 442
Kommotion, 214
Kong, 277
Kookie, Kookie (Lend Me Your Comb), 80
Kookie Little Paradise, 86

La Bamba, 395, 622
La Bomba, 606
La Dee Dah, 47
La Paloma, 628
La Plume De Ma Tante, 312
La Vie En Rose, 418, 671
Ladders Of Love, The, 244
La-Do-Dada, 294
Lady, 344
Lady Came From Baltimore, The, 165
Lady Luck, 500
Lady Madonna, 194
Lady Of Spain, 237
Lama Rama Ding Dong, 216
Land Of 1,000 Dances, 350, 486
Landlord, 363
Landlord Blues, 312
Language of Love, 397
Lara's Theme From Dr. Zhivago, 659
Large Large House, 479
Last Chance To Turn Around, 488
Last Dance, The, 403
Last Date, 149, 651
Last Leaf, The, 92
Last Minute Miracle, 562
Last Night, 414
Last One To Know, 246
Last Tango In Paris, 6
Last Time I Saw Her, The, 85
Last Word In Lonesome Is Me, The, 18
Lasting Love, 435
Lately, 668
Laughin & Clownin, 104
Laughing Boy, 652
Laughing On The Outside (Crying On The Inside), 565
Laughter In The Rain, 554
Laura, What's He Got That I Ain't Got, 41, 368
Laurie, 376
Lavender Blue, 565, 616
Lawdy Miss Clawdy, 500, 589
Lay Down Your Arms, 111
Lay Lady Lay, 234, 322
Lay Some Happiness On Me, 417
Lay-Away, 322
Lazy Elsie Molly, 107
Lazy Lady, 194
Lazy Mary, 443
Lazy River, 164
Lazy Summer Night, 256
Leah, 461
Lean Jean, 287
Leap Frog, 3

Learnin' The Blues, 569
Leave Me Alone, 198, 645
Leave My Kitten Alone, 392, 499
Leavin' On Your Mind, 123
Leaving Here, 307
Leaving On A Jet Plane, 483
Left Arm Of Buddha, 29
Left Right Out Of Your Heart, 469
Legend of Sleepy Hollow, The, 441
Lemon Tree, 395, 482
Leroy, 551
Let A Man Come In And Do The Popcorn (Part 1), 67
Let A Man Come In And Do The Popcorn (Part 2), 67
Let Her Go, Let Her Go, Let Her Go (Don't Cry, Joe), 569
Let It Be Me, 144, 226
Let It Ring, 170
Let It Snow! Let It Snow! Let It Snow!, 442
Let Me, 522
Let Me Be Good To You, 601
Let Me Be The One, 471
Let Me Be Your Teddy Bear, 496
Let Me Belong To You, 314
Let Me Call You Sweetheart, 672
Let Me Get To Know You, 12
Let Me Go Home, Whiskey, 430
Let Me Go, Lover! 62, 469, 649
Let Me Go The Right Way, 594
Let Me Go To Him, 644
Let Me In, 554
Let Me Love You, 104
Let Me Tell You Babe, 134
Let Me Try Again (Laisse Moi Le Temps), 570
Let The Bells Keep Ringing, 12
Let The Four Winds Blow, 194
Let The Good Times In, 417
Let The Good Times Roll, 104, 462, 563
Let The Little Girl Dance, 49
Let Them Talk, 392, 519
Let There Be Drums, 454
Let There Be You, 241
Let This Be A Letter (To My Baby), 663
Let True Love Begin, 134
Let Yourself Go, 66, 497
Let's Be Lovers, 492
Let's Call It A Day Girl, 629
Let's Dance, 444
Let's Get It On, 269
Let's Get Lost, 442
Let's Get Together, 432
Let's Go, 540
Let's Go Again, 24
Let's Go Calypso, 202
Let's Go Get Stoned, 104
Let's Go, Let's Go, Let's Go, 24
Let's Go Steady Again, 554
Let's Go Steady, 142
Let's Hang On, 257
Let's Have A Party, 327
Let's Kiss And Make Up, 636
Let's Limbo Some More, 107
Let's Lock The Door, 334
Let's Love, 424
Let's Make Christmas Merry, Baby, 430
Let's Move And Groove Together, 452

Let's Put The Fun Back In Rock 'n' Roll, 88
Let's Start All Over Again, 470
Let's Stomp, 138
Let's Take An Old-Fashioned Walk, 136
Let's Think About Living, 398
Let's Try It Again, 407
Let's Turkey Trot, 388
Let's Twist Again, 107
Let's Work Together, 294
Letter Full Of Tears, 362
Letter, The, 425
Letter To An Angel, A, 115
Letter To The Beatles, A, 256
Liar, 519
Licking Stick-Licking Stick, 66
Lie To Me, 41
Liechtensteiner Polka, 651
Life, 498
Life Is A Song Worth Singing, 424
Life Is But A Dream, 212, 292
Life's A Holiday, 642
Life's Too Short, 367
Lifetime Of Loneliness, A, 181
Light Of Love, 377
Lightnin' Strikes, 114
Like I Love You, 80
Like Long Hair, 521
Like Strangers, 226
Like The Big Guys Do, 532
Lili Marlene, 420
Lily Maebelle, 623
Limbo Dance, 96
Limbo Rock, 96, 107
Limelight, 46
Linda, 332
Linda Lu, 557
Linda On My Mind, 618
Ling, Ting, Tong, 105, 241, 365
Lion Sleeps Tonight, The, 606
Lips Of Wine, 654
Lipstick & Candy & Rubber Sole Shoes, 371
Lipstick On Your Collar, 260
Lisa, 48, 234
Lisbon Antigua, 432, 524
Listen Here, 292
Listen Lonely Girl, 424
Little Altar Boy, 161
Little Bit Now, A, 409
Little Bit Of Soap, A, 227, 333
Little Bitty Girl, 544
Little Bitty Pretty One, 169, 293, 400, 407
Little Bitty Tear, A, 323, 327
Little Black Book, 172
Little Blue Man, The, 341
Little Blue Riding Hood, 263
Little Boy Blue, 220
Little Boy (In Grown Up Clothes), 257
Little Boy Sad, 78
Little Boy, The, 39, 156
Little Brass Band, The, 555
Little By Little, 68
Little Coco Palm, 642
Little Darlin, 183, 275
Little Darling (I Need You), 268
Little Deuce Coupe, 31
Little Devil, 554
Little Diane, 188

Little Dipper, 448
Little Dog Cried, A, 534
Little Drummer Boy, The, 93, 567
Little Egypt, 129
Little Feeling, A, 551
Little Girl I Once Knew, The, 31
Little Girl Of Mine, 120
Little Girl, 622
Little Green Apples, 470, 574
Little Gypsy, 7
Little Honda, 31
Little Latin Lupe Lu, 358, 525
Little Less Conversation, A, 497
Little Love Can Go A Long, Long Way, A, 203
Little Marie, 44
Little Mary, 193
Little Miss Stuckup, 492
Little Miss Sunshine, 535
Little Musicians, 666
Little Old Lady, The, (From Pasadena), 332
Little Old Wine Drinker Me, 417, 440
Little Pedro, 461
Little Pigeon, 435
Little Pixie, 365
Little Queenie, 44, 48
Little Red Rented, Rowboat, 201
Little Red Riding Hood, 45
Little Red Rooster, 142
Little Sandy Sleighfoot, 172
Little Serenade, 507
Little Shoemaker, The, 270, 666
Little Side Car, 370
Little Sister, 497
Little Star, 220
Little Things Mean A Lot, 329, 348
Little Things, 277
Little Too Much, A, 301
Little Town Flirt, 556
Little Turtle Dove, 658
Little White Cloud That Cried, The, 511
Little White Lies, 341
Little Young Lover, 319
Live For Life, 344
Live It Up Part 1, 322
Live Wire, 416
Livin' Above Your Head, 334
Livin' Dangerously, 403
Livin' In The Life, 322
Living A Lie, 419
Living A Little, Laughing A Little, 580
Living For The City, 105, 668
Lizzie Borden, 438
Locking Up My Heart, 420
Loco-Motion, The, 388
Loddy Lo, 107
Lolita Ya-Ya, 631
Lollipop, 111
Lollipops And Roses, 344, 484
Loneliest Night, The, 159
L-O-N-E-L-Y, 637
Lonely Again, 18
Lonely Avenue, 103
Lonely Blue Boy, 618
Lonely Blue Nights, 539
Lonely Boy, 12
Lonely Boy, Lonely Guitar, 214
Lonely Bull, The, 5

Lonely Chair, 500
Lonely For You, 589
Lonely Guitar, 13
Lonely Is The Name, 167
Lonely Island, 141
Lonely Man, 496
Lonely Nights, 299
Lonely One, The, 214
Lonely Saturday Night, 265
Lonely Street, 301, 654
Lonely Surfer, The, 457
Lonely Teardrops, 315, 663
Lonely Teenager, 187
Lonely Weekends, 524
Lonely Winds, 207
Lonesome Number One, 273
Lonesome Old House, 273
Lonesome Town, 453
Lonesome Whistle Blues, 356
Long Ago (And Far Away), 135, 581
Long Distance Call, 647
Long Green, 236
Long John Blues, 646
Long Legged Girl, 497
Long Line Rider, 165
Long Lonely Nights, 9, 177, 407, 637
Long Promised Road, 31
Long Tall Sally, 58, 390
Long Time Coming, 212
Longest Walk, The, 448
Longing For You, 62, 160
Look At Me Girl, 629
Look Away, 434
Look For A Star, 296, 430, 628
Look Homeward Angel, 251, 511
Look In My Eyes, 101
Look Into Your Heart, 262
Look Of Love, 279
Look What They've Done To My Song, Ma, 105
Lookin' For Love, 139, 624
Lookin' For My Baby, 212
Looking Back, 134
Looking For Love, 260
Looking Through The Eyes Of Love, 488
Looking With My Eyes, 644
Loop De Loop, 603
Loosers Weepers—Part 1, 328
Lord's Prayer, The, 136
Losing You, 375
Losing Your Love, 518
Lost, 79
Lost In The Shuffle, 448
Lost John, 197
Lost Love, 26
Lost Someone, 66
Lotta Lovin', 635
Louie Louie, 358
Louisiana Blues, 647
L-O-V-E, 134
Love, 379
Love All The Hurt Away, 262
Love and Marriage, 565, 569
Love Bones, 597
Love Bug, 344
Love Bug Leave My Heart Alone, 416
Love Came To Me, 188
Love Can't Wait, 529

Love Child, 594
Love Don't Love Nobody, 580
Love Finds Its Own Way, 363
Love For Sale, 399
Love I Lost, The, 52
Love I Saw In You Was Just A Mirage, The, 437
Love In A Home, 170
Love In The Shadows, 554
Love Is A Golden Ring, 368
Love Is A Many-Splendored Thing, 144, 249, 539
Love Is All We Need, 91, 161, 218
Love Is Better In The A.M., 597
Love Is Blue, 420
Love Is Funny That Way, 664
Love Is Here And Now You're Gone, 594
Love Is Like An Itching In My Heart, 594
Love Is Me, Love Is You, 261
Love Is Strange, 428
Love Is The Sweetest Thing, 548
Love Letters In The Sand, 58
Love Letters, 378, 497
Love, Love, Love, 126, 183
Love Machine Pt. 1, 438
Love Makes The World Go 'Round, 12, 137
Love Man, 514
Love Me, 319, 496
Love Me All The Way, 652
Love Me (Baby Can't You Love Me), 511
Love Me Forever, 251, 659
Love Me Good, 582
Love Me Now, 41
Love Me Tender, 96, 496
Love Me To Pieces, 144
Love Me Warm And Tender, 12
Love No One But You, 337
Love Of A Boy, The, 672
Love Of My Life, 226
Love Of My Own, A, 601
Love Or Leave, 580
Love Potion No. 9, 126, 129
Love She Can Count On, A, 437
Love So Fine, A, 109
Love Somebody, 170
Love The One You're With, 322
Love Theme From One Eyed Jack, 234
Love Theme From Romeo & Juliet, 410
Love Theme From The Sandpiper, 39
Love Theme From The Godfather, 420, 655
Love Walked In, 244, 305, 647
Love We Had, The (Stays On My Mind), 177
Love Will Find A Way, 181
Love With The Proper Stranger, 344
Love You Most Of All, 141
Love You So, 306
Loveliest Night Of The Year, The, 370
Lovely Lies, 410
Lovely, Lovely, 107
Lovely One, 258
Lover Boy, 120
Lover Come Back, 171
Lover, 377
Lover Please, 407
Lovers Always Forgive, 362
Lovers By Night, Strangers By Day, 246
Lover's Concerto, A, 627

Lover's Island, 51
Lovers Never Say Goodbye, 244
Lover's Question, A, 407, 514
Lovers Who Wander, 188
Love's Been Good To Me, 569
Love's Street And Fool's Road, 76
Lovesick Blues, 149, 316
Lovey Dovey, 126, 365, 407
Lovin' Touch, 186
Loving You, 165, 496
Loving You More Every Day, 328
Lowdown Popcorn, 67
Lucille, 207, 226, 391
Lucky Devil, 190
Lucky Ladybug, 47
Lucky Lips, 70
Lullaby Of Love, 267
Lullaby Of The Leaves, 631
Lumberjack, 41

Mack The Knife, 164
Mad Love, 647
Madeira, 432
Madison, The, 71
Madison Time, 73
Madrid, 134
Magic Fingers, 238
Magic Man, 6
Magic Moments, 137
Magic Moon, 513
Magic Tango, The, 666
Magic Touch, The, 490
Magic Wand, 196
Magnificent Seven, The, 84
Maharaja of Magador, The, 442
Main Theme From Exodus, 411
Main Title And Molly-O, 327
Majestic, The, 188
Make Believe It's Your First Time, 637
Make Believe Wedding, 94
Make It Easy On Yourself, 79, 644
Make It Funky, 67
Make Love To Me!, 582
Make Me A Present Of You, 647
Make Me Belong To You, 380
Make Me Forget, 544
Make Me The Woman That You Go Home To, 363
Make Me Your Baby, 380
Make Someone Happy, 137
Make The Music Play, 644
Make The World Go Away, 18, 672
Make Yourself Comfortable, 626
Makin' Love, 531
Makin' Whoopee, 104
Making Memories, 368
Mama, 260
Mama Didn't Lie, 61
Mama Doll Song, The, 469
Mama Don't Allow, 538
Mama From The Train, 469
Mama Guitar, 144, 371
(Mama) He Treats Your Daughter Mean, 70
Mama Look At Bubu, 32
Mama Said, 562
Mama Sang A Song, 62
Mama, Teach Me To Dance, 280

Mama Told Me Not To Come, 487
Ma-Ma-Ma Marie, 270
Mama-Oom-Mow-Mow, 528
Mambo Baby, 70
Mambo Boogie, 466
Mambo Italiano, 124
Mambo Rock, 287
Mambo Shevitz, 155
Mame, 6, 17, 165
Mamma And A Papa, A, 587
Mam'selle, 568
Man And A Half, A, 486
Man Chases A Girl, A, 238
Man In Black, 94
Man Or Mouse, 389
Man Upstairs, 583
(Man Who Shot, The) Liberty Valance, 488
Man With The Banjo, The, 7
Man With The Golden Arm, 424
Manana, 377
Mandolins In The Moonlight, 137
Manhattan Spiritual, 467
Manish Boy, 647
Man's Temptation, 97
Many A Time, 373
Many Tears Ago, 260
Many Times, 237
March From The River Kwai & Colonel Bogey, 432, 445
March Of The Siamese Children, 23
Marching Thru Madrid, 5
Margie, 193
Maria, 424, 659
Maria Elena, 396
Marianne, 274, 305, 322, 396, 424
Marie, 258
Marie's The Name His Latest Flame, 497
Marina, 282
Marlena, 256
Martinique, 180
Marvelous Toy, The, 438
Mary Ann Regrets, 323
Mary Ann Thomas, 264
Mary Don't You Weep, 327
Mary In The Morning, 420
Mary Lee, 505
Mary Lou, 295
Mary's Boy Child, 32
Mary's Little Lamb, 166
Mashed Potato Time, 557
Mashed Potatoes U.S.A., 66
Mashed Potatoes, 4
Master Blaster, 668
Master of Eyes, 262
Matador, The, 93, 368
Mau-Mau, 642
May You Always, 403
Maybe, 101, 137
Maybe Baby, 153
Maybe I Know, 279
Maybe Just Today, 629
Maybe Tonight, 562
Maybellene, 43
Me And Bobby McGee, 382
Me Japanese Boy I Love You, 277
Mean Little Woman, Rosalie, 535
Mean Old World, 454

Mean Woman Blues, 461
Mecca, 488
Meditations, 59
Mediterranean Moon, 513
Medley: My Girl, Hey Girl, 629
Medley—You Keep Me Hangin' On/Hurt So Bad, 181
Meet Me At The Twistin' Place, 448
Meet The Lady, 322
Meeting Over Yonder, 319
Melancholy Music Man, 525
Melodie D'Amour, 7
Melody Of Love, 90, 249, 627
Melting Pot, 57
Memories, 497
Memories Are Made Of This, 207, 417, 591
Memories Of You, 124, 250, 666
Memphis, 44, 64, 404
Memphis Soul Stew, 157
Mercy Mercy Me (The Ecology), 269
Mercy, Mercy, 147
Mermaid, The, 368
Merry Christmas, Baby, 44
Merry-Go-Round, 343
Merry-Go-Round Waltz, 444
Mess Of Blues, A, 496
Message To Michael, 644
Metro Polka, 368
Mexican Drummer Man, 5
Mexican Hat Rock, 15
Mexican Shuffle, The, 5
Mexico, 446
Michael, 4, 304, 395
Michelle, 628
Mickey's Monkey, 437
Midnight, 12
Midnight Cowboy, 234
Midnight Flyer, 134
Midnight In Moscow, 23
Midnight Lace, 139
Midnight Mary, 487, 494
Midnight Sky Part 1, 322
Midnight Special, 225, 573
Midnight Stroll, 520
Midnight Train To Georgia, 363
Mighty Love Pt. 1, 580
Mighty Good Lovin', 437
Mighty Good, 453
Miller's Cave, 26
Million And One, A, 161, 417
Million Miles From Nowhere, A, 40
Million To One, A, 102, 315
Milord, 63, 164
Mini-Skirt Minnie, 486
Minute You're Gone, The, 330
Mio Amore, 244
Miracle, A, 20
Miracle Of Love, 533
Miss Ann, 391
Miss You, 155, 448, 564
Missing, 403
Missing You, 485
Mission Bell, 64
Mister And Mississippi, 469
Mister Fire Eyes, 285
Mister Sandman, 249
Mister Tap Toe, 170

Mistrustin' Blues, 466
Misty, 424, 500, 587, 633
Misty Blue, 18
Mo' Onions, 57
Mockin' Bird Hill, 469, 477
Mockingbird, The, 254, 259, 262
Model Girl, 422
Mohair Sam, 524
Molly, 276
Moments To Remember, 254
Mona Lisa, 134, 618, 671
Money, 358, 363, 591
Money Honey, 206, 496
Money Tree, The, 653
Money Won't Change You, 66
Monkey Time, The, 368
Monkey-Shine, 48
Monster Mash, 486
Monsters' Holiday, 486
Moody Blue, 498
Moody River, 59
Moody Woman, 80
Moon Over Naples, 347
Moon River, 79, 410
Moon Talk, 137
Moon Was Yellow, The, 569
Moonglow & Theme From Picnic, 95, 589
Moonlight And Roses, 161
Moonlight Bay, 207
Moonlight Gambler, 368
Moonlight Love, 137
Moonlight Serenade, 527, 637
Moonlight Sonata, 410
Moonlight Special, 587
Moovin' 'N Groovin', 214
More, 137, 161, 664
More And More, 655
More I See You, The, 444
More Love, 437
More Money For You And Me, 256
More Than The Eye Can See, 420
Morgen, 530
Moritat (A Theme From The Three Penny Opera), 315, 478, 651
Mornin Mornin, 277
Morning After, 414
Morning Side Of The Mountain, The, 218
Most Beautiful Girl, The, 524
Most Beautiful Words, The, 517
Most Of All, 446
Most Of All/The Door Is Still Open To My Heart, 144
Most People Get Married, 469
Mostly Martha, 152
Mother Nature, Father Time, 41
Mother, Please, 86
Mother Popcorn (Part 1), 67
Mother-In-Law, 349
Motorcycle, 603
Moulin Rouge Theme, The, 411
Mountain Of Love, 198
Mountain's High, The, 184
Move Two Mountains, 343
Movin', 48
Movin' On, 176
Mr. Bass Man, 158
Mr. Blue, 246

Mr. Businessman, 587
Mr. Custer, 632
Mr. D. J. (5 For The D. J.), 262
Mr. Dream Merchant, 79
Mr. Happiness, 422
Mr. Jaws, 277
Mr. Lee, 52
Mr. Livingston, 632
Mr. Lonely, 285, 637
Mr. Lucky, 410
Mr. Magic Man, 487
Mr. Pitiful, 514
Mr. President, 277
Mr. Sandman, 111
Mr. Songwriter, 586
Mr. Success, 569
Mr. Sun, Mr. Moon, 522
Mr. Wonderful, 377, 626
Mrs. Robinson, 57
Ms. Grace, 619
M.T.A., 358
Muddy Mississippi Line, 277
Mule Skinner Blues, 233
Mule Train, 248, 367, 442
Multiplication, 164
Mumblin' Mosie, 467
"Murder," He Says, 564
Music, Maestro, Please, 368
Music! Music! Music!, 6, 62, 554
Music To Watch Girls By, 152, 655
Muskrat Ramble, The, 87, 403
Mustang Sally, 486
Mutual Admiration Society, 18, 63
My Babe, 525
(My Baby Don't Love Me) No More, 175
My Baby Don't Dig Me, 104
My Baby Left Me, 496
My Baby Loves Me, 416
My Baby Must Be A Magician, 421
My Baby's Coming Home, 477
My Believing Heart, 329
My Best Friend's Wife, 12
My Blue Heaven, 193, 214
My Bolero, 160
My Bonnie Lassie, 7
My Boomerang Won't Come Back, 202
My Boy, 498
My Boy Flat Top, 36
My Boyfriend's Back, 10
My Bucket's Got A Hole In It, 453
My Cherie, 420
My Cherie Amour, 668
My Claire De Lune, 373
My Coloring Book, 348, 588
My Dad, 484
My Daddy Knows Best, 420
My Darling, 102
My Dearest Darling, 328
My Devotion, 442
My Ding-A-Ling, 44
My Dream, 490
My Dream Come True, 551
My Dreams, 375
My Elusive Dreams, 524, 637
My Empty Arms, 663
My Empty Room, 385
My Eyes Adored You, 625

My Favorite Song, 272
My Favorite Things, 6
My Foolish Heart, 91, 179
My Friend, 238
My Girl Friend, 83
My Girl Has Gone, 437
My Girl Josephine, 194
My Girl Sloopy, 386, 633
My Guy, 652
My Happiness, 260
My Heart Became Of Age, 13
My Heart Belongs To Only You, 637
My Heart Cries For You, 104, 160, 439, 565, 671
My Heart Has A Mind Of Its Own, 260
My Heart Is An Open Book, 190
My Heart Is Yours, 294
My Heart Reminds Me, 583
My Heart Would Know, 420
My Hearts Desire, 212
My Heart's On Fire, 49
My Hero, 51
My Home Town, 12
My Juanita, 150
My Kind Of Girl, 442
My Last Date With You, 168, 329
My Life, 661
My Little Angel, 254
My Love, 134
My Love For You, 424
My Love Forgive Me, 281
My Love, My Love, 329
My Love Will Never Die, 98
My Lover's Prayer, 514
My Lovin' Baby, 218
My Melancholy Baby, 218
My Melody Of Love, 637
My Memories Of You, 292
My Merry-Go-Round, 452
My Mistake, 269
My Old Car, 199
My One Sin, 134, 250
My Own True Love, 115, 210
My Part/Make It Funky, 67
My Prayer, 490
My Pretending Days Are Over, 177
My Real Name, 194
My Shoes Keep Walking Back To You, 439, 501
My Shy Violet, 434
My Sometimes Baby, 352
My Song, 2, 262
My Special Angel, 300
My Story, 660
My Summer Love, 542
My Sweet Potato, 57
My Tani, 65
My Thang, 67
My Town, My Guy And Me, 279
My Treasure, 305
My True Carrie Love, 134
My True Confession, 41
My True Love, 551
My True Story, 338
My Truly, Truly Fair, 160, 439
My Way, 41, 498, 569
My Way Of Life, 569

My Whole World Is Falling Down, 375
My Wish Came True, 496
My Woman My Woman, My Wife, 529
My World Is Empty Without You, 594

Nadine, 44
Nag, 288
Name Game, The, 222
Namely You, 109
Nancy, 568
Nathan Jones, 594
National City, 343
Natural Born Lover, 194
Natural Woman, A, 262
Nature Boy, 134, 164, 568
Naughty Lady Of Shady Lane, The, 7, 50
Near You, 659
Nee Nee Na Na Na Na Nu Nu, 198
Need To Belong, 79
Need You, 467
Need Your Love, 264
Need Your Love So Bad, 392
Needles And Pins, 180
Neither One Of Us, 363
Nel Blu Dipinto Di Blu (Volare), 440
Nervous Boogie, 270
Never, 212
Never Be Anyone Else But You, 453
Never Dreamed You'd Leave In Summer, 668
Never Give You Up, 80
Never Had A Dream Come True, 668
Never In A Million Years, 552
Never Let You Go, 239
Never, Never Leave Me, 652
Never, Never, 338
Never On Sunday, 111, 146
Never Turn Back, 302
Nevertheless, 14, 434
New Girl In School, The, 332
New In The Ways Of Love, 218
New Mexican Rose, 256
New Orleans, 54, 306
New York's My Home, 167
Next Door To An Angel, 554
Next Door To The Blues, 328
Next In Line, 92
Next Hundred Years, The, 420
Next Kiss, The, 618
Next Time You See Me, 389
Nice 'N' Easy, 569
Night, 663
Night Has A Thousand Eyes, The, 629
Night Life, 202
Night Lights, 134
Night Train, 66, 297, 638
Nightingale, 355
9,999,999 Tears, 376
Ninety Nine Years, 439
Ninety-Nine And A Half, 486
Ninety-Nine Ways, 313
Nip Sip, 126
Nitty Gritty, The, 222, 363
No, 586
No Arms Can Ever Hold You, 270, 637
No Chemise, Please, 282
No Help Wanted, 202
No If's—No And's, 500

No Love (But Your Love), 424
No Love Have I, 487
No Matter What Sign You Are, 594
No Money Down, 44
No Night So Long, 645
No, No, No, 102
No, Not Much, 254
No One, 104, 375
No One But You, 7
No One Knows, 189
No One To Cry To, 104
No One Will Ever Know, 535
No Other Arms, 58
No Other Arms, No Other Lips, 111, 249
No Other Love, 137, 581
No Particular Place To Go, 44
No Pity (In The Naked City), 663
No Shoes, 310
Nobody But You, 117
Nobody Cares, 645
Nobody Knows What's Goin' On, 109
Nobody Loves Me Like You, 244
Nobody Wins, 375
Nobody's Baby Again, 417
Nola, 477, 656
Non Dimenticar, 134
Norman, 602
North To Alaska, 311
Not Enough Indians, 417
Not Me, 465
Not One Goodbye, 448
Not One Minute More, 517
Not Too Young To Get Married, 53
Nothing But Good, 24
Nothing But Heartaches, 594
Nothing Can Change This Love, 141
Nothing Can Stop Me, 97
Nothing New (Same Old Things), 194
Nothing Takes The Place Of You, 41
Nothing's Too Good For My Baby, 668
Now And For Always, 289
Now And Forever, 347
Now I Know, 344
Now Is The Hour, 591, 653
Now That I Need You, 170, 367
Now That You've Gone, 586
Now You Know, 393
Nowhere To Run, 416
Number One Man, 98
Nut Rocker, 29
Nutbush City Limits, 614
Nuttin' For Christmas, 247, 263, 278
N'yot N'yow (The Pussycat Song), 136

O Dio Mio, 13
O' Falling Star, 253
Ode To Billie Joe, 73, 157
Oh, Babe!, 501, 582
Oh! Baby, 337, 401
Oh Baby Doll, 44
Oh Baby Don't You Weep, 66
Oh, Boy!, 153
Oh! Carol, 554
Oh Happy Day, 85, 253, 651
Oh How I Miss You Tonight, 48
Oh Julie, 149
Oh, Little One, 551

Oh Lonesome Me, 93
Oh Lonesome Me / I Can't Stop Loving You, 273
Oh Me Oh My, 262
Oh Mein Papa, 376
Oh My Maria, 238
Oh! My Papa, 237
Oh No, Not My Baby, 68
Oh, Pretty Woman, 461
Oh, Rock My Soul, 483
Oh, What A Day, 177
Oh What A Dream, 70
Oh What A Fool, 318
Oh, What A Night, 176, 177
Oh What It Seemed To Be, 94, 568
Oh Why, 598
Oh-Oh, I'm Falling In Love Again, 534
Okefenokee, 87
Ol' MacDonald, 569
Ol' Man River, 508
Ol' Race Track, The, 434
Old Cape Cod, 469
Old Enough To Love, 454
Old Lamplighter, The, 70
Old Master Painter, The, 369, 569
Old Oaken Bucket, The, 546
Old Payola Roll Blues, The, 263
Old Philosopher, The, 372
Old Rivers, 62
Old Shep, 496
Old Smokey Locomotion, 388
Old Soldiers Never Die, 442
Old Spanish Town, 33
Ole Buttermilk Sky, 48
On A Clear Day You Can See Forever, 424
On An Evening In Roma, 417
On And On, 363
On Bended Knees, 301
On Broadway, 207
On Campus, 277
On London Bridge, 582
On My Word Of Honor, 352, 490
On Sunday Afternoon / The Masquerade Is Over, 292
On The Dock Of The Bay, 177
On The Rebound, 149
On The Street Where You Live, 160, 238, 655
On This Side Of Goodbye, 525
On Top Of Old Smoky, 232, 442, 648
On Top Of Spaghetti, 275
On Treasure Island, 591
Once In Awhile, 110, 469
Once Upon A Time, 269, 531
Once You Hit The Road, 645
One Boy, 576
One Boy Too Late, 122
One Broken Heart For sale, 497
One Day Of Your Life, 655
One Dozen Roses, 564
One Fine Day, 109, 355
One For My Baby, 39
One Girl, 434
One In A Million, 490
One Kiss Led To Another, 129
One Kiss Too Many, 18
One Love, One Heart, 250
One Man Woman / One Woman Man, 12

One Mint Julep, 104, 126
One More Chance, 42
One More Heartache, 268
One More Town, 359
One Night, 496
One Night Affair, 80
One Of A Kind (Love Affair), 580
One Of The Lucky Ones, 73
One Of Us (Will Weep Tonight), 469
One On The Right Is On The Left, The, 93
One Piece At A Time, 94
One Rose, 63
One Scotch, One Bourbon, One Beer, 430
One Step At A Time, 374
One Stop At A Time, 68
One Summer Night, 161, 183
One Track Mind, 381
One Way Love, 207
One Who Really Loves You, The, 652
Onion Song, The / California Soul, 269
Only Because, 491
Only In America, 334
Only Love (Can Save Me Now), 76
Only Love Can Break A Heart, 488, 637
Only Love Is Real, 355
Only Love Me, 373
Only One Love, 289
Only Sixteen, 141
Only The Lonely, 330, 461
Only The Strong Survive, 80
Only Those In Love, 645
Only You, 46, 305, 490, 493
O-o, I Love You, 176
Ooby Dooby, 461
Ooh Babe, 186
Ooh! My Soul, 391
Ooh Poo Pah Doo, 614
Ooh Poo Pah Doo—Part II, 304
Ooh Rocking Daddy, 446
Ookey Ook, 480
Oo-La-La-Limbo, 162
Ooo Baby Baby, 437
Oooh-Oooh-Oooh, 500
Oop-Shoop, 152
Oowee, Oowee, 137
Op, 310
Open Up My Heart / Nadine, 177
Open Up The Back Door, 430
Operator, 362
Opus 17 (Don't You Worry 'Bout Me), 257
Orange Blossom Special, 93
Orange Colored Sky, 134
Organ Grinder's Swing, The, 574
Organ Shout, 146
Our Anniversary, 559
Our Day Will Come, 542, 625
Our Everlasting Love, 543
Our Love Is Here To Stay, 647
Our Song, 344
Our Winter Love, 379, 502
Our World, 604
Out Of Limits, 413
Out Of My Mind, 604
Out Of Sight, Out Of Mind, 241, 385, 592
Out Of This World, 109
Out In The Cold Again, 400
Outside My Window, 246, 668

Outside The Gates Of Heaven, 114
Over A Bottle Of Wine, 418
Over And Over, 293
Over And Over Again, 446
Over The Mountain, Across The Sea, 340, 636
Over The Rainbow, 179
Over The Weekend, 491

Padre, 16
Pain In My Heart, 514
Painted, Tainted Rose, 419
Painter, 114
Palace Guard, 454
Palisades Park, 87
Pamela Throws A Party, 520
Papa Don't Take No Mess P.1, 67
Papa Loves Mambo, 137
Papa-Oom-Mow-Mow, 528
Papa's Got A Brand New Bag, 66, 514
Paper Doll, 433
Paper Roses, 72
Paper Tiger, 602
Paradise, 616
Paralyzed, 496
Part Of Me, A, 115
Part Of Me That Needs You Most, The, 334
Part Time Love, 363, 597
Partin' Time, 352
Party Doll, 364, 372
Party Lights, 116
Party Time, 435
Party's Over, The, 171
Pass Me By, 377
Passing Strangers, 626
Patches, 376
Patricia, 137, 494
Patricia Twist, 494
Patsy, 551
Patti Ann, 149
Patty Baby, 88
Payback, The, 67
Pay Back, 328
Paying The Cost To Be The Boss, 353
Peace In The Valley, 496
Peace Of Mind, 63, 352, 522, 664
Peaches 'N' Cream, 317
Peanut Butter, 411
Peanuts, 388, 524
Pearl, 535
Pearly Shells, 323
Peek-A-Boo, 83
Peggy Sue, 31, 308
Pennies From Heaven, 572
Penny A Kiss, A, 565
Penny Nickel Dime Quarter, 152
People, 619
People Are Talking, 298
People Are Talking/Your Way, 298
People Get Ready, 319
People Like You, 238
People Tree, 167
People Will Say We're In Love, 568
Pepe, 214
Pepino The Italian Mouse, 443
Pepino's Friend Pasqual, 443
Pepper-Hot Baby, 405, 448
Peppermint Twist, 173

Percolator (twist), 46
Perfect Love, A, 20
Perfidia, 249, 631
Personality, 500
Pet Me, Poppa, 124
Peter Gunn, 14, 214
Petticoats Of Portugal, 327, 628
Philadelphia, 353
Philadelphia, U.S.A., 459
Philly Dog, 414
Pick Up The Pieces, 601
Pickle Up A Doodle, 63
Picnic, 403
Pictures In The Fire, 59
Pied Piper, The, 656
Pin A Medal On Joey, 166
Pineapple Princess, 13
Pink Chiffon, 608
Pink Panther Theme, 410
Pink Pedal Pushers, 482
Pink Shoe Laces, 586
Pipeline, 99
Pitter Patter, 68
Pittsburgh, Pennsylvania, 439
Place In The Sun, A, 668
Plain Jane, 164
Plantation Boogie, 174
Play A Simple Melody, 581
Play It Fair, 22
Playboy, 420
Playing For Keeps, 496
Plaything, 605
Plea, The, 101, 337
Please, 316
Please Accept My Love, 352
Please Don't Ask About Barbara, 629
Please Don't Go, 198
Please Don't Leave Me, 193, 247
Please Don't Stop Loving Me, 497
Please Don't Talk To The Lifeguard, 90, 509
Please Forgive Me, 2
Please Help Me I'm Fallin', 202, 393
Please Hurry Home, 352
Please Love Me Forever, 95, 218, 637
Please Love Me, 352
Please Mr. Johnson, 83
Please Mr. Postman, 420
Please Mr. Sun, 218, 511
Please, Please, Please, 66
Please Say You Want Me, 549
Please Say You're Fooling, 104
Please Send Me Someone To Love, 446
Please Stay, 207
Please Tell Me Why, 663
Pledge Of Love, 608
Pledging My Love, 2, 62, 290
Pocketful Of Miracles, 569
Pocketful Of Rainbows, 296
Poco-Loco, 271
Poetry In Motion, 604
Poinciana, 372
Point It Out, 438
Point Of No Return, 403
Point Of Order, 263
Point Panic, 595
Pointed Toe Shoes, 482
Poison Ivy, 129

Pokomo, 244
Pomp And Circumstance, 351
Pony Express, 162
Pony Time, 107, 147
Poor Boy, 496, 542
Poor Butterfly, 305
Poor Dog (Who Can't Wag His Own Tail), 391
Poor Fool, 614
Poor Jenny, 226
Poor Little Fool, 453
Poor Little Rich Girl, 373
Poor Man's Roses, A, 469
Poor Me, 193
Poor People Of Paris, The, 29, 651
Pop Pop Pop-Pie, 560
Pop That Thang, 322
Popcorn, The, 67
Pop-Eye, 573
Pop-Eye Stroll, 414
Popeye The Hitchhiker, 107
Popeye Waddle, 147
Pops, We Love You, 269, 668
Popsicle, 332
Popsicles And Icicles, 449
Port Au Prince, 524
Portrait Of My Love, 373, 606
Portugese Washerwomen, 89
Potato Peeler, 285
Poverty, 49
Prayer And A Juke Box, A, 385
Pretend, 28, 134, 414
Pretend You Don't See Her, 621
Pretty Blue-Eyes, 373
Pretty Boy Lonely, 470
Pretty Little Angel, 150
Pretty Little Angel Eyes, 375
Pretty Little Baby, 268
Pretty Paper, 461
Price, The, 75
Pride, The (Part 1), 322
Pride And Joy, 268
Primrose Lane, 642
Princess, 267
Princess And The Punk, The, 410
Princess In Rags, 488
Priscilla, 142
Prisoner Of Love, 66, 136
Private Eye, 461
Problems, 226
Promise Me A Rose, 73
Promise Me, Love, 654
Promised Land, 44, 498
Promises, Promises, 644
Proud, 149
Proud Mary, 76, 614
Proud One, The, 625
P.S.: I Love You, 305
Psycho, 300
P.T. 109, 172
Puff The Magic Dragon, 483
Punish Her, 629
Puppet On A String, 497
Puppy Love, 12, 380
Purple Haze, 188
Purple People Eater Meets The Witch Doctor, The, 577
Purple People Eater, The, 669

Push And Kick, The, 623
Pushover, 328
Pussy Cat, 7
Put A Light In The Window, 254
Put A Little Love In Your Heart, 181
Put A Ring On My Finger, 478
Put Your Arms Around Me Honey, 193
Put Your Head On My Shoulder, 12, 379
Puzzle Song, The, 222

Quando, Quando, Quando, 59
Quarter To Three, 54
Queen Of The Hop, 164
Queen Of The Senior Prom, 434
Question, 500
Quicksand, 416
Quicksilver, 170
Quiet Village, 180
Quite A Party, 236

Race Is On, The, 344
Race With The Devil, 635
Rag Doll, 257
Rag Mop, 6
Rags To Riches, 38, 592, 643
Ragtime Cowboy Joe, 110
Rain In My Heart, 569
Rain Rain Go Away, 636
Rain, Rain, Rain, 368
Rainbow '65, 97
Rainbow, 97
Rainbow At Midnight, 535
Raindrops, 117
Raining In My Heart, 291, 309
Rainy Night In Georgia, 41
Raised On Rock, 498
Rama Lama Ding Dong, 216
Rambling Rose, 134, 136, 407
Ram-Bunk-Shush, 191, 631
Ramrod, 214
Rang Tang Ding Dong, 95
Raspberries, Strawberries, 358
Rat Race, 207
Raunchy, 264, 346, 628
Rave On, 308
Raw-Hide, 669
Razzle-Dazzle/Two Hound Dogs, 287
Reach Out For Me, 644
Reaching For The World, 52
Ready For Your Love, 559
Ready Teddy, 391
Real Live Girl, 4
Real Pretty Mama, 430
Real Wild Child, 322
Reality, 67
Reap What You Sow, 587
Rebel-'Rouser, 214
Record, The, 354
Red Red Wine, 161
Red River Rock, 341
Red River Rose, 7
Red Roses For A Blue Lady, 161, 347, 442, 456
Red Sails In The Sunset, 134, 194, 313, 491
Reelin' And Rockin', 44
Reet Petite, 663
Reflections, 594

Release Me, 387
Remember Diana, 12
Remember Me Baby, 212
Remember Me I'm The One Who Loves You, 417
Remember Then, 212
Remember When, 456, 491
Remember You're Mine, 58
Repeat After Me, 469
Respect, 262, 514
Respectable, 321
Return To Me, 417
Return To Sender, 497
Reveille Rock, 341
Revenge, 40
Reverend Mr. Black, 359
Rhapsody In The Rain, 114
Rhinestone Cowboy, 85
Rhythm, 368
Rhythm Of The Rain, 92
Rib Tips, 654
Ricochet, 62
Ride!, 557
Ride Away, 462
Ride, Ride, Ride, 375
Ride The Wild Surf, 332
Ride Your Pony, 199
Riders In The Sky, 322, 442, 651
Ridin' The Wind, 608
Right Or Wrong, 327
Right Time, The, 104
Ring Of Fire, 93, 214
Ring-A-Ding-A-Ding, 546
Ring-A-Ding-Doo, 386
Ring-A-Ling-A-Lario, 534
Rinky Dink, 145
Rip It Up, 287, 391
Rise, 6
River Deep-Mountain High, 614
River Stay 'Way From My Door, 569
Riverboat, 670
Road Hog, 397
Road Runner, 186
R-O-C-K, 287
Rock & Roll Music, 31, 44
Rock A While / Lipstick, Powder And Paint, 615
Rock And Roll Is Here To Stay / School Boy's Romance, 162
Rock And Roll Rhapsody, 249
Rock And Roll Waltz, 583
Rock Around Mother Goose, 278
Rock Around The Clock, 287
Rock Island Line, 144, 197
Rock Love, 247
Rock Me In The Cradle Of Love, 557
Rock 'N' Roll Heaven, 525
Rock N' Roll Party, 501
Rock Night, 272
Rock Steady, 262
Rock Your Little Baby To Sleep, 364
Rock-A-Billy, 439
Rock-A-Bye Your Baby With A Dixie Melody, 261, 381
Rocka-Conga, 15
Rock-A-Hula Baby, 497
Rockhouse II, 104
Rockin' Around The Christmas Tree, 374

Rockin' Blues, 466
Rockin' Chair, 193
Rockin' Crickets, 312, 532
Rockin' Ghost, 50
Rockin' Good Way, A, 41
Rockin' In The Jungle, 223
Rockin' In The Same Old Boat, 49
Rockin' Little Angel, 574
Rockin' Robin / Over And Over, 169
Rockin Shoes, 7
Rocking Goose, 341
Rocking Pneumonia & The Boogie Woogie Flu, 573
Roll Over Beethoven, 44
Rollin' And Rockin', 44
Romeo, 284
Ronnie, 257
Ronnie Call Me When You Get A Chance, 228
Room Full Of Tears, 207
Rooming House Boogie, 430
Rosanna's Going Wild, 93
Rose And A Baby Ruth, A, 289
Rose Mary, 193
Rose, Rose, I Love You, 368
Roses Are Red, 636
Rosie Lee, 427
Rotation, 6
Round And Round, 137
Roundabout, 261
Route 66 Theme, 524
Rovin' Gambler, 248
Roving Kind, The, 439, 648
Rubber Ball, 629
Rubberband Man, The, 580
Ruby, 29, 104, 297, 641, 671
Ruby Ann, 529
Ruby Baby, 188, 207
Rudolph The Red-Nosed Reindeer, 83, 110
Rudy's Rock, 287
Rules Of Love, 465
Rum And Coca-Cola, 442
Rumble, 669
Rumors, 149
Rumors Are Flying, 418
Run Red Run, 129
Run, Rudolph, Run, 44
Run, Run, Look And See, 314
Run, Run, Run, 594
Run Samson Run, 554
Run To Him, 629
Run To My Lovin' Arms, 650
Runaround, 246, 519
Runaround Sue, 187
Runaway, 556, 651
Runnin' Out Of Fools, 262
Running Bear, 330, 499
Running Scared, 461
Rusty Bells, 375

'S Wonderful, 139
Sacred, 94
Sad Eyes, 213
Sad Mood, 141
Sad Movies (Make Me Cry), 378, 602
Sad, Sad Girl And Boy, 319
Sad Tomorrows, 395
Sadie, 580

Sail Along Silvery Moon, 628
Sail On Sailor, 31
Sailor, 393
Sailor Boy, 109
Saints Rock 'N Roll, The, 287
Sally, Go 'Round The Roses, 336
Sally Was A Good Old Girl, 194, 395
Same Old Hurt, The, 323
Same Old Me, The, 439
Same Old Saturday Night, 569
Same One, The, 40
Same Thing It Took, 319
Sam's Song, 89
San Antonio Rose, 149
Sand And The Sea, The, 134
Sandy, 188, 287
San-Ho-Zay, 356
Santa & The Satellite, 74
Santa And The Touchables, 277
Santa Baby, 361
Santa Claus Is Coming To Town, 256
Santa Claus Is Watching You, 587
Santo Natale, 653
Sassafras, 427
Satin Pillows, 637
Satisfaction, 438, 514
Satisfaction Guaranteed, 52
Saturday Night (Is The Loneliest Night In The Week), 568
Saturday Night At The Movies, 207
Saturday Night, 455
Sausalito, 420
Save All Your Lovin' For Me, 375
Save It For Me, 257
Save The Last Dance For Me, 207
Save Your Kisses For Me, 637
Saved, 22
Saving My Love For You, 2
Say Has Anybody Seen My Sweet Gypsie Rose, 464
Say It Loud—I'm Black & I'm Proud, 66
Say Man, 186
Say Man, Back Again, 186
Say Wonderful Things, 470
Say You Love Me, 319
Say You're Mine Again, 137
Say You're My Girl, 461
Scarlet Ribbons, 70
Scarlett O'Hara, 651
School Day, 44
School Is In, 54
School Is Out, 54
Scotch And Soda, 359
Sea Cruise, 247
Sea Of Heartbreak, 273
Sea Of Love, 485, 556
Sealed With A Kiss, 314, 637
Searching, 86, 129, 305
Seattle, 137
Second Fiddle Girl, 401
Second Fiddle, 583
Second Hand Love, 260
Second Honeymoon, 93
Second Time Around, The, 569
Secret Agent Man, 631
Secret Love, 170, 446, 588
Secret, The, 407

Secretly, 379, 534
Security, 328
See Saw, 262, 446
See Saw/When I'm With You, 446
See See Rider, 22
See The Funny Little Clown, 276
See You In September, 600
See You Later Alligator, 287
Seein' The Right Love Go Wrong, 344
See-Saw, 144
Send For Me, 134, 271
Send Me Some Lovin', 141, 391
Send Me The Pillow You Dream On, 70, 393, 417, 604
Send One Your Love, 668
Sentimental Me, 6, 14
Separate Ways, 498
September In The Rain, 647
September Song, 508
Serenade Of The Bells, 581
Sermonette, 517
Set Me Free, 387
Settle Down, 482
Seven Days, 152, 407
"7-11," 277
Seven Letters, 354
Seven Little Girls Sitting In The Back Seat, 225
Seven Lonely Days, 272
Seven Minutes In Heaven, 493
Seven Years, 319
Seven-Day Weekend, 54
Seventeen, 36, 202, 247
Sex Machine (P1), 67
Sexy Ida, 614
Sexy, Sexy, Sexy, 67
Sexy Ways, 430
Shadow Of Your Smile, The, 507
Shadows, 243
Shadrack, 40
Shag, The, 284
Shake A Hand, 2, 70, 479
Shake A Tail Feather, 239
Shake Hands And Walk Away Crying, 114
Shake, Rattle And Roll, 287, 615
Shake, Shake, Shake, 663
Shake Sherry, 140
Shake, The, 142, 413, 514
Sha-La-La, 562
Shame On Me, 25, 326
Shame, Shame, Shame, 402, 516
Shanghai, 170
Shangri-la, 161, 170, 250, 379
Share Your Love With Me, 49, 262
Sharing You, 629
Shazam, 214
Sh-Boom, 113, 152
She Belongs To Me, 454
She Called Me Baby, 524
She Can't Find Her Keys, 484
She Cried, 334, 379
She Lets Her Hair Down, 488, 606
She Said Yes, 486
She Say (Oom Dooby Doom), 183
She Thinks I Still Care, 498
She Understands Me, 604
She Wants T'Swim, 107
She Was Only Seventeen, 529

Sheik Of Araby, 443
Sheila, 535
She'll Never Know, 375
Shelter Of Your Arms, The, 167
Sherry, 256
Sherry Don't Go, 379
She's A Fool, 278
She's A Heartbreaker, 488
She's Everything, 198
She's Got Everything, 223
She's Got You, 122
She's Lookin' Good, 486
She's Not You, 497
Shifting, Whispering Sands, The, 202, 627
Shimmy Like Kate, 461
Shimmy Shimmy, 465
Shimmy, Shimmy, Ko-Ko-Bop, 385
Shine, 367
Ship Of Love, 458
Ship That Never Sailed, The, 90, 628
Shirl Girl, 456
Shirley, 549
Shish-Kebab, 415
Shoes, 41
Shoo-Be-Doo-Be-Doo-Da-Day, 668
Shoo-Fly Pie and Apple Pan Dowdy, 565
Shoot It Again, 63
Shop Around, 437
Shoppin' For Clothes, 129
Short Fat Fanny, 657
Short Shorts, 541
Shortnin' Bread, 33
Shotgun Boogie, 248
Should've Never Let You Go, 554
Should I, 249, 591
Shout, 173, 321
Shout and Shimmy, 66
Shout! Shout! (Knock Yourself Out), 413
Shrimp Boats, 582
Shrine of St. Cecelia, 292
Shu Rah, 194
Shut Down, 31
Shutters And Boards, 642
Shy Away, 265
Sick And Tired, 193
Side By Side, 583
Side Car Cycle, 543
Sidewalk Surfin', 332
Signed, Sealed & Delivered, 66, 202
Signed, Sealed, Delivered I'm Yours, 668
Silent Lips, 272
Silhouettes, 183
Silhouettes/Daddy Cool, 513
Silly Boy, 379
Silly Little Girl, 596
Silly Ol' Summertime, 455
Silver Star, 257
Silver Threads & Golden Needles, 580
Simply Call It Love, 97
Sin, 249
Since I Don't Have You, 326, 572
Since I Fell For You, 524, 650
Since I Found A New Love, 597
Since I Lost The One I Love, 319
Since I Made You Cry, 527
Since I Met You Baby, 313, 330
Since You Showed Me How To Be Happy, 664

Since You've Been Gone, 407
Sincerely, 12, 257, 403, 446
Sing Boy Sing, 546
Singin' On A Rainbow, 20
Singing Hills, 628
Singing The Blues, 439, 529
Sink The Bismarck, 311
Sinner Man, 395
Sir Duke, 668
Sister Sookey, 613
Sittin' In The Balcony, 131, 174
Sittin' On The Dock Of The Bay, 157, 514
Sitting In The Park, 588
Six Boys And Seven Girls, 73
Six Days On The Road, 209
Six Nights A Week, 150
634-5789, 486
16 Candles, 150
Sixteen Reasons, 586
Sixteen Tons, 248
Sixty Minute Man, 196
Skinny Minnie, 287
Skokiaan, 14, 254, 287, 415
Slaughter On Tenth Avenue, 631
Sleep, 59, 392
Sleep Walk, 548
Sleepy-Eyed John, 311
Slippin' And Slidin', 391
Sloop John B, 31
Slop Time, 560
Slow Twistin', 107
Slow Walk, 19, 190
Smack Dab In The Middle, 104
Smackwater Jack, 355
Small Sad Sam, 405
Small World, 424
Smile, 39, 134, 234, 672
Smoke Gets In Your Eyes, 491
Smoke Rings, 477
Smoke Stack Lightning, 666
Smokey Joe's Cafe, 531
Smokey Joe's La La, 520
Smokie (Part 2), 48, 191
Smoky Places, 145
Smooth Operator, 627
Snap Your Fingers, 300
Sneakin' Around, 352
Snow Flake, 518
Snowbound For Christmas, 172
So Close, 40
So Deep, 375
So Excited, 353
So Far Away, 355, 474
So Fine, 235
So High So Low, 22
So In Love, 407, 469, 565
So Long, 70
So Long Baby, 556
So Long, Dearie, 17
So Many Ways, 40
So Much, 385
So Much Love, 354, 619
So Rare, 199
So Sad, 226
So Sad The Song, 363
So Strange, 337
So This Is Love, 94

So Tired, 582
So Tough, 94, 365
So What, 48
So Wrong, 123
Soft, 191
Soft Summer Breeze, 183, 301
Soft Winds, 647
Softly, As I Leave You, 569
Soldier Boy, 252, 562
Solitaire, 38
So-Long, 193
Some Changes Are For Good, 645
Some Day, 368
Some Day Soon, 238
Some Enchanted Evening, 136, 334, 568, 581
Some Kind Of Wonderful, 207
Some Kind-A Earthquake, 214
Some Kinda Fun, 444
Some Things You Never Get Used To, 594
Somebody Bad Stole De Wedding Bell, 361
Somebody Else Is Taking My Place, 420
Somebody Like Me, 18
Somebody Stole My Gal, 511
Somebody To Love, 164
Somebody Touched Me, 365
Somebody Up There Likes Me, 137
Somebody's Gettin' It, 597
Somebody's Sleeping In My Bed, 597
Someday, 352, 442, 517, 546
Someday We'll Be Together, 594
Someday (You'll Want Me To Want You), 434
Someone, 424
Someone Is Watching, 76
Someone Somewhere, 389
Someone To Come Home To, 7
Someone To Love Me, 629
Someone To Love, 249
Someone You Love, 134
Somethin' Bout You Baby I Like, 85
Somethin' Else, 131
Somethin' Stupid, 570
Something, 57
Something Good, 601
Something Happened, 12
Something He Can Feel, 262
Something Old, Something New, 478
Something's Gotta Give, 403
Something's Gotta Give/Love Me Or Leave
   Me, 167
Somethings' Got A Hold On Me, 328
Something's On Her Mind, 257
Something's Wrong, 193
Sometime, 581
Sometimes I Wonder, 368
Sometimes You Gotta Cry A Little, 49
Somewhere, 452, 619
Somewhere Along The Way, 134, 373
Somewhere In Your Heart, 569
Somewhere My Love, 139
Somewhere There's A Someone, 417
Son Of Hickory Holler's Tramp, The, 574
Son Of Rebel Rouser, The, 214
Song For A Summer Night, 432
Song, For You, A, 655
Song From Moulin Rouge, 232
Song Of The Barefoot Contessa, 666
Song Of The Sparrow, 432

Song Of The Dreamer/Don't Stay Away Too
   Long, 238
Sooner Or later, 319, 424
Soothe Me, 567
Sorry (I Ran All The Way Home), 318
Soul Dance Number Three, 486
Soul Dressing, 57
Soul Hootenanny, 97
Soul Power, 67
Soul Serenade, 157
Soul Time, 222
Soul Twist, 157
Soul-Limbo, 57
Soulville, 647
Sound of Music, The, 469
Sound Off, 442, 616
South Street, 465
Southern Nights, 85
Southtown, U.S.A., 190
S.P. Blues, 313
Spanish Eyes, 420
Spanish Flea, 6
Spanish Harlem, 157, 262, 353
Spanish Lace, 403
Spanish Nights And You, 261
Sparrow In The Tree Top, 439
Special Occasion, 438
Speed Ball, 587
Speedo, 83
Speedy Gonzales, 59
Spend The Night In Love, 257
Spill The Wine, 322
Spinning A Web, 269
Spinning Wheel, 67
Spinout, 497
Spirit In The Dark, 262
Splish Splash, 164
Spring In Manhattan, 39
Spring Rain, 58
Springer, The, 176
Squeeze Her—Tease Her, 663
St. George And The Dragonet, 263
St. Louis Blues Mambo, 409
St. Therese Of The Roses, 643
Stagger Lee, 500, 535
Stag-O-Lee, 486
Stairway To Heaven, 554
Stand By Me, 283, 353, 389
Standing On The Corner, 254, 417, 434
Star Is Born, A, 186
Star Love, 492
Star You Wished Upon Last Night, The, 405
Starbright, 424
Stardust, 569, 599, 643
Starlight, Starbright, 552
Starry Eyed, 589
Stars And Stripes Forever, 367
Start Movin', 435
Stay, 7, 256, 658
Stay And Love Me All Summer, 315
Stay Away, 497
Stay Away From Me (I Love You Too Much),
   368
Stay In My Corner, 176
Stay With Me, 569
Stayin' In, 629
Steam Heat, 469

Steamroller Blues, 498
Steel Guitar & A Glass Of Wine, A, 12
Steel Men, 172
Step By Step, 150
Steppin' Out, 521, 554
Steps 1 And 2, 551
Stewball, 483
Stick Shift, 207
Sticks And Stones, 104
Still In The Dark, 615
Sting Ray, 540
Stir It Up, 452
Stir It Up And Serve It, 535
Stolen Love, 565
Stoned Love, 594
Stoned To The Bone, 67
Stood Up, 453
Stop And Think It Over, 137, 159
Stop! In The Name Of Love!, 594
Stop Look And Listen, 109
Stop Monkeyin' Aroun', 201
Stop The Music, 562
Stop The Wedding, 328
Stormy Monday Blues, 49
Stormy Weather, 578
Story From My Heart And Soul, 352
Story Of My Life, The, 529
Story Of My Love, The, 12, 617
Story Of Three Loves, 297
Story Untold, A, 152, 458
Straight A's In Love, 93
Straight Life, The, 277
Straighten Up Your Heart, 380
Straigten Up And Fly Right, 133
Stranded In The Jungle, 82, 335
Stranded In The Middle Of No Place, 525
Strange, 122
Strange Are The Ways Of Love, 284
Strange Feeling, 587
Strange I Know, 420
Strange Things Are Happening, 80
Stranger In Paradise, 39, 249, 418
Stranger In Town, 556
Stranger In Your Arms, 629
Stranger On The Shore, 46, 207, 654
Strangers In The Night, 569
Streak, The, 587
String Along, 7, 229, 454
String Around My Heart, 120
Stripper, The, 539
Stroll, The, 183
Stubborn Kind Of Fellow, 268
Stuck On You, 496
Stupid Cupid, 260
Such A Day, 401
Such A Night, 206, 497
(Such An) Easy Question, 497
Suddenly There's A Valley, 284, 371, 434, 582
Sugar Dumpling, 142
Sugar Moon, 58
Sugar Shack, 275
Sugar Sugar/Cole, Cooke & Redding, 486
Sugarbush, 170
Sugartime, 403
Sukiyaki, 546
Summer. . . ., 277
Summer And Sandy, 279

Summer Breeze (Part 1), 322
Summer Dreams, 403
Summer Love, 329
Summer Sand, 464
Summer Set, 350
Summer Sounds, 281
Summer Sweetheart, 7
Summer Wind, 456, 569
Summer's Gone, 12
Summer's Love, 26
Summertime, 141, 412, 588
Summertime Blues, 131
Summertime, Summertine, 330
Sun Arise, 293
Sun Is Shining, The, 516
Sunday And Me, 334
Sunday Barbecue, 248
Sunday Kind Of Love, A, 179, 292, 332, 650
Sunday, Monday Or Always, 568
Sunday Morning Coming Down, 94, 587
Sundowners, The, 628
Sunflower, 85, 586
Sunny, 554
Sunrise, Sunset, 659
Sunset Strip, 587
Sunset To Dawn, 466
Sunshine Girl, 238
Sunshine Lollipops And Rainbows, 279
Super Bad, 67
Super Woman, 668
Supernatural Thing (Part 1), 354
Superstition, 668
Surf City, 332
Surf Party, 107
Surfer Girl, 31
Surfer Joe, 595
Surfer's Stomp, 413
Surfin', 31
Surfin' Bird, 610
Surfin' Safari, 31
Surfin' U.S.A., 31
Surrender, 136, 496
Susie Darlin', 398, 535
Susie-Q, 294
Suspicious Minds, 497
Suzy Baby, 628
Swamp Girl, 367
Swanee River Rock, 104
Sway, 417, 544
Swearin' To God, 625
Sweet And Lovely, 599
Sweet Annie Laurie, 616
Sweet Chile, 669
Sweet Darlin', 416
Sweet Dreams (Of You), 123
Sweet Dreams, 273
Sweet Harmony, 438
Sweet Home Chicago, 389
Sweet Impossible You, 375
Sweet Lips, 448
Sweet Little Rock And Roll, 44
Sweet Little Sixteen, 44, 382
Sweet Little You, 554
Sweet Memories, 655
Sweet Nothin's, 374
Sweet Old Fashioned Girl, A, 63
Sweet Pea, 535

Sweet Seasons, 355
Sweet Sixteen, 352, 615
Sweet Sixteen Bars, 283
Sweet Stuff, 439
Sweet Sugar Lips, 348
(Sweet Sweet Baby) Since You've Been Gone, 262
Sweet, Sweet Lovin', 491
Sweet Sweetheart, 629
Sweet Talkin' Guy, 109
Sweet Thursday, 424
Sweet Violets, 565
Sweet Young Thing Like You, 104
Sweeter Than You, 453
Sweetest One, 150
Sweets For My Sweet, 207
S-W-I-M, 264
Swingin' Daddy, 365
Swingin' Gently, 283
Swingin' Safari, A, 628
Swingin' School, 544
Swingin' Shepherd Blues, The, 365, 539
Swingin' Sweethearts, 278
Swiss Maid, The, 556
Switch-A-Roo, The, 24
Symphony, 581

Ta Ta, 407
Taboo, 399
T'Ain't Nothin' To Me, 129
Take A Closer Look At the Woman You're With, 487
Take A Fool's Advice, 134
Take A Look, 262
Take A Message To Mary, 226
Take Care Of Your Homework, 597
Take Five, 72
Take Good Care Of Her, 91, 641
Take Good Care Of My Baby, 629, 637
Take Me Back To Toyland, 134
Take Me Back, 385
Take Me For A Little While, 366
Take Me In Your Arms And Love Me, 362, 477
Take Me In Your Arms, 652
Take Me (Just As I Am), 76
Take My Heart, 419
Take My Love (I Want To Give It All To You), 393
Take Some Time Out For Love, 322
Take These Chains From My Heart, 104
Take This Heart Of Mine, 268
Take This Hurt Off Me, 147
Takes Two To Tango, 17
Talk Back Trembling Lips, 604
Talk Of The School, 330
Talk That Talk, 663
Talk To Me, 569, 592
Talk To Me Baby, 13
Talk To Me, Talk To Me, 392
Talkin' To The Blues, 398
Talking About My Baby, 319
Tall Cool One, 642
Tall Oak Tree, 77
Tall Paul, 13
Tallahassee Lassie, 87
Tammy, 7, 522
Tango Of The Drums, 29

Taste Of Honey, A, 6, 39, 180
Taste Of Tears, 424
Te Amo, 327
Tea For Two, 599
Tea For Two Cha Cha, 200
Teach Me Tonight, 172, 582, 647
Teach Me Tonight Cha Cha, 172
Teacher, Teacher, 424
Teacher's Pet, 171
Tear, A, 402
Tear Drop, 548
Tear Drops, 9
Tear Fell, A, 63, 104
Teardrops From My Eyes, 70
Teardrops In My Heart, 27, 63
Teardrops On Your Letter, 24
Tears, 637
Tears And Laughter, 647
Tears And Roses, 420
Tears From An Angel, 563
Tears Keep On Falling, 621
Tears Of A Clown, The, 438
Tears On My Pillow, 385, 403
Tears, Tears, Tears, 354, 430
Teasable Pleasable You, 365
Teasin, 503
Teen Age Idol, 454
Teen Angel, 186
Teen Beat, 454
Teen Queen Of The Week, 87
Teen-Age Crush, 546
Teenage Heaven, 131, 158
Teenage Love, 400
Teenage Meeting, 144
Teenage Prayer, 411, 590
Teenage Sonata, 141
Teenager In Love, A, 189
Teenager's Romance, A, 453
Teen-Ex, 70
Tell Her For Me, 641
Tell Her (You Love Her Every Day), 569
Tell Him, 227
Tell Him I'm Not Home, 326
Tell Him No, 610
Tell It Like It Is, 655
Tell It On The Mountain, 483
Tell It To The Rain, 257
Tell Laura I Love Her, 485
Tell Mama, 328
Tell Me, 184
Tell Me A Story, 368
Tell Me Baby, 434
Tell Me So, 463
Tell Me That You Love Me, 193
Tell Me The Truth, 664
Tell Me Why, 35, 152, 237, 249, 497, 591, 637
Tell Me You're Mine, 269
Tell The World, 176, 490
Tell The World How I Feel About 'Cha Baby, 52
Telling Lies, 193
Telstar, 608
Temptation, 226, 507, 659
Ten Commandments Of Love, The, 385, 446
10 Little Bottles, 53
Ten Little Indians, 31
Ten Lonely Guys, 59
Ten Long Years, 352

Tender Trap, The, 569
Tenderly, 124, 347
Te-Ni-Nee-Ni-Nu, 291
Tennessee, 332
Tennessee Flat-Top Box, 93
Tennessee Stud, 18
Tennessee Waltz, The, 138, 142, 247, 265, 469,477, 581
Tequila, 48, 96, 488
Tequila Twist, 96
Te-Ta-Te-Ta-Ta, 349
Texan & A Girl From Mexico, A, 73
Texas Lady, 478
Thank You And Goodnight, 10
Thank You Baby, 562
Thank You For Calling, 582
Thank You Pretty Baby, 40
Thanks A Lot, 375
That Boy John, 506
That Evil Child, 353
That Girl Belongs To Yesterday, 488
That Greasy Kid Stuff, 284
That Happy Feeling, 347
That House On The Hill, 430
That Lady, 322
That Lovin' You Feeling Again, 461
That Lucky Old Sun, 17, 104, 367, 442
That Old Black Magic, 167, 501, 544
That Old Feeling, 348
That Sunday, That Summer, 134
That'll Be The Day, 153
That's A Lie, 104
That's All, 248, 454
That's All I Want From You, 447, 647
That's All I Want, 169
That's All There Is To That, 134
That's All You Gotta Do, 374
That's Alright, 389
That's Amore, 417
That's For Me, 581
That's How Heartaches Are Made, 645
That's How Much I Love You, 58
That's It—I Quit—I'm Movin' On, 141
That's Life, 569
That's Life (That's Tough), 266
That's My Desire, 98, 367, 554
That's My Little Susie, 622
That's My Pa, 669
That's Old Fashioned, 227
That's The Way Boys Are, 278
That's The Way Love Is, 49, 268
That's What Girls Are Made For, 580
That's What Love Is Made Of, 437
That's What My Heart Needs, 514
That's What The Nitty Gritty Is, 222
That's What You're Doing To Me, 196
That's When I Cried, 345
That's When It Hurts, 354
That's When The Music Takes Me, 554
That's When Your Heartaches Begin, 496
That's Why, 663
That's Your Mistake, 658
Them That Got, 104
Theme For Young Lovers, 232
Theme From A Summer Place, The, 232, 379, 631
Theme From Ben Casey, 624

Theme From "Charlie's Angels," 410
Theme From Dixie, 214
Theme From Dr. Kildare, 96
Theme From Goodbye Again, 234
Theme From Hatari, 410
Theme From Harlow, 637
Theme From Lawrence Of Arabia, 234
Theme From Love Story, 410
Theme From My Three Sons, 651
Theme From New York, New York, 570
Theme From Picnic, 415
Theme From Silver City, 631
Theme From Taras Bulba, 79
Theme From The Apartment, 234
Theme From The Dark At The Top Of The Stairs, 264
Theme From The Great Imposter, 410
Theme From The Proud Ones, 310, 524
Theme From The Threepenny Opera, A, 17, 297, 627
Theme From The Unforgiven, 146
(Theme From) Valley Of The Dolls, 644
Themes From The Man With The Golden Arm, 409
Then Came You, 580, 645
Then He Kissed Me, 156
Then You Can Tell Me Goodbye, 18
There Are You, 20
There Comes A Time, 551
There Goes My Baby, 207
There Goes My Heart Again, 194
There Goes My Heart, 329
There Goes The Lover, 97
There I Go, 442
There Is, 176
There Is Something On Your Mind, 406
There It Is, 67
There I've Said It Again, 141, 442, 637
There Must Be A Way, 329
There Oughta Be A Law, 428
There She Goes, 642
There Was A Time, 66, 97
There Will Never Be Another You, 444
There Won't Be Anymore, 524
There'll Be No Teardrops Tonight, 39
There's A Big Blue Cloud, 137
There's A Girl, 332
There's A Gold Mine In The Sky, 58
There's A Moon Out Tonight, 88
There's Always Me, 497
There's No Fool Like A Young Fool, 313
There's No Other, 156
There's No Tomorrow, 418
There's Nothing I Can Say, 454
There's Only One Of You, 254
There's Only You, 536
There's Something On Your Mind, 412
These Arms Of Mine, 514
These Foolish Things Remind Me Of You, 643
These Foolish Things, 66
These Hands (Small But Mighty), 49
These Things I Offer You, 626
They Don't Make Love Like They Used To, 18
(They Just Can't Stop It) The Games People Play, 580
They Say It's Wonderful, 136, 568
They Were Doin' The Mambo, 442

They're Coming To Take Me Away, Ha-Haaa, 451
Thing Of The Past, A, 562
Things, 164
Things I Didn't Do, The, 137
Things In This House, The, 165
Things We Did Last Summer, The, 228
Think, 66, 67, 242, 262, 375
Think I'll Go Somewhere And Cry Myself To Sleep, 420
Think It Over, 154
Think Me A Kiss, 407
Think Of The Good Times, 334
Think Twice, 40
Thinking Of You, 109, 237
Third Finger Left Hand, 533
Thirty Days, 43
This Bitter Earth, 647
This Empty Place, 644
This Friendly World, 229
This Girl's In Love With You, 644
This Guy's In Love With You, 6
This I Swear, 572
This Is All I Ask, 39, 323
This Is it, 518
This Is Love, 12
This Is My Country, 319
This Is My Love, 473
This Is My Story, 271
This Is The Beginning Of The End, 144
This Is The Night, 624
This Is The Thanks I Get, 401
This Land Is Your Land, 378, 455
This Little Girl, 54, 188
This Little Girl Of Mine, 226
This Little Girl's Gone Rockin', 70
This Love Is Real, 663
This Magic Moment, 207, 334
This Old Heart, 66
This Old Heart Of Mine, 321
This Ole House, 124
This Should Go On Forever, 42
This Time, 563
This Time I'm Gone For Good, 50
This Town, 569
Those Lazy-Hazy Days Of Summer, 134
Those Oldies But Goodies, 386, 457
Thou Shalt Not Steal, 184, 397
Thousand Miles Away, A, 298
Thousand Stars, A, 671
Three Bells, The, 70
Three Coins In The Fountain, 249, 569
Three Hearts In A Tangle, 66
Three Nights A Week, 193
3 O'Clock Blues, 352
Three O'Clock In The Morning, 347
Three Stars, 174
Three Steps To The Altar, 559
3,000 Miles, 314
Three Wishes/That's The Way It Goes, 292
Three Window Coupe, 526
Thrill Is Gone, The, 353
Tic Toc, 4
Tick Tock, 422
Tie A Yellow Ribbon, 464
Tie Me Kangaroo Down, Sport, 293
Ties That Bind, The, 40

Tiger, 229
Tiger Lily, 202
Tijuana Jail, The, 358
Tijuana Taxi, 6
'Til, 10, 232, 659
'Til I Kissed You, 226
Til Then, 119, 305, 434
Till Death Do Us Part, 61
Till I Waltz Again With You, 62
Till The End Of Time, 135
Till Then, 305, 434
Till There Was You, 73
Time After Time, 247, 444
Time Alone Will Tell, 261
Time And The River, 134
Time Is Tight, 57
Time Machine, 163
Time Marches On, 290
Time, The, 645
Time Was, 244
Times Of Your Life, 12
Tina Marie, 137
Ting-A-Ling, 126
Tiny Tim, 22
Tip Of My Fingers, The, 18
Tip On In, 291
Tit For Tat, 67
Titanic, 19
T.L.C. Tender Love And Care, 534
To A Sleeping Beauty, 172
To Be A Lover, 97
To Be Alone, 305
To Be Loved (Forever), 480
To Be Loved, 663
To Be Young, Gifted & Black, 567
To Each His Own, 368, 418, 491, 619
To Get To You, 642
To Give (The Reason I Live), 625
To Know Him, Is To Love Him, 598
To Know You Is To Love You, 353, 637
To Love Again, 249
To The Aisle, 243
To The Door Of The Sun, 420
To The Ends Of The Earth, 134
To Wait For Love, 6
Today, 455
Today I Met The Boy I'm Gonna Marry, 397
Today's Teardrops, 454
Together, 260
Together Again, 104
Together We Can Make Such Sweet Music, 580
Togetherness, 20
Tom Cat, 538
Tom Dooley, 358
Tomboy, 137
Tonight, 234, 238
Tonight (Could Be The Night), 630
Tonight I Fell In Love, 606
Tonight I Won't Be There, 641
Tonight I'll Say A Prayer, 280
Tonight My Heart Will Be Crying, 238
Tonight My Love, Tonight, 12
Tonight Tonight, 427
Tonight We Love, 418
Tonight You Belong To Me, 378, 476

Tonight You're Gonna Fall In Love With Me, 562
Tonight's The Night, 76, 109, 562
Too Bad, 354
Too Busy Thinking About My Baby, 268
Too Close For Comfort, 280
Too Hot To Hold, 368
Too Late Now, 172
Too Late To Turn Back Now, 41
Too Late To Worry, Too Blue To Cry, 84, 387
Too Many Fish In The Sea, 420
Too Many Rivers, 375
Too Much, 496
Too Much Lovin' 242
Too Much Monkey Business / Brown Eyed Handsome Man, 44
Too Much Of Nothing, 483
Too Much Talk, 522
Too Much Tequila, 96
Too Much, Too Little, Too Late, 424
Too Old To Cut The Mustard, 124
Too Pooped To Pop, 44
Too Soon To Know, 462
Too Young, 134
Too Young To Go Steady, 134, 469
Toot, Toot, Tootsie (Good-Bye), 444
Top 40, News, Weather & Sports, 186
Topsy I, 132
Topsy II, 132
Tore Up Over You, 430
Torquay, 236
Torture, 336
Tossin' And Turnin', 381
Touch, 594
Touchables In Brooklyn, 277
Touchables, The, 277
Tower Of Strength, 402
Tower's Trot, 327
Town Without Pity, 488
Toy Soldier, 257
Tra La La, 22, 272, 614
Tra La La La Suzy, 172
Traces / Memories Medley, 379
Tracks Of My Tears, The, 437
Tracy's Theme, 539
Tragedy, 246, 315, 648
Train Of Love, 13
Trains And Boats And Planes, 644
Transfusion, 458
Transistor Sister, 87
Travelin' Man, 453, 668
Travelling Stranger, 385
Treasure Of Love, 407
Treasure Of Your Love, 533
Treat Me Nice, 496
Treat My Baby Good, 164
Tree In The Meadow, A, 653
Trees, 302, 491
Triangle, 284
Tricky, 415
Trolley Song, The, 442
T-R-O-U-B-L-E, 498
Trouble In Mind, 262, 646
Trouble In Paradise, 150
Trouble Is My Middle Name, 636
Trouble Man, 269
Trouble With Harry, The, 29

Troubles, Troubles Troubles / I Want To Get Married, 352
True Blue Lou, 39
True, Fine Mama, 391
True Grit, 84
True Love Goes On And On, 323
True Love Never Runs Smooth, 488
True Love, True Love, 207
True True Happiness, 604
True True Love, 20
Truly, Truly, True, 375
Truly Yours, 580
Trust In Me, 139, 328, 469
Try, 263
Try A Little Kindness, 84
Try A Little Tenderness, 262, 514
Try It Baby, 268
Try Me, 66
Try The Impossible, 9
Try To Remember / The Way We Were, 363
Trying, 305
Tucumcari, 534
Tuff, 86
Tulips And Heather, 137
Tumbling Tumbleweeds, 628, 659
Tunes Of Glory, 432
Tunnel Of Love, 171
Turn Around, 184
Turn Around, Look At Me, 84
Turn Back The Hands Of Time, 237
Turn Me Loose, 229
Turn On Your Love Light, 49, 382
Turn The World Around, 18
Turn Your Radio On, 587
Turvy II, 132
Tutti-Fruitti, 58, 390
TV Is The Thing (This Year), 646
TV Mama, 615
Tweedlee Dee, 22, 272
Twelfth Of Never, The, 423
Twelve O'Clock Tonight, 171
Twenty Four Hours From Tulsa, 488
Twenty-Four Hours Of Sunshine, 444
Twenty Miles, 107
26 Miles, 255
Twilight, 470
Twilight Time, 491, 654
Twinkle Toes, 462
Twist And Shout, 321
Twist-Her, 48
Twist It Up, 107
Twist, The, 24, 107, 264
Twist, Twist Senora, 54
Twistin' All Night Long, 162
Twistin' Bells, 548
Twistin' Matilda, 577
Twistin' Postman, 420
Twistin' The Night Away, 141
Twistin' U.S.A., 162
Twistin' White Silver Sands, 48
Twistin' With Linda, 321
Twixt Twelve And Twenty, 58
Two Different Worlds, 446, 536, 650
Two Faces Have I, 114
Two Fools, 20
Two Hearts, 58, 105
Two Kinds Of Teardrops, 556

Two Lovers, 652
Two Of A Kind, 602
Two People In The World, 385
Two Sides To Every Story, 328
Two Thousand, Two Hundred Twenty-Three Miles, 469
Two Tickets To Paradise, 41
Tzena, Tzena, Tzena, 160, 432

Uh! Oh! Part 2, 459
Uh-Huh, Oh Yeah, 373
Uh-Huh-Mm, 330
Um, Um, Um, Um, Um, Um, 368
Unbelievable, 519
Unchain My Heart, 104
Unchained Melody, 29, 290, 302, 525, 625, 639
Under The Boardwalk, 207
Under The Moon Of Love, 375
Understand Your Man, 93
Understanding, 104
Underwater, 265
Unforgettable, 134, 647
United Together, 262
Universal Soldier, 84
Unless, 237, 439
Unsquare Dance, 72
Untie Me, 596
(Until Then) I'll Suffer, 401
Until You Come Back To Me, 262
Untrue, 154
Unwind, 587
Up A Lazy River, 674
Up In Heah, 614
Up On The Mountain, 408
Up On The Roof, 207
Up The Ladder To The Roof, 594
Up Tight (Everything's Alright), 668
Up Until Now, 511
Ups And Downs, 522
Uptown, 156, 461
U.S. Male, 497
Use Your Head, 652
Utopia, 267

Vacation, 260
Vagabond Shoes, 160
Valencia, 418
Valerie, 427
Valley Of Love, 613
Valley Of Tears, 193
Valley Of The Dolls, 157
Valley Valparaiso, 232
Vanessa, 666
Vanishing Point, 413
Vanity, 109
Vaquero, 236
Vaya Con Dios, 207, 477
Velvet Glove, The, 666
Velvet Waters, 425
Venus, 20
Venus In Blue Jeans, 115
Verdict, The, 241
Very Precious Love, A, 7
Very Special Love, A, 432, 452, 522
Very Special Love Song, A, 524

Very Thought Of You, The, 393, 454
Vesti La Giubba, 370
Village Of Love, 425
Village Of St. Bernadette, The, 654
Viva Las Vegas, 497
Voice In My Heart, 280
Voice In The Choir, A, 420
Voices, 247
Volare, 403, 417, 420, 544
Voodoo Woman, 277
Vows Of Love, The, 470

Wabash Blues, 638
Wadda-Do, The, 613
Wade In The Water, 6
Wah Watusi, The, 465
Wait A Minute, 129
Wait And See, 193
Wait For Me, 492
Wait 'Til My Bobby Gets Home, 397
Waitin' For The Train To Come In, 377
Waitin' In School, 453
Wake Me, Shake Me, 129
Wake Me When It's Over, 654
Wake The Town And Tell The People, 29, 91
Wake Up Everybody (Part 1), 52
Wake Up Little Susie, 226
Wake Up Susan, 580
Walk A Mile In My Shoes, 577
Walk Away, 442
Walk Don't Run, 631
Walk Easy My Son, 80
Walk Hand In Hand, 418, 654
Walk Like A Man, 256
Walk On By, 626, 644
Walk On The Wild Side, 40, 573
Walk On With The Duke, 97
Walk Right Back, 226
Walk Right In, 538
Walk Slow, 392
Walk, The, 402
Walk-Don't Run '64, 631
Walkin' After Midnight, 122
Walkin' Blues, 430
Walkin' Miracle, A, 223
Walkin' My Baby Back Home, 134, 511
Walkin' With Mr. Lee, 4
Walking Along, 183
Walking Dr. Bill, 352
Walking In The Rain, 334, 537
Walking Proud, 373
Walking The Dog, 601
Walking The Floor Over You, 58
Walking To New Orleans, 193
Wall, The, 533
Wallflower, The, 328
Walls Have Ears, The, 469
Waltzing Matilda, 534
Wanderer, The, 188
Wang Dang Taffy-Apple Tango, The, 58
Wang Wang Blues, 6
Wanted, 137
Wanting You, 659
War And Peace, 160
Warm Up To Me Baby, 60
Warmed Over Kisses, 314
Was It Good To You, 322

Washed Ashore, 491
Washington Square, 634
Wasn't The Summer Short, 424
Watch The Flowers Grow, 257
Watching Scotty Grow, 277
Watergate, 277
Waterloo, 327
Watermelon Man, 401, 547
Watermelon Song, 248
Watusi, The, 633
Way Down, 498
Way Down Yonder In New Orleans, 87
Way I Am, The, 663
Way I Walk, The, 551
Way Of A Clown, The, 507
Way Over There, 437
Way You Look Tonight, The, 379
Ways Of A Woman In Love, The, 93
Wayward Wind, The, 284, 527
We All Need Love, 232
We Belong Together, 529
We Can Make It Together, 585
We Can Make Music, 535
We Can Work It Out, 668
We Go Together, 332 446
We Got Love, 544
We Gotta All Get Together, 522
We Have Love, 647, 663
We Know We're In Love, 279
Wear It On Our Face, 176
Wear My Ring Around Your Neck, 496
Weary Blues, 403
Wedding Bells (Are Breaking Up That Old
    Gang Of Mine), 249
Wedding Bells, 298
Wedding Boogie, 466
Wedding, The, 111, 625
Week End, 357
Weight, The, 181, 262
Welcome Home Baby, 562
(Welcome) New Lovers, 58
We'll Have It Made, 580
Well I Told You, 101
Well, I'm Your Man, 604
Well Now Dig This, 339
Well-A, Well-A, 563
Wendy, 31
Wendy Wendy, 250
We're A Winner, 319
We're All Alone, 625
We're Getting Careless With Our Love, 597
We're Rolling On, 319
West Of The Wall, 238
Western Movies, 460
We've Come Too Far To End It Now, 438
We've Got Honey Love, 416
Whami, 404
What A Diff'rence A Day Makes, 387, 647
What A Dream, 469
What A Guy, 506
What A Party, 194
What A Price, 194
(What A Sad Way) To Love Someone, 198
What A Surprise, 422
What A Sweet Thing That Was, 562
What A Walk, 381
What About Me, 273

What Am I Going To Do Without Your Love,
    416
What Am I Gonna Do, 115
What Am I Living For, 105, 618
What Am I Living For/Hang Up My Rock And
    Roll Shoes, 661
What Are You Doing New Year's Eve, 463
What Are You Doing Sunday, 464
What Color Is A Man, 637
What Do I Care, 93
What Do You Want, 628
What Does A Girl Do, 50, 562
What Good Am I Without You, 269
What Have I Got Of My Own, 395
What In The World's Come Over You, 551
What Is A Teen Age Boy, 217
What Is A Teen Age Girl, 217
What Is Love, 492
What Is Truth, 94
What It Comes Down To, 322
What Kind Of Fool (Do You Think I Am), 596
What Kind Of Fool Am I, 167, 281
What Kind Of Love Is This, 173
What My Baby Needs Now Is A Little More
    Lovin', 67
What Now, 97
What Now My Love, 6
What The World Needs Now Is Love, 181
What Time Is It, 338
What To Do With Laurie, 122
What Will Mary Say, 424
What Would I Do, 428
What Would You Do, 518
What You Gave Me, 269
What'cha Gonna Do, 207
What'd I Say, 104, 164, 382, 497
Whatever Lola Wants, 565, 626
Whatever Will Be, Will Be, 170
Whatever You Want, 79
What's A Matter Baby, 672
What's Easy For Two Is So Hard For One, 652
What's Going On, 269
What's Gonna Happen When Summer's Gone,
    87
What's He Doing In My World, 18
What's Made Milwaukee Famous, 382
What's So Good About Good-Bye, 437
What's The Matter With You Baby, 269
What's The Reason I'm Not Pleasing You, 193
What's The Reason, 216
What's The Use Of Breaking Up, 80
What's The Use?, 511
What's Your Name, 196
Wheel Of Fortune, 22, 583, 646
Wheel Of Hurt, The, 420, 653
Wheels, 591, 628
When, 348
When A Boy Falls In Love, 91, 142
When A Woman Loves A Man, 387
When I Fall In Love, 379
When I Get Through With You, 123
When I Grow Too Old To Dream, 609
When I Grow Up (To Be A Man), 31
When I See You, 193
When Joanna Loved Me, 39
When My Blue Moon Turns To Gold Again, 496
When My Dreamboat Comes Home, 193

When My Little Girl Is Smiling, 4, 207
When Rock 'N' Roll Comes To Trinidad, 134
When The Boy In Your Arms, 260
When The Boys Get Together, 576
When The Lights Go On Again, 442
When The Lovelight Starts Shining Through His Eyes, 594
When The Saints Go Marching In, 193
When The Ship Comes In, 483
When The Swallows Come Back To Capistrano, 58
When The White Lilacs Bloom Again, 310, 627, 651, 673
When We Get Married, 203
When Will I Be Loved, 226
When Will I Know, 289
When You Dance, 334, 613
When You Lose The One You Love, 653
When You Loved Me, 375
When You Walk In The Room, 180
When You Were Sweet Sixteen, 136
When You Wish Upon A Star, 189
When You're Hot, You're Hot, 515
When You're #1, 97
When You're Young And In Love, 421, 543
Whenever He Holds You, 277
Where, 491
Where Are All My Friends, 52
Where Are You Going, 80
Where Are You, 647
Where Did I Go Wrong, 557
Where Did Our Love Go, 594
Where Did The Good Times Go, 184
Where Did They Go, Lord/Rags To Riches, 498
Where Did We Go Wrong, 625
(Where Do I Begin) Love Story, 655
Where Does Love Go, 550
Where Have All The Flowers Gone, 359
Where Have They Gone, 572
Where Have You Been All My Life, 4
Where I Fell In Love, 88
Where Love Has Gone, 344
Where Or When, 189, 379
Where Peaceful Waters Flow, 363
Where The Boys Are, 260
Where There's Life, 95
Where Were You (On Our Wedding Day), 500
Where's The Playground Susie, 84
Whiffenpoof Song, The, 152
While You Danced, Danced, Danced, 272
Whip It On Me, 304
Whipped Cream, 5
Whispering, 599
Whispering Bells, 179
Whispering Winds, 469
Whispers, 664
Whistling Organ, The, 145
White Christmas, 207, 508, 568
White Cliffs Of Dover, 450
White Rose Of Athens, The, 90
White Silver Sands, 48, 536
White Sport Coat, A, 529
Whither Thou Goest, 477
Who Are They To Say, 172
Who Are We, 284
Who Are You, 353

Who Can I Turn To, 39, 644
Who Cares, 194, 273
Who Else But You, 20
Who Gets The Guy, 644
Who Is Gonna Love Me, 644
Who Loves You, 257
Who Loves You Better (Part I), 322
Who Needs You, 254
Who Put The Bomp, 410
Who Stole The Keeshka, 424
Who Will The Next Fool Be, 49
Whole Lot Of Shakin' Goin' On, A, 107, 382, 618
Whole Lot Of Shakin' In My Heart, 437
Whole Lotta Loving, 193
Whole Lotta Woman, 506
Whole Lotta' Love, 352
Wholy Holy, 262
Who's Afraid Of Virginia Woolf, 574
Who's Gonna Take The Blame, 438
Who's In The Strawberry Patch With Sally, 464
Who's Making Love, 597
Who's Sorry Now, 260
Who's That Knockin', 271
Whose Heart Are You Breaking Tonight, 260
Why, 20
Why Baby Why, 58
Why Can't You Bring Me Home, 334
Why Do Fools Fall In Love, 183, 400, 411, 591
Why Do I Love You So, 604
Why Do Kids Grow Up, 508
Why Do Lovers Break Each Others Hearts, 53
Why Do You Do Me Like You Do, 120
Why Don't They Understand, 289
Why Don't You Believe Me, 210, 329, 469
Why Don't You Fall In Love With Me?, 564
Why Don't You Write Me, 324
Why I Sing The Blues, 353
Why I'm Walkin', 327
Why Was I Born, 160
Why'd You Wanna Make Me Cry, 586
Wichita Lineman, 84
Wiederseh'n, 420
Wiggle, Wiggle, 1
Wiggle Wobble, 143
Wild, 557
Wild Cherry, 109
Wild Honey, 31
Wild Horses, 137
Wild In The Country, 496
Wild Is The Wind, 424
Wild One, 416, 544
Wild Weekend, 532
Wild Wild Young Men, 70
Wildwood Days, 544
Will Power, 142
Will You Be Mine, 595
Will You Love Me Tomorrow, 257, 562
Willie and The Hand Jive, 467
Wimoweh, 648
Win Your Love For Me, 141
Wind In The Willow, 582
Wind, The, 181, 337
Windows Of The World, The, 644
Windy, 270
Wings Of A Dove, 314
Winter Wonderland, 136

Wipe Out, 595
Wisdom Of A Fool, 241
Wish You Were Here, 237
Wish You Were Here, Buddy, 59
Wishful Thinking, 385
Wishing For Your Love, 640
Wishing It Was You, 261
Witch Doctor, 555
Witchcraft, 497, 569, 579
With A Little Bit Of Luck, 232, 582
With All My Heart, 546
With My Eyes Wide Open I'm Dreaming, 469
With Open Arms, 447
With Pen In Hand, 277
With The Wind And The Rain In Your Hair, 58
With These Hands, 237
With This Ring, 491
With You On My Mind, 134
With Your Love, 551
Without A Song, 290
Without Her, 6
Without Love, 262
Without Love (There Is Nothing), 104, 407
Without You, 238, 604
Wives And Lovers, 344
Wizard Of Love, 399
Wizard, The, 534
Woe Is Me, 83
Woke Up This Morning, 352
Wolverton Mountain, 356
Woman, A Lover, A Friend, A, 663
Woman I Love, The, 352
Woman In Love, A, 249, 368
Woman's Got Soul, 319
Woman's Love, A, 601
Wonder Like You, A, 453
Wonder Of You, The, 484, 497
Wonderful Dream, A, 409
Wonderful Girl, 243
Wonderful Guy, A, 653
Wonderful Summer, 643
Wonderful Time Up There, A, 58
Wonderful World, 141
Wonderful! Wonderful!, 423, 619
Wonderful You, 534
Wonderland By Night, 73, 347, 501
Won't Be Long, 261
Won't You Come Home Bill Bailey, 164
Woo Woo Train, 623
Woodchoppers Ball, 166
Wooden Heart, 201, 637
Woo-Hoo, 532
Words, 58
Words Of Love, 183
Work Song, The, 6
Work To Do, 322
Work With Me Annie, 430
Workin' For The Man, 461
Working Class Hero, 535
Working In The Coal Mine, 199
Working My Way Back To You, 257, 580
Workout Stevie, Workout, 667
World, 67
World I Used To Know, The, 535
World Is Waiting For The Sunrise, The, 477
World Of Lonely People, The, 73
World Outside, The, 249, 250

World Through A Tear, The, 554
World We Knew, The, 569
World Without Love, A, 544
Worried Guy, 604
Worried Life Blues, 389
Worried Life, 353
Worried Man, A, 358
Worried Mind, 14
Worry, 604
Worryin' Kind, The, 546
Would I Love You (Love You, Love You), 170,
    418, 469
Would It Make Any Difference To You, 328
Wouldn't It Be Nice, 31
Wow Wow Wee, 10
W-P-L-J, 251
Wreck Of The "John B," The, 534
Wringle, Wrangle, 297, 472
Writing On the Wall, The, 641
Wrong For Each Other, 655
Wun'erful, Wun'erful, 263

Ya Ya, 199
Yakety Sax, 507
Yakety Yak / Zing Went The Strings Of My
    Heart, 129
Yeah Yeah, 294
Year Ago Tonight, A, 150
Years, 456
Years From Now, 663
Yeh-Yeh, 547
Yellow Bird, 399, 434, 651
Yellow Dog Blues, 163, 408
Yellow Rose Of Texas, The, 263, 432
Yep, 214
Yes I Do, 75
Yes I Want You, 313
Yes, My Darling Daughter, 564
Yes, My Darling, 193
Yes Sir, That's My Baby, 453, 554
Yes Tonight, Josephine, 511
Yessiree, 552
Yes-Sir-EE, 586
Yester Love, 438
Yesterday, 104
Yesterday And You, 629
Yesterday I Had The Blues, 52
Yesterday Once More, 580
Yesterday's Hero, 488
Yester-Me, Yester-You, Yesterday, 668
Yet . . . I Know, 373
Yield Not To Temptation, 49
Yogi, 323
You, 15, 268
You Alone, 137
You Always Hurt Me, 319
You Always Hurt The One You Love, 301, 433
You Are Beautiful, 424
You Are Mine, 20
You Are My Destiny, 12
You Are My Love, 329
You Are My Sunshine, 104, 341
You Are The Only One, 453
You Are The Sunshine Of My Life, 668
You Baby You, 120
You Beat Me To The Punch, 652
You Belong To Me, 210, 417, 469, 582

You Better Know It, 663
You Better Know What You're Doing, 500
You Better Move On, 4
You Bug Me, Baby, 657
You Can Depend On Me, 374
You Can Have Her, 290, 525,
You Can Have Him, 644
You Can Never Stop Me Loving You, 604
You Can Run, 79
You Can't Be True Dear, 401, 470
You Can't Get To Heaven On Roller Skates, 341
You Can't Hurry Love, 594
You Can't Judge A Book By The Cover, 186
You Can't Let The Boy Overpower The Man In You, 326, 437
You Can't Lie To A Liar, 378
You Can't Sit Down, 201
You Can't Sit Down—Part 2, 620
You Cheated, 560, 573
You Do, 442, 565, 653
You Done Me Wrong, 193
You Don't Have To Be A Baby To Cry, 89
You Don't Have To Be A Tower Of Strength, 401
You Don't Have To Go, 515
You Don't Have To Say You Love Me/Patch It Up, 497
(You Don't Know) How Glad I Am, 664
You Don't Know Girls, 384
You Don't Know Me, 104, 497, 621, 650
You Don't Know What You've Got, 198
You Don't Love Me Anymore, 454
You Don't Need Me For Anything Anymore, 375
You Don't Owe Me A Thing, 511
You Don't Own Me, 278
You Don't Want My Love, 654
You Excite Me, 20
You Gave Me A Mountain, 368
You Gave Me Peace Of Mind, 578
You Got Me Walking, 663
You Got That Touch, 330
(You) Got What I Need, 550
You Got What It Takes, 343
You Gotta Make Your Own Sunshine, 554
You Haven't Done Nothin', 668
You Keep Me Hanging On, 486, 594
You Know I Love You, 352
You Know It Ain't Right, 305
You Left The Water Running, 401
You Lied To Your Daddy, 596
You Light Up My Life, 355
You Little Trustmaker, 619
You Lost The Sweetest Boy, 652
You Made Me Love You, 134
You Mean Everthing To Me, 554
You Met Your Match, 668
You Must Believe Me, 319
You Must Have Been A Beautiful Baby, 164
You Need Hands, 280
You Need Love Like I Do (Don't You), 363
You Never Can Tell, 44
You, No One But You, 368
You Painted Pictures, 578
You Put It On Me, 353
You Really Know How To Hurt A Guy, 332

You Send Me, 63, 141
You Should'a Treated Me Right, 614
You Stepped Into My Life, 456
You Sure Love To Ball, 269
You Take My Heart Away, 166
You Talk About Love, 271
You Talk Too Much, 247, 346
You Threw A Lucky Punch, 97
You Turned My World Around, 570
You Upset Me Baby, 352
You Wanted Someone To Play With, 368
You Went Back On Your Word, 407
You Were Made For Me, 141
You Were Mine, 236
You Were Only Fooling, 160, 582
You Win Again, 194, 382
You You You, 7, 91
You, You, You Are The One, 6
You'd Be So Nice To Come Home To, 564
You'd Be Surprised, 384
You'll Answer To Me, 469
You'll Lose A Good Thing, 401
You'll Never Get Away, 62
You'll Never Get To Heaven, 644
You'll Never Know, 568
You'll Never Never Know, 490
You'll Never Walk Alone, 290, 366
Young Abe Lincoln, 144, 312
Young And In Love, 184
Young And Warm And Wonderful, 39
Young Blood, 129
Young Boy Blues, 353
Young Emotions, 453
Young Folks, The, 594
Young Love, 152, 279, 313, 329, 587
Young Lovers, 478
Young School Girl, 193
Young Wings Can Fly, 542
Young World, 453
Young-At-Heart, 569
Your Baby's Gone Surfin', 214
Your Cash Ain't Nothin' But Trash, 126
Your Cheating Heart, 104, 329, 628
Your Friends, 117
Your Heart Belongs To Me, 594
Your Kisses Kill Me, 280
Your Last Goodbye, 149
(Your Love Keeps Lifting Me) Higher And Higher, 664
Your Ma Said You Cried In Your Sleep Last Night, 186
Your Nose Is Gonna Grow, 149
Your Old Stand By, 652
Your Other Love, 244, 260
Your Own Back Yard, 188
Your Precious Love, 269
Your Teen-age Dreams, 424
Your True Love, 482
Your Unchanging Love, 268
Your Used To Be, 375
Your Wonderful Sweet, Sweet Love, 594
You're A Lady, 464
You're A Sweetheart, 392
You're A Wonderful One, 268
You're All I Need To Get By, 262, 424
You're All I Need, 49
You're All I Want For Christmas, 367

You're Breaking My Heart, 160
You're Following Me, 137
You're Gonna Hurt Yourself, 625
You're Gonna Miss Me, 260
You're Gonna Need Magic, 290
You're Gonna Need Me, 401
You're Good For Me, 75
(You're) Having My Baby, 12
You're In Love, 284
You're Just In Love, 137
You're Looking Good, 117
You're Making A Mistake, 491
You're My Driving Wheel, 594
You're My One And Only Love, 453
You're My Remedy, 420
(You're My) Soul And Inspriation, 525
You're Nobody Till Somebody Loves You, 417,
    647
You're Sensational, 569
You're Sixteen, 78
You're So Fine, 232
You're Still My Baby, 661
You're The Apple Of My Eye, 255
(You're The) Devil In Disguise, 497

You're The One, 421, 579
You're The Only World I Know, 330
You're The Reason I'm Living, 164
You're The Reason, 216, 577
You're Throwing A Good Love Away, 580
Yours, 401
You've Been An Angel, 352
You've Been Cheatin', 319
You've Been In Love Too Long, 416
You've Got Me Dizzy, 516
You've Got To Love Her With A Feeling, 356
You've Lost That Lovin' Feelin', 525, 644
You've Never Been This Far Before, 618
You've Really Got A Hold On Me, 437
You've Still Got A Place In My Heart, 417

Zazuera, 6
Zip Zip, 183
Zip-A-Dee Doo-Dah, 53
Zoom, 83
Zoop, 105
Zorba The Greek, 6
Zorro, 111

PHOTO CREDITS

1, ABC/Dunhill. 3, Chess. 7, RCA. 8, Chess. 9, The Angels. 11, Tommy Edwards. 13, RCA. 17, RCA. 19, Tommy Edwards. 21, Atlantic. 23, King. 25, RCA. 28, Columbia. 30, The Beach Boys. 33, RCA. 34, Kriegsmann. 36, RCA. 37, King. 38, Columbia. 40, Kriegsmann. 41, Mercury. 43, Chess. 45, Tommy Edwards. 46, Atlantic. 47, Kriegsmann. 54, John Apostole. 56, Atlantic. 59, King. 60, Tommy Edwards. 63, Columbia. 64, Columbia. 69, Kriegsmann. 71, Columbia. 73, Columbia. 76, Atlantic. 77, Mercury. 79, Tommy Edwards. 81, Modern Records. 83, Kriegsmann. 85, Kriegsmann. 87, Kriegsmann. 93, Columbia. 99, Earl Lewis. 100, Kriegsmann. 103, Atlantic. 106, Kriegsmann. 108, Columbia. 111, Tommy Edwards. 112, Kriegsmann. 113, Columbia. 115, Kriegsmann. 116, Tommy Edwards. 118, Emil Stucchio.

119, Herb Cox. 121, Columbia. 121, Columbia. 124, Columbia. 125, Atlantic. 127, Atlantic. 128, Atlantic. 130, Tommy Edwards. 132, Columbia. 133, Kriegsmann. 136, RCA. 140, RCA. 143, Columbia. 146, Kriegsmann. 147, Columbia. 148, RCA. 151, Mercury. 155, Bruno of Hollywood, J.J.K. Copy Art. 156, Bruno of Hollywood, J.J.K. Copy Art. 157, Atlantic. 159, Columbia. 161, Columbia. 165, Atlantic. 168, RCA. 170, Columbia. 171, Columbia. 176, Chess. 178, Mercury. 182, Mercury. 184, Warner Brothers. 185, Chess. 188, Columbia. 191, King. 192, Kriegsmann. 195, Kriegsmann. 195, Kriegsmann. 197, Kriegsmann. 205 (top), Kriegsmann, 205 (bottom), Atlantic. 206, Kriegsmann. 208, Richard Blandon. 210, Columbia. 211, Kriegsmann. 213, RCA. 215, Jim Maderitz. 217, Tommy Edwards. 219, United Artists. 220, RCA. 221, Columbia.

223, Roulette. 224, Tommy Edwards. 225, Kriegsmann. 228, Fabian. 230, Atlantic. 231, Columbia. 233, United Artists. 237, RCA. 239, RCA. 240, Kriegsmann. 242, Kriegsmann. 244, Zeke Carey. 245, United Artists. 250, Columbia. 254, Columbia. 257, Mercury. 258, Columbia. 259, Tommy Edwards. 263, King. 273, RCA. 274, Columbia. 275, Atlantic. 276, Kriegsmann. 279, Mercury. 280, Columbia. 281, Columbia. 283, RCA. 285, Columbia. 286, Kriegsmann. 288, Columbia. 289, RCA. 290, Columbia. 292, Kriegsmann. 294, Tommy Edwards. 295, Columbia. 298, Kriegsmann. 299, Tommy Edwards. 301, RCA. 302, Kriegsmann. 303, Columbia. 306, Columbia. 308, Bruno of Hollywood, J.J.K. Copy Art. 311, Columbia. 313, Kriegsmann. 315, ABC-Paramount. 316, Atlantic. 317, Joe Frazier. 319, Atlantic. 321, RCA. 325, Kriegsmann.

326, Columbia. 331, United Artists. 333, United Artists. 339, Kriegsmann. 340, Kriegsmann. 343, Kriegsmann. 344, Kriegsmann. 345, Jimmy Jones. 348, RCA. 351, Kriegsmann. 354, Atlantic. 355, RCA. 356, Columbia. 357, Atlantic. 359, Kriegsmann. 360, Columbia. 362, Kriegsmann. 364, Tommy Edwards. 366, Columbia. 369, Columbia. 371, Kriegsmann. 373, Kriegsmann. 374, Brenda Lee. 376, Atlantic. 378, RCA. 380, Bobby Lewis. 382, Mercury. 383, RCA. 385, Kriegsmann. 387, Atlantic. 389, RCA. 391, Columbia. 392, Kriegsmann. 394, King. 395, King. 396, Columbia. 400, Kriegsmann. 402, Columbia. 405, King. 405, RCA. 406, Atlantic. 409, RCA. 415, Kriegsmann. 421, Kriegsmann. 423, Columbia. 426, Jerry & Bob Scholl. 428, Kriegsmann. 429, King. 431, Columbia. 433, Kriegsmann. 435, Columbia. 436, Kriegsmann. 439, Columbia.

441, Chess. 443, Kriegsmann. 445, Kriegsmann. 447, RCA. 450, Contrera & Cracolici. 453, Willie Nelson. 455, Columbia. 460, Tommy Edwards. 462, RCA. 463, Columbia. 465, Kriegsmann. 466, King. 467, RCA. 468, Mercury. 471, Tommy Edwards. 472, Tommy Edwards. 474, Chess. 476, Tommy Edwards. 477, Bruno of Hollywood, J.J.K. Copy Art. 478, Mercury. 479, Dootone Records. 481, Tommy Edwards. 483, Kriegsmann. 484, RCA. 487, Kriegsmann. 489, Mercury. 492, Tommy Edwards. 493, Tommy Edwards. 494, RCA. 495, RCA. 499, Banner Talent, Dave Zaan, Lloyd Price. 502, Columbia. 510, Columbia. 512, Hal Miller. 513, Atlantic. 515, Columbia. 516, Kriegsmann. 517, Kriegsmann. 518, RCA. 521, Columbia. 523, Mercury. 528, Columbia. 533, Columbia. 534, Kriegsmann. 536, Columbia. 537, Ronnie Spector. 541, Joe Villa.

543, 20th Century Fox. 547, Columbia. 549, Columbia. 551, RCA. 553, RCA. 556,

Kriegsmann. 558, Kriegsmann. 561, Kriegsmann. 564, RCA. 566, Billy Horton. 572, The Skyliners. 575, Columbia. 576, Columbia. 583, RCA. 585, Columbia. 586, Tommy Edwards. 588, Chess. 590, Tommy Edwards. 593, Kriegsmann. 598, Modern Records. 599, Atlantic. 602, Columbia. 606, RCA. 607, Columbia. 609, Tommy Edwards. 611, Chess. 613, Kriegsmann. 615, Atlantic. 616, Kriegsmann. 617, Tommy Edwards. 618, Columbia. 621, Columbia. 622, Hal Roach. 627, Kriegsmann. 629, United Artists. 632, Atlantic. 633, Columbia. 635, Bruno of Hollywood. J.J.K. Copy Art. 636, Columbia. 639, Dave Rick. 641, Columbia. 643, Tommy Edwards. 645, Atlantic. 646, Mercury. 649, Columbia. 651, Warner Brothers. 655, Columbia. 656, Tommy Edwards.

657, Specialty. 659, Kriegsmann. 660, Atlantic. 661, Kriegsmann. 663, Jackie Wilson. 665, Columbia. 667, Kriegsmann. 669, Tommy Edwards. 674, United Artists.